Services
Marketing
Management

F

Services Marketing
Management

A Strategic Perspective

Second Edition

Hans Kasper
Piet van Helsdingen
Mark Gabbott

JOHN WILEY & SONS, LTD

Other Wiley Editorial Offices

John Wiley & Sons, Inc., 111 River Street, Hoboken, NJ 07030, USA

Jossey-Bass, 989 Market Street, San Francisco, CA 94103-1741, USA

Wiley-VCH Verlag GmbH, Boschstr. 12, D-69469 Weinheim, Germany

John Wiley & Sons Australia Ltd, 42 McDougall Street, Milton, Queensland 4064, Australia

John Wiley & Sons (Asia) Pte Ltd, 2 Clementi Loop #02-01, Jin Xing Distripark, Singapore 129809

John Wiley & Sons Canada Ltd, 22 Worcester Road, Etobicoke, Ontario, Canada M9W 1L1

Wiley also publishes its books in a variety of electronic formats. Some content that appears
in print may not be available in electronic books.

Library of Congress Cataloging-in-Publication Data

Kasper, Hans.
Services Marketing Management : A Strategic Perspective. – 2nd ed. / Hans
Kasper, Piet van Helsdingen, Mark Gabbott.
p. cm.
Subtitle on 1999 ed.: An international perspective.
Includes bibliographical references and index.
ISBN 0-470-09116-9 (pbk. : alk. paper)
1. Service industries – Marketing – Management.   2. Customer
services – Marketing – Management.   I. Helsdingen, Piet van.   II. Gabbott, Mark.
III. Title.
HD9980.5.K375 2006
658.8–dc22   2005034528

British Library Cataloguing in Publication Data

A catalogue record for this book is available from the British Library

ISBN-13 978-0-470-09116-6
ISBN-10 0-470-09116-9

Project management by Originator, Gt Yarmouth, Norfolk (typeset in 9/13pt Garamond ITC).
Printed and bound in Great Britain by Scotprint, Haddington, East Lothian.
This book is printed on acid-free paper responsibly manufactured from sustainable forestry
in which at least two trees are planted for each one used for paper production.

CONTENTS

DETAILED TABLE OF CONTENTS

PREFACE

Services marketing is about people, especially caring about people. Their needs – from customers as well as employees – have to be met (and more effectively than the competitors meet them) in order to create real value to all the stakeholders. This 'care-issue' appears to be the most critical element in the culture of market-oriented service organizations and is our starting point to focus on those issues critical in delivering excellent service quality.

We believe that in the coming years the effective and efficient management of five topics will help inform the positioning of every service organization. These five topics are therefore used as the guiding principles throughout our text. They are:

■ Market orientation;
■ Assets and capabilities;
■ Characteristics of services;
■ Internationalization; and
■ Value: the service experience in order to actually create value to all the stakeholders.

Market orientation can be defined in various ways; basically, it refers to understanding the market behaviour of customers and competitors and applying that information in the company effectively in order to be different from other suppliers. More and more academics, business men and women and consultants realize that although market orientation looks simple it is very hard to implement correctly. Also some parts of an organization's market orientation are so self-evident (e.g., knowing what the customer wants) that managers overlook them and forget to pay attention to the basics.

The *assets and capabilities* relate to the internal strengths of the service organization; they are indispensable to implement the organization's market orientation. Customer-based assets are also critical, which is in line with our emphasis on market orientation. In today's literature on strategic management such assets and capabilities receive a lot of attention, next to the key success factors in the market.

The *characteristics of services* are another fundamental issue that in our consultancy work we have noticed is easily overlooked. It is our firm belief that once you forget to look at the basics you try to develop a strategy that becomes much too complex. Another issue that is fundamental today is *internationalization*. No company exists in isolation and many service organizations act in an international arena. Even a small local bar or coffee house will be affected by the entrance of Starbucks in their local high street.

Finally, customers and organizations exchange money and ask for great services; this trade-off will result in the value customers perceive and shareholders require. So, understanding, creating and delivering value to customers, the firm and all the other stakeholders is the main reason to include this fifth principle in our book.

The application of these five principles in a strategic and operational context must be based on the relationships between service provider and customer. Since services is a people's business, the human side of the service enterprise is critical next to newly introduced technologies like utilizing e-services and the Internet. For the (inter)national service organization to be effective requires inspiring leadership that reveals the soul of service.

In our wide overview of this subject, many different perspectives have been taken into account. For instance, we focus on the importance of relationships as well as the relevance of the marketing mix in services. We have not taken one perspective to look at service quality, but different ones. The focus on assets and capabilities is unique to a textbook on services marketing.

'Managing the service organization' is an important theme throughout thix text – for instance, in terms of leading, motivating and even assessing/evaluating employees (and customers). Overall, much attention is given to 'people' as one of the most important assets in services marketing management.

Objectives and Target Audience

The objectives of this second edition are to provide an extensive overview of services marketing management based on the international literature and to provide up-to-date information about managing service organizations.

The main target group will be advanced undergraduate students and graduate students in the UK, Europe and Australasia. The textbook can also be used in management development programmes (as the present authors did successfully with the first edition of the book) and post-graduate programmes. We expect our target groups to be familiar with the basics of management, strategic management, marketing, finance, accounting, human resources management and internationalization strategies.

We hope the reader will:

1 Gain a proper understanding of services marketing management in a national and international context;
2 Be able to manage a market-oriented service organization; and
3 Be able to deliver excellent service quality at a price – leading to long-term relationships with customers, employees, shareholders and other stakeholders.

New to the Second Edition

The new edition is a very thorough revision of the first edition, integrating not just additional topics, but a new approach and a completely revised structure. We have also made the second edition more relevant to readers outside the USA by including many more examples from the UK, mainland Europe and Australasia. We have also chosen not to focus just on research from the UK and USA, but also to draw on literature from the Netherlands, Belgium, Germany, France, Spain and Scandinavia, for example.

The new theme of assets and capabilities is a challenging one, as we encountered in discussions with students and companies. In particular, the four groups of assets (customer-based, internal-based, distribution-based and alliance-based) and the four groups of capabilities (inside-out, outside-in, spanning and networking) provide the reader with new and unique insights on services marketing management not published before.

In this second edition electronic services are discussed at length. In the future they will partly be an alternative to services provided via the traditional channels, partly they offer complete new service opportunities. This holds also for the new topic of business-to-business services which in our contacts with companies was often mentioned as important, especially since in many product-oriented companies margins on their products are shrinking and profits can only be made via the services. However, many of these companies are very technically oriented and not (yet) customer or market oriented. Therefore, they not only need to make this shift from technique oriented to market oriented but also from the traditional break and fix services to a more pro-active, interaction-oriented service provider during the life cycle of the products. The typology of business-to-business services that we have used in this edition fits very well to the general service typology that we developed in the first edition. So the distinction between the next four kinds of services remains:

- Standard core services;
- Standard augmented services;
- Customized core services; and
- Customized augmented services.

Structure of the Book

We have chosen to focus on the first three parts of the first edition giving it a clear strategic orientation (hence the title of this new edition contains the word 'strategic'). Market orientation, service quality, the integration of HRM and marketing, and the internal strengths in terms of assets and capabilities are important building blocks providing the fundamentals of strategic services marketing management. These fundamentals are the starting point to create the service experience the consumer actually perceives. The present part on the marketing mix is much shorter than in the first edition.

From a methodological and educational/learning perspective we hold it is important to first sketch an holistic picture of the field of services and the many developments that take place in that domain. This is why we chose to start with a first chapter focusing on what is going on in the world of services. In this way you are first confronted with all the relevant trends and situations in the actual world of the phenomenon that you are studying. After reading such a general overview, the reader will be better equipped to understand the contents of the book, the concepts introduced, the nuances made and the links between concepts (in theory and practice).

The book contains three parts, which in the way they are structured follow the line of understanding, creating and delivering value. Creating value is the ultimate goal to all the service organization's stakeholders:

■ Part 1: Understanding creation in services;
■ Part 2: Creating value in services; and
■ Part 3: Delivering value through the actual service experience.

Part 1 is on understanding services marketing management and the relevance of focusing on value, and consists of these three chapters:

1 The world of services;
2 The fundamentals of services marketing management; and
3 Buyer behaviour and segmentation.

Part 2, on creating value, consists of the next four chapters:

4 Service relationships and brands;
5 Service quality;
6 Market strategies for service organizations; and
7 Internationalizing services.

Part 3 is on creating the actual service experience as the way to create and communicate value to the stakeholders. To discuss the relevant topics we developed these five chapters which are reflecting the seven Ps of services marketing:[1]

8 Services and e-services;
9 Service innovation;
10 People, process and physical evidence;
11 Place, promotion and price; and
12 Implementation, performance and control.

In essence all five guiding principles will come to the fore in each chapter. The link between the three parts with these 12 chapters and the five guiding principles is shown in Figure P1.

The Pedagogical Structure and Layout

Services Marketing Management: A Strategic Perspective can be used in classroom teaching as well as for self-study activities. Therefore:

■ The goals of the whole book and the goals of each chapter are stated clearly;
■ The book is easily accessible, well-structured and attractive;
■ It has a clear writing style;

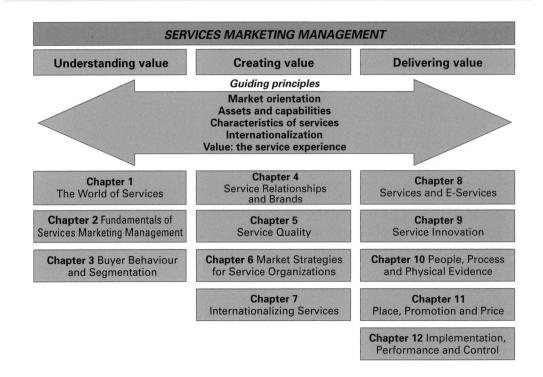

Figure P.1 Contents of Part 1 related to the other parts of the book

- The link between theory and practice is always present;
- It is based on literature from all over the world; and
- The text possesses incentives to test one's own knowledge and skills.

These pedagogical considerations are reflected in the layout of the book. Every chapter:

- Starts with an image illustrating real world services marketing;
- Gives a clear overview of the chapter's objectives;
- Contains Service Practice Boxes: real life examples that illustrate points in the text when needed;
- Ends with a summary that is closely linked to the objectives stated at the beginning of the chapter; and
- Provides a full set of revision questions and practical assignments.

We have included six full length cases at the end of the book, with accompanying questions, offering you the opportunity to apply what you have learned and solve real life problems of service companies. They are grouped together because they do not specifically hinge on the theory from one chapter, although they focus on some particular topics. We hope that the cases also contribute to a more holistic approach of the services business you are working in or intend to work in.

Our book is supported by a website at *www.wileyeurope.com/college/kasper* providing lecturers with suggested solutions to all the end of chapter questions and case study questions. All the figures and tables from the book are also available as PowerPoint slides. Extra cases will be available on the website for students.

Acknowledgements

Since the first edition, Wouter de Vries Jr has left our team and Mark Gabbott from Monash University in Australia has joined us. Many thoughts and ideas Wouter had developed in the first edition have remained. Nevertheless, the three of us have developed a whole new book with a lot of new insights from all over the globe.

Our work 'in the market place' has given us a lot of problems to think about. We hope our ideas and suggestions will clarify these problems and provide solutions to marketers and other managers in services organizations to solve these challenges. The feedback that we got from our students during classes where we tested some of our ideas was great. This holds also for the comments managers made during the management development programmes where we were able to discuss and test our ideas on excellent services marketing management. These valuable comments have contributed to the topics discussed and the way we structured this text. Our publisher also invited many academics to review the draft text of the chapters. Their valuable suggestions and comments were of great help in developing this text. We appreciate their efforts.

Having two non-native English speakers in the team, it was quite a job to turn the draft texts into one coherent, well-reading English text. We greatly appreciate the work Janine Hendry from Monash University has done to improve the quality of our text. We would like to thank our students who have contributed one way or another to this text. Many of them wrote an MBA thesis that formed the basis for some sections in our book.

Prof. Allard van Riel, Université de Liège, contributed to our chapter on services and e-services; thank you, Allard, for writing the section on e-services.

We would like to mention especially Fieke Schopenhouer who did a lot of work with respect to the tables on assets and capabilities in Chapter 6 and in putting the references together. Next, a word of special thanks goes to Julia Valkova who worked on the service practices in Chapters 1, 7, 11 and 12. Moreover, she prepared the website case on ING Direct. We also would like to thank Tom van de Molengraft, Sanna Sutter and Hendrik-Jan Lugtmeijer, students of the Master Programme Business Administration and Marketing, who contributed to the cases and examples in those chapters.

Finally, we have to express our great gratitude to the Wiley team that helped us tremendously to get this book published. We admire their knowledge of the business and their patience with us as a team of academics whose strongest competence is not always sticking to the planning. We could not have accomplished this project without the great support of Anneli Anderson, Sarah Booth, Trisha Dale, Deborah Egleton, Rachel Goodyear and Steve Hardman. Thanks a lot.

Hans Kasper, Maastricht
Piet van Helsdingen, Amsterdam
Mark Gabbott, Melbourne

1 Chapters 8 and 9 refer to the well-known P of product. Chapters 10 and 11 each discuss three Ps.

All reasonable efforts have been made to trace the copyright owners of third party material included in this book. In the event of any omission of acknowledgement, copyright owners are invited to contact the Higher Education Division at John Wiley & Sons Ltd, so that they can be acknowledged in future editions of the book or request that such material be removed from future editions.

Part 1
Understanding Value Creation in Services

This book is about services marketing management. Services marketing is about caring about people; nothing more, nothing less. Therefore, the book is composed of three parts, all referring to the value that customers and other stakeholders are looking for. The three parts are about

- understanding
- creating
- delivering

that value.

We have chosen five topics as the guiding principles throughout all three parts of this book:

1. The service organization's market orientation;
2. The service organization's assets and capabilities;
3. The characteristics of services;
4. Internationalization in the service sector; and
5. Value created in the actual service experience.

Part 1 focusses on understanding the domain of services marketing management. This part starts with an overview of 'the world of services' revealing what is happening in the services business. This overview shows what the empirical phenomenon is that we are discussing. Then we can continue to elaborate on the fundamentals of services marketing management. Services will be defined as well as the concepts of marketing and management. These concepts will be elaborated upon in order to be able to define the service organizations' market orientation. In Chapter 3 we will discuss the many typical features of consumer behaviour and services, in general and for specific market segments. These are the building blocks for the general framework that service organizations may apply to create value for their customers and other stakeholders. It all hinges upon the ultimate and high quality service experience.

Once we know these basics we can pay attention to creating, developing and maintaining relationships, brands, service quality, satisfaction, strategies to go to market and the internationalization aspect of the service business in Part 2. This sets the framework for the creation of value at a strategic level.

In turn, that all provides the basis to create the ultimate service experience. The delivery of value through the actual service experience will be presented in Part 3. A wide variety of subjects are needed to create value through those service experiences in terms of services (be it traditional services or e-services); service innovations; people, processes and physical evidence; place, promotion and price; and the final implementation and control.

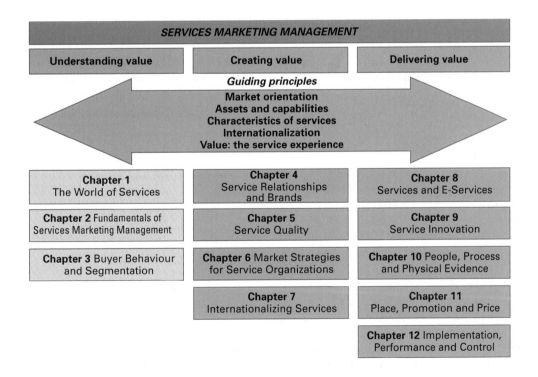

Figure P.1   Contents of Part 1 related to the other parts of the book

Chapter 1

The World of Services

Reproduced by permission of Mobile.de, Germany

Learning objectives

At the end of this chapter you will be able to:

1 Define the scope of the service sector

2 Discuss the importance of mapping trends in a service environment

3 Explain how the environment impacts on service businesses

4 Describe what is meant by the term environmental mapping

5 Apply environmental mapping at three levels:
   - The macro environment (DRETS-factors),
   - The sector environment (marketing-related service trends), and
   - The direct market environment

6 Translate an environment map into strategic activities relating to a service business

7 Write a strategic marketing plan for a service business

1.1   Introduction

SERVICE PRACTICE 1.1

Scanning the Future[1]

Forecaster Peter Francese has identified several trends which are expected to dominate the coming years. Western consumers are changing. Trend forecasts should help businesses gauge which sectors are most likely to benefit from the dominant trends of the year. Several of these shifts have been developing for some time and will not come as a surprise. Others are just becoming evident and may have a major impact on business.

There is no longer an average consumer. In the past year millions of people have lost their jobs and subsequently cut back on their purchases, and yet many more affluent people have continued to spend freely on new cars, second houses and other luxury goods. Consumer spending is still growing but the rate of growth has varied significantly from year to year depending on shifting wants and needs.

Baby Boomers are getting older and they have a large influence on consumer spending. Some of them, because of their higher educational attainment are more likely to remain fully employed as they enter their sixties. This is good news for restaurants and travel industries. Health and fitness businesses striving to help Boomers look younger are also likely to do very well over the next decade.

Higher educational achievements, especially among women, support the trend of an increasing number of jobs requiring more intellectual than physical skills. It is projected that in the future 25% more women than men will be in college and the long-term impact is an increase in women's lifetime earning power.

In Latin America there will be a decline in the number of jobs created to accommodate teenagers. Therefore, many of them will try to find jobs in the USA in the service sector, resulting in an anticipated increase in emigration from Latin America to the USA. This will put a higher premium on managers speaking Portuguese and Spanish. Hispanics now represent one-third of the population in California and Texas with a median age of 25.8 years, nearly 13 years younger than that of the non-Hispanic white population in the USA. Hispanics have larger households and spend more on food and clothing for children. Thus, metro areas with growing numbers of Hispanics are likely to benefit from higher than average retail sale. Over time, more than half the children in US public schools will either be Hispanic, African American, or Asian.

As life expectancy increases, workers are retiring later. One of the consequences will be that pensions and pension funds will continue to grow. Manual and clerical workers are increasingly outnumbered by knowledge workers. Information is the primary commodity in more and more industries today. Services are the fastest-growing sector of the American economy (and not only in the USA).

The degree to which each of these trends will affect firms that sell consumer goods or services depends on who their customers are and how firms adapt to shifts in their client base. Firms that are best aware of how customers are changing have the biggest opportunity to adjust successfully.

Reprinted with permission from the November 2002 issue of *American Demographics*. Copyright, Crain Communications Inc. 2004

Services marketing management is about servicing people. In fact, it is about caring about people as we will explain in this text. People as individuals, as households, as employees in companies. It encompasses both the profit and not for profit sectors.

Services usually deal with intangibles; things that you cannot hold, touch nor see before you use them. Services refer to deeds, processes and experiences. Ownership of services is generally not possible. You as a customer experience a service and you will decide whether you are satisfied with it or not. Satisfaction is based on the quality of the process of delivering the service and the actual outcome of the service delivery process.

The services sector encompasses a wide variety of industries such as hotels, entertainment, transportation, information, leisure, plumbing, after sales services for products, professional services. The sector also encompasses publicly offered services, like education, police, fire brigades, pension funds, army and taxation services.

Most of this book hinges upon the services offered by the market sector. However, many of the ideas presented can also be applied to the public sector. The basic principles of marketing apply in this sector as well. Although a real market does not exist in the public sector because citizens should get what they are asking for; this assumption is basic to marketing.

This chapter is aimed at giving you an overview of the services sector. Having read this chapter you will better understand why the marketing and management of services is such a crucial activity for firms. Many examples throughout the book refer to the topics discussed in this chapter.

The services sector is constantly changing and is sometimes difficult to predict. The only thing that is certain about the future is that people keep trying to predict it.[2] Although not every forecast will be realized, and not every American trend will apply to the rest of the world, the fact is that each organization that wishes to survive will have not only to understood the environment but will have to adapt to this environment.

This chapter illustrates that the dimensions of the services sector are changing and growing. Mapping sustainable societal changes or trends, such as the ones outlined in Service Practice 1.1, is an important tool for survival of service businesses. These trends indicate opportunities and threats to the sector and to services businesses.

Environmental mapping should be done periodically as trends are rapidly changing. Together with the analysis of the internal strengths or core competencies environmental mapping will form the basis of the corporate strategy of the service firm. Environmental mapping will systematically chart the external factors influencing the service business.

This chapter provides a basis for the corporate and marketing strategy of a service provider. By doing so, we utilize the environment theory which sees the company as an open system interacting with its environment and striving towards the survival of the organization.[3]

The environment theory is based on the idea of periodically scanning the external factors surrounding the organization in order to develop, adjust and implement an adequate company policy. Mapping the environment means collecting and analysing information about relevant trends in the environment of the organization.

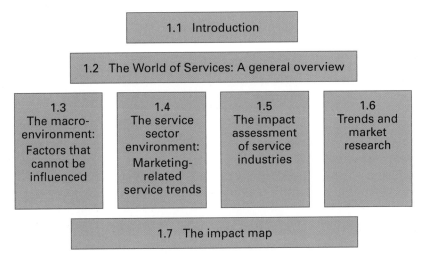

Figure 1.1   Chapter outline: the world of services

Before environmental mapping can commence the organization needs to have a general idea of the services sector within its particular country or market. The relative size of a country's services sector correlates highly with the stage of economic development. More specifically, the macro factors in any society are important when organizations seek to develop and implement marketing strategy.

At the service sector level there is a tendency to combine certain trends which relate to services and then apply these trends to entire sectors. In such situations the external analysis of the industry environment will result in an overview of developments shaping the future in various service industries. The whole scanning process of the service environment should be done from an international perspective.

In short, this chapter will chart the strategic map of a service firm's success. Figure 1.1 shows the outline of this chapter as well as indicating the various layers a service organization must consider when developing strategy.

1.2   The World of Services: A General Overview

Nowadays services are the dominant sector in many countries, especially in OECD countries. However, differences in economic development will impact on the present size of the services sector in any country (see Figure 1.2).

The Services Sector in Any Country

From an historic perspective the agricultural sector and the manufacturing sectors have declined in many countries while the services sector has grown. In the countries of the Organization for Economic Co-operation and Development (OECD), the contribution of the

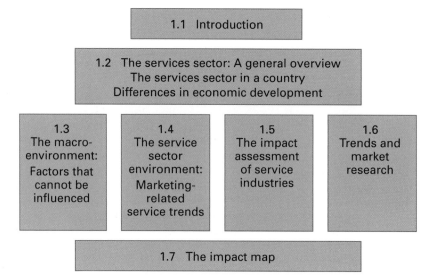

Figure 1.2   A general overview

services sector to gross value added per country in 2002 ranges from 53.4% in Korea to 79.0% in Luxembourg.[4] In terms of employment, the 2003 data reveal that on average in the OECD countries 68.6% of employment is in the services sector, ranging from 43.4% in Turkey to 78.3% in the USA.[5] In terms of its contribution to gross value added (or approximately gross domestic product measured in terms of value added), we see the services sector's share increase in most of the OECD countries (except for Ireland and Canada). More detailed information is presented in Table 1.1.

In all OECD countries (except Portugal), the percentage of people employed in the profit and public services sector has increased between 1993 and 2003; and you can see the differences in development per country all over the world – large increases for instance in Turkey, Korea, France and Luxembourg, while the figures for 2003 for Canada are largely static.

Differences in Economic Development

The data in Table 1.1 holds for all OECD countries. Most OECD countries are western, industrialized and wealthier. The services sector is small in many developing or less developed countries. In those countries even basic services remain elusive, according to a World Bank report.[6] These countries need economic growth, financial resources, reforms and innovations in the services that contribute to positive health and education outcomes. The lack of basic services, such as education, health care, water, energy and sanitation, blocks economic development and wealth creation for a large part of the population. But even if such services did exist the World Bank report concludes that these 'services are failing poor people; in access, in quantity, in quality'. For it appears that services are unequally distributed among the population. In Nepal for instance, 46% of education spending accrues to the richest fifth, only 11% to the poorest. In India the richest fifth receives three times the

Table 1.1   Figures on services worldwide

Country	Services' contribution to gross value added 1992 (in %)	Services' contribution to gross value added 2002 (in %)	Civilian employment in the services sector 1993 (in %)	Civilian employment in the services sector 2003 (in %)
Australia	68.3	71.2	71.1	74.8
Austria	63.9	65.6	57.9	64.8
Belgium	67.8	71.7	70.2	73.8
Canada	68.1	63.8[a]	74.0	74.7
Czech Republic	45.8	56.7	48.7	55.8
Denmark	69.8	71.2	68.5	72.9
Finland	64.6	64.6	64.5	68.5
France	67.5	72.1	67.8	73.0
Germany	62.0	69.2	57.6	65.6
Greece	64.0	69.5	54.5	61.1
Hungary	58.9	65.3	56.5	60.8
Iceland	59.3	61.8[b]	65.8	69.6
Ireland	55.0	54.7	59.9	65.8
Italy	64.1	69.0	58.2	62.9
Japan	59.9	68.0	59.8	66.6
Korea	47.6	53.4	52.5	63.6
Luxembourg	70.6	79.0	67.9	77.2
Mexico	65.2	69.6	51.9	58.7
Netherlands	66.5	71.6	72.2	76.6
New Zealand	65.1	67.8[c]	66.0	69.5
Norway	62.7	60.4	71.3	74.7
Poland	52.2	66.9	43.7	53.0
Portugal	63.3	67.4	55.4	54.7
Slovak Republic	57.3[d]	63.8	–	55.9
Spain	62.4	67.0	59.1	63.6
Sweden	68.4	70.0	71.0	75.2
Switzerland	–	–	67.5	72.0
Turkey	50.8	57.5	34.9	43.4
United Kingdom	66.3	72.1	68.5	75.2
United States	72.0	75.6	73.2	78.3
G7	–	–	66.7	72.8
EU-15	–	–	62.7	68.5
OECD Total	–	–	–	68.6

Source: **This table is based on data mentioned in OECD (2004), *OECD in Figures, 2004 edition, Statistics on the Member Countries,* OECD, Paris.**

Key: **a 2000; b 2001; c 1998; d 1993; – Not available**

curative health care subsidy than the poorest in the population. In Morocco, where more than 60% of the population has access to safe water, only 11% of the poorest fifth do. In some countries the absenteeism rate among service providers is quite high and even when doctors are present, poor patients may be treated badly.

Another way in which services fail the poor is through lack of demand. Poor people often do not send their children to school or take them to a medical clinic because they have to work, it is too costly and even subsidies to travel are spent on other, more needed products. Even where the services are free, many poor people cannot afford the time it takes to travel. In Cameroon for example it is on average 8 kilometres to the nearest primary school or 23 kilometres to the nearest medical facility. The World Bank study also indicates that education or health facilities are located physically closer to wealthier people.[7]

1.3 The Macro Environment: Factors that Cannot be Influenced

All organizations are influenced by macro factors in their environment. Although a few large companies are sometimes able to influence a number of these factors, these forces remain constant for most companies.[8] This section deals with five uncontrollable influences in the macro environment of an organization (see Figure 1.3). These are as follows:

■ demographic (D);
■ regulatory (R);
■ economic (E);
■ technological (T); and
■ social factors (S).

An extensive overview of the relevant trends and developments can be found on the website

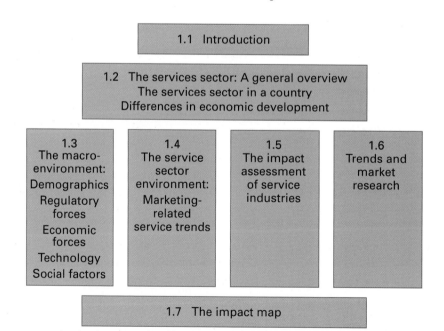

Figure 1.3 The macro environment

of our book; here we will mention them briefly. Their impact will be discussed at length in the next sections.

To simplify matters, all these factors combined will be abbreviated to DRETS. Sometimes these factors are also labelled as the PEST or STEP factors representing the political, economic, social and cultural, and technological factors. We have put the political factors among the regulatory forces and distinguish between demographic and social factors. We think that demographics can help determine a company's strategy. For example less (or more) people, means less selling (or more).

Demographic Factors (Drets)

The demographic environment of the service sector has changed considerably during the past decades. The major demographic trends are: population growth, increase in the number of households and decrease in the number of household members in most industrialized countries, greater life expectancy, dejuvenation and population ageing; better education; increase in the number of multiracial societies particularly in North America, Australia and in major parts of Europe. Depending on your business, these developments may be seen as threats or opportunities.

SERVICE PRACTICE 1.2

Ageing Chances for Service Providers[9]

The 'economics of ageing' is based on the idea that the populations in western countries are getting older. Sometimes this is called 'the double greying'. The Woodstock generation, the Baby Boomers who were born from 1946 to 1964, is going grey. The elderly are now living longer.

This sector of the population are generally thought of as spendthrifts and they aren't saving enough for their retirement. Social security payments may not be there to help out as the system buckles with too few workers supporting too many retirees. The swelling ranks of the elderly will send medical costs spiralling out of control. These days, the mantra 'we can't afford it' echoes from Senate hearings to corporate boardrooms.

But there are strong reasons that suggest that the age apocalypse will never arrive. Instead, a series of broad, mutually reinforcing changes in the economy will make ageing populations much more of an economic asset than before.

One striking transformation is how companies now use information technologies to raise productivity, which makes it easier to fund the social security and health care bills that are squeezing for example the American wallet today. People are also productive far longer in an information and services economy. Healthier lifestyles and medical advances should postpone disability among the elderly.

In the USA, until recently, a nursing home was one of the few alternatives for those who were finding it difficult to run their own household. In the past decade, however, 'assisted' living centres for those who needed some help have been gaining in popularity. At the moment, many are quite expensive, although competition should bring prices down over time.

The Heritage Club in Denver has both independent apartments and assisted living, and some of the homes also have nursing facilities. Companies like Philips Medical Systems are developing special products for people to check their own health, or special ICT-based devices to live and stay longer at home rather than being 'transferred' to a home for the old aged.

Reproduced by permission of Business Week

Regulatory Factors (dRets)

Governments both directly and indirectly have a strong influence on the commercial operations of service providers. The influence of government on services businesses may be divided into a number of separate influences. We mention the following: political and legal (both regulation and deregulation); flexibility of the labour factor; commercialization of education and health care; and self-regulation and other regulating forces.

Political and legal factors

Political and legal factors include the leanings of the government in power, for example are they conservation or liberal. Legislation, jurisprudence and decisions taken by various governmental bodies, including the North American Free Trade Association (NAFTA) and the European Union (EU) are other factors. There is a shift of regulatory power from national governmental bodies toward supra-national governmental bodies such as the EU. The European Commission plays an important role in controlling service businesses to determine whether they follow the rules, as Service Practice 1.3 reveals. It is not only market forces that guide competition.

SERVICE PRACTICE 1.3

EU Cites Telecom-Rule Offenders[10]

The European Commission warned 10 countries for failing to implement European Union telecommunication rules, another sign of its difficulties in getting its 25 members to fully open up their markets.

The commission said Germany, Italy, Latvia, Malta, the Netherlands, Austria, Poland, Portugal, Slovakia and Finland had received the first of two warnings needed before taking action at the European Court of Justice. The 10 countries have been identified as having given insufficient powers to their national telecom regulator or failed to impose certain requirements, such as allowing consumers to switch operators and keep their phone numbers. Such number portability remains unavailable in Latvia, Malta and Poland.

Under German law, the telecom regulator is required to impose the same requirements for prices and interconnection on small municipal telecom companies in cities such as Cologne as on incumbent national giant Deutsche Telekom AG. The EU wants the regulator to be allowed to take into account differences in structure and size.

The ten offenders now have the opportunity to address the commission's concerns and avoid a court case, said Martin Selmayr, a commission spokesman. The commission has launched legal action against seven other EU nations on similar issues. Four of these – against Belgium, Luxembourg, Greece and France – are now before the European Court of Justice.

Economic Factors (drEts)

Economic forces have an important influence on company policies. This third category of macro factors encompasses among other things: the development of the Gross National Product (GNP) and the changes in consumer's income; changing expenditure patterns; the country's stage of economic development and the value of the national currency.

In many industrialized countries, the 'Baby Boom' generation (the people born between 1946 and 1964) is increasingly being forced to save for their pensions. No doubt, this change in expenditure will influence service sectors such as health care, the tourist industry and financial services such as mutual funds and other investment vehicles. In the short term, this has a negative impact on the turnover of many other goods and services. In the longer term, with an anticipated shortage of young labour, the prices of the services that retirees want, notably in health care and leisure, will experience material inflation. The scarcity of labour will be reflected in higher wages, which will be needed to attract workers to the professions that serve the expanding population of retirees. Thus, the outcome could be a surge in real wages in the service sector and a continuing surge in medical costs.[11] In Service Practice 1.4 we see however that not all Baby Boomers are the same.

SERVICE PRACTICE 1.4

Not All Baby Boomers Are the Same[12]

The majority of US Baby Boomers are optimistic, active and participate in a wide range of activities. This is what comes up from a recent US study by the Chicago-based C&R Research Inc. However, within this group different segments can be found, implying different responses in terms of products and services from marketers. The segments are:

☐ 'Looking for balance' Boomers – about 27% of the Boomers fall into this very active and busy segment. They long for time-saving products and services. They desire experiences, for instance in the travel and food-related businesses;

☐ 'Confident and living well' Boomers – about 23% of all Boomers fall into this segment with the highest income of all four segments. They relish the chance to be the first to purchase a new product or service. They are technology oriented and care about what is stylish and trendy. Travelling and luxury goods and services are important to this group of 'innovators and early adopters';

☐ 'At ease' Boomers represent 31% of all Boomers. They are at peace with themselves and do not worry about the future, job security or financial security. They express the lowest interest in luxury and do not travel that much. These traditional Boomers are the most home-centric and family oriented of all Boomer segments;

☐ 'Overwhelmed' Boomers are the smallest Boomer segment (19%). They have the lowest income of all Boomer segments, worry about the future and financial security. They are the least active of all, but health is a big concern for them. They have the least social contacts and the lowest acceptance of new technologies of all Boomer segments.

Technological Factors (dreTs)

In the last few decades, the western world has been flooded with all sorts of technological developments which have had a strong influence on the services environment. The last century has seen an acceleration of technological developments with products like the PC, telefax. The services they provide were still unknown in the 1960s, not to mention electronic mail (e-mail) and the Internet which only developed during the 1990s.

Children in today's industrialized world cannot imagine that their parents lived in a world in the beginning of the 1990s, without a PC at home and the access to e-mail, chat rooms and the Internet that the home PC provides.

In the 1980s at the dawn of the fax age (a tremendous invention at that time) facsimile machines were the size of washing machines. The fax was such new and unfamiliar technology that one senior editor said, in all seriousness: 'This is confidential. Fax it in an envelope.' Now it would be an encrypted attachment. Technologies are rapidly enfolding and the adoption process of consumers and businesses alike is much faster than in the past.

Here, we can distinguish between technological developments and the emergence of ICT, the integration of information technology and telecommunications. Nowadays, ICT plays a crucial role in supporting relationships between customers and suppliers in many service industries. Many professional services are ICT-based.

A major technological breakthrough such as the development of the chip allows for the rapid manufacturing of numerous new goods which, in turn, form the basis for developing new services. To illustrate:

- Mobile phones simplify the accessibility of professional service providers who are en route most of the time;
- (Wireless) modems make it possible for insurance agents to advise their clients or submit a quotation on the spot. While travelling, consultants or managers of large companies can remain informed on the latest company news through e-mail;
- Help desks and self- service desks have been introduced due to ICT developments. Many machines can service themselves by automatic links to these help desks, implying that service engineers do not have to come anymore to solve problems;
- The Internet has created a total new way of distribution and communication, addressing world audiences with the push of a button. In many industrialized countries now more than half of the number of households is connected to the Internet facilitating information search, compare product offerings, e-dating, e-(re)tailing and e-ticketing. The growth of the Internet is expected to continue especially in newly industrialized countries;
- The impact of e-business and m-business is rising.

Service Practice 1.5 reveals more of the impact ICT had on society. Through ICT (but also due to other factors) many service industries converge as the examples given above and in Service Practice 1.5 illustrate.

SERVICE PRACTICE 1.5

Information Technology Impacts on Business and Society[13]

An exciting future is waiting for us. Technological trends within IT that may impact our life according to Bergner *et al.* (2002) are:

☐ *Faster, more powerful and cheaper*: Extrapolating trends reveal hardware, networks and software will become faster, more powerful and cheaper in the next couple of years;

☐ *Smaller and more mobile*: In exploring the planets, for instance, all systems used by humankind have become smaller and more mobile, especially computer-based systems. Mobile phones, Internet connected PC wireless laptops and Apple's IPod represent consumer examples. This trend is mostly demand-driven;

☐ *Higher degree of interoperability, integration and standardization*: Standards help companies to preserve investments and enhance quality. Increasingly, business processes are supported by software solutions and more and more departments of the companies are supported by computers. More universal, programmable and embedded systems are being used in diverse service industries as insurance, health care and car maintenance;

☐ *More intelligent and applicable*: Due to immense processing power, modern systems are able to include a much larger variety and amount of information and thus to demonstrate increasing levels of 'intelligence'. Consequently, the necessity for sophisticated human/computer interfaces arises (which, again, is a demand-driven trend).

But how will this all affect (un)employment, the dependence on technology, individualization and communication?

The foregoing leads us to social factors, the last set of macro forces to be mapped.

Social Factors (dretS)

The final DRETS factor concerns the social and cultural environment that encompasses the prevailing values, traditions and trends in society. Typically, these tendencies are influenced by the four external environment factors mentioned earlier (demographics, regulation, economics and technology). That is why we will elaborate on them a little more than on the other four factors.

The following social tendencies have also contributed to the growing demand for services: individualism and rising customer expectations, sensationalism, women working outside the home, a shorter working week, the complexity of society, care for health, concern about environmental issues, and the trend towards more convenience.

Individualism is the luxury of rich societies.[14] In poorer societies the power of tradition and survival is so great, that the individual gets no chance whatsoever to become fully self-reliant. The need of the group(s) to which the person belongs usually prevails.[15] In many developing countries people are losing their economic and social roots. In the suburbs of the big cities the individualistic trend has brought the concept of 'survival of the fittest' instead of the more social family and traditional ties of the past.

Individualism is fuelled by:

- the demographic force of growing number of smaller families and elderly people;
- the growing number of singles in the cities (either for a short time or as a pause in-between living together) postponing marriage or as a result of a divorce, single mothers and fathers.[16]

The cost of individualism, is rather high to a society. Driving with fewer passengers, the increasing demand for housing, and single package designs are only a few of the effects. This trend, however, does not mean that everybody wants to act on their own. On the contrary, it seems that more and more sub-groups exist in today's society, each having their own behaviour, norms, values, opinions and brands.

Sensationalism refers to the growing need of consumers to experience the unexpected. Films and TV programmes are becoming more explicit and in some cases increasingly more violent. Programmes such as *Big Brother* have been very successful for their producers, attracting large audiences. Reality TV programmes such as *Fantasy Island* and *Pop Idol* are attracting large markets around the world. The combination of reality TV, targeted commercials, paying audiences and SMS paid voting has proved to be a lucrative business format for the television networks.

Extreme sports such as bungee jumping are becoming more popular and consumers are searching for 'off the beaten track' travel destinations to quench their thirst for new and exciting experiences. However paradoxical it seems there is also an increasing demand for adventure and security, with a rise in popularity of organized adventure package tours, for those who yearn for safer versions of excitement.

The degree of female labour force participation varies in each country. Female labour force participation was for a long time very much higher in Eastern Europe and Sweden than in other countries; however women working outside the home has now become common around the globe.[17] Services responding to these developments have tended to concentrate on activities that the woman working outside the home, or her partner, no longer can or wishes to do:

- Food preparation, specifically buying prepared meals or having the food delivered to the home;
- Day care for children and elderly parents;
- Delivery for items ordered by phone or the Internet;
- Domiciliary services such as house cleaning, dry cleaning and ironing.

Most Europeans are working less and less. In Europe, the tendency to shorten working hours, at least for a period, seems to be coming to an end. People nowadays have much more leisure time than 30 years ago, leisure time that is filled with new activities. Services which appear specifically to profit from this are:

- Tourism; which includes hotel stays and travel, as well as amusement fairs and theme parks;

- Education including self-improvement classes, evening-classes and adult education classes;
- Toys and sports equipment.

Society is becoming more complex. Structures that used to be transparent are disappearing and new forms of cohabitation are emerging. Unwed mothers are living besides earning couples who have living-apart-together relationships, and someone benefiting from a job release scheme plays cards with a father who is on parenthood leave.

The simplicity of times past, when in every village one could ask for advice from the vicar, the JP or the headteacher, has had to make room for a broad range of organizations delivering these services more or less professionally. Nowadays, people address themselves to marriage counsellors, psychoanalysts, tax consultants or insurance agents. Finding a date via the Internet is growing as an alternative to meeting people in the pub.

The interest in our health has also led to an explosive growth in those services. The emphasis on leading a healthy life has stimulated industries in the fields of health food, fitness and recreation. From an organizational perspective this trend has evolved into fitness centres, squash courts, weight loss centres (Weight Watchers, Slender You, Manhattan), aerobics and body-shaping schools. Tomorrow's food will not only be healthier but also spicier and more flavourful than today's.[18] Here, the demographic composition is the key factor. In western countries, over the next 25 years, Baby Boomer's taste buds will be dulling and most populations will be more ethnically diverse.

Consumers want more convenience and comfort. They want to both order and consume their services at home. A number of services that have been able to capture this trend are still in their infancy but will become more important as the 21st century proceeds. These are services such as Internet banking, tele-shopping, e-retailing, e-commerce, e-dating, or studies by way of the Internet.

Time usage and energy expenditure (efforts) are central to the convenience concept. Both have an opportunity cost, in monetary and non-monetary terms. The consumer or firm (in the B2B market) have choices as to how their time is spent. For example a customer could choose to visit service provider's premises or to have the service provider visit them. Time usage can be viewed as either an investment or a cost.

SERVICE PRACTICE 1.6

Different Kinds of Convenience Wanted

Customers value both access convenience and transaction convenience argue Berry, Seiders and Grewal.[19] Access is important because so many services require the consumer's participation. They state that firms can improve access convenience by:

- ☐ Offering consumers multiple ways to initiate service, including the use of self-service technologies;
- ☐ Separating required front front-end administrative tasks in time and place from the benefit-producing part of a service, such as allowing consumers to reserve a rental car online;
- ☐ Bringing the service to the consumer rather than bringing the consumer to the service;
- ☐ Reducing consumers' time and effort in moving the core service (such as buying a home) to functionally related services (such as mortgage financing and homeowners' insurance).

Transaction convenience according to these authors is important because waiting is especially unrewarding to consumers. Consumers will judge time usage as a cost over investment.

This section dealt with most of the macro environment factors and the embedded trends on a stand-alone, one-dimensional basis. From a marketing perspective, the growing number of healthier seniors living longer will drive the customization trend. This is just one example of how trends come together.[20]

1.4 The Service Sector Environment: Marketing-Related Service Trends

The early 1990s was a period during which large companies like IBM and American Airlines were struggling to survive. Enormous cost-cutting programmes were swiftly executed by companies worldwide. Not for profit companies too were unable to avoid this development. Massive amounts of dismissal notices were the order of the day. 'Back to the core business' was a slogan one often heard.

The government had related questions. What are the core tasks of a government? How can government bodies operate more efficiently? How may they become (more) market oriented and deliver better quality? All types of service organizations had to react to the growing complexity surrounding them.

Inspired by Lovelock's dynamics of change, many factors underlie the ongoing transformation of service management that is taking place in a highly developed economy.[21] Ten years later the trend is again fully visible. The focus on core business parallels with outsourcing and offshoring. The phenomenon of offshoring – exporting jobs, often service jobs – tops the political agenda. This section examines the trends resulting from the interplay of macro environmental factors in the world, which are especially pertinent to strategy and, within the strategic arena, especially relevant to services marketing strategy.

These trends in the environment apply to the service sector as a whole. As a consequence they have practical use for individual companies establishing their marketing policy or as input while developing new services. As we will see later in this chapter, the impact of each macro and service sector marketing-related trend is different for each company (see Figure 1.4). The services trends are accommodated in the following six groups and considered as marketing-related trends which pertain to services:

■ Internationalization;
■ The rise of commercial principles such as gaining self-sufficiency, privatization and unbundling of services;
■ The implications of focussing on core business and down-sizing, outsourcing, offshoring, and specialization;
■ Up-scaling in core activities including mergers, acquisitions, co-operation and franchising;

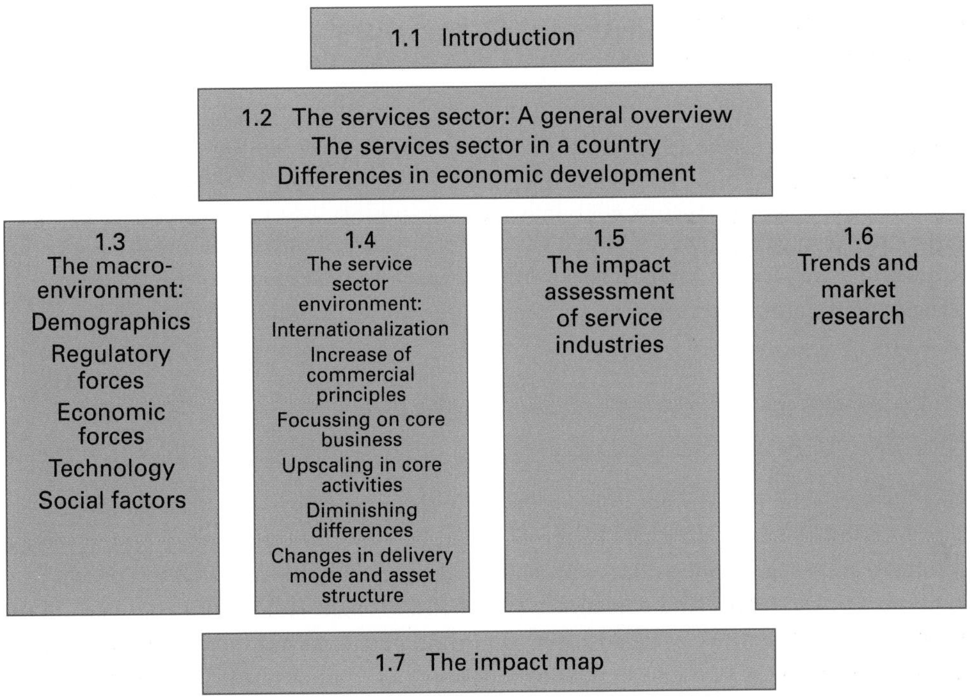

Figure 1.4   The service sector: marketing-related trends

■ Diminishing differences between services and goods as well as between ownership and non ownership;

■ Changes in asset structure and delivery mode including delivery via technology, (dis)intermediation and self-service.

Internationalization

The internationalization of services has risen steeply. The same hotel chains, fast-food restaurants, airlines, rental companies, auditing firms, advertising agencies and financial services can now be found all over the world. This trend is reinforced by both the media and ICT.

All over the world more than four billion people watch American films and television programmes or listen to English-language music. Every local culture, wherever it may be, is being Americanized as a result. The other side of the coin is that local societies and cultures may lose their identity. This internationalization is not only fuelled by media and changes in technology. Deregulation, competition, financial markets and many other globalization drives have a major impact on the internationalization of services. As we believe that the internationalization trend and its underlying factors influence many service industries, we shall analyse this trend in detail in Chapter 7.

The Increase of Commercial Principles

Applying commercial principles in both profit and not for profit service industries is on the increase. This trend is visible throughout the world. Accountable management and focussed goals are key issues. In the private sector offering profit services, this trend is identified through a strong focus on creating shareholder value and business units gaining more self-sufficiency or independence within a central framework of objectives and strategies. More client decisions are made at lower levels in the organization and closer to the market. Privatization and unbundling services for competition are expressions of this trend in the public sector.

Shareholder Value and Sustainability

In many instances the focus is not only on the strategy or actions of the firm, but on the short-term results obtained. In financial terms, it can be viewed as the impact on the value of the company to its shareholders. Recently, managing for (shareholder) value has drawn a lot of attention. 'Cooked books' and sometimes even fraud brought large companies both in the USA and Europe to the brink of bankruptcy or beyond. It should not be forgotten that satisfied customers (based on excellent service quality) are a prerequisite to achieving profits and, hence, shareholder value. The one-dimensional view toward shareholder value and the outcry of society against the rewards of top management solely bound with shareholder value have brought attention to the notion of sustainability. With sustainability, we refer here to sustainability of profits (in contrast to focussing on short-term profits and windfalls), adequate corporate governance and to the sustainability of resources.

Gaining Self-Sufficiency

Business units that gain self-sufficiency by becoming autonomous units have led to the tendency towards independence and autonomy. A fruitful basis for gaining self-sufficiency seems to be at hand everywhere. On a worldwide scale, large companies and governments are trying to streamline their activities. First of all, firms try to become more efficient by focussing on their core business, downsizing or 'mean and lean' production. Two developments that go further in this respect are privatization in the case of a state company and unbundling of (public) services.

Privatization

Across the world governments have loosened their grip. Bureaucrats still run important segments of economies, particularly in developing countries. In these countries, large state-owned sectors can be significant impediments to growth. The word 'privatization' was first used in Britain to denote a policy in which nationalized companies were sold off to private ownership. Applying the theme of commercializing government services, a less far-reaching option of service delivery in the public sector has emerged. An Australian study covering four case studies, found that aspects of 'in-house' commercialization, government bodies and departments operating semi-independently with their own profit/loss account may present a compelling alternative to adopting the more dramatic approach of privatization or large-scale contracting out of government services.[22]

Unbundling Services for Competition

Like privatization, unbundling services fits within the rapidly changing regulatory environment. Politics and governments think differently about public enterprises than a few decades ago. The unbundling of public services for competition attracts global service providers. Should one company provide all telephone services including local, long distance, cellular and data transmission, or should the divisions of the telecommunications business be unbundled into separate enterprises?[23] Similar questions could be raised for the most efficient way to generate, transmit and distribute power by utilities or public transport. Typically, the unbundling of public services is accompanied by arrangements between public ownership and private operation in the form of leases, concessions and short-term contracting-out services or fully fledged privatization.[24]

While it is true that much of the public sector is experimenting with unbundling, other industries in particular, once competition has been established, are returning to the idea of bundling services. A good example is telephone operators offering all telecommunication both voice and data (fixed line, mobile, including Internet access) services through one supplier.

Focussing on Core Business

Focussing on the core business is a trend that also can be observed in the service sector. It implies typically downsizing. Later on it appears that enterprises scale up their (newly defined) core activities. Important ways to pursue downsizing or downscaling are: spinning off units which senior management view as not belonging to the core activities, specialization and outsourcing. During the last two decades the trend to focussing on core business has led in many industries to spin-offs or outsourcing of such diverse activities as cleaning, security and information technology. This development creates tremendous opportunities for service companies operating in these industry sectors.

Even within the service sector, organizations such as banks and hospitals have followed the trend of outsourcing their non core activities. Offshoring is the export of white-collar jobs offshore. It is not just routine, repetitive jobs that are exported. Initially call centre jobs moved from the West to India. But increasingly, higher level professional services, including computer software development, architectural drawing, accountancy and financial analysis, have moved to India, Eastern Europe and countries such as the Philippines and Vietnam where labour costs are much lower.

Outsourcing and Offshoring

The trend toward the contracting out of non core activities has been facilitated by laws governing dismissal. In continental Europe and Australia, it is not easy for employers to dismiss permanent staff and to rehire them when things are going better. Although in some countries (as a consequence of the globalization trend) changes in labour laws are under way, these options are available right now by contracting-out activities.

For many large companies the solution to these labour law constraints may well be found in *downsizing*. The trend towards contracting-out seems to run parallel with this development of downsizing and *specialization*, that is focussing on the core competencies of the firm and/or services with the greatest market potential.

Commodity services such as security, cleaning, gardening and catering are commonly contracted out to specialized firms. During the 1980s, more complex speciality services such as corporate information systems also started to become outsourced. Companies such as Eastman Kodak announced outsourcing contracts with IBM, Business land and DEC. In 2003, ABN AMRO Bank decided to outsource its global wholesale banking IT to EDS in the USA. Other companies who have outsourced include American Airlines who outsourced their catering.

One particular form of outsourcing leads to shared service centres (SSCs). SSCs can be defined as separate entities that are accountable for a particular result while delivering services to operational entities like business units of one or more organizations on the basis of well defined service level agreements (SLAs). A service level agreement is a contract between the client and the supplier of a service. This contract usually includes the following: intention statement; description of the service; the approval process for meetings regarding the contract; description of conditions; performance criteria (including acceptable and not acceptable service levels); identification of the users of the service; and responsibilities of client and supplier and actions that need to be undertaken under specific circumstances (e.g. if required service levels are not achieved).[25] More and more types of services can be covered in a SLA and/or executed by a SSC. These services can be things like finance and administration/bookkeeping, management control, juridical and fiscal matters, human resource management, sales and marketing, purchasing/procurement, ICT, assembly, logistics, facility management, and even R&D. SSCs are regarded as a way to reduce the high costs of decentralized business, create synergies, increase professionalism and quality in supporting processes, increase productivity, enhance control of outsourcing, create strategic flexibility and increase knowledge sharing throughout the organization. It is also in line with the present need for a greater accountability of managers and employees.[26]

Offshoring or the export of white-collar service jobs abroad is more than labour arbitrage. It reflects education levels as well as lower wages in some developing countries. India, China, Malaysia and the Czech Republic are the top four countries in management consultant A.T. Kearney's global ranking of outsource destinations. But Singapore, Canada and New Zealand are among the top 12 because they offer highly educated workforces with excellent infrastructure and low-risk business environments.[27] A recent publication of a PA consulting group showed that 66% of the businesses felt the benefits they expected from their outsourcing contracts had been either only partially realized or not realized at all. While using offshore jobs, service firms, such as telecoms, IT firms, banks and insurance companies may start their own subsidiary, outsource the tasks via an outside firm which operates abroad or set up a joint venture with another company.

There are two trends at work. One is companies setting up new facilities of their own in countries such as India, or companies passing activities onto third parties. The joint venture is in fact a combination of the two. While the first – managing your own workers at a distance –

is demanding, the second, which is ensuring that someone else's employees are working effectively, is far more difficult.

Trends and counter trends do exist, for outsourcing is emerging in some countries but not in others, as Service Practice 1.6 illustrates.

SERVICE PRACTICE 1.7

Trends in outsourcing[28]

Call centres and other business support services are expanding in many corners of the globe from Manila to Estonia as companies weigh the availability of skills and workers.

Before the Internet arrived, the southern Philippine town of Davao was the kind of place where gun-toting vigilantes hunted down communist guerrillas in the streets, says James Hookway in the *Wall Street Journal Europe*. Like much of the Philippines, Davao is steeped in Americana. The city's linkage to US pop culture seems to help make many Filipinos adept at outsourcing work. Beside, these people understand American and American English. In situations where their language skills are inadequate US firms like 3G Communications Inc. are more than happy to start education projects in conjunction with local authorities to improve these skills.

Nearshoring is similar to offshoring. However in nearshoring the call centre is located closer to the targeted customers of the businesses. Nearshoring may well be an alternative to offshoring.

Swedish-based Transcom Worldwide SA decided that Eastern Europe could emulate India as a base for establishing call centres. Mr Keith Russell, Transcom's CEO, says 'The idea is to market a combination of India-like cheap labour with strong skills in English and other European languages and a sensitivity to western culture. Many European companies don't feel comfortable doing business with someone as distant geographically and culturally as India.'

Up-scaling in Core Activities

In a number of sectors, especially once an organization has a clear view of its core business, we see scaling up. This is often seen in combination with a concentration of the sector and internationalization. Examples of the clustering in sectors are insurance, banking and professional services such as accountants, consultants, lawyers and public notaries. A larger number of operations can be reached in various ways, as we will see in Chapter 7. Up-scaling in the service industry is typically concentrated on or around the core activities of companies.

Co-operation

In the past decade, the trend toward co-operation between companies has undeniably increased. Whereas McKinsey & Company is seeking expansion by establishing their own offices (and promoting their mutual co-operation), other local management consulting groups are tapping into their membership network of independent bureaus abroad to carry out international assignments.

Every month we read about new strategic alliances between parties nobody ever expected to co-operate. Recent examples of partnering between very different companies can be found everywhere. Philips has developed jointly with the coffee brand DE (Douwe Egberts, part of

Sara Lee, the America-based company) a new coffee machine using the DE coffee pads. Other partnering includes Heineken and Krupps (home beer tap), Philips and Robijn who developed plastic patches filled with fluid to help with ironing.

This co-operation reminds us of the early days of photocopiers, where sale of special copy paper by the provider maintained the long-term profitability of the photocopier manufacturer.

Strategic partnering and strategic (commercial) alliances are common in the airline and telecom industries.[29] Flight code sharing among airlines is an attractive option to optimize yields. At present, the cost of coordination and co-operation seem to be less than the 'cost of competition'. Co-operation can be actively sought by parties or more or less compelled by circumstances such as the high cost of R&D or government regulation. Whenever there is a public EU tender, Brussels encourages companies from different countries to form a consortium. Co-operation and competition are no longer at odds with each other.

Franchising

A franchise chain attempts to present itself to the consumer as a cohesive unit by providing a consistent level of service through all outlets. According to Lovelock (1991), the major growth is in the franchising of so-called 'business formats', in which almost every aspect of the business is specified by the franchising organization; from the shop's design up to and including the training of its employees. A general prerequisite to a proper functioning of a franchise organization is that both parties are willing to co-operate and trust each other. Opportunistic behaviour will be detrimental here.[30]

Most franchising chains operate in the B2C market. Fast-food restaurants, hairdressers, DIY stores and photocopy centres are well-known examples. Other service providers which do not necessarily operate from a shop or outlet include the pest control company, Rentokil, and the drain-cleaning company in the UK, Dyno-rod, use unified vans and uniforms in house colours to demonstrate consistency. Franchising is more than an alternative in the service sector, as Chapter 11 on distribution will show.

Diminishing Differences

Existing boundaries between services and goods as well as between ownership on the one side and rental, leasing or collective property are diminishing. Is a computer company a supplier of goods or services? How important is ownership? Can we enjoy the total usage of a good without owning it?

Diminishing Borders between Services and Goods

Service profit centres within industrial enterprises are changing the image of world famous companies. Additional services, once designed to support the sale of physical goods – such as consultancy, credit, transportation and delivery, installation, training, maintenance and repair – are now offered by manufacturers as independent profit-generating services.[31] These services are often sold to clients who opted for rival services. IBM, once well known for its mainframe computer, is now mainly a service provider. This notion of diminishing boundaries between goods and services can be referred to as 'bundling'. Bundling is concerned with the aggregation of physical goods or core services with other supporting services; the success of bundling has contributed to the diminishing of borders between service and goods.

Growth in Leasing, Rentals and Collective Property

Leasing and rentals represent a marriage between the service sector and the manufacturing sector.[32] An increasing percentage of business and individual consumers think that they can enjoy a physical product without necessarily being the owner. From a sociological perspective friends and neighbours will generally not notice that you are not the owner of, say, your new car, and as such ownership is no longer considered to be as important as it once was. Ownership does not necessarily enhance someone's satisfaction with a product.

The increased demand for commercial leasing is tax-driven; because leasing costs are deductible while investments can only be depreciated. Alongside the tax benefits there is an argument that management can focus on their core business instead of on their equipment or cars and that it is sometimes easier to lease rather than to borrow or to attract capital. Commercial leasing is also considered to be convenient for employees and management as only a little of management time needs to be devoted to this type of non core activity.

On the supply side, leasing is attractive to many banks and other finance companies as they can generate higher margins on this type of business. Besides a nice return on investment this type of financing offers producers of capital goods a route to enhance their market share. In some emerging countries, leasing may even be an important medium-term financing, as an alternative to buying or renting.

Leasing companies have apparently increased their ownership shares in North American and Western Europe's fleets of vehicles and copying machines, formerly owned by the companies. Nowadays even kitchens and gardens can be leased. Tools, audio and video equipment rentals are available. Crockery and even toilets can be rented for special events. The rental section in the *Yellow Pages* provides an impressive array of things that people can rent.

Changes in Delivery Mode and Asset Structure

Technology is dramatically changing the way services are purchased, processed and delivered. The Internet and (mobile) telephones are important alternatives to physical contact. Call centres have standardized the way products are serviced. Technology, customer demand and high personnel costs are main drivers to increasing the service participation of the client (self-service). This has left opportunities for personalized services for customers who can afford it.

Changes in Delivery Mode

Technology has changed the distribution of many services. Delivery via technology is the game of the day. The personal touch is replaced by the technological touch (partly). In some services it is the add-on services which are being delivered by technology, in other cases the complete core service is available via a technological interface. Examples of service add-ons are information on your account balance via the telephone or the Internet, information by telephone about the number of collected air miles or after sales service for software or hardware problems. By spinning off services some companies have even repositioned after sales services as their core business. Core services such as payment transactions, insurance, investment funds, travel, books and other shopping can now be performed via the Internet. The use of 'computerized services' is partly determined by consumers' willingness, capability and motivation to use these services.[33]

The advantages of technology to both the service provider and client are generally obvious. For the service provider these advantages include: cost savings; speeding up responsiveness; standardization of processes and delivery (however, the service itself can be still be customized); and access to a larger market. Travel agencies and consumer banks have all enjoyed these advantages. For consumers the advantages are: convenience of the Internet; and a reduction in the consumer efforts and costs (e.g. travelling to the service provider, searching through all brochures, choosing their own time). Easy access to a number of alternative service offerings is another advantage for the consumer or business searching the Internet.

Despite these advantages the increase in technology has also spawned an increase in competition by providing an increasing reach of competitors and more information about prices to the customer. Presence on the Web is almost a precondition of business for many services. Alongside this increase in competition is the growing number of viruses and spam which are still a threat to the Internet.

Many large service businesses will maintain a number of distribution channels for their service delivery. Each of these channels will exist side by side, in some cases each targeting a different market. An insurance company might sell through direct mail, bank branches and independent agents.

Self-Service

During the past 20 years numerous services have increased the level of client participation in manufacture and delivery of the service. Advances in technology have facilitated this increase in client participation. Other drivers of this trend include pricing (at the demand side), lower costs (at the supplier side), social acceptance and convenience. Sometimes self-services will even give the impression of a higher service level; as in the case of a breakfast buffet in a hotel where the guests may choose from a selection of foods in their own time. The cash dispenser, direct insurance, electronic banking, home-schooling (a legal right in the USA), as well as having consumers collect their own trays in the school or company restaurant are all forms of self-service as is photocopying one's own documents. The youth hostel concept was initially based on this principle of doing things yourselves. Technological intermediation and self-service will fundamentally reconfigure the service encounter and thus alter the customer–supplier relationship.[34]

Changing Asset Structures

Service providers such as banks no longer need to own the branches through which they serve their clients. Hospital managers are also asking themselves whether they need to own a hospital, and whether or not owning a hospital building actually results in the provision of excellent patient care. In many cases a specialized company owns the real estate and another provides the building maintenance and the third is the client organization. This structure is very common within the hotel sector with management companies stepping in to operate the hotel, the buildings of which are owned by companies such as banks or developers.

As in other industries not only are asset structures changing, but also assets are being substituted by information. The increasing technology component in many service industries has changed the asset structure. Consumer services based on franchising concepts such as key-cutting or shoe repairs will require investment in equipment, furbishment, a cash register and a PC; the service will also expend fixed costs such as rent, bookkeeping and wages.

As noted these trends, combined with the macro factors discussed in section 1.3, account for the growth (or sometimes the decline) of the service sector. Organizations that regularly assess their environment appear to be more successful within their sector more often as they will be more aware of any changes in their environment and as such upgrade their strategic planning and decision making more expediently. They are also likely to operate more effectively in relation to government matters and upgrade their sector and market analysis accordingly.

1.5 The Impact Assessment of Service Industries

Service industries and as a consequence individual services businesses are influenced by events that have taken place across the globe (see Figure 1.5). Just consider for one moment how the tourism sector and individual airline businesses operating in that sector worldwide faired following 9/11. The aim of this section is to give the reader a systematic approach to assess the environment of the services sector, the industries within the services sector, and the services businesses that operate within the industry. These results will then be captured in an impact map. The overview is aimed at giving the reader a global impression (and no more than that) of how some of the largest and most interesting service industries are converging worldwide.[35]

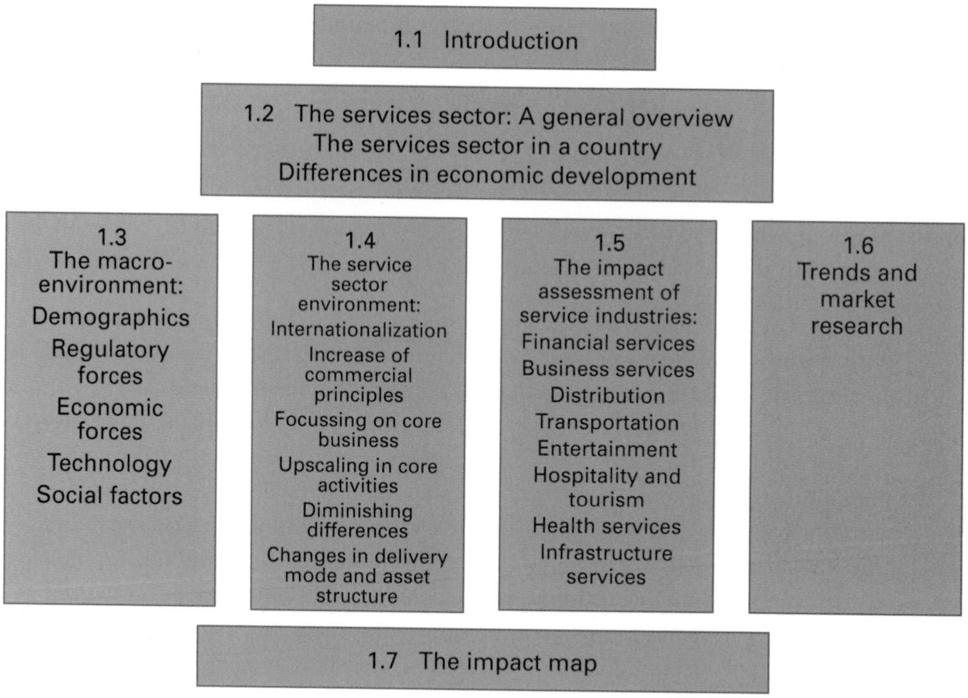

Figure 1.5   The impact assessment of service industries

Financial Services

On the surface the financial sector seems to be in turmoil. This sector, worldwide, is experiencing saturated markets, rapidly changing technologies, globalization, deregulation and increased competition. However the sector is still seen as an important sector. In 1996 financial services were 13% of the US economy and contributed nearly half of US pure-service revenue.[36] Only the most dominating trends in retail banking, corporate banking, insurance and securities will be reviewed.

Retail Banking

During recent years, a dramatic shift in retail banking has taken place in the USA, Western Europe and some countries in Asia. Whereas in the past retail banking was virtually impossible without having a local personal presence, other options are now becoming available. These options offer a more cost-effective alternative for banks servicing the retail market internationally. As retail banking is a mature market in most countries, consumers have more information about the characteristics and prices of financial services. Because these services are very much alike, the focus of retail banks is now on reducing costs in combination with a higher degree of automation. 'Bricks and mortar' branches have become an expensive way of expanding. Traditional discussions in banks about issues such as security, labour costs, rental costs and expensive management time are gradually taken over by discussions about issues like 'which technology is most user friendly' and 'until what hours telephone-banking employees have to work at night (in shifts) and at weekends to back up the computer (voice)'. Sophisticated bank-o-mats from which customers can deposit funds, transfer funds and withdraw funds are becoming more widely available. Point-of-sale terminals and retailers which allow customers to pay with their local bank cards or credit cards instead of cash are now popular. The growth of direct service provision, either as add-ons to existing accounts or as stand-alone operations, is visible around the globe. Telephone banking, call centres, Internet applications and other devices of electronic banking are now common in this sector. The Internet is seen as an alternative mechanism, for paying bills, trading securities, balance checking and for gathering information about financial services. Currently, e-banking and in particular Internet banking is found everywhere, while all finance houses have websites.

The availability of software packages for direct banking and other types of electronic banking allows banks and non bank competitors – such as retailers, software houses, credit card organizations, insurance companies and even car manufacturers or companies such as GE-Capital – to avoid the route of expensive expansion via branches. In other words, established banks have become more vulnerable to leaner and more innovative competitors or well-known players from other industries (brand and assortment extension). Niche players try to conquer profitable slices of markets when they feel they have competitive advantages over the more traditional retail banks. By offering their services via different distribution channels, established banks must work harder to protect their core business.

The outsourcing or contracting-out of non core bank services including security, catering, transport and other facilities is, next to technology and distribution changes, the third major trend in retail banking. In recent years, discussions have started as to whether information systems, or parts of them belonging to the core strategic strengths of banks, could be contracted out.

A fourth trend is deregulation. In the past 20 years many countries including Australia and New Zealand have deregulated their financial services markets. Prior to deregulation there were four banks operating in the Australian market; currently in excess of 100 foreign banks operate in Australia.

As a fifth trend, we note the privatization of state banks. This is occurring in Asia, South America and Central and Eastern European countries.

Globalization, although not so visible in corporate banking, is the final trend that we will talk about in retail (consumer and SME) banking. American Express, HSBC-group and Citigroup are all examples of financial services providers who have successfully globalized. Mature markets, technological developments and deregulation in many countries have led to increased competition; consequently banks operating in mass markets will have to concentrate on cost savings in order to stay competitive. These and other factors have resulted in an increasing number of acquisitions and mergers throughout the sector. This has resulted in redundancies in the banking industry.

In terms of employment the retail banking sector is shrinking. Staff reductions in retail banks are significant.[37] Outsourcing and off shoring underpin this development. Much of the impetus for takeovers stems from first a fear factor; that is, individual players are frightened of being left behind or unwanted or being taken over; second from ambition where size and capital are the dominant forces; or third from the genuine desire to increase shareholder value, assuming that economies of scale and synergies exist in both revenues and costs.

In many countries such mergers and acquisitions have led to oligopolistic market structures. Fair competition issues such as supervision on pricing and limits to consolidation are now important issues in many countries.

Corporate Banking

Whereas the advantages of globalization are less profound in retail banking, they are certainly present in corporate or wholesale banking. To be a relationship bank for a multinational, a bank should have sufficient resources to enable it to finance the company around the globe. Organizational selection criteria, used when selecting a relationship bank or so-called first tier bank, include the bank's ability to create 'added value' for the organization, access to relatively inexpensive local funding and placement power in case of securitization.

These requirements suggest that corporate banks seeking relational status with major multinational corporations require strong capitalization, good market knowledge and the ability to network with clients, other banks and financial advisers. For these reasons, (particularly in the 1990s) we saw takeovers of several specialized merchant banks in the UK by continental banks.

Technology has a major impact on the successful operation of these newly merged financial wholesale institutions. E-mail and Intranet connections between employees, sophisticated dealing rooms, video conferencing in order to coordinate strategic activities, online information from data providers such Telerate, Reuters and Bloomberg are just a few of the most obvious developments.

Relationship marketing and networking are crucial tools to survive in this highly competitive industry. As customized solutions are the key, highly qualified, well paid and strongly motivated staffs are a condition *sine qua non* for long-term success.

The Web offers both a threat and an opportunity to corporate banks and everyone involved in financial activities such as lawyers, accountants, venture capitalists and stockbrokers. For example, to small companies selling stock has always been a cumbersome undertaking. By appealing directly to investors via the Internet, firms can raise money without spending a fortune on expensive underwriters such as banks or venture capital houses. By selling shares or bonds directly to investors over the Internet the cost of raising money has been substantially lowered.[38]

Leasing is a burgeoning business. As a vehicle for financing purchases of capital equipment and other items leasing has been growing worldwide since the first independent leasing company was established in the United States in the 1950s. According to estimates of the IFC (a subsidiary of the World Bank), leasing supports global sales of vehicles, machinery and equipment. It amounts to an eighth of the world's private investment. Around the globe, including the emerging markets, leasing has now been perceived as an effective means to broaden the access to medium- and long-term financing.[39]

Securities

The securities and commodities exchange markets are adding more technology, allowing members to trade at distance even from outside the country. The implication of this is that the operations are no longer location-bound. The pressure is on commodities exchanges to operate more globally. For example, traditional trading houses are disappearing around the world. Either they have been acquired by larger banks or fund managers, or will be pushed out of business by their larger competitors. At the same time, demand forces them to change their strategy. Trading houses have to concentrate their market focus if they are small or, as part of a large entity, to integrate their activities and do more things for their customers. Partly as a reaction to this internationalization, stock and commodity exchanges have started a kind of internationalization process as well. Recently, EURONEXT, a merger between the stock exchanges of Paris, Amsterdam and Brussels was formed. Other European stock exchanges may join later or will choose another partner.

Insurance

With 'Bancassurance' or 'All-finanz', one financial institution combines banking and insurance services. The putting together of a bank and an insurance company offers potential cross-selling based on vertical integration (especially when an insurance company starts using the whole bank's network as its distribution channel). This tendency towards an integrated approach of all financial services is visible in several European countries.[40] However, not every bank or insurer sees the advantages of such an integration. For instance, banks may choose to operate as an intermediary of insurance providers rather than as a producer, and thus position themselves as independent advisors. Much depends on whether customers prefer to have all these financial services performed by one company. This makes them very dependent on one supplier.

On the distribution side, direct marketing of motor policies has become enormously popular in the USA and UK since the introduction of shopping-around for cut price deals by telephone in the mid-1980s and Internet Direct Insurance in the late 1990s. This new distribution trend in insurance will no doubt conquer new markets. The trend is fuelled by comparison sites which are able to compare terms and conditions of the various policies.

As deregulation sweeps its way through the world, internationalization is another force changing the landscape of the security sector. After the opening up of Japan's insurance sector in 1997 and the gradual opening up of the Chinese and Indian markets, foreign insurers are in overdrive now to move in to these lucrative markets. This will press existing institutions into becoming more cost-efficient. In theory, a fully deregulated Japanese financial market would lead to a 60% decline in profits.[41] Foreign competition in many countries will certainly heat up, bringing better deals to the consumers.

As a whole, the international financial markets have changed and will further change the conditions for service businesses. Easier access to information about the credit-worthiness of companies, deregulation, and internationalization of both the financial institutions and their clients in the service sector and the increasing use of technology are the main reasons.

Business Services in General

The business-to-business sector is one of the fastest-growing sectors of activity in industrialized countries.[42] In the USA, business oriented services grew more than 88% over the period 1988–2000, this resulting in a growth of almost 6.8 million people. Similar figures can be found for other industrialized countries.

Business services can be classified in sub-sectors on the basis of several criteria. One of these criteria relates to the functions performed for the customer or firm.[43] According to this classification, business services can be grouped as follows:

1   Management and administrative services, which include management consultancy, legal services, accounting and fiscal advice.
2   Production services such as architectural, engineering, operational leasing, repair and maintenance, packaging and quality control.
3   Research-related services such as contract research, and R&D.
4   Personnel-related services including vocational training, labour recruitment and the supply of temporary labour.
5   Information and communication services such as data banks, software services, technical computer services, advanced telecommunications services and express mailing.
6   Marketing services including advertising, sales promotion, market research, direct marketing, public relations, export promotion and fairs and exhibitions.
7   Operational services such as industrial cleaning, security services and linguistic services.

A recent US study on 'who sells professional services' revealed that, in 69% of the companies investigated, sales executives, who were primarily responsible for selling products, were selling these professional services. The other employees that were selling professional services were:

■   professional service consultants (40%);
■   dedicated service salespeople (31%);
■   dedicated professional services salespeople (31%);
■   practice leaders (27%).[44]

Many sales executives, particularly product salespeople, sell professional services. This often leads to a product oriented approach to selling services in which the professional services are approached from a technical point of view, not from a customer or marketing point of view. Given this organizations like the Association for Services Management International (AFSMI) still has a mission to complete, especially when it turns out that in the maintenance and repair sector (often a large part of the after sales services of manufacturers) a shift is going on from the typical 'break and fix' services to building professional services capabilities.[45] For this to occur corporate culture has to change as well.

A company sample survey on the use of externally provided business services within the European Community, covering users from all economic sectors, revealed that 40% of business services are entirely externally subcontracted.[46] External (business) services pertain to industrial and other professional buyers outside the company. Almost a third of all business services are provided exclusively in-house. In other words, these are internal services pertaining to the customers within the company. The remainder (27%) are provided as a combination of in-house and external services. The degree of externalization varies with type of business services, size and country.

The importance of business services for the economy in the USA is similar in Europe. In Asia, the growth in this sector is impressive. Different factors explain the rapid growth of business services. First of all, total demand increases quickly as the whole economy expands.

Second, as the business environment is becoming more complex, management needs specialists to cope with legislation, taxes, market research and personnel matters. The ever-increasing complexity of the legislation, production and distribution systems, and the widespread adoption of information-related functions are the main factors here.

Even without the hefty requirements of the environment, companies may also need additional temporary specialists to carry out all the business tasks as they have an insufficient workload to keep these people busy permanently. For reasons of efficiency and expertise, the opportunity to hire skilled staff temporarily or on a semi-permanent basis is welcomed. Because of the relatively low barriers to entry at the supply side, the increase in the number of business-to-business firms may be explained by young entrepreneurs, freelancers and people who have recently been laid off by their firms.

In observing the market structure of business services, one should note that a large number of small units and, at the same time, a limited number of very big, mainly international companies exist. The sectors in which a large number of firms employ more than 50 employees are engineering consultancy, accountancy, market research, testing, inspection, quality control and some operational services. Many business firms operate on a regional or national scale. Some very specialized industrial and professional service firms are international by nature as the home country offers only a limited customer base. Moreover, they have to follow their clients when they internationalize. Concentration in most worldwide business services industries is undoubtedly growing. Smaller units are linking up within the country, transnationally across Europe or Asia and even more globally as the development of legal, management, accounting and advertising services shows (also referred to as 'professional services'). This tendency is expected to continue as a 'natural' consequence of deregulation, following clients abroad, and changing information technology. It will all lead to a growing interest in mergers, acquisitions, partnerships and alternative business formats such as franchising in this dynamic sector of today's western economies.

Distribution

The distribution sector is a very large services sector in terms of both output and employment. In 1990, the distribution sector accounted for nearly 40% of employment in the EU, USA and Japan. The role and structure of the distribution sector, which includes retailing and wholesaling activities, has changed dramatically over the past 40 years.[47] And now, e-tailing is taking over part of the business of retailing. There is a diversity of retail formats ranging from speciality stores to hypermarkets, embracing supermarkets, department stores, discount stores and catalogue sales. They differ in their degree of providing services.

Local planning laws and opening hours are two important regulatory differentiators between countries. Local planning, strong relationships between manufacturers, wholesalers and distributors, strengths of established supermarket chains and local lobby groups of established retailers also explain for a large part why the hypermarket is not widespread over Europe and Asia.[48] Regarding opening hours, there has been a recent trend toward extending opening hours on week days and at the weekend in many countries where shopping has traditionally been limited to 40 hours a week or less.

The drive towards cost savings has increased the significance of logistics, including computer ordering by phone and lean production techniques that were born in the manufacturing sector, such as 'just-in-time' and 'zero-stock' in distribution. These factors have a major impact on the layout as well as on the size of retailer outlets. Supermarkets have taken business from smaller shops, selling food and non food convenience goods in most countries. For most traditional entrepreneurs the consequences were that they had to adapt by investing in larger sales units, joint procurement and selling formats, joint labelling of name and articles, or become a franchisee, specialize, sell out or disappear. The others survived as small shop owners, delivering personal service by knowing their clients by name, offering a rather broad but limited assortment against relatively high prices resulting in lower annual sales. Some of them become specialized niche players located in the proximity of the large retailers. Remarkable is the start-up of immigrant entrepreneurs in many places around the western world, often filling in the gaps traditional shop owners leave after ending their own business or the gaps not met by the large retailers. In spite of the limiting forces in some countries the trend is towards larger and more specialized stores. Recently, during the period of slow economic growth, the successful US and French hypermarket formula (Wal-Mart, Carrefour) and the German discount formula (in Europe e.g. Lidl and Aldi) has been gaining ground.

Environmental issues are becoming more important as the preference of consumers for 'natural or green' is gaining momentum. The role of the national government (and EU) in the packaging industry is further proof of increasing environmental awareness among regulators.

The fun aspect of shopping will gain importance in face-to-face retailing and as a way to spend growing leisure time. On the other hand where almost no personal contact with the service provider is needed, home shopping and virtual shopping are gaining market share. Clients, at certain times, will appreciate the convenience of not actually visiting the store. So, two seemingly opposite trends may occur at the same time.

Transportation

In the transportation industry, the two main subjects to be transported are freight and passengers. The transport options vary between road, rail, water and air. Increase in demand for transport services is, in general, strongly related to overall economic development around the world and the individual countries where companies are located.[49] Outsourcing, off shoring and near shoring impact on transportation as well.

Road Transport

The road transport industry is changing from a general haulage type of service towards modern logistic services consisting of sophisticated transport and distributive services (physical distribution and materials management). This change will involve several structural changes. On the one hand, a process of concentration and co-operation in this fragmented market will take place. On the other hand, a rise in market niches for specific specialized services by small companies will emerge. As a consequence of regulatory and technological factors, an increased professionalism of the sector is visible. Expert knowledge is also required by manufacturers and retailers either as they centralize their stockholding at a national or cross-country scale (depending on the size of their activities) within value chains in order to achieve economies of scale or require reliable sophisticated transport partners to implement just-in-time techniques.

In more and more countries, such as Switzerland, Austria and the Netherlands, the combination of transport via road and rail and/or water is more environmentally acceptable to the public than purely transport by road. Multimodel transportation systems are being set up for instance in industrial zones where containers can be switched easily between ships, trains and trucks. Increasing congestion and pollution is making road transport unpopular and expensive.

Rail Transport

Aside from in the US, governments of various countries are moving toward the privatization of railways. This has happened in different ways. In the UK authorities created a separate vehicle for the rail infrastructure management and (competing) train transport operators, by dividing freight and passengers (both approaches also involve unbundling) or by privatization of the whole formerly state-owned company. Governing, managing and controlling all these separate entities, is needed badly, to secure the quality and safety that has to be delivered to the public. Eventually, the railway industry may benefit from this trend. With growing attention toward the environment, the positioning of rail transport is improving. The flexibility of the train deserves special attention. Both passengers and freight need transport from door to door, which the train cannot offer. Therefore, efficient combinations with other transportation modes will make the train a more attractive alternative than at present. With substantial investments in (international) high speed rail links, rail will become more attractive for medium range transportation needs in many countries. Also, trains can compete with planes over shorter distances. Total travelling time is almost the same by train as plane when you have to go from downtown Manhattan to downtown Boston. From an environmental perspective inland waterways offer an attractive solution for the transport of bulk freight and to a lesser extent container and roll-on roll-off cargoes.

Shipping

Everyone who follows the share prices of major shipping companies at the stock exchanges has experienced that this trade is a very cyclical one. The shipping industry is highly fragmented with some large companies specializing in bulk or containers. In particular, container shipping is characterized by an ongoing process of concentration. In 1998 there were six major alliances. However, the takeover of Sea-Land by the relative outsider Maersk will no doubt trigger new mergers. Globalization without the emergence of containerization is hard to imagine. Standardization is the key format behind containerization. The shipping industry is an international one, faced with low profitability as a result of overcapacity and fierce competition.

Strategic moves of shipping companies to counter this situation include: co-operation on some lines, focussing on deep sea shipping; niche marketing such as specialized bulk transport; short-distance shipping intended to cover many harbours with self-equipped vessels for container loading and unloading; door-to-door transport either by self or by means of strategic alliances; and/or heavy attention on logistics and added value for augmented services.

Air Transport

Whereas the American deregulation in the airline industry took place in the late 1970s, this process recently started in most other countries and in trading blocs. Deregulation and liberalization of markets will no doubt lead to more competition and a shake-out of inefficiently operating airlines (e.g. PAN AM). Low-cost airlines like South Western, Ryan Air and Easy Jet are popping up around the globe. Current responses by existing airlines to the challenge of new foreign entrants in, up till now, still heavily regulated home markets will include: cost reductions (personnel and operating); higher loading/occupancy rates both for passengers and freight; concentration (mergers and acquisitions); collaboration and partnerships, e.g. in maintenance of carriers, code-sharing, reservation systems, joint marketing, etc.[50] Many established airlines now operate their own low-cost carriers under a different label.

In no other industry does fortune appear to change so quickly as in the air business. The airline industry is a cyclical one. Now, it seems that the cycles are becoming shorter, making it more difficult to plan a long-term strategy. In 2004 Air France and KLM merged their operations. In fact Air France took over the old established Royal Dutch Airlines. However, some countries continue to restrict FDI to minority stakes. The most active investors are airlines from Western Europe, pursuing different geographical strategies by means of equity links. Strategic alliances and mergers between airlines of different parts around the world are other well-known strategies to increase economies of scale and subsequently yield per mile (both in passenger traffic 'seats' and freight 'tonnage'). But even then it appears that some airlines are hard to sell. For, selling insolvent national carriers such as Malev (Hungary), Olympic Airlines (Greece), LOT (Poland) or Alitalia (Italy) has proved nearly impossible for some countries, due largely to the airlines' symbolism for national sovereignty. Not long ago, flying the flag was more important than making a profit. The years of state aid have led to inefficient operations with coddled and bloated work forces.[51]

Entertainment

All over the world, public broadcasters are in retreat from the onslaught of new commercial channels. Perhaps with hindsight, public service broadcasting will seem a freak of technology; for a rare half-century, it was possible for one medium to communicate the same material to most of a country's population.[52] This observation indicates that public broadcasters that are heavily dependent on licence fee revenues have to change their business to survive. One could even ask how legitimate it is to request a licence fee from the public if people watch fewer and fewer of their programmes. Cutting costs of overheads and production, diminishing bureaucracy, investment in programmes, investment in digital transmission, increased broadcasting hours, expanded services, reducing overcapacity and increased co-operation between national public broadcasters are only part of the answer to competing more successfully with commercial television and radio. Most governments are searching for ways to reduce their budgets and tax burdens to their inhabitants. To reduce the number of public broadcasters to one or to zero fits both desires. Public broadcasters face an additional problem, as we see that financial muscle and income from advertising allows commercial broadcasters to successfully bid on major sport and other events, luring even more viewers from public television. Privatization, scaling down or focussing on core business on particular subjects (e.g. sports or news and its background stories) may be the only solution in the long term. In the long run, of all the parties involved, satellite TV promises great opportunities with channels reaching pan-regional audiences in different parts of the world.

The competition in the whole industry will be stifled by the scaling up, concentration and integration of production and distribution of entertainment. A combination of environmental changes and industry characteristics has resulted in the globalization of the media industry. In particular, large media companies have snapped up their rivals both in the entertainment industry and its distribution channels. Driven by saturation in their home markets, competition and changes in technology, US firms are very active in this concentration wave. For example, the combination of Walt Disney and Viacom is combining the production of film with distribution via television stations, cable networks and satellite TV. Sony has entered the entertainment market from the other end, namely from hardware. Sony films and Playstation, combining hardware and software, are now an integral part of its business. Recently, music companies including Universal Music, Warner and EMI have shed assets to offset a five-year decline in music sales. Piracy, including Internet downloading of music and filmmovies, has much contributed to this decline. The global music industry has launched lawsuits in various countries against Web-users who copy illegally over the Internet. On the production side, the game is still to find the creative talent and good scenarios.

Hospitality and Tourism

The accommodation market is cyclical, where firms benefit from the upturns in the economy but suffer in recessions. The hospitality industry includes tourism, hotels and restaurants. This industry is still fragmented. However, in accommodation (and to a lesser extent the restaurant business), we notice a trend to universal business formats. This takes place sometimes through full ownership, sometimes via joint ventures or franchising. Concentration, in particular in the hotel business, is noticeable.

The accommodation market is highly segmented. High end segment names include Mariott, Four Seasons, InterContinental, Hilton (Europe) and Conrad. The target groups of Hilton in the USA are more dependent on market opportunities and the size/type/location of the hotel than on one single well-defined market segment. The Flamingo Hilton Las Vegas, for example, caters to middle market tour and travel patrons, while the Las Vegas Hilton targets conventions and high spending guests. Hilton's Nevada properties serve different customer groups. Outside Las Vegas, the Reno Hilton targets the middle market and conventions, while the Flamingo Hilton-Laughlin targets the budget market. Holiday Inn finds itself in the middle of the full service accommodation market.

Around Europe, hotel chains focussing on the low (budget) end of the market have been rapidly developed. Accor, operating under various labels such as Formule 1, Novotel and Ibis, is an important player. As in the rest of the world, in many Asian countries, the hotel market is dominated by local and foreign moguls. For many chains, the fee income from management and franchise contracts provides a stable earnings stream. The occupancy rate of rooms and beds is crucial in this industry. Overcapacity in many countries is driving down industry margins. Exceptions to this rule are often found in the emerging markets, including former Eastern-bloc countries, where prices for western-style rooms are still high, until more high end hotels enter the market and occupancy rates are now starting to fall. It is obvious that events such as 9/11, the 2003 SARS epidemic in Asia and the economic climate are underlying factors which heavily influenced occupancy rates in the past. Though economic trends may be predicted reasonably well (extrapolation and periodical wave approach) forecasting the events to happen (e.g. by means of embryo predicting approach) is difficult as the practice shows.

Tourism has become an important source of income for many countries around the world. In Asia alone, Indonesia, Malaysia, Thailand, India and Sri Lanka are all well-known holiday destinations. The same holds in the Caribbean, for Aruba and Barbados. Less well known is the fact that, since Vietnam opened to visitors, international travellers have taken a keen interest in the country. Singapore now aims to transform itself into a culture hub. In Hong Kong, the importance of the total service sector has surpassed that of the industrial one. Within the service sector tourism was and is important in terms of national income. Tourism spreads its wealth among many different people within the society, especially when tourists are not booked into holiday resorts owned by large companies' conglomerates. Because the foreign buyer is visiting the service provider, it can be seen as a way of exporting services while staying at home. Projections of economists in Australia show that tourism, alongside manufacturing, will be the two main money-makers for the country in the coming years.

Countries cannot take income from tourism for granted. This has been experienced by the Mediterranean region. This centre of the world's 'sun, sea and sand' holiday lost its market share in the late 1980s and early 1990s. Bad service quality, high prices and old facilities are partly to blame. Service innovation, promotion, investments in infrastructure, market segmentation and co-operation between private entrepreneurs and governments should provide an answer to this. While focussing on different market segments, Portugal and Spain are currently portraying their golf courses to show that they have more than sun and beaches. Thus, in marketing terminology these countries, at an aggregated level, are changing their positioning in the leisure business, their segmentation, their product offering and their service concept.

Health Services

The ageing of the world population, breakthroughs in the medical diagnostic and research front, the increasing price of health services (often in relation to other goods and services) all contribute to an increase of (public and private) spending on health care. In 2001, the United States devoted 5.8% of its GDP to health, as against 6.4% in Canada, 7.3% in France, 7.9% in Germany, 5.9% in Japan, and 5.6% in the United Kingdom.[53] Health costs are a major concern of governments in the United States and other industrial countries. The ageing of their populations and the surge in new medical techniques and medicines are vital reasons. At the same time, health care costs are becoming increasingly relevant for middle-income developing

1.1 Introduction

1.2 The services sector: A general overview The services sector in a country Differences in economic development

1.3 The macro- environment: Demographics Regulatory forces Economic forces Technology Social factors	1.4 The service sector environment: Internationalization Increase of commercial principles Focussing on core business Upscaling in core activities Diminishing differences Changes in delivery mode and asset structure	1.5 The impact assessment of service industries: Financial services Business services Distribution Transportation Entertainment Hospitality and tourism Health services Infrastructure services	1.6 Trends and market research

1.7 The impact map

Figure 1.6 Trends and market research

1 *Extrapolation* is based on assuming the continuity of current and past trends in the future – for example, demographic shifts, the increasing regulatory power of supra-national bodies such as the EU, the steady evolution of hardware.

2 *Crossover* is an approach based on the observation that many trends are a combination of current realities – for example, predicting small improvements, changes or forecasting long term the combination of computers and telecommunication.

3 *Demand-driven* approach is a prediction concept that assumes people will invent and build the things and services they want. Examples include convenience-driven services and flat screen monitors.

4 The *embryo* method assumes most dominant macro trends and technologies once started small. Successful technologies have been invented, researched and developed for some time at universities or other research institutes. Also, stand-alone social events, economic events and regulatory try-outs may become mainstream. The embryo theory is however difficult to apply as it is most uncertain to predict which events will lead to major trends.

5 *Analogy*, another related method, predicts the time a new trend needs to mature, based on analogous series of events in the past. This seems, for example, to apply to object databases whose history and development roughly repeats the history of relational databases. The problem with this approach is that e.g. consumer trends and new technologies seem to be maturing much faster than in the past.

6 *Periodical waves* prediction is based on the observation that many macro factors and marketing-related service trends have a cyclic nature. Well known are the seven rich years and seven poor years which are noted in the Bible, Kondratieff's model of economic long-term economy due to new technologies, and the fashion look which seems to repeat itself in cycles. In this model a part of a macro factor, e.g. ICT, is seen as causing a wave. The difficulty of predicting the periodical wave is that, even if we are able to identify the wave, it is hard to predict exactly what the new wave will bring.

7 *Market research* (varying from an entrepreneur's sound intuition to scientifically sound quantitative or qualitative research) is the systematic gathering, recording and analysing of data to provide information useful to marketing decision making. Though market research is predominantly a demand-driven tool, it may also, for example by means of analysing secondary data, be a help for the other approaches to predict the future. In subsequent chapters we will deal with more characteristics of market research.

1.7 The Impact Map

So far, we have analysed the generic trends within the macro factors, the marketing-related services trends, and the forces within the market of the service provider. At this stage, all these factors and embedded trends are translated for a particular company into an Impact Map.

By means of an example this section assesses the environment of the insurance industry. In this case, the business unit of a life-insurance company in the Netherlands selling 'collective' life insurance to enterprises (Table 1.2). For this reason, also the implications within the value chain (e.g. the insurance intermediary forms part of the analysis) are taken into account. Based on the five DRETS factors relevant to trends in the macro environment and in the service industry, the trends in the service environment and in the life insurance business itself are being mentioned briefly. Next, it is shown in what way they impact on the insurance company. Because the activities described in the last column in the Impact Map should converge with the strategic and marketing objectives of the company (to be discussed in Chapter 6), the formulated actions could be at this stage only of a preliminary and indicative nature.

Like in many other service industries in a slow growing economy, the trend towards individualization, sophisticated ICT-application, increased transparency enhances personalization of (life insurance) services. The challenge is to be as much as standardized in the back-office (low-costs) and too be as much as personalized or customized in the front-office (to suit customer needs). Moreover, the final column labelled as *actions* should be followed by the name of the person who is responsible for the activity, required budget, other means (e.g. names and time involved of staff members and ICT-sources) and the date when the activity should be completed. However, even it in its rudimentarily form, management can employ the outcome of the Impact Map as a Marketing Management Agenda.

As the reader will notice many factors have a national angle. For example the structure of three pillars, consisting of a governmental funded basic pension, an industry linked pension and a voluntary individual (or company based) scheme are typically for the Dutch insurance environment. This is different from e.g. Germany. When a service organization or its advisor prepares the Impact Map for a similar business unit of an insurance company in another

Table 1.2 Impact map of an insurance company in the Netherlands

Factors	Trends	Macro level impact	Sectors level impact	Micro level impact Impact for value chain	Provisional actions value chain
Demographic factors	• Ageing • Fewer youngsters	1.1 Budget pressure of government 1.2 Number of working people decreases	2.1 Premium supplementary pension increases 2.2 Premium volume collective pension market decreases	3.1 The pension gap becomes bigger 3.2 Individuality and desire for flexibility increase 3.3 Increasing control requirements 3.4 Collective pension market becomes smaller 3.5 Central role of consumer in value chain (currently, the insurance agent) 3.6 Market transparency increases 3.7 High investments (in systems and back office) 3.8 The role of technology will become more prominent	• Concentrating on the client • To combine the IT-information • Defining the strategy • To strive for partnership and alliances • To offer products which are more flexible and customized • Increase of scale by means of mergers, acquisitions, purchase of client portfolios and developing new market segments • Forecast on cost savings • Because of value based approach of the whole organization the difficult issue arises of 'invest now, harvest now'
Regulatory factors	• Equal treatment of women and men with regard to pensions • Pension agreement between the labour unions and employers • Annual government budget and the EU	1.3 Entitled to lower claims 1.4 Withdrawing government 1.5 Funding of pensions in all three pillars gets more difficult 1.6 More control 1.7 The government should meet the criteria of the EU Growth and	2.3 Individualism stimulated through withdrawing government 2.4 'Level playing field' 2.5 Pension gap bigger 2.6 More and intense competition on current pension market	3.9 Revenue and margins under pressure 3.10 Small sized competitors disappear 3.11 Competition will become more focussed (both company and consumer)	

continued

Table 1.2 *(cont.)*

Factors	Trends	Macro level impact	Sectors level impact	Micro level impact *Impact for value chain*	Provisional actions value chain
	● Stabilization pact with regard to government budgets in EU	1.8 Country legislation to consider international law trends in this area	2.7 Complicated government legislation		
Economic factors	● Economic situation and outlook ● Economical structure ● Return	1.9 Trade-off between economic outlook and social policy 1.10 Slow economy and unfavourable outlook are motives to reduce expenditures drastically 1.11 Necessity to increase labour participation 1.12 The 2nd and 3rd pillar are sensitive for interest fluctuations 1.13 Financial stability of the country is strongly dependent on value of total amount of pensions	2.8 Decreasing return 2.9 Increased responsibility for insurers 2.10 Small competitors disappear from the market 2.11 Focussing on lowering costs	*Impact on the Business Line 'Life insurance Collective'* Manage according to the following core values: 1 Satisfaction of company, employee and intermediary in the value chain 2 Collaboration 3 Controlling efficiency in processes, internal and external 4 Focus on costs and quality	Actions business line: ● Defining the strategy ● To strive for partnership and alliances ● To adjust procedures and systems to the wishes and needs of the final consumers ● Information to be available to both partners and consumers
Technological factors	● Technology	1.14 On this level 'value added' is difficult to define	2.12 Technology input to support and improve business processes 2.13 Technology input as communication means	*Three central issues on micro level:* 1 Focus on end-consumer 2 Technology and technological innovation are becoming more crucial for success	
Social factors	● Social ● Labour mobility	1.15 Heterogeneous preferences 1.16 Both participants and employers require more flexibility 1.17 Stimulus for individuality	2.14 To match the individual situation 2.15 Individuality at the expense of collectivism	3 Increasing competition from larger competitors	

country, naturally it will lead to different implications. As a consequence, it will trigger different activities.

Summary

This chapter focussed on the components of a service organization's business environment affecting its strategy and operations.

Dynamic changes in the macro environment can be labelled as the DRETS-factors. They include:

- Demographic factors;
- Regulation (in some sectors) and further deregulation (in other sectors);
- Economic factors;
- Technological developments; and
- Social and cultural factors.

A number of marketing-related trends in the service sector indicate the possible direction of company growth in the next decade. Internationalization is the first, although to many service providers it is slippery ground to tread on. The need for more efficiency urges governments and companies to be(come) self-supporting (privatization and contracting-out).

Service companies in various sectors from entertainment to banking and from tourism to auditing have reviewed their corporate and marketing strategies during recent years as a result of globalization, market and technological changes. In many service industries, we see the impact on the strategies (and employment) of major service firms caused by closely linked issues of privatization, deregulation and liberalization.

In this chapter, these issues are combined under the phrase 'the urge of increasing commercial principles around the globe'. Technology, market and competition drive service industries into convergence. The amalgamation of telecommunication, hardware (computer and consumer electronics) and content (entertainment and information) is a well-known example. Less known perhaps is the convergence of retail banking and insurance in many countries as well as shopping and entertainment. Throughout the world, low cost competitors are entering deregulated markets. Unbundling services, a flexible work force and the Internet, facilitating e.g. e-ticketing, are contributing to this phenomenon.

Increasing commercial principles, focussing on core business is a marketing-related trend, often leading to downsizing e.g. by spinning off subsidiaries. On the other hand, scaling up in the same core business by means of internal growth, mergers, acquisitions, strategic alliances or strategic partnering is another marketing-related trend. Diminishing differences between products and services and changes in asset structure of service companies and the delivery mode they choose are the fourth and fifth service trends. The growth in leasing and rentals, as well as in collective ownership, are interesting developments in the service sector. It is obvious that in many industries delivering services electronically (e.g. by telephone or the Internet) is dramatically changing the landscape.

Consumers are empowered by means of the Internet and new intermediary (Web-based) channels. Together with the trend towards the commodification of services, it raises fundamental questions about the roles of professionals and consumers during the service encounter. This counts for medical doctors, lawyers, notaries and real estate brokers alike. Where possible, the marketing-related service trends should be translated into strategic policies and definite ideas on new services.

The results of the external analysis of the service environment, resulting in an 'Impact Map' for a service industry of a service provider, will be utilized while carving out the corporate strategy, the marketing strategy, developing new services and the planning of the other marketing instruments in chapters still to come. Insight in the world of services shows that issues which occur or have occurred in a particular service industry could be applied in another industry to get a competitive advantage. In this way, service firms can learn from one another to satisfy shareholders, customers and other stakeholders by providing excellent service quality.

Now that we have seen this general overview of what is happening in the world of services, you have become (more) familiar with that world. In turn, this eases your understanding of strategic management in the services business, especially when you do realize what are the fundamentals of services (which is the topic of the next chapter).

Questions

1. Which environmental factors together form DRETS? Give examples of each of the factors identified.
2. What type(s) of service provider(s) would be interested in the rate of fluctuation of the national currency?
3. Why should a service provider analyse macro factors which are beyond the organization's control?
4. What social trends partly account for the growth of the service sector?
5. What other trends are relevant to the growth of the service sector?
6. Give a description of disintermediation. In which service industries may this phenomenon play a role?
7. Why is information and information technology so important to service firms?
8. Outsourcing has been mentioned on various occasions in this chapter.
   a What are the reasons for and consequences of outsourcing as mentioned in this chapter?
   b What are the reasons and consequences of offshoring?
9. Why does privatization of governmental services take place? What is your opinion regarding this phenomenon?
10. Discuss briefly the major reasons explaining the explosive growth of leasing. State your opinion whether this growth will continue.

Assignments

1. Make, on the basis of your own case study, an impact map of a specific company. Use tendencies, trends and macro and service sector factors that play a role in determining the strategy of a particular service provider you selected yourself.

2. Discuss the major developments in one of the following industries:
   ☐ financial services,
   ☐ business services in general,
   ☐ distribution,
   ☐ transport,
   ☐ travel,
   ☐ entertainment,
   ☐ hospitality,
   ☐ health services,
   ☐ infrastructure services.
   a What can be said about concentration in these industries?
   b What is happening in those industries in your own country?
3. Is there a kind of convergence in the financial sector worldwide? If so, describe the convergence and its roots.
4. When firms define their markets in a different way, this may open up new opportunities. Give some examples for service industries defining their markets in a different way.
   ☐ Do you see an individual company in a service industry in your own country which has become, based on one or more environment trends, a national champion in your own country?
5. List the ten biggest organizations within three service industries selected by you.
   a Indicate by means of scanning articles and interviews why the top three of each industry are successful.
   b Analyse the way they are coping with the macro trends and marketing-related service trends.
6. Select a service organization which you know well.
   a Assess the service environment and its impact on this organization.
   b Utilize for this assignment the format of the services 'Impact Map' as developed in this chapter.

Endnotes

1 This Service Practice has been based to a large extent on Peter Francese, 2002/2003.

2 Example used by Margaret Crimp, 1985.

3 In this view on the organization theory, the external environment of the organization is viewed in its entirety as an 'independent' source. As a consequence, the environment influences the organization.

4 OECD, 2004, pp. 22–23.

5 OECD, 2004, pp. 6–7.

6 See the Overview section in World Development Report, 2004.

7 These facts and conclusions stem from the Overview section in the World Development Report, 2004.

8 In Chapter 7, we will see that the most recent ideas of gaining a competitive advantage are based on the ability of a firm to shape its own external environment, e.g. trends in its own industry. The competitors have to follow. We will not elaborate on that idea at present.

9 *Business Week*, 1994, 19 September.

10 Based on Sandra Plas, 2005, p. A3.

11 Arnott and Casscells, 2003, p. 23.

12 This Service Practice is based on Dick Chay, 2005, p. 24.

13 Bergner *et al.*, 2002.

14 According to some trend watchers, e.g. P. Schnabel, 1999.

15 In Chapter 3 we will see that, in terms of national cultures, richer societies have a more individualistic culture whereas poorer societies, relying more on groups and belonging to the group, have a more collectivistic culture.

16 Poiesz and Van Raaij, 2002.

17 We do not refer here to some tribal societies where women usually do all the work and educate children.

18 Gardyn, 2002, p. 34.

19 Berry, Seiders and Grewal, 2002, pp. 1–17.

20 Rosenbloom, 2001, p. 375.

21 Lovelock, 1991, p. 2.

22 Brown, Ryan and Parker, 2000, p. 206.

23 Question of the Authors of the 1994 World Bank report.

24 Unbundling is even able to offset the advantages of economies of scale and scope. The latter occurs when it is cheaper for a provider to produce and deliver two or more services jointly than for separate entities to provide these services individually. Unbundling promotes new entry and competition. The benefits of cost-minimizing behaviour under competitive pressures can easily outweigh the gains from economies of scope. Unbundling makes cross-subsidies – between lines of business or customers within enterprises offering multiple services – more transparent. It identifies more precisely the subsidies needed to deliver services to the poor and/or remote customers, and improves management accountability. The World Development Report 1994, *Infrastructure for Development* is clear on this. The trend is unmistakable: unbundling of infrastructure services is proceeding at a brisk pace.

25 See for example, Sturm *et al.*, 2002; and Lewis, 1999.

26 See for example Strikwerda, 2003; Bergeron, 2003; and the Corporate Executive Board, 2000.

27 This paragraph is based on two articles in the Financial Times by Andrew Balls and Christopher Swann, 2004; and Michael Skapinker, 2003.

28 This Service practice is based on James Hookway, 2005; and John W. Miller, 2005.

29 Sometimes partnerships stop after a while. For instance, Qantas sold their 19% share in Air New Zealand for strategic reasons in the beginning of 1997.

30 See e.g. Kasper, 1994.

31 Also, those who were initially service providers are increasingly entering into the production of tangible goods if the market demands them. Thus the success of the film *Jurassic Park* by Steven Spielberg brought about a veritable craze of goods. So, the reverse trend can be seen as well.

32 Lovelock, 1991.

33 Kasper, 1997, pp. 38–39.

34 Laing *et al.*, 2002, p. 491.

35 Many of these observations have been based on a joint study done by some of the leading European economic institutions about Europe in 1998 (see Baker, 1994 on the ERECO Report, Market Services and European Integration, 1993) as well as various World Bank reports, OECD publications and our personal experiences.

36 Mulligan and Gordon, 2002, p. 31.

37 The projected staff reduction in retail banking of as high as 50% by 2005 draws on Coopers & Lybrand who conducted more than 50 interviews with senior bank executives. It indicates not only a sharp reduction in staff but also a change in the skills employees will require, according to Richard Waters, 1995.

38 Internet offerings, 'On-line capitalism', New York, *The Economist*, 23 November, 1996, p. 98.

39 See Kathy Holzmann, 1996, p. 1.

40 Not everywhere (yet), i.e. in the USA, regulators allow banks and insurance companies to join forces.

41 See William Dawkins, 1997.

42 To some people, this industry even has become of age; see James Alexander, 2004.

43 Vogler-Ludwig and Hofmann, 1993, p. 383.

44 See James Alexander and Mark Hordes, 2005.

45 See James Alexander, 2004.

46 Commission of the European Community, 1988.

47 Baker, 1994, pp. 306–310.

48 Nevertheless, the French Carrefour group has been successful with their hypermarkets in Taiwan; the same holds for the Dutch Makro group (which sold part of its foreign business to the Metro group, based in Germany).

49 Most observations of this sector are based on Baker's ERECO Report, 1994.

50 Still this can take a long time and large amounts of money as the continuous subsidizing of Air France by the French Government shows.

51 Keith Johnson and Marton Dunai, 2005.

52 In radio where lots of new services have become freely available, the BBC's share has dropped from 66% in 1990, when commercial radio was deregulated, to just 50%.

53 OECD, October 2002.

54 Burns, 2000.

55 Bergner *et al.*, 2002, p. 2.

56 Popcorn, 1992, pp. 8–31.

57 This overview of approaches predicting the future is based on Bergner *et al.*, 2002, pp. 2 and 3.

Chapter 2

Fundamentals of Services Marketing Management

70,000 trucks and buses
660 hp
120 countries
3 letters: MAN

COMMERCIAL VEHICLES | INDUSTRIAL SERVICES | PRINTING SYSTEMS | DIESEL ENGINES | TURBOMACHINES

If you have strength and substance you can get things moving. With an annual production of 70,000 vehicles, MAN is one of the biggest commercial vehicle manufacturers in Europe. MAN trucks transport millions of tonnes of goods every day. What's more, MAN has built up further future-oriented competence fields in mechanical engineering and services. Almost 250 years of innovative strength have made MAN one of the leading suppliers of industrial goods in Europe. And a performer on the stock market too. Isn't it good to know that sustained action yields long-lasting success?

Engineering the Future.   MAN

Reproduced by permission of MAN AG

Learning objectives

At the end of this chapter you will be able to:

1 Define services

2 Discuss the basic characteristics of services

3 Understand the concept of market orientation

4 Apply the essentials of strategic management in (international) service organizations

5 Define the concept of value creation to the firm's stakeholders

6 Understand the need for relationship marketing

7 Explain the relevance of managing the marketing assets and capabilities in service organizations

8 Define the essential features of a market oriented strategy in a service company

9 Explain why services marketing management can be defined as managing people

2.1   Introduction

One Day We'll Fly Away?

The airline industry is a very important part of the service sector. While 9/11, the wars in Afghanistan (2002) and Iraq (2003) and SARS (2003) may have temporarily decreased the number of airline passengers, in general there has been an increase in the overall number of airline passengers worldwide. However, this increase has not been consistent across all airlines. Certain routes (for instance from Europe to Asia) or airlines (many in the USA and Europe) have run into severe financial problems due to a sharp decline in passenger numbers, whereas other airlines have performed very well and have even seemed to benefit from these world events. Each airline will react differently to the challenges created by the external environment and will subsequently serve their customers in different ways. Various ways to create customer and stakeholder value seem to exist simultaneously. Have a look at what some airlines are doing.[1]

Singapore Airlines (SIA) is famous for its service excellence. It has been one of the most profitable airlines in the world for a long time; however SIA's first quarter results in 2003 were negative. This was due to a decline in passenger numbers which occurred as a result of the events mentioned above. SIA provides a large number of high quality services to its customers. These services are supported by a large number of internal processes such as service maintenance, training, empowering employees and complaint handling. Each of these processes has been designed to support excellent customer service, thus creating a 'wow effect' which consist of a bundle of service surprises.

EasyJet, South West Airlines and Ryanair are all low budget airlines. During 2002 and 2003 each of these airlines saw their number of passengers, market share and financial results improve. The low fares on these airlines were achieved through the careful management of costs. Cost could be reduced by: outsourcing maintenance and repair; using only one type of aircraft; flying to regional airports; providing inexpensive and convenient 'no-frills' service, whereby the passengers pay separately for any extra services above the bare minimum; increasing occupancy rates per plane because the planes have no requirement for a galley; and minimizing the time at the gate between arrival and departure.

Companies like Singapore Airlines have a value-added strategy: they provide a wide range of high quality services additional to the core service of transporting people from one place to another. The low budget carriers on the other hand provide their core service with a minimum of other additional services. These airlines focus on their core activities with the objective of increasing their return on investment (ROI).

Airlines such as SIA apply a strategy of differentiation while the low budget airlines have a strategy of cost leadership. Both companies aim to create value for their customers, but do it in a different way.

Much has to be done to create a high quality service experience such as that provided by SIA, as described in Service Practice 2.1. The airlines have to perform a large number of activities to satisfy their passengers. As a consequence the airlines must have the right balance of assets and capabilities. This book will describe how the management of assets and capabilities can create excellent service quality which generates value to both the customer and the other stakeholders. It is our belief that the firm's market orientation is an important contributor to accomplishing value-driven objectives. We will demonstrate that the essence of delivering excellent service quality is not difficult to define; however, the actual delivery of that excellent service quality can be difficult to implement.

Essentially, services marketing management is about people; customers as well as employees. Sometimes, technology is added to this personal interaction and sometimes technology can even replace the service employee. When technology is used to replace people, organizations must focus their activity on their systems to ensure that they are designed to provide this caring process.

A lot of skills, activities, knowledge, performances, efforts, deeds, systems and processes are necessary when implementing processes which focus on people. Thus the question that needs to be considered here is how can this caring, servicing, adding value or creating value, be achieved when technology is used to replace people? Is it really possible to achieve the goals of all the parties; the customer, the company and other stakeholders simultaneously? We are convinced it is. Although it is not a matter of magic, it must be a matter of managing the appropriate assets and capabilities in service organizations.

Developing and implementing these assets and capabilities is a challenge to a market oriented service provider. This means motivating the company's employees to serve the customer well through the delivery of excellent service quality. The outcome of this will be satisfied customers that may be retained over a lifetime. Satisfied customers and satisfied employees 'go hand in hand in service business' and can create shareholder value. That is why we put so much emphasis on the assets and capabilities the market oriented service provider can use to create a high quality service experience for their customers. However it is important to also discuss relationships, customer relationship management, strategic management, human resources, processes and the instruments of the marketing mix in the context of services marketing management.

SERVICE PRACTICE 2.2

A Great Many High Quality Service Offerings

At the core of all airline operations lies the airline's ability to maintain on-time arrivals and departures. Alongside this core service offering lie many other important service components, such as luggage handling, ticketing or in the case of a full service airline such as KLM, the provision of a meal. Online service providers such as Amazon.com serve their customers by answering their requests quickly and delivering the products ordered efficiently and effectively. Insurance companies such as Allianz focus on providing their customers not only with appropriate policies but also information. Banks such as ING are delivering service 24/7 to their customers over the Internet, and this increasingly is expected. Even heavy machinery manufacturers like John Deere are competing on service, by providing an after sales break down service. Universities are increasingly being asked to provide a wide array of services, including the provision of online courses. Everywhere we look there are organizations providing a greater number of high quality services, and in areas where we may not traditionally have looked. Increasingly it is the provision of these services that is defining the nature of the competitive activity.

This chapter contains an overview of the domain of services marketing management. First we have to define services in order to understand what assets and capabilities have to be managed to create value to all the stakeholders. This value is premised on an organization delivering a high quality service experience to its customers. Section 2.2 deals with the definition of services and discusses the characteristics of services.

Services can be described in many ways; we provide an overview of the many ways to classify them. Section 2.3 provides an introduction to managing services: strategic management, creating value, relationship management, the necessary assets and capabilities, and as well the need to match demand and supply in service industries will be discussed.

In section 2.4 we build on our discussion of managing services and discuss the basics of marketing services: market orientation, customer expectations, quality perceptions, the internal organization, employees, key success factors, competitive advantage, and market oriented cultures. The findings from all the sections are brought together in section 2.5 – our perspective on market oriented services marketing management to create the ultimate service experience to the customer (Figure 2.1).

2.2   What are Services?

Organizations in many different industries offer services. For example, schools offer education while hospitals offer medical care. Public utilities offer natural gas, electricity and water. Some services are provided by non profit organizations, others by profit oriented organizations. Manufacturers of fast moving consumer goods, such as soup, may offer a recipe forum and they may also have a complaint handling department. Manufacturers of durables, such as washing machines, may also offer services such as user instructions, repair and maintenance.

In some instances companies deliver services to consumers (B2C services), in other instances businesses deliver services to other businesses (B2B services). Nevertheless, in all instances delivering excellent service quality and creating value for the customer is the cornerstone of success.

In our view, caring about people is a prerequisite to both excellence and to creating customer value. However it is important to consider that even within one industry sector, for example the hotel industry, the same service can be provided in a variety of ways. An organization's service positioning can be a major point of differentiation in a given industry.

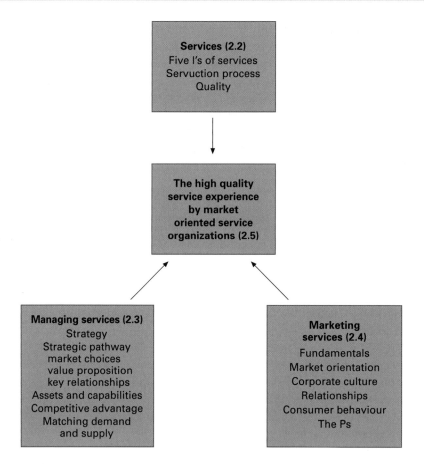

Figure 2.1   Chapter outline: the relations between the building blocks

Differentiation can be achieved through the manipulation of the organization's marketing assets and capabilities.

Service Practice 2.3 shows us how the Ritz Carlton chain of hotels uses excellent service quality as a positioning tool.

SERVICE PRACTICE 2.3

Ladies and Gentlemen of the Ritz Carlton

Ritz Carlton Hotels have a comprehensive service quality programme that is an integrated part of the marketing and business objectives.

Characteristics of the programme include participatory executive leadership through information gathering, coordinated planning and execution, and a trained workforce that is empowered 'to move heaven and earth' to satisfy customers. Of these, committed employees rank as the most essential asset of the company. All employees are schooled in the company's 'Gold Standards' which set out Ritz Carlton's service credo and the basics of premium service. According to a company brochure the corporate motto is 'ladies and gentlemen serving ladies and gentlemen'.

This way of looking at providing services is completely different from the experience we all have once in a while when employees in other service organizations consider serving the customer an obligation. The Ritz Carlton shows it really can be different.

On the other hand the French hotel chain Formule 1 also serves their customer well. Formule 1 provides a simple service for overnight stays. The hotels are often located in business areas and near major airports. During the day a receptionist will welcome the guests and take forward reservations. However the hotels offer no room service and bathrooms are generally cleaned automatically. Booking via the Internet is quite usual. When guests arrive late they have to book their room via their credit card at the entrance of the hotel and nobody shows them the way to their room.

Both Formule 1 and the Ritz Carlton offer excellent service quality. Both approaches satisfy their target market. Ritz Carlton achieves service excellence through the provision of an individualized customer management programme. Formule 1 achieves service excellence through the provision of a tightly managed service process. Both strategies are supported with appropriate pricing strategies.

Defining Services

The services marketing literature contains many definitions of services.[2] However there are some common features in all of these definitions. At first, these commonalities refer to the fact that services deal with something that is intangible. This means that it is difficult to hold or to stock services. Moreover, the buying of services does not necessarily result in the ownership by means of a physical transfer of the object. Rather, it creates a bundle of benefits during and/or after the interaction between the service provider and the customer that results in a particular experience for the customers.

Services refer to efforts, deeds or processes consisting of activities or a series of activities performed by the service provider, quite often in close co-operation and interaction with the customer. Technology, especially information and communication technology (ICT) may facilitate these processes. Services may be added to 'things' (after sales services, complaint handling, training, maintenance of a copier) or exist as services on their own; for example, teaching or medical care. Based on this, we can now construct our definition of services: *Services are originally intangible and relatively quickly perishable activities whose buying, which does not always lead to material possession, takes place in an interactive process aimed at creating customer satisfaction.*

The Basic Characteristics of Services

In general, services are intangible. The intangibility feature is most dominant when defining services. It determines the other characteristics of services; simultaneous production and consumption, heterogeneity and perishability. Given the lack of material possession, the inability to own a service is also considered to be a characteristic of services. Consequently, creating a service usually requires the presence and participation of the customer during the production and consumption of the service. This two-sided human influence on the service often leads to a fluctuating quality of the service. Thus, controlling service quality, motivating employees to deliver excellent service quality and the introduction of technology (especially ICT) are some of the important ways to avoid heterogeneity in service quality.

These characteristics of services are frequently referred to as the five I's of services.[3] The five I's are intangibility, inseparability, inconsistency, inventory and inability to own. Each of these characteristics are considered to be relative. Each of these characteristics will exist in all services, but some will be more important than others depending on the service.

- Intangibility: as a degree of (in)tangibility;
- Inseparability: as a degree of simultaneous production and consumption;
- Inconsistency: as a degree of heterogeneity;
- Inventory: as a degree of perishability; and
- Inability to own: as a degree of (lack of) ownership.

Intangibility: The Degree of (In)Tangibility

Services are an activity or an experience and not a thing. It is often difficult for customers to understand the elements of an activity and as such service organizations generally try to make their intangible offer as tangible as possible. This will help to reduce the perceived risk that a customer may feel when buying a service, especially buying a service that is new to the customer. Many services cannot be provided without tangibles. How could transportation services be provided when there were no planes, trucks, cars, boats or trains? How could a hospital function without advanced technological equipment and beds? However, we believe that intangibility determines the four other characteristics of services. Looking at services this way, the demarcation line between goods and services becomes rather diffuse.[4]

The intangibility continuum visually demonstrates the degree of intangibility (Figure 2.2). This continuum is based on Shostack's (1977) idea of the goods–services continuum. The continuum ranges from tangible goods to intangible services; our continuum ranges from services to goods. In this way, Figure 2.2 better demonstrates the importance of services and the service sector in western economies. It also makes clear that services are not a particular kind of goods.

Inseparability: The Degree of Simultaneous Production and Consumption

Generally the consumer of a service will have to participate in the production of that service. We generally know exactly who taught us at school, who cuts our hair, what our doctor's name is and who serves us in the pub. In many cases, the consumer can not only pinpoint who provided the service, but will often know the service provider personally. In most cases the service process can only start when the customer is present. It is for example quite impossible to get a haircut without actually going to the hairdresser, or conversely having the hairdresser come to you.

This personal contact in services has generated the terms 'interactive consumption' and 'interaction process'. Interaction in services will take place during the service encounter where both the customer and the employee have to perform particular roles and activities. The roles performed in a service setting are based on the notion that there are a set of implicit scripts each pertaining to a particular service environment, for example the office

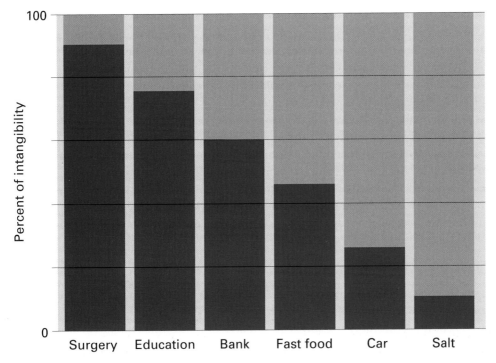

Figure 2.2 Degree of intangibility: service–goods continuum

reception, theatre or classroom. These scripts become clear through experiences with the service provider or in some situations can be communicated in advance. Even Internet services do not exclude this interaction – the notion of service performance according to a script. If a consumer does not insert the correct words, search engines like Google cannot perform the right job.

Inconsistency: The Degree of Heterogeneity

Service production involves both a service provider to produce the service and the active participation of the customer in the service production process. The service environment is also important in creating the right atmosphere in which to produce the service. An appropriate service environment will help to facilitate appropriate customer facilitation in the service production process. This means that standardizing services is quite difficult, raising questions such as:

■ Who controls the customer?
■ Who tells the customer what (s)he is expected to do? and
■ What is the influence of time on service quality?

A service provider has to constantly balance employee control and the customer's perceived needs. Heterogeneity is a given in all service delivery situations, even when companies try to standardize their service operations through the use of manuals and employee training. Automation and reducing the role of people in these processes cannot completely reduce the impact of people and environment on service quality. For example, the automated teller machine (ATM) provides a standardized service to bank customers, but even the ATM is programmed and used by people and this will create variation.

People and time cannot be separated from one another during the service production process. The time that a customer has to spend on a service delivery can vary between service purchases episodes. For example a customer may take an afternoon off work to visit the hairdresser and be happy to spend the entire afternoon receiving the services; on another occasion the same customer may be very short of time but still want to receive the same services. This affects their willingness to participate extensively in the service process. The work of a service provider is quite complicated and is compounded by things such as the mood of the customer which may change each time they purchase the service.

Inventory: The Degree of Perishability

If a service becomes more and more intangible, the opportunities to store the service decrease, in other words the degree of perishability increases. Services which are perishable cannot be kept in stock. Not being able to store services creates the complexity of matching demand and supply. Managers in service organizations have to face fluctuations in demand or in capacity. These fluctuations may have an impact on the service delivery. Managing these fluctuations to increase efficiency, to reduce cost or to increase sales is crucial in service organizations. Meeting customer needs is an appropriate objective for a service organization but it is inefficient to set capacity on the maximum level of demand, as it will be difficult for the organization to consistently meet this level of demand, and subsequently may result in a strain on the organizational resources. Thus, the capacity of a public swimming pool will never be based on the busiest day. That is why many service providers deliberately strive for minimizing unused capacity in quiet times and 'no sales' in busy times. However, that may cause problems as Service Practice 2.4 reveals.

SERVICE PRACTICE 2.4

Demand and Supply for Electricity

During the 1980s public utilities such as electricity companies had a lot of overcapacity; that is, they produced more electricity than they sold. This situation remained because government or public business had little need to be efficient, moreover they had no competition. The government deemed it important to have that overcapacity available in case it was needed. Security in delivering electricity was regarded as a public task and the public sector agreed on the price to be paid for that utility.

Now that the electricity market has been privatized in many countries, many electricity producers have replanned their production capacity. The stock of electricity has been reduced. The production capacity has become very vulnerable to peaks in demand. Increased demand leads to increasing prices on the spot market for energy, and production problems in one plant may lead to a chain of reactions in other electricity production plants. This can lead to stress in the production plants and may result in production equipment malfunctioning.

In 2003 discussions started as to whether the private firms served the customer, including households, organizations and not for profit organizations, well. These topics were raised as some of the main reasons for the shortages in electricity in California and again in Europe during the very hot summer of 2003, and the 14 August 2003 blackout in the USA and Canada where we saw about 50 million people without electricity for an extended period of time.

Inability to Own: The Degree of (Lack of) Ownership

As stated in our definition of services, buying services does not always result in a transfer of title. Services refer to deeds and processes; so what do you own when you have taken a 14-day package tour to Brazil or when you have bought a life insurance policy? When you rent a car or an apartment you do not own the car or the apartment by definition. Still you transfer money and get some right to use the car or stay in the apartment. Once you have taken a class in services marketing, you may have internalized the knowledge transferred; however, when you buy a book on services marketing, you own it.

Some Nuances of the Five I's

Although our definition of services seems to fit reality well, we have to make some changes and discuss the following issues to fully understand what services are about. Discussing the following questions provides some challenges to the common notion of services:

- What does the inability to own a service mean?
- Are services really intangible?
- What is a bundle of benefits?
- What does the experience mean? and
- What does the interaction mean?

What Does the Inability to Own a Service Mean?

As we have stated, services are intangible. This implies that they cannot be stored or transferred. Therefore, no physical delivery of title can occur with respect to chairs in a theatre, seats in an aeroplane or rooms in a hotel. However this does not always hold true. In some situations, the result of the service encounter may be that the customer has something of a tangible nature, like an airline ticket, or a travel code when tickets are booked on line, money from the bank, an insurance policy or the marketing consultant's report. It should be realized though that the prime goal of these transfers is not the possession of something tangible. With insurance, the possession of a policy is not the core service, but the security provided in case of illness or a fire at home. The marketing consultant's report as such is not as important as the consultant's advice written down so as it can be reread, stored or shared with others. In many situations the outcome of the service process may be partly tangible in nature. In such situations there seems to be a transfer of title but in essence the nature of most services makes the transfer of title superfluous.

Christopher Lovelock and Evert Gummesson believe that a new services paradigm should be developed.[5] Although many authors believe the intangibility feature of services is *the* fundamental characteristic of a service, it is also proposed that the lack of ownership is the most fundamental of all of the characteristics.

We contend that services involve a form of rental *or* access *in which customers obtain benefits by gaining the right to use a physical object, to hire labour and expertise of personnel, or to obtain access to facilities and networks. (p. 34)*

In this rental/access paradigm 'services are presented as offering benefits through access or temporary possession, rather than ownership, with payments taking the form of rentals or access fees' (p. 37). In this way of thinking manufactured goods can form the basis of services as well as what we have always considered as typical services.

Are Services Really Intangible?

Many services are intangible. However, the demarcation line between tangibility and intangibility is not always easy to discern. A particular activity can be service focussed, such as teaching. However this same activity, undertaken in a different context, can be part of a more tangible offering; for example teaching someone how to use a new computer. In this example, the teaching or service component is merely a component of the total offer.

To a certain extent this is in line with the three types of products Kotler (1994) identified, these being: the core product, the tangible product and the augmented product. In Kotler's model, the augmented product is seen as the comprehensive product embracing the other two plus all the additional services provided such as installation, after sales, repair and maintenance.

It is important to distinguish between core services and augmented services. Augmented services are defined as the core service plus the additional (or supporting) services. The core service is generally intangible, while the additional service will support the core service and in many cases will function to 'tangibilize' the intangible core service offer.

Some services cannot be provided without a tangible component. You cannot fly without an aircraft. The common notion of intangible services may be challenged; often some degree of tangibility is involved or even needed to produce the service.

What is a Bundle of Benefits?

Fitzsimmons and Fitzsimmons (1994, p. 24) discuss the concept of the 'service package'. It is defined as 'a bundle of goods and services provided in some environment'. The phrase 'bundle of benefits' is important in understanding consumer behaviour. It is a reflection of what consumers expect from a service. What is in it for me? How will it satisfy my needs and wants? How will it solve my problem or contribute to maintaining or improving my lifestyle or status? There are many consequences associated with the buying of services.[6]

The bundle of benefits and the way services are delivered are aimed at creating a wonderful experience for the customer. Excellent service quality is a crucial means to accomplish customer satisfaction. Customer satisfaction is a necessary but not sufficient condition to create loyalty. Some customers will be satisfied with a simple standard service; for example a bed in a Formule 1 hotel will suffice, while others prefer an augmented service such as that on offer at the Ritz Carlton hotel. Sometimes the bundle of benefits is very small and sometimes it consists of many benefits. In the end, it is the bundle of benefits that creates customer value.

What Does the Experience Mean?

Services provide benefits. These benefits as experienced by the customer are intangible. Customer experience to receive the desired benefits (outcomes) takes place during a process of interaction, which is referred to as the service encounter. The service encounter is where the customer and service provider meet and both contribute to the production of the service. The customer, while co-producing the service, perceives what is going on and what the result will be. This experience is very subjective and determines to a large extent how the customer feels after the service delivery.

More and more, experiences are regarded as a profitable way of creating value for the customer, especially with the experience economy.[7] As we move further into the 21st century and many people work hard, the quest for experiences is increasing; especially as highly educated people with hectic jobs seem to have a huge need for unexpected positive experiences.

The consumer will also have expectations about the service experience. It is crucial for service organizations to meet and preferably exceed expectations. Satisfied customers may return to your organization, at least they are more likely to either return and tell others of the positive experiences. It sounds self-evident, but many service organizations forget this simple truth: 'The essence of service marketing is service. Service quality is the foundation of services marketing.'[8]

What Does the Interaction Mean?

In many cases, the production and consumption of services take place at the same moment. This means that the production and consumption occurs simultaneously and cannot be separated. This has been explained by Eiglier and Langeard (1987) who developed a concept referred to as the servuction process.

The servuction process describes the process of service production, indicating the simultaneous production and consumption of services. A model of the servuction process can be seen in Figure 2.3. In viewing the diagram you will see two main components. The first of these components identifies a part of the service production that is visible to the customer. This is the part of the service production process where the customer interacts with employees that are called the 'front office personnel'. The front office personnel and their activities are supported by the invisible part of the service provider: the back office personnel, which is the second component of the servuction process model. Direct contact between the service provider and the customer is essential.

During these events, referred to as the servuction process, the actual service delivery takes place. Within the servuction process 'the moments of truth' occur where the organization actually shows what they can do and how they meet expectations set. Because customers will

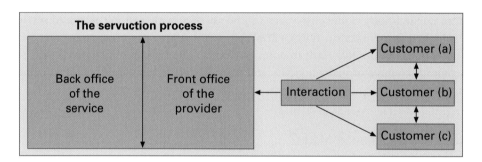

Figure 2.3 The servuction process

evaluate a service in part from the service environment, the physical setting and the atmosphere become relevant to the customer. The physical setting is the area in which the mutual interaction between customers and service providers takes place, as well as the area where the other customers impact on the final outcome of the service delivery process.

Customer A will be affected by the presence and the actions of customers B and C. For example, your own experiences at a restaurant or during a holiday (and thus your experienced quality) may be heavily affected by the other guests' behaviour. For a service provider, it is hard to control this part of the process. A hotel manager is not able to control the behaviour of his or her guests and as such must implement strategies to ensure that noisy guests do not impact upon the overall satisfaction of guests wanting a romantic weekend away.

Technology and automation, such as the ATM, have resulted in the number of personal contacts decreasing. Consequently, the lasting moments of truth become more and more important. The impact of this on service providers is that all elements of the service process have to be managed to ensure that each element is performed as it should be, the first time.[9]

The borderline between front office and back office is not fixed within a particular service organization, this line may change over time. Setting and changing this line is also a matter of internal structure of the service organization and hence affects human resource management. Thus the open kitchen in a restaurant as part of the visible front office can be a component of the restaurant's positioning strategy.

The service interaction process is also described in terms of the service encounter. This allows for the metaphor of considering the service delivery as drama or as a play with various actors all having their own script and roles to play. Using this metaphor, the physical setting is seen as a theatre with the stage, the back stage area and the area where the audience enjoy the show.[10] The servuction process refers to human encounters in both a profit and a non profit setting. People interact with one another, unless technology is used as a substitute for this interaction.

Interaction offers the opportunity for employees and clients to start building relationships with one another through the service encounters. Building these relationships is important for several reasons:

■ It offers the opportunity to learn about each others' wishes, whims, preferences, capabilities, opportunities. This may sharpen the knowledge of the expectations about the other 'party involved in the interaction'; and

■ existing relationships may function as a means to keep customers. Consider here the terms, loyalty, churn, and switching.

The second aspect relates to the premise that services are inherently relational. Christian Grönroos states: 'Understanding relationship marketing or marketing based on customer relationship management becomes a necessity for understanding how to manage a firm in service competition.'[11]

Classifying Services

Not all services are the same. It is therefore important to understand the nature of different services. Consequently, different management approaches need to be considered across the broad spectrum of services. Classifying services is a way of helping us to understand the varied nature of services.

Many authors have made typologies or classifications of services.[12] We have grouped many of these typologies. We hold that it is possible to describe services with respect to the following ten criteria:

1 Ownership;
2 Intangibility;
3 Service firms in the profit sector versus service organizations in the not for profit sector;
4 Markets and industries;
5 Internal and external services;
6 The service delivery process;
7 The customer's buying behaviour;
8 The relationship between the service provider and the customer;
9 The service provider's skills, knowledge and capacity; and
10 The physical site of the service delivery.

The first six criteria are strategic in nature, while the latter four are operational and are concerned with the service delivery process. All these ways of looking at services can be used to describe the services from competitors and compare them to one's own services. Competitive positions will be revealed as well as the opportunities to develop new services and bring them to the market successfully. For instance, when descriptions of a group of similar universities demonstrate that all of the universities have a system of classroom teaching, opportunities for a new way of teaching may be found utilizing technologies which could result in new approaches to teaching such as action-based learning or problem-based learning.

In relationship to *ownership*, we have stated that varying degrees of ownership may occur. Some services may be rented, leased or owned. You may rent vehicles, power tools, formal clothing; you may rent a car, an apartment, a team of management consultants; or you may rent admission to a museum, theatre or spa; or you may rent access to a network of telecommunications or banking services.

With respect to classifying services along their degree of *intangibility* we can say the continuum ranges from very intangible or pure services to very tangible, pure goods. In between these two extremes we find services with supporting services and goods; for example information boxes in tourist areas, as well as goods with accompanying services, such as after sales services and instructor's manuals. In fact, pure goods are canned services; a cup is the means to provide the service of drinking, a chair provides the service of sitting or even relaxing.[13]

The distinction between service organizations in the *profit and not for profit sector* refers to the basic problem of 'who sets the price' or 'who regulates the service offering'. Are prices set by the marketplace as in the profit sector, or via self-regulation in the industry or by public authorities? In other words, it hinges upon the difference between marketable and unmarketable services, which is also labelled as the difference between private services, merit services and public services.

Services can also be classified according to their *markets and industries*. Usually markets refer to the geographical area that is involved, for example the local market, the country or the world. Or to industrial markets versus consumer markets. Industries refer to the Standard Industry Codes (SICs) used in many statistics to define services at the industry level such as electricity, gas and water supply; construction; hotels and restaurants; financial intermediation; education or public administration.

Services can be provided both to an organization's customers and to customers within the organization such as the employees. This is the well-known distinction between *external and internal services*. In the literature on internal marketing and quality management the idea of internal customers has been developed; employees and departments are regarded as each other's customers and suppliers. This may enhance the internal market orientation and internal service quality, but also relates to the question of which services will be bought outside the organization and which will be produced by the organization itself. It is essential to understand that the level of internal quality determines the level of the external quality; mistakes made inside the company will affect the quality the external customer receives.

The *service delivery process* is another way to classify services strategically. Here we can think of the strategic decisions on the role the customer is expected to play in the servuction process. For example, is the service delivery process capital intensive, labour intensive, people-based or equipment-based? Is the service based on one-time contacts or episodes versus long-term relationships or contracts? Is the customer's presence and participation always needed when providing the service or not? Is the service delivered on the customer's premises or on the provider's premises? And finally, is the service tailormade or a standardized delivery?

After these classifications based on more strategic considerations are made, we can now turn to classifying services along operational considerations. These are the considerations involved in providing the actual service.

Services can also be classified according to the *customer's buying behaviour*. What kind of problem solving behaviour is required? In consumer markets we can speak of extensive, limited or routine problem solving behaviour; in industrial markets about new task, modified rebuy or straight rebuy. It is also important to distinguish between speciality, shopping or convenience services, or to look at the degree of perceived risk involved. Is perceived risk high, low or non existent for the target group of customers? Finally we must consider the consumer participation in the production of the service to a larger or smaller degree.

The kind of *relationship between the service provider and the customer* is another way of classifying services. Now concrete questions have to be asked, such as: will there be a formal or informal relationship between the service provider and the customer? Will the service be provided in an ongoing relationship, for example is the service subscription-based or will it be provided casually? Is the service membership-based or not? Is the service interactive or not? Are we at the beginning or end of the relationship life cycle? Is true loyalty at stake or not?

The *service provider's knowledge, skills and capacity* can also be used as a way of understanding services. This is dependent on whether or not the service provider has the appropriate characteristics to act in a market oriented way and deliver excellent service quality. But how is this done? How flexible is the service provider's capacity? How customized or standardized is the service delivery? Are the services delivered by one employee or by a group of interchangeable persons? Which assets and capabilities do they possess to deliver excellent service quality? Moreover, we can think of the distinction between knowledge-based services, facilitating services, people-based, property-based or information-based services.

Finally, the actual *physical site of the service delivery* is a criterion to classify services. Here we look at the distribution network of the service company; for example is the distribution intensive, selective or exclusive? Is the service delivered at a single site or is it a multiple site service? Is the servuction process location-bound or are the services transportable? Does the customer have to travel to the service provider, such as attending a class at university, or does the service provider have to travel to the customer, such as a home visit by a doctor? Is personal contact always needed or is remote interaction via telephone or e-services feasible? How important is the design of the servicescape (the environment where the service delivery takes place)? Are services delivered personally or in a group?

What you also can see from all these classifications and examples is that (just as with products) there is some kind of core of the service surrounded by one or more supplementary services. Christopher Lovelock developed the idea of the 'flower of service': the heart of the flower is the core services, the petals round the core are the supplementary services.[14] The many supplementary services that exist are either:

- ■ Facilitating supplementary services that facilitate use of the core product or are required for service delivery, like information, order taking, billing and payment; or
- ■ Enhancing supplementary services that may add extra value for customers, like consultation, hospitality, safekeeping, exceptions and special requests.

There are many ways to describe, analyse and classify services. Each method refers to a different way of looking at specific aspects of services. However, none of these aspects can be separated from one another and as such a more holistic approach is needed to take many or all of them into account. From our value creating perspective we maintain that it is important to focus on the degree of customization required by the customer because this will reflect whether standard services or customized services will be offered.

The supplier's view of services marketing management tends to consider core services versus augmented services; that is, the core service plus all the supplementary services added to the core service. In this text we will often refer to the following four types of services (Figure 2.4):

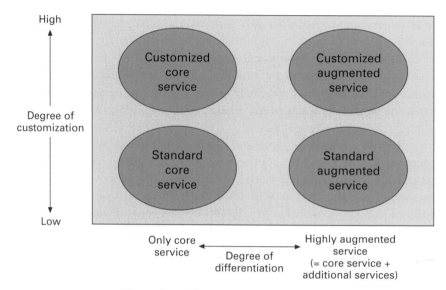

Figure 2.4 The taxonomy of service

Reprinted from *Market-led Strategic Change*, Nigel Piercy, pp. 146, Copyright 1997, with permission from Elsevier

1 *standard core services* such as dry cleaning, take home pizza, Mister Minit, Formule 1 hotels, McDonald's and low budget carriers;

2 *standard augmented services* such as Pizza Hut, Days Inn, toll free numbers, Marriott hotels, Singapore Airlines economy class;

3 *customized core services* such as doctors, accountants, Internet services, mail order houses, KLM business or royal class on daily routes;

4 *customized augmented services* such as specialized lawyers, Ritz Carlton hotels, Four Seasons hotels, five star resorts, private jets.

In Chapter 1 we outlined the importance of the services sector across the developed nations. The contrast between the services sector in developed nations and the services sector in developing nations is vast, and as such the types of service listed above will have different contexts across countries.[15]

2.3 Managing Services

This book will discuss services marketing management. However before we discuss marketing issues in depth we have to discuss the basics of management and strategy. This will be done in this section.

Strategic Management

Strategic management is that set of managerial decisions and actions that determines the long-run performance of an organization. It entails all of the basic management functions;

that is, the organization's strategies must be planned, organized, put into effect, and controlled.[16]

In other words,

A strategy is the pattern or plan that integrates an organization's major goals, policies, and action sequences into a cohesive whole. A well-formulated strategy helps to marshal and allocate an organization's resources into a unique and viable posture based on its relative internal competencies and shortcomings, anticipated changes in the environment, and contingent moves by intelligent opponents.[17]

There seems to be quite some confusion about the proper use and content of the term 'strategy'. In order to avoid this confusion it is important to know from which perspective strategy has been defined.[18] Strategy can be viewed from five perspectives; namely, strategy is a

■ Plan: some sort of consciously intended course of action, a guideline (or set of guidelines) to deal with a situation;

■ Ploy: a specific manoeuvre intended to outwit an opponent or competitor;

■ Pattern: consistency in behaviour;

■ Position: a means of locating an organization in an environment. Here, strategy is the mediating force between the organization and its environment, between the internal and external context. It hinges upon the chosen combination of service, market and technology;[19] and

■ Perspective: here strategy refers to the ingrained way of perceiving the world. It looks inside the organization. In this perspective, strategy is to the organization what personality is to the individual. In the rest of our book we will label this perspective as the organization's culture or the corporate culture to distinguish it from the other four strategic perspectives.

These five perspectives are not contradictory to each other nor are they mutually exclusive. Rather, they are linked to each other. Whatever strategic perspective will be taken, it is crucial to know what sets an organization apart, what is its distinctive edge, its competitive advantage, its unique offering. This uniqueness is based on the organization's core competencies or capabilities. It is commonly accepted that an organization should strive for a sustainable competitive advantage, an advantage that is hard to imitate. Such an advantage will create the value to the many stakeholders of the organization such as customers, employees, shareholders.

Market Strategies

One way to look at the process of determining the organization's market strategy – for example, making decisions on positioning and defining the overall direction of an organization in each of its various target markets – is to apply Nigel Piercy's model, the

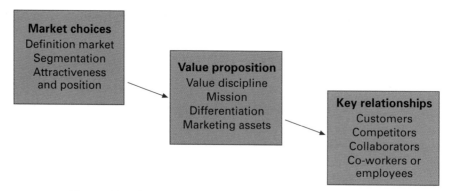

Figure 2.5   Our way of looking at the strategic pathway

strategic pathway.[20] According to Piercy, market strategy centres on making decisions on three main issues, namely:

■ Market choices;
■ The value proposition; and
■ The key relationships that drive the strategy.

Market choices refers to decisions on the exact definition of the market, the segmentation of the market, the attractiveness of the market to the organization and the position to be achieved.

The value proposition is based on the content of the organization's mission statement, its competitive differentiation and the marketing assets, which contain among others the brands and the brand equity or value. We add here the value discipline (see second box in Figure 2.5) which reflects which one of the three value disciplines the service firm has selected.

Creating value for the customer is a capability that can be implemented in three ways. Some customers, such as individual households, segments of customers or companies, demand low priced products, while others favour innovations or close contacts with their suppliers.[21] This made Michael Treacy and Fred Wiersema develop the three value disciplines namely:

■ Operational excellence;
■ Product leadership; and
■ Customer intimacy.

Customer intimacy fits best with organizations offering customized products and services, while product leadership fits best to firms always being at the edge of developing high quality new products and services, whereas operational excellence suits best to producing low cost standard products and services.[22]

Organizations should focus on one of these three value disciplines and excel in one of them while the other two value disciplines are comparable to what is common or standard in the industry within which they operate. Consequently, the three disciplines are not mutually exclusive. All three value disciplines can create value for the customer, not only customer intimacy. Some customers find their value in buying at discounters like Aldi, Lidl or low priced retailers like Wal-Mart, while others find value in buying at more expensive retailers like Nordström, Bijenkorf, Bloomingdale's or Selfridges. So, different segments search for different qualities and values.

Finally, the key relationships with customers, competitors, collaborators such as other firms in the distribution channel – namely market research agencies, accountants, banks, advertising agencies – and co-workers and employees are crucial in developing the organization's market strategy.[23]

Managing Relationships

More and more marketing academics and managers recognize that relationships between people and organizations are crucial in today's competitive environment. These relationships can be regarded as valuable assets that can be managed in a way that is hard to imitate and can thus be used to create a sustainable competitive advantage.

Many service providers like to have long-term formal relationships with their customers. Such relationships create long-term value to the firm and quite often consist of barriers to exit which make it difficult for a customer to leave or switch to another supplier. That is why insurance companies love to have ten-year contracts with their insured or why publishers like to have subscriptions for a year or longer.

Marketing managers could ask themselves what kind of long-term formal relationships they would like to have with their customers. To be successful however, they should also know what kind of long-term formal relationships customers want; increasingly customers are frustrated when tied into a long-term relationship with a service supplier, particularly when it is difficult to leave that relationship, as is often the case with say Internet service providers.

The capability of managing relationships can be evaluated from two perspectives:

1   Starting, building, maintaining and ending relationships;
2   Starting, building and maintaining profitable relationships.

At first glance both perspectives seem to look the same. However, the emphasis on the profitability of the relationships differs. The first perspective encompasses on the one hand the relationships that not for profit organizations may have with their target segments (despite their 'profitability' or costs compared to benefits) and on the other hand, it will fit into every organization's way of giving content to its social responsibility.

The second perspective focusses on profitable relationships. It is very simple to say that an organization should focus on creating and maintaining profitable relationships, but defining what is profitable can be difficult. For example, a bank may have customers who are not profitable now but may develop in the future, such as students. What should an organization do with a customer who creates a temporary loss? How much attention does a customer need in order to transform into a profitable customer? If these efforts prove to be great then it may mean that the organization will end the relationship. To determine whether or not to end a relationship an organization such as a bank may identify the profitability of their customer base and stimulate unprofitable customers to leave by increasing the price of various banking services for this segment. This will be done while simultaneously focussing on their profitable customers. This can be achieved only if the organizational accounting system is one in which profitability per customer or market segment can be identified.

Customer relationship management (CRM) focusses on customer interaction over a long period of time; transactions are one-off interactions with the firm. In CRM knowing the customer is crucial. ICT databases with such information capabilities can now be easily developed. Loyalty programmes are one way to implement CRM. The lifetime value of the customer is very important to the service provider. This may be helpful in making the trade-off between the short-term and long-term profitability of the customer,[24] particularly when an organization is considering rationalizing its unprofitable customers.

We mentioned two perspectives on managing relationships. In both perspectives, concepts such as trust, commitment, satisfaction, benevolence and mutual interdependence come to the fore. Managing relationships with all partners in the distribution channel, not only the customer but also the suppliers and other collaborators, may be one of the service provider's core competencies or capabilities in creating and maintaining its sustainable competitive advantage.

Managing relationships to create a sustainable competitive advantage does not only refer to managing the relationships with customers or suppliers, but also with employees and co-workers. Given the complexity of the relationships which need managing in the service organization, internal marketing becomes a more critical component of the marketing strategy. Satisfied employees are a great asset to the organization, especially in the service sector where much of the business is people's business. Since there seems to be a clear impact from service employees' behaviour on the customer's satisfaction, it is crucial to be aware of this effect.

The idea of the service profit chain hinges upon the notion that creating satisfied customers and creating satisfied employees goes hand in hand; in both cases loyalty to the organization will increase. In the case of dissatisfied customers and employees, loyalty will decrease and switching to competitors will increase.[25]

In recent years this thinking has extended into the development of the value profit chain.[26] This model is based on the premise that when the company cares about its employees these employees will then extend this care to their customers who will then care about the company by doing things such as buying shares, buying the products and services, and recommending the firm to others. This model hinges upon the concepts of creating customer value, employee value and shareholder value simultaneously.

Assets and Capabilities

Alongside the technical knowledge about the services in a particular industry – for example, factual knowledge on wine and food in the hospitality industry – and the skills, competences, capabilities of the employees, the systems of the organization, the procedures and formal and informal organizational structures are critical when determining how a service will be delivered. These skills however must sit alongside the skills of the customer which are required to co-produce and deliver the service.

As the services sector is usually regarded as a people's business, many of these skills refer to the skills of the service provider. Since these skills belong to the employees of the firm, they could simply be labelled as assets, while the way they are applied could be called the capabilities of the firm. In other words, they can be regarded as the resources the service firm possesses. In that sense, this section is based on the ideas expressed in the resource-based view of the firm.[27] The assets and capabilities come to the fore in the strategic pathway's second box (marketing assets) and third box (managing the key relationships) in Figure 2.5.

Applying this way of thinking to the marketing domain means that marketing assets are the resource endowments the firm has acquired or built over time and can be deployed to create the competitive advantage in the marketplace. They can be tangible as well as intangible, the intangibles being the most difficult to imitate, but sometimes the most important ones to create a sustainable competitive advantage. They can be customer-based, distribution- or supply chain-based, internal organization-based or alliance-based:

■ Customer-based assets are for example brand name or reputation, credibility with customers, level of customer service and relations with key customers.

■ Assets with respect to distribution or the whole supply chain refer to the relations with suppliers, the distribution network, the distribution approach, or the relations with the channel intermediaries.

■ Internal assets are for instance the cost advantage achieved in the servuction processes, the marketing information systems, the cost control systems or copyrights and patents.

■ The alliance-based assets refer to co-operation with strategic partners and the sharing of knowledge or other resources.

The marketing capabilities are the glue that binds the assets together and facilitates their effective deployment in the marketplace. They can be differentiated into inside-out, outside-in, spanning and networking capabilities.[28]

Inside-out capabilities refer to internal operations that might be used to create value to the customer; they hinge upon the organization's internal resources and capabilities like financial management, human resources management, operations management, cost control, technology development, controlling the servuction processes, integrated logistics or marketing management.

Outside-in capabilities refer to the use of marketing information, understanding customer needs, creating relationships or maintaining and enhancing them; they help to understand the changes that take place in the marketplace in order to operate more effectively in the chosen market segments.

Spanning capabilities refer to the capabilities to integrate the inside-out and outside-in capabilities; among other things they have to have the ability to launch new services, to set the right prices, and to control order fulfilment, purchasing, service recovery, internal communications, and processes to develop new services and products.

Finally, the networking capabilities refer to the ability to manage relationships with suppliers, pooling expertise with strategic partners, sharing mutual trust with strategic partners and sharing mutual commitment and goals with strategic partners.[29]

Matching Demand and Supply

Managing demand and supply requires special skills in the service sector since services cannot be stored. In fact, the economic conditions of centuries ago, when people consumed what they had produced themselves, still count. Storing products has made life easier and production companies can benefit from this basic feature of tangible products. Since this is not the case for services, service providers have to find other ways to match demand and supply.

Capacity management can be directed at managing and controlling demand as well as supply.[30] Pricing services can be a very effective tool here. For example, electricity can be priced so that there are different prices for supply at different times of the day. Similarly there are different tariffs for using Internet lines during the day and night, or off-peak prices in tourist destinations.

Understanding customer behaviour is another way to match demand and supply in the short or long run. Understanding the market is crucial as it is important to understand what customers prefer at what time. The supply of services can be controlled for instance by hiring part-time workers, such as having more waiters during peak hours; sharing capacity with other service providers, for example when one hotel is full, a hotel will often refer you to another hotel with which they have made such arrangements; or increasing the participation of the customer in the service delivery process, such as having a customer fill out their own loan application forms in a bank.

Managing waiting times is another way to better match demand and supply. All elements of the marketing mix can be applied in matching demand and supply.[31] In this perspective, relationships with customers and elements of the marketing mix can be regarded as the assets, while managing these assets refers to the service provider's capabilities to match demand and supply.

The interplay of all the assets and capabilities in matching demand and supply determines the ultimate service quality delivered and thus customer satisfaction, employee satisfaction, and sales and profits in the short run. In other words, they contribute to the value created for many different stakeholders such as customer value, employee value and shareholder value. And value can be created in many ways as indicated by the three different value disciplines.

Value to the Stakeholders

The key success factor when developing strategy for services is value. Value can be expressed through both quality and pricing. Alongside value, marketers must also consider how relationships can be maintained with customers through the development and implementation of relationship marketing strategies. Finally, a service firm's image or reputation must also be considered as critical components of any services marketing strategy. A well-positioned corporate image can be particularly important to first-time buyers.[32]

These key success factors or core competencies resemble the marketing-based assets and the outside-in and spanning capabilities. Having them is one thing; having a competitive advantage is another thing. The most important issue is whether they all lead to a better performance.[33] Excellent performance will lead to higher customer value.

Customers however are not the only stakeholder in organizations. An organization has many stakeholders. Creating value for one of the stakeholders may conflict with the value created for other stakeholders. In many banks today, value-based management is dominating the firm putting emphasis on the financial results by creating shareholder value in the short run. Customers might start complaining about a banking service in circumstances where many banks are closing down branches. In this situation customers may be more inclined to switch. Conflicts may arise between accomplishing goals in the short run and long run as well as between the interests of the many stakeholders. Taking a broad, holistic perspective may help in solving this problem.

Focussing on stakeholder value affects the way an organization evaluates both its performance and the performance of its employees. It means that not only financial but also non financial indicators have to be used to evaluate the performance. Financial indicators such as revenue, cost, profit, return on investment, expenses on R&D and training and the value of stock as well as non financial indicators such as market share, customer satisfaction, complaints and compliments, customer loyalty, employee absenteeism, company image and reputation can be all applied to assess the organization's performance from various perspectives.

The balanced score card can be a useful instrument to integrate the various aspects of performance.[34] In this respect, socially responsible behaviour by companies has been emphasized more and more. Managers who like to evaluate the company's performance according to the balanced score card quite often have conflicting views with those who like to evaluate the company's performance based on shareholder value. In such situations a board has to decide which system will be used, and this will be dependent upon the organization's mission.

The next section will show that a real market oriented firm will probably benefit the most from using the balanced score card. In Holland, the Rabo Bank, a co-operative bank uses the balanced score card approach, while banks such as ABNAmro and ING use value-based management, focussing on shareholder value.

In the long term there should be no reason for conflict between marketing and shareholder value. Peter Doyle holds a very clear position in this respect:

The illusion of conflict has occurred because many managers have confused maximising shareholder value and maximising profitability. The two are completely different. Maximising profitability is short term and invariably erodes a company's long-term competitiveness. It is about cutting costs and shedding assets to produce quick improvements in earnings. By neglecting new market opportunities and failing to invest, such strategies destroy rather than create economic value. Strategies aimed at maximising shareholder value are different. They focus on identifying growth opportunities and building competitive advantage. They punish short-term strategies that destroy assets and fail to capitalise on the company s core capabilities.[35]

Now that we have discussed the most important characteristics of services and managing services in broad terms, it is time to turn to marketing. Let's have a look at what is marketing all about.

2.4 Marketing Services

This section discusses the fundamentals of marketing and its impact on service organizations. Important concepts discussed here include market orientation, customer expectations, quality, the internal structure and the employees, and finally the key success factors for service organizations. But first of all, we have to define what marketing is. The latest definition of the American Marketing Association on marketing is the following one:

Marketing is an organizational function and a set of processes for creating, communicating, and delivering value to customers and for managing customer relationships in ways that benefit the organization and its shareholders.[36]

This definition includes short-term transactions as well as taking a long-term relationship perspective, which would allow an organization to take a marketing orientated perspective. It allows for both focussing on relationships and the implementation of marketing mix instruments to create value (the benefits) during and after exchange processes. According to the AMA, marketing management can be defined:

Marketing management is the process of setting marketing goals for an organization (considering internal resources and market opportunities), the planning and execution of activities to meet these goals, and measuring progress toward their achievement.

In this definition the resources and opportunities refer also to the assets and capabilities we mentioned, the market orientation, the internal processes to deliver internal and external service quality to create the ultimate service experience.

However, misperceptions about marketing do exist. We have encountered the fact that many organizations that start their marketing practices, especially service organizations, have a misperception of the discipline. 'Marketing' is a word that is widely bandied about. Sometimes, it is supposed to be the cure for all problems organizations face in the marketplace. Advertising would then be the solution to the problem of low sales. We all know real life in the marketplace is not that simple.

The Image of Marketing

In discussions concerning marketing, one often finds people defining marketing as nothing more than a trick that is used to sell goods and services. Sometimes, people see marketing as a trick designed to sell products people do not even want to buy or use. Marketing, then, is very much associated with pushing and persuading people to buy goods and services they do not really want or need. Marketing is quite often associated with terms such as advertising, consumers, market research, sales, products, and other forms of communication.[37] Such public opinion was quite common in the 1970s and early 1980s. These opinions started to appear in studies about consumer attitudes towards marketing and consumerism.[38] Even today these ethical opinions come up anew in discussions on health care; for instance, to what extent are fast-food restaurants, catering companies at schools and manufacturers of snack foods encouraging unhealthy forms of eating? Should they not show their corporate social responsibility and discourage unhealthy behaviour or provide warnings associated with eating too much fast food?

Our conclusion from these findings concerning the image of marketing is that there are minimal associations of marketing with strategic activities such as market orientation, quality, segmentation, need satisfaction, strategy, relationships, servicing, or specific marketing assets and capabilities. Contrary, very visible operational issues are dominant. The important longer-term issues upon which every marketing strategy should be based are lacking in the current, popular view of marketing. Therefore, we will focus attention to the following fundamentals of marketing.

Underlying all marketing strategy, marketers should consider:

■ Market orientation;
■ Customer expectations and quality perceptions;
■ Organizing the marketing effort and employees; and
■ Key assets and capabilities.

These should then form the holistic framework from which the operational actions that are now associated with marketing, can be applied. Without such a framework it is hard to bring marketing into action and create value.

Market Orientation

Market orientation is based on five benchmarks in the market. These are:

1 The customers or the chosen target segments;
2 The competitors;
3 The partners in the distribution channel;
4 All the other collaborating organizations; and
5 The service provider itself.

Each of these elements interacts with a particular market. The organization should provide services which actually satisfy the needs, wishes, whims and preferences of present and future customers. In order to accomplish this difficult and complex mission an organization should select an appropriate target group. The activity of focussing on these customers is called the organization's customer orientation. This customer orientation is linked to the chosen value discipline: customer intimacy, product leadership or operational excellence. Customer orientation may also lead to providing different services for different customers or segments. In terms of Michael Porter's generic strategies, it is possible to speak here about differentiation strategies and/or focus strategies.

The organization's own services should create more value than those services offered by competitors. The customer should then ascribe a higher quality–price ratio or value to the organization's service than to the competitors'. In order to realize this, a company should know:

1 Which services customers perceive as competing services;
2 Which other organizations currently or potentially produce these services;

3 In which way are they produced, including how much and what kind of customer participation is required; and

4 What are competitors likely to do in the near future.

In short, the organization should know when, where and how consumers perceive them as different from their competitors. What do consumers regard as the companies' unique selling or service points and which guide their decision making? Only when the company knows this, can it position itself on the grounds of quality or price. Quality–price ratios quite often have to do with the costs and cost structure of the company. So, to a large extent, this item has to do with Michael Porter's strategy and ideas about cost leadership. On the other hand, quality related to the price to be paid can also be defined as value.

George Day took a similar way of reasoning when he argued that 'Competitive superiority is revealed in the market as some combination of superior customer value and lowest delivered cost' and:

The essence of competitive advantage is a positioning theme that sets a business apart from its rivals in ways that are meaningful to the target customers. The most successful themes are built on some combination of three thrusts:

☐ *better (through superior quality or service);*
☐ *faster (by being able to sense and satisfy shifting customer requirements faster than competitors); and*
☐ *closer (with the creation of durable relationships).*

The task for management is to simultaneously find a compelling theme and ensure continuing superiority in the skills, resources, and controls that will be the source of this advantage over target competitors.[39]

It is essentially a capability of market oriented organizations to properly use market information. When information is considered as a crucial asset, market orientation can be defined as done by Kohli and Jaworski (1990): 'the organization wide generation of market intelligence pertaining to current and future customer needs, dissemination of the intelligence across departments and organization wide responsiveness to it'.[40]

The generation of intelligence focusses on collecting relevant market information. The dissemination of intelligence spreads the information across an organization. Every employee should have relevant market information and an external orientation toward the market referred to as market sensing capabilities, instead of only having a perspective on internal procedures. The result of the generation and dissemination of the relevant information has to be that departments and people work closely together or at least co-operate. When the information is available, a corporate strategy, a marketing strategy and a positioning strategy can be formulated for each target group of customers.[41]

The combination of the visions of customer orientation and competitor orientation culminate in the concept of market orientation.[42] The other partners in the distribution channel, such as the suppliers and the institutional customers and the other organizations with which the service provider is collaborating, determine the actual service offering, its quality and hence the market offering. High quality relationships with all these partners in the

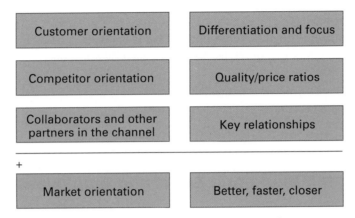

Figure 2.6   Market orientation: more value

distribution channel and in the whole process of delivering the service co-determine the final service quality and hence the value created to the stakeholders (see Figure 2.6).

Based on this, we will use the following broad definition of market orientation:

Market orientation is the degree to which an organization in all its thinking and acting (internally as well as externally) is guided by and committed to the factors determining the market behaviour of the organization itself and its customers. The right internal and external actions, then, will create the benefits and value for the organization's customers and other stakeholders.

Customer Expectations and Quality Perceptions

As part of the market orientation, marketers have to pay attention to the expectations of customers and how they perceive quality.

The first issue relating to customer expectations is dealing with the fact that customers should know in advance what the service organization can do for them or may mean for them. Creating appropriate expectations is important for the service provider in order to avoid customers having expectations that cannot be met. The service provider, therefore, has to communicate with customers in relation to what to expect and what not to expect from the organization. This is not a matter of manipulating the market but a matter of providing fair and honest information. Often wrong, false or unjustified expectations will lead to dissatisfaction. In turn, dissatisfaction will often lead to brand switching, complaining or negative word-of-mouth communication. Certainly, it will not lead to a high degree of brand loyalty or repeat purchases, let alone long-lasting relationships between company and client. Managing customer expectations and providing fair and honest information, therefore, are important features of services marketing management in order to create value to the stakeholders.

The issue of quality perception is important because the customer's evaluation of the service is determined to a large extent by the employee's behaviour. Every employee, including front as well as back office employees, contributes to the service quality as customers experience it. The final quality is determined by the weakest part of the quality chain. It is possible to distinguish between three kinds of quality. Christian Grönroos (1990b, 2000) mentioned the first two in the list, we have added the third one:

1 The technical quality: *what* is being delivered?;
2 The functional quality: *how* is it delivered?; and
3 The relational quality: *who* delivers the service?

Organizing the Marketing Effort and Employees

The service industry is an industry where people can have very intense relationships. Quality is mostly determined by *who* delivers the service; this forms the relational quality. Trust and understanding are very important in service delivery processes, even in Internet-based relationships where the personal contact in a physical sense is lacking. Relationship marketing is a crucial topic in services marketing management, and leads to establishing strong relationships based on trust and commitment. The affective or emotional component of commitment plays a decisive role in continuing relationships.

Each employee has to realize that out of a first contact a lifelong relationship can be born. The first contact is the start of the relationship life cycle. During this life cycle, the intensity of the relationship may change due to requirements in needs, preferences, whims and external contingencies. This has to be reflected in the employee's service attitude.

The interplay between employees and customers sets special requirements on controlling the service delivery and managing and assessing the employees. Therefore, human resource management and motivating people is such an essential element in providing high quality services. That is why the P of personnel is often mentioned as the first P of the services marketing mix. Other instruments are process, product (service), place, promotion (communication), price and physical evidence. These will be elaborated upon in the final part of this book on 'creating the service experience'. For, all these operational Ps make the final service the customer encounters provided the organization has the right systems (on information or delivering the service). So, being a market oriented service provider is much more than just having a marketing department; it implies all employees act in a market oriented way. That calls for a market oriented culture.

Market Oriented Cultures in Service Organizations

Corporate culture refers to the norms and values deeply rooted in an organization.[43] They are the shared values or shared beliefs. These are about how people do things around here. Quite often they are taken for granted, in the sense that it is self-evident that employees behave in a particular way although these norms and shared values can differ between countries. Hofstede (1991) defines corporate culture as 'the collective programming of the mind which distinguishes the members of one organization from another'.[44]

This conceptual definition is operationalized by looking at culture via 'the shared perceptions of daily practices'.[45] The capability of defining and managing the service organization's culture is therefore an essential issue for a market oriented culture in a service organization.

A market oriented corporate culture appears to be a results oriented, employee oriented, professional, open and pragmatic culture. Partly, control should be tight: goals and targets should be set and well communicated to employees so that their performance can be compared to these goals. On the other hand, service providers should also be empowered. This requires a loose control system. People can be empowered only when they are aware of the overall strategic framework and set goals.[46]

Care for people, both customers as well as employees, is a dominant feature of a market oriented culture. Companies having such a culture also possess high ethical standards and do business accordingly. Meeting customer preferences is much more important than applying rules. Consequently, many governmental bodies and bureaucratic agencies such as privatized public utilities have to make big changes when they want to become market oriented. A mind shift for the employees and top management is then needed. Market oriented firms also stress a long-term orientation over a short-term orientation. Such an organization is open and the employees find risk taking self-evident. They are empowered and are able to accept the responsibility to act accordingly.

These cultural characteristics are the foundation for their marketing strategy. These marketing strategies are dominated by a strong drive to be the best, thorough knowledge about present and potential customers and competitors within the market, clear marketing goals and a positive attitude towards risk taking in developing new services. Moreover, such a culture is characterized by meeting the needs of the customers via targeted marketing strategies, and setting marketing goals accordingly. These goals are clear and well communicated throughout the company in which management provide example by showing how employees should work and treat the customer. Their style of leadership in showing this role model can be characterized more as a democratic, coaching style of leadership. A market oriented company is permeated with the marketing philosophy and is aware of providing excellent after sales services. Within this company, the various departments cooperate and exchange market information deemed relevant to other departments automatically.

2.5 Market Oriented Services Management: Our Perspective

In our view, market oriented service organizations have a unique culture in which their assets are implemented via specific capabilities to create value to the customer and the other stakeholders.

Such a *culture* is characterized by a sincere concern and care about people, ethics, results, goals, long-term orientation, risk taking, empowerment and pragmatically meeting customer needs. This can be translated into thorough market knowledge, clear and internally well-communicated target group specific marketing goals, developing new services, democratic and coaching styles of leadership, with adjustments to specific contingencies, management role models, better quality of services and after sales services, and excellent co-operation and exchange of market information between departments.

The market orientation perspective sets the framework for how employees and the partners in the marketing channel will think, act, and consequently treat their customers in giving meaning to their external orientation and service attitude.

Many assets and capabilities are needed to create a better value, performance and sustainable competitive advantage. Sometimes these assets are labelled as the key success factors of service organizations: value for money, excellent and close relationships between service provider/employee and the customer/client, quality in services and performance, the organization's reputation and brand name/brand equity, competitive pricing.

All these can reduce the customer's perceived risk with regard to the intangible service and ultimately create value to all stakeholders. To be effective, the market orientation should live throughout the whole service organization and not only in the sales and marketing department; consequently, all the employees in the back office, in the front office and of course top management should be permeated with this way of thinking and acting. The customer is not the only stakeholder for whom value has to be created; also employees and shareholders are crucial to accomplish goals and act in a socially responsible way by paying attention to the people, the planet and the company's profit. Or, to put it differently, sustainable services are a prerequisite for sustainable profit to survive in the domestic and international marketplace.

In implementing this philosophy, it should be customized in an integrated or holistic way to the specific needs of the chosen customer segments. Some customers just want a simple, standardized, no-frills, core service while others want very augmented, personalized services. Therefore, a market oriented service provider can create value for its customers and other stakeholders by offering various types of services, as we distinguished:

1 Standard core services;
2 Standard augmented services;
3 Customized core services; and
4 Customized augmented services.

Each service provider needs to decide which of these four services they will provide. Organizations must balance customization and differentiation to develop their positioning in the customer's mind. Organizations must also ensure that their selected value discipline is well communicated among employees. Some service providers focus on customer intimacy and like to provide customized augmented services while others perform in terms of operational excellence and provide low cost standard core services.

For all four types of services it will be important to identify how conveniently these services are co-produced. In other words, how much time and effort consumers have to spend on buying and using a service.[47] Consumers spend time and effort deciding on accessing, transacting for and benefiting from a service. The content of this process may differ for each of the four service types distinguished. We also think it is important to notice that this convenience may largely differ between the wide range of existing services in different countries. Nevertheless, a trade-off between costs and benefits will always be made.

So, after the overview of what is happening in the world of services in Chapter 1, we have now laid down the fundamentals of our view on strategic services marketing management in a domestic or international context. To further develop your understanding of services marketing management we will discuss the following topics in this book:

- buyer behaviour and segmentation (Chapter 3);
- service relationships and brands (Chapter 4);
- service quality (Chapter 5);
- market strategies (Chapter 6);
- internationalization (Chapter 7);
- services and e-services (Chapter 8);
- service innovation (Chapter 9);
- people, process and physical evidence (Chapter 10);
- place, promotion and price (Chapter 11); and
- implementation, performance and control (Chapter 12).

Summary

The phrase 'strategic services marketing management' comprises many sub-topics:

- Strategic management refers to that set of managerial decisions and actions that determine the long-run performance of an organization. It entails all of the basic management functions; that is, the organization's strategies must be planned, organized, put into effect, and controlled;
- Services are originally intangible and relatively quickly perishable activities whose buying, which does not always lead to material possession, takes place in an interaction process aimed at creating customer satisfaction;
- Marketing refers to an organizational function and a set of processes for creating, communicating and delivering value to customers and for managing customer relationships in ways that benefit the organization and its stakeholders.

Our view on market oriented services management underlies strategic services marketing management.

The five I's of services relate to their intangibility, inseparability, inconsistency, inventory and inability to own. There are a number of nuances about these five I's, which must be considered when developing strategy.

Services can be classified along ten different criteria. The first six are more of a strategic nature while the latter four are more of an operational nature:

1   Ownership: owning, leasing or renting;
2   Intangibility;
3   Profit or not for profit organizations;
4   Markets and industries;
5   Internal and external services;
6   The services delivery process;
7   The customer's buying behaviour;
8   The relationship between the service provider and the customer;
9   The service provider's skills, knowledge and capacity; and
10 The physical site of the service delivery.

The market choices made by the service provider, the value proposition and the key relationships they want to accomplish will make up the strategic pathway as a means to define the organizational market strategies.

The organization's assets and capabilities are crucial to accomplish these goals. Four types of marketing assets:

1 customer-based,
2 distribution-based,
3 internal-based and
4 alliance-based

and four types of capabilities

1 inside-out,
2 outside-in,
3 spanning and
4 networking

have been distinguished.

The service organization's market orientation is reflected in its culture of caring about people, ethics, results, goals, long-term orientation, risk taking, empowerment and pragmatically meeting customer needs. This is translated in marketing terms into thorough market knowledge, clear and internally well-communicated target group specific marketing goals, developing new services, democratic and coaching styles of leadership with adjustments to specific contingencies, management role models, better quality of services, after sales services, and an excellent co-operation and exchange of market information between departments. This market oriented culture and practice should live throughout the whole organization in order to create value to the customer in all its relationships. That sets the framework to really act in line with the adage: services marketing management is about people, especially caring about people, customers as well as employees. And service quality is the foundation of services marketing.

Questions

1. What are the key elements in defining services?
2. Define what is meant by the following terms:
   a value discipline
   b market orientation
   c strategic management
   d strategic marketing.
3. How are the terms listed in Q. 2 linked together?
4. Why can service marketing management be circumscribed as 'caring about people'?
5. Using examples to illustrate, summarize the characteristics of a market oriented service company.

6. What are the key success factors of the service companies you regularly use?

7. Using a company that you regularly use as an example, describe what you consider to be their most important assets and capabilities?

8. Describe the five I's of services.

9. In considering intangibility, can you identify any circumstances where a service might not be intangible?

10. What is meant when it is stated that all five I's are relative characteristics?

11. How could information technology improve the service delivery process and partly 'solve the inventory problem'?

12. What is meant by the term 'strategic pathway'?

13. Which four types of services are to be distinguished in this book?

Assignments

1. Download the World Development Report (2004) *Making Services Work for Poor People*. The report concludes that 'services are failing poor people specifically in access, in quantity, in quality.'
   a Why is this occurring?
   b How different is the situation in Bangladesh, Bolivia, Chad, India or Nigeria?

2. Source OECD statistics, for gross domestic product (GDP).
   a Compare the GDProduct and the number of employees in the various service industries in the USA, the UK, the Netherlands, Germany, Australia, New Zealand, Spain and Italy.
   b What can you conclude from these figures? How different is the situation in 2000, 1975 and 1950?

3. Identify two companies; one that that you consider delivers excellent service quality and another that you consider very poor services quality.
   a Describe the excellent service, detailing why you consider the services to be excellent.
   b Describe the poor service detailing why you consider the service to be poor.
   c What are the main differences between the two companies?

Endnotes

1 Based on Kangis and O'Reilly, 2003; and Wirtz and Johnston, 2003.

2 Christian Grönroos (2000, p. 46) defines a service as 'a process consisting of a series of more or less intangible activities that normally, but not necessarily always, take place in interactions between the customer and service employees and/or physical resources or goods and/or systems of the service provider, which are provided as solutions to customer problems.' Philip Kotler (1991) defines services as: 'any act or performance

that one party can offer to another that is essentially intangible and does not result in the ownership of anything. Its production may or may not be tied to a physical product.' John Bateson (1992) argues: 'The goods/service dichotomy is a subtly changing spectrum, with firms moving their position within this spectrum over time. A good example of a good/service dichotomy is Domino's Pizza, a home-delivery pizza chain. Is the customer buying goods (a pizza) or a service (a guaranteed arrival within 30 minutes)? and 'The word service should be read with the following caveat: to the extent that the benefits are delivered to the consumer by a service rather than a good.' Valarie Zeithaml and Mary Jo Bitner (2003, p. 3) hold that 'in the most simple terms, *services are deeds, processes and performances*'. Their broader definition, which is in line with this simple one, is: 'services include all economic activities whose output is not a physical product or construction, is generally consumed at the time it is produced, and provides added value in forms (such as convenience, amusement, timeliness, comfort or health) that are essentially intangible concerns of its first purchaser.' Ray Fisk, Stephen Grove and Joby John (2000) simply state in their book on interactive services marketing: 'Service is a deed, a performance, an effort.'

3 Berkowitz *et al.* (1986, pp. 608–610) discussed the first four I's; we have added as the fifth I the inability to own (based on the 2004 Lovelock and Gummesson article).

4 That is a major reason for Grönroos to take the service perspective in his book published in 2000. The following statements are important in his way of reasoning. 'Every firm, regardless of whether its core product is a physical good or a service, whether the firm is operating on consumer markets or business-to-business markets, has the option of taking a service perspective.' (p. 4) 'A service perspective means that the role of service components in customer relationships is seen as strategic ... Service competition is a competitive situation where the core solution is the prerequisite for success, but where the management of a number of services, together with the core solution, forms a Total Service Offering and determines whether or not the firm will be successful.' (p. 6) Recently, this topic has also been discussed in Vargo and Lusch (2004), who regard this service perspective as the new dominant logic in marketing (instead of the dominant logic of focussing on tangible goods). We hold that tangible products like a chair offer in fact the service of 'a means to sit or relax'. So products are 'canned services'; see also section 2.2.

5 Lovelock and Gummesson, 2004, pp. 20–41.

6 Peter and Olson (1993), discuss the functional and psycho-sociological consequences of buying, which can be either positive or negative. If these consequences are positive we talk about the benefits of a service. We may speak about perceived risk when the consequences are negative. So a service may have positive (benefits) as well as negative consequences for a consumer. Perceived risk will turn out to be one of the core issues in the analysis of consumer behaviour with respect to services.

7 Horovitz, 2000, pp. 24–26; Pine and Gilmore, 1999.

8 Berry and Parasuraman, 1991, p. 4.

9 This is also the basic idea of quality management these days.

10 Bitner, Booms and Tetreault, 1990; Zeithaml and Bitner, 2003, pp. 45–47; Grove, Fisk and Bitner, in Swartz, Bowen and Brown, 1992.

11 Grönroos, 2000, pp. 6–8.

12 A detailed overview of those classifications is provided in the first edition of our *Service Marketing Management*, Chapter 2. Christopher Lovelock's 1983 study is one of the most well-known studies in this field.

13 See also endnote 3.

14 See for instance the detailed description of this flower in Lovelock and Wright, 1999, pp. 177–194.

15 World Development Report, 2004.

16 Robbins and Coulter, 2002, p. 198.

17 Quinn, 1980, in Mintzberg *et al.*, 2003, p. 10.

18 Mintzberg *et al.*, 2003, pp. 2–16.

19 We 'translated' the well-known phrase of Abell and Hammond (product, market, technology combination) here into service-market-technology combination.

20 Piercy, 1997, pp. 137–147; 2002.

21 Treacy and Wiersema, 1995.

22 The concept of the value disciplines will be further elaborated upon in Chapter 6.

23 All the topics mentioned will be elaborated upon in our text; especially in Chapter 6.

24 This will be elaborated upon in Chapter 4. However, we would like to mention here that the total of the discounted lifetime values of all the firm's customers can be regarded as the firm's customer equity. This concept not only encompasses brand equity but also value equity and retention equity. These ideas have been developed by Rust, Zeithaml and Lemon, 2000.

25 Heskett, Sasser and Schlesinger, 1997. This idea will be elaborated upon in Chapter 6.

26 Schlesinger *et al.*, 2003; Maister, 2001.

27 See for instance Grant, 1991; Hunt and Morgan, 1995, 1996.

28 Day, 1994, 1999; Hooley, Saunders and Piercy, 1998, 2004.

29 Hooley, Saunders and Piercy, 1998. Sometimes these four types of capabilities are classified slightly differently and named market sensing, market relating and strategic thinking capabilities (Day, 1994, 1999). Market sensing capabilities relate to reading and understanding the market, while market relating capabilities hinge upon creating and maintaining relationships with customers; the strategic thinking capabilities allow the organization to align its strategy to the market and help the organization to anticipate market changes.

30 This section is largely based on Heskett, Sasser and Hart, 1990.

31 This will be discussed further in Chapter 12.

32 Hooley, 1992; Alsem and Hoekstra, 1994. More detailed results from this study are presented in the first edition of our Service Marketing Management, in Figure 1.6.

33 Hooley, Greenley and Fahy, 2001.

34 The concept of the balanced score card will be further explained in Chapter 12.

35 Doyle, 2000, p. 3.

36 This definition can be found on the AMA's website.

37 For more details, see Kasper, 1993 or Kasper, Van Helsdingen and De Vries Jr, 1999, pp. 20–22.

38 See Barksdale and Darden, 1972; Barksdale *et al.*, 1982; Interview/IPM, 1974 and 1981; Gaski and Etzel, 1986; Varadarajan and Thirunarayana, 1990.

39 Day, 1990, p. 29.

40 Kohli and Jaworski, 1990; Kohli *et al.*, 1993; Jaworski and Kohli, 1993; Diamantopoulos and Hart, 1993; Langerak, 2001.

41 See e.g. McNaughton, Osborne and Imrie, 2002; Esteban *et al.*, 2002; Kasper, 2002; Matear *et al.*, 2002.

42 Narver and Slater, 1990; Slater and Narver, 1994a, 1994b.

43 Corporate culture has been a widely studied issue the past 20 years, since Peters and Waterman, 1982, concluded that a customer orientation is one of the characteristics of excellent companies and their culture. Deal and Kennedy (1982) use two dimensions to describe the culture of a corporation, namely the risks implied in the business activities (which may be high or low) and second, the speed of obtaining feedback on the results of decisions made (this feedback from the market may be fast or slow).

44 Hofstede, 1991, pp. 180, 182–183.

45 Hofstede's research depicted six dimensions to describe organizational cultures: process orientation versus results orientation; employee orientation versus job orientation; parochial versus professional; open system versus closed system; loose control versus tight control; and, normative versus pragmatic.

46 Kasper, 1995, 2002.

47 See Berry, Seiders and Grewal, 2002.

Chapter 3

Buyer Behaviour and Segmentation

Make customer interactions seamless with BT's networked IT services.

In the digital networked economy your customers want to choose where, when and how they contact you and they expect an exceptional level of service every time.

BT's networked IT services can help you serve your customers more efficiently by giving you a single view of all the communications you have with them. This enables you to increase customer satisfaction. Because of its expertise in networked IT services, BT can also help your organisation improve its operational flexibility, enabling customer service staff to be located anywhere and still work effectively. This makes you more competitive.

To discover more about BT's networked IT services, go to **bt.com/networkedIT**

BT
More power to you

Reproduced by permission of BT, Me Company and St. Lukes

Learning objectives

At the end of this chapter you will be able to:

1 Explain consumer behaviour with respect to services

2 Differentiate between the buying behaviour in business-to-business markets and the buying behaviour in consumer services markets

3 Describe the impact of culture on buying and using services

4 Explain the impact of emotions on buying and using services

5 Explain the role of perceived risk in buying services

6 Describe and apply the ways in which markets for services can be segmented

7 Explain the importance of positioning in services

8 Illustrate which factors are important to customers in the relationships with their service providers.

3.1   Introduction

Are All People Created Equal?

George Orwell once wrote 'all animals are created equal' in his book *Animal Farm*. Is it possible to change this to 'are all people created equal and therefore behave the same?' Clearly *no*, and yet this is the same premise upon which many marketers base their marketing strategies.

In the airline sector business travellers have different needs than those travelling purely for pleasure, however it is difficult to lump all business travellers together and assume that they all want the same thing. It is easy to assume that all business travellers will care about is departure and arrival times, and in-flight services, cost being largely irrelevant. However this is clearly not the case. Many organizations see cost as a clear driver when selecting business travel, and in that sense many business travellers may exhibit choice behaviour closer to those travelling for pleasure. We may have all been created equal but clearly our execution of this equality will differ over time, between purchase events and purchase types.

The services consumer is fickle and the drivers to their behaviour will differ between purchase moments even when they purchase the same service. In Chapter 1, we found that within industrialized countries of the OECD the services sector accounted for a very large part of the country's gross domestic product. In this chapter, we will consider the services consumption of individuals, households and organizations and demonstrate how it might differ between various segments. This understanding of the buyer is critical to define the market oriented service provider's strategy. This knowledge is part of the customer-based assets mentioned in Chapter 2; the way it is practised refers to some of the firm's marketing capabilities.

Consumers (individual persons, households, companies as well as not for profit organizations) buy and use products and services to both satisfy their needs and to accomplish goals, thus achieving a level of satisfaction. The decision a consumer makes to buy a particular service will be influenced by many circumstances, the most important of which will be individual characteristics. A list of characteristics which are deemed to influence consumer behaviour can be found in Figure 3.1. In general, actual consumer behaviour is determined by cognitions and affect. We hold that in buying services, the affective factors will probably play a very critical role because of the intangible nature of services. Reducing perceived risk by only providing more cognitive information will not be sufficient since service quality is determined to a very large extent by factors relating to the social interaction between customer and service provider.

Of all of the characteristics listed in Figure 3.1,[1] culture is the core underlying factor impacting on consumer behaviour. We will start this chapter with a discussion of culture

Situational factors	**Psychological factors**	**Social factors**
Physical environment	Perceived risk	Culture and subcultures
Social environment	Perception	Reference groups
Economic environment	Motivation	Family
Demographics	Development	Opinion leaders
Time	Attitude	Social class
Reason to buy	Personality	
Buyer's mood	Lifestyle	

Figure 3.1   Characteristics deemed to infuence consumer behaviour

because differences in culture can affect the context of the strategy of service firms.[2] Second the intangibility of services will be discussed in relation to its impact on consumer behaviour. Finally we will discuss the issue of perceived risk. This will assist understanding of the relationship between the consumer and the service provider. Although a service provider understands consumer decision making styles and knows how to segment the market and position its offering, consumers may act in a way not expected (dysfunctional behaviour). Figure 3.2 provides a chapter outline.

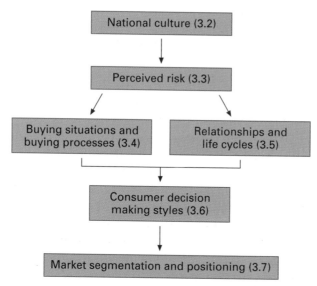

Figure 3.2   Chapter outline

3.2   National Cultures

An organization's operations will be impacted upon by the cultural environment within which the organization is operating. Differences in national cultures should be taken into account when developing strategy. National culture can influence both the internal operations of the organization as well as the external operations. Some of these differences will be:

- Different customs or rites;
- Different reactions to colours, words, sounds or symbols; or
- Different ways of looking at parents, at authority in working relations or at relations between customer and service employee.

The Impact of National Culture

Geert Hofstede is one of the world's leading authors on culture. He has studied the national culture of 64 countries and he defines culture as: 'the collective programming of the mind which distinguishes the members of one group or category of people from another.'[3]

Hofstede argues that cultural differences manifest themselves in various ways. Hofstede defined culture on five dimensions. They are defined in Figure 3.3. These dimensions are:

- Masculinity versus femininity (MAS);
- Individualism versus collectivism (IDV);
- Uncertainty avoidance (UAI);
- Power distance (PDI); and – the subsequently added dimension of;
- Long-term orientation versus short-term orientation (LTO).

Hofstede computed scores for each of the dimensions. These scores may range per dimension from zero to a little over 100. The scores for the countries are presented in Table 3.1. All these scores should be interpreted as relative scores: one country's culture is, for instance, more individualistic than another country's culture. Comparing scores will show you which cultures are more or less similar and which are completely different. This may affect the success of internationalization strategies in services to a certain extent.

It is also possible to see which countries look alike when their positions on all factors are taken into account simultaneously. This indicates which country's consumers have similar norms and values. In Figure 3.4, we present the graphical results of a correspondence analysis performed on the data for the 64 countries and the four dimensions.[5]

In this perceptual map, three cultural 'outliers' can be found: Denmark, Slovak Republic and Guatemala. Denmark has relatively low positions on three out of four dimensions: masculinity (high on femininity), power distance and uncertainty avoidance. Guatemala on the other hand, scores very high on uncertainty avoidance, while the Slovak Republic scores relatively high on both masculinity and power distance.

This map reveals, for instance, that the cultures of many English speaking countries are similar because cultural closeness is related to similarity in language. Similarly the Scandinavian countries are grouped together. You can also decipher that many of the wealthier western countries are located at the left side of the graph where more dominant scores on individualism can be found. It has been shown that there is a rather high correlation between wealth (defined as income per capita) and individualism.

Feminine dominated cultures can be found on the lower side of the graph; these are the Scandinavian countries, Estonia, the Netherlands, Portugal and Slovenia. In these countries the caring element is typical for the whole society. This will impact on services delivery because

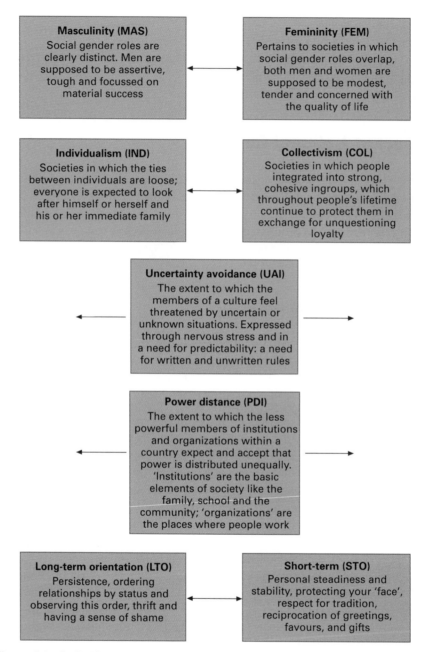

Masculinity (MAS)
Social gender roles are clearly distinct. Men are supposed to be assertive, tough and focussed on material success

Femininity (FEM)
Pertains to societies in which social gender roles overlap, both men and women are supposed to be modest, tender and concerned with the quality of life

Individualism (IND)
Societies in which the ties between individuals are loose; everyone is expected to look after himself or herself and his or her immediate family

Collectivism (COL)
Societies in which people integrated into strong, cohesive ingroups, which throughout people's lifetime continue to protect them in exchange for unquestioning loyalty

Uncertainty avoidance (UAI)
The extent to which the members of a culture feel threatened by uncertain or unknown situations. Expressed through nervous stress and in a need for predictability: a need for written and unwritten rules

Power distance (PDI)
The extent to which the less powerful members of institutions and organizations within a country expect and accept that power is distributed unequally. 'Institutions' are the basic elements of society like the family, school and the community; 'organizations' are the places where people work

Long-term orientation (LTO)
Persistence, ordering relationships by status and observing this order, thrift and having a sense of shame

Short-term (STO)
Personal steadiness and stability, protecting your 'face', respect for tradition, reciprocation of greetings, favours, and gifts

Figure 3.3   Definitions of the cultural dimension developed by Geert Hofstede

high quality service delivery may be self-evident in these countries while it has to be learned in other countries.[6]

Figure 3.4 also depicts the difference between geographical distance and cultural difference. For example it is interesting to note the reach of positions between Belgium, Germany and the Netherlands compared to the relative closeness between the United States, Australia, Great Britain and Ireland.

National Culture and Services

When we see the present trend toward substituting labour by technology in many service situations, one may question whether the acceptance of self-service operations will be the same in different cultures. Today, we see that self-service technologies are accepted in industrialized countries. As such, individualism is the most important cultural dimension in these countries. Cultures scoring high on power distance will have a greater expectation that others will provide services; their willingness to engage in self-service delivery will be reduced.

A similar point can be made for countries with a high uncertainty avoidance score; then for instance, the risk of trying new services will be high. Uncertainty avoidance may be a cultural trait inhibiting the use of services due to the risk of its intangibility. Consequently, in countries with a high UAI score, service providers have to develop sophisticated communication strategies in order to overcome this barrier. This is especially true with respect to accepting new services or new service technologies. It has been speculated for instance that the higher the UAI score, the more hesitant people may be in accepting new technologies. That is why we will discuss in a later section of this chapter the concept of the technology readiness index (TRI). The TRI considers such things as the communication of technology use as well as role clarity as precursors to the acceptance of technology.[7]

In cultures scoring high on power distance and masculinity (the upper right part of the graph in Figure 3.4) reliability and responsiveness are less important in determining service quality, while assurance and the tangible features of services are very important. Showing off coupled with some kind of security seem to be important here. On the other hand, in cultures scoring low on power distance but high on individualism (the lower left part of the graph in Figure 3.4), reliability and responsiveness are valued highly in determining service quality. This information assists marketers in selecting those service quality dimensions appropriate to the country that they are operating in.[8]

In the first section we mentioned that belonging to a particular reference group may affect an individual's consumer behaviour. That notion can also be applied here in terms of whether or not someone belongs to the in-group or the out-group. Belonging to the in-group is a very important issue in the cultural dimension of collectivism. A study in Europe revealed average ethnocentrism scores for Belgium (28.7), Great Britain (30.3), Spain (34.1) and Greece (37.8).[9] Comparing these scores with the Hofstede scores on collectivism for these four countries reveals that a higher score on ethnocentrism goes with a higher score on collectivism.[10]

In feminine cultures caring is a value shared among all people, while this is not the case in masculine societies. Consequently, serving people may be a more natural trait in feminine cultures; in other cultures it has to be learned to a larger extent (and is probably more difficult to implement). The same might hold when introducing relationship management. This may be easier in cultures where group feeling or femininity is valued highly. It is self-evident in those cultures to think and act in terms of relationships; this is quite uncommon as a natural trait in masculine and individualistic societies. Therefore, it might be more difficult to implement relationship marketing in the USA for instance.[11]

Table 3.1 **Scores of 64 countries on five dimensions reflecting their national culture as computed by Hofstede (1991, 2001)[4]**

Country	PDI	IDV	MAS	UAI	LTO
Argentina (ARG)	49	46	56	86	–
Australia (AUL)	36	90	61	51	31
Austria (AUT)	11	55	79	70	31
Bangladesh (BAN)	80	20	55	60	40
Belgium (BEL)	65	75	54	94	38
Brazil (BRA)	69	38	49	76	65
Bulgaria (BUL)	70	30	40	85	–
Canada (CAN)	39	80	52	48	23
Chile (CHL)	63	23	28	86	–
China (CHN)	80	20	66	30	118
Colombia (COL)	67	13	64	80	–
Costa Rica (COS)	35	15	21	86	–
Croatia (CRO)	73	33	40	80	–
Czech Republic (CZE)	57	58	57	74	13
Denmark (DEN)	18	74	16	23	46
Ecuador (ECA)	78	8	63	67	–
Estonia (EST)	40	60	30	60	–
Finland (FIN)	33	63	26	59	41
France (FRA)	68	71	43	86	39
Germany (GER)	35	67	66	65	31
Great Britain (GBR)	35	89	66	35	25
Greece (GRE)	60	35	57	112	–
Guatemala (GUA)	95	6	37	101	–
Hong Kong (HOK)	68	25	57	29	96
Hungary (HUN)	46	80	88	82	50
India (IND)	77	48	56	40	61
Indonesia (IDO)	78	14	46	48	–
Iran (IRA)	58	41	43	59	–
Ireland (IRE)	28	70	68	35	43
Israel (ISR)	13	54	47	81	–
Italy (ITA)	50	76	70	75	34
Jamaica (JAM)	45	39	68	13	–
Japan (JPN)	54	46	95	92	80
Korea (KOR)	60	18	39	85	75
Malaysia (MAL)	104	26	50	36	–
Malta (MLT)	56	59	47	96	–
Mexico (MEX)	81	30	69	82	–
Morocco (MOR)	70	46	53	68	–
Netherlands (NET)	38	80	14	53	44
New Zealand (NZL)	22	79	58	49	30
Norway (NOR)	31	69	8	50	44
Pakistan (PAK)	55	14	50	70	0
Panama (PAN)	95	11	44	86	–
Peru (PER)	64	16	42	87	–
Philippines (PHI)	94	32	64	44	19

Poland (POL)	68	60	64	93	32
Portugal (POR)	63	27	31	104	30
Romania (ROM)	90	30	42	90	–
Russia (RUS)	93	39	36	95	–
Salvador (SAL)	66	19	40	94	–
Singapore (SIN)	74	20	48	8	48
Slovak republic (SLK)	104	52	110	51	–
Slovenia (SLV)	71	27	19	88	–
South Africa (SAF)	49	65	63	49	–
Spain (SPA)	57	51	42	86	19
Sweden (SWE)	31	71	5	29	33
Switzerland (SWI)	34	68	70	58	40
Taiwan (TAI)	58	17	45	69	87
Thailand (THA)	64	20	34	64	56
Turkey (TUR)	66	37	45	85	–
United States (USA)	40	91	62	46	29
Uruguay (URU)	61	36	38	100	–
Venezuela (VEN)	81	12	73	76	–
Vietnam (VTN)	70	20	40	30	80

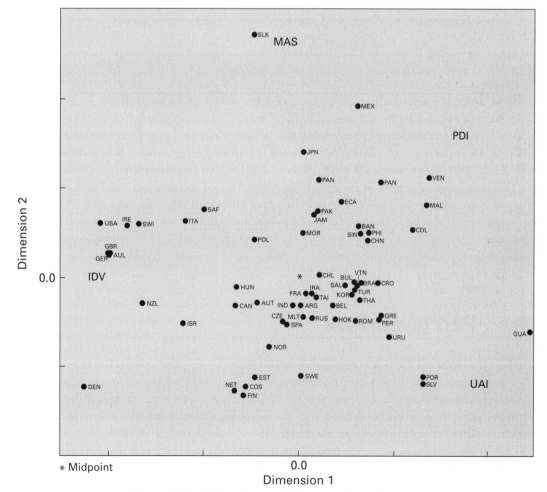

Figure 3.4   Cultural map of the countries of the world

SERVICE PRACTICE 3.2

Business Travellers' Cultural Background and Actual Behaviour[12]

Business executives who travel frequently from both eastern cultures such as Singapore, Hong Kong, Thailand, Taiwan, the People's Republic of China, India and western cultures such as Australia, Canada, United Kingdom, United States and Scandinavian countries are likely to differ quite dramatically in the way they evaluate complex services like luxury hotels.

Westerners might be more likely than their Asian counterparts to evaluate a complex service based on the tangible cues presented by the physical environment. Asian business travellers might expect more personalized service, while western business travellers whose core values tend to include fun and enjoyment might regard the hedonic dimension of the consumption experience as more important than do their Asian business counterparts, whose value structures tend to reflect a greater sense of duty.

As a partial explanation for these findings, we can say

In general, Asian cultures are characterized by large power distances, and because status differences are expected and accepted within most Asian cultures, the role of the service employee is clearly seen by Asians as to provide service. Asian institutionalization of the traditional service concept further enhances the importance of service in the Asian customer's overall evaluation of a service organization.

National culture, ethnocentrism and country-of-origin effect are factors that are very important in offering services worldwide. Their impact on the acceptance of (new) services should not be underestimated. Quite often this impact is not easy to measure because it takes place implicitly and unconsciously. Nevertheless it impacts on consumers' decisions and thus affects the firm's performance. We will show in this chapter how these concepts work and impact on consumer behaviour in service industries. One of the dimensions of national culture is uncertainty avoidance. This is quite closely linked to the issue of perceived risk which relates to the basic characteristic of services: intangibility. We will discuss perceived risk now.

3.3 Perceived Risk

Perceived risk means the risk consumers perceive when buying and using particular services. Due to intangibility, it is hard to evaluate services in advance of purchase. Nor is it always known in advance what the outcome will be. These factors create uncertainty for the services consumer and thus the risk associated with the purchase will increase. You can imagine this risk may differ between services you really like to buy (a new fashionable haircut, going to the latest movie) versus 'unsought services' (like a funeral insurance, wills, etc.). There are many types of perceived risk.

Different Types of Perceived Risk

Risk comes in many guises. The risks associated with purchasing a service are: financial risk; functional risk; physical risk; social risk; psychological risk; lifestyle risk; time risk; and environmental risk.[13] Each of these risk factors are outlined in Table 3.2.

A consumer's total perceived risk in certain purchase situations or in the participation in the service delivery process consists in principle of a mixture of these eight different kinds of

Table 3.2   Risk factors in services

Risk	Possible effects
Financial risk	Uncertainty as to whether consumers pay more than they should pay. So, there is doubt about the quality–price relation. Consumers cannot always determine all of the costs associated with producing a service. Sometimes it is difficult to make a comparison between the performance of an intangible service and the money they have to pay for the service delivery. Besides it is possible that the consumer is willing to pay a certain additional amount of money (= premium price) just for 'accessing the name of the service provider', without an actual performance.[14]
Functional risk	Uncertainty as to whether the service really offers what it should provide. This has to do with the question of whether the service is in line with expectations. Does the fire insurance policy really cover what one hoped for when being confronted with fire damage now?[15] Because it is often difficult to standardize services, consumers cannot always rely on their own experiences with comparable services to reduce functional uncertainty. In these situations customers need help or advice from others: family, friends or independent bodies like consumer unions or consultants (e.g. brokers). Even today with much information available on the Internet where you can do a lot of the comparative testing yourself, we see more and more intermediaries come up to provide you information on the best buy of your mobile phone or home mortgage.
Physical risk	Concern about the safety of the service delivery. Might the service or the service delivery process cause any damage to others or the self? This can play a role when taking skiing lessons or learning to parachute.
Social risk	Concerns about the way in which the environment of the consumer will react to the choice of a certain service or particular service provider. Will the reaction be disapproving or approving; does the choice of services provider fit in with the consumer's self-perception? For a consumer may feel anxious about a choice of restaurant, when taking a group of business associates out to dinner.
Psychological risk	Psychological risk is an extension of social risk. It concerns the uncertainty that a bad choice will damage the consumer's image. This uncertainly might centre on the consumer's anxiety that consumer and service provider might not like each other personally.
Lifestyle risk	Lifestyle risk is much like the social and psychological risk, but concerns the expected or actual consequences for one's own lifestyle. In particular the consumer is anxious that their lifestyle be maintained when using specific services.
Time risk	Time risk refers to the uncertainty that the time spent searching for a service is wasted when the chosen service or service provider does not perform according to expectations. This also has to do with the customers' decision about their allocation of time available, based on the costs of their time.[16] Another time risk concerns the time in which a consumer has to make a decision about the intangible service or the unknown service delivery process. Is that time enough or must a choice be made in a short time?
Environmental risk	Environmental risk concerns the uncertainty of consumers about the possible damage the service or service delivery process may cause to the environment (energy and materials used during the service delivery process by airlines; environmental pollution when going to the service provider). Nowadays, this risk is becoming increasingly important in the decision making process of consumers.

risk. Because of the intangible nature of service, this risk may be considerable. This risk not only concerns the choice of the right service and/or service provider but also the expected positive and negative consequences of this choice, including both the benefits and risks.

Although the total perceived risk could be constructed from the risk outlined, this does not imply that every type of risk will always be felt to the same extent or is equally as important. Of course, this can vary among services or service delivery processes. Stated differently, perceived risk is a relative concept; it can occur to a greater or lesser extent. Perceived risk is also dependent on earlier experiences. Therefore perceived risk may diminish over time when more positive experiences have been achieved.

The notion that perceived risk is not necessarily equally high for every customer has several implications. For example, the extent of perceived risk varies among customer groups; different kinds of services; different buying situations and various cultures. So, the degree of perceived risk can be used as a way to segment the market.

Groups of customers with a high perceived risk will choose from only a limited number of familiar services; often they will be highly brand loyal. In contrast, customers with low perceived risk will experience no difficulty in choosing from many different alternatives and more often show variety-seeking behaviour. The perceived risk towards different kinds of services can vary; it will be different in the case of life insurance compared to a cinema ticket. Perceived risk also varies among different kinds of buying situations, such as:

- Extended problem solving behaviour;
- Routine buying behaviour; and
- Limited problem solving behaviour (modified buying)[17]

or its counterpart in business-to-business markets of:

- New task;
- Straight rebuy; and
- Modified rebuy.[18]

How Can Customers Reduce Perceived Risk?

Consumers can reduce perceived risk in many ways.[19] The most common behavioural strategy is to search for information about the service prior to making the purchase decision. This will come from consulting friends and acquaintances or from being informed by sales and front office personnel. Often, the service organization's reputation and image are used. Advertisements or research findings published by consumer unions are also used.

Perceived risk can be difficult to reduce because a customer does not always know exactly where to look or what the cost and benefits of the service will be. Furthermore, a customer does not know for sure whether all the communication initiated by the service organization is a proper reflection of reality because advertising usually presents an idealized view.

In the case of a first-time buy (a new task), this uncertainty will be higher than in the case of a rebuy situation. Therefore, brand loyalty, store loyalty or supplier loyalty (sometimes resulting in some firms having the status of preferred supplier) are behavioural strategies suitable for reducing these uncertainties.

Customers can also use price as a quality indicator and thus as a measure to reduce the perceived risk. Most customers assume a higher price indicates a better service. Sometimes, an uncertain consumer searches for the most expensive service as a solution. In this situation the customer assumes that you don't get something valuable cheaply. This is not always the case, especially in less informed markets. Price does not always have to be the best indicator of the perception of quality. Another way of reducing perceived risk is to purchase a service that comes with a warranty, a guarantee or a well-known service recovery policy.

Finally, due to services' intangibility, raising the tangibility of a service may be the simplest way to reduce perceived risk. That way of reasoning is true as such but it is also quite simplistic, as the next Service Practice 3.3 shows.

SERVICE PRACTICE 3.3

Is it Simply a Matter of Increasing Tangibility to Reduce Perceived Risk?[20]

Michel Laroche and his colleagues found that there is more than just one kind of intangibility to services. They studied a number of services such as pizza restaurants (Pizza Hut), hairdressing services and checking accounts at the Royal Bank of Canada. They distinguished between three kinds of intangibility:

1   physical,
2   mental,
3   generality.

On the physical intangibility scale (referring to the extent to which a good cannot be touched or seen; it is inaccessible to the senses and lacks a physical presence), pizza restaurants were perceived as the most tangible service, being much more physically tangible than haircuts or banking services.

Haircuts and pizza dinners were seen as very tangible on the mental intangibility scale (this scale refers to the fact that a good or service can be physically tangible, but difficult to grasp mentally). On the generality scale (which refers to the customer's difficulty in precisely defining or describing a particular good or service) haircuts were seen as the most tangible in this respect.

They also distinguished between five types of perceived risk (financial, time, performance, social and psychological). It appeared that the physical intangibility of these services was not related to any of these five dimensions of perceived risk. However, both mental intangibility and generality were significantly related to four out of the five types of perceived risk investigated here: financial, time, performance and psychological but not to social risk.

We conclude from this that merely increasing a service's tangibility does not work to reduce perceived risk. A service provider should especially focus on communicating to the customer and providing information to enhance the 'clarity of the description' of the service, the service delivery process, the script in the service encounter and, role clarity rather than just making it more tangible in a physical way.

3.4 Buying Situations and Buying Processes

Buying Situations

Consumers can face different buying situations. There is for example a difference between a new or initial purchase and a repeat purchase. This difference concerns the knowledge the buyer has of the characteristics of the intangible service or about the presumed participation in the service delivery process. During an initial purchase cycle everything is new, relatively unknown and, therefore, a high perceived risk exists. During a decision about a repeat purchase, experiences in previous service encounters can play a role in helping to reduce the perceived risk.

Buying Bundles of Benefits

Services are a bundle of attributes, which consist of a number of characteristics. Each of these characteristics has a certain benefit or value for the consumer. In fact, consumers judge the buying process of a service in terms of its consequences with respect to the service outcome and the service process. Peter and Olson defined these consequences as 'the specific outcomes that happen to a consumer when the service is purchased and used or consumed'.[21] In turn, these consequences are determined by the many attributes of services and service delivery processes; and these attributes are aimed at achieving a particular need fulfilment. Moreover, these 'consequences' can have both a positive and a negative impact or meaning for the consumer. Therefore, the consequences of buying services and participating in service delivery processes can be classified as positive consequences (perceived benefits) and negative consequences (perceived risks). Simply stated, when consumers buy services, they buy bundles of benefits which satisfy their needs.

From Five Stages to Three Stages

The well known five stage model of the buying process can easily be applied to services. This model can be seen in Figure 3.5.

This process will vary with respect to the buying situation. All the factors from Figure 3.1 may impact on this decision making process. Three types of buying situation have been identified.

- Extensive problem solving behaviour (EPS);
- Restricted problem solving behaviour (RPS); and
- Routine buying behaviour (RBB).

With EPS, all stages will be passed through, with RBB only the final two stages. If this model of buying process considers the characteristics of services including the interaction between

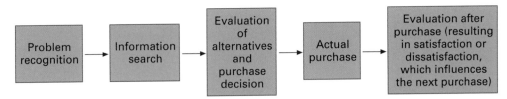

Figure 3.5   The five stage model of buyer behaviour

consumer and producer then the buying process of services can be described in three stages, namely:

■ The pre-purchase stage, which comprises the first three of the five stages mentioned above;
■ The consumption stage, which corresponds to the fourth stage. Here, it consists of the servuction process of the service delivery in which the customer participates; and
■ The post-purchase evaluation stage, which partly determines the satisfaction or dissatisfaction of the customer about the complete service delivery (the fifth stage).

The three stages are shown in Figure 3.6. We will elaborate on each of these stages in the following section.

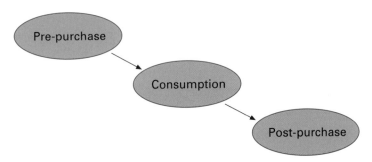

Figure 3.6   The three stages in the buying process of services

Pre-Purchase Stage

In the pre-purchase stage of the buying process the consumer is looking for an answer to a problem. In searching for information the consumer will use the information sources and experiences of others to assist in the evaluation of the alternatives available. The consumer is searching for information about the service provider, the services and the service delivery process. Because services are intangible and the market is not transparent, the consumer does not always know exactly which aspects are important in choosing a particular service or service provider. In choosing, consumers may rely on, among other things:

■ Their own needs, wishes and experiences from the past with this and other service providers;

- Word-of-mouth (from both consumers and service providers); and eventually
- Objective sources like advice or results of comparative testing by (national or international) consumer groups.[22]

Besides this, the image of the service provider plays an important role in the decision making process. The image or reputation of a service provider can give the consumer a sense of trust and security. A logical business consequence is that organizations invest in guarding their image. This image or reputation issue is also relevant in starting a relationship in professional business-to-business services.[23]

Another way of looking at this search behaviour is determined by the kind of attributes used. Here, we consider search attributes, experience attributes and credence attributes. Search attributes are attributes that the consumer can judge easily prior to the service delivery. Usually, they involve tangible aspects that are physically visible to the consumer. Credence attributes by contrast can be judged only a long time after the actual service delivery (only a long time after an operation do you know whether it has been successful or not) and are therefore based on trusting people delivering the service. Experience attributes are positioned in between these two extremes of the (in)tangibility of service attributes. They are also quite difficult to evaluate in advance and mostly they can be experienced only during or shortly after the service delivery. Both the experience and credence attributes are more people-based than equipment-based.[24] Products (and thus the selling of the products by retailers) like clothing, jewellery and houses have many search attributes. Services providers such as car dealers, restaurants, travel agencies, hairdressers and child care centres have many experience attributes, while computer repairers, consultancy services, medical diagnosis and church services have high credence attributes.[25]

Consumption Stage

The consumption stage is where the actual service delivery and service encounter occur. At the consumption stage the entire service process is evaluated and overall levels of satisfaction with the service are determined. During this phase of the consumption process the service consumer will also determine whether or not to continue the service relationship.

In this stage, it becomes clear whether consumers are really getting the benefits they were hoping for or expecting. 'The benefits bought by a customer consist of the experience that is delivered through an interactive process.'[26]

During and after the service experience it becomes clear what the benefits of the purchase and use of the service are; that is, the value to the customer. That is why we will discuss the marketing mix in the service business under the heading of 'creating the service experience' in Part 3 of this book. The actual moments of truth may appear to be very short; nevertheless, the experience attributes will now become visible to the consumer.

Post-Purchase Stage

In the post-purchase stage, consumers review and evaluate the complete service delivery. At this very point, the consumer can determine whether or not they have received the desired benefits in terms of quality or value. The outcome of this evaluation may not be 'available' after the service experience, but rather may take some time to emerge. At the end of this evaluation the overall level of consumer satisfaction will emerge.

Satisfaction[27]

When consumers of services realize that their expectations are not met, disconfirmation will occur. This may be a positive disconfirmation when actual experiences exceed expectations or a negative disconfirmation when expectations are above actual experiences. This will lead to two situations, respectively resulting in perception of high service quality or a lack of service quality. Moreover, when expectations are met, confirmation of expectations is at stake, also leading to a positive quality judgement. Because service quality is such an important topic in services marketing management we will discuss it extensively in Chapter 5. Here it is important to note that the further subjective evaluation of the service quality leads to satisfaction or dissatisfaction, respectively.

Satisfaction hinges upon the evaluation of the complete consumption experience during all the stages we discussed including what happens before, during and after the service experience. Satisfaction can be measured with the level of service received and the satisfaction with the service recovery actions if you have a complaint that is resolved. Consequently, it is necessary to look at the emergence of satisfaction about services in many ways.

We can distinguish between overall satisfaction and satisfaction with the various parts of the service delivery process, with the service encounters that may have taken place, and also with the servicescape. It is important to consider the customers' relationships with the services provider and the services environments as well as their relationships with other customers in the servicescape. Experiences with one part of the service delivery process may affect satisfaction with other parts. Think of bad experiences at the hotel check-in that may affect your own standard for your expectations about the room and the quality of the bed or dinner. Such carry-over effects were also found in studies about museums in Sweden and the Netherlands for instance where the satisfaction with one part of the exhibition partly impacts on the satisfaction with other parts or facilities in the museum (restaurant, shop, entrance, etc.).[28]

Richard Oliver[29] proposes as a definition:

Satisfaction is the consumer's fulfilment response. It is a judgment that a product or service feature, or the product or service itself, provided (or is providing) a pleasurable level of consumption-related fulfilment, including levels of under- or overfulfilment.

Expressing satisfaction or dissatisfaction with services can be done in many ways after the quality of the service has been evaluated. The first decision consumers have to make is whether they really want to express their (dis)satisfaction. In order to do so, they must be motivated and capable and have the opportunity to express it. When consumers do not think it is worthwhile, they do not express their dissatisfaction; for instance, when they think that the effort to write a complaint letter costs more time and money than the expected results.

A study of the Stockholm Sweden public transport company identified an interesting division between complaints and compliments. Compliments focussed upon interpersonal interactions between customers and employees while complaints focussed on reliability, punctuality, design and space in the vehicle and simplicity of information.[30]

Satisfaction can be expressed via positive word of mouth, giving compliments to the service provider, and via loyalty to the brand, the shop or the dealer. In the latter case, the relationship between customer and service provider is continued. Service quality, mutual trust and responsiveness are other important factors determining satisfaction and the continuation of the bond between the customer and the service provider. This implies it is critical to look further afield than merely reviewing satisfaction.[31]

In most cases it is too simple to state that satisfaction will automatically lead to repeat purchases or to brand, shop or dealer loyalty. Loyalty refers to situations in which consumers continually rebuy the same brand whenever a new buying situation occurs. The buying situation is biased in the sense that not all alternatives are taken into account but there is a choice to continue buying a particular service.[32]

Satisfaction is a necessary precondition, but is insufficient to provide a full explanation as to why some buyers are brand loyal. Commitment and involvement with a particular service will also play a critical role, as does the elaboration on the choice made and experiences found. Commitment can be defined as 'the pledging or binding of an individual to his/her brand choice.'[33]

A consumer becomes committed to a particular service brand after extensive and explicit decision making processes and evaluative processes of the service experience. Then, committed buyers will be truly loyal when they buy the brand again. When this commitment is lacking, repeat buying may occur, but then it will be based on inertia or ease of buying. Customers who buy on the basis of inertia can easily switch to another brand or service provider. They do not have a strong relationship with that service provider and are not so motivated for that particular brand nor did they elaborate on their choice. This made us distinguish between two kinds of satisfaction (manifest and latent) and two kinds of brand loyalty (true and spurious). Latent satisfaction will lead to spurious loyalty, while manifest satisfaction will lead to true loyalty.

In Figure 3.7 we are talking about commitment in general. In more detail, three types of commitment can be distinguished:

1 Affective commitment, which refers to a desire-based attachment to the service provider such that you would like to continue the relationship.
2 Continuance or calculative commitment, which refers to a cost-based attachment: you have to continue the relationship, switching is too costly.
3 Normative commitment, which refers to an obligation-based attachment to the service provider: you ought to continue the relationship.

Especially, affective and normative commitment affect loyalty in a positive way and switching in a negative way, while calculative commitment quite often has a negative impact on loyalty (but also on switching). This holds for B2C as well as for B2B situations.[34]

This distinction will also help you better understand the relationship between satisfaction and company performance. Although we know such a relationship is a positive one (the higher the satisfaction, the better the financial performance), repurchase intentions do not

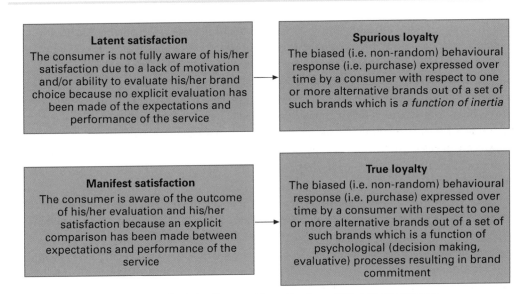

Latent satisfaction
The consumer is not fully aware of his/her satisfaction due to a lack of motivation and/or ability to evaluate his/her brand choice because no explicit evaluation has been made of the expectations and performance of the service

Spurious loyalty
The biased (i.e. non-random) behavioural response (i.e. purchase) expressed over time by a consumer with respect to one or more alternative brands out of a set of such brands which is *a function of inertia*

Manifest satisfaction
The consumer is aware of the outcome of his/her evaluation and his/her satisfaction because an explicit comparison has been made between expectations and performance of the service

True loyalty
The biased (i.e. non-random) behavioural response (i.e. purchase) expressed over time by a consumer with respect to one or more alternative brands out of a set of such brands which is a function of psychological (decision making, evaluative) processes resulting in brand commitment

Figure 3.7   Satisfaction and loyalty: two different processes

always exactly come true. This may be due to the fact that the purchase intentions belonging to these two kinds of loyalty differ as well.

Managers should focus on having consumers evaluate and elaborate their choices to become truly loyal. That will enhance the fact that service quality leads to service loyalty while this relationship is mediated by service satisfaction.[35] Moreover, the impact of trust, bonds, switching barriers, involvement, etc. has to be included to get an even better understanding of the relevant processes underlying these relationships in B2C as well as in B2B situations.[36]

When consumers are dissatisfied, they can undertake different kinds of action. Factors such as the seriousness of the problem, the anger aroused, the amount of money involved and the personal importance of the service codetermine whether the dissatisfaction will be expressed or not.

The first action to express dissatisfaction is in fact 'to do nothing at all'. This happens quite often, especially when it is not seen as a worthwhile investment to express it. In these situations it may be easier to switch to another supplier than to voice the dissatisfaction. The seeking redress propensity (SRP) is a critical moderating factor in this process of taking action or not. It refers to feeling apt to openly and directly stand up for one's own consumer rights (or, conversely, their propensity to avoid this behaviour).[37] Consumers do vary in levels of assertiveness, aggressiveness and willingness to express their dissatisfaction. The higher the SRP, the more likely is complaining behaviour.

The most common reasons for switching service providers are related to core service failures such as mistakes or a series of mistakes during one service encounter or over a period a decrease in service levels; billing problems; and 'service catastrophes' such as service failures which cause damage to the customer's person, family, pets, belongings or losing time or money.[38] A second group of reasons relates to issues about behavioural interpersonal failures in the service encounter such as uncaring, impolite, unresponsive and unknowledgeable service employees. A third group of reasons relates especially to prices (to high, unfair, increasing or deceptive pricing). Fourth, inconvenience may be at stake, relating to inconvenience to the location, hours of operation and waiting time. Finally, competition and ethical issues form the fifth group of reasons to switch.

Voicing a complaint is another important tool dissatisfied customers of services can use. Complaints are industry specific as you can imagine. Many complaints about insurances can be attributed to a lack of information. In banking, usually a very contact intensive service industry, many complaints refer to contact personnel's behaviour and waiting; this may change when Internet banking use increases. Most complaints about medical services deal with the core service, the care provided, people's behaviour, and incorrect or unclear billing. Also in postal services, many complaints are about the on-time delivery of the mail and the 'good condition it should be in'.

When consumers feel their complaints are not solved adequately, they may become dissatisfied about this complaint solving process. Then a double deviation may occur when service recovery processes fail after a service failure has occurred.[39]

Most of the research on satisfaction has been done in consumer markets. It is also an important topic in the relationship between organizations in the B2B sector. In a study on financial B2B services it appeared that share of wallet (SOW, which is defined as the percentage of the volume of total business conducted with the firm by a client organization within a 12-month period) is indeed positively associated with satisfaction.[40] However, the relationship is not linear; there is an optimum in this relationship.[41]

Share of wallet does not automatically increase with increasing levels of satisfaction. It may even go up and down with increasing levels of satisfaction (this is also true for consumer services). Consequently, managers should be well aware of this relationship; otherwise they may think it is important to increase customer satisfaction assuming that it will always result in a higher share of wallet. Especially in this B2B financial services market it appears that this relationship also differs for various buyer groups or members of the purchasing unit at the buying company.

Business-to-Business Services

In the business-to-business (B2B) world the same decision making process holds as depicted in the previous section, the major difference being that more people are involved in the decision making process within the B2B environment. Here the decision making unit (DMU) plays an important role. The DMU will be composed of gatekeepers, users, purchasers, influencers, buyers, deciders. Within a company like Philips Medical Systems sometimes a simple distinction between choosers and users at its customers' has been made in this respect. Each of these people will play a different role. For sellers it is important to know who is playing what role. Satisfaction may differ for people playing each specific role because they represent different interests. The buyer wants the lowest price, the user will focus on ease of use while other people focus on the lowest cost of repair and maintenance.

At the sellers side, the problem solving unit (PSU) consists of a team of specialists from various disciplines like production, sales, marketing, customer services, engineering, research and development, logistics, and finance. They can offer all the company's knowledge, skills and capabilities to serve the client and the client's DMU during the whole process of buying the service. The members of the DMU at the buyer's side and the members of the PSU at the

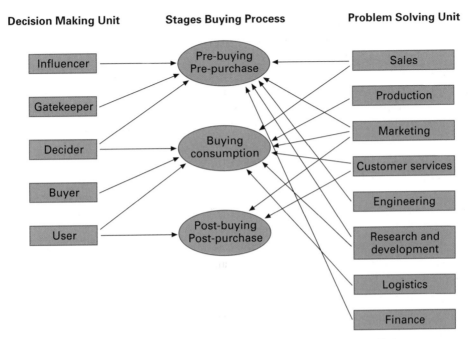

Figure 3.8 Decision Making Unit and Problem Solving Unit

seller's side have to interact with one another. The kinds of contacts may differ during the stages of the buying process, as Figure 3.8 shows.

On the supplier's side in B2B relations we see more and more that the customer services department evolves from a 'break and fix' service to a critical boundary spanning role in the continuation of the relationship. For these service engineers are 'the face' of the service provider; they make the services come true, they interact with the buyer's employees and can detect present and future needs. More over, more services like training, software updates and finance can be offered through the customer services department. As a service to the equipment used, these after sales services are critical during the life time of the equipment.[42]

Within the B2B sector we are seeing increasingly that the traditional purchasing function has evoled into professional supply management. Then professional supply managers are responsible for making purchase decisions across a range of services and products.[43] Services like this may also include professional services representing a high knowledge content such as management consultants, lawyers, accountants, advertising agencies, market researchers and technical engineering. It is critical that all these organizations are market oriented and service focussed. That is why James Alexander and Mark Hordes prefer to use the term S-business which 'refers to the services-focused, services-measured, and, indeed, services-driven organization, regardless of whether it also builds and sells products.'[44]

Organizations buy services for a wide variety of reasons. They can be grouped into three main categories:

1 the buying organization does not have the capability to perform the service effectively and with the required quality;

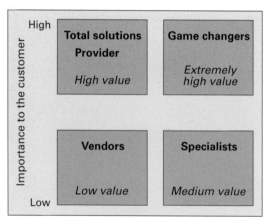

Figure 3.9   Four types of service providers and their value to the customer

2 the buying organization does not have the scale or ability to perform the service efficiently;

3 the buying organization does not have enough capacity to perform the service.

In fact, it is a matter of a make or buy decision, that is, can the service be produced in-house or should it be purchased?

You may recall that we developed a typology of services in Chapter 2 based on the degree of customization and the degree of differentiation. James Alexander and Mark Hordes developed a similar typology for B2B service providers representing for instance the value potential of each type of services provider from the customers' eyes. Their dimension of 'importance to the customer' resembles our dimension of customization, while their dimension of 'uniqueness of offerings' resembles our dimension of differentiation. The resulting matrix is shown in Figure 3.9.

Vendors usually offer services that are not unique and that have less importance to the customer, therefore their value to the customer is rather low. The opposite holds for the game changers, offering highly unique offerings that are mission-critical to customers. Consequently, the value of such a relationship is extremely high for the customer. The other two types of service providers offer services of lower value than the game changers but of higher value than the vendors.

This model, however, does not include two dimensions that are also very important in running a service business, namely the profit impact and the supply risk of the buying company. These have been taken into account in the model developed by Kraljic.[45] When you take a good look at Figure 3.9 and 3.10 you will see that the four types of service buying and selling situations in each figure overlap. With respect to services we can explain this model as follows. The profit impact of the goods and services bought can be analysed in terms of the volume purchased, the percentage of total cost, the impact on business growth, and the impact on service quality or the strategic value of the service to the final service. Supply risk is quite a complex concept; it refers to many different factors such as terms of availability, on-time delivery, reliability, number of suppliers, competitive demand, make-or-buy opportunities, storage risks and possibilities for substitution. The buying service organization

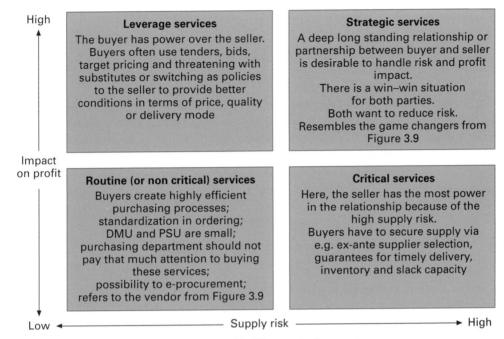

Figure 3.10   The Kraljic matrix for services

may have high or low scores on each of these dimensions. Each cell in the 2x2 matrix now shows how the buyer and seller could interact with one another.

In business markets the relationship between the supplier and the customer is founded on the interpersonal interaction that takes place in that relationship. The network of all the existing relationships, assets, capabilities, technologies and competencies of both the customer and supplier firm and the final offering are all aspects that need to be considered.[46] It also sets specific requirements on the behaviour of contact employees. The seller should know what buyers expect from their sales representatives in order to be really market oriented. According to customer companies the key traits of good industrial service representatives in the USA are:

being people-oriented, responsive, knowledgeable, and hard to ruffle … Under specific conditions other characteristics take on greater importance, for example negotiation ability for those working primarily with commodity-type products or analytical ability for those working in high tech focussed markets.[47]

In more tactical terms, the key traits are:

■ good listener;
■ knows where to get data;
■ handles stress well;
■ responds quickly;
■ is a problem solver;
■ is polite;

- is sensitive;
- is patient;
- enjoys people; and
- gets along with people.

Many of these traits will come to the fore in our discussion on the dimensions of service quality in Chapter 5; they appear to be critical in delivering excellent service quality. However, service representatives themselves have a different view on these traits. They think for instance that the skill of being a good listener is less important to the customer than the customers actually value. Again, knowing customer needs is a prerequisite to be market oriented and to developing and maintaining the mutual relationship in the long run.

3.5 Relationships and Life Cycles

Since service delivery is characterized as an interaction process between supplier and customer, the relationship between the two is very important. A trusted relationship is another means of reducing perceived risk. Creating, building and maintaining relationships is an important capability of market oriented service organizations to create that trust along the whole life cycle of the relationship.

Relationships are one of the variables to be used in classifying services. Relationships can be formal or informal; or continue in the long term versus short-term, one-shot transactions. In the services sector, many relationships are long term. For example you may have had the same doctor, dentist or physiotherapist for many years. Many of these relationships have a certain degree of temporarity in common and as such we consider the life cycle of the relationship to be an important issue. The chosen marketing strategy and mix may be of help in giving content and meaning to that relationship.[48] In discussing relationships it is important to realize that some people like to engage in relationships while others are more hesitant. The willingness to engage in relationships or relationship proneness is a personality trait of the buyer and one that organizations should take into account when approaching customers. Buyer relationship proneness can be defined as a buyer's relatively stable and conscious tendency to engage in relationships with sellers of a particular product or service category.[49]

Relationships Between Service Providers and Customers

Market oriented service providers are not focussing on a single transaction with consumers. Their main objective is starting, developing and maintaining relationships with customers. In some situations, it may also mean that relationships are ended, e.g. when the service provider cannot meet customer's specific demands (any longer) or when the supplier's goals are no longer met. In other words:

Relationship marketing concerns attracting, developing, and retaining customer relationships. Its central tenet is the creation of 'true customers' – customers who are glad they selected a firm, who perceive they are receiving value and feel valued, who are likely to buy additional services from the firm and who are unlikely to defect to a competitor. True customers are the most profitable of all customers. They spend more money with the firm on a per-year basis and they stay with the firm for more years. They spread favorable word-of-mouth information about the firm, and they may even be willing to pay a premium price for the benefits the service offers.[50]

Companies with such customers will have lower marketing costs. Customers favour such relationships. In the service business, customers want to have a partner whom they can trust and whom they feel cares about them. A caring culture is one of the central elements of a market oriented organization. A caring culture sets the framework for closer and more personalized contacts in the extreme situation: one-on-one contacts, where fully customized services can be provided. But you can imagine that the degree of caring may differ for the four types of situations described in Figures 3.9 and 3.10. In the situation of a vendor selling routine services to the customer the relationship may be completely different from the game changer–seller mission-critical, very unique services. The latter case may call for more intensive relationships while switching for cost reasons may occur more easily in the vendor situation.

Of course, it is interesting to know if and how long-term relationships impact on the firm's performance. It has been shown for instance that, in the long run, relationship oriented business service firms can achieve higher returns on investment than transaction oriented firms. Long-term client relationships however do not improve productivity at the relationship oriented firms; but help business service firms to resist price pressures from their customers and add more value to their services over time.[51]

Relationships are not static phenomena. Rather, they are characterized by dynamics and change over time, as Service Practice 3.4 indicates.

SERVICE PRACTICE 3.4

What Kind of Relationship Do You Want?

Kotler (1994) defined five different levels of relating to customers. Redefined in terms of services they can be described as follows:

1 *Basic*: the salesperson sells the service but does not contact the customer again;
2 *Reactive*: the salesperson sells the service and encourages the customer to call if he or she has any questions or complaints;
3 *Accountable*: the salesperson phones the customer a short time after the sale to check whether the service is meeting the customer's expectations. The salesperson also solicits from the customer any service improvement suggestions and any specific disappointments. This information helps the company to continuously improve its offering;
4 *Proactive*: the company salesperson phones the customer from time to time with suggestions about improved service use or helpful new services;
5 *Partnership*: the company works continuously with the customer to discover ways to effect customer savings or help the customer to perform better.

These five types of relationship were used in a study with respect to the relationships car owners have and would like to have with their car dealer.[52] In a study among 1038 car owners of the Japanese brand Mitsubishi the researchers found that:

☐ 55% of the Mitsubishi car owners wanted to keep the relationship in the future as it was now;
☐ 40% wanted to have a more intense relationship than at this very moment; while only
☐ 5% wanted to have a less intensive relationship.

The study also indicated that car owners having (or preferring) a less intensive relationship were less brand loyal, less dealer loyal but more price sensitive than those car owners having (or preferring) a more intensive relationship.

In addition to the dynamics revealed in Service Practice 3.4, relationships go through a certain development, comparable with the well-known life cycles of products or organizations. So, there is a life cycle for services and a life cycle for service providers.

Life Cycles of Organizations and Relationships

Within the life cycle of a service we like to distinguish three different types of life cycles: the traditional life cycle; the relationship life cycle; and the family life cycle.

The traditional life cycle is comparable to the product life cycle. The change points or transition points are the critical moments of choice at which the organization moves from one stage to the other. The following stages can be distinguished: introduction and survival in the short-term, expansion, consolidation, further growth, maturity and decline.[53]

The relationship life cycle shows us four stages in the relationships of (business-to-business) services:[54]

■ *Selection* (interest, pre-relationship phase, getting to know each other, pre-purchase);
■ *Development* (purchase, repeat purchase, development, initiation, post-pitch, test stage, initial phase);
■ *Maintenance* (involvement, integration, continuation, maturity, growth phase, troubled phase, constant phase); and
■ *Termination* (end relationship, decline phase, termination phase).

Commitment, trust (to reduce perceived risk), satisfaction, quality and various kinds of bonds and switching barriers are all factors contributing to the success of a relationship in the business-to-business as well as in the business-to-consumer business. We will elaborate on these issues to a fuller extent in Chapter Five.

The family life cycle charts the household needs for services in time as a consequence of, for example, family composition, wishes, income and the like. Service providers should take this into account when developing marketing strategies to suit particular segments and households. Insurance companies or brokers, knowing their insured very well, can really benefit from such a family life cycle approach. A lot of relevant data on the demographics and spending patterns of their customers can often be detected very easily from their own company records.

Still Staying?

Once relationships have been created the customer will stay for a shorter or longer period with the service organization. Sometimes they stay after a deliberate decision, sometimes they just stay out of ease or inertia. In fact the same processes occur as we have seen in the section on satisfaction and loyalty where we distinguished between manifest and latent satisfaction leading to true and spurious loyalty. But will all dissatisfied customers switch? In an Australian study among dissatisfied customers of financial services, it appeared that many customers still stayed with their financial institution for their savings, cheque, credit or personal loan accounts. The main reasons for this inertia were: all financial institutions are similar, the switching process is too complex and costly in terms of transfer fees, and the time required to make the change.[55]

In its extreme, (satisfied) customers may stay for the rest of their life. This has given rise to the concept of the customer lifetime value: what is the worth of the customer taking into account all his or her future spending on the company's services? For companies this expected value may also function as a decision criterion in situations when the possibility occurs that the customer may leave or switch to another supplier. This value can be counted in retailing as well as in banking, for instance, when (small) complaints have to be solved. If these complaints are not solved satisfactorily, customers may leave and consequently the firm is more harmed in its sales and profits than when the complaint was solved. So, how well the relationship is can be revealed at different moments in time.

We have been talking about consumers and their behaviour as if they are one homogeneous group. It is typical in marketing to know that this is not the case. This has led to the concept of market segmentation, which will be discussed later in this chapter. Here, we will first focus on different ways of decision making by consumers, for that also appears to be related to dealing with perceived risk.

3.6   Consumer Decision Making Styles

Consumer Decision Making Styles

In section 3.4 we showed the three stages of the decision making process in buying services. How consumers actually make these decisions may be called their decision making style. Such a decision making style is in fact the basic buying decision making attitudes consumers adhere to.[56] Such a style is assumed to hold for consumers irrespective of the products or services they buy (luxury goods or basics; expensive or cheap products; standard core services or augmented customized services). But, since every customer is unique, different customers may possess different decision making styles. In other words, a consumer decision making style can also be described as: 'a patterned, mental, cognitive orientation towards shopping and purchasing, which constantly dominates the consumer's choices resulting in a relatively-enduring consumer personality'.[57]

Table 3.3   Decision making styles

Decision making style	Description
Perfectionism/high quality consciousness	These consumers search for the highest or very best quality products and services; they are careful, systematic buyers and compare products
Price–value consciousness	These consumers shop carefully for the lowest or sale prices, they search in this way value for money
Brand consciousness	This kind of consumer is expected to buy expensive, well-known brands because they believe that the higher the price, the better the quality
Novelty-fashion consciousness	These consumers are novelty seekers who find seeking out new things pleasurable. They like fashion products, shop less carefully, are quite impulsive and are not so price sensitive
Confused by over choice of brands, stores, and consumer information	Such consumers are confused about the quality of different brands and by all the information available. Friends – as a reference group or as a group to reduce perceived risk – are likely to influence these consumers' decisions. This kind of consumer could be regarded as support-seeking decision makers
Recreational, hedonistic shopping conciousness	These consumers find shopping pleasant. They like to shop for fun
Impulsiveness	This kind of consumer does not plan their shopping or buying. They appear to be quite unconcerned with how they spend or value money
Habitual, brand loyal	These consumers have their favourite brands, outlets and stores and use these habitually

It reflects 'a mental orientation characterizing a consumer's approach to making choices'.[58] In general, eight consumer decision making styles can be distinguished, as shown in Table 3.3.

Many studies have been done to test this US typology in other countries to see whether the typology can be generalized across countries, cultures, products and services. Most of these eight styles come to the fore although some new or slightly adjusted decision making styles were found. These additional styles pinpointed the effective use of time, energy and information in determining the decision making style.[59] In other words, the way people perceive and value time is also reflected in their decision making style.

All these decision making styles were found in studies concerning the purchase of personal goods such as clothes and jewellery. The decision making styles of males and females differ. In a Dutch study, male consumers appeared to be focussed on the price–value relationship: they want value for money (be it during sales or not).[60] So, gender may be a criterion to segment the market. Recently, a UK study was done among male respondents about their decision-making styles.[61] The decision making styles for men were:

1 confident brand and quality seekers (26% of the population);
2 fashion and brand uninterested (22%);
3 reluctant perfectionists (15%);

4 confused, time-energy conserving (14%);

5 quality and value seekers (13%); and

6 recreational, trendsetters (10%).

This seems to suggest that each customer has one decision making style. That need not be the case. One style may dominate. You yourself will also see that your way of decision making does not completely and always fit to one of these styles. Decision making styles may also differ per product or service. This may be relevant for fashion retailers for instance, as a Chinese study revealed. Seven decision making styles were found researching consumers buying clothes.[62] Differences were made with respect to buying domestic brands, imported brands or both. It appeared that Chinese consumers preferring to buy foreign, imported brands score high on the styles of brand loyal, hedonistic, quality conscious, brand conscious and fashion conscious. Consumers preferring domestic brands score high on the styles of confused over choice and price consciousness. So, retailers can use the shopping orientation to segment the market. The first group spends a lot on clothing while the latter does not.

SERVICE PRACTICE 3.5

Decision-making Styles and Buying Financial Services

A study in the UK financial services sector revealed in a very practical way of determining if and how consumers' decision-making styles differed for current accounts, insurance products, credit products and investment products.[63]

Most UK consumers open their current accounts and buy their credit-based services at the branch itself, whereas insurance-based services are mostly bought via the telephone or at the branch.

UK consumers buy their investment-based services via a wide variety of channels: at the branch, by telephone and post, and visits at home. They also indicated that they use a wide variety of sources of information to come to their buying decision of investment-based service. These sources included professional advice, friends or family, advertising, the financial press and the Internet.

Information sources used in opening a current account are mainly friends or family and advertising. Professional advice, friends or family and advertising are the main sources of information used in buying insurance- and credit-based services.

UK consumers use a large number of channels and information sources to buy investment-based services. For all other financial services mentioned in the study they have a more limited, focussed decision making style with respect to channels and information sources used.

You may recall that consumers differ in the way they can cope with perceived risk. A consumer's perception of risk will also correlate with their decision making style. In a Dutch study on banking services such as personal accounts and credit cards, it appeared that the behaviour of impulsive buyers was negatively correlated with perceived risk, meaning that the more impulsive you are the less perceived risk you experience. The more impulsive consumers did not elaborate on their choice; consequently they are less likely to demonstrate a high level of loyalty.

Customers who prefer buying well-established brands, also referred to as brand conscious consumers, were highly correlated with perceived risk. This implies that they need the security of brands.[64] From a marketer's perspective these consumers are more likely to demonstrate a high degree of brand loyalty.

Insight into the service organization's customers' decision making style will help marketing managers improve their offer and the communication of that offer to the selected target groups. Decision making styles are also used to make the consumer's decision making process more efficient. These heuristics may contribute to consumers' use of time. It is possible then to view time efficiency as a new way of marketing services in the experience economy where people are perceived to be time poor.

Time

Time is of particular importance in the servuction process. Time is needed to ensure that the actual service delivery takes place. Customers have to be present during the services delivery and sometimes have to wait before or during this. Even a consumer changing their bank will have to give up their time in order to facilitate their desired outcome. The previous section showed that time is one of the most important reasons people choose to stay with a bank that they are otherwise dissatisfied with.

People perceive and value time in a different way. These differing perceptions of time may lead to different time styles for different consumers.[65] In a French study, various time styles were found.[66] Time styles can be regarded as the relationship between personality traits and time. Persons and groups of persons may have a common representation and evaluation of time. A distinction can be made for instance between people valuing time as economic time ('time is money'), and people's orientation towards time in terms of

> *past orientation, future orientation, time submissiveness (the capacity to comply with schedules) and people's feeling of uselessness of time (related to the belief that one's own time has little value or purpose).*[67]

People with an economic time orientation want to be served quickly.

Since time is a scarce commodity in many western countries many time saving products and services have been developed. Companies providing services such as pet sitting, plant watering, wedding advising, personal shopping and house cleaning are booming. Valarie Zeithaml and Mary Jo Bitner call it the 'antidote to time deficiency'.[68] In B2B markets we call it outsourcing, but you will see it is also happening in consumer markets.

In the Netherlands some studies have been undertaken in which a distinction has been made between consumers with high and low levels of income and purchasing power versus consumers with a lot of leisure and free time and consumers without this time. High income consumers without free time will be vulnerable and are thus more likely to buy in time saving services.

The inability to store services means that waiting is quite common. Quite often waiting times can induce customer dissatisfaction, especially when the wait is unexpected.[69] Emotions such as anger then play a critical role in determining the final (dis)satisfaction with the service and the resulting propensity to complain or repurchase. You can imagine that waiting is perceived differently whether you are in a good mood or in a bad mood.

Emotions and Mood

Time is important in service delivery processes, especially with respect to waiting. People perceive waiting times, shopping trips or service processes to be shorter when they are in a good mood. When people are in a good mood they will spend more engaging in the specific activity.[70] In general, atmospherics in the servicescape affect the financial and non-financial performance of the service organization. Appropriate atmospherics can lead to a better financial performance. Music likeability for example impacts on the consumer's subjective evaluation of the wait-length and mood. Emotions and mood are critical. The two are not the same as Bagozzi has pointed out:[71]

> *by emotion we mean a mental state of readiness that arises from cognitive appraisals of events or thoughts; has a phenomenological tone; is accompanied by physiological processes; is often expressed physically; and may result in specific actions to affirm or cope with the emotion, depending on its nature and meaning for the person having it; ... and is typically intentional (i.e. it has an object or referent).*

and

> *by convention mood is conceived to be longer lasting (from a few hours up to days) and lower in intensity than an emotion ... [moods] are generally non intentional and global or diffused ... and are not as directly coupled with action tendencies and explicit actions as are many emotions.*

Emotions affect satisfaction in either a positive or negative way. Emotions can be expressed in different ways and magnitudes in various cultures. The Plutchik scale[72] has often been used in measuring emotions. It consists of seven items:

1 Anger;
2 Sadness;
3 Acceptance;
4 Disgust;
5 Expectancy;
6 Surprise; and
7 Anxiety.

The impact of emotions is a critical element in the service experience. Emotions can have a positive or negative impact. Positive emotions are emotions felt as: attentive, alert, concentrated, joyful, delighted and happy. Negative emotions are felt as: downhearted, sad, discouraged, enraged, angry, mad, scared, fearful, afraid, regretful and disappointed.

Positive emotions influence two aspects of employee behaviour in creating both the encounter and relationship satisfaction in stores. That is employee specific attributes such as competence, authenticity, age, experience and gender, and interaction-induced behaviours such as mutual understanding, extra attention and meeting minimum standards.[73] Positive emotions moderate the relationship between satisfaction and loyalty with respect to extended services in the case of high involvement settings. This does not occur in low involvement services.[74] In other words, positive emotions enhance the relationship between satisfaction and loyalty.

Emotions affect people's mood.[75] A study of German tourists on the Canary Islands found that these tourists expressed different moods on different days of their holiday; happiness increased gradually during their stay but dropped dramatically on the day of departure. Therefore, we doubt whether it is really the best to have vacationers fill in their satisfaction questionnaire on the day of departure; the results may be biased by such a mood effect. Mood also fluctuated during the day depending on whether or not the respondent was categorized as a 'morning type' and 'evening type'. Every day during the whole holiday the mood of extrovert people was higher than for introvert people.

Acceptance of New Technologies

At the beginning of this chapter we emphasized how the intangibility of services determined perceived risk. The perceived risk of new technologies may be rather high to some consumers, but probably not to the early adopters. More and more services are based on a technological interaction between the consumer and the service provider. Some people enjoy this, others not. Technology readiness is an important construct to understand consumer behaviour in buying and using technology-based services.

> *The technology-readiness construct refers to people's propensity to embrace and use new technologies for accomplishing goals in home life and at work.*[76]

Four components reflect different aspects of the acceptance or non-acceptance of a new technology. In a later study they were condensed to two dimensions, as shown in Table 3.4.[77]

Table 3.4 Dimension of technology readiness		
Components	*Description*	*Dimensions*
Optimism	A positive view of technology and a belief that it offers people increased control, flexibility, and efficiency in their lives	Technological positivism
Innovativeness	A tendency to be a technology pioneer and thought leader	Technological positivism
Discomfort	A perceived lack of control over technology and a feeling of being overwhelmed by it	Technophobia
Insecurity	Distrust of technology and scepticism about its ability to work properly	Technophobia

Table 3.5	Technology readiness segment profiles in the UK				
Cluster	Size	Gender	Age	Education	Income
Explorers	27%	Men	Late 20s/early 30s	High	High
Pioneers	32%	Women	Older than 35	Low	Average
Skeptics	20%	Men	Younger than 45	Average/high	Average
Laggards	21%	Women	Older than 45	Low	Low

Parasuraman[78] maintains: 'Optimism and innovativeness are drivers of technology readiness, whereas discomfort and insecurity are inhibitors.' People scoring high, medium and low on the technology readiness indicator show different behaviours in accepting and not accepting new technologies that are in line with the behaviours expected: a high TRI-score goes along with a high degree of accepting these innovations and new ways of offering services.

Parasuraman and Colby[79] identified five clusters of US consumers based on their TRI scores:

The first people to adopt are the Explorers, who are highly motivated and fearless. The next to adopt are the Pioneers, who desire the benefits of new technologies but are more practical about the difficulties and dangers. The next wave consists of two groups; Skeptics, who need to be convinced of the benefits of new technologies, and Paranoids, who are convinced of the fruits but unusually concerned about the risks. The last group, Laggards, may never adopt unless they are forced to do so.

Tsikriktsis[80] found only four clusters in a similar UK study: the Paranoids were not represented in the UK. The four segments found in the UK have different sizes and are dominated by different demographic variables, as shown in Table 3.5.

Self-Service Technologies

Nowadays consumers can use many service delivery modes to access a service. In general customers have to make a choice between being served or serving themselves using a self-service technological interface with the service organization. Self-services are services such as the ATM, the ticket vending machine at railway stations, a self-service petrol station, telephone banking, the automated hotel check out at a Formule 1 hotel, or online investment trading.

For service providers it is sometimes quite hard to convince customers to use these new technologies. It seems to be risky to them while they also have to master a new service process in which they are the co-producer. In self-services the customer generally must take responsibility for their own level of satisfaction. Given this, the customer's technological readiness will determine their overall readiness to use and adopt the self-service.

The trialling of a new service seems to be determined by four factors.[81] These factors are:

1 role clarity;
2 extrinsic motivation;
3 intrinsic motivation; and
4 ability to use the new technology.

Recently it was shown that image congruence has a significant impact on consumer attitudes and the adoption of new services such as mobile banking. Image congruence refers to whether there is a fit between consumers' self-image and the image of an innovation.[82] All in all, customers must perceive the value of the new offering before they accept it.[83]

Self-services are important in both the B2C and B2B markets. The services in B2B markets are such services as: line supply ordering, reservation systems, payment transfer, help desks, display, shipment tracking and downloading information. In Canada the sources of satisfaction of self-services in B2B are: improved speed in turn-around time, improved process efficiency, saved time and cost, reliability of the system, convenience and quick help via Web-based transactions. The sources of dissatisfaction are: technology failures, transaction process problems, post-transaction problems, customer services problems such as a long wait online, user-unfriendliness, lack of prior notice and customer fault.[84]

The potential hazard of self-service is that it may create more distance between the customer and the service employee and company. Many banks are now aiming to reverse the trend to more self-servicing because they feel that they are loosing contact with their customers. Customers seemingly prefer interpersonal contact when more difficult financial questions have to be solved. These developments offer less opportunities for cross-selling and may reduce customer loyalty because the social bonds are weakened. A Norwegian study on this topic concluded that:

> *self-service without a minimum of personal interaction may well have a negative effect on customer loyalty because the important social-bond mechanism is removed. Unless other loyalty mechanisms are created and integrated into self-service systems, the long-term effect of self-service without personal interaction is likely to be reduced customer loyalty. Thus, personal service and personal relationships between customers and employees are even more important when simple and repetitive tasks are automated.*[85]

Online shopping utilizes much of the new self-service technology. A wide variety of factors will determine whether consumers shop on line or not.[86] The intention to shop online is determined by the attitude toward online shopping which in turn is determined by the usefulness, ease of use and enjoyment of online shopping. Demographic variables and personality characteristics also play a critical role. On average, younger consumers, men, higher educated people and higher income people tend to shop more online compared to older consumers, women, lower educated and lower income people. Personality traits like expertise, self-efficacy and need for interaction play a role as well. Moreover, situational factors like time pressure, lack of mobility, geographical distance, need for special items and attractiveness of alternatives determine the use of online shopping.

Products and services that do not need personal interaction or products that the consumer does not need to trial prior to purchase are suitable for online shopping. A customer's previous experience with respect to billing, product information, method of payment, delivery terms, risk involved, privacy, security, personalization, visual appeal, navigation, entertainment, and their evaluation will impact on whether or not a customer will continue to shop online after initial trial. Lack of trust is one of the most commonly cited reasons for consumers not to shop on the Internet.

Dysfunctional Behaviour

When consumers do not accept the new technology, we may describe this as 'negative consumer behaviour' since consumers are not doing what they are expected to do. However the direct cause of not using the new technology may be found in the consumer's cognitive nature, affective nature or due to the environment.

Cognitive reasons may be a perceived lack of control, a perceived higher risk, a lower self-efficacy, a greater effort to be made, or a longer waiting time. The affective reasons can be formulated as consumers feeling lonelier, fearing an interaction with a machine or having a negative attitude towards dealing with a machine. Environmental reasons could be that the machine is out of order; that customers do not have the correct coins to pay, or that the machine is located in a dark or unfriendly spot. Indirect causes have to do with the supposed flexibility, complexity and reliability of the technology. Past experiences contribute to accepting the innovation or not.[87]

Many of these reasons can be easily applied to the acceptance of for instance ATMs and ticket vending machines at railway stations. In fact, these customers show dysfunctional behaviour. We can define this behaviour as 'actions by customers who intentionally or unintentionally, overtly or covertly, act in a manner that, in some way, disrupts otherwise functional service encounters'.[88]

Dysfunctional behaviour impacts on customer-contact employees through emotions and physical effects, on customers themselves through spoilt consumption effects and the domino effects on behaviour of other consumers and the service organization via direct and indirect financial costs.

3.7   Market Segmentation and Positioning

Segmentation

A well-developed segmentation of the market has to be in line with the strategic choices made by the service provider. As shown in Chapter 2, segmenting the market is one of the crucial steps in the model of the strategic pathway. All well-known segmentation variables – such as gender, income or other socio-economic and demographic variables – and psychographics can be applied. A prerequisite however is that this also ends up with viable, homogeneous groups of customers, which can be clearly separated from other customer groups. These groups should be served in a market oriented way (see Chapter 6).

In this section we will elaborate on some of the specific issues of market segmentation in the service industry. All of the variables to be used in classifying services could be used in segmenting the market as well. Each of these variables provides a different way of looking at the way customers interact with these services. Segmentation of the services market may be based on the score on the technology readiness index, the decision making style, the required participation in the service delivery process, the stage in the family life cycle or the degree of perceived risk (see section 3.3 on perceived risk in general and section 3.6 on the impact of perceived risk on using self-services technologies in particular).

A UK study segmented the market of financial services in terms of the consumer's degree of uncertainty (high or low) and their degree of involvement in those services (high or low).[89] Consumers in the low uncertainty and low involvement segment may be fully aware of the service and know a lot about it. As a result they are disinterested in the service or they perceive it as a simple service, even a commodity service, for example a current bank account. These customers will be loyal to the bank out of inertia. The bank then may have some kind of a simple relationship marketing programme to keep them on board. It is important however that banks determine their earnings from these customers as this will give them an idea of what services could be automated.

Consumers in the high uncertainty, high involvement segment will seek advice, especially when they do not have enough knowledge about special or augmented services. They will be very dependent on the bank and will probably favour a rather close and personal relationship with their financial counsellor or account manager.

Segmenting Customer Markets

Segmentation can be based on one variable, however it is more common to use a combination of variables. For example we know that the decision making styles between men and women differ, therefore it would be appropriate to overlay gender with decision making style to develop an appropriate segmentation in say the retail clothing market.

Psychological variables, psychographic variables and lifestyle can also be used to segment services markets. A promising development in this area is the domain specific segmentation, in which the specific use of a particular service in a certain situation and in a specific moment is the segmentation criterion.[90] In fact, this has to do with specific behaviour in specific situations. Domain specific segmentation deals essentially with need fulfilment. In other words it deals with segmenting the market along the required desired benefits.

Another development in segmentation is related to the different ways people perceive time. Some people spend more time in memories and past situations while others concentrate on current issues and yet others will turn their thoughts to events that may or may not take place in the future. Past-orientated people are more conservative, sentimental and brand loyal. Present-orientated people have a quick reaction/stimulus process and are therefore more impulsive and uninterested in long-term projects. Future-orientated people are likely to be more adventurous and creative and to be risk-takers. They switch more and like to test new services, and as such are more likely to be innovators or early adopters. When you look back at the four different segments of TRI consumers, you will recall that the degree of adoption of service innovations can indeed be used to segment the market within a country. However, segmenting international markets on the basis of perceived risk may also be due to cultural differences, specifically the difference in uncertainty avoidance.

It is also possible to segment the market based on the actual value the customer has to the organization. This may be in the long term the life time value of the customer or in the short run their generated cash flow or contribution. To the service provider it will be self-evident that segments of valuable customers are important, especially when these turn out to be profitable customers. More and more banks would like to focus on profitable customers; particularly as there is greater pressure to generate shareholder value and value-based management. Such a management philosophy requires banks to have the administrative procedures and systems to allocate costs to individual customers or segments so as they can calculate the profitability of these customers in as much detail as possible. If this can not be done it is not a net profit per customer that is computed but a (gross) contribution margin. Activity-based costing or direct product profitability can be used to calculate these margins.

Johnson and Leger have developed a model to analyse the profitability of customers.[91] They introduced the concepts of customer inertia, customer value and potential value. The idea of customer inertia reflects the fact that some customers do not want or need a relationship. In other words, their relationship proneness is low or non existent.[92] These customers may buy some services for a shorter or longer period of time, but these services are not that crucial to be a part of their lifestyle. The idea of customer value hinges upon those customers on top of the total customer pyramid who spend a lot of money on services. If this spending is compared to their potential value the company can decide on what to do to attract them.

The customer base can be divided in four segments:

1 Customers with a high share of wallet.
2 Customers with a low share of wallet.
3 Customers with a high profitable lifetime duration.
4 Customers with a low profitable lifetime duration.

From an economic point of view the service company may abandon customers scoring low on both dimensions. They may outsource these customers or decrease marketing expenditure in these segments. Customers scoring high on both dimensions should be pampered to keep them on board; they can be rewarded via loyalty programmes or personal attention. Customers with a low profitable lifetime duration but a high share of wallet could be approached with a lot of cross-selling activities via selected marketing programmes. Customers with a high profitable lifetime duration but a low share of wallet should be kept away from competitors, especially where they have other services.

In our opinion, segmentation based on dynamic behavioural criteria like benefits sought, decision making style, observed uncertainty, perceived risk or time perception corresponds more closely to the actual behaviour of customers. The advantage of the behavioural segmentation approach is that these criteria reflect individual factors which in turn determine the decision making style of a customer. A market-oriented service provider segments the market in this way. This applies to both B2B services as well as B2C.

Segmenting Business-to-Business Markets

B2B markets in services are characterized by decision making units, problem solving units and networks of relationships between organizations and employees.[93] When customers do not succeed within the existing supplier relationships they start searching for new ones. The uncertainties they are facing have to do with need uncertainty, market uncertainty and transaction uncertainty. Some relationships are high involvement and others low involvement; some are long standing while others are quite new. In fact, all the crucial terms describing B2B marketing could be used in segmenting the market:

■ Relationships, including relationship duration, relationship strength, and relationship involvement;
■ Interaction, which includes the interaction degree and the persons involved in the DMU;
■ The network of relationships, these can be seen as a portfolio;
■ The resources and technologies of both supplier and customer companies;
■ The abilities, problems and uncertainties of both supplier and customer companies; and
■ The offerings of the supplier and the solutions for the customer next to traditional criteria such as sales, preferred supplier, geographic distance, reliability in deliveries or reaction time.

Service providers can also use the matrices developed in Figures 3.9 and 3.10 to segment the market. They segment the market based on the relevance of the products and services to the buying company. Knowledge about the dimensions used in these matrices – such as importance to the customer, uniqueness of the offering, impact on profit and supply risk – may also be used to bring about some changes in the segments, especially when the service provider recognizes that being dependent on the customer may harm their own company or future viability.

Positioning

Segmenting a market is the first step in developing appropriate strategy; once segmented, organizations need to consider positioning. Positioning can be defined as the mental place a service holds in the mind of the consumer relative to the nearest main competitor.

> *Positioning is not what is done to the service, it is what is created in the minds of the target consumers; the service is positioned in the minds of these consumers and is given an image.*[94]

An image can be defined as the total impression a customer or group of customers has about an object, a service or a service provider or an organization and its employees. Such an impression consists of more than just facts. Facts, feelings, customs, attitudes, expectations and perceptions plus all the associations of a person or group will result in the final image formation. An image can be based on either a quick first impression or a thorough analysis of and elaboration on all facts and feelings surrounding the object.[95] An image always has a subjective evaluation component. This subjectivity is expressed not only in the specific position of a service relative to other services, but also in the number of competitive services and in the ways these are deemed important to a customer. After all, customers subjectively determine what and who are viewed as services' competitors. Therefore, it is important to know what customers perceive as competitive services rather than what the service organization assumes the competitors are. Perceptual mapping is a tool to visualize the relative positioning of different services on specific attributes. This results in a positioning map.

A service provider can consider, on strategic grounds, whether their positioning is the desired one and what position it should aim to accomplish. If such an objective is clear the strategy can be designed to assist the organization in reaching this goal.

The identity of the service organization and its image are two different concepts. The identity refers to what the firm wants to be, how it wants to be seen in the market place. The image reflects the actual opinions of the customers about the firm, its services and the quality of the services. The identity is the norm, the plan and the goals set by the supplier while the image reflects the actual situation, the actual perception of the customer or other stakeholder groups. Identity and image may differ; the service organization should strive for congruence between both.

SERVICE PRACTICE 3.6

Peru's Identity and Image[96]

PromPeru is the promotion commission of Peru. Its job is to promote Peru as an attractive tourism destination. In tourism, destination image can be defined as the sum of the actual beliefs, ideas and impressions of individual destination objects, as well as the actual overall impression a person has of a destination. A destination's identity can be viewed as the desired image of the destination, as set by tourism service providers, operators and tourism boards, which is communicated to the general public and specific target groups.

According to PromPeru, the destination identity of Peru should be based on three building blocks: history, nature and living cultures. Peru's prime archaeological sites – like Machu Picchu, the Nasca lines, the historic city of Cusco, the 2500-year-old Chavin ruins, the huge adobe capital of the Chimu empire Chan Chan, the historic centre of Lima, and the Rio Abiseo National Park – are crucial in attracting international tourists. Biodiversity and nature are other key features of the identity alongside folklore, dances, music, cuisine and handicrafts.

Results from a qualitative and quantitative study in Germany, one of Peru's primary target markets, revealed that most Germans were quite unfamiliar with Peru; they had not visited the country before and knew only a little bit about it from the news and literature. It turned out that attributes like weather, nature and culture contributed in a positive sense to the image of Peru. The tourism infrastructure, the political and economic instability and poor perceived safety factor had a negative effect on the image.

Those Germans who had been to Peru expressed a much more positive image about Peru than the ones who had not been there.

Targeting

Market segmentation will lead to defining various segments in the market. Positioning refers to the position of the service brand in the minds of the customers given the position of other service brands. The examples provided on segmenting the market described how identifiable segments can be found. How these segments are approached by the service organization reflects their targeting strategy, specifically the different strategies developed for each segment.

Heavy users have to be targeted differently from lighter users. The high involvement/high uncertainty segment in financial services has to be treated differently from the low involvement/low uncertainty segment. Profitable lifetime duration customers need a different treatment from less profitable lifetime customers. Tourists with a lot of knowledge about the country to visit will need another amount of information on that country than those who know hardly anything about that particular country. So, after defining the specific segments chosen to target and counting the number of target markets the service provider can decide whether they will implement a differentiated or a niche strategy.

Country of Origin

The study on the image of Peru demonstrated that some Germans base their image of Peru on a general perception of the country or just any South American country. The image of Peru in Germany originated from a kind of halo construct, in which an overall impression is based on some stereotyping or generalizations that are not based on actual knowledge or experiences. When the image is based on factual knowledge and a thorough evaluation of that knowledge, the image could be regarded as a summary construct.[97] From a marketing perspective, stereotypes are much harder to change than factual misunderstandings.

Attitudes about a particular country may affect the perceived quality and purchase value of services from that country. This may hold for individual households buying services as well as for organizations.[98] When these attitudes are negative, this will negatively affect the service quality of services rendered by companies from that particular country. This may then be a barrier for customers to spend their holidays in that country or to companies entering that foreign market. The opposite may hold in other instances.

Many issues are hard to evaluate in the services sector and as such it can be expected that country of origin (COO) will be one of the attributes consumers use to evaluate the service from a particular international service provider. It may be used as a proxy for quality, trust and reliability. Some countries may be evaluated more positively than others. COO may be a variable determining the perception of the technical, functional and relational quality of a service organization. For international service providers, the home country image will affect the image of their own company.[99] If the image is positive then they can benefit from it, conversely a negative image can be a disadvantage. In these situations a large communication effort is needed to change that image. COO can be used to make the intangible service of a foreign service provider 'more tangible'; consumers can also use COO as a search attribute in the first stages of their decision making process.

Ethnocentrism

While COO refers to the impact of the image of a country on buying foreign services, ethnocentrism has to do with favouring services and products from one's own country over foreign products and services. Ethnocentrism can be defined as: 'the beliefs of consumers in a particular country about the appropriateness, indeed morality, of purchasing foreign-made services'.[100]

Using the concept of ethnocentrism will improve the understanding of how consumers and corporate buyers compare domestic services with foreign-made services. It shows how and why their judgements may be subject to various forms of bias and error. Highly ethnocentric consumers are probably most inclined to accentuate the positive aspects of domestic services and to discount the virtues of foreign-made items. Non ethnocentric consumers will evaluate services on their own merits without taking into account the country from which the service provider originates. Highly ethnocentric consumers will consider buying foreign services as wrong arguing that it will hurt the domestic economy, and that it is unpatriotic.

Stated differently, 'consumer ethnocentrism gives the individual a sense of identity, feelings of belongingness, and ... an understanding of what purchase behaviour is acceptable or unacceptable to the in-group.'[101] The degree of ethnocentrism may not only vary per country but also per region within a country; usually older people, less educated people and lower income people tend to be more ethnocentric than younger, higher educated and higher income people. Ethnocentrism is a way of valuing the 'in-group' (the group with which an individual identifies) and not valuing the 'out-group' (those regarded as the opposite of the in-group). This brings us back to the distinction between the national cultures that we discussed at the beginning of this chapter.

Summary

Consumer behaviour with respect to services has several unique aspects, all emerging from the intangible nature of services. The internationalization of service industries makes this even more complex as we must now consider differences in consumer behaviour across various countries. This requires analysing the different cultural characteristics in these countries and assessing the cultural distances, which are often different from the geographical distances. This is important because coping with uncertainty, which is inherent in the perceived risk, will differ between cultures. This is partly because the barriers to entry can be caused by ethnocentrism.

Moreover, the 'country-of-origin' effect may play a role in accepting services offered by foreign companies. This all may impact not only on the eight types of perceived risk, but also the three different types of intangibility will also impact on perceived risk. The three different types of intangibility are physical intangibility, generality and mental intangibility.

Uncertainty avoidance and perceived risk are crucial elements in providing services in an international context. Many ways exist to reduce perceived risk. Consumers' time perception affects the servuction process as well as the mood customers are in. Emotions are rather important in the process of buying and evaluating services, especially when consumers are dissatisfied about the services offered. Many ways to express (dis)satisfaction about services have been found. Satisfaction does not always lead to loyalty; distinguishing between two processes is important here. There is a relationship between manifest satisfaction and true loyalty and between latent satisfaction and spurious loyalty.

The services market can be segmented on the basis of socioeconomic and demographic variables, as well as on the basis of the typical characteristics of services and on our classification criteria. The benefits and perceived risks can be used as segmentation variables especially when these segmentation variables match the policy of a market oriented service provider. We favour psychographics and more dynamic, behavioural criteria over more static criteria like income or age to segment the market.

The image of a service or service provider can differ between each segment. The positioning of services can be shown by a perceptual map. From these positions, strategic consequences can be drawn and specific targeting strategies developed.

In order to be able to analyse the buying process of services, the following classification has been made:

- pre-purchase stage;
- consumption stage; and
- post-purchase stage.

Different decision making styles have to be known to understand consumer behaviour well. At least eight styles were found in various studies. These styles can also be applied in the services sector. These different styles are also linked to differences in perceived risk. More perceived risk and a more perfectionist style go hand in hand, whereas the more impulsive customers are the less risk they perceive. The technology readiness index helps explain why some people accept new (self-) service technologies and others do not.

The interaction between a service provider and a customer can be analysed within the framework of ongoing relationships. This holds even more for business-to-business services with their DMU and PSU than to business-to-customer services. In B2B markets the process of purchasing has evolved into a process of supply (chain) management. The focus then is not on one short-term transaction but on a long(er)-term relationship. The dynamics in these relationships should be analysed carefully in order to be a truly market oriented service provider. This relationship paradigm is preferred over a strong and sole focus on the marketing mix.

In our view, the different service marketing mix instruments should support and enhance the relationship between the client and the service provider. The relationship concept also applies to analysing modified and straight rebuy situations and the different positions in the portfolio of products and services industrial companies buy. This paradigm can be applied also to the issues of starting, developing and maintaining relationships in the case of new task buying situations. Building relationships is one of the many ways to reduce customers' perceived risk.

Questions

1. Why should one distinguish between search, experience and credence attributes in services?
2. Describe the eight categories of perceived risk.

3. Describe how each of the categories of perceived risk (described in Q2) are related to the various kinds of intangibility.
4. Summarize the main arguments as to why service organizations should focus attention on their reputation and image.
5. Outline the main consequences to the organization, with respect to consumer behaviour if the organization fails to maintain a positive image.
6. Describe the ways in which customers can reduce perceived risk with respect to their buying and using services.
7. Using your university or a bank to illustrate, describe the kinds of activities that you engaged as you passed through your own decision process in buying their services for the first time.
8. What is meant by the terms 'customer satisfaction' and 'customer dissatisfaction'?
9. Describe how the terms 'customer satisfaction' and 'customer dissatisfaction' can be expressed.
10. Describe the relationship between satisfaction and loyalty.
11. Explain the term 'benefit segmentation', detailing why it could be useful to service providers.
12. Explain why market oriented service organizations prefer not to use their own perceptions about the market (competitors and consumers) but rather the customers' perceptions about service attributes and competitors.
13. Describe how to define and operationalize national culture.
14. Explain what you perceive to be the link between COO and ethnocentrism.
15. Describe the various consumer decision-making styles.

Assignments

1. Using the data from Table 3.1, describe the culture of your own country.
   a Where is your country's culture positioned in Figure 3.4?
   b In the data and Figure 3.4, you will see countries with similar countries close to your own.
   i Does that positioning make any sense to you?
   ii Why/why not?
2. In this chapter we used some examples that focussed on the image and identity of holiday destinations. Describe the image and identity of your own country as a holiday destination.
3. Describe the kind of business-to-business services a large chemical firm like DSM, Hofman La Roche, or BASF would use.
   a What do they actually outsource?
   b Why do they outsource?
4. What decision-making style fits best to your own behaviour in buying services? How do you see that reflected in your buying of:
   a banking services?
   b cinema tickets?
   c holidays?

5. What would you recommend PromPeru to do to change its image in Germany and to attract more visitors from Germany?
   a What kind of tourists should they attract?
   b Make a rough outline for a marketing plan for PromPeru on the German market.

Endnotes

1 See for instance Peter and Olson, 2002, or Kotler, 1996.

2 Riddle, 1992.

3 Hofstede, 1991, p. 5. The definitions of the first four dimensions can be found respectively on pp. 82–83, 51, 113 and 28.

4 The scores presented here can be found in Hofstede, 1991 and 2001, and in De Mooij, 2004. See also Usunier, 1992. When the correspondence analysis would be performed for the countries having scores on all five dimensions, only 35 countries could be taken into account. Now we can show this graph for 64 countries which provides more information.

5 This picture is different from the one in the first edition of our book. This is mainly due to the increasing number of countries involved and changes in the way the statistical package to perform correspondence analysis has developed over the past ten years. When we performed the initial analyses, correspondence analysis was a separate statistical package, now it is part of SPSS.

6 In that respect, it is worthwhile to note that one of the leading schools in services marketing management is the Nordic School with well-known scholars like Christian Grönroos and Evert Gummesson.

7 This conclusion has been drawn on the basis of the results found in the study by Meuter, Bitner, Ostrom and Brown, 2005.

8 These conclusions are based on the results found in studies performed by Matilla, 1999; Furrer, Shaw-Ling and Sudharshan, 2000; Shaw-Ling, Furrer and Sudharshan, 2001; and the way some of these results are presented in Zeithaml and Bitner, 2003.

9 The maximum ethnocentrism score obtained could be 50 in this study by Steenkamp (1993).

10 At the end of this chapter we will deal with the concept of ethnocentrism in a more detailed way.

11 Some proof for this statement is the fact that initially the literature on relationship marketing has been developed in Scandinavia by the Nordic School who proposed it as an alternative for implementing marketing via the manipulation of the various marketing mix instrument in a very competitive way.

12 This Service Practice is based on Matilla, 1999.

13 Gemünden, 1985; Suchard and Polonsky, 1991.

14 In our discussing of pricing in Chapter 11, we will return to the question how price can act as an indicator for quality of services.

15 Note that this is a different use of the word 'functional' than at the end of Chapter 2.

16 The monetary and non monetary cost of the consumer involved in searching for services will be discussed in Chapter 11 on pricing.

17 Peter and Olson, 1993.

18 Hutt and Speh, 1992.

19 Assael, 1987; Schiffman and Kanuk, 1987.

20 This Service Practice is based on Laroche, Bergeron and Goutaland, 2001, and Laroche, McDougall, Bergeron and Yang, 2004.

21 Peter and Olson, 1993, pp. 92, 93, 97.

22 See also the SERVQUAL-model of Parasuraman, Zeithaml and Berry (1988), discussed in Chapter 5.

23 See e.g. Venetis, 1997.

24 This shows the usefulness of applying our classification of services from Chapter 2 here.

25 Many of these examples are also mentioned in Zeithaml and Bitner, 2003, pp. 36–37. They have defined these as search, experience and credence qualities instead of attributes.

26 Bateson, 1992.

27 This section is based to a large extent on the work of Oliver, 1997; Oliver and Burke, 1999; Cronin and Taylor, 1992; Bloemer, 1993; and Bloemer and Kasper, 1995.

28 See for instance Bitner and Hubbert, 1994; Danaher and Mattsson, 1994; and De Ruyter, Lemmink, Wetzels and Mattsson, 1997.

29 Richard Oliver, 1997, pp. 13–14.

30 Friman and Edvardsson, 2003.

31 For an example in the US health care sector, see Blackwell *et al.*, 1999.

32 The definition of loyalty that we will use in this text is based on the well-known definition of Jacoby and Chestnut, 1978.

33 Kiesler, 1968, p. 448; and Lastovicka and Gardner, 1978, p. 90.

34 Venetis, 1997; Bansal *et al.*, 2004.

35 Caruana, 2002.

36 Ranaweera and Prabhu, 2003; Venetis and Ghauri, 2004; Gounaris, 2005; Lam *et al.*, 2004.

37 Chebat, Davidow and Codjovi, 2005; Richins, 1983.

38 Keaveny, 1995; Roos, 1999.

39 Bitner, 1990.

40 See Keiningham, Perkins-Munn and Evans, 2003.

41 For a comprehensive overview, see Anderson and Mittal, 2000.

42 For further reading on the relationship between the buyer's DMU and the seller's PSU, see Rossomme, 2003.

43 Axelsson and Wynstra, 2002, p. 19.

44 Alexander and Hordes, 2003, p. 2.

45 Kraljic, the director of the Düsseldorf McKinsey Company office, has presented this view at various conferences and in his *Harvard Business Review* article of 1983.

46 See e.g Ford *et al.*, 2004.

47 Oliva and Lancioni, 1996.

48 These and similar ideas have been developed to a large extent in Scandinavia by Grönroos (1990a) and Gummesson (1987) with respect to services and by the Industrial Marketing and Purchasing (IMP) Group with respect to business to business marketing (see, for instance, Häkansson, 1982; Ford, 1982, 1990, 2004).

49 Odekerken-Schröder, 1999; De Wulf *et al.*, 2001.

50 Berry and Parasuraman, 1991, p. 133.

51 Kumar, 1999. One should realize that this study focusses on the output of the relationship and not on the process of service delivery.

52 Lemmink, Rohs and Schijns, 1994.

53 All marketing textbooks show what marketing strategy and mix fit best in every stage of the product life cycle or service life cycle.

54 Karin Venetis' overview (1997) is based on studies in the BtB services sector, like Grönroos, 1982a, 1982b; Wackman *et al.*, 1987; Yorke, 1988; Szmigin, 1993; Sharma, 1994; and Halinen, 1994. Within brackets we mention the terms used by other authors than Venetis.

55 White and Yanamandram, 2004.

56 Walsh *et al.*, 2001.

57 Sproles, 1985.

58 Sproles, 1985.

59 Sproles and Kendall, 1986; Hafstrom *et al.*, 1992; Durvasula and Lysonski, 1993; Lysonski and Durvasula, 1996; Fan and Xiao, 1998, Mitchell and Bates, 1998; Walsh *et al.*, 2001; Canabal, 2002; Kozlova, 2003. The time and energy conserving style fits to consumers who 'let their fingers do the walking' in the sense that they consult consumer magazines, compare ads before they buy and save energy by shopping at the same stores (Hafstrom *et al.*, 1992; Mitchell and Bates, 1998). This style resembles the brand conscious and habitual, loyal styles mentioned before. The time consciousness style is characterized by consumers indicating to shop deliberately always at the same shop because it is efficient, taking the time to shop carefully for the best buys and not making fast shopping trips. Quite often they need help in making their decision (Fan and Xiao, 1998). The information utilization style (Fan and Xiao, 1998) is comparable to the confused by overchoice style; however, these consumers indicate being able to process and take advantage of the information provided. The store loyal style is typically for consumers who indicate going to the same stores each time they shop (Mitchell and Bates, 1998). Consumers with a variety-seeking decision-making style regularly change brands, have fun in buying something new and exciting and like to shop for a variety of brands (Walsh *et al.*, 2001). It is remarkable to see that these 'new' styles are found in these studies although the questionnaire is basically the same in all studies; nevertheless, the factor structure differs by country.

60 See MBA thesis of Zhanna Kozlova, Universiteit Maastricht, 2003.

61 Bakewell and Mitchell, 2004.

62 Wang, Siu and Hui, 2004.

63 Howcroft, Hewer and Hamilton, 2003.

64 This is based on the masters theses of Joost van der Pas, 2004 and Esther van Es, 2004.

65 See for instance Morello, 1988; Bergadaà, 1991; Mowen and Mowen, 1991.

66 Usunier and Valette-Florence, 1991 and 1994; Durrande-Moreau and Usunier, 1999. Given these different time styles, time styles can be used also as a way to segment service markets.

67 See Durrande-Moreau and Usunier, 1999, p. 175.

68 Zeithaml and Bitner, 2003, pp. 34–35.

69 See for instance Casado Díaz and Más Ruíz, 2002.

70 See Beverwijk, 2003; Cameron, Baker, Peterson and Braunsberger, 2003; Mowen and Mowen, 1991; Usunier and Valette-Florence, 1991, 994.

71 Bagozzi *et al.*, 1999, pp. 184–185.

72 Plutchik, 1980.

73 Van Dolen *et al.*, 2004; Zeelenberg and Pieters, 1999.

74 Bloemer and De Ruyter, 1999.

75 This assumption was made in a German study about the mood of German tourists during their stay at the Canary Islands. The study was done by Roth and Silberer, 2000.

76 Parasuraman, 2000. Here it is assumed that technology impacts on all the relationships between the customers, the employees and the service organization. A 36-item scale has been developed to measure consumer's technology readiness quite easily, resulting in the four components mentioned in Table 3.4.

77 Tsikriktsis, 2004.

78 Parasuraman, 2000, p. 311.

79 Parasuraman and Colby, 2001, p. 59.

80 Tsikriktsis, 2004.

81 Meuter, Bitner, Ostrom and Brown, 2005; Curran, Meuter and Surprenant, 2003.

82 Kleijnen, de Ruyter and Andreassen, 2005.

83 Nijssen *et al.*, 2003.

84 Pujari, 2004.

85 Selnes and Hansen, 2001, pp. 87–88.

86 Perea y Monsuwè *et al.*, 2004.

87 See MBA thesis by Karin Verschuren, Universiteit Maastricht, 1996.

88 Harris and Reynolds, 2003.

89 Beckett, 2000.

90 Van Raaij and Verhallen, 1994.

91 Johnson and Leger, 1999.

92 See Odekerken-Schröder, 1999, and De Wulf *et al.*, 2001.

93 Ford, 2004, p. 80.

94 This definition is similar to the definition of positioning products provided by Dibb *et al.*, 1994, p. 89.

95 The two kinds of images referred to can also be described as a halo construct and a summary construct respectively. See also the section on Country of Origin.

96 This Service Practice is based on Pascal Beckers' MBA thesis, Universiteit Maastricht, 2003. Definitions of image and identity in the tourism industry are based on Crompton (1979) and Echtner and Ritchie (1991).

97 Han, 1989.

98 This section is based on Ahmed and d'Astous (1994) and Papadopoulos and Heslop (1993).

99 The most often mentioned explanatory variables in COO studies are: involvement or familiarity with the product or service category; knowledge about that particular country; experience and expertise in making buying decisions; individual or group decision making (e.g. households or businesses); presence of other extrinsic cues; education, income and gender. Since the COO cue is a representation of a particular image of a country, we believe several scaling techniques may be applied to measure COO. To us, the semantic differential scale can be used to that end. It will indicate the underlying feelings of consumers with respect to services from a particular country. Given the words used in the semantic differential scale, this technique will reveal also something about the norms and values attributed to services from a particular country. The semantic differential scale usually ranges from 1 to 7.

100 Shimp and Sharma, 1987, p. 287.

101 Shimp and Sharma, 1987, p. 280.

Part 2
Creating Value in
Services

Services marketing management is about caring about people; nothing more, nothing less. These people can be customers, employees or managers and CEOs in service organizations. This second part of the book hinges upon the strategic aspects of creating value to customers and the other stakeholders. The preceding part was on understanding value creation while the next part will be on the actual delivering of that value. Also in this part you will see that the five guiding principles will be discussed in the three chapters:

1 The service organization's market orientation;
2 The service organization's assets and capabilities;
3 The characteristics of services;
4 Internationalization in the service sector; and
5 Value created in the actual service experience.

The three chapters in Part 2 focus upon the following subjects: creating, developing and maintaining relationships; brands; service quality; satisfaction; strategies to go to market; and the internationalization aspect of the service business. This sets the framework for the creation of value at a strategic level.

In turn, that all provides the basis to create the ultimate service experience which will be the topic of part three.

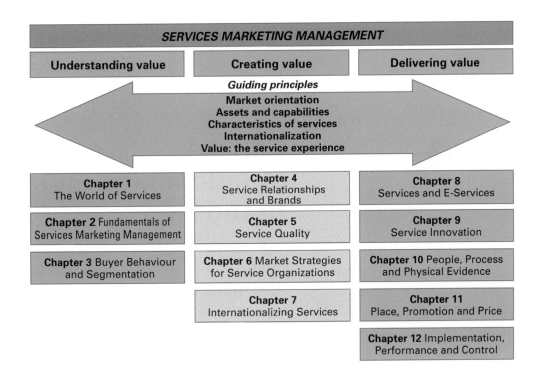

Figure P.2 Contents of Part 2 related to the other parts of the book

Chapter 4

Service Relationships and Brands

You and us. The longer the relationship, the clearer the view.

At UBS we're committed to long-term relationships with our clients. We believe it's the only way to understand your needs, deliver trusted advice and create lasting value. So we work with you to build your business for the future. Whether it's strategic advice and investment ideas, debt or equity, structured products or foreign exchange – by anticipating your changing needs, we can deliver the relevant solution from across the firm. We'll be there, over time, every time. www.ubs.com/investmentbank

You & Us UBS Investment Bank

Learning objectives

At the end of this chapter you will be able to:

1 Distinguish between a transaction and a relational approach to services

2 Understand the meaning of interaction

3 Identify the different forms of interaction that occur in a service setting

4 Describe the key relational constructs of trust, commitment and understanding

5 Appreciate different relational forms

6 Understand the importance of service loyalty and categorize customers according to their loyalty characteristics

7 Describe the main features of a CRM programme

8 Explain the main steps in building a brand

9 Understand some of the problems in managing service brands.

4.1   Introduction

Hanging Out Online[1]

One of the greatest phenomena of recent times is the ever-increasing number of us now using computers. We know that young people are hooked on these products of the modern age, but these days large numbers of the older generation – many of whom are drawing their pensions – also have a computer and know how to use it.

Last month an elderly friend of mine booked a ticket to Valencia with Virgin Express, added the hotel booking and even arranged a hire car from the website with no assistance whatsoever. Only a year ago he was convinced that computers were a scourge of the modern age and that he was too old to bother with them anyway. These days you can't get him away from the machine.

He is not alone. More and more people are finding that being able to surf the Web allows them to shop around for the best prices, and the airline industry has been one of the first to feel the full effects of this quiet revolution. The impact of Virgin Express has been that in 2004 nearly 70% of all our flights were booked via our website and this number looks set to grow even higher this year. This means that the vast majority of customers flying with us today will have shopped around on the Web and decided that Virgin Express offers the best value to the destination of their choice.

In making their decision they will have considered not just the low prices that are on offer, but also the fact that with Virgin Express you get to travel to and from major airports. This is very different from some of their competitors who fly from secondary airports, some many kilometers away from the intended final destination and with only basic passenger and operational facilities. If you never expected to end up in the proverbial middle of nowhere, landing in a secondary airport can be a pretty frustrating experience.

The same goes for having to push your way onto the aircraft in order to get a seat. With Virgin Express you are given assigned seating and a comprehensive choice of in-flight options, including additional legroom. What's more, you get to fly with an airline with a punctuality record second to none in the world. You can change your booking at a reasonable cost right up until a day before departure and, best of all, you get looked after by the most friendly and caring cabin crew in the sky.

What more could you want? Don't bother with the answer, because I know what it is – you want even lower prices! Virgin Express is trying, with first-minute fares as low as €19 before taxes. You can't get much cheaper than that.

So, if you are not yet in the 70% who buy online, maybe it is time for you to think about joining the majority by surfing to www.virgin-express.com every time you want to fly Europe.

When we purchase something as a customer, or on behalf of an employer, we are undertaking an exchange which involves a wide variety of interactions. At the core of the commercial transaction is the exchange of money for goods and services but in addition we are engaged in a series of social and functional interactions often with numerous people; for example, sales staff, delivery personnel and service providers. We are engaged in using and interacting with processes and technology which allow us to gain the benefit of the service; for example, automated teller machines (ATMs), mobile phone services, and order and payment systems. We are interacting with and responding to the environment in which the transaction takes place; for example, retail premises, public spaces and other customers. While we know that this series of interactions all form part of a service product, they comprise something quite beyond a simple transaction. They can be viewed as the total customer experience and many of these interactions are the reason why we choose different suppliers, continue to go back to specific suppliers and build our understanding of the brand. In this way both relationships and branding impact directly upon customers' perceptions of trust and risk and enhance the likelihood of customer loyalty over time.

Perhaps the most significant shift in approach when considering services is moving from a transactional mindset most usually associated with physical goods to a relational mindset more appropriate to services. This is both in terms of the consumption of a specific service event, as well as the consumption of service events over time. This shift in focus is entirely consistent with the nature of the service product which tends to be delivered over time, with the way in which the product is delivered (which is mainly through human interaction) and current business practice which has identified considerable benefits from building customer relationships. According to Bain Consulting, a 5% increase in customer retention can increase profits by 25%–95%. In other words it costs a lot to acquire a customer and even then many of the relationships are unprofitable, so it is better to identify the best and make sure they stay.

Consumers engage in a variety of different commercial exchanges with organizations which range from the transactional (the discrete exchange of money for a service) to the relational (a series of exchanges over time).[2] A more detailed distinction between the two is 'time', i.e. transactional exchanges have a start point and an end point, and they comprise a simple exchange which usually takes place in a short period of time. Relational exchanges have a start point but may not have a clear end point and usually take place over an extended period comprising many different interactions. Some sectors of the economy are dominated by transactional exchanges where due to the characteristics of the market or product there is little opportunity to develop relationships. This is most likely where the offering is commoditized, meaning that there is very little perceived difference between suppliers of the same product. In other sectors of the economy relational exchanges are the norm, such as financial services, utilities (gas, water and electricity) and healthcare services. This is supported by Coviello and Brodie (1998) who argue that this continuum is characterized at one end by industrial commodities where the products are tangible, and each exchange is transactional, it being a one-off sourcing of the product almost entirely focussed upon the cheapest price. At the other end of the continuum are intangible products (our legal services example) with a high degree of relational exchange. This relational form is characterized by multiple exchanges and the development of a variety of different obligations between the two parties involved.

In this chapter we will consider the basis of service relationships, different types of interaction, and the management of customer relationships. Finally we will look at brands and specifically service brands as the platform upon which service relationships are built. This is depicted in Figure 4.1.

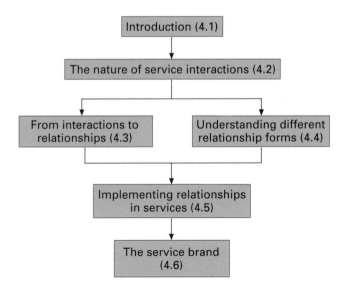

Figure 4.1 Chapter outline: the nature of service interactions

4.2 The Nature of Service Interactions

The prime event in any service delivery is called the 'service encounter' and this simply describes the physical contact event between service provider and customer. Different services have different degrees of contact between customers and providers and this was clearly articulated by Lovelock (1992) who described three levels of contact: high, medium and low.

- High contact services require customers to physically visit the service provider, whose physical presence is an essential part of the service delivery. For example medical services, hairdressing, restaurants, counselling and psychological services.
- Medium contact services are those where the physical presence of the customer is often required but not for the duration of the service. Customers often have limited contact with personnel such as providing transaction details or providing guidance. For example you might take your car to an exhaust replacement garage. You still have to visit the premises to book the car in and may wait while the work is done or go back some time later when the service is complete. This category of medium contact is highly associated with retail services such as pharmacy and dry cleaning but equally with procuring business services such as market research or consulting where an initial meeting is sufficient to scope the service prior to final delivery.
- Low contact services are those where there is very little, if any, physical contact between the service provider and customer. This is a growing category of service and includes a wide range of services which have changed their contact characteristics as well as services which have developed as a result of changing technology. In the former case we can observe traditionally medium contact services migrating via technology to low contact services. For example, Internet shopping and telephone banking are migrations

from medium contact to low contact. The automated booking of cars into servicing centres, automated maintenance requests from photocopiers and computers, and even self-check-in at airports are further examples of the trend from medium to low contact. Technology itself has spawned new service formats within the low contact group for instance via mobile phones, which form a conduit to a range of subscription services, access to self-service vending machines, and transport alerts.

We'll concentrate for the moment upon medium to high contact services as we continue to consider the role of people and processes in building relationships. Within the medium to high contact situation we need to return to the idea of the service encounter and the notion of interaction. This is not only the prime interaction between the customer and the specific service provider, but a whole series of other activities which take place when a customer physically interacts with a service. Gummesson[3] describes four key interactions that comprise the service encounter and these combine to form the service experience. The precise interactions identified by Gummesson are between frontline staff and customer, customer and customer, customer and service environment, and finally customer and delivery system or process.

Customer-to-Service Provider Interaction

This is perhaps the most obvious and direct interaction that takes place, and describes the coming together of two people to co-create the service. What is often not recognized is the importance of the discourse that occurs between them and the consequences of failed versus effective communication. In any interaction with other people we communicate on a variety of different levels. We communicate by talking to one another, we communicate through what we wear, we communicate subliminally through non verbal behaviours, we communicate through our tone of voice and our accent. There is an assumption that interaction is straightforward but the communication of two individuals represents the interplay of many different aspects of behaviour. Where the interaction 'works' it is deemed to be effective, both parties develop a degree of reciprocity and trust as they learn to collaborate to produce the service event. Some have observed that this is a process of recruitment by the service organization of the customer into becoming a 'partial employee', working themselves to deliver their own service. However, where the interaction is flawed in some way the two parties may start to become antagonists and the service outcomes may never be achieved or, if they are, aren't satisfactory in their delivery. While training and sensitivity can reduce the chances of antagonism, high stress situations often mean situations can rapidly deteriorate and service personnel must be able to manage interactions effectively. At the very least they need to be aware of the fact that some customers will not like them and subsequently they will not be able to achieve extraordinary satisfaction from them.

Customer-to-Customer Interaction

Services vary according to the degree to which customers interact with each other. In a medical consultation for example there is very little customer-to-customer interaction since the consultation is private. In some clinics, patients are deliberately kept away from other patients through the use of separate entrances, or specified appointment times. However this type of isolation from other customers – which often occurs in professional services, services to the person or low contact services – is not the norm. In high to medium contact services, customers interact and in some circumstances the delivery of the service requires that they interact. For example, in a nightclub there is no expectation that the proprietor will dance with every customer, nor a comedian perform for each individual in the theatre. The service itself requires other customers to help deliver aspects of the experience. In other circumstances interaction with other customers takes place just because others are in the vicinity. This might include other passengers on a train, other members in a queue for tickets, other patrons in a restaurant. In most cases this interaction is fairly insignificant but occasionally it can destabilize the service. Consider the impact of a fellow airline passenger with smelly feet, bad breath and bad wind upon those seated close by. Or the customers who are noisily complaining about the bad service they have received as you are queuing up to receive it. In most circumstances customer-to-customer interaction is difficult to predict but, where it is problematic, service personnel must have strategies and responses ready.

Customer and Service Environment Interaction

There is long theoretical tradition which supports the impact of the environment upon behaviour.[4] This is also true in service situations and the interaction between a service customer and the service environment can impact directly upon the service experience and the attainment of service outcomes. There has been an increasing emphasis upon the design of service environments across the world and the relationship between the look and feel of the environment and elements of the service. Some services use design to differentiate their service. McDonald's restaurants use red and yellow colours, the big M of the 'golden arch' and the uniforms of its staff to engender certain brand expectations and reassurances about the service. In the same way, a lawyer might use wood-panelled offices, law books, potted plants and muted colours to suggest reliability and conservative professionalism, or bright lights, and white colours in pharmacists to suggest hygiene and medical environments. Service environments can also be designed to prompt certain behaviours; queue dividers for instance prompt customers to form queues for service, or a desk by a restaurant entrance prompts customers to wait for seating. Self-service food dispensaries are designed for linear flow, checkout islands prompt payment. Some retail chains such as Ikea operate on constrained flow designs to encourage customers to browse, others on free flow designs to encourage directed browsing, and still others provide waiting areas, check-in areas and form filling areas all designed to manage interaction between customers and the service.

Service Process Interaction

Behind every service, the glue that holds the people, products, environment and technology together is the service process. It is the process that provides the necessary coordination of effort into the delivery of a service for customers. Aspects of a service process might include booking a service rather than just turning up, the benefit being that demand is managed and customer requirements and service requirements predicted, for example a beauty salon. The process might dictate the need to complete some sort of form before the service to speed up the interaction. This allows the service provider to concentrate upon delivery rather than information collection such as in the case of issuing a passport or visa. Equally the service process will dictate when payment is made, either before the service is delivered, at the end or as different elements are delivered. In some services the process relies upon service personnel having access to critical information, being able to respond to requests or the facility to customize delivery to improve service outcomes.

The interaction between the service system, service personnel and service customers impacts upon both employee and customer satisfaction. In the best service systems, customers will be unaware of its operation, interacting with the process is simple, convenient and intuitive. If systems are difficult to interact with, they can mitigate against great personal service. For example when leaving some countries in Asia and South America you need to pay an exit tax which requires queuing at a separate counter often at a different part of the airport. You will have to pay in cash only and then proceed to check-in. Regardless of how helpful the check-in staff are, you won't be checked in until you pay the exit tax and no one will tell you about this process until you have queued up to check in. If processes are easy and convenient to use they can support outstanding service by becoming so natural and expected that the customer isn't aware of them. At a simple level processes may be represented by a sequence of events, such as entering a PIN number in an ATM and then selecting a transaction, an account and a monetary amount. More complex systems might include purchasing an airline ticket, providing proof of identity, recording baggage, allocating a seat, ordering special meals and connecting flights. These are complex processes but require simplicity, convenience and reliability. Service personnel are also included in this form of interaction because often poorly designed systems can fail them too. How many times have you waited while a service employee tries to find your order in their computer, or can't find your name, or can't work out how much to charge you, or when you should come again? The service system can also be used as a source of competitive advantage. Dell's ordering system, British Airways ticketing, Domino's pizza ordering system, Credit Agricoles' online banking and Tesco's self-checkout are all attempts to leverage competitive advantage through the service process.

Customers interact with service organizations at a variety of different levels as shown in Figure 4.2 but relationships spring from a single source and that is mutual recognition and obligation. At a simple level we may recognize our service provider, or they may recognize us and engage in some form of social exchange. You are more likely to develop a relationship with long-term personal service providers such as doctors, teachers and lawyers who you recognize and who recognize you. You will be less likely to develop a relationship with a call centre operator, an animated ATM avatar or an Internet website.

4.3 From Interactions to Relationships

A relationship approach implemented by an organization is characterized by exchanges which are reciprocal, committed and long-term. These attributes have been generally assumed to provide both organizations and customers with a range of benefits:[5]

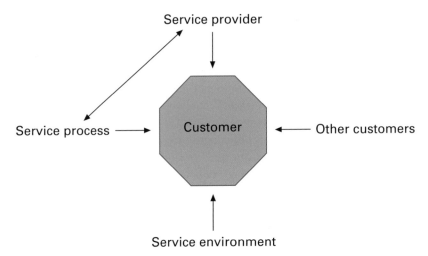

Figure 4.2 Interactions with the customer

■ To the customer accrue social benefits associated with recognition and familiarity, knowledge benefits associated with knowing what to expect and how to optimize their own use of the service, transactional benefits associated with customization, priority, possibly discounts, lower search costs, and more targeted communication; and

■ To the organization accrue benefits associated with loyalty, positive word of mouth, higher switching costs for customers, lower marketing costs, and greater opportunities for up-selling and cross-selling.

The services marketing literature was one of the first to recognize the applicability of the relationship marketing approach. This was due to the relationships developed between individual customers and service personnel.[6] Where these relationships were positive and ongoing, customer satisfaction grew. In turn, these satisfied customers tended to be more loyal to the service organization, recommended the organization to others, tended to be more forgiving of service failures and devoted more of their purchasing in that category to the service firm. In this sense customer satisfaction was a key intervening step between interactions and all the positive benefits associated with long-term relationships.[7]

Customer satisfaction is driven to a large extent by the outcome of interactions between customers and service providers. As a consequence, in order to achieve higher levels of aggregate customer satisfaction, service organizations should focus upon developing long-term and close relationships with their customers. In this way they could acquire and maintain a competitive advantage in the marketplace. This supportive stance for relationship building was also seen in the business marketing literature which was developing a view of business to business transactions as sequential interactions forming stable dyads (or pairings). These business relationships were characterized by trust between parties, mutual goals, a sense of commitment, satisfaction and a willingness to adapt to each other.[8] Dyads or pairings include relationships with customers, suppliers, channel members and distributors to form a network of interrelated stakeholders.[9]

The first thing to note is relationships will exist only if both parties want them to exist. This refers to the concept of relationship proneness developed in the previous chapter.

Examples of organizations developing complex relationship programmes which are then foisted upon unsuspecting customers are fortunately a rarity. So relationship development has to be approached carefully and in recognition that there must be reciprocity, i.e. both parties must develop the relationship together. There are still organizations which use huge resources attracting a customer for the first time, but once they have made a sale, look for the next new customer and ignore the ones they have already. You can find evidence of this when you use some automated phone systems: Option 1 if you are new customer, Option 2 if you are a retailer and want to stock our product, Option 3 if you are interested in becoming a franchisee and Option 4 to find out about our new products. Some banks have come under criticism for not allowing existing customers to transfer to new cheaper accounts and some mobile phone offers only apply if you are transferring your service to them.

The benefit of focussing upon the customers that you have already is to develop their relationship with you. To try and develop trust and satisfaction, attention must be given to the emergence of social bonds and ultimately commitment and loyalty. The benefits of doing this are many and include:

- *The reduction in cost of sale* It costs anywhere between five and 30 times less to service an existing customer than a new customer. With existing customers there is no need to advertise to the whole market nor go through a long period of getting to know what they want from you.
- *The capture of the customer's lifetime value* If you concentrate on customers coming back then you can get access to the aggregated revenue of that customer over their lifetime. If every time you wanted to purchase a mobile phone service you went to the same provider, add up what your business would mean to them over your lifetime of using a mobile phone. There are a number of different methods of calculating lifetime value (LTV) but all relate to the accumulated margins aggregated over successive service or product renewal.
- *Opportunity to cross- and up-sell* Once a customer is known then other services can be presented to them, or existing services customized precisely to their needs. Often customers are prepared to pay extra for customized, augmented or upgraded services such as hotel rooms, credit cards or mobile phone accounts.
- *Improved market information* The more a customer interacts with you the better you get to know them, what they require and how to satisfy them. Using existing customers some organizations have been able to identify whole new markets based upon usage patterns they hadn't observed before.

Principles of Relationships

Although a number of definitions have been presented, we can say that a relationship is the process of developing mutual understanding and the mutual creation of value with customers over the lifetime of an association. This definitional statement points to the development of a number of important principles upon which a relationship (as opposed to an interaction) is based. These are understanding, trust, collaboration, commitment and adaptation, which characterize the transition from an interaction to a relationship. We will consider each one in turn.

Understanding

The first principle is that the customer and the organization must understand each other. In consumer markets this merely restates the basic marketing principle of understanding customer needs, wants and desires. However it also places a responsibility upon the organization in communicating what it offers. This understanding is not restricted to the specific circumstances of consuming the service, but recognizes the importance of context. For instance selling a customer a bank loan may satisfy their need, but allowing them to change their repayment amounts or frequency due to changed family circumstances will show an understanding of consumption context. In industrial markets, understanding the customer's business is critical in the selling of a wide range of customized machinery, business services and goods, many of which have to be tailored exactly for the client.

Trust

Trust is at the core of any relationship and implies many different obligations and expectations for the participants to that relationship. It has been suggested by a number of authors that trust is the key to any long-term relationship and once established unlocks a whole series of other relational benefits such as commitment and loyalty. Trust has been conceptualized in a number of different ways. Trust is 'a willingness to rely upon an exchange partner'.[10] In other words being comfortable that they will support you in what you do. This is particularly important in relationships between businesses, for example in a supply chain where companies have to rely upon each other to deliver their products. Alternatively trust is considered to be an expectation of dependability in delivering upon promises.[11] From a customer point of view trust can be placed in a service provider based upon experience. For instance you have grown to trust a specific provider or service organization to deliver services to you. Equally you can develop trust without experience; you might trust an airline even though you haven't flown with them, or a particular manufacturer, a service company like a bank or a particular service brand. In relationship terms, good relationships exhibit high levels of trust between the partners and there is evidence that high trust relationships are associated with open communication, a willingness to take risks and information sharing.

Collaboration

The second principle is that both the customer and the organization must collaborate with each other in order to gain mutually beneficial outcomes from exchange. If we take any human relationship, its success depends upon the parties working together. At a simple level collaboration can be seen in the interaction between the customer and service provider which in turn leads to the development of friendships which supercede commercial relations. These are often referred to as social bonds and can be extremely strong ties between a business and its customers. Unfortunately they tend to be non transferable in the sense that they are between specific individuals. This may mean that they are lost when an employee leaves. In consumer markets, collaborative relationships usually refer to circumstances which are characterized by customer loyalty, where customers are satisfied and therefore return. But collaboration can also emerge in online environments where the customer is involved with the product specification; such as the case in ordering a Dell computer, product design such as some fashion clothing sites, or online banking advice such as that provided by Citibank. In industrial markets collaboration is evident at all stages of consumption from specification through to implementation or order receipt. Collaboration can occur in the specification of manufacturing plant, outsourced services such as payroll or IT, in contract terms such as regular deliveries of stationary, or in creative activities such as advertising campaigns or packaging design.

Commitment

The terms 'commitment' and 'trust' are often used together and the research would appear to make very fine distinctions between the two. Only the presence of both will lead to efficiency, productivity and effectiveness in relationships.[12] Commitment is defined simply as the enduring desire of a customer to maintain and develop a supplier relationship. In other words the relationship is so important that the parties will make extra effort to protect and nurture it. In these circumstances high commitment is associated with a number of effects: increased willingness to forgive small failings, willingness to sacrifice short-term benefit in favour of long-term gain, and a willingness to invest in the relationship through information sharing. As you can see, commitment also has a tendency to overlap with definitions of loyalty.[13] In circumstances where customers and service providers display commitment to each other the relationships are likely to be very strong and to persist for an extended period of time. In the previous chapter we saw that commitment is critical in determining true loyalty.

Adaptation

Possibly the most important aspect of relationship marketing and one that is often overlooked is the importance of change and the ability to adapt to it. Relationships change, and often provider organizations are slow to adapt to customer change and as a consequence relationships break down. In order to avoid this, customers and organizations must constantly be sensitive to changing circumstances. This form of market sensing is critical to market oriented service providers. Consumers may face changed household circumstances, increases or decreases in income, or be more or less susceptible to competitors. An organization which professes a relationship marketing approach will have systems in place to detect these subtle changes and be able to respond to them. Similarly in industrial markets customers will change their requirements, go through contract reviews, enter new supply arrangements or change their operations. This in turn will alter their consumption patterns and will require a reconfiguration of the product(s) supplied.

Service principles when applied to a series of transactions may completely change the way a company looks at its market which in turn may lead to radical changes in the way they operate and the services they supply. We can summarize the potential transition effects of changing from a transaction to a relationship approach as:

1 Generating long-term value for customers and in so doing reap winwin outcomes for both relationship partners.
2 Recognizing the role of customers in helping the organization to define and develop services and products.
3 Providing a focus upon the long-term alignment of business systems, products, services, people and technology directly to customers.
4 Recognizing the importance of a customer's lifetime value, i.e. the aggregation of their business with the company rather than any single transaction.
5 Building relationships with other stakeholder organizations to generate a network of providers through the value chain.

As you can appreciate, relationships have a number of distinct benefits and are generally considered to be superior to transaction-based exchange. However it is difficult sometimes to fully appreciate the large range of relationship forms which operate and it is dangerous to treat all relationships the same. In the next section we will consider some of the characterizing differences in commercial relationship forms.

4.4 Understanding Different Relationship Forms

In the preceding section we considered the importance of interaction and we looked at the various forms of interaction which occur during a service encounter. We then looked at some characteristics of that interaction which will engender the development of a relationship. We often talk about relationships between people and places, people and inanimate objects, and people and ideas. There are many different forms of relationship and the best way to describe them is to contrast relationships on different dimensions. The dimensions which we have chosen are individual versus collective, and obligated versus non obligated.

Individual Versus Collective

When we describe relationships in the commercial domain they are almost always between people. We can think of individual-to-individual relationships such as that between a client and their lawyer, or between a patient and their doctor, or between a customer and their hair stylist. These are the simplest and most easily comprehended relationships. However the idea of commercial relationships can be expanded to include 'collective' relationships. This collective includes the organization, firm, company or retail outlet which often contain our individualized relationships. In some circumstances the identity of the person we deal with is more important than the collective i.e. the company. These circumstances often occur in professional services where individual professionals often take clients with them when they move firms because their personal relationship is stronger than the collective relationship. In other circumstances the collective relationship is more important than the individual. Take for example an airline where it is the service organization you have the relationship with rather than any particular person/service provider. This applies to many retail services where you start to build a relationship independent of the specific service provider such as restaurants, supermarkets, bars and clubs as well as some healthcare clinics.

Obligated Versus Non Obligated

Relationships come in many different forms. Sometimes we have the power to enter them, change them and end them, while at other times we have no choice at all. In the commercial domain some relationships are constructed formally where the parties sign an agreement to undertake certain tasks or responsibilities. Here the parties have no choice as to the relationship once the agreement is signed. An example would be an industrial contract to supply outsourced IT services. The service provider once signed up will be in a relationship with the contracting firm until the contract ceases. Obligated relationships tend to be very functional although the parties can develop very close personal relationships over time. They also characterize a large number of industrial networks such as supply chains and distribution channels. In consumer markets obligated relationships are few in reality although some household utilities are still obligated, such as those which serve a single geographical area, or where the market is still highly regulated or supply is from a monopoly.

By contrast we can think of non obligated relationships which we enter and leave according to how we feel. This type of relationship occurs with the regularity of contact, such as repeated transactions over time and is distinguished from obligated relationships by the freedom the customer has to terminate the relationship at any time. You might think of a relationship with a specific retail store, restaurant, mobile phone company or airline. Non obligated relationships are not exclusive, i.e. you can have relationships with a number of service providers. It is worth noting that many service organizations have non obligated relationships with their customers but would like to engender a perception of permanence in the hope that customers view them as obligated. Take for example a bank or a mobile phone company. In the case of the bank you are free to leave when you wish although it might be incredibly difficult to close accounts, cancel direct debits, pay off and transfer credit cards and ATM cards. In this sense some service relationships which are non obligated take on the characteristics of obligated services. Because of these switching costs, mobile phone contracts used to be quite punitive if you decided to cancel or change your contract but are becoming much more flexible. These relationships are obligated, that is they are based upon a contract but are taking on the characteristics of non obligated.

4.5 Implementing Relationships in Services

As we have seen above, relationships are complex and comprise activities at multiple levels, from individual service personnel and sale staff, to organization-wide initiatives such as strategic alliances. Where there has been some debate though is whether relationships which comprise those characteristics we have described above can be 'managed' in the sense that the service organization can implement processes to attract, maintain and enhance customer relationships. Some would argue that they cannot, others that they can, but the debate has been focussed upon the success of different marketing solutions all focussed upon enhancing the measurable aspect of a relationship: loyalty. Here we will provide some additional thoughts on loyalty from the relational perspective next to what you have already seen in Chapter 3.

Customer loyalty has been treated in two different ways by service researchers. The first is to treat loyalty as purely behavioural such as repeat purchase behaviour.[14] The problem with this approach is that it will also include a group of customers who are called 'spuriously loyal'. These are customers who display repeat purchase behaviour but only because they have no choice. If there were a choice they would leave. This lack of choice or inertia is either because there is no competition or they cannot access an alternate provider. Organizations which are interested purely in repeat behaviour are often referred to as focussing upon 'retention'.

The second approach is to treat loyalty as a combination of both a behavioural component (i.e. repeat purchase behaviour) with a positive attitudinal component (i.e. liking or preference), but this too has its problems. First, a customer may be a repeat purchaser but is prevented from visiting for some reason. They are still attitudinally loyal but without repeat purchasing they are not visible, nor are they financially valuable to the organization. Second, the attitudinal component is often difficult to isolate. The positive attitude may be towards a person, the service brand, a specific retail outlet or a specific product. In sum it is difficult to identify with any degree of certainty a 'loyal customer' as opposed to a 'retained customer'. However, we can identify some attributes of loyal customers which may help identify the truly loyal:

- They engage in positive word of mouth (i.e. make recommendations, and provide reports of good experience).
- They have a resistance to switch suppliers (i.e. given the opportunity, they exercise the choice to stay).
- They identify with the service or a particular service provider (i.e. feeling and espousing a sense of belonging such as using the prefix 'my', and defending the service against criticism).
- They show great commitment to the service provider and are manifest satisfied (see Chapter 3).
- They have a relative preference for the service over competitors (i.e. faced with all the market offers they believe that your service offer is superior).

A number of authors have presented variations upon how to develop loyal customers.[15] We present here a variant on these approaches based upon a loyalty pyramid. The benefit of this approach is that the pyramid represents the reductionist nature of loyalty. What we mean by this is that not everyone is going to become a loyal customer so, as loyalty gets stronger and stronger, the proportion of customers in each loyalty category declines. At the bottom of the pyramid are prospects which include the whole market for the product. Some of those prospects may become customers, i.e. transact with you. Once they are customers, over time they may develop into clients which is a recurrent or repeat customer. The next level of loyalty in the pyramid is to become a supporter and then finally an advocate, ambassador, evangelist or partner (see Figure 4.3).

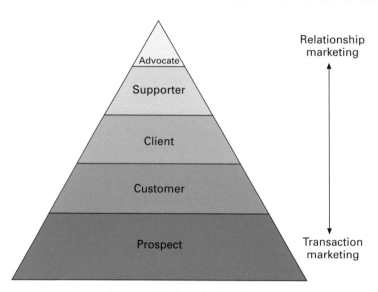

Figure 4.3 Loyalty levels

The important point to note is that up until the customer stage there is nothing new. The company can use traditional marketing techniques to attract service customers. The departure from transaction-based marketing is managing and developing the relationship from the customer level upwards. This requires an approach which is aimed at developing a relationship with the customer but within the context of increasing loyalty. This approach has become known as customer relationship management (CRM).

Customer Relationship Management

Some have argued that this is a contradiction in terms, because any relationship which is managed can't be a relationship between equals, which is a necessary requirement for any relationship to exist. However, accepting that the terminology of CRM is ambiguous it has become recognized as a powerful corporate methodology. CRM encompasses all activities undertaken by an organization to identify, select, develop and retain customers.

CRM has developed into a multi billion dollar industry simply due to the application of database and interactive technology to the process. In the past, CRM was principally applied to business markets where the smaller number of customers (often numbering less than 20) allowed marketers to manage relationships with a degree of intimacy and continuity within a relatively stable business customer group. The benefits of this approach were so evident that many organizations wanted to transfer the methodology to consumer markets. Since consumer markets meant customer numbers in the millions, this presented a different challenge and was really only possible by utilizing databases and technology to track, trace and store customer data.

In terms of getting closer to customers, to start to build relationships, the first thing that is required is understanding, and that requires information. The current solution to this is to generate some form of centralized customer database. The database or data warehouse contains records of each customer's interactions with the organization. In general terms all the interactions between a customer and the organization are drawn to a central point. These interactions are organized by customer rather than product or location. Customers are sometimes difficult to define; they might include individual consumers, agents, dealers, channel partners, etc.

There are structural problems in determining who is able to update the information, how often records are maintained and whether additional sources of information are added to the organization's data. For instance a customer record might also contain details of credit ratings, location, lifestyle or ownership data which have been supplied from external sources and add 'colour' to the organization's interaction record. The data warehouse in turn must be accessible by all service personnel who interact with customers so that they can use the data to plan and predict more accurately customer requirements.

Once the data warehouse has been constructed the organization can then start to analyse the data to identify particular insights relevant to the organization's operations. This might be an analysis based upon customer profitability where high profit customers are worth more investment in terms of relationship building than low profit customers. Or alternatively that customers with a particular profile but currently low profitability might show good potential for increasing spend. The analysis might be focussed upon product forms with services offering little benefit to the organization while unpopular services contribute a large return. Such analysis might suggest a repositioning or the reconfiguring of a service. For instance an airline focussing upon the profitability of individual flight segments may identify a low profit route and consider eliminating the flight segment. Analysis of the data warehouse might suggest that this particular route is used by high value customers as a connection between airport hubs and therefore the case to remove the flight might subsequently destroy value for the whole network.

Additional analysis might focus upon using customer data to focus upon the future rather than the past, in other words to forecast behaviour. It might be important for a service to try and predict on the basis of past evidence what characteristics are associated with a customer about to defect to a competitor or more likely to upgrade to a higher value service, or respond to a cross-selling opportunity. Credit card companies often use sophisticated forecasting to assess credit risk or likely defection based upon credit balances, promptness of payment or number of transactions per card. This type of forecasting can also provide security protection by alerting the organization to unusual spending patterns that might indicate a card or card number may have been stolen. An even more advanced approach may allow data to be used across different services and different suppliers if they have integrated data management. For instance a customer arriving at a hotel might be upgraded because the airline they flew on had been delayed. Alternatively, a hire car company might allow an extended rental because the hirer had contacted an airline to delay their departure date.

SERVICE PRACTICE 4.2

Virgin Active is a group of health clubs which recently acquired 85 new clubs in South Africa. After a new CRM system was implemented the organization was able to share customer information worldwide. If someone joins one of the health clubs in South Africa, they are able to walk into a Virgin Active club anywhere in the world and their membership history will be known and they can also access their exercise regime. Membership renewal can also be managed through the club which the customer uses rather than the club which was originally joined. In this way the organization can offer a truly global and seamless service.

Clearly different organizations have different objectives and will likely deploy CRM differently. What we do know is that CRM creates many challenges to an organization as it tries to develop ongoing relationships with target customers. We can identify four challenges which we will consider in more detail: how to identify customers, how to distinguish different customer types, how to develop customer relationships and how to retain customers.

Identify

The first task of a CRM system is to be able to identify customers given the goal of the CRM policy. This applies to existing customers as well as new customers or those specifically targeted to recruit. This might seem quite a simple task and in some circumstances it is. This is especially true where the customer has to identify themselves. This is the case when visiting a doctor, opening a bank account, or buying an airline ticket. But what about a theatre? A restaurant? Or a post office? In these circumstances customers don't need to identify themselves. Here, the service provider must design some method of identifying customers. Examples might be introducing membership or discount cards which have to be applied for and provide a constant connection to the individual. Other techniques include recruiting customers to a mailing list via a promotional campaign, starting a phone booking system where customers have to identify themselves, or staging a competition which requires an entry form to be completed and may also use purchase or usage receipts as qualifying information. More sophisticated techniques include the capturing of credit card details, the registering of phone numbers through caller ID systems, the capturing of cookies on the Internet, or broad profiling through postcode. Some call centre technology can piece together an identity from randomly collected information such as date of birth, house number and postcode. Any one of these methods can be used to provide a customer's identity. These identities are then compiled into a customer database.

Select

The second task once a customer database has been populated is to add details of the customer's buying behaviour as well as attitudinal and other information if available. This additional information may also be used as the basis for selection. There are a number of techniques for profiling customers but the three main approaches are customer profitability; CLV or customer lifetime value; and recency, frequency and monetary value (RFM) analysis.

1 *Customer profitability* is the difference between the revenues earned and the costs associated with the customer relationship during a specified period.[16] This approach is based upon the observation that some customers cost more to service than others. If the revenue received per customer is the same then the overall customer contribution to

SERVICE PRACTICE 4.3

The example below is from a hotel which has allocated its revenues across a year to different types of customer. By allocating the costs associated with each customer type a profit yield can be calculated as a percentage of the revenue figure. From this you can see that the most profitable customer group is Conferences and the least profitable group are Bands. This type of information would allow the hotel to try and build relationships with those who are booking conferences and either discourage or increase the price for bookings by bands.

Customer type	Annual revenues	Assigned costs	Profit %
Travel Agent	564 000	356 000	36.8
Business direct	78 000	82 000	(5.1)
Commercial	217 000	193 000	11.1
Individual	67 000	56 000	16.4
Bands	22 000	32 000	(45.5)
Weekend break	113 000	93 000	17.7
Own package	12 000	8 500	29.2
Group	76 000	82 000	(7.9)
Conference	55 000	32 000	41.8
Concession	23 000	29 000	(26.1)
Bar	370 000	430 000	(16.2)
Food	393 000	404 000	(2.8)

profit is different. Differences in cost might be generated by some customers phoning in more often, demanding customization which means they take longer to service, or requiring follow up visits to resolve problems. Clearly, depending upon what the organization decides to cost and how those costs are calculated, the profitability will be different. Nevertheless it does provide indicative data regarding different customer contributions to profit.

Customer profitability analysis also provides the possibility of calculating customer gross margin, which is the difference between revenue received and cost of service provided. Some organizations are able to calculate these figures for each individual which allow them to select out those customers for special attention and those whose gross margin is negative and should receive less relational benefits. Many of these calculations depend on the service organization's accounting system. Is it possible to allocate all costs to the different market segments, or just part of the costs? Obviously, it is most attractive to have some kind of activity-based costing or direct costing to allocate these costs properly.

2   *Customer lifetime value* is a method of calculating the present value of the future cash flows attributed to the customer relationship.[17] Various implementations of this approach include: discounted cash flow, and net present value of the cash flow. In simple terms this is a calculation based upon the expected flows of revenue from a finite relationship. For example if a car manufacturer were able to ensure that a single customer was to buy

SERVICE PRACTICE 4.4

In the example below a mobile phone provider has four different plans in column 1. The number of customers on each plan is given in column 2. The estimated lifetime of a mobile phone customer in this analysis we assume is five years. According to the company the different plans have a different attrition rate. Customers on plan A have a much higher likelihood of renewing their plan each year (0.65) while the customers in plan D are quite unlikely to stay for five years. The company has calculated that over the five-year lifetime the profits on each plan are given in column 5. Using a simple CLV calculation Col 2 × Col 5 × Col 4 = CLV, the company can see that investing in retaining customers on plan B is much more profitable than investing to retain customers on plan D.

Service type (Col 1)	Number of customers (Col 2)	Estimated lifetime (L) (Col 3)	Estimated probability of (L) (Col 4)	Profit over lifetime (Col 5)	CLV
Plan A	1345	5 yrs	0.65	3350	2.9 m
Plan B	3678	5 yrs	0.52	2660	5.1 m
Plan C	2786	5 yrs	0.23	6442	4.1 m
Plan D	2915	5 yrs	0.11	8034	2.5 m

every one of the cars they acquire in a lifetime from them, then the CLV would be the present value of the aggregated revenue for the life of the customer. This approach is not normally applied over a real lifetime, but usually over a shorter period, for instance a year, or five years. This technique allows the organization to discriminate between a customer who is likely to buy the service twice in five years, relative to a customer who is likely to buy 20 times in five years. Clearly if we were able to keep the latter customer our revenue or value will be higher. As a consequence the cost of relationship enhancement with the latter customer must be considered relative to their CLV.

3 *Recency, frequency and monetary value* This approach as the name would suggest is a method of categorizing customers based upon three key behavioural variables. These are: recency, frequency and monetary value. Recency is the time that has elapsed since the customer made their last purchase. The more recent the purchase the higher the score on this variable. The second is frequency, the total number of purchases made by that customer in a predefined period of time. The more frequent the purchase behaviour relative to other customers then the higher the score on this variable. Finally monetary value, simply that customers who spend more per transaction gets a higher score. The figure is moderated by frequency, where the average purchase amount is equal to total spend in year divided by number of transaction in year. This analytic is usually implemented by literally scoring individual customers in a customer database and for some organizations this is the driver of relationship building investments. This analytic has gained support in a variety of different settings, from catalogue and direct mail to Internet and e-tailing. The customers who score highest on all three variables are, and are likely to remain, the most valuable customers. Those with low scores on all three

		Actual loyalty in buying behaviour (= behavioural RFM dimensions)	
		High (very valuable)	Low (= less valuable)
Perceptions/ attitude of relationship (= attitudinal dimension)	High (= strong)	Friends	Sympathetics
	Low (= weak)	Functionalists	Acquaintances

Figure 4.4　The relation perception and loyalty matrix

variables are the least valuable customers. The high value group have been associated with higher response rates to direct mail, higher sales per year, highest profitability per customer and highest number of visits to online purchase sites.

However, these RFM-proxies for actual buying behaviour may not be sufficient to define the strength of the relationship between a supplier and a customer properly (see Figure 4.4).[18] Thinking in terms of the strength of a relationship is important because the stronger the relationship, the more difficult it will be to break it (e.g. the less likely it is that customers will switch). Researching the strength of a relationship also requires looking at the way in which customers perceive and evaluate the relationship: their attitude towards the relationship with the supplier based on, for example, their committment to the supplier. So, the (actual buying) behavioural dimension reflects the economic value of the relationship to the supplier, while the (attitudinal) perceptual dimension reflects the customer's value for the relationship. To keep it simple, the values of both dimensions may vary between high and low. This can be depicted in the relation perception and loyalty matrix (RLM) which is shown in Figure 4.4.[19]

Service organizations can now use their databases with actual data about consumer buying behaviour and perceptual data on how customers perceive and evaluate the relationship, to segment their market into four segments, as shown in Figure 4.4.[20] These RFM data on actual buying behaviour may also be stated in terms of the customer(s) profitability to the service firm, e.g. as a return on investment (ROI). Then, customers with a high ROI are considered to be very valuable to the firm.

The customers in the four parts of the matrix have been labelled as friends, sympathetics, functionalists and acquaintances. Friends are customers who are very loyal to the organization and perceive themselves as having a strong relationship (commitment) with the organization. As these customers make above average contributions to the ROI and/or profit of the company, from the company's economic or financial point of view, these customers are very valuable. Sympathetics perceive themselves to have a strong relationship with their supplier. However, their sympathy is scarcely expressed in their behaviour. So, in spite of the fact that they have good feelings towards the organization, they hardly contribute to the ROI and/or profit of the

SERVICE PRACTICE 4.5

A small stockbroking firm had recently moved its account information onto a database. The individual brokers were complaining that they were spending so much of their time talking to and advising clients that they were getting behind in their trading and market report work. To make things worse, many of the customers they were spending time with didn't seem to make many share trades, and those who were eager to trade couldn't get through to speak to their broker. The marketing manager had decided that the firm needed some assessment of their customers 'worth' in order to focus the relationship development task on high potential value customers.

Each individual customer record was assessed according to a simple RFM scoring system. The scores allocated were 1 for low to 10 for high, over trades in the previous 18 months. An extract is given below:

Name	Portfolio value	Last trade recency	Last 18 months frequency	18 months avg. value of trade
Smith, A.	1 678 900	1 week (9)	53 trades (10)	$14 500 (9)
Patel, B.	167 000	6 months (2)	4 trades (1)	$2 400 (3)

The analysis produced a small cohort of about 40 customers who scored above 9 on each of the three measures (see Smith above). The marketing manager also used the scoring to categorize the database into four other groups. Group 1, the high value cohort with 9 or more on each metric, were given their own priority telephone number to reach the brokers, were able to execute trades within eight hours and were able to run deficit accounts for 24 hours. They were also given a daily value update and alerts on moving stocks. Group 2 was given a weekly portfolio update, were contacted once per week by the broker to alert them to significant changes to share values and to alert them to potential share purchases. Group 3 were contacted weekly by e-mail only, Group 4 were contacted every three months with a newsletter and portfolio statement. Group 5 were contacted to assess their current status and discuss whether the stock broking firm was the right one for them.

company. Functionalists perceive a weak relationship with their supplier but are of great economic or financial importance to the organization. These customers show a weak commitment towards the organization. Nevertheless, they mght still buy repeatedly, e.g. because of bonds as a result of a contract (a matter of calculative commitment). Acquaintances are customers neither perceiving a strong relationship, nor being of any economic or financial importance to the organization at a particular moment. However, these customers can be exploring a new relationship with this firm or consider ending the existing relationship.

Analysing the actual distribution of customers over those four segments will reveal whether this is also the preferred distribution, whether all kinds of promotional activities have to be performed to let customers move from one segment to another in order to create a larger group of true loyal customers. The various strategies mentioned in Chapters 6 and 7 as well as the elements of the marketing mix can be used to that end.

When data about individual customers are present, a service provider can check whether customers move from one segment to another. Banks and insurance companies can investigate these dynamics quite easily by looking at their client's records. These shifts will affect long-term customer relationship profitability,[21] for customers do not provide the same profitability at every moment during their relationship with the service provider. In using this profitability perspective, the prime interest lies in understanding the cash flow effects on handling customer relationships in the long run; what are the revenues from and costs of serving a specific customer?[22] The key for effective relationship marketing management is an understanding of the customer's value creation process, which occurs at different levels of interaction during the relationship. The service encounter comes to the fore at various moments during this period. Therefore, a distinction can be made between the relationship, the episode and the actual action. A relationship consists of a number of episodes. Episodes are complete service events as seen from the customer's point of view, like an overnight stay at a hotel or a rafting holiday of two weeks. Actions are service elements or activities within an episode, like checking out or making a reservation. The quality of each action adds up to the total service quality of an entire episode, which in turn affects the quality of the relationship. This way of reasoning indicates that the relation between service quality and profitability is a complex one.[23]

Develop

The third task of CRM is to develop customers, quite simply to move them up the pyramid either one or two steps. Analysing the distribution of customers within the pyramid will reveal whether this is the preferred distribution, or whether promotional activities need to be used to get customers to promote themselves. Since customers are identified it might be possible to invite them back more frequently, or to offer them specific incentives in the form of discounts or bundled offers. These are offers where the primary service is offered with supporting services such as a cinema ticket with free popcorn or car parking. Clearly developing a relationship is a complex strategic process and dependent upon the industry and more importantly the type of relationship the organization wants with its customers. Evidence would suggest that if the right tool is chosen a small promotional offer can yield significant lifts in frequency and monetary value.

There are four broad types of relationship development; push, pull, purchase and plug. All CRM activity is a variant of one of these approaches.

■ *Push* is primarily aimed at pushing a customer toward a particular outlet or service provider. The key to push is location and visibility and this approach is often used by service organizations whose service is similar in many respects to competitors. Examples might be promotional invitations to local outlets or offices, specialized service offerings to specific locations based upon customer profile, or exclusive provision for members.
■ *Pull* is clearly aimed at drawing customers to the service by the tailoring of the service to their requirements, either through delivery, environment or service personnel. Increasingly alliances are being used to pull customers through by using such activities as

cross-promotional offers, tie-ins or coupon redemption in consumer markets. In business markets trading terms, new product or simply notification of availability can provide pull.

■ *Purchase* strategies are not used specifically for any particular product class but relate to financial or reward groups such as Visa, American Express, Air Miles, Fly Buys, or programmes like Nectar in the UK. The key is to provide customers with a range of purchase opportunities that closely fit the profile of the customer. Hence each customer will be offered a different portfolio of products and services.

■ *Plug* approaches as the name suggests are directed at products which are in over supply. In a services setting one of the characteristics of services is that they are perishable; if they are not used they cannot be stored for later consumption. Hence plug loyalty is for directing customers to utilize services at low demand times, or when service provision is plentiful. Bars and restaurants offer discounts early in the evening, car repair shops might offer fixed price servicing, or special evening rates, weekend prices at hotels, or flights on Christmas Eve.

Retain

The fourth element in CRM activity is retention. Strong relationships are often exit barriers for customers and entry barriers for competitors. Therefore, it is very important to know why customers want to have a relationship with a service provider and why they want to maintain, strengthen or weaken the existing relationship. The key here is to be able to read the customer and respond accordingly in order to retain them. If customers wish to be left alone then pestering them with questions and offers will only make them feel manipulated, question the motivation of the organization and reject the notion of a relationship. At the core of retention is building a wall around your customer such that competitors can't see them (or more precisely they are not worth focussing upon because they will remain loyal) and your customers can't see your competitors (or more precisely they aren't in the market for an alternative supplier). We can achieve this wall in number of ways but two approaches are common; building switching barriers and by rewarding transactions.

Switching barriers are often used in highly competitive markets such as telecommunications, finance and hospitality. They come in many forms but in essence they attempt to reduce the benefit of moving by increasing the cost of moving. For example in Australia the telecommunications providers bundle their services together, and customers receive a discount for having mobile, landline, Internet and cable from a single supplier. Suppose now a new mobile phone entrant offers a great deal on a new mobile. To switch would mean losing the combined discount so even though you would have cheaper mobile, you would lose the discount on the other services thereby making them more expensive. In many European countries people are hesitating to subscribe to such a bounded offer because of the 'risky dependence' on one supplier for all these services. The deal from the new entrant would have to be really good to compensate for losing the discount. Banks tend to apply charges to move loans to new suppliers or add additional interest when changing products. In business markets switching costs may be in the form of having to retrain a new supplier, losing an integrated system or losing partnered sourcing.

Rewarding transactions refers to the many different forms of loyalty programmes which operate around the world. In consumer markets the most well known are those which are

SERVICE PRACTICE 4.6

O2 Churn Drive[24]

O2, a mobile telephone company, will introduce a range of initiatives to increase loyalty among its 14.2m customers in the UK. These include a pledge to give pre-pay customers 10% of their top-up payments back every three months. The network will also offer 50% extra text messages and calls for life to post-pay customers who have been with the network for more than one year. The strategy focusses exclusively on existing customers to stop them switching to another network. O2 was also badly affected by customers buying a pre-pay O2 phone, using up the credit and then buying a competitors SIM card.

run by airlines in collaboration with credit card companies or by retail chains. Here the customer accumulates points or other notional credit through transactions which can then be redeemed either for additional services, discounts or products. The theory behind loyalty programmes is very appealing but there are also some dangers especially because the cost of the programme is often funded by a margin reduction, or excessive redemption; for example demand for airline seats can cause service delivery problems.[25]

The idea of building relationships with customers is not new; indeed it has been a feature of Nordic service research since the early 1960s. Some authors[26] suggest that relationship marketing is just a restatement of the basic marketing principles of keeping customers coming back and represents a renaming not a new approach. Whatever its genesis, the focus upon customer relationship building has kept service organizations thinking about their service in the long term and thinking about developing valuable and consistent delivery. But despite all the investment and effort, one feature of current consumer economies is the difficulty in building a distinctive voice. One technique to develop distinctiveness is concentrate upon building a brand, a summary of what the company sells, what the company does and what the company is. In total, a brand can help in the process of building trust, consistency and expectations which are at the heart of relationships.

4.6 The Service Brand

At the same time as relationship marketing emerged in the marketing literature, so too did the recognition of the importance of brands. As these two threads have developed they have become closer to one another and now the brand is often seen as a major relationship builder between a service organization and its customers. Brands are not just what a company sells or delivers, they are what a company does in every circumstance, and more importantly what a company represents to its employees and its markets. From the organization's perspective brands are increasingly seen as valuable market assets and an essential source of differentiation in markets which are becoming saturated with similar service offerings. For the consumer, brands have a number of important functions such as identifying the provider of a service,[27] reducing search costs,[28] reducing perceived risk, and signalling quality.[29]

Characteristics of Brands

According to Van Riel *et al.* the research into service brands has been slow to develop because service organizations have not been recognized as distinctive in terms of brand management.[30] In other words the activity of developing and maintaining a brand in respect of a physical good is not perceived to be different in any important respect from the developing and maintaining of a service brand. Some research is now beginning to emerge[31] but the field is still dominated by physical goods. As a consequence it is worth reviewing the general approaches to branding which can be generalized across product types before we look in more detail at service branding.

De Chernatony and McDonald provide an eight-category typology of brands which serves as a useful introduction to some of the issues associated with brands and provides an explanation of why branding is so often a confusing concept to grasp.[32] The taxonomy comprises eight functions or purposes of brands. These are as follows.

Brands as a Sign of Ownership

There has been considerable emphasis on who owns a brand. Originally it was the manufacturer who owned the brand; for example washing powders, chocolate bars and cars. Increasingly these brands are now subservient to distributor brands such as retailers, who have developed their own brands that are arguably more powerful than the manufacturers'. In simple terms the ownership of a brand determines who undertakes the marketing activity associated with it. In services, there is often little distinction between manufacturer and distributor since the service is provided at the point of consumption. The brand indicates some sense of responsibility by the owner. Telstra owns the telephone network in Australia. The network capacity is also leased out to other providers. If you sign up with Optus, you are still using the Telstra network but Optus is responsible for the service you receive.

Brands as a Differentiating Device

By applying a name or logo or distinctive package to a product, manufacturers were able to distinguish or differentiate their product from similar products. In today's market, with more experienced customers and more sophisticated marketing just about every product or service is identified by the owner, or provider. As a consequence differentiation can be maintained only by generating additional points of difference; that is, things that identify it over and above the name, logo or livery. These are often quite conceptual, such as 'youthful', or 'reliable', 'high quality' or 'convenient'. For instance, Virgin as a service brand has become differentiated on the basis of its 'youthfulness and irreverence', Qantas on the basis of its safety record, Ryanair on the basis of value for money. Developing distinctive features of a service brand are operationalized through consistent communications, through service personnel, through service processes and where the service is delivered.

Brands as Functional Devices

This refers to the opportunity to associate the brand with certain functional attributes or capabilities. For instance the FedEx brand is associated with speedy and accurate delivery; 7Eleven is associated with 24-hour convenience, American Express with its global coverage and insurance protection, and Domino Pizza with prompt delivery 'delivered in 20 minutes or it's free'. Functional attributes are as yet an undeveloped opportunity for service brands since they are a method of tangibilizing the intangible service. They can provide real and measurable experiences for customers.

Brands as Symbolic Devices

In some markets customers realize significant benefits from the 'badge' value of a brand; that is, the ability to show others the brand they have bought or are using such as a handbag, a car or piece of clothing. For services this is often difficult since the service leaves little residual impression. You might have paid a fortune for a haircut from a Paris salon but no one who sees your hair will be able to appreciate who cut it. Credit card companies have pushed this further by trying to associate their credit card service with particular types of people, global sports personalities, adventurers and business executives. Revealing the card, a symbol of the service provider is as close to 'badge value' that many services can come.

Brands as Risk Reducer

Customers are assumed to view purchasing as a trade-off between risk and benefit. When a customer is faced with a purchase choice, they will gravitate toward the solution with the lowest risk and the highest gain. In these circumstances the brand becomes a risk reducing device. Faced with a wide and complex choice set, customers can make it simpler by focussing upon the brands they like or trust as opposed to comparing the details of the different offers. In services, especially those associated with the person, or money, the risks might be quite high and a recognized brand will often relieve a great deal of tension for the customer by simplifying the choice. By knowing what risks are perceived by customers (and we have mentioned eight different risks in Chapter 3), the service organization can tailor communications to provide explicit risk reduction values.

Brands as a Shorthand Device

Customers have limited memory capability and considering the large volume of information they have to process every day they tend to bundle information into 'chunks'. These chunks are tagged so that they can be retrieved quickly in appropriate circumstances. A brand is a useful information tag. In this way customers can collect relevant bits of information associated with a service and recall them all by reference to the brand. This may be at the point of purchase, or on viewing an advertisement, or experiencing a service.

Brands as a Legal Device

Because brands are so valuable to the organization, the brand name or logo can be used to protect the product or service from copying. In the case of physical goods this is relatively straightforward with a large body of legal protection provided to prevent counterfeiting, misleading packaging, similar names and in some cases copying of business models and sounds. Service brands however are even more open to copying since a service event is not legally protectable. Other mechanisms such as distinctive service environments, service scripts for personnel and service documentation have to be relied upon.

Brands as a Strategic Device

A brand is seen to embody everything that the organization stands for. As a consequence the brand is also a mechanism for pursuing specific market strategies. Repositioning a brand can in effect change the organization's reputation and share price. The brand can be an opportunity to enlarge the service business such as adding service products under a well-recognized brand, or attacking incumbents in new markets. For the service business, a well-recognized and well-respected brand can provide a platform for growth. Marks and Spencer, a well-regarded retail brand, was able to branch out into financial services, investment advice and insurance.

Based on this overview of De Chernatony's and McDonald's ideas you will recognize that brands may perform different functions for the consumer and supplier of services. In general, they perform a function of reduction to customers: reducing search costs, risks, etc. To service providers, they perform a function of facilitation: facilitating new service introductions, promotions, segmentation, premium pricing, etc. They can be regarded as symbols around which relationships are built. This applies also for the consumer market as well as to the business-to-business market. The reason for this is quite simple. Since services are intangible, customers have difficulties in assessing services and service quality. Consequently, it is important for service providers to add an important role in services in general. This role may even be more important in the first phase of the life cycle of the service or in the first stages of the relationship life cycle. For, then, services have to be bought for the first time and consumers have to go through all the phases of their decision making process. In many instances emotional factors play a decisive role in buying services. This activity is often associated with a high degree of perceived risk. Then, the brand names of firms with an excellent reputation provide trust and security about quality, consistency and reliability and contribute to the perceived benefits. Brands not only have such a security function, but also an associative function for customers. Then, the combination of various signals and symbols results in association in the customer's mind. These associations may have a positive or negative meaning to the customer about the services intended to buy. Brands have an economic function as well. This hinges upon the efficiency improving character of brands as perceived by customers. Now, they have to remember only a small number of services/brands. This makes the decision making process much easier, as alternatives do not have to be assessed every time one wants to buy a service. Brand loyalty is a very relevant concept here. Brands may also have an expressive function, in the sense that by using such a brand the customer expresses a particular lifestyle or status. Additionally, there is the social-adaptive function of brands. Customers of a particular service may want to imitate a particular lifestyle or want to identify themselves with a particular sub-group in society.

In business-to-business services, brands also perform several functions for the industrial customer. In these markets, the industrial buyer is not always the very rational, well-informed customer often assumed. Here, emotions also play a role. Brands have a security function as well as an expressive function. Moreover, in these markets brands have a continuity function. The brand name, reputation and image of the service provider guarantees the delivery of these services in the future and hence a continuity of one's own firm.

Brands have also a particular meaning and function for the suppliers of services in consumer and business-to-business markets. Now, branding may change services from commodity services into identifiable and well-recognizable services. Branding then has a differentiation function for the service provider. This is a way to avoid price competition and sometimes even charge higher prices in particular market niches. A higher prestige credit card company can also charge higher membership fees; then branding facilitates the cash-generator function. The security function of brands leads to brand loyalty and hence a more stable market share for the service provider arises. Brands have a communication function for the service provider: an umbrella featured in the logo of insurance companies strengthens the impression of security. Many service firms have only one brand name for all their services. Strong brand names then offer opportunities for successful 'brand and line extension'. This relates to the life-cycle and differentiation functions of brands. In the retail sector, brand names are also associated with a particular amount of power in the distribution channel.

Brands are important in the relationship between customers and service providers. They can even act as 'relationship partners', often helping to resolve or address important personal issues. Seven attributes are essential to creating and maintaining high quality, enduring bonds. These are:

1 life and passion (consumers feel affection and passion for the service or are obsessed by it, and may experience separation anxiety if the service is not available);
2 self-concept connection (using this service brand helps consumers address a life issue on level one or two of the service hierarchy; see Chapter 8);
3 interdependence (the service brand is inextricably woven into the consumers' daily lives and routines);
4 commitment (consumers stick with the service through good and bad times);
5 intimacy (consumers describe a sense of deep familiarity with the service and an understanding of its attributes);
6 partner quality (consumers seek certain positive traits in the brand as if it were a best friend, such as dependability, trustworthiness, accountability); and
7 nostalgic attachment (the service brand brings back positive memories).

Brand Building

The task for the service marketer is to build a brand and build it in such a way that it is relevant to the customer and represents the relationship that the service organization wishes to develop with its customers. Keller (2002) provides a comprehensive model of how to build a brand and these steps can inform the process of developing a service brand. It comprises four building blocks which form the basis of a brand. These are identity, meaning, response and relationships.

Identity

To achieve an identity, customers must be able to recall and recognize the brand as well as linking it to the product category where it competes. Two associated concepts are brand depth and brand breadth. Depth refers to how easily customers can recall or recognize the brand while breadth refers to the range of purchase situations where the brand comes to mind. In other words to have an identity the brand must have both 'top of mind' position and sufficient 'mind share'. Clearly the more visible your brand the more depth you are likely to generate. Intensive advertising or sponsorship campaigns can provide a speedy acquisition of identity.

Meaning

In order to provide a brand with meaning it must be characterized by a set of values. Customers will be more drawn to brands that are perceived as having an image encompassing values congruent to their own (actual or aspired to) and it is primarily through the behaviour of customer contact employees that this occurs.[33] In essence the successful service brands are underpinned by their organizational values and as a consequence developing and maintaining these values is the prime driver of meaning, i.e. something that the brand stands for in the customer's mind. You can make a distinction between core values and peripheral values.[34] Core values are constant and drive overall activity; for instance values such as service quality, security, or innovation represent core values. As Kapferer noted, 'A brand grows over a long period by remaining consistent.'[35] Peripheral values are those which change over time and adapt to new market circumstances. Current market sentiment might require a focus upon corporate social responsibility through arts sponsorship, or low environmental emissions, or 24-hour access to facilitate global trading.

A brand can be defined as:

> *an identifiable product, service, person or place, augmented in such a way that the buyer or user perceives relevant, unique added values which match their needs most closely.*[36] *Furthermore, the success of a brand results from being able to sustain these added values.*

The development of meaning is achieved by a range of brand associations. Situations, representations or experiences can all present opportunities to associate messages with the brand which then provide meaning for customers. Broadly, meaning can be distinguished in two ways. The first is through associations based upon functional attributes of the product; for instance in services this might be efficiency, price, speed of delivery, or elements of the experience. Second, meaning might be communicated through consistent imagery such as a colour, idealized users or spokespersons, or history and heritage. Meaning must be assessed relative to strength of association, favourability of association and uniqueness of association.

Response

The third building block of a brand is the response by customers. A lot of the branding literature focusses upon what the organization believes without a recognition that customer perceptions of the brand are equally if not more important. Customers' responses can be broken down into brand judgements and brand feelings. Brand judgements focus upon customers' opinions of the service brand; this might be simply whether it is reliable, high quality, consistent or easy to use. These brand beliefs are often associated with the functional qualities of brands. By contrast brand feelings relate to subconscious reactions such as being a fun experience, whether the service experience is enjoyable or whether service personnel embody the core brand values.

Relationship

The final step is the level of personal identification between the customer and the brand and Keller refers to the concept of brand resonance to capture the degree of synchronicity between customer and brand. Sometimes this is called 'value congruence': the degree in which the values of the customer and the service are congruent. This synchronicity comprises four elements. The first is the degree of behavioural loyalty which might be measured via devices such as RFM. Second, the degree of attitudinal attachment which will distinguish between those customers who buy out of necessity, versus those that 'love' the brand. Third, the degree of brand community associated with buying, which is the basis of 'kinship' or recognition with other brand users. The final element is the degree of customer engagement engendered by the brand. This might be measured by the customer involvement in related magazines, websites or fan clubs.

These four building blocks together will determine the 'equity' of the brand. It is important to emphasize that each of the four building blocks referred to above are interdependent. There is no value in focussing upon the communication of meaning if there isn't any brand recognition, nor upon building relationships if the response to the brand is one of aversion.

Problem with Service Brands

As noted above, service branding is a relatively new topic for marketing researchers and the distinctive features of service branding are still being explored. However what is emerging is at least some recognition that service brands are different. One of the key differences in terms of branding is the degree of separation between how a service is delivered and what is delivered. (You will discover in Chapter 5 that these two dimensions are also referred to as technical and functional quality). Customers often use the how to develop expectations of what will be delivered. For organizations where these two parts of the service are synchronized, they can avoid circumstances of over promising or under delivering since they have control. Take for example a life insurance policy; the 'how' is developed when the policy was taken out, the forms, signing of documents, etc. The 'what', i.e. the insurance pay out on death, may not occur for many years. As a consequence there is considerable distance between brand promise and brand reality.

Branding in this environment is very difficult since every service interaction will test the organization's ability to deliver on its 'brand' promise. This means that for every interaction with the service organization, every 'moment of truth', service employees must exhibit elements of the brand's personality and be true to the brand promise. Virgin Airlines in Australia operates under the brand name Virgin Blue coined primarily because its red livery had already been taken by the established market leader Qantas Airways. Virgin Blue positioned its brand as youthful, slightly irreverent and fun. The staff they employ, the uniforms they wear, the service they provide all exhibit these characteristics and serve to reinforce the corporate brand. This relationship between the service organization and its service providers requires viewing the service brand as organization-wide, in other words as a corporate brand.[37] The service brand as corporate brand requires a degree of control over how the service employee presents the brand to customers. As Reichheld and Teal (1996) observed, communicating the brand to employees is probably far more important than communicating it to customers. The personal experience that the customer receives will cement the relationship with the brand and therefore the customer will need to trust that the employee represents the brand accurately. Staff training such as providing scripts or interaction rehearsal can help to improve consistency. Equally, briefing staff about the nature of the brand communications received by customers is important. If you are telling customers that they will 'be received with a friendly smile' then it's imperative that staff know this before the campaign is executed.

An added complexity is where the service organization is relying upon other organizations to deliver the service such as alliance partners, third party providers or contractors. Here there may be many different 'brands' interacting, hopefully consistently but often in competition. Travel services may have little control over individual hotel owners, insurance companies may have little control over medical assessment services or recruitment agencies over the staff that they place.

This problem of consistency, added to the problem of control, serves to make service branding extremely difficult to execute. In addition the interrelationship between the product and the service provider suggests that the corporate service brand is the more appropriate direction for service organizations rather than trying to brand specific service products. There has been little evidence that the extensive attempts by some financial institutions for instance to develop product-based brands have had any market effect. In customers' minds they are dealing with a bank, an airline and insurance company, a hospital, and not a specific component of those services. While service branding remains a critical issue for service managers there is no doubt that the principles of branding already developed for physical products combined with human resource management (HRM) techniques will provide the basis for unlocking the service branding puzzle. The HRM perspective is critical here as well since the (frontline) employees are the ones who really live up the brand.

Summary

In this chapter we have looked at the concept of relationships in services which are at the heart of the service product. Our acquisition of physical products is often about a simple economic transaction, we pay the money and we get the product. We can often accomplish this with very little effort. We don't have to talk to anyone, we don't have to reveal who we are, or even what we want with the product. By contrast when we acquire a service we do have to talk to people, we often have to reveal who we are and to some extent explain what we require of the service. Once we engage in consumption in this way we are starting to interact and interaction relationships develop. We can understand interaction by looking at the many different forms it takes within a typical service setting, with people, processes, other customers as well as the service provider. Interaction though is just the start and for relationships to develop there must be evidence of developing understanding, trust and commitment. Over time, through collaboration and adaptation the relationship will develop, providing benefits to both service suppliers and service customers. Due to the recognition of the importance and value of relationships to the organization they require a degree of recognition and management. This is to try and encourage relationships to develop, to improve those relationships over time and to leverage those relationships for both the customer and the organization. In consumer markets where there are likely to be a large number of customers the application of technology through databases and data mining has spawned 'customer relationship management' as a powerful corporate methodology to develop relationships, loyalty and customer interaction.

In the last part of the chapter we considered branding and its role in the creation of relationships between organizations and customers. Branding has received a great deal of attention in recent years as organizations have sought to create brands with distinct personalities in order to differentiate their offering in an increasingly cluttered market. Brands are very complex entities which require very careful management. In the services context brand development has not been easy primarily because customers interact on many different levels and with many different parts of the product. Because brand development relies to a great extent upon consistency the management task for services is considerable. This has led to an increased focus upon corporate branding rather than individual product brands which in services have provided little customer recognition.

Questions

1. Describe the four main sources of interaction for a customer.
2. Identify the benefits of a relationship to the customer and to the organization.
3. Explain why service organizations focus upon existing customers.
4. Explain what is meant by 'commitment'. How does this relate to loyalty?
5. What is trust? Is it a valuable attribute for customers?
6. Distinguish between individual and collective relationship forms.
7. What are the four attributes of loyal customers?

8. Explain the difference between customer profitability and customer lifetime value.
9. What are the eight functions of a brand?
10. Describe the main problems with managing service brands.

Assignments

1. Develop a list of five services with which you are familiar for each of the high, medium and low contact service types suggested by Lovelock (1992).
2. Write down all the things a service organization does which to you indicate that you have a relationship with them. Separate out those things which relate to a transaction and those which do not.
3. List the relationships which you have with service organizations which are obligated. Under what circumstances would you consider ending these relationships?
4. In the example given for customer lifetime value, what marketing actions do you think the mobile phone provider should take in respect of those customers on plan D?
5. Make a list of the top ten service brands in your country.
   a Find an example of the advertising for each of them
   b Identify the associations which the advert is making with the brand.

Endnotes

1 Burrows, 2005, in his column in the *Virgin Express Inflight Magazine.*

2 Dwyer *et al.*, 1987.

3 Gummesson, 2002, p. 67.

4 For examples of service applications, Greenland and McGoldrick, 2005: Ward, Davies and Kooijman, 2003; Foxall and Greenley, 2000.

5 Hennig-Thurau *et al.*, 2002.

6 Möller and Halinen, 2000.

7 Berry and Parasuraman, 1993; Grönroos, 1990b.

8 Ford, 1984; Wilson, 1995.

9 Anderson *et al.*, 1994; Easton, 1995.

10 Moorman, Deshpande and Zaltman, 1992.

11 Morgan and Hunt, 1994.

12 Morgan and Hunt, 1994.

13 Bansal, Irving and Taylor, 2004; Pritchard, Havitz and Howard, 1999.

14 Gwinner *et al.*, 1998.

15 Christopher, Payne and Ballantyne, 1991; Gummesson, 2002; Griffin, 1997.

16 Pfeifer, Haskins and Conroy, 2005.

17 Jain and Singh, 2002; Reichheld and Teal, 1996; Hughes, 1997.

18 Schijns 1996, 1998

19 The discussion of this RLM-matrix heavily depends on Schijns (1996). As Schijns (p. 28) states, the framework for this model is not new, as it is rooted in models of Hoekstra (1993), Krapfel *et al.* (1991), and Strandvik and Liljander (1994b), and is analogous to the relative attitude–behaviour relationship of Dick and Basu (1994). However, measuring relationship strength by relationship commitment (Wilson, 1999, 1995), and using relationship strength as the attitudinal dimension are non-relational.

29 For the sake of simplicity only 4 segments are mentioned. It is self-evident that more segments can be found when each dimension is subdivided into more than two.

21 Storbacka, 1994.

22 Storbacka, 1994. The following remarks stem from Strandvik and Storbacka (1996) and Liljander and Strandvik (1995).

23 See also our section on the Service Profit Chain.

24 Adapted from *Marketing* (UK), 23 March 2005, p. 2.

25 Uncles, Dowling and Hammond, 2003.

26 Petrof, 1997.

27 Lassar *et al.*, 1995.

28 Biswas, 1992.

29 Van Janiszewski and Osselaer, 2000.

30 Van Riel *et al.*, 2000.

31 De Chernatony and Dall'Olmo Riley, 1999; De Chernatony, Drury and Segal-Horn, 2002; O'Cass and Grace, 2004.

32 De Chernatony and McDonald, 2003.

33 Davies and Chun, 2002.

34 De Chernatony and Segal-Horn, 2004.

35 Kapferer, 1997, p. 169.

36 De Chernatony and McDonald, 2003.

37 This is supported by King, 1991; Ambler and Barrow, 1996; and Schultz and De Chernatony, 2002.

Chapter 5

Service Quality

**YOUR
OPERATIONS
SPAN THE GLOBE.
WE CAN MAKE
THAT LESS OF
A STRETCH.**

You want to seize opportunities that come from operating in
many markets. Our international network delivers world-class
financial expertise to your doorstep, so you're able to achieve
your ambitions no matter how far and wide they take you.

www.wholesale.abnamro.com

Making more possible   ABN·AMRO

Learning objectives

At the end of this chapter you will be able to:

1 Describe the main perspectives on quality

2 Illustrate the difference between quality and satisfaction

3 Describe the disconfirmation model of service quality

4 Distinguish between technical and functional quality

5 Appreciate the operation of the SERVQUAL Model

6 Describe the basis of the six sigma approach

7 Appreciate some of the managerial problems in implementing service quality

5.1   Introduction

SERVICE PRACTICE 5.1

Excellent Quality: Mission Impossible?

The legendary basketball player Michael Jordan is famous for 'flying' under the basket. Perhaps even more legendary in the USA is baseball player 'Babe' Ruth, who in 1927 held the home run record of 60 in a 154-game season.

Emile Zatopek, marathon runner from the former Czechoslovakia, was called the 'locomotive'. He was known for his revolutionary constant speed. Now, 50 years after his sporting career, Zatopek plays a key role in an Adidas advertising campaign.

In June 1988, the Dutch Football Team played in the European Championship Final in Munich. Russia was the opponent. During the second half of the game, Marco van Basten scored an almost impossible goal. The Dutch press described this goal as the 'miracle of Munich'.

All these sportsmen have in common is that they have achieved the seemingly impossible. In sports terminology, this is often associated with quality. Fortunately, in service delivery, quality does not necessarily relate to the impossible. However, accomplishing unexpected things contributes to quality to a great extent.

Customers will always look for quality. Quality is one of the main drivers of customer satisfaction as we saw in Chapter 3. Therefore quality is a natural pursuit for any organization seeking a source of competitive advantage. However, when you think about it a bit more, you start to realize that this oversimplifies what is a very complex issue. For example, what is quality? Can every customer see it? If so, is it the same for every customer? How does it relate to the price paid or the value extracted from the service? In the case of physical goods which have a degree of standardization and are able to be compared, these issues are complicated enough. When applied to services, where the product is heterogeneous, intangible, inseparable, perishable and difficult to own, quality becomes very difficult to comprehend and even more difficult to implement and manage. This way of reasoning explains why this chapter is positioned here in our book.

For any organization, improving the quality of their service costs money and so they need to know where to focus resources to make the best impact. They need to understand the relationship between investment in service quality and the return on that investment, through profitability or loyalty for example. Put simply, most organizations are seeking to deliver the highest quality of service to the largest number of customers over the longest period of time at the lowest unit cost. For the customer, quality is perception and like most perceptions differs in subtle ways from objective reality. Before consumption, it is generally understood that customer perceptions are a function of their prior experience with the service or similar services, their individual opinion, reaction to other people's opinions and communications such as advertising. Taken together these combine to generate expectations about the service performance. During consumption, customers react to service delivery events, such as the attitude of sales staff, the environment where the service is delivered, their involvement in service delivery, or the behaviour of other customers. Finally, after consumption there is a process of reflection on the outcome, an assessment of the service, such as education or health services, in respect of its enduring value. These are just some of the issues which make the study and implementation of service quality intellectually and managerially challenging.

Given the problems of pursuing quality for a service organization one might question whether it is worth the effort but service quality is not pursued as an outcome in its own right but because of its association with satisfaction and through this to profitability and customer retention. Current research has expanded the range of potential benefits from a high quality service to include: *Recommendedion Benefits of usi of service quality*

- Creating competitive advantage by insulating customers from competitors. This is due to customer inertia. If the service delivered is perceived to be of equal or higher quality than that of competitors then there is no motivation for customers to defect regardless of poaching tactics.
- Lowering customer recruitment costs occurs due to the positive word of mouth from existing customers who provide a free recruitment service for those organizations fortunate enough to have satisfied customers. Equally, by spending less on attracting new customers (because fewer of them defect to competitors) marketing expenditure can be directed at ensuring existing customers are happy.
- Promoting positive word of mouth and reputation occurs as customers talk about the service to others. Customers regularly poll other people in their work and social networks about consumption experiences looking for re-assurance that their provider is as good as everyone else's, looking for status associated with having found a better provider than others and looking for alternative suppliers if current businesses aren't providing satisfaction.
- Improved financial performance is a natural corollary of increased customer loyalty, reduced customer recruitment spend and positive word of mouth.
- Reduced staff turnover although widely canvassed has only limited empirical support. However, the argument goes that as customers are more satisfied and less likely to complain they also exhibit 'helping' behaviours and are more forgiving of service failures, and the extended time available through higher loyalty rates allows for more enduring service relationships.

These benefits represent substantial advantage to an organization that can provide a service of quality. The problem of course is how to do it. This chapter considers some of the general issues about quality, focuses upon service quality and presents the main ways in which service quality is operationalized for managers (Figure 5.1).

5.2   What is Quality?

The application of quality to the management of services is a relatively recent phenomenon and the way that it has been achieved is to draw upon and adapt a number of approaches

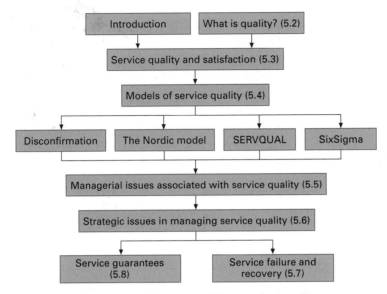

Figure 5.1   Chapter outline: service quality

already in use in other contexts. Before we can investigate service quality specifically, we need to understand the various definitions and approaches to quality that exist in the wider social and business environment. This will allow some understanding of where current issues in the application of quality to services have arisen. We know that quality can be viewed from many different points of view. Garvin (1988) presented five different approaches to understanding quality which are a good summary of the different ways quality is viewed as well as providing a framework for appreciating some of the problems associated with service quality. These different ways of looking at quality are:

■ Transcendent-based
■ Attribute-based
■ User-based
■ Manufacturing-based
■ Value-based.

Transcendent-Based Quality

According to this approach quality cannot always be defined and is partly the result of individual rather than shared experience. This ability to understand what something is but not be able to describe it is characteristic of something known as an 'epiphenomenon'. The way we get around this problem is to use either comparators or attributes. For instance as an individual we know what we find beautiful, but it's difficult to describe to someone else without reference to something (a comparator), e.g. this piece of jewellery is more beautiful than that piece. In service terms we might be able to say that service experience was better than this service experience but not be able to explain why. What this means is that quality cannot be defined precisely, it is a simple unanalysable property we learn to recognize only through experience. When we apply this approach to services you can immediately see that many service experiences are transcendent. It is impossible to describe exactly why they felt so good. Was it the way the waiter anticipated your every need? The way the airline ensured you were comfortable on your flight? Or maybe the speed with which your insurance claim was processed? There are a large number of subtle events and reactions, many of which are hardly noticed, which can nevertheless make a difference to service quality.

Attribute-Based Quality

'Quality is zero defects – doing it right the first time.'[1]

The attribute-based approach maintains that quality is a direct outcome of the number of features or attributes of a product. Take the example of a mobile phone. If one phone has a colour screen, Bluetooth, polyphonic ring tones and interchangeable covers while the other phone has a black and white screen, no Bluetooth, no ability to download polyphonic ring tones and no alternative covers then they are by definition different quality, but the issue is which is higher. Under the attribute-based approach the product with more attractive attributes is higher quality. So in this example the first is higher quality than the second. This approach suggests that quality is an objective and absolute term and therefore measurable. The problem of course is that the characteristics of services prevent 'side by side' comparison not just because you can't experience two similar services at the same time but because many service attributes are identifiable. Similarly, even if you could identify all the attributes of the services you were assessing your assessment wouldn't be complete until the service ended, or the service benefit was finally revealed.

User-Based Quality

'Quality is fitness for use, the extent to which the product successfully serves the purpose of the user during usage.'[2]

From this perspective, quality is simply determined by the customer and, as you might recognize, this approach is entirely consistent with a marketing orientation. The problem of course is that this approach to quality is highly subjective because every user has a different view of quality. In reality what we are dealing with is perceived quality, which is not a totally reliable indicator of actual quality. To a great extent this is a problem for a market oriented organization because on the one hand they want to please their customers but on the other they can't produce n different variants for n customers in order to secure individual quality requirements. The only exceptions to this are where we offer the ultimate form of an augmented customized service or when technology is involved such as online services. Here, customization is individualized and can be very low cost. Equally some membership-based CRM activities use customization as a means of securing individualized quality assessments. For instance, ensuring hotel rooms have guests' favourite pillows drawn from their profiles, or in the case of very high value services such as large industrial service contracts where the service is almost entirely customized to buyer specification. User-based quality would certainly be held up as the most market focussed, and provides a stated link between quality and organizational performance. It also motivates companies to ask customers about quality but does little to help in the production of quality outcomes.

Manufacturing-Based Quality

'Quality is conformance to requirements.'[3]

Quality following this approach is considered entirely in terms of conformity to a previously set standard. Since every manufactured product must meet a finite number of specifications as a function of the manufacturing process, quality is measured simply by conformance, with divergence considered a decrease in quality. In Europe you might see a stylized 'e' on some packaged goods. This is a quality-based mark which indicates that over one hour of production the product conforms on average to the weight stated. Similar specifications may be set for services such as answering the phone within three rings, not having to queue longer than two minutes, invoices sent out within five days, or maintenance contract call-out times for IT equipment. There are many services that rely upon this approach simply because it resolves many of the measurement issues associated with service performance. If a manager can specify what a service should be like, such as speed between different process points, information provided to customers, or the provision of tangible outcomes then the service can be assessed relative to these specifications and relative quality determined.

Value-Based Approach

'Quality is exceeding what customers expect from the service.'[4]

The value-based approach sees quality simply as a function of customer benefit relative to price or cost. In simple terms quality is assessed as the difference between a customer's investment in acquiring or consuming a product relative to the enjoyment, benefit or satisfaction they will yield. In reality this approach is a version of the user-based approach because the customer makes the determination of value. It is conceivable that if we were to compare two similar products side by side, they would be assessed as having different 'quality'. For instance, a tee shirt bought in your local supermarket may satisfy the same functional requirement as a tee shirt bought in a boutique except for the value obtained from wearing an exclusive brand attached to the boutique rather than any intrinsic difference in the tee shirts. The point here is that often the perceived value of something is derived from a complex assessment of both product and customer attributes. The value-based approach to assessing service quality can be seen in broad attempts to differentiate service provision relative to price charged. For instance, different classes of service are used to define different value propositions in a wide range of services. In airline travel, everyone gets to the same destination at the same time but the service level is different depending upon the different 'class' of travel. Similarly in many countries you will pay higher bank charges to be served by a bank employee rather than via the Internet or ATM bank machine.

As you can see quality is an ambiguous term. On the one hand, everybody knows what quality is for them but it is very difficult for us to know what quality means for someone else and that in essence is the problem for marketing management. Whatever product an organization offers to the market be it physical or service-based they can never know precisely how its quality will be assessed. The issues which relate to services can be identified by going back to the service characteristics you are already familiar with and using them to identify some further specific issues.

Service Quality and the Five Characteristics of Services

Service Quality and the Inability to Own

Since services cannot be owned you cannot determine its quality once you 'possess' the service. However, some services can be rented or leased; then you can evaluate the service quality somewhat earlier. In all instances, the quality of the process of delivering the service will be critical.

Service Quality and Intangibility

Intangibility prevents customers from being able to make comprehensive assessments of many services before, during or after delivery. Some parts of the service may be visible (such as the service provider), some may be comparable between service organizations (such as the physical environment) but many will remain unknown before and even after the service has occurred. For example, when you undergo surgery you have no idea what happened, or indeed how well the surgery was performed and hopefully will never need to question it. Similarly when a business employs a consultant or a financial advisor it is sometimes difficult to assess exactly what is being offered and more importantly what has actually been delivered.

Service Quality and Inseparability

The third important characteristic of services when considering quality is that of inseparability. The customer's involvement in the delivery process will impact upon both real and perceived quality. Take the example of a psychotherapist who relies upon interaction with you to help solve your problems. If you don't interact or aren't honest in your interaction then the psychotherapist really can't deliver the service you require. As a consequence you might perceive the quality of the service received to be low. Similarly business services rely heavily upon clear and unambiguous specification by the client company to ensure that they meet the desired outcomes. If that specification is ambiguous or incomplete there is a danger that delivery will be considered inadequate. As a general rule more interaction between customers and the service organization should improve quality but this is dependent upon a range of issues such as clear communication, responsiveness to requests, and volume of contacts, etc.

Service Quality and Heterogeneity

Heterogeneity (variability) impacts upon quality from both the organizations' and customers' perspectives. For the organization, variability makes the definition and implementation of precise quality standards very difficult to achieve and if staff slavishly follow them it makes the service less responsive to customers' demands and therefore lower quality. For the customer, variability simply means that sometimes the service will be outstanding and other times will be disappointing. The issue for both organization and customer is to ensure delivery falls within a boundary, i.e. there is a minimum level guaranteed and a maximum level manageable. In business-to-business services this boundary is usually enshrined in some sort of service or delivery specification which in turn is part of the trading contract. However it is not possible to specify every aspect of the service such as the individual performance of the personnel involved and as such variability is evident even in the most rigidly specified service.

Service Quality and Perishability

An important characteristic of services is that they represent a performance usually by a service provider and therefore often cannot be stored. While in some circumstances it is possible to keep capacity in readiness for service delivery, this does not represent a store of finished service products. We can't buy an hour of an actor's performance in the last night of a play and store it in a warehouse until we want to view it (unless we tape it). Perishability means that the service has to be consumed at the time it is offered. Sometimes a service is so popular that many customers want to consume it at the same time thereby restricting its supply and putting staff under pressure. This might cause some customers to suffer in a long queue or cramped conditions, altering their assessment of service quality. Alternatively a service might be needed instantaneously, such as an ambulance or fire service which requires it to be available to everyone 24 hours a day, or IT support for large corporate systems. Any delay in provision will impact upon an assessment of quality. The fluctuations in supply, demand, as well as urgency will impact upon service quality.

5.3   Service Quality or Satisfaction?

From the section above it should be evident that service quality is a complex and ephemeral concept which makes it all the more interesting that academics and organizations around the world have pursued service quality with an almost evangelical enthusiasm. The outcome of this work has been a number of frameworks or models which have been applied to services as a means of understanding and ultimately managing improvements to service quality. However, before we start this consideration of service quality models we have to deal with a consistent confusion, which is the relationship between service quality and customer satisfaction. We could leave it until the end of this chapter but it is important enough to consider head-on and make some remarks in addition to what we already said about it in Chapter 3.

In simple terms quality refers to some attribute of what is offered, provided, produced whereas satisfaction or dissatisfaction refers to a customer's reaction to that offer. In this sense they are separate; quality is something that an organization is responsible for, whereas satisfaction is in the customer's domain, it is an experience. However these two concepts are clearly related in that we might use customer response (satisfaction or dissatisfaction) as a means of assessing whether quality has been delivered. In fact this is entirely consistent with user-based quality assessment as described above, and is consistent with a marketing-based approach. As customers we can have perceptions of service quality without having actually experienced the service. We might think for instance that staying at the Dorchester Hotel in London or travelling first class on an airline would allow us to experience high service quality even though we haven't stayed there, or travelled first class. By contrast satisfaction has to be experienced; it cannot be imputed by assumption. So using the same examples, you can't say that you are satisfied with staying at the Dorchester Hotel unless you actually have done so, or that you were satisfied with travelling first class unless you had actually experienced it. Your reaction to a service is not solely derived from the service itself. It might have something to do with the environment in which the customers find themselves, how the customer is feeling at the time, whether they understand what is happening or not, other customers' actions which might be irritating them, etc. To summarize, we can determine satisfaction only first hand and, if we were satisfied with the experience, that satisfaction may derive from a whole range of things, both the service quality as designed by the hotel and airline and our reaction to elements of the service experience not designed by the service organization.[5]

Because of the interrelatedness of quality and satisfaction it is often difficult to treat them separately. You will not be surprised to learn that many of the models of service quality we consider below are actually based upon customers' or users' assessments of a service. It is worth digressing here to note that some authors view perceived quality as similar to an ongoing attitude whereas satisfaction is transaction specific. There is also some evidence to suggest that satisfaction is a prerequisite of perceived service quality, i.e. you only perceive quality if you are satisfied first. These issues are worthy of consideration and suggest that there is yet more discussion and research needed to clarify this. However, because the dominant perspective on service quality is what customers think, customer reactions (i.e. satisfaction and dissatisfaction) are considered as integral to service quality. As a consequence we will consider quality holistically rather than separating the two perspectives of organization and customer.

It is also worth noting at this point the range of services to which service quality can be applied. One often underexplored area of services is those which are sold between businesses as we tend to focus on services that we know or have experienced. In terms of communicating the operation of service quality models we will be using the usual selection of consumer service examples simply because most people will have experienced them. However, we shouldn't forget business-to-business services such as IT service contracts, maintenance, and the enormous array of professional services such as management consultants, market research, auditing, legal services and building and engineering reports. These services are often very high value amounting to hundreds of thousands or occasionally millions of euros. As such there is often scope to customize the service to a degree impossible in consumer services. Here, the perception of quality, as one may recall from Chapter 3, is often the responsibility of a purchasing group, a contract manager, or in some professional services the main board of the company; even shareholders can be involved in the case of auditing, or legal problems. With a large number of people involved, and complex service delivery processes B2B services aren't good exemplars of normative service quality approaches. But we would urge you to consider the application of these broad quality approaches to the B2B arena.

Because we are interested in how service quality is managed we will now review the main measurement techniques and their association with satisfaction. Finally we will consider some of the main management issues associated with service quality such as return on quality, satisfaction and dissatisfaction, and service failure and recovery.

5.4   Models of Service Quality

While it would be desirable to review all the approaches to service quality we will focus upon those which have the greatest applicability and widest use in business and academic circles. The models we have chosen are: first, the disconfirmation model;[6] second, the perceived quality model;[7] third, SERVQUAL;[8] and, finally, SixSigma designed by Motorola which is becoming a dominant approach in many organizations. Clearly each model has its supporters and detractors and you are encouraged to read the large number of articles and reviews associated with each.

The Disconfirmation Model of Service Quality

The application of quality to the services context was driven in part by the early studies of Oliver (1977), and Olshavsky and Miller (1972) which were based in turn on early research by Carlsmith and Aronson in 1963. The first part of this approach is to recognize that individuals (or in our case customers) are not blank sheets of paper but approach events, including purchases, with some expectation of what will occur. For instance if someone invites you to a party you may not know precisely what is going to happen but you will have some expectations of what will happen. When we actually experience an event (in our case a service transaction), we understand it through our perception of what happened. In simple terms we are assessing the service relative to what we expected. In doing so, we are dealing with an assessment of the actual service experience and our reaction to it and so in this instance we can make the link between quality and satisfaction. If what we experienced was better than we expected, then according to this model we are satisfied, if it is worse than we expected then we are dissatisfied. This doesn't say much about the actual quality of the service experience, only its perceived performance relative to our expectations. Nevertheless expectations and the subsequent performance are fundamental to current conceptualizations of service quality.

Expectations (E)

The concept of expectations has been widely used in many consumer studies and we will come back to them later when we consider SERVQUAL, but very little is known about what determines expectations, how these expectations are formed and how stable they are over time. Research on expectations[9] raised some concerns about terminology. Specifically what do we mean by the term? Is an ideal, an expected or a minimum level tolerable? We do know they are based on individual norms, values, wishes, needs, etc.[10] and we know therefore that expectations are very individualistic. This obviously is a problem in terms of disconfirmation since even if service delivery is absolutely identical between two individuals there is a good chance that expectations will be different and therefore satisfaction levels are also different. Also, we know that expectations are not stable and may change over time, possibly minute by minute but also over longer time periods, due to changing personal circumstances such as family life cycle, income levels, educational achievement or increasing aspiration levels. But expectations are also affected by the interaction of a person with social reference groups, general media, observation of specific situations, interaction with service providers, and other customers, etc. which brings individual experience to bear upon service quality assessment.

Berry and Parasuraman (1991) discuss two levels of expectations and conclude:

> *Our findings indicate that customers' service expectations exist at two different levels: a* desired *level and an* adequate *level. The desired service level reflects the service the customer hopes to receive. It is a blend of what the customer believes 'can be' and 'should be'. The adequate service level reflects what the customer finds acceptable. It is, in part, a function of the customer's assessment of what the service 'will be', i.e. the customer's* predicted *service level.*

The difference between the desired service level and the adequate service level is called the zone of tolerance which can be considered to be a zone of acceptability. In focus group interviews, considerable variation in customers' tolerance zones was found between various services, between various service attributes, and also between events, i.e. the zones vary (expand or contract) over time, even for one particular service. Based upon their conceptual model, we can see four main determinants of expected service which consists of the two levels of desired service, and adequate service.

Individual Sources

The antecedents of a desired service outcome are referred to as enduring service intensifiers. These are stable personal factors that underpin an individual's attitude to a service generally. These include views on fairness, social interaction, politeness, non verbal communication styles and perceptions of self. The antecedents of adequate service are called transitory service intensifiers which are usually situational things which alter the enduring intensifiers. These are temporary, usually short-term individual factors such as the urgency of the service need, particular service requirements, the perceived attractiveness of service alternatives, perceived service role and a range of immediate factors such as weather, time pressure, etc.

Environmental Sources

Impacting upon the determination of desired service is a range of derived service information comprising explicit service promises from the organization such as advertising, leaflets, personal selling. A range of implicit service promises are being communicated by the

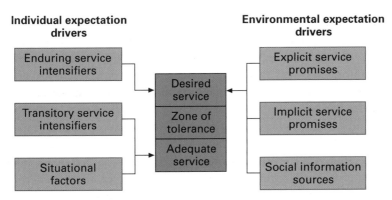

Figure 5.2   Determinants of the zone of tolerance

opulence of offices, impression given by sales staff, prices charged, etc. Added to these are social sources of information provided via word of mouth, observation, general media portrayals of service, etc.

We can put these three sets of determinants together to explain their impact upon the zone of tolerance (see Figure 5.2). As you can see, the formation of expectations is particularly complex and almost impossible to manage from the organization's perspective. A point to note though is that expectations can be positive, in that we are looking forward to an event, but equally they can be bad, i.e. we aren't looking forward to the event. In either case when we arrive at the service event, or our service transaction, we do so with some predisposition toward it. Service organizations often ask customers to provide their broad expectations, for instance:

In a good local supermarket what is the maximum number of people you would expect to be ahead of you in the queue at checkout?

☐ *None.*
☐ *1 person*
☐ *2 people*
☐ *3 people*
☐ *More than 3.*

The answer to this question would help a new retail supermarket measure expected queue depth across different supermarket offerings and position their service accordingly. However for a single service organization attempting to measure their actual service quality the data has to be complemented by actual experience. This we refer to as performance.

Performance (P)

The second part of the disconfirmation approach is making an assessment of what is actually received or experienced. In quality terms, the expectations provide the specification and then the performance provides the service production. The problem with performance from the customer's point of view is that it all depends upon the individual's perception. Very often as we have seen the characteristics of services mean that it is very unclear exactly what has been received. Take education for example, your immediate service experience is assessed based upon your perception of your current experience. But the wider issue associated with quality is that you may not be able to perceive many of the benefits accruing to you. For instance you may assess your educational experience to be outstandingly good but five years from now you might realize that your education didn't prepare you as well as you had thought. The same issues relate to health – great bedside manner of the doctor but no long-term relief from your ailment – or even stockbroking with great personal service but an underperforming investment portfolio.

The assessment of what actually happens in service delivery is subject to many of the same sources of variance as expectations. Individuals react differently to different things, according to their needs (conscious and subconscious), their personality and their (selective) perceptions of events. These differences account for different tolerances to things like queues, social interaction with service providers, time delays, specification of customization requests, or reaction to other customers, etc. In addition there is often an opportunity to compare service directly with other customers as many services are performed in public. For instance, in a retail environment the service is transparent; if you believe that the person in front of you in the queue got quick service, and yet you received very slow service, then your perception of the performance will be affected. This is different from a situation where you are in a waiting room, in which case you have no idea about the service delivered to the patient or customer before you and have often little opportunity to discuss experiences with others.

So what has this got to do with service quality? Simply that a customer derived quality assessment based upon the disconfirmation model will depend upon a comparison of expectations relative to performance. Clearly there are a number of different outcomes that can emerge from this comparison.

- *When expectations are exceeded (E < P)* This is the easiest and most desirable state for an organization; where expectations are exceeded. This provides the basis of positive confirmation of which the outcome is beyond satisfaction and closer to customer delight.[11] Perceived service quality is high.
- *When expectations are not met (E > P)* In this circumstance perceived service quality is low and the organization would expect to have a dissatisfied customer.
- *When expectations are met (E = P)* In this instance the customer will assess the quality of the service to be satisfactory or so you might predict. In fact it's not that simple. Suppose you expected really poor service quality and it was poor service quality. Does that make you satisfied with the service quality you received? While it is not clearly specified, the Berry and Parasuraman quote above helps us to understand the intricacy of the measurement problem. Expectations contain both adequate and desired components and therefore adequacy expectations, if confirmed through experience, don't mean satisfaction, just confirmation. By contrast desired expectations, if disappointed, mean dissatisfaction. Hence the poor service expected and poor service delivered does not necessarily mean satisfaction.

The Nordic Service Quality Model

Clearly the disconfirmation approach is a very powerful one for service managers because it provides a customer referenced method for assessing something which is innately difficult to assess. Disconfirmation has had a huge impact upon service quality and has been subject to a series of refinements. The first of these was from Grönroos (1982a, 1982b) who presented a variant model of service quality. Grönroos identified that services are not one big amorphous event but comprise different components which interact to determine overall quality. The key contribution here was to identify what he termed technical quality and functional quality.

Technical quality refers to a dimension which describes what the customer gets as the outcome of their interaction with the organization. Services are designed to produce an outcome and therefore we can think of the quality of services varying according to the outcome received. In many services this outcome or technical quality can be measured to a degree by the customer. For instance, a hotel service provides a room and a bed, an airline provides transportation to a destination, a transport firm moves goods from manufacturer to customer. However this is not the only quality that counts towards the customer's perception.

Functional quality refers to a dimension which describes the process by which the technical quality is delivered to the customer. This includes the demeanour of the service providers, the environment in which it is delivered, and the behaviour of other customers, etc. In our examples quoted above, hotels differ according to the attentiveness of staff, or the facilities in rooms, airlines differ according to airport facilities and in flight comfort and service, and transportation differs according to speed of delivery and care. We can think of many services where the technical quality is similar between organizations but the functional quality is what makes the difference (Figure 5.3).

One interesting observation from Grönroos is that:

an acceptable technical quality can be thought of as a pre-requisite for a successful functional quality. On the other hand, it seems as if temporary problems with the technical quality may be excused if the functional quality is good enough.[12]

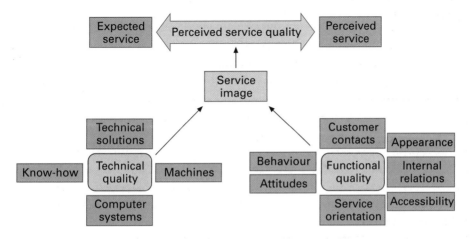

Figure 5.3   Perceived service quality

Adapted from Grönroos, 1982, *Strategic Management and Marketing in the Services Sector*, p. 79, reproduced by permission of Christian Grönroos.

	Technical	Functional
Person-based	• Response to illness • Quality of interaction with staff	• Time with doctor • Rapport with doctor • Information and diagnosis
Organization-based	• Availability of appointment times • Practice administration	• Waiting times • Continuity of care • Home visits • Physical facilities

Figure 5.4 Assymetrics

This observation refers to an evident asymmetry between dimensions of service which basically means that good performance on one aspect isn't always a compensation for bad performance on another. This is an important consideration when we come to look at more comprehensive service quality models.

Research conducted in the health service context provides further evidence of this asymmetry.[13] Using similar dimensions to those included in the Grönroos model the following distinction shown in Figure 5.4 was evidenced in relation to personal and organizational aspects of primary healthcare.

In this research two key dimensions emerged: those focussed upon personal aspects of the service and those focussed upon organizational or process elements of the service. It was clear that, in assessing the quality of service from a doctor, unless the technical elements were present then the inclusion of the functional aspects made no difference to the assessment of service quality. For instance if the quality of the interaction with staff (booking clerks, reception staff, etc.) was poor, then good time with the doctor, good rapport, good information and diagnosis were irrelevant in assessing overall service quality. But if interaction was good then the other three components did contribute to service quality in customer's assessment. This asymmetry is important in understanding how to improve service quality; unless the basics are right, no amount of investment in the service will improve quality in the customers' minds. Many organizations waste resources by focussing upon 'feel good' factors in service delivery; better quality napkins, nicer menus, staff uniforms, etc. to improve service quality when the problem is that the service is just inattentive and it takes too long to get a meal. The behavioural side is often much more critical than the technical side. That is why we sometimes separate the second dimension into a functional one and a relational one. Then the relational quality especially captures all elements deemed relevant in the personal relationship and interaction between the service employee and the customer.

The SERVQUAL Model of Service Quality

The SERVQUAL approach to service quality engineered the most profound shift in our understanding of both consumer and organizational responses to the problem of managing service quality. Since 1985 the three original authors, Len Berry, Parsu Parasuraman and Valarie Zeithaml, have published a variety of research initiating, developing and improving their original model. One consequence of their writing is that there are now over 5500 research articles on this model, which makes the task of summarizing the approach for this book quite difficult. Nevertheless, we should start where the researchers started and that was with service customers.

Service Quality Dimensions

A consistent theme in the field of service quality is the problem of identifying what comprises a service in order to determine the dimensions of the service which customers use to assess quality. Remember, the disconfirmation approach didn't really specify any service components in particular, treating expectations as holistic. The Grönroos model went further, and categorized two sets of service product attributes (technical and functional) and SERVQUAL started by trying to develop a more comprehensive understanding of service quality dimensions. The original qualitative interviews produced a set of ten dimensions:

- Tangibles: The appearance of physical facilities, equipment, personnel, etc.
- Reliability: Ability to perform the service dependably and accurately
- Responsiveness: Willingness to help customers
- Competence: Possession of the required skill/knowledge to perform the service
- Courtesy: Politeness, respect, consideration and friendliness
- Credibility: Trustworthiness, believability, and honesty
- Security: Freedom from danger
- Access: Approachability and ease of contact
- Communication: Keeping customers informed
- Understanding: Making an effort to know customers

As you can see nine of these dimensions relate to what Grönroos termed functional quality and only one relates to technical quality. As a consequence, what we are dealing with here is very much how a service is delivered rather than the detail of what is delivered. The research continued into a second phase where the ten dimensions were collapsed into five. These five have become dominant in service quality research. They are often referred to as the RATER dimensions:

- Reliability: Ability to perform the service dependably and accurately. For example the consistency in meeting service promises which could include keeping schedules or appointment times, completing tasks on time, ensuring that outcomes are met.
- Assurance: Which includes competence, courtesy, credibility and security. This dimension would include staff training in the use of tools and knowledge of their service processes, customer interaction, and the perception that the service is competent and not going to harm anyone. This has also been seen to include brand names, and reputation.
- Tangibles: Appearance of physical facilities, equipment, and personnel. The elements of the service environment impact upon perceived service quality for instance cleanliness of premises, staff appearance and the appropriateness of things like computers, phones and décor.

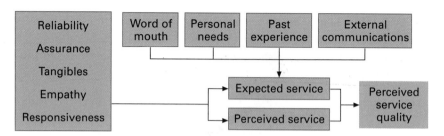

Figure 5.5   The SERVQUAL model

■ Empathy: This includes access, communication and understanding. This composite dimension is really about the communication style of the service organization through its service personnel, its communications including leaflets, instructions, signage and people management.

■ Responsiveness: Willingness to help customers. This refers to the ability of the service to respond to individual customer requirements such as specifying delivery times, altering aspects of the delivery process, and ensuring that customers remain involved.

An interesting result of the analysis was that these dimensions remained relatively stable across different service sectors, with reliability consistently coming out top, followed by responsiveness, assurance, empathy and tangibles. It is possible for individual organizations to ask customers to allocate relative weightings to these different dimensions to produce some representation of the relative importance of the five dimensions for their organization which may be used to direct investment.

The full SERVQUAL model (Figure 5.5) contains a large part of the disconfirmation approach already discussed – the disconfirmation between expected service and perceived service derive perceived service quality. However that process is influenced by the four externalities word of mouth, personal needs, past experience and external communications which impact upon the formation of expectations. The five dimensions of service quality drive the disconfirmation.

In simple terms the SERVQUAL model defines quality as the difference between customers' expectations and perceptions of the service delivered. To measure quality, the respondents are asked to answer two sets of questions, dealing with the same subject. These define the two disconfirmation components. For example, customers of a bank are asked:

■ Employees in excellent banks will . . .
■ Employees in bank XYZ do . . . .

Customers complete these two questions on a 7- (or 5- in Europe) point Likert scale, indicating the degree to which they agree with the statement. As you can see this defines the comparison, i.e. excellent banks confirm the expectation, and bank XYZ confirms the perceived or actual service.

For each service dimension and for the total service, a quality judgement can be computed according to the following formula:

$$\text{Perception} - \text{Expectation} = \text{Service Quality}$$

Or

$$P - E = Q$$

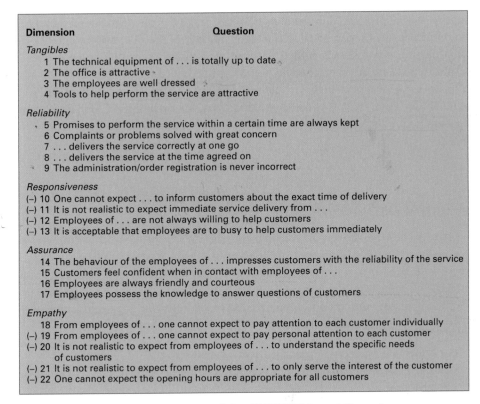

Dimension   **Question**

Tangibles
1 The technical equipment of . . . is totally up to date
2 The office is attractive
3 The employees are well dressed
4 Tools to help perform the service are attractive

Reliability
5 Promises to perform the service within a certain time are always kept
6 Complaints or problems solved with great concern
7 . . . delivers the service correctly at one go
8 . . . delivers the service at the time agreed on
9 The administration/order registration is never incorrect

Responsiveness
(–) 10 One cannot expect . . . to inform customers about the exact time of delivery
(–) 11 It is not realistic to expect immediate service delivery from . . .
(–) 12 Employees of . . . are not always willing to help customers
(–) 13 It is acceptable that employees are to busy to help customers immediately

Assurance
14 The behaviour of the employees of . . . impresses customers with the reliability of the service
15 Customers feel confident when in contact with employees of . . .
16 Employees are always friendly and courteous
17 Employees possess the knowledge to answer questions of customers

Empathy
18 From employees of . . . one cannot expect to pay attention to each customer individually
(–) 19 From employees of . . . one cannot expect to pay personal attention to each customer
(–) 20 It is not realistic to expect from employees of . . . to understand the specific needs of customers
(–) 21 It is not realistic to expect from employees of . . . to only serve the interest of the customer
(–) 22 One cannot expect the opening hours are appropriate for all customers

Figure 5.6   22 items of the SERVQUAL questionnaire

There is some debate about the intricacies of the measurement system,[14] but the overall essence of the formula allows for continuous adjustment from a customer determined benchmark. The very best service quality would conceivably be +6, i.e. 7 on performance minus 1 on expectation, and the worst service quality would –6, i.e. 7 on expectation minus 1 on performance.

The total service quality can now be measured, using the five dimensions mentioned before: tangibles, reliability, responsiveness, assurance and empathy. Service quality can be measured by these five dimensions via 22 questions. These 22 items are mentioned in Figure 5.6.

The expectation question (fill in: 'excellent company') concerns the excellent company in the industry. The perception question (fill in: 'company X') relates to the firm whose service quality is examined. So as an example let us assume bank A is the bank a customer perceives as an excellent bank (the expectation), and the customer rates bank B. With repect to the expectations question, 'Bank A is attractive', and with respect to actual perception, 'Bank B is attractive'.

To provide for some managerially actionable outcomes Zeithaml and Bitner (1996) suggest that zones of expectation tolerance for each of the five dimensions of service quality be plotted for the organization. Subsequently the service quality outcomes from SERVQUAL are plotted on the same basis. The outcome is one where the zone of tolerance between desired and adequate service provides a target and the actual service quality provides a measure of where the organization's service quality is located on each of the five service dimensions.

The next phase of the research, now that the service quality evaluation criteria were resolved, was to understand how and why service quality failures occurred. This was an attempt to work backwards to help service organizations use the information gained to understand service failures. This process of engineering the organization to manage service quality is based upon the concept of gaps or sequential failures between expectation and performance.

Internal Gaps in the SERVQUAL Gaps Model

The next step in the research was to consider the causes for possible quality differences. Therefore, not only users, customers, consumers and/or buyers are asked to participate, but employees and managers as well. The model assumes that differences between the service desired by the customer and the service finally delivered by the service provider may be caused by systemic disconfirmations which comprise the following four gaps (see Figure 5.7):

Gap 1: consumer expectation – management perception gap. In formulating its service-delivery policy, management does not correctly perceive or interpret consumer expectations;

Gap 2: management perception – service quality specification gap. Management does not correctly translate the service policy into rules and guidelines for employees;

Gap 3: service quality specification – service delivery gap. Employees do not correctly translate rules and guidelines into actions; and

Gap 4: service delivery – external communications gap. External communications – promises made to customers – do not match the actual service delivery.

The SERVQUAL model shows the relationship between the external Gap 5 (perceived quality as experienced by customers) and the internal Gaps 1–4. Gap 5 depends on the size and direction of the four disconfirmations associated with the delivery of service quality on the marketer's side. If Gaps 1–4 are reduced, then service quality can be improved. A particular strength of this approach is to examine whether the organization's views are in line with customers' views about quality. If these two perspectives differ widely then the company will have opinions about service quality quite different from those of consumers. To be able to deliver excellent services, it is necessary to bring the customer's perception and the employee's perception together.

Research into the relative importance of the internal Gaps 1–4 shows that Gap 3 and Gap 4 are particularly important in this, suggesting that organizations should concentrate their efforts and tools on factors that influence these areas. Specifically, hiring qualified personnel, providing the right tools or equipment, giving employees more freedom of action, stimulating team work, introducing procedures for an optimal co-operation between, especially, the marketing department and the operational department and providing true, fair information.

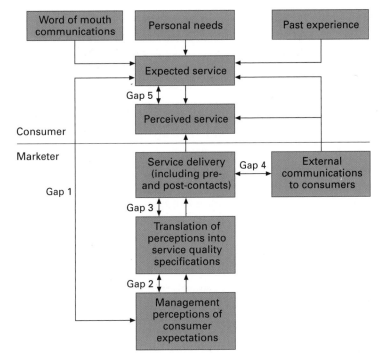

Figure 5.7   The SERVQUAL model

Using Gaps to Identify Causes of Poor Service Quality

Using the four gaps identified in the SERVQUAL model, we will now discuss the factors explaining or contributing to a failure to deliver the expected service quality.[15]

Gap 1: Factors causing a customer expectation – management perception gap

- First, managers may think that they understand their customers' needs and do not invest in marketing research. This is especially dangerous for customer expectations are changing rapidly, often weekly, such as in the case of mobile telecommunications, entertainment, or supply chain partnerships.
- Second, managers may spend too little time in gaining first-hand knowledge of their customers and may have too little contact with customer experience.

SERVICE PRACTICE 5.2

Mercedes-Benz discovered that their senior managers had forgotten what it was like to purchase a car because as senior employees they were provided with one. Similarly senior Vodafone managers who are provided with a phone had rarely experienced purchasing a mobile phone since they started with the company. Some service organizations let their (top) managers perform as front office employees for a certain period per year. Managers of Hertz have to stand behind the desk to rent cars and bell boys in the Marriott Hotel are managers on a weekly 'training' course. Australia

Post has members of their marketing department work for a period every year in a local post office. In this way, managers are placed in a positon where they have close contact with customers and hopefully better understand customers.

- The third factor that may cause Gap 1 is the number of layers of management between top managers and customer-contact personnel: i.e. the organization's hierarchy. Larger organizations have more layers and this may cause inadequate communications.
- The larger the number of layers between management and contact personnel, the less objective the information will be that finally reaches management. On each level, the information will be interpreted differently and passed on to the next level.

Gap 2:   Factors causing a difference between management perception and service quality specification.
- First, there may be a lack of management commitment to service quality. It's very easy for managers to talk about service quality as something they wish to achieve, but in reality they are assessed upon their commercial performance, such as profitability, revenue generation or cost reduction. These objectives are more easily formulated and results are more easily measured by senior managers and as a consequence other objectives may receive less attention.
- A second factor that can play a role is the degree of goal setting. Even if there is some commitment to service quality within the organization it may not as yet have resulted in clear guidelines and standards. It's very easy to preach to staff about service quality but quite a different matter to specify in detail what it means to the individual service provider. For instance, answering the phone quickly, introducing yourself, listening skills, appearing approachable, speed of resolution, etc. The detail is the most difficult part of the process of implementing service quality across an employee group.
- The third factor is the degree to which the service can be appropriately standardized. In some services it is possible to specify almost exactly what will happen. Indeed some organizations have pursued standardization to such an extent that almost every action and interaction with customers is carefully scripted. However, for some services we expect customization, such as medical or healthcare where we value responsiveness and empathy; these services don't standardize well since every person will require a different service.
- The last factor is the perception of feasibility. This is a description of managers' perceptions of the extent to which meeting customer expectations is possible. Management knows that customers have certain expectations, but employees have the impression that meeting these expectations is not possible. This impression may be caused by employees lacking in confidence, ability or insight, which in turn can be caused by a lack of organizational capabilities, skills or resources.

Gap 3: Factors causing a difference between service quality specification and what is actually delivered.

This gap refers to the difference between service quality specification and the service delivery actually undertaken. This occurs primarily when employees are unable or unwilling to perform the service at the level designated by the organization. Factors accounting for the degree of difference between design and delivery standard are varied but they are all associated with some aspect of the firm's operations and in particular service personnel management.

- Teamwork – Inadequate teamwork is reflected in the lack of co-operation with colleagues or managers, and the extent to which employees feel personally involved or committed to the service role;
- Employee–job fit – Lack of employee-job fit reflects the extent to which an employee is unable to perform the service adequately. Is the employee suited for the job?
- Technology–job fit – The appropriateness and adequacy of the tools or technology employees use to perform their service roles;
- Perceived control – The extent to which employees perceive they are in control of their jobs and have the necessary flexibility to serve their customers;
- Supervisory control – Output control systems (i.e. number of customers served) are often inappropriate for measuring employee performance relating to delivering quality service;
- Role conflict – Role conflicts may occur when employees are expected to cross-sell services to the customer while the time to serve a customer is limited. Employees may be torn between the company's expectations and the desire to serve the customer;
- Role ambiguity – Employees may be uncertain about what management expects from them with regard to their job and efforts, and how to satisfy those expectations. Employees should have an accurate understanding of what is expected from them.

Obviously, organizing a service company internally is a very complex matter, in which a variety of interests and relationships play a role. Despite this complexity, managers must try to stimulate employees to function as a team to achieve high quality service delivery. Management must therefore create conditions for a maximum job performance. Role conflict and role ambiguity do not contribute to job satisfaction and thus lead to low quality performance.

Gap 4: Factors causing a difference between what is communicated to customers and what is actually delivered.

This gap mainly results from management's propensity to over promise. Customer expectations are enhanced by external communications but these must be accurate. If, after a service encounter the customer is disappointed because the promised service did not match the service delivered then the disconfirmation of the customer's expectations and therefore dissatisfaction is entirely the organization's fault. In addition, ineffective horizontal communication between employees responsible for the company's external communication and advertising, and operational personnel within an organization, may result in inaccurate instructions and procedures for front office employees. These employees should have a clear and timely understanding of the promises made in the advertising campaign, to be able to deliver the service that matches the image presented (and know them before they are communicated to the customers).

SERVICE PRACTICE 5.3

These are examples of communications gone wrong which have caused customer complaints:

Description: 'Fitness Suite'
Reality: Two ancient rowing machines in a basement

Description: 'State of the art presentation equipment'
Reality: A flip chart and an overhead projector

Description: Within easy reach of the airport
Reality: An hour by taxi

Description: Business facilities
Reality: Complimentary hotel stationery and a payphone

Some Criticisms of SERVQUAL

Despite and probably because of the dominance of this approach to service quality there have been many criticisms of the SERVQUAL. These have ranged between authors' overall rejection of the approach on philosophical grounds to small technical disagreements mainly about measurement and the ability to reproduce some of the results. Buttle (1996) summarized these criticisms and suggested two overall sets of issues: theoretical and operational. We present them here to provide a degree of balance; as in service quality just like marketing there are few incontrovertible truths.

Theoretical

Under the theoretical heading, SERVQUAL would appear to be subject to two criticisms. The first is that it is based upon the disconfirmation approach which we discussed above. The problem is that this disconfirmation format also underlies customer satisfaction. Therefore SERVQUAL is actually measuring satisfaction and not quality. This criticism is a difficult one to get around and it has been suggested that this confusion which is at the core of SERVQUAL has contributed to the conceptual confusion surrounding satisfaction and quality. The second criticism is that the outcome of SERVQUAL is not a quality measure *per se*, but is actually a customer attitude to the service measure. Therefore it is not something which should be used by organizations to alter or adjust operations. Finally there is the issue of the gaps, which while 'intuitively appealing'[16] don't actually add anything to our understanding since the differences themselves are very unreliable and are artificially derived.

One variation upon SERVQUAL which suggested an alternative approach was published by Cronin and Taylor in 1992. This criticism was highly theoretical and highly significant although it has achieved less notoriety. The essential difference is the absence of expectations in the SERVPERF model which ignores the disconfirmation approach. According to this research, service quality is best measured only by the perceived performance of the service on the same 22 items and follows the 'service quality as attitude' approach. In terms of application Cronin and Taylor also allow for what they term a weighted SERVPERF. This may provide an opportunity for applying different weights to the 22 service attributes.

Operational
The main issues under operational criticisms are associated with measurement. The first thing to note is that the measurement of expectations is central to this model but the lack of clear definition, the volatility of expectations over time and the imprecision of the form of expectation as they relate to a service event make the core of the model highly unstable. Added to this are the practical issues of a dual administration, i.e. asking the questions of the same people twice, can lead to confusion and boredom; the lack of scale labelling for points 2–6, which may promote polarity of answers; and the model looks to be not as stable as first thought. Critics go on to point out that the explanatory power of the model in terms of variances extracted all point to some degree of imprecision in measurement. Organizations implementing this approach must also consider the importance of the service dimensions. For instance in legal services there may be a tendency for customers to weight the décor more highly than empathy. If the service environment looks like a lawyer's office, then this may be more important to the perception of service quality than aspects of the lawyer's interaction. Clearly each service context is likely to have different attribute weights and these may need to be generated from independent research.

The criticisms can be summarized as:

■ the basic question of whether it is necessary to measure expectations at all;[17]
■ the way expectations are measured;[18]
■ the reliability and validity of using difference scores;[19]
■ the dimensionality of SERVQUAL;[20]
■ the number of items in the SERVQUAL scale.[21]

The SixSigma Model of Service Quality

An alternative way to look at service quality is essentially to ignore it and to focus upon what is really important, customer satisfaction. Many organizations have come to the conclusion that pursuing service quality as a managerial input and then putting it together with a model for assessing service quality outputs such as SERVQUAL is just too difficult. What is really required is a consistently inductive model where customer satisfaction drives the service delivery. It is no good for example specifying delivery of documentation within three working days, measuring your performance against that measure and focussing resources upon ensuring performance if customers don't think it's important. By using customers to continually update the quality drivers of a service this approach ensures the changing drivers of quality among customers are reflected in organizational activity.

SixSigma relates to the elimination of defects and you will recognize this approach from our summaries of different quality definitions. The aim is to achieve six sigma deviations from the mean which represents 3.4 defects per million. The reason for its inclusion here is that defects have been broadly defined to include defects in service process, and within the methodology the critical driver is not just to perform without fault but to perform according to customer determined criteria.

SixSigma is a highly structured and integrated programme for developing customer orientated business processes. The method was developed by Motorola in the 1980s after engineers had concluded that the ability to produce zero defects was one thing but that the outcome of a zero defects product might not actually satisfy their customers, which would rather defeat the object of zero defects in the first place. Therefore both quality and customer requirements had to be integrated into a single approach and the link between them was the service process.

SERVICE PRACTICE 5.4

When, applying the SixSigma method to their sales department, CCG Pty Ltd discovered that the critical to quality attribute according to customers was 'receiving the correct order', the company worked backwards to determine the impact of incorrect orders, such as incorrect inventory levels, customer complaint handling, reordering, etc. The company then invested in their order systems to allow customers to place orders directly and verify the order before dispatch. This reduced cost significantly, but at the same time improved customer satisfaction.

The key thought is to map the specific processes involved in delivering service to the customer. Hence a large part of the SixSigma approach is process mapping. There are many possible approaches to process mapping, including blueprinting, system mapping and information tracking. While grounded in manufacturing, its application has spread to many large service organizations and over the next few years is likely to emerge among some of the major global service providers. The method is based upon a five-part process: define, measure, analyse, improve and control (DMAIC), with the first stage dependent upon a 'critical to quality' (CTQ) metric which is the customer's definition of what is most relevant to them. For instance if getting food within 15 minutes of an order is critical for a restaurant then the order process is engineered to achieve that end. The organization determines which activities drive the CTQs and works backwards through their processes to analyse their systems, set performance metrics and implement process controls to ensure customer orientated performance.

SERVICE PRACTICE 5.5

Example (DMAIC) for a House Cleaning Service

Define: What defects are there in our house cleaning service? Which is the defect most complained about?
The company has detected that many customers are dissatisfied with the quality of the floor cleaning on tiled surfaces. After cleaning a white dusty residue is evident.

Measure: Why does this occur? How big a problem is this?
Examine how many houses have tiled floors, find out what products are used by the cleaners and possibly understand when and how often tile floors are cleaned. Compare this with the incidence of complaint.

Analyse: Examine the data to identify any unusual patterns

Following the data collection, one cleaner who has a large number of tile floors has no complaints, in fact many compliments about the quality of the cleaning work on tiled surfaces.

Improve: What can we do to improve overall quality?

The company got the cleaner to explain how the tiles were washed and what the cleaner did to get such a great finish. This was then communicated to all other cleaners.

Control: How can we ensure that the improvement is maintained?

All cleaners and new employees were issued with a cleaning manual that specified the best cleaning approach for different types of floor finish. Complaints re tiled floors reduced by 80% and customer satisfaction with cleaning service rose by 63%.

The impact of the method has been significant with clear contribution toward profitability and customer satisfaction. In a very real sense SixSigma captures and resolves a lot of shortcomings noted in the service quality literature. Notice the explicit link between what an organization does in terms of service performance (actual service delivery) and customer satisfaction. Note also how the method automatically includes performance measures and more importantly implicitly includes an element of return on investment. The implementation of SixSigma has been championed by major corporations and a significant amount of support material has been produced to aid in implementation.

5.5 Managerial Issues Associated with Service quality

So far we have considered some of the approaches to quality, applied them to service quality and examined some of the main models used to understand service quality. In the next section we look at some of the managerial implications of service quality such as how customer data can be collected, designing a simple audit tool and some fundamental questions about the financial implications of pursuing a service quality approach.

Collecting customer data

Today, more and more organizations practise customer research to detect whether customers are satisfied with the service delivered, providing opportunities to change the service delivery, if needed. In this way, it is possible to really improve quality. Important indicators to be investigated include loyalty, repeat purchases, cross-selling, satisfaction, complaints and compliments received. Complaints always receive a lot of attention in quality programmes. In order to get this kind of information, customers should express their opinions, attitudes, satisfaction, dissatisfaction, etc. Complaints are an important source of information. The number and nature of complaints gives an indication of the quality perception of customers.

If the registration and analysis of complaints are performed properly, the service provider can determine which aspects of the quality perception do not meet customer expectations and adjust them. It can also be determined upon which aspects of quality management the focus should be set for the next few months.

However, a problem is that not everyone who has had bad experiences or was dissatisfied will voice a complaint. As we saw in Chapter 3, a high proportion, if not the majority, will not complain but simply never use the service again. Therefore, it is not possible to control quality on the basis of complaint registration only. In addition to other sources (for example, customer research), complaint information is essential: for dissatisfied customers, it is easy to express the reasons for their discontent. Satisfied customers will find it more difficult to describe why they are satisfied.

SERVICE PRACTICE 5.6[22]

In a recent study of restaurant complaints in Hong Kong the most cited motive to complain was to 'seek corrective action', followed by 'ask for an explanation' and 'seek an apology'. Surprisingly 'seek compensation' and 'seek redress' did not feature highly. In the initial emotionally charged situation of complaining about a service it is important for managers to explain what happened, make it right and apologize rather than worry about compensating customers or giving them a discount on their meal.

Some cautionary points about driving service quality through complaints have to be made. The first is that the objective is not necessarily to reduce complaints, i.e. more complaints doesn't necessarily mean you have low quality – it could in fact be the reverse. Some organizations actively pursue complaints, with rewards and incentives to increase the number of people coming forward. Why? Because this allows the organization to adapt on a short time scale to investigate service quality failings, and means that the customer feels that their dissatisfaction has been heard and acted upon. The second cautionary note is that complaints tend not to be very representative since only 10% of customers generally voice complaints. As a consequence changing the service at the behest of a complainer can risk alienating the rest of the customer base. Finally complaints and dissatisfaction generally will always be present and may to a degree be a normal part of market adjustment. Specifically your service may be targeted to a different segment, hence those that come to you inadvertently have a higher propensity toward dissatisfaction.

Many techniques can be used to detect satisfaction and dissatisfaction about services. Usually, questionnaires are used to gain a general insight. These will normally have a rating scale which allows organizations to track aspects of their service delivery over time. Chakrapani (1998) summarized some of the measurement problems associated with service quality research which are worth reviewing. Qualitative research may be very useful here.

Comparative Service Quality

If customers get poor service from all competitors in an industry then poor service is the norm. Any attempt to measure relative performance will be thwarted since any scoring will regress toward the mean, i.e. scores will tend to 5 and 6 on a 10-point scale. This does not indicate that the service received is 'average' in relative terms; just that customers see mediocre service as 'normal' and are accustomed to it. In some industries the situation is even more confusing where, because of long experience in one form of delivery, any attempt to improve the service immediately results in a lower performance score because consumers are moved out of their comfort zone and are required to 'learn' the new service.

Satisfaction

Any service provision will generate a segment of satisfied customers, which automatically inflates the mean satisfaction score across all customers. Since all customers do not demand or expect the same level of service, there will be some whose expectations are so low that they are quite satisfied. Depending upon the market this may be a sizeable group again thwarting any argument to improve or invest in a service on the basis of dissatisfaction.

Perception

It is difficult to get customers to identify what would conceivably constitute great service because they rarely think outside their current experience. This problem has been identified before especially in new product development, where an innovation once introduced is highly regarded but before it was introduced no one mentioned it as desirable. This is a real problem in new service development.

Culture

Many large global organizations adopt universal service quality standards which then allows for ease of management and comparison across countries. Service quality perceptions and expectations will differ from country to country and therefore there is a contradiction between standardized customer surveys which are suitable for global comparison.

Mid Points

For many customers a service is satisfactory, i.e. it meets all their requirements and they are happy. Applying a 10-point scale to this situation is difficult since customers tend to rate a service at say 5 points out of 10 to indicate that they are effectively ambivalent, i.e. not 'dissatisfied' but also not 'overly delighted'. This confusion in terminology is difficult to break since we assume that a satisfied customer will put down a 10 out of 10 rating and this effect deflates true service quality measurement.

Return on Quality

There is a consistent theme throughout the literature on service quality and reflected in practitioner interest and activity that the pursuit of quality service will bring with it happy and loyal customers. These customers in turn will spend a greater share of wallet, carry your reputation far and wide through word of mouth and keep coming back. This tacit understanding is characteristic of many management and marketing initiatives but the question for managers is whether in fact the pursuit of service excellence actually delivers. More simply does more money spent mean more quality delivered, and is this true for every level of expenditure? The answers to these questions have only recently been pursued under the heading 'return on quality'. Put simply, quality costs money and pursuing ever higher levels of quality may not in fact deliver any benefits, only higher cost. The first study to consider return on quality (ROQ) and provide some measurable performance of service quality improvements relative to investment was conducted by Rust, Zahorik and Keiningham in 1995. In order to provide an operational method for linking quality and a financial return they stated four principles:

Quality is an Investment

Organizations undertake expenditure on staff training, process mapping, complaint handling and service specification in order to secure a return. As such the initial expenditure is made to secure an outcome.

Quality Efforts Must be Financially Accountable

Funds to invest in service quality has an opportunity cost, i.e. if we spend money on improving the quality of service we can't spend it on buildings, shareholders' dividends or advertising and promotion. Therefore any organization needs to be clear about why they are spending money on service quality and the appropriateness of the expenditure. In operational terms the expenditures must be financially defensible.

It is Possible to Spend Too Much on Quality

Across a large organization the sums involved in the pursuit of service quality can be large. The question that must be asked is whether the customer actually detects the improvements. You can think of investment in staff and training, a good service environment and competent technology to secure a rise in perceived service quality. However, is the additional expenditure on fresh flowers at reception, staff uniforms with gold buttons and the very latest computers actually going to raise perceived quality any higher?

Not All Quality Expenditures Are Equally Valid

Service quality is a combination of many things and investment in each component must be judged according to its impact upon overall service quality. Different customer groups weigh different aspects of the service differently and we know that sometimes small innovative investments, such as free samples of food, giveaway pens and even the gift of the comb used while cutting your hair can enhance the perception of quality in different service settings.

The ROQ approach relies upon evidencing a link between service quality and a series of performance criteria such as customer satisfaction, share of wallet, market share or revenue. This is achieved through quasi experimentation, such as tracking customer satisfaction in a single location and manipulating an aspect of the service delivery. A whole series of these allow for the specification of simple relationships. The analysis then provides a series of linked effects; for instance, improved satisfaction leads to higher retention, which provides higher share of wallet and increased profitability. The process of implementing ROQ also relies upon a series of steps starting with a preliminary audit which includes customer data relating to the current market offering, a market analysis looking at competitor offerings and broad market descriptors.

The second stage is an opportunity analysis, using the data gathered in step one to identify where improvements to the market offer can be made. This is especially important in areas of the service where a competitor's customers rate quality more highly than your own. The opportunities identified must then be financially valued to asses the required investment and the likely return. The third step is to undertake a small test of the quality improvement identified possibly using an experiment. For instance in one store you might decide to get your service personnel to recite a welcome script, and test whether this improves the quality perceived. Using this data we can move to the fourth step where the organization can assess a range of pretested initiatives whose performance is measured using a variety of financial and market metrics such as yield, revenue lift per customer, market share and penetration, etc. Finally the initiatives chosen can be rolled out with clear metrics on likely cost, revenue performance, profitability and a final retune on quality metric.

5.6 Strategic Issues in Managing Service Quality

In this section we consider some broad strategic issues which managers need to be aware of in their pursuit of service quality. These have been grouped under three headings: market segmentation, competitor intelligence and resources.

Market Segmentation

It is possible to identify market segments with quite different service quality expectations. Many managers overlook this fact when reviewing service quality initiatives. Quite simply it may be that the segmentation approach is too broad and the expectation variation within each segment too wide. As a consequence no amount of adjustment to the service will satisfy everyone equally. As a consequence a regular review of the positioning of the service offering needs to be undertaken. This review will also need to assess general improvements in expectations. One of the often cited problems of great service companies is that quality improvements serve to raise customer expectations to a point where they are unsustainable. You can imagine trying to outdo customer expectations every time they transact with you in order to secure satisfaction but eventually you can go no further. In these circumstances it is important to identify neglected areas of service, which provide opportunities to positively surprise customers, thereby maintaining interest.)

Competitor Intelligence

By measuring customer satisfaction about competitor' services, further insight into the relative position of competitors can be gained. Remember it is not illegal or unethical to ask questions about competitors' market offerings and this is sometime overlooked. Market research can identify those aspects of service quality where you are higher or lower than your competitors and can provide useful strategic input when deciding upon long-term investment or development plans. This however is a relatively formal process and managers should not overlook the opportunity to use their own personal experience as a basis of market intelligence. The key issue is not to fall into a responsive strategic posture where you end up copying or replicating competitor activity. The advantage in pursuing your own customer research and your own service quality response is that your market positioning is difficult for others to replicate. In service quality terms it is better to base your quality improvements upon close dialogue with customers than upon close dialogue with competitors.

Resources

So far in considering service quality we haven't touched upon the issue of resources, specifically the trade-off between human and technological. When we think of services we automatically think of people, restaurant staff, doctors, etc. There is no doubt that the people part of the service is a critical one. In this respect service quality is ultimately driven by people, specifically your service personnel, and even the most carefully specified and managed services can fail where people aren't fully involved in quality initiatives. Simple things from the human resources management domain, such as incentives, working conditions, good team management and reliable technical support, can make big differences to service quality and customer satisfaction in the short term. In the long term, having committed, well-trained and motivated staff reduces recruitment costs, reduces training costs, improves corporate knowledge and builds stable customer relationships. However, we shouldn't overlook the emergence of technological solutions to the service quality problem. One of technology's side effects is that in order to operate it requires very clear task specification. Think of your local ATM; it does a few things but it does them well and reliably 24/7 which is a high quality service for those tasks it can undertake. There has been increasing pressure upon organizations to utilize vending type machines, Internet sites and e-commerce applications as cheaper and more reliable options for service delivery of simple tasks and thus creating no or fewer variations in service quality of standardized core services. This leaves expensive human staff more time to deal with more complex service tasks in augmented customized services. Ultimately the decision about the human/technology mix must be dependent upon your customers' reaction and the service dimensions they value.

SERVICE PRACTICE 5.7[23]

SDL

With an increasing number of companies trading internationally, there has been a corresponding extension of supply chains to target customers across the world. Research would suggest that customers are four times more likely to buy a product presented to them in their own language. With the opportunities for extending into more diverse geographic areas offered by Internet ordering and delivery the ability to target customer groups with communications in their own language has increased the demand for global translation services.

SDL Sheffield Ltd runs one of the largest translation services in the world. Translating about 150 languages, it specializes in delivering a high quality, fast turnaround service to companies engaged in overseas trade. In order to improve its service quality the company wanted to offer an even faster service but also to lower its costs allowing them to make the service attractive to a larger market by offering lower price translation to small businesses. Traditionally someone needing a translation service would identify a company through a telephone directory or by recommendation, would call a translator, describe the job, wait for a quote, negotiate a price and then send off the text or recording. The objective was to improve service quality by offering instant quotes and instant submission of materials thereby speeding up the service.

SDL developed Click2Translate.com, a website which offers instant online ordering and pricing of translation services with facilities for file upload and storage. The company offers three levels of service: instant machine translation, edited machine translation and premium priced professional services. Customers merely upload the document or digital files, select the required language they wish to translate from and into, select their desired level of service and get an instanteous price and delivery date.

The success of Click2Translate.com has seen the business grow by 100% and opened up new areas of business including employee manuals, mobile phone games and website translation. By careful analysis of the number of steps required to place an order, process time was further reduced with an increase in service quality and customer satisfaction.

Source: Department of Trade and Industry, *www.dti.gov.uk* Crown Copyright material is reproduced with permission of HMSO and the Queen's Printer for Scotland

5.7 Service Failure and Recovery

This chapter has dealt with service quality and has highlighted the importance of customer perception as well as organizational action in maintaining customer satisfaction. However we must also recognize that services are variable and that some customers will believe that the service quality was below that which they expected. This is termed a service failure. Solving customer complaints satisfactory is an essential part of a market oriented service provider. There is also a financial argument to do so. It has been shown that the stock market value of Spanish banks decreases significantly once their names are published in an annual report of the Spanish Central Bank because the Central Bank has received complaints about those banks.[24] Research has indicated that service failures emanate from many different areas of the service but three categories of failure were identified.[25]

Failures in the Delivery System

These failures refer to a specific set of outcomes which link the service process to service personnel. In simple terms the service fails to deliver but the critical point is how employees actually respond to these events. The three dominant failures which emerged from the research were, first, service unavailability (i.e. a desk which is closed, a facility that has broken down or no longer available). Slow service refers to queues, unreasonable delay or simply a staff member wasting time. The third category was core service failures, i.e. things which went to the heart of the service, a train breaking down, baggage being lost, undercooked food, etc. Quite often this refers to the technical quality discussed above.

Failures in Response to Customer Requests

These failures were split into two distinct types. The first are 'explicit requests' and relate to special medical or dietary needs, expressed preferences such as seating in a restaurant, customer errors such as a lost key or PIN number, and disruptive events such as those associated with other customers. The more interesting category is 'implicit requests'. Here the customer may expect the service personnel to understand that they need something but it is not forthcoming. For example if you spill a drink in a restaurant you might expect the service personnel to bring you a cloth without you asking. Similarly in business services if a machine breaks down you might expect them to come and fix it even if you don't specifically tell them to. So, this may hinge upon technical and functional qualities.

Failure through Employee Actions

The final category of failure refers to unexpected actions on behalf of the employees. Service personnel may display a lack of attention to the customer, may display behaviour perceived to be dismissive, unfair, dishonest or just rude. Often service personnel may deliver all the necessary components of the delivery process but do so with a 'don't care' attitude and that is enough for the customer to arrive at the conclusion that the service has failed. Thus a bad functional or technical quality.

Despite the academic research in this area we can probably think of a thousand different examples of where services have gone wrong. In simple terms we respond to failure by attribution, assessment and action.

Attribution

Attribution describes the process of allocating blame – whose fault is it? It may be that we blame the service personnel, we may blame the service process and feel sorry for the service provider, and we may blame ourselves because we failed to do something. Alternatively we might blame the failure on something or someone outside the organization's control.

Assessment

Once we have determined blame we then make an assessment of the severity of the failure. Some failure we blame upon the service provider but decide that it isn't really important and do nothing about it. Alternatively we might think the failure is very important and want some form of redress.

Action

The third aspect of response to service failure is what to do about it; this is action. We may walk out never to return; we might cancel an order and never do business with the firm again. We might complain or engage in service disruption or other forms of retaliation.

As managers we have to accept that if a customer thinks the service has failed then it has failed. This issue for the manager is whether they can do something about it. Many customers who believe that a service failure has taken place will not communicate that to the service provider. Despite all the organization's attempts to find out whether we are happy, we often hide our dissatisfaction. It is estimated that only 10% of customers who are unhappy will communicate or 'voice' that dissatisfaction to the organization but 90% of those who don't complain will complain to friends, family or colleagues. So the first issue is getting customers to communicate to your company. This might be via feedback questionnaires, random polling, follow-up phone calls, or even simply talking to clients.

Let's assume that a customer has voiced a complaint and now a response must be made. This is the service recovery phase. To make an effective recovery effort, organizations need to know their customer.

Execute Recovery Appropriately

Specifically, they have to execute recovery appropriately. Service failures will affect all customers but some customers are more important to you than others. If you know how important they are, you can avoid the situation where a low value customer gets great recovery, while a high value customer gets poor recovery and never comes back. Some firms, especially in business-to-business markets, keep a score or rating system for customers, which allows them to choose appropriate responses to failure which are measured by cost or as a proportion of expected revenue or income per period. In many instances customers don't require anything more than an apology or an explanation of what happened and too often organizations go to excessive lengths to reimburse customers and forget the apology. It is important therefore to know what the customer expects.

Treat Recovery as a Process

From the organization's point of view, service recovery efforts are a process. They should start with an immediate response; the faster a firm responds to the problem the better the recovery message to the customer. This has implications for the amount of discretion. Employees have to deduct items from a bill, provide replacement services or compensation. The next stage is to investigate why the failure occurred and whether there is something that can be done to avoid it happening again. Finally, the customer should be contacted again to explain what happened and to reassure them that it won't happen again. This learning and reassurance cycle is often ignored with organizations assuming a quick response and an apology is enough. And then the customer gets even more angry, perceives increased injustice and becomes even more dissatisfied. Then it is for sure: this really is a lost customer. A 'double deviation' scenario should be avoided.[26]

5.8 Service Guarantees

Over the last few years service organizations have started to adopt the idea of a customer service guarantee.[27] Guarantees have been around for a long time and traditionally were promises to replace goods or to refund money when faulty goods were returned. This idea is not so easily applied to services. Suppose you were getting your hair cut and the cut you received was bad. Would you want that hairdresser to do it again? Probably not. If a consultant was employed by your company to undertake a specific project and they didn't do a good job, would you want them to have another go? Probably not. Service guarantees are usually framed in terms of monetary compensation and are closely linked to overall service quality performance. Research by Hart (1988) and Hart, Schlesinger and Maher (1992) concluded that service guarantees can provide management with a mechanism to provide superior service quality, respond quickly to changes in market demand and solve service problems quickly and cheaply. By using guarantees, firms are able to learn from customer complaints, are forced to respond to customer feedback and are able to monitor failures. It has been suggested that any guarantee must be unconditional, easy to understand and communicate, easy to invoke and the outcome easy to collect so that they offer real value to the customer. There are three types of guarantees that are used in relation to services.

Implicit Guarantees

These are unspoken and unwritten but nevertheless represent an agreement between an organization and its customers. They might be based upon past practice, such as responding to complaints, getting compensation, returning goods or where possible repeating the service for free. The fact that the guarantees are not explicit suggests that there is a spirit of co-operation and mutuality and is a very powerful benefit. However, they can also have their drawbacks; specifically they take time to develop, can be abused by customers and if not respected can terminally impact upon the firm's reputation.

Outcome Guarantees

These relate to specific service outcomes rather than apply to the service as a whole. The benefit of these outcome guarantees is that they can be linked directly to service quality efforts. For example in SixSigma programmes the CTQ events can form the basis of explicit customer guarantees. The type of outcome guarantees vary greatly by sector but those such as Domino Pizzas 'delivery in 20 minutes otherwise its free' or the FEDEX 'overnight delivery' are most recognizable. The drawback to these guarantees is that they can appear pretty trivial to customers and can suggest that the firm is only confident about certain specific aspects of its service.

Unconditional Guarantees

This service guarantee promises complete customer satisfaction and full refunds or no cost solutions. These guarantees are very powerful marketing tools and communicate complete confidence in the service. If the value of a guarantee is measured by its reduction in the perceived risk of failure then this form is the most likely to encourage customers to transact. The benefit to the firm is that they have to monitor and deliver to a customer determined service quality to avoid expensive payouts. Similarly where the guarantee is invoked these circumstances can be used to learn more about how to improve the service such that it is always optimal. However as you can anticipate, there are some drawbacks. As a completely open ended guarantee some customers can abuse them and the firm has little opportunity to discriminate between real and bogus claims. Other drawbacks may be the suggestion that the firm is desperate, is trying to recover from a catastrophe or has to charge a lot for their service so that they can afford to pay out under any circumstance.

Service Practice 5.8 is an example of an unconditional guarantee from a bank, SouthTrust. The guarantee is notable in that each guarantee component is backed up with a payment. The issue here is whether the guarantee is so unconditional that it encourages 'cheating'. Certain individuals will always cheat on unconditional guarantees such as this.[28] This behaviour has been identified as a major obstacle to more generous service guarantees.[29]

SERVICE PRACTICE 5.8[30]

SouthTrust Satisfaction Guaranteed

We realize that no one is perfect, however, we do have high expectations of ourselves. When we don't deliver to our high standards, we feel we owe you a full and satisfactory recovery.

We guarantee:

☐ Accuracy. If you find a mistake we've made, let us know. We'll correct the error and credit your account $10. This includes errors on any transaction, statement or check order.

☐ Responsiveness. If you have questions or problems with any SouthTrust account, call or come by. If we cannot answer immediately, we promise to follow up with you by the end of the day, or we'll credit your account $5.

☐ Reliability. If a SouthTrust ATM is out of service when you try to access your SouthTrust account, just tell us when and where. We'll credit your account $3.

☐ Courtesy. If you feel one of our representatives has been less than courteous, please notify the manager so we can address the situation. Additionally, you will receive $5.

Summary

At the beginning of this chapter we considered the nature of the trade-off that organizations have to make in any decision to pursue quality. We also know that the characteristics of services make quality particularly difficult to define in relation to services. However when service managers talk about service quality they do so by drawing upon a range of established quality perspectives which were summarized as transcendent-based quality, attribute-based quality, user-based quality, manufacturing-based quality and value-based quality. These approaches are all reflected in how service managers approach the problem of service quality. However there are still some areas where there is a degree of confusion and despite the large amount of research published the relationship between service quality and customer satisfaction is still not firmly established. We suggested that the only real distinction is that service quality is an attribute of the organization's market offer, whereas satisfaction is the individual customer's reaction to that offer.

Having discussed the main conceptual issues, definition and scope we then moved on the look at four different service quality models. The first is the disconfirmation model in which service quality is directly related to customer satisfaction. In this model quality is implied if the customers' expectations of the service experience beforehand are exceeded by the service when it is delivered. The second model was a slight variation which described different types of service attributes, i.e. functional qualities and technical qualities, and that we must distinguish in our deliberations of service quality between what a service delivers relative to how it was delivered. Third, we looked at SERVQUAL, the main service quality approach you will find in the academic literature. This is a combination of different parts, taking in disconfirmation and different service attributes and linking them together with management activity through a gaps framework. Finally we briefly described the SixSigma approach to quality, which is an organizational change model driven by customer demand.

In the final section we looked at some managerial issues associated with service quality; specifically the problems associated with collecting customer data and the problems which have to be recognized when analysing customer responses. Staying in the managerial domain we consider the problems of balancing service quality with profitability through the ROQ approach. Finally we considered a series of strategic issues which are often ignored and which we consider are critical to implementing service quality.

Questions

1. Name the five approaches to quality presented by Garvin (1988).
2. What approach to quality is implicit in the SERVQUAL model?
3. What is the difference between service quality and satisfaction?
4. What are the two components of the disconfirmation model?

5. What drives the formation of expectations?
6. Explain what is meant by asymmetry in respect of technical and functional service attributes.
7. What does RATER stand for?
8. Which gap in the SERVQUAL approach deals with differences between service quality specification and actual service delivery?
9. What does DMAIC stand for in the SixSigma approach?
10. Name three forms of service guarantee.

Assignments

1. Find as many definitions of quality as you can. Make a list of the common words used and see if you can come up with a better definition.
2. Think of a recent visit to a retail store, and on a piece of paper prepare two separate columns. In one column write down those things which you liked about the service you received. In the other column write down those things which you disliked about the service you received. If you were the manager of the store how would you resolve the items on the 'dislike' list?
3. Choose a service organization in your locality that you are unfamiliar with and list your expectations about the service you would receive. Put a score against each of the expectation items. If you can, visit the company and score the service you actually received.
4. Categorize functional and technical qualities for three different services. Do you agree that the relationship between them is asymmetrical?
5. Design a service guarantee for your services course. Include elements of compensation for any failures. Now, view yourself as the provider of the course. What changes would you make if any?

Endnotes

1 Parasuraman, Zeithaml and Berry, 1985.

2 Juran, 1974.

3 Crosby, 1983.

4 Zeithaml, Parasuraman and Berry, 1990.

5 If we were lucky enough to stay at the Dorchester or travel first class on an airline and we received excellent service and were totally satisfied, then we could say that in that instance service quality and satisfaction are synonymous for us.

6 Oliver, 1980.

7 Grönroos, 1982a, 1982b.

8 Parasuraman, Zeithaml and Berry, 1988.

9 Miller, 1979.

10 See Woodruff, Cadotte and Jenkins, 1983.

11 See Rust, Zahorik and Keiningham, 1995.

12 Grönroos, 1982a, p. 43.

13 Gabbott and Hogg, 1995.

14 Teas, 1993.

15 This section is heavily based on upon the references listed in Grönroos, 1990b, pp. 58–65 and on Zeithaml, Bitner and Gremmler, 2005.

16 Babakus and Boller, 1992.

17 See Cronin and Taylor, 1992.

18 See Teas, 1993.

19 Teas, 1993.

20 See Grönroos, 1984.

21 See Buttle, 1996, and the overview in Kasper *et al.*, 1999.

22 Heung and Lam, 2003.

23 Adapted from www.dti.gov.uk/bestpractice 2005.

24 See Casado Diaz, 2005.

25 Bitner *et al.*, 1990.

26 Casado Diaz, 2005.

27 See Fabien, 2005.

28 Wirtz and Kum, 2004.

29 Chu, Gerstner and Herst, 1998.

30 http://www.southtrust.com/st/aboutus/QualityService, accessed June 2005.

Chapter 6

Market Strategies for Service Organizations

More power.

There's a new global standard in express delivery, freight and logistics. DHL can now offer you more performance, more service and more options in more than 220 countries. So whatever your needs, we can meet them. Visit us at **www.dhl.com** to get the power of DHL behind your business.

Reproduced by permission of DHL International

6.1   Introduction

Turbulence in a Relaxing Industry[1]

Thanks to a rising tide of aging Baby Boomers who are determined to look good as long as they can, the US spa business has been surging since the 1990s. The business includes a broad range of facilities from day spas to hotel spas and luxurious spa resorts. The number of spas has been growing at a very fast rate the past few years. However, recently the US spa industry has become a very competitive industry, the business is consolidating, it was hit hard by the 11 September terror attacks. Consequently, it isn't a relaxing experience to these service providers anymore.

In 2000, North Castle Partners, a private equity firm, bought the US chain of Elizabeth Arden Salons and Day Spas as well as the Chicago-based 26-store Mario Tricoci Hair Salons & Day Spas. The Arden clientele consisted of socialites and other affluent women. While Arden's business mostly revolved around massages and facials, Tricoci's expertise was in trendy haircuts, manicures and pedicures. North Castle Partners acknowledged the trend for spas, the democratization of the day-spa industry (the industry is attracting more men, more younger – working women and a different kind of middle aged woman than the traditional Arden clientele) and the preferences of the increasing number of Baby Boomers. They intended to transform its spas from hair salons that offer a few extra services into something more akin to mini luxury hotels. However, developing and implementing a new strategy, the integration of the two companies and the creation of a successful chain of spas has proved to be a big challenge, especially in this era. Problems that occurred refer to a wide range of issues.

Executives of the two companies tussled over who was in charge as the two operations struggled to integrate. Mr David Stoup, the former CEO of Arden, was responsible for running the combined operation, while Mr. Tricoci, the founder of his own business, was made president, reporting to Mr Stoup. These two men quite often disagreed. There was a lack of focus and too many chiefs. North Castle executives seemed to favour Tricoci because it was more profitable than Arden. The individual spa operations were much more rationalized, for instance by discouraging spa workers from talking directly with clients when they weren't rubbing, buffing or polishing. Employees did not like this way of working.

One goal of this rationalization was to encourage loyalty to the spa itself, rather than to individual employees (because the company recognized that if employees left, they could take clients with them once the personal bond was too strong).

The 11 September attacks led to a sharp slowdown in the business and in difficulties in securing new financing to help meet growth targets, including a fast growth in outlets. In 2001 Mr Stoup stood aside to Mr Richards, a former top executive of the Four Seasons Hotels Inc. chain and Starbucks Corp. Mr Richard's new strategy focusses on improving the results of the Arden part of the company with less dependence on independent-minded hair stylists and selling more profitable spa services. They target more men who are more likely to opt for premium services when buying gifts, like gift certificates. Arden also introduced a centralized online booking system and a rewards program. New spas that will be opened the coming years will be named 'Red Door' Spas, referring to the portal of Elizabeth Arden's famous Fifth Avenue location, but not explicitly using the Arden brand anymore.

Image, quality and close links with key customers are among the most important key success factors and competitive advantages of service companies. Image is the maintenance of the organization's positioning in the market. This is supported by the actual behaviour of contact personnel, the role of employees, and service quality. Front office employees are the face of the company and as such will have a determining impact on the delivery of quality. Quality is a key driver of strategy within service organizations, and will support the development and implementation of relationship marketing strategies.

The development of strategy is about creating value for the organization's stakeholders, such as the customers, employees and shareholders. This value will arise through the differentiation of your service offering over that of your competitors. This difference can occur in many ways; for example, the content of the service, the way the service is being offered, the employees, the relationships with key customers, the service quality or the niche that you are operating in within in the market. Within this way of reasoning it is quite obvious that this chapter of market strategies is positioned at this moment in our book.

In this chapter we will elaborate on corporate and marketing strategies in service organizations. In particular, we will focus on market strategies. We start with some basic issues about creating value in market oriented service organizations and establishing the link between market orientation and performance. Alongside this we will look at the impact of leadership and social responsibility. That sets the tone for the firm's market orientation which in turn sets the framework for the way value can be created to the customer. The assets and capabilities service companies need to create a competitive advantage and a competitive position will be discussed. All these topics are the basics to build up our view on the strategic pathway; a model used to define the market strategies needed for market oriented service organizations to be different than their competitors. Both generic and marketing strategies build up these market strategies. The service profit chain as well as the balanced score card show the many links between the critical parts of service companies' market strategies (see Figure 6.1).

6.2   Creating value in market oriented service organizations[2]

SERVICE PRACTICE 6.2

Key Success Factors in Services

Service quality, close links with key customers, the company or brand reputation, competitive pricing, performance and speed of reaction to customer requirements are the key success factors of

Figure 6.1   Chapter outline

many European service organizations. In the UK, the market leaders in services actually claim to have a competitive advantage on performance, after sales service, personal selling, quality, close links with key customers and reputation. The Dutch market leaders in services claim to have a competitive advantage especially in reputation, quality, close links with key customers and performance.

When the market leaders are compared to other service firms, it appears that, in the UK, the leaders differ from other service companies in only two respects. The leaders have significantly higher scores on performance and advertising/promotion than the other service firms. In Holland, quite a different picture emerges there, the market leaders have more often a competitive advantage than the other service firms in: company/brand reputation, product/service quality, close links with key customers, distribution coverage, prior market research, advertising and promotion.

The PIMS database (Profit Impact of Marketing Strategy) contains data about service firms in the USA. The most important determinant of success in US service industries is a service company's image and reputation. A positive image can reduce risk and increase market share.[3] Other important conclusions of the analysis of the PIMS data are:

1   Forward integration increases market share and has a significant and positive impact on financial performance;
2   Alternatively, backward integration strategies do not seem to affect a firm's market or financial performance *per se*;
3   Service quality did not have a direct effect on service provider's financial or market results, but it did lower a firm's strategic or business risk;

4 A firm's reputation and service image not only increase market share but also lower business risk. Therefore, it appears that while managerial perceptions of service quality may impact on actual service quality, this study shows that it is the firm's reputation and perceptions of service image that ultimately drive performance;

5 Synergy of business operations and marketing activities increase market share, improve financial performance and lower business risks;

6 High market shares appear to be double-edged swords according to the results of this study. On the one hand, high shares improve the financial position of a firm; on the other hand, they also increase its risk levels;

7 In contrast to conventional wisdom, customizing services actually increases market share; and

8 Sales promotions appear to have a positive effect on firm's risk levels. In contrast, advertising has a negative effect on profitability but has a positive effect on relative market share as it lowers a firm's risk level.[4]

Republished with permission, Emerald Group Publishing Limited. *http://www.emeraldinsight.com/jsm.htm*

Firms are always looking for ways to create a competitive advantage and deliver value to all their stakeholders. Market leaders are constantly looking for ways to 're-invent their business' so as to differentiate their offers as well as to meet their customer needs. Figure 6.2 outlines how market orientation and performance can assist organizations achieve their objectives.

In the services business, market orientation and financial performance are positively linked to each other. The same holds for the link between market orientation and non financial performance. This latter link is even stronger than the first one mentioned, indicating the highly relevant managerial task of securing satisfied employees in a services business, for, one of the most critical non financial performance indicators appeared to be the level of employee satisfaction and retention.[5]

Customers as well as competitors, and the firms' own assets and capabilities are leading in defining market strategies aimed at creating superior value to the customers and other stakeholders. Creating value can be done in various ways. Often, it is based on five principles used to accomplish a lean organization in which all waste is banished and wealth created:[6]

1 Define the value of the service offering from the customer's perspective. The customer's perspective is crucial. It determines what the customer considers as value and warrants spending money on (even if this is counterintuitive to the company).

2 Identify the values streams for each service and service delivery process. Analyse it from a customer's perspective and banish all waste. Analysing the supply chain can be very beneficial here.

3 Organize around processes instead of batching and queuing (e.g. analyse the whole process of coming to a hospital and going through all investigations and tests from the

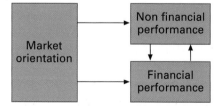

Figure 6.2 Market orientation and performance

patient's perspective and avoid waiting times for the customer during a one-day visit instead of letting the patient return for every test on different days – and wait for months for the outcome of all the tests).

4 Respond quickly to the pull of the product, service or after sales service through the supply chain. Just as in retailing where scanning bar codes offers the opportunity to re-order directly what has been sold, a service employee in a garage or public utility (gas, electricity) may order right away what spare parts have been used in repairing the equipment. We could even go one step further: when we have an idea of what should be replaced, we can order it before we go to the customer. This would decrease storage cost to a very large degree (but could increase delivery cost).

5 The drive to be the best, the pursuit of perfection in all things, to excel (which is a crucial feature of a market oriented service organization).

In such a lean organization all waste is banished and wealth created for the stakeholders. This will not be done automatically; however, the conditions to create value to all stakeholders have been set. One of the present-day requirements to give content to these conditions refers to the concepts of leadership, social responsibility and market orientation in service organizations.

We have stated before that an open, people oriented culture is fundamental to the culture of market oriented service organizations.[7] That contributes to accomplishing the organization's goals to be the best and deliver excellent service quality. What basic traits of leadership are necessary in such organizations?

Leaders in a service organization have a large impact on the company's culture. Many leadership styles can be found in the literature on management and leadership.[8] In general,

market-oriented service organizations probably need leaders (or a team of leaders) acting as employee-oriented leaders with a concern for empowered people, achievement-oriented leaders, democratic or laissez-faire leaders, and leaders with a delegating, participative, supportive or coaching style. Autocratic and instrumental leaders may be typical for non-market-oriented cultures.[9]

However, in routine service delivery processes or in processes where it is important to follow strict procedures or when a lot of guests have to be served a banquet or dinner, quite an autocratic or instrumental, transactional style may be necessary to best serve the customer. Leadership styles are contingent on the situation.

Leadership and the values that are highly valued in service organizations are fundamental to get the employees' commitment to delivering excellent service quality. As Len Berry has found out in his research, great service companies have values or, even better, have a soul, which underlies their strategies and daily actions. Excellent service companies have seven core values in common: excellence, innovation, joy, teamwork, respect, integrity, and social profit.[10] The delivery of these concepts hinges upon effective human resources policy setting the conditions to fully exploit creativity and the drive to be the best by each employee of the organization.

Leaders' and founders' norms and values also determine the service organization's social responsibility. The triple P concept is rather popular. The three Ps are: people, planet and profit. The company's activities are not only directed at accomplishing an appropriate profit for its shareholders and continuity, but should be directed by the three Ps. It has been shown in New Zealand that the more market oriented firms are, the more they have written codes of ethics, guiding employee behaviour.[11] Ethics discussed with respect to the consequences of company actions in many respects, are for instance:

- Not only towards the people in general (are you really getting what you pay for?), but also with respect to serving minorities (especially those with less purchasing power would be confronted with higher interest rates). Think about the dilemma a tour operator may be confronted with when they know particular groups of their customers only want a package tour to Thailand or Brazil just to have sex (especially when it is with children; would you organize a trip for that kind of people?).

- Planet: depletion of resources and pollution of the environment. See for instance discussions in countries like Malaysia or Brazil where the area with rain forest or jungle decreases due to almost unlimited cutting down of trees for reasons of exporting or constructing new highways for economic development and tourism, and where unexpected consequences of landslides or changes in climate occur.

- Politics: varying from discussions on the ethics of lobbying and paying civil servants to get things done to doing business in countries with authoritarian, un-democratic or human rights violating regimes.

- Accounting, book keeping and banking malpractices (because of all the scandals about for instance Enron in the USA, Ahold in Holland, Parmalat in Italy).

- Marketing malpractices (promising more than can be kept in advertising, misleading advertising, misleading trade practices towards consumers, etc.).

One of the issues in discussions on ethics and social responsibility refers to whether it is enough for service companies to just obey the law or whether service companies (or whole service industries) should take responsibility voluntarily and define their standards for appropriate service business practices. Where and when for instance banks, insurance companies, casinos or lotteries do not take responsibility, should the government take corrective action and formulate laws?

   What position managers choose in these discussions is determined not only by industry standards in a particular country but also by their own view of organizing society, their political opinion and their own norms and values. People with broadly left wing views often prefer governmental action quite quickly, while people with right wing views prefer to have the market correct the excesses. In Europe, the European Commission is actively developing policies to protect the customer and fight misleading trade practices. In 2004 the Commission had formulated directives to build a European network of organizations to protect the consumer in all countries of the EU. Cheating the customer may seem to be beneficial in the short run for some service companies to survive in the competitive arena; it will certainly not be viable in the long run.

   While many companies do not use their assets and capabilities to deliver excellent service quality in a market oriented way, the performance of many service organizations would benefit from being (more) market orientated.[12] This is especially important for service organizations as their performance and success depends to a large degree on person-to-person interaction.[13]

   We have seen that starting, building and managing excellent relationships with key customers is one of the essential assets and capabilities of market oriented service organizations. The culture of a market orientated service organization is one that cares about people: customers, competitors, employees, the partners in the distribution channel (suppliers in the supply chain) and the other collaborating organizations such as market research agency, advertising agency and accountancy firms.

Delivering excellent service quality and thus creating value to the customer will lead to better performance, both in terms of financial and non financial indicators. This requires clarity on goals and a well-developed (internal and external) communication policy. Also, market orientation and two other concepts are linked together, namely the learning perspective and the innovation perspective. More market orientation, more learning and more innovation go hand in hand or support each other and will lead to a better performance.[14] But even more factors or contingencies are at stake as shown in the following three examples.

The market orientation of Belgian and Spanish insurance companies is determined not only by one general factor of market orientation they have in common, but also by the unique characteristics of the industry in each country. The Spanish insurance industry for instance has more growth opportunities than the Belgian one, which is reflected for example in a greater competitive rivalry.[15]

In distribution channels:

market orientation is a way of instilling and promoting trust in a channel relationship, which then leads to greater co-operation and commitment. Greater relationship commitment ultimately results in enhanced organizational performance, which then works to further improve market orientation; thus, the cycle continues.[16]

A New Zealand study showed that 'market orientation both has a direct contribution to performance and also contributes through innovation, with innovation mediating the contribution'.[17] Probably the process goes like this: market orientation leads to better market performance, in terms of sales, market share, customer satisfaction that in turn leads to better financial performance. Or, as has been found in the accounting literature: non financial performance indicators (like for instance customer satisfaction) impact heavily on financial performance (like for instance return on investment and profits).[18] Also, market orientation and customer satisfaction are positively correlated: more market orientation and more customer satisfaction go hand in hand.[19]

Usually, the features of existing service organizations are discussed in textbooks. However, many people start their own business in the service industry. What can be said about these start-ups? How do they perform? What challenges do they encounter? Have a look at the following Service Practice 6.3.

SERVICE PRACTICE 6.3

Successful Service Start-Ups[20]

In the period 1995–1998, 1500 people started their own new business in the Maastricht area. In analysing their success or failure, we took a sample of 800; 354 firms responded, of which 27 were not in business anymore. A little more than 43% were active in the business-to-business services sector: consultancy, coaching and training, advertising and communications, direct marketing and mailing services, ICT, software development and book keeping; 9% were in the business-to-consumer services.

The average age of the new entrepreneurs in the services sector was 36 years when they started their own business and 71% were males. Of these, 93% had a middle or higher education degree; most of them had a job and relevant working experience in the business when they started their own company. Some 80% said they were well prepared to start the business due to the consultancy of the Chamber of Commerce in Maastricht; the Chamber was very helpful in developing a business plan, warned of the dangers of starting a business and discouraged people if they had the impression that the risk would be too high.

The main reasons these people gave for wanting to start their own business were: the independence, the challenge, a long-lasting wish to start an own business and a general interest in the field.

The major difficulties at the start were: building the customer base, developing and delivering the service offer, arranging finance, building capital, and managing the administration and finance.

After a few years the major issues to emerge were: the long working hours, problems in hiring the right staff, the physical location and building the customer base.

The qualitative part of the study consisted of 16 personal interviews. Those interviews revealed the three key success factors of these B2B service start ups as:

☐ The network and relations the entrepreneur had when starting the business and to keep it going;
☐ A high level of knowledge of the field (the technical quality);
☐ Customization (customer orientation, flexibility and quality).

Innovation and learning were not mentioned as separate issues, but resulted from the combination of these three success factors. Leadership was also not mentioned because most of these companies were still very small: most of them consisted of only one to four people.

The conclusions drawn suggest that two types of B2B service firms exist:

☐ The younger not so innovative firms offering core (and quite standard) services via discrete transactions; and
☐ Older firms who are more innovative offering augmented and more customized services on a continuous basis.

Perhaps this is a natural pattern of growth in the company life cycle for service start-ups.

Many of the topics discussed here about the relationship between market orientation and performance refer to the service firm's assets and capabilities. However just being aware of these relationships is not enough. More important is to manage processes in such a way that service organizations can become more market oriented, perform better, be service leaders and practise their social responsibility to all stakeholders. Organizations have many stakeholders, and each of these stakeholders will have a different idea as to how value is to be created within the organization. We have previously discussed value-based management[21] and as such we will continue discussing a model that can be used to define those market strategies aimed at creating value, the model of the strategic pathway.

6.3   Our Strategic Pathway

In Chapter 2 we developed our version of the strategic pathway as originally developed by Nigel Piercy. Here we will elaborate on this model for use in decision making processes in service organizations (see Figure 6.3).[22]

This model provides a structured process helpful in defining corporate strategy and marketing strategy in service organizations in general, jointly termed as market strategies. However, it can also be applied to defining corporate and marketing strategies with respect to each of the four different types of services developed in our taxonomy; namely the standard core service, the standard augmented service, the customized core service and the customized augmented service (see also the examples given in Chapter 2 and 3).

Defining market strategies hinges upon the decisions that have to be taken to determine:

■   the positioning of the organization; and
■   the overall direction of the service organization (as a whole and for each of its strategic business units) in each of its various target markets.

The model consists of three parts: market choices, value proposition and key relationships. The first box in the model of the strategic pathway is called 'market choices' and relates to four items:

1   The process of *defining the market* relates to how the service organization selects a piece of the marketplace and identifies it as their market. Defining the market can be done in many ways. How a service is defined determines what and where the specific market is.

2   The process of *market segmentation* relates to how the service organization identifies groups within the market as the targets for their service offerings. Chapter 3 showed the many ways to segment the market.

3   Determining *market attractiveness* hinges upon the degree to which an opportunity in the market (segment) fits with the goals and capabilities of the service organization.

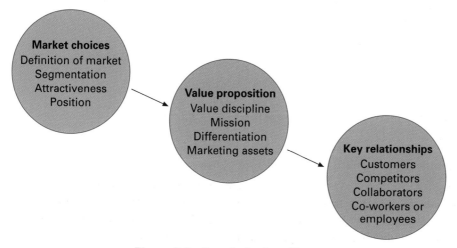

Figure 6.3   Our strategic pathway

4   Finally, determining the required or *planned market position* relates to how well the service organization believes they can do in the market or chosen segment.

Appropriate market and business intelligence is needed to collect, interpret and diffuse the relevant information throughout the service organization. Market research is a very valuable input to that part of being market oriented.

The second component of the model refers to the 'value proposition', which identifies the activities that an organization must undertake in order to build and sustain a strong competitive position in a market or a market segment. An organization's value proposition can be determined by answering the following questions:

1   *Value discipline*: What does the service organization consider to be the way they feel most comfortable to create value for their customers? In other words, how do we prefer to please the customer: is that operational excellence, product leadership or customer intimacy?

2   *Mission of the service organization*: What does the service organization want to be or want to stand for? What function do we want to perform for them? What is our *raison d'être*? It also relates to clearly answering the question, 'What are we good/best in for our customers?': Why should they choose us instead of another service organization to meet their needs? On the other hand, the mission – once properly formulated with the right adjectives – gives the actions a particular loading, creates an atmosphere and sets the tone for the internal and external communications.

3   *Competitive differentiation*: In which respects is the service organization different from the competitors, not only in the organization's own eyes, but especially in the eyes of the beholder: the customers? What differences do they see or perceive?

4   *Marketing assets* refer to the competitive advantages in the service firm's intangibilities, like the customer-based assets, the distribution (or supply chain)-based assets, the internal-based assets and the alliance-based assets (see Chapter 2).

These four items encompass the fundamental activities necessary to manage a service organization. You probably realize that value discipline and mission are closely linked to the organization's culture, leadership and social responsibility. The capabilities deal with the way all four items are implemented and put into action.

The final component in the strategic pathway model refers to the company's key relationships with four groups of partners, namely;

■   Customers;
■   Competitors;
■   Collaborators; and
■   Co-workers or employees.

Here we like to recall that starting, building and maintaining profitable relationships with customers is one of the critical capabilities of a market oriented service organization. Such capabilities bind the assets and facilitate their effective deployment in the marketplace. Capabilities relate not only to the relationships with customers, but also to the relationships with the collaborating partners in the distribution channel or supply chain, with the employees and with the competitors.

Once a service organization has realized that the activities identified in the model reflect the basic building blocks for formulating strategy, ensuing discussion can focus on the 12 subjects that are mentioned in the strategic pathway.

The strategic pathway applies many concepts from the literature on strategic management, strategic planning, marketing management and marketing planning. Although in a slightly different order, it focusses on the process of strategic planning. This includes scanning the environment, setting goals and strategies, implementation, and feed back and evaluation on the positions achieved leading to eventual adjustment of the goals and strategies set.

6.4 Competitive Advantage and Competitive Position

Accomplishing and keeping a competitive advantage is crucial to an organization's success. Well-developed and executed market strategies are needed to create a competitive advantage. Such market strategies can only be developed following consideration of the firm's assets and capabilities. The firm's assets and capabilities are an operationalization of its market orientation. The links between these concepts will be discussed in this section.

With respect to the service organization's competitive advantage two topics are crucial. First, what is the content of the competitive advantage and what is it composed of? Second, an organization must consider the sustainability of the competitive advantage and how the advantages are protected. Following on from this, how easy is it to imitate or copy the competitive advantages?[23]

These four factors may create a competitive advantage for service firms:

1 Competitive assets and capabilities that are hard to imitate (e.g. no access to specific resources like company experience based on the ideas of the learning curve; it takes a long time to build the particular competitive advantage; it is hard to tackle how the competitive advantage has been built);
2 The knowledge and skills of employees and managers;
3 Switching costs too high for the customers or the value of the offering is very high to those customers; and
4 Legal protection through copyrights and patents.[24]

The competitive position can be defined as the combination of the benefits offered to the target market and thus emerges from the service quality, supporting services, price, innovation, uniqueness, customization, speed of delivery or decision making or response time, and responsiveness.[25] Service firms can position themselves in five ways:

1 Customize the offering based on the strength of the relationship with individual customers, knowledge of the customer's needs, speed of delivery and responsiveness to customer requests and enquiries;

2 Offering an accepted price/quality ratio based on comparing the value of the service offering (especially the technical quality) to the price that has to be paid;

3 Offering a unique service;

4 Offering a high level of supporting services which often reflects the functional and relational quality;

5 Creating an innovative offer.

When you relate these five ways of positioning to our typology of services in Chapter 2, you will recognize that customization is at stake in our typology and in this overview. The other four ways of positioning here relate one way or another to the differentiation dimension of our typology. In that way, our typology can be applied realistically to service firms' positioning strategies.

Finally, organizations need to consider the link between performance, competitive position and competitive advantage. It is important to consider whether or not a competitive advantage actually results in a better performance, particularly in relation to the overall performance of the competition.[26] As said, a service firm's market orientation determines its financial and non financial performance. And, non financial performance determines financial performance. Not all four assets or all four capabilities are important in determining the firm's competitive advantage or competitive position. The most important assets and capabilities in creating a competitive advantage and competitive positioning are the customer-based assets, the alliance-based assets, the internal-based assets, the outside-in capabilities and the spanning capabilities. So, these should receive full attention of service organization's management in order to create value to the stakeholders and survive in today's turbulent marketplace.

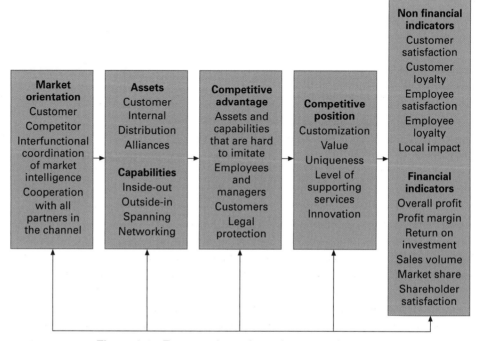

Figure 6.4 From market orientation to performance

6.5 Assets and Capabilities

We have referred often to the service firm's assets and capabilities. Here we will go deeper into that topic and see in what assets and capabilities international service firms have a competitive advantage.[27] Results from an international 12-country study among B2B and B2C service firms are presented in Table 6.1. It contains the mean scores for all the service firms answering the following question:

Here is a list of marketing assets and capabilities supplied by other managers. Please indicate on which of these you believe your company has an advantage over competitors and on which competitors have an advantage over you (1 = strong competitor advantage; 2 = competitor advantage; 3 = no difference; 4 = our advantage; 5 = our strong advantage).

Interpreting the results, it can be assumed that average scores of more than three indicate the own firm has an advantage over competitors according to the managers who completed the questionnaire.[28] In general it seems service firms in many countries have quite a competitive advantage with respect to the customer-based assets, the outside-in capabilities and the inside-out capabilities. Generally, this conclusion holds for all four customer-based assets (credibility in the market, superior levels of customer service and support, relationships with key customers, and the company or brand name and reputation). The outside-in capabilities refer to being good at understanding what customer needs and requirements are, and respectively being good at creating, maintaining and enhancing relationships with key customers or customer groups; the inside-out capabilities are good operations management, strong financial management and effective human resources management. With respect to these inside-out capabilities, in many countries service firms have a greater competitive advantage in operations management than in marketing management; it seems as if they do understand the market better than competitors but are not really that better in using information about markets, customers and competitors. This is in line with the finding that service firms in many countries do not have a competitive advantage in the asset of superior marketing information systems. Perhaps the quite good networking and relationship management capabilities might reveal all the necessary information to run the business. This will be especially true for B2B service firms where smaller numbers of clients and close relationships might diminish the need for formal market research.

The results also indicate that in most countries the service firms do not have a substantial competitive advantage on the internal-based assets (superior marketing information systems, copyrights and patens, cost advantage in production, and superior cost control systems) compared to the competitive advantage on the other assets or capabilities. This seems to hold especially for service firms in Hungary, Poland, Slovenia, Finland and Germany.

You may recall that many of these assets and capabilities relate to the characteristics of market oriented service organizations such as managing relationships, collecting market intelligence and understanding the market and service quality. When you look at the figure in more detail you will also see that a firm's competitive advantage occurs with respect to internal communication, but is not that high on effective new service development, the distribution channel, and cost and controlling the service organization's cost.

Very broadly speaking, it seems that service firms have competitive advantages in the external, marketing domain but not that much competitive advantage in the internal domain

Table 6.1 Assets and capabilities of service firms, BtC and B2B in 12 countries

ASSETS	United Kingdom	Ireland	Austria	Finland	New Zealand	Australia	Hungary	Poland	Slovenia	Greece	The Netherlands	Germany
Customer-based assets												
Company or brand name and reputation	3.9	4.0	3.8	3.8	4.0	3.9	3.5	3.7	3.9	4.2	3.8	3.9
Credibility with customers due to being well established in the market	4.1	4.2	4.1	4.0	3.9	3.9	3.7	3.7	3.9	4.2	3.9	4.3
Superior levels of customer services and support	4.0	3.8	3.9	4.1	3.9	3.9	3.8	3.4	3.9	4.3	3.7	3.8
Relationships with key target customers	4.0	3.9	4.0	3.8	3.9	3.9	3.9	3.6	4.1	4.1	3.6	3.9
Internal-based assets												
Cost advantage in production	3.1	3.2	3.2	3.3	3.1	3.2	3.3	2.9	3.0	3.1	3.1	3.1
Superior marketing information systems	3.1	3.0	3.0	2.9	3.0	3.1	2.8	2.7	2.9	3.3	2.9	3.0
Superior cost control systems	3.2	3.2	3.4	3.4	3.3	3.3	3.0	3.0	3.3	3.4	3.1	3.5
Copyright and patents	3.0	3.2	3.0	2.9	3.1	3.0	2.8	2.9	2.9	3.4	3.1	2.6
Distribution or supply chain-based assets												
Good relationships with suppliers	3.6	3.6	3.4	3.4	3.6	3.6	3.4	3.2	3.7	3.9	3.5	3.5
Extent or nature of the distribution network	3.3	3.4	3.1	3.5	3.3	3.4	3.0	3.1	3.2	3.5	3.4	3.1
The uniqueness of our distribution approach	3.3	3.3	3.1	3.2	3.3	3.5	3.1	2.9	3.2	3.6	3.5	3.0
Relationship with distribution channel intermediaries	3.2	3.3	3.2	3.4	3.1	3.3	3.2	3.1	3.2	3.3	3.1	2.9

Alliance-based assets

	United Kingdom	Ireland	Austria	Finland	New Zealand	Australia	Hungary	Poland	Slovenia	Greece	The Netherlands	Germany
Market access through strategic alliances or partnerships	3.3	3.3	3.5	3.1	3.5	3.5	3.2	3.2	3.3	3.6	3.4	3.4
Shared technology through strategic alliances or partnerships	3.2	3.2	3.2	3.3	3.3	3.3	3.1	3.0	3.2	3.5	3.3	3.2
Access to strategic partners' managerial know-how and expertise	3.3	3.3	3.4	3.2	3.3	3.4	3.0	3.2	3.2	3.6	3.3	3.2
Access to strategic partners' financial resources	3.1	3.1	3.0	3.0	3.0	3.1	2.9	2.8	3.1	3.1	3.2	2.5

CAPABILITIES	United Kingdom	Ireland	Austria	Finland	New Zealand	Australia	Hungary	Poland	Slovenia	Greece	The Netherlands	Germany
Inside-out												
Strong financial management	3.7	3.7	3.4	3.3	3.7	3.7	3.2	3.4	3.3	3.9	3.6	3.6
Effective human resource management	3.6	3.4	3.5	3.1	3.5	3.4	3.3	3.3	3.6	3.8	3.5	3.6
Good operations management expertise	3.9	3.7	3.9	3.3	3.8	3.7	3.5	3.4	3.7	3.8	3.6	3.8
Good marketing management ability	3.7	3.5	3.6	3.0	3.6	3.6	3.0	3.0	3.4	3.7	3.3	3.6
Outside-in												
Good at using information about markets, customers and competitors	3.6	3.4	3.3	3.1	3.5	3.4	3.3	3.0	3.4	3.7	3.3	3.4
Good at understanding what customer needs and requirements are	4.1	3.9	4.0	4.0	4.0	4.0	3.6	3.8	4.0	4.1	3.7	4.2

continued

Table 6.1 (cont.)

CAPABILITIES	United Kingdom	Ireland	Austria	Finland	New Zealand	Australia	Hungary	Poland	Slovenia	Greece	The Netherlands	Germany
Good at creating relationships with key customers or customer groups	4.1	3.9	3.9	3.7	4.0	3.9	3.8	3.5	4.0	4.1	3.4	4.0
Good at maintaining and enhancing relationships with key customers	4.1	4.0	3.8	3.8	3.9	3.9	3.8	3.5	3.9	4.2	3.5	4.1
Spanning												
Ability to launch successful new products	3.4	3.4	3.5	3.2	3.4	3.4	3.1	3.3	3.6	3.7	3.0	3.5
Good at setting prices which attract customers and achieve financial goals	3.4	3.5	3.2	3.2	3.4	3.2	3.4	3.2	3.3	3.4	2.8	3.7
Good at communicating internally across the organization	3.4	3.3	3.6	3.1	3.5	3.4	3.4	3.0	3.7	3.8	3.3	3.6
Effective new product/service development processes	3.3	3.2	3.2	3.4	3.3	3.2	3.1	3.1	3.2	3.6	3.1	3.4
Networking												
Ability to manage relationships with suppliers	3.5	3.5	3.4	3.3	3.5	3.5	3.5	3.3	3.5	3.7	3.3	3.6
Good at pooling expertise with strategic partners	3.3	3.5	3.6	3.4	3.4	3.3	3.3	3.3	3.4	3.7	3.3	3.7
Good at sharing mutual trust with strategic partners	3.3	3.4	3.6	3.5	3.5	3.4	3.4	Not asked	3.6	4.0	3.5	3.9
Good at sharing mutual commitment and goals with strategic partners	3.3	3.4	3.6	3.5	3.4	3.4	3.4	3.5	3.5	3.8	3.4	3.8

of cost and controlling cost. In other words, this distinction more or less relates to two (of the three) generic strategies Michael Porter defined: the differentiation strategy and the cost leadership strategy.[29]

6.6   Generic strategies to Go to Market

The strategic pathway can be used as a tool to assist in the development of market strategies. Usually, market strategies focus on developing a new service for an existing market, while developing and maintaining a competitive advantage. Alternatively the other view starts from the service firm's own strengths, key success factors or core competencies. Here, the belief in one's own strengths is the starting point and what the company believes they can accomplish based on their own 'potential and energy' within the firm. In practice it is not a matter of choosing one of the two market strategies. Both perspectives are highly relevant for a market oriented service company and fit into our approach of a market oriented service firm having its own assets and capabilities (Figure 6.5).

Belief in Own Strengths and Capabilities: The Perspective from Within

When undertaking a competitive analysis, firms should consider the competencies that the firm has accumulated in order to perform well. Hamel and Prahalad (1994) concluded that companies should 'search for new functionalities or new ways of delivering traditional functionalities'.[30] In such circumstances they will be able to shape the future of their industry. This view is in line with our approach of services functions and benefits to consumers mentioned in Chapter 3 and the belief in own assets and capabilities.

   An example of this way of thinking is given in the health care research ADK case study at the end of the book. Here, it suffices to say that ADK had to change its thinking dramatically from promoting its functional attributes to its technology's benefits. It appeared that the technical capabilities will not create interest in ADK's service unless they are directly tied to benefits recognized by the client.[31]

   Hamel and Prahalad are convinced that a clear vision on the future is the most important competitive advantage an organization can have. In their opinion, that vision should lead to a strategy of 'getting in front' of the future instead of 'catching up' with the present. Being an industry leader is not enough; shaping the future of an entire industry is what it should be all

Internal strengths	External opportunities
Assets	DRETS factors
Capabilities	Market structure, competitors
Key success factors	Market developments
Core competency	Consumer behaviour
Shape your own future	Forces impacting on competitive position
Competitive advantage due to own strengths	Market position, market share

Figure 6.5   Internal strengths and external opportunities

about.[32] And that requires a clear vision. Such a vision also relates to what opportunities the company expects to happen in the external world.

In other words, service organizations must be motivated, able, willing and have the opportunity to create breakthroughs that are hard to follow or imitate by competitors in order to survive and find their own position in the market.[33] Other scholars in services management emphasize the need for creating close relationships. This will result in a high degree of customer loyalty due to the customer value delivered. Such a situation could be achieved through the development of strategies based on delivering value for customers mostly achieving both low cost and significant differentiation.[34]

The Market and Competitors: The External Perspective

SERVICE PRACTICE 6.4

The Mobile Telephone Market[35]

In many countries, one or a few suppliers dominate the cellular or mobile telephone market leading to market structures of oligopoly, duopoly or monopolistic competition. Companies in such markets typically show behaviour as proposed in the textbooks on micro economics: e.g. they set high prices, realize high margins, have to take each other's actions into account in defining their own strategy and anticipate those actions. Such a situation attracts new entrants or forces governmental bodies to take corrective actions. Both actions originate from high consumer prices and/or high margins.

The Australian mobile telephone market is dominated by one large player, Telstra, which currently holds 70% of the mobile telephone market in Australia. The revenue from this business accounts for almost 40% of all of Telstra's revenue, so maintaining their market share is crucial to their longer-term revenue projections. Newer entrants into this market such as Singtel's Optus have found the competition tough going but are slowly making ground in this highly profitable and fast-growing market. However the market is changing from a monopoly to a duopoly and now many new competitors such as Vodafone are entering this competitive market. With this change, consumers are enjoying increasingly competitive pricing, and more customer service. The market while highly regulated is becoming fiercely competitive, particularly as the market structure changes; no longer can a government owned business enjoy such market dominance.

The European Commission acts as a consumer watchdog, particularly when consumers are being charged too high a price. At the end of 2004 and the beginning of 2005 it was found that in Ireland Vodafone and mm02 controlled 94% of the mobile market, and that their revenue per customer was 50% higher than the EU average. The European Commission tends to force down these tariffs in Ireland and other countries. The Commission is also investigating whether European service providers charge unfairly high prices for 'roaming calls' – the calls that their customers make and receive outside their home countries. Similar actions such as occurred in Ireland may be expected in France, Germany or Italy where also two companies have a joint market share of more than 70% in the cellphone market in September 2004:

France:	83.4%	(Orange 48.1% and SFR 35.3%)
Italy:	78.6%	(TIM 43.0% and Vodafone 35.6%)
Germany:	77.2%	(T-Mobile 39.5% and Vodafone 37.7%)

While the market structure itself will impact on the competitive position of a firm, many other factors must also be considered. Michael Porter has developed an industry analysis tool to detect the specific characteristics of the forces impacting on the competitive position of organizations. These market forces are:

1 *Competitive rivalry* which relates to the strength of the company compared to the impact of the competitors;
2 *Potential entrants* which may challenge the existing market situation especially when they perform more effectively or efficiently than our company;
3 *The bargaining power of suppliers*;
4 *The bargaining power of buyers* which may directly affect the service firm, as such good relationships with these organizations are crucial to prosper; and
5 The threat of substitute services should be taken into account.

SERVICE PRACTICE 6.5

Analysing Competitors in the Airline Industry

It is often difficult to get an accurate picture of the competitive situation within an industry. For example in the airline industry it might appear at first glance that KLM are direct competitors with Air France, and yet both airlines are merged now and belong to the SkyTeam air alliance.

Airline alliances are conglomerates of airlines that share not only passengers but also airline lounges, facilities and booking systems. A passenger may think that they are booking a flight with say British Airlines, but when it comes to fly they may be flying Qantas. Airline alliances are an example of co-operation, and their existence makes it very difficult for those outside of the airline sector to actually determine what airlines are competing and what airlines are co-operating. In all, the airlines are hoping that through the alliance they can use their sheer size to dominant specific sectors of the market. The three main airlines alliances are the Star Alliances, SkyTeam and One World.

Another tool, developed by Porter to help marketers understand the market within which they are operating, is called the 'three generic strategies'. These strategies are defined as cost leadership, differentiation and focus. Sometimes it seems as if the idea exists that a market oriented strategy only fits to a differentiation or focus strategy because the focus is on the customer. This is quite strange, for the other part of market orientation (competitor orientation) is important to cost leaders; they have to watch competition carefully. Therefore, it is not a matter of either/or but a matter of both to create value to the customer by a market oriented service organization.[36]

Service companies are interested in achieving above average profits by delivering superior value to their customers. Sometimes, this profit motive can be achieved via the lowest cost servuction process. At other times, it can be achieved via successfully differentiating services that can be sold at a premium price. In both cases, it is important to realize that the internal structuring of the servuction process and the skills and knowledge of the employees are decisive factors that are hard to imitate and thus contribute to creating the competitive advantage.

The generic strategies of cost leadership and differentiation fit best when the target market is broad. For cost leadership the competitive advantage is to be found in lower cost of the servuction process (so in producing and delivering the service), while for differentiation it is to be found in offering different services to each of these broad(er) target segments. Each segment must be viable and profitable to the service firm. When the target market is narrow, a focus strategy is best. Focus strategies can be either cost focus or differentiation focus. When we integrate the two perspectives discussed in this section, we provide some more insights into the assets and capabilities of firms following a generic strategy of cost leader, differentiation and focus.

Given the critical differences between a cost leader, a focus and a differentiation strategy, it is obvious that the assets and capabilities of service firms pursuing such a strategy differ as well. From the study reported in Table 6.1 we can briefly conclude that the service firms had quite a competitive advantage on all the customer-based assets, irrespective of their chosen strategy. So, they all indicate having competitive advantages with respect to their credibility with customers, superior levels of customer service and support, relationships with key target customers and the company or brand name and reputation. This seems to be a condition for every service organization, irrespective of its strategy, to survive in the marketplace. Next, the cost leaders in particular reported competitive advantages on the inside-out capability of strong financial management and the cost advantage in production (as one of the internal-based assets); this reflects their internal financial cost orientation. On the other hand, the service firms applying a differentiation and focus strategy had quite some competitive advantages on the outside-in capabilities of being good at creating, maintaining and enhancing relationships and were good at understanding what customer needs and requirements are. This reflects their external, marketing orientation. There were hardly any large differences for the other assets and capabilities.

Focus Strategy

An organization cannot fulfil all functions for all people at all times as has been stressed in developing the concept of the value discipline. Organizations focussing their service on one type of client or providing one well-executed service for more segments achieve both lower costs and higher service levels. The discipline of market leaders relates to their ability to choose a clear group of customers and narrow their focus to dominate the market.[37] In other words, a combination of low costs, high quality and strong focus may lead to higher productivity.[38] This unique combination deserves some additional attention here.

A focus strategy is also typical for niche players; in their relatively small market they offer a very specialized, often limited number of services to their target market. Sometimes, large companies can also provide specialized services via a focus strategy; then often they have founded their special company or strategic business unit to that end. More important is the fact that the number of limited service suppliers is increasing today; these LSPs challenge the established general service providers (GSPs). We expect this process to happen in many industries where niche players seek for the markets not (sufficiently) serviced by the larger general service providers.

GSPs and LSPs

Established airlines like British Airways, Lufthansa and Delta Airlines are challenged by two types of newcomers in the market. First, companies like Virgin, easyJet and Southwest provide low costs ('no frills') services. Second, charter companies delivering customized airline services for business trips and incentive travel. The same applies to a universal bank such as CitiGroup. Financial service providers offering a very limited range of products are threatening these large institutions. For example, Schwab (a direct discount broker) offers a limited range of investment products mainly via the Internet and telephone to all investors. Specialized Internet brokers in many western markets offer new online services for 24-hour-a-day investments in the stock market. They all are serious rivals for the established general banks. On the other hand, there are also investment banks specializing in an industry such as high-tech or biotechnology offering very customized corporate finance advice (such as mergers, acquisitions, capital raising, financial engineering) to and about firms in this limited segment.

Both types of newcomers are an extreme form of focussed strategy. The LSPs focus on either a specific range of services or a specific market segment. Their structure is less complex than a GSP and more dedicated. Both forms try to steal market share from the GSP. The demand driven incumbents focus on client needs. They provide a combination of customized and standardized services to meet the specific needs of their well-defined target group. This is the consequence of their market driven orientation resulting in a pull concept.

The established companies in various service industries, offering their broad spectrum of services to a wide range of customers (many segments), have to reconsider their strategic options. Either they can join the race, start such a specialized operation themselves or improve their existing activities in which costs, relationships (loyalty management), processes and multi-distribution channels are important aspects.

The Heskett Typology of Generic Strategies for Service Firms

James Heskett elaborated on the generic strategies of Michael Porter for the service sector and defined the next three generic strategies:

■ strategies producing low-cost services;
■ strategies producing highly differentiated services; and
■ strategies producing highly differentiated low-cost services.[39] (See Figure 6.6)

Concerning the operationalization of strategies producing low-cost services you may think of

■ Seeking low cost clients (think of South West Airlines, Ryanair or Formule 1 hotels);
■ Standardizing customized services; or

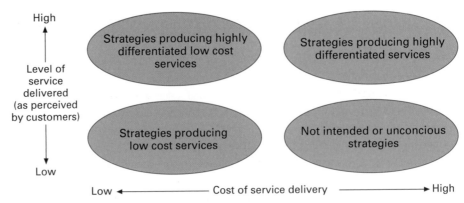

Figure 6.6   Alternative competitive strategies in the service sector

- Reducing the human factor in the service delivery process (for instance by increasing the technology part).

Strategies producing highly differentiated services may be put into action via;

- Making the intangible more tangible (think of the atmospherics in department stores, the interiors and coloured brochures of banks or the buildings of accounting firms);
- Customizing standard services (think of bartenders knowing and welcoming their clientele by name as a way of customizing while focussing on cost);
- Quality control (see the previous chapter);
- Attention for training and the value-added per employee (also as a part of the firm's quality standards);
- Managing customer expectations (as long as customers perceive higher quality and satisfaction, even if cost and prices have been raised, their increased value perception is the only thing that really counts. Of course, the service firm should know its clients' price elasticity of demand and manage customer expectations).

Strategies producing highly differentiated low cost services focus on the challenging combination of diversifying services and reducing cost. This can be accomplished for instance by:

- Introducing do-it-yourself services (quite often used in the finance and insurance industry by direct marketing offerings);
- Developing a membership base (many publishers like Elsevier Science Publishing or telephone companies do so and create relationships);
- Leveraging of scarce talents and skills (accountants and management consultants do so by coupling seniors to less paid juniors);
- Substituting assets with information (look at retailers where stock is diminishing and scanning the barcodes encourages the just-in-time delivery);
- Managing the service triangle (this implies managing the three corner stones of: the (image of the) service company itself; the contact/front office employees who actually

serve the customer and the customers themselves – their expectations and their role in
the service encounter script);
■ Simply focus on one core service by limiting the number of services.

Standardized services typically occur more to the left side of Figure 6.6, where low cost is the
major characteristic. Customized services usually are highly diversified and this implies higher
costs in general, for both the client and the service organization. These customized services
are positioned at the upper right side of Figure 6.6.

To fit in with our typology of services developed in Chapter 2, the Heskett model should be
adapted slightly. Both axes are labelled differently but represent, in essence, the same
phenomenon in ours as in Heskett's approach. Heskett's dimension of 'level of service
delivered' (as perceived by customers) has to do with the individual's assessment of whether
the service fits their personal needs or not. This is more or less equal to our concept of
customization. Heskett's dimension of 'cost of service delivery' ranges from low to high. These
costs depend to a large extent on the complexity of the service and the service delivery
process. This complexity varies as long as more features are added to the core service. In
general, augmented services will be more complex than just the core service alone. This is
reflected in the degree of differentiation between core services and augmented services, the
second dimension of our framework. Now, the fourth strategy that we initially called the
unintended strategies can be replaced by the intended strategy of producing highly
differentiated services at more cost and higher prices customers are willing to pay for. This
may sound as an irrational strategy; the most important thing though is whether customers
perceive it as delivering more value to them, for instance in terms of status. Then customers
are willing to pay for it.

Now that we have discussed our own typology of services and the typologies Michael
Porter and James Heskett have developed with respect to generic strategies and seen in
which respects they are (more or less) similar, we can put it all together. This is shown in
Figure 6.7.

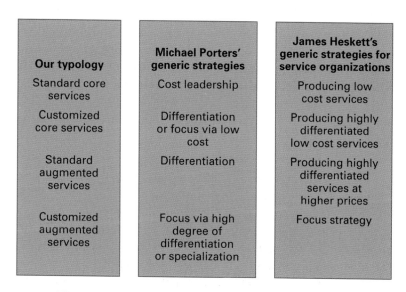

Figure 6.7   Generic strategies: putting it all together

The Ansoff Matrix for Service Firms' Growth and Development

In addition to what has been discussed so far, some other generic strategies for growth and development can be mentioned. To achieve the central goal of the organization it is essential to look at the strategic service/market combinations. A choice should be made from these combinations. In principle, organizations can grow in four ways.[40] Applied to services, this results in the following picture (Figure 6.8).

A company will grow initially by reinforcing the current existing market position, by further penetrating the existing market (*market penetration*). This is achieved by persuading current customers to buy more, attracting non users in the current market and/or getting competitors' customers to switch. A second option consists of developing new services for the existing market (*services development*). Accountants usually follow this strategy, by constantly introducing new services (which in service organizations are often called 'products') for their current clients. Tax consultants, company auditors and automation consultants also try to throw each other 'the ball'. By developing new policies themselves, the offspring of the original accountant get more and more non audit clients. A third possibility is offering the present service to a new market. This means expanding the market with existing services (*market development*). This may mean new market segments within a marked geographical area, but it could also mean new geographical (international) market segments. An increasing number of service providers however seem to be capable of successfully exporting their service formula. The last option of the matrix is *diversification*. This means rendering new services for new markets. As in other sectors, this strategy can be dangerous since both services and markets are new to the company.

Next to the dimensions of service and market, *technology* can be added as a third dimension. This can be included when defining the business of a new service firm and consequently in developing its strategy. Changes in technology offer new opportunities for service firms. In Chapter 1, we pointed out the impact of IT and the substitution of labour by equipment, automation and technology. Now that it can be used to create new services and markets, technology enables you to serve customers better and distinguish yourself from competitors. But also new services industries come up, like mobile telephones, information services and even brokers and comparative testing via the Internet. Sometimes, these are called 'e-strategies for growth'. So, let us elaborate on e-strategies based on the Internet technology.

E-strategies can be used in various growth strategies. In fact, the value of this type of

Services Market	Present	New
Present	Market penetration	Services development
New	Market development	Diversification

Figure 6.8 Services/market combinations in the Ansoff matrix

strategy here is in controlling time, distance and complexity in servuction processes.[41] They require specific knowledge, creativity and relationships from service providers and their employees, but also offer new opportunities to them and to their customers. For instance, customers can be contacted much more easily, customers can respond much quicker and administrative processes can be performed in an easier way than in situations without ICT. With respect to time, customers can control their own patterns of spending time much better: they can now perform their banking activities at the time they like.

SERVICE PRACTICE 6.7

Barclays to Expand Asian Trading[42]

Barclays Capital plans to roll out its electronic trading system for bonds and swaps into Asia – a move that the bank hopes will significantly boost market liquidity, particularly in US dollar interest rate markets. Hoping to be the first in the Asian region to offer this service, Barclays hopes it will increase their credibility with clients.

When the system went live on 14 February 2005, it was the first time that investors had the opportunity to hit live bid and offer screen prices for treasury and agency bonds and swaps during Asian trading hours and could trade in larger amounts and at better prices than they had before. The bank's clients in Europe and the USA were also able to use the system to trade during Asian hours, showing that physical distance does not play a role anymore.

With respect to distance, geographical distances can be met much more easily. You no longer have to go to the travel agent to book your trip; that can be done easily via the Internet. In terms of complexity ICT now allows for actions that were at one time impossible; for example, providing a quick response to a customer request or determining direct product profitability at a detailed level of groups of services provided or even at the level of individual customers.

Next to growth strategies, development strategies can be distinguished, such as stability strategies, withdrawal strategies and combined strategies.[43] Service organizations may develop more or less gradually via internal growth, merger, horizontal or vertical (backward and forward) integration, joint ventures and franchising (the latter especially in international retailing or in the hospitality industry). The combination of a standardized formula, central financial agreements and fast growth via a multisite strategy makes it difficult for competitors to imitate. But it is not always that simple, for insufficient adaptation to local circumstances is one of the reasons why international retailers such as Marks and Spencer and Virgin Music Stores have failed on the continent in Europe.[44] Franchising is also a relatively easy entry mode in internationalization strategies of service providers and could have helped Marks and Spencer or Virgin to avoid the problems they have encountered by starting their own greenfield operations in various countries outside the UK. Another example refers to the merger of the two largest telecom operators in Sweden and Norway, Telia and Telenor. It was shown that historical sentiments, feelings and emotions, which were not handled well in this case, were the main cause of the merger's failure in 1999 despite perceived similarities in national culture, corporate practice and language.[45]

A stability strategy is used by companies that are satisfied with their present situation; they cannot grow anymore because the market is saturated or they do not want to grow anymore because they consider 'small is beautiful'. Often the owners/entrepreneurs find their leisure time more important than making more money or growing and having many more personnel and the accompanying problems.

If a company's financial performance is constantly under pressure, a withdrawal strategy may be the only choice. Of course, there are other possible reasons. A turn around strategy occurs if the organization tries to change rigorously to be a more effective and efficient operation. A disinvestment strategy means that an enterprise sells a part of its business. Disinvestment, or sell-off, usually occurs when a company is in trouble or when it re-orientates to its core business. Stated in a positive way, we should say that rather than disinvesting or liquidation the entrepreneur is harvesting.[46]

SERVICE PRACTICE 6.8

Much Needs to Be Done to Survive[47]

In 2005 Swiss International Air Lines continues with its actions to reduce cost and make the company profitable again. After the 2003 lay-off of 3000 jobs, another 15% reduction of its workforce will take place in order to regain profitability. But more needs to be done to turn the 2004 loss into profits again, for instance:

- ☐ the regional fleet of aircraft will be reduced by up to 13 aircraft (about one-third of their fleet), by mid-2006;
- ☐ services will be maintained by outsourcing many loss making routes to lower cost 'partner' airlines, continuing the policy that already led to shifting routes to such carriers as Cirrus Air, Denim Air and Styrian Spirit;
- ☐ all Basel-based services will be outsourced, along with two or three loss making Geneva routes;
- ☐ a low cost subsidiary to handle regional services will be considered;
- ☐ a renegotiation of contracts with suppliers will occur;
- ☐ Swiss remained committed to standardizing its regional fleet on Embraer 170 and 190 aircraft.

It will not be a surprise that unions reacted angrily to these plans when Christopher Franz, chief executive of Swiss, announced them.

Very large service organizations such as banks, insurance companies, accountants and government organizations often follow a combination of strategies. Their environment is so dynamic and they have so many strategic business units operating in so many markets at the same time that it forces them to follow this strategy. In the past 20 years, the financial world has been in a tremendous turmoil. The changes all occurred at American, Asian, European and worldwide level most of the time, and not at the national level of a single country. These structural changes in the financial world are illustrated by four factors: clients becoming more demanding and more professional; more expensive funding and smaller returns on investments; improved technology; and changes in legislation.[48]

The Wheel of Servicing

This model reflects the dynamics in service industries.[49] The different stages of entry, trading-up and vulnerability can be applied here as a tool to analyse a service company's life cycle:

■ *Entry:* Most service providers probably start on a small scale and try to deliver services that are as tailored as possible. These services are targeted to a specific market segment with unique expectations. Quite often, services are not yet very complex.
■ *Trading-up:* As the life cycle of the service organization continues, the tailored core service delivery process becomes more efficient and/or new features are added. It will become more complex, on the one hand, and/or more efficient, on the other. So, two ways of development can be distinguished: one in the direction of more efficient core services (standard core services) and one in the direction of customized augmented services.
■ *Vulnerability:* After a time, competition increases and competitive prices are of utmost importance. This may be the case for both situations described in the trading-up stage. The important task now is how to cope with this competition. A further trading-up may be the case leading to a higher and even more specialized level of tailor-made augmented services.
■ Another way is to harvest and leave the industry or try to survive in the cut-throat competition by becoming more cost efficient. Quite often, this means that new low cost service providers may enter the industry and find more niches.

In this way, the coming up of LSPs fits in this 'wheel of services' concept: they are eating away market share from GSPs, in particular when these established firms are not cost conscious and do not adapt their marketing mix (Figure 6.9).

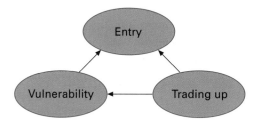

Figure 6.9 The wheel of servicing

Variety Strategies and Loyalty Strategies

It is a common belief that customer loyalty is decreasing.[50] An overwhelming choice (created by companies themselves), the availability and easy application of information, individualism and commoditization (many products and services, even luxury ones, look almost the same) are among the causes of a declining loyalty.[51] The increasing opportunities to choose offered by the suppliers are, in fact, the outcome of strategies aimed at offering variety to customers and to perfectly fit the needs of a particular market segment. A high-variety strategy ultimately leads to perfect customization: a unique offer for (each individual) customer. On the one hand, customers like to seek variety. Curiosity, learning, internal needs due to satiation, natural survival instinct, changing needs over time (family life cycle, aspiration level) or just out-of-stock situations may cause this variety-seeking behaviour.[52] Probably, the perceived variety by customers is the ultimate issue for companies to differentiate the offer. This will determine to a large extent whether customers do accept the (wide) variety or not.[53] On the other hand, customers like to reduce perceived risk, seek security and decrease the cost of looking for and buying new services. Then the service organization can put all efforts in meeting the challenge of creating loyalty. So, instead of customized variety, customized loyalty may be the purpose of relationship marketing. Here, five principles may apply:[54]

1   Focus on specific types of customers (e.g. the most profitable ones);
2   Focus on creating value, not on reducing price;
3   Focus on building loyalty, not just reducing churn;
4   Systematically prioritize efforts based on financial goals like ROI; and
5   Create social and psychological bonds balanced with the financial requirements.

All kinds of relationship strategies and programmes may help to decrease switching behaviour and increase loyalty behaviour. However, one should keep in mind that too much loyalty or too much variety may be too much for the customer (no freedom, too much choice) and the supplier (too high costs, too wide an assortment). So, the proper balance should be found between loyalty and variety.

6.7   Marketing Strategies to Go to Market

Going to the market requires a combination of the generic strategy chosen and the specific marketing strategy related to that overall framework. In this section we turn away from the generic strategies and go on to the marketing strategies as one of the functional areas within the company that can be used to go to the market. We do recognize that a market orientation is not the exclusive property of the marketing or sales department, rather the whole organization should be permeated by it. So, these marketing strategies as well as the strategies in the field of human resource management or operations research should fit into that basic philosophy as well. All the generic strategies discussed and the marketing strategies that still have to be discussed help in defining the exact strategy to go to market: the chosen market strategy based on the strategic pathway.

Market Positions, Assets, Capabilities and Strategies

Not all service industries are the same in structure. The market positions taken by the firms rendering services may be very different. Some companies are small, others have a dominant position in the market; some have a strong position in many assets and capabilities while others specialize in one particular respect. Some have strong financial resources and can stand competition for a long time, while others are almost bankrupt (and easily thrown out of the market by a single price reduction of the main competitor). So, service firms may have the position of market leader, market challenger, market follower or market nicher.[55] And for our discussion on strategies, it is important to know if and how these four types of service firms differ with respect to having a competitive advantage on their assets and capabilities.

Here, the *market leader* is the firm with the largest market share in a particular service industry; usually it leads other firms in price changes (like for instance the interest rates in the mortgage market), new service introductions, distribution coverage and promotion spending. They can implement many different ways to maintain their leading position, for instance in expanding the total market (finding new users, show new ways of using the service or just more usage, like more billing minutes for cellular phones), protecting their market share (via various defensive tactics) or expanding their market share. Kotler *et al.* (2004) cite a study done by Fred Wiersema revealing the four mindsets that a number of market leaders like Cisco, eBay, Nokia, Bell, Yahoo, General Electric, Wal-Mart, Mercedes Benz and Intel 'have in common:

1 They create a larger than life presence and stay out front in the customers' mind;
2 They seek out customers who stretch their capabilities;
3 They make sure that customers realize the full value of their offers and innovative solutions; and
4 They act boldly and take the initiative even though this involves risks and they gain the respect and support of their customers.'

We can add that many of these commonalities are also the characteristics of market oriented service organizations.

Market challengers are the runner-up service providers in a particular service industry that are fighting hard to increase their market share. They may attack the market leader or some other firms in the industry and in doing the latter they avoid attacking the leader. Many ways of attacking can be found: frontal, flanking, encirclement, bypass or guerrilla attack. Often they attack by providing lower prices or more services.

Market followers are also runner-up firms in a service industry; however, they want to hold their market share without rocking the boat. They are not the meek followers, but are still active. They deliberately do not want to be the first in the market, are not that innovative, but follow others (often the leader or other innovative service providers). They come later with modified services that are not hindered by the shortcomings of the first movers (teething troubles). They may clone exactly, imitate to a large degree or adapt the leader's offering, often by some slight quality improvements. By definition they will never have first mover advantages.

Market nichers are the service providers in an industry that serve small, well-defined segments that the other service providers overlook or ignore. They are the specialists, often the ones offering the customized, augmented services from our typology. They can specialize in many ways: end-use, customer type (small target market or even individuals), quality–price ratio, etc. Some of them are active in multiple niches. As within the overall market, a service provider can also be the leader, the challenger or the follower in a niche market.

Concerning specific assets and capabilities, all these types of firms have an advantage over their competitors. It appears that for the leaders, challengers and followers in the overall market and in a niche market, service firms indicate having a greater competitive advantage in the four types of assets mentioned before than in the capabilities.[56] As before, service firms have a larger degree of competitive advantage in the customer-based assets than in the other assets irrespective of their position in the market. However, it turns out that especially the market leaders (in the overall market and in a niche market) indicate having a stronger competitive advantage on the service firm's:

- customer-based assets, like company or brand name and reputation, and credibility with customers due to being well established in the market;
- internal-based assets, like superior marketing information systems;
- distribution-based assets, like extent or nature of the distribution network, and uniqueness of the distribution approach;
- alliance-based assets, like market access and shared technology through strategic alliances or partnerships;
- spanning capabilities, like the ability to launch successful new services, and an effective new service development process.

So, these empirically found characteristics of market leaders' assets and capabilities are in many respects in line with the features of the market leaders and market oriented organizations discussed before.

In many instances the challengers in the niche market have similar competitive advantages to the two groups of market leaders. Moreover, challengers (especially in the overall market) seem to be better at understanding customer needs and requirements than the other firms. Quite often niche players in general seem to have a competitive advantage in the relationship management domain.

In many cases the followers in a niche market do not have that strong competitive advantage. That may be self-evident; they follow firms in a particular niche, especially when they are meek followers. It appears that they scored for instance lowest of all on a possible competitive advantage on copyrights and patents.

Firms having one of these three positions in the (overall or niche) market may use a wide variety of strategies to deal with their competitors. In focussing on the competitor, 'marketing warfare' comes to mind; search for weak spots in a competitor's performance and focus marketing attacks on those weak spots. Searching for weaknesses may be successful, as the following examples show. At the beginning of the 1980s, Digital Equipment Corporation (DEC) was able to take advantage of IBM's weakness to produce and market small computers. Burger King was also successful at that time in attacking McDonald's with its broiling, not frying concept. However, many of the advantages from that time have vanished and new ways to attack have to be found today.

There are four tactical ways to lead a marketing war:

- Defensive tactics;
- Offensive tactics;
- Flanking tactics; and
- Guerilla tactics.

Defensive tactics are the most appropriate for the market leader. If the market leader is not constantly innovative, the competitor will be. The market leader always has to react to important movements of the (smaller) competitors. They may be challengers or niche players, to a larger extent than the market leader, thus satisfying specific customer needs to a greater extent than the market leader.

Offensive tactics can be used when you find that your own service organization is number two or three in a specific service industry. Typically, challengers should use an offensive strategy to attack the market leader. First, you must search for blind or weak spots in the strategy of the market leader (excellent marketing information systems are needed then). Then, you must concentrate the attack on this weak spot. Keep in mind that you should start the attack on a small front at first; later on, the battlefield can be broadened.

Flanking tactics are the most innovative way to lead a marketing battle. The three principles of this tactic are:

■ A good flank attack should be made in an indisputable area;
■ A tactical surprise must be a necessary part of the plan; and
■ Continuing the action is as important as starting the attack itself.

Guerilla tactics have proved to be quite successful in history. The most important assumptions of such a tactic are:

■ Search for a segment in the market small enough to defend. Focus or niching is in fact the strategy to apply here;
■ No matter how successful you become, never act as a market leader. Leaders are always the ones to challenge and attack;
■ Stick close to the market and keep overheads low; and
■ Be prepared to withdraw immediately if the situation requires such a change.

We think this attacking approach does not always fit well with the culture of a market oriented service firm. With this approach, a service firm may run the risk that the customer will be forgotten, because of the sole focus on the competitor, let alone the relationship with the customer. Relationship marketing and retention strategies emphasize co-operation, trust, benevolence and commitment between service organizations and customers as well as networking. Such an approach is very different from the war-seeking and conflict approach. However, it appears to be very useful to know something about this 'war approach' when a service organization is confronted with 'war-minded' competitors or when the organization has become very unresponsive to developments in the market place. Then, it may be a suitable way to 'wake them up'.

Relationship Marketing and the Portfolio of Relationships

Creating, developing and maintaining excellent relationships is one of the key assets, capabilities or success factors of market oriented service firms. The present emphasis on relationship marketing is not only based on a shift from short-term to long(er)-term orientation. It is also based on a shift from offensive marketing to defensive marketing. This means a shift from attracting or conquering new customers to keeping and protecting the existing customers.

The key for effective relationship marketing management is an understanding of the customer's value creation process and the strength of the relationship. This requires appropriate information. Many service organizations are lucky in that they possess large data bases with the history of their clients. Then, banks and insurance companies can check whether customers' value changes along the relationship. Customers do not provide the same profitability at every moment during their relationship with the service provider. In predicting future customer profitability, present customer profitability is often used. However, a recent American study in the banking industry revealed that 'a substantial amount of variation in 1-year a head customer profitability is left unexplained by current customer profitability'.[57] This implies many more factors should be taken into account to count customer lifetime value.

In using this profitability perspective, the prime interest lies in understanding the cash flow effects on handling customer relationships in the long run; what are the revenues from and costs of serving a specific customer? It is also relevant to know how this profit has been created. Is it based on one-time transactions or on the basis of contractual relationships? These are ways to look at the service organization's portfolio of present and future profitable and non profitable customers. The information on the non profitable customers may be used to skip them from the firm's customer base. However, it may be that for strategic reasons some loss creating customers are kept, hoping for better results in the future. That is why many students receive attractive offers from banks, hoping that they will be profitable accounts once they have graduated and buy more services.

As shown in Chapter 4, relationships can be defined by focussing on the economic and behavioural side of a relationship and on the strength of the relationship. Both dimensions may vary between high and low, as depicted in the relation, perception and loyalty (RPL) matrix which is shown in Figure 4.4. Service organizations can now use their database with actual data about consumer buying behaviour and perceptual data on how customers perceive and evaluate the relationship, to segment their market into four segments. When the recency, frequency and monetary value (RFM) data on actual buying behaviour are stated in terms of customer(s') profitability to the service firm (e.g. as a return on investment – ROI – or as a lifetime value), customers with a high ROI or lifetime value are considered to be very valuable to the firm. The customers in the four parts of the matrix have been labelled as friends, sympathetics, functionalists and acquaintances.

Analysing the actual distribution of customers over those four segments will reveal whether this is also the preferred distribution, and whether all kinds of promotional activities have to be performed to let customers move from one segment to another in order to create a larger group of true loyal customers. The generic strategies and marketing strategies mentioned as well as the elements of the marketing mix can be used to create value, but also human resources management strategies should not be overlooked here.

SERVICE PRACTICE 6.9

The Personal Touch in the Relationship

Employees and customers are the actors in a service relationship. Episodes and actions give the personal touch, which will be much greater in customized augmented services than in standard core services. In the latter, automation can often replace the personal touch. Where automation and technology have been used to replace employees, employees can no longer be 'used' to develop and maintain a strong relationship with the organization's clients. In these situations other means have to be applied to assist in the maintenance of customer relationships. One can see that many banks, insurance companies, car manufacturers, car importers and car dealers all publish magazines to communicate to their present customers about new services and new types of service offers. They also institute customer satisfaction programmes to measure satisfaction levels. Just calling them 'customers' often gives customers the feeling that the firm cares about them. Such an approach is often highly valued by customers, in consumer markets as well as in industrial service markets. The personal touch then is substituted by a printed (or telephone) touch due to changes in technology. All these activities are aimed at keeping or retaining customers.

Keeping customers is also important in business-to-business service relationships, where the difference between the outcome of the process of delivering services and the process itself are important variables determining service quality and hence maintaining the relationship.[58]

Studies in the advertising industry reveal that the intentions of companies to keep the relationship with their ad-agency mainly depended on the existing degree of affective commitment which, in turn, is largely determined by the professional business service quality, trust, and negatively by 'stuck bonds'. The professional business service quality is mainly determined by three factors, namely

- ☐ the outcome quality for example of an advertising campaign;
- ☐ the soft process quality, which is the clients' evaluation of the interactions with and the treatment of the customer during the service production process; and
- ☐ the competence, which is the clients' evaluation of the competence and expertise displayed during the service production.[59]

This demonstrates that the personal touch is important in keeping clients long term.

Retention strategies are strategies that aim to maintain relationships with customers. More and more, it becomes clear that in mature markets keeping customers is much cheaper than attracting customers from competitors. When all companies are stealing customers from each other in a saturated market, it means that they all invest in stealing from one another and one may doubt whether this is a rational strategy from a macro perspective. For, the cost of winning customers will result in higher consumer prices. Therefore, the goal of retention strategies is to keep customers and sell more services to existing customers through techniques such as cross-selling. Most of the time, this also implies investing in the knowledge of the customer. It is a way of creating bonds with customers.

Four Types of Customers and Four Types of Service Providers in the B2B Sector

In Chapter 3 we mentioned various models for the B2B services sector. You may recall the vendors, the total solutions provider, the specialists and the game changers from Figure 3.9 as the service providers fitting to the specific needs of their customers. Here we will elaborate on that taxonomy and show you how these four service providers differ in their market strategy. For each of the four types of service providers we will show what their typical customers want, how that buying firm acts and how the service provider responds (Table 6.2).[60]

This way we have provided you with more insight into the way B2B service providers may respond to the specific needs of their customers from a strategic point of view. The critical metrics at the end of each box at the supply side refer to the critical metrics that have to be used to evaluate the supplier's performance. Next, it is interesting to see if and how top performing firms differ from low performers.

Top performance can be measured for instance in terms of high gross margins and large part of total sales from professional services. Such top performers (TP) in the B2B services sector in the USA differ significantly from the low performers (LP) in four respects:[61]

- TPs are smaller (small is beautiful and seems to create a competitive advantage over larger and probably older, more established and perhaps less adaptive firms).
- TPs' senior management has defined building professional services capabilities as a business priority to a much larger extent than LPs. They also have implemented it; it has become part of the company's culture and thus they do not have to pay that much explicit attention to it anymore.
- TPs implemented to a much larger degree a niche strategy. So, differentiation might contribute to the higher performance levels. LPs implemented to a larger degree a lean and mean strategy (referring to the cost – leader? – approach) or no strategy at all.
- TPs emphasize to a much larger degree than LPs' business advisory services, which by definition address higher business needs and are therefore regarded as more valuable. Customers may be willing to pay more for such services thus leading to higher margins.

In terms of best practices, TPs among others have a professional services strategy that aligns very well with the overall business strategy; they know very well how they differentiate from competitors, have a professional service strategic plan in place and segment professional services' clients by profitability. You see many of these items are similar to key traits of market oriented service organizations.

Let us end this chapter by looking in a more detailed way at service firms' performance from a strategic point of view. We will broaden the perspective again to service firms in general (and not only the B2B sector).

6.8 The Service Profit Chain

On various occasions we have talked about the link between customer satisfaction and employee satisfaction. The two are closely linked in service organizations. They mutually

Table 6.2 Customer needs and service provider's strategy in the B2B sector

Customers of Vendors	*Suppliers as Vendors*
● Offering's importance to customer: low ● Offering's uniqueness to customer low ● Offering's value potential: low ● Customer expectations: meet my specifications, make it easy for me to buy, give me the lowest price ● Actual buying is done by supporting functions like Purchasing ● Buying strategy: shop	● Strategy: Lean and mean ● Value proposition: adequate performance, low cost, no hassle ● Services offerings: product support services and/or professional services ● Drivers for success: efficiency ● Assets and capabilities: process optimization, appropriate use of technology ● Critical metrics: cost of sale, cost of delivery, customer acceptance

Customers of Total Solutions Providers	*Suppliers as Total Solutions Providers*
● Offering's importance to customer: high ● Offering's uniqueness to customer: low ● Offering's value potential: high ● Customer expectations: reliability, one-stop shopping, acceptable solution ● Actual buying is done by buying committee with senior management sponsors ● Buying strategy: negotiate	● Strategy: Big bang ● Value proposition: total package from a reliable supplier ● Services offerings: total solutions ● Drivers for success: breadth of offerings/assortment ● Assets and capabilities: high level selling skills, engagement management competency ● Critical metrics: project profitability, customer satisfaction

Customers of Specialists	*Suppliers as Specialists*
● Offering's importance to customer: low ● Offering's uniqueness to customer: high ● Offering's value potential: medium ● Customer expectations: provide the best-of-class services, give me options, do not take advantage of me ● Actual buying is done by subject matter experts ● Buying strategy: investigate (other suppliers and substitute services) constantly and compare	● Strategy: Niche ● Value proposition: world-class capabilities in selected areas ● Services offerings: product support services and/or professional services ● Drivers for success: deep knowledge of selected topic or field ● Assets and capabilities: expertise of employees, proprietary knowledge management system ● Critical metrics: market penetration, retention of key employees

Customers of Game Changers	*Suppliers as Game Changers*
● Offering's importance to customer: high ● Offering's uniqueness to customer: high ● Offering's value potential: extremely high ● Customer expectations: improved business performance through innovation ● Actual buying is done by top management ● Buying strategy: partnering between buyer and seller to get the job done 'world class'	● Strategy: Breakthrough ● Value proposition: game-changing propositions that no one else can provide ● Services offerings: professional services ● Drivers for success: constant innovation ● Assets and capabilities: the best and the brightest in the field ● Critical metrics: key client retention, managing the talent process

determine each other. Finally, it results in that customer loyalty and employee loyalty go hand in hand in service organizations. Remember that both may strengthen each other; however, they may also weaken each other. That is why it is so important in service organizations to look at this link. For, the personal interaction is so decisive in many kinds of service organizations.

The service profit chain shows the interaction between the satisfaction and loyalty of both groups of people involved in the service encounter (customers and employees) to the company and its service, resulting in greater profits due to high(er) productivity (greater commitment and less role stress or ambiguity and better service quality).[62] Usually the model's reasoning starts with the notion that the internal service quality within the service organization determines the external service quality on the market.[63] So, employees' satisfaction with their jobs and the other elements of the operating process within the company (productivity, structure, etc.) affects the quality of the service delivered (the value of the service to the customer), which in turn leads customers to be satisfied and loyal (or not), which positively affects revenues, revenue growth and profitability. And this in turn affects employee satisfaction again resulting in an ongoing process in which employees and customers affect one another. This is quite self-evident for the service encounter during the servuction process where both sides interact with one another (Figure 6.10).

You can imagine that these processes are very complicated and difficult to prove in reality. However, a meta-analysis of many studies on (elements of) the service profit chain provides some evidence for the following chain of effects.[64] Three topics heavily impact on an employee's job satisfaction and affective commitment to the company:

■ the interface between the employee and the job;
■ the interface between the employee and the manager; and
■ the interface between the employee and the organization.

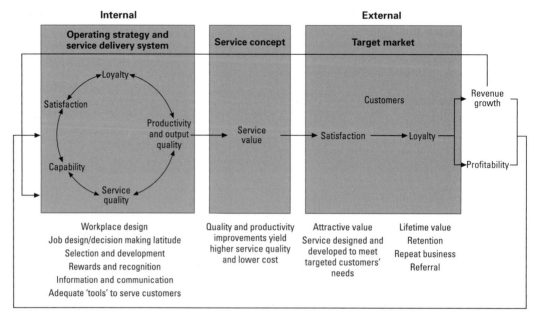

Figure 6.10 The service profit chain

The absence of role stress, the presence of autonomy to perform the task, and feedback on the tasks completed determine the employee–job interface in a positive way. An excellent relationship between supervisor and employee as well as the presence of an atmosphere of affective support and care about the employees has a positive impact on the employee–management interface. Perceived organizational support is the factor affecting the employee–organization interface; it hinges upon the employee's belief that the organization values their efforts and cares about their well-being. So, it hinges again upon the issue of care about people that we have described as one of the basic features of a market oriented culture.

Many studies support the hypothesis that the more positive customer evaluations are, the better the financial performance will be (as measured in terms of profitability, return on assets, return on investment, revenue per customer, market share and sales volume). According to the basic notion of the service profit chain, this affects employee's satisfaction and loyalty again.

In service organizations many concepts and disciplines have to be linked together in order to be market oriented and create excellent service quality. Consequently that impacts on the specific characteristics of controlling the service business. Using only a financial perspective will be insufficient.

6.9 Strategies, Performance and Our Balanced Score Card

In many instances, a service organization's goals and performance are formulated in financial terms such as return on investment, profits and sales. Accountants and controllers have realized that these financial figures reflect developments from the past. These past data are also the outcomes of a whole process in the organization and at the market. What is needed though is prospective future oriented information to develop strategies and evaluate company performance. Therefore, information is needed also about the processes within the company and the company strengths or weaknesses, for then it is possible to change processes – if necessary – to create a greater value to the stakeholders.

To meet these various perspectives, Kaplan and Norton have developed the concept of the balanced score card.[65] This score card tracks the key elements of a company's strategy, from continuous improvement and partnerships to teamwork and global scale. In that sense, it can be used as a means serving two purposes:

1   To develop strategies; and
2   To control the business.

We modified the original idea of the balanced score card slightly to create a better fit in order to get a balanced perspective on the whole service organization's performance. Within the balanced score card, six perspectives of company performance have been defined:

1   The financial perspective: to succeed financially, how should we appear to our shareholders?

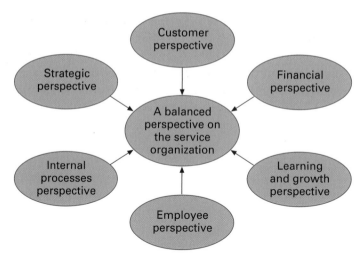

Figure 6.11 Our balanced score card

2 The customer perspective: to achieve our vision, how should we appear to our customers? How do customers perceive us?

3 The internal business process perspective: to satisfy our shareholders and customers, what business processes must we excel at?

4 The learning, innovation and growth perspective: to achieve our vision, how will we sustain our ability to change, innovate and improve?

5 The employee perspective: to achieve our vision, how should we appear to our employees? How do our employees perceive us (e.g turnover, job satisfaction, commitment, organizational citizenship, absenteeism, etc.)? and

6 The strategic perspective: will our strategic goals be met? How about our strategic position relative to our peer competitors? How about our own strengths, skills, core competencies, key success factors, assets and capabilities and chosen value discipline?[66]

Every service organization (be it in the profit or not for profit sector) can define for each of the perspectives shown in Figure 6.11 the relevant criteria to evaluate performance. Especially key performance indicators have to be found to provide information on the key success factors, core competencies and critical assets and capabilities of the organization.

Summary

Defining and developing a service organization's strategy is the main theme of this chapter. The model of the strategic pathway can be used here. It contains three parts:

1 Market choices (defining the market; market segmentation; market attractiveness; and planned market position);

2 Value proposition (value discipline; mission; competitive differentiation; and marketing assets); and

3 Key relationships (customers; competitors; collaborators; and co-workers or employees).

It is advantageous for service firms be market oriented. There is a strong positive relationship between market orientation and financial performance as well as between market orientation and non financial performance.

The organization's assets and capabilities are important when developing strategies to go to market. First, competitive advantages will be created when assets and capabilities are hard to imitate. Moreover, the unique knowledge and skills of employees and managers, high switching costs, high value to the customer and legal protection through copyrights and patents all create competitive advantage.

Service firms can position themselves in five ways:

1 Customized offering;
2 Offerings with an accepted price quality ratio (= value);
3 Offering unique services;
4 Offering a high level of supporting services; and
5 Innovative offerings.

From the four groups of assets and the four groups of capabilities, the critical assets and capabilities to create competitive advantages and competitive positions are:

- Customer-based assets;
- Alliance-based assets;
- Internal-based assets;
- Outside-in capabilities;
- Inside-out capabilities; and
- Spanning capabilities.

Many of these assets and capabilities refer to creating, developing and maintaining relationships with (key) customers. Relationship management is very critical to service a firm's successes.

Service firms may apply a generic strategy of cost leader, differentiation or focus. In practice, it appears they all have developed a competitive advantage on the customer-based assets (e.g. the credibility with customers, superior levels of customer service and support, relationships with key target customers and the company or brand name and reputation). Cost leaders also have competitive advantages on the inside-out capability of strong financial management and the cost advantage in production; differentiators and focussed firms have also competitive advantages on the outside-in capabilities of being good at creating, maintaining and enhancing relationships and good at understanding what customer needs and requirements are.

Service firms may have reached a position of leaders, challengers or followers in the overall market or in the niche market they have chosen. Market leaders (in the overall market and in the niche market) appear to have clear competitive advantages in:

- Customer-based assets (company or brand name and reputation, credibility with customers);
- Internal-based assets (marketing information systems);
- Distribution-based assets (extent, nature and uniqueness);
- Alliance-based assets (market access and technology); and
- Spanning capabilities (effective development and launch of new services).

Other concepts or tools that can be used to develop and implement strategies are:

- Generic strategies like producing low cost services, highly differentiated services and highly differentiated services at low cost;

- Market penetration, services development, market development and diversification (Ansoff);
- E-strategies;
- The wheel of servicing (entry, trading up and vulnerability);
- Variety strategies; and
- Loyalty strategies.

With respect to vendors, total solutions providers, specialists and game changers, the specific characteristics of the customers and the service providers are linked together providing insights in the buying and selling of services in B2B markets. Also the critical metrics in evaluating the service firm's performance have been mentioned. They differ for each of the four situations. Top performers are relatively small, apply a niche strategy, focus on business advisory services and their top management see the capabilities as business priority.

The service profit chain and the balanced score card can be used to evaluate and assess a service firm's performance. We have emphasized six perspectives for this performance evaluation:

- Financial;
- Customer;
- Internal business process;
- Learning, innovation and growth;
- Employee; and
- Strategic perspective.

Questions

1. Describe what would you consider as the key success factors of service organizations.
2. Define what is meant by the term market strategies.
3. Describe the difference between a generic strategy and a marketing strategy.
4. Using an example to illustrate, describe the unique assets and capabilities of a service organization that will lead to a competitive advantage.
5. Describe what you perceive as being the main differences and similarities between the results for the 12 countries in Table 6.1.
6. Describe the way in which assets and capabilities differ for:
   a market leaders;
   b followers;
   c challengers (in the overall and niche market).
7. Define market orientation.
8. Describe the leadership style required in a market orientated firm.
9. Describe how a 'higher degree' of market performance affects corporate performance.
10. Explain why relationship marketing is so important in services marketing. Does your answer differ for the B2C and the B2B sectors?
11. Explain the specific elements of evaluating and assessing a service firm's performance via:
    a the service profit chain; and
    b the balanced score card.

12. What is the difference between a GSP and an LSP?
13. Given our conclusions about the assets and capabilities of service firms applying a strategy of cost leader, differentiation and focus,
    a What assets and capabilities are critical to a GSP?
    b What assets and capabilities are critical to an LSP?
14. What are the critical metrics for:
    a vendors?
    b total solutions suppliers?
    c specialists? and
    d game changers?
15. Explain why the metrics listed in question 14 are the critical metrics.
16. Describe the concept of the wheel of servicing.

Assignments

1. Make a graph of the chain of effects found in empirical studies on the service profit chain as described in section 6.8. What is your main conclusion from this graph on managing a service organization?
2. Which companies are part of the alliances mentioned in Service Practice 6.5? How has that changed in the past five years?
3. How can a bank stimulate variety-seeking behaviour among its private investment clients? How can an airline encourage loyalty in its freight segment (not the passenger part of its business)?
4. Search for the mission statement of a bank and one charity in your own town.
    a Write them down.
    b Are the statements clear to you?
    c Are the statements clear to the company employees? Why or why not?
    d Do the statement guide the employees' daily behaviour?
    e How do the statements fit with the assets and capabilities of those organizations?
5. Collect the annual reports of some banks, hotel chains and consultancy firms.
    a Do these firms use the balanced score card?
    b Can you analyse their performance in applying the balanced score card yourself to these reports?
    c What conclusions can be drawn about their performance in the various perspectives?

Endnotes

1 This Service Practice has been based on Beatty (2005).

2 This section is based to a large extent on Kasper (2002).

3 The authors themselves maintain that study is still exploratory; data about consumer and industrial services are pooled by Bharadwaj and Menon (1993). We would like to add that the reader should also be aware of the fact that many scholars have also critized the PIMS-database and analysis in some respects.

4 Bharadwaj and Menon, 1993, pp. 31–32.

5 See a forthcoming paper by Kasper *et al.*, 2006a, 2006b, with the results of a four-country study on the relationship between market orientation and (non) financial performance.

6 We follow here the way Piercy (1997, p. 18) elaborates on the work of James P. Womack and Daniel T. Jones (1996).

7 See Chapter 2.

8 See for instance Blanchard, Zigarmi and Zigarmi (1985); Quinn (1988); Dessler (2002); or Robbins and Coulter (2002). We can think of democratic, autocratic, laissez-faire, employee oriented, production oriented, supportive, participative, achievement, coaching, transactional, transformational, charismatic or facilitator, and many more.

9 Kasper, 2002, p. 1054.

10 Berry, 1995.

11 Gray, Matear and Matheson, 2002.

12 This conclusion could be drawn from a meta analysis of many studies on market orientation and performance (also in service industries) carried out by Esteban, Millán, Molina and Martín-Consuegra (2002). See also Vorhies, Harker and Roa (1999).

13 Cano, Carrillat and Jaramillo, 2004.

14 Hurley and Hult, 1998; Han, Kim and Srivastava, 1998; Baker and Sinkula, 1999.

15 Lado, Maydeu-Olivares and Rivera, 1998. In total, 34 Belgian and 32 Spanish insurance companies were involved in this study.

16 See the UK study by Siguaw, Simpson and Baker (1997), p. 25.

17 Matear, Osborne, Garrett and Gray, 2002.

18 See e.g. Ittner and Larcker, 1998; Banker *et al.*, 2000; and Nager and Rajan, 2001.

19 See Esteban *et al.*, 2002.

20 Kasper and Bloemer, 2000.

21 See Chapter 2.

22 This section is based to a large extent on Nigel Piercy (1997, 2002). As said, we adjusted the original model to a certain extent.

23 This question would be the typical question of looking at sustainability when we look at it from the perspective of the resource-based view of the firm. See for instance Hunt and Morgan (1995); Hunt and Morgan (1996); Hunt (2001).

24 Kasper, Bloemer, Kyriakopoulos, Hooley and Greenley, 2004.

25 See endnote 24.

26 These factors occurred after exploratory factor analysis of the 11 topics of financial and non financial performance that were taken into account. These two factors explain more than 70% of the total variance. See Kasper *et al.* (2004).

27 This section draws upon the first results of an international study in 12 countries initiated by Graham Hooley and Gordon Greenley. Papers by Kasper *et al.*, 2005, 2006a, 2006b, 2006c.

28 The answers are self-reported opinions by managers of the respective firms.

29 Porter, 1980.

30 Hamel and Prahalad, 1994, Chapter 12.

31 Roth and Amoroso, 1993.

32 Remember this is more than just being a market leader with all its key success factors discussed in the previous pages. However, imposing such a vision on the whole industry is quite difficult. Firms realizing service breakthroughs are well on the way to shaping the future of an entire industry. Probably, this 'stage' is easier to accomplish.

33 Heskett, Sasser and Hart, 1990.

34 Heskett, Sasser and Hart, 1990, p. 261.

35 This Service Practice is partly based on Jacoby and Pringle (2005).

36 This way of reasoning is in line with the ideas of George Day about a market oriented company as expressed in our Chapter 2.

37 Treacy and Wiersema, 1995.

38 Heskett, 1986.

39 We use James Heskett's framework as a starting point for the discussion in this section, add some of our own insights to it, and use our own terminology at certain points to avoid confusion.

40 Ansoff, 1965. The technology dimensions in this section stems from Abell (1980).

41 Tiggelaar, 1999.

42 This Service Practice is based on McDonald (2005).

43 See e.g. Johnson and Scholes, 1988.

44 Hinfelaar, 2004.

45 See Fang, Fridh and Schultzberg, 2004.

46 This is also one of the possibilities associated with one of the positions in the GE-matrix used in strategic planning.

47 This Service Practice is based on Simonian (2005).

48 These issues have been discussed in Chapter 1.

49 The wheel of servicing can be regarded as an application of the well-known wheel of retailing developed by McNair in the 1950s.

50 It not only occurs in consumer behaviour but also in political behaviour (e.g. floating votes) and the church.

51 These causes are mentioned in Schriver (1997).

52 Kahn, 1998. In a commentary Lehmann (1998) questions whether the basic assumption really holds that more variety is always better.

53 In the retail world, it appears the procurement department has an important say here. They decide what will be put on the shelves.

54 Duboff and Sherer (1997) mention the first four; we have added the fifth.

55 See for instance Kotler, Brown, Adam and Armstrong (2004). Remember that the positions we talk about here is a completely different concept from positioning discussed in the previous sections. Here we discuss the four positions a firm can have in the market; positioning refers to the position of the firm or brand in the mind of the customer.

56 These conclusions are based on the prelimary results of the studies done by Kasper *et al.* mentioned in endnotes 24 and 27.

57 Campbell and Frei, 2004.

58 Payne, 1993.

59 Venetis, 1997.

60 This section is based to a very large extent on Alexander and Hordes (2003). Sometimes we have used some terms that are more in line with the concepts we used in our book.

61 These results are based on Alexander (2004).

62 Heskett, Jones, Loveman, Sasser and Schlesinger, 1994; Heskett, Sasser and Schlesinger, 1997.

63 See also Palmer (2005), section 8.3.

64 This chain of effects is based on our interpretation of the results published in Sandra Streukens' 2005 PhD.

65 Kaplan and Norton, 1992.

66 Based on these ideas and realizing the importance of brands (especially in the service sector as one of the key success factors) we can understand that Slater, Olson and Reddy (1997) developed the idea of the strategic score card encompassing the next five perspectives (and their operationalization): 1 All strategies; 2 Customer intimacy; 3 Product leadership; 4 Operational excellence; 5 Brand champion. It would go too far to elaborate upon this.

Chapter 7

Internationalizing Services

Reproduced by permission of ABN AMRO

Learning objectives

At the end of this chapter you will be able to:

1 Evaluate the international services sector

2 Discuss the motives which may lead a service firm to internationalize

3 Formulate the management of assets and capabilities within the international services sector

4 Distinguish between service standardization and service adaptation

5 Discuss the theory of internationalization of foreign markets

6 Describe the different entry barriers

7 Describe the different entry strategies

7.1   Introduction

Market Opportunities in India. Here's how to Grab Your Share[1]

For 60 years, Vilas Vitha's family has sold vegetables in a narrow lane in central Bombay. Now he has added a new sales tool, a mobile phone. The 24-year-old, who earns €90 per month, is the first in the family to own a mobile phone and he is using it to arrange home deliveries for customers. As more working-class Indians like Mr Vitha go mobile, India's cellular market is finally fulfilling its potential. Lower prices and rising incomes are translating into explosive growth. In 2005 the expectations are for 56 million users, which will double in 2006. That is turning India to one of the hottest markets for hand-phone makers, telecom equipment suppliers and investors. There are two million new subscribers per month.

Lucent Technologies Inc. and Nokia have already identified India as a key market. The government has ended a feud between two categories of telecom licence holders. The resulting competitive landscape means cheaper prices for consumers.

For foreign investors, the remaining hurdle to the Indian market is the cap on foreign investment in local telecom concerns which currently stands at 49%. The government will increase the cap to 74% after assessing the risk associated with foreigners controlling telecom ventures and political manoeuvering. There is still a widely held opinion that the telecom sector badly needs foreign funds as the potential growth is estimated to jump from 30 million to 200 million subscribers in three to four years.

The Indian new middle class are called 'zippies' – young Indians who walk around with a zip in their stride, oozing with attitude, ambition and money. They are the representatives of India's burgeoning middle class, which outnumbers the entire US population. Indian consumers are buying everything from imported computers to cell phones and clothes. According to some preliminary forecasts, the 487 million middle-class Indians will spend an additional $420 billion during the coming four years. The new business opportunities are facilitated via introducing new credit policy and fiscal reforms, eliminating trade restrictions on industries such as textile and pharmaceuticals and implementing business friendly laws.

Summarizing, there is a little secret that you do not make money in India until your product or service does make sense for the masses; these are the hundreds of millions of people earning as little as US$3 per day.

Cultural barriers, poor infrastructure and government restrictions all make the business with India a challenge. The 'Beginner's Guide to Indian Marketing' looks like the following:

☐   *Scale down*: While American customers favour large containers, Indians save cash by buying smaller quantities. Revlon have sold more bottles of nail polish after reducing the size of their nail polish bottles.

☐ *Price for mass appeal*: UTStarcom found that spending constraints trickle down; it had to design cheaper network switches to sell to local phone companies.

☐ *Tailor products to Indian tastes*: since Subway started to offer a separate vegetarian counter and a specialized 'Indian Delights' menu, they opened 27 new stores within the last three years.

☐ *Localize your message*: Pepsi was not successful in using the same commercials aired elsewhere. However when Pepsi recruited the local box-office star Shahrukh Khan, sales immediately took off.

☐ *Find a good partner*: tap into the booming local chains. The local branches of Food World or Pantaloon are favoured places for the Indian middle class. Distribution through these outlets is viewed positively.

The terms 'globalization' and 'internationalization' are often used interchangeably. Both terms indicate that national boundaries are becoming less important across the world, even in service industries which have often been locally bound. Internationalization refers to organizations operating offshore whereas globalization encompasses a broader scope including the convergence of demand and supply in many areas around the world.[2] In essence, the difference between globalization and internationalization is not that important here, since we intend to focus on service organizations starting their international activities. So, both concepts will be used interchangeably here. This chapter is aimed at discussing the unique challenges service organizations encounter when they go international, with a specific focus on the impact of international on an organization's strategy.

After introducing the global services environment in section 7.2, this chapter shows the importance of managing the basic characteristics of services in an international setting (section 7.3). For example, are companies able to export intangibles? How can firms deal with standardization or adaptation; and how can service quality be managed abroad?[3]

Service organizations will have to assess their resources in order to develop the assets and capabilities to be able to manage the service features successfully in foreign markets. Section 7.4 documents the assets and capabilities of market oriented international service providers; what is unique for them compared to what we learned about assets and capabilities in general in Chapter 6? Section 7.5 is about the organizational impetus to internationalize as well as the main theories relevant to services organizations considering internationalization.

After understanding why organizations internationalize and having knowledge of the available strategic options, companies will have to consider the barriers to entry in specific markets, after which, it can choose a particular entry mode (section 7.6). The next section of this chapter introduces features of the internationalization strategies. Finally we make some remarks on the (im)possibility of internationalizing location bound and intangible services. The outline of this chapter is given in Figure 7.1.

7.2 The Global Services Environment

Many authors have raised the question as to whether services really can be imported or exported. The characteristics of services determine the predominantly 'local' structure of

Figure 7.1   Chapter outline

service firms. Intangibility leads to services' close buyer–supplier interactions. The 'service encounter argument' refers to the need for the physical presence of both parties during the service encounter. This will complicate the internationalization process in services. But is this really the case? Can this international physical distance be bridged? The following statistics prove it must be feasible indeed. How this can be done, will be the topic of this chapter.

Table 7.1 gives an overview of the international services trade (exports and imports) within the OECD countries.[4] We added two columns indicating which countries are net exporters and net importers of services. There are more countries that can be labelled as net exporters than as net importers of services in this group of 29 OECD countries. Net exporters are for instance France, United Kingdom, United States, Luxembourg and Turkey, while for instance Germany, Japan, Canada, Korea and Portugal are net importers of services.

Service exports, covering things like transport services, travel, other commercial services and government services, between OECD countries, accounted for just over 80% of total OECD exports. The largest destination region is the EU with 46%, followed by NAFTA with 21% of service exports. The OECD Asia and Oceania countries mainly trade with Asia and Oceania (over 3% of world exports) and American (3% of world exports) countries.

When we take a closer look at the OECD totals mentioned in Table 7.1, we can break down total exports and imports to three main sectors of transport, travel, finance and insurance, and the remaining other services. The following data are found and shown in Table 7.2.

Travelling and transport are two large service sectors, as you can see. In travelling you may think of holidays and business trips but also of commuting to work. With respect to transport you may think of air lines (Varig or Virgin), shipping cargo (Dutch P&O Nedlloyd which merged with Danish Maersk), busses (e.g. Eurolines), trains (Deutsche Bundesbahn or Amtrak) as well as of transportation via pipelines of commodities such as oil and gas.

Table 7.1 Services exports and imports in OECD countries in 2002

Countries	Imports in billion US$	Exports in billion US$	Net exporter of services	Net importer of services
Australia	18.1	17.9		X
Austria	34.2[a]	35.1[a]	X	
Belgium	35.9	37.3	X	
Canada	42.5	37.2		X
Czech Republic	6.3	7.0	X	
Denmark	25.1	27.1	X	
Finland	8.2	6.5		X
France	68.2	85.9	X	
Germany	150.1	105.6		X
Greece	9.8	19.9	X	
Hungary	7.2	7.8	X	
Iceland	1.1	1.1		
Ireland	40.3	28.2		X
Italy	63.1	59.6		X
Japan	107.7	65.7		X
Korea	35.6	28.1		X
Luxembourg	13.6	20.4	X	
Mexico	17.7	12.7		X
Netherlands	56.9	55.7		X
New Zealand	4.7	5.1	X	
Norway	16.4	19.2	X	
Poland	9.2	10.0	X	
Portugal	6.7	9.8	X	
Slovak Republic	2.3	2.8	X	
Spain	37.7	62.3	X	
Sweden	23.8	23.7		X
Switzerland	15.2	29.4	X	
Turkey	6.2	14.0	X	
United Kingdom	106.9	129.6	X	
United States	227.4	288.7	X	
G7	765.8	772.3		X
EU-15[b]	690.8	706.9	X	
OECD total	1208.3	1253.6	X	

Notes:
a. including services not allocated by type of service
b. including estimates of data which may not be separately available for individual countries

Table 7.2 Breakdown of total exports and imports of services in OECD countries, 2002

Sectors	Percentage of total exports	Percentage of total imports
Transport	23.5%	– 21.6%
Travel	27.9%	27.5%
Finance and insurance	7.3%	9.5%
Other services	41.3%	41.3%

Many of the arguments in favour of internationalizing services will outweigh the risks of internationalization. Changes in information technology appear to be a major driving force behind the rapid growth of service internationalization.[5] Recent changes in technology make it possible to export services and organize the accompanying international marketing activities in a different way from one or two decades ago. In this respect, it is important to stipulate the differences between knowledge/information-based services and resource-based services.[6] Knowledge and information-based services are easier to export than resource-based services, because they contain a large technology component.

In some industries, demand may trigger the internationalization of services to these countries. Business travellers and companies may expect the same high quality service from hotels and airlines the world over. It may also be that service providers are forced to internationalize when their national clients internationalize in order to be able to deliver their service world wide. In essence, we mentioned here the two basic options service firms have in internationalizing;

1 seek your own market, or,
2 follow your client and be there.[7]

Basically, these are the answers to the questions raised at the beginning of this section.

Export and internationalization are important not only to the survival of many large service companies but also small and medium sized service firms. The reason is simple; this strategic growth option offers tremendous potential for enhancing sales growth, increasing efficiency and improving quality.[8] For instance, the emerging markets of Brazil, Russia, India and China are offering attractive growth options to international service providers with well-known brand names.

SERVICE PRACTICE 7.2

Storm over Globalization[9]

In 1820, 85% of the world population lived on US$1 per day. In 1950 this figure dropped to 50%; in 1980, 30%. Currently it is 20%. Infant mortality rates have decreased from 18 per 1000 in 1950 to six per 1000 in 1995. Alongside this, illiteracy has decreased from 74% in 1926 to 52% in 1948 to 20% today. Such advances are related to the process of liberalizing and globalization.

In 1950, 30% of the population were living in democratic regimes; nowadays this is already 60%. Incomes have increased and working hours have decreased. In 1870 the average employee in Western Europe had one hour of work for each two hours of leisure (1 : 2). In 1950 the proportion was 1 : 4, and now it is 1 : 8. The capitalism spread however is uneven across the world.

Forty years ago South Korea was economically similar to Zambia and Taiwan. The income *per capita* in Zambia in 2000 was US$880 per annum and in Congo US$1500 per annum, whereas it was US$16 500 per annum in Taiwan and in South Korea US$12 600 per annum. The economy in Asiatic countries continues to open, while most economies in Africa are run under protectionism, which has a negative impact on development.

Although the market is not perfect, it is a better manager than government in distributing goods and services. The trade barriers of the West are heavily criticized. The poor countries can sell anything to the West but because of trade barriers, their own products become automatically much more expensive.

Around the world, support for free trade is weak at best, and the World Trade Organization (WTO) is copping the blame for the perceived evils of globalization. It is under attack from trade unions, greens and even consumer groups, all of whom say its rules advance big companies' global ambitions at the expense of jobs and the environment. They also attack the WTO for being secretive and unaccountable. Such arguments will gain ground unless the case for globalization is made with renewed vigour.

Despite the huge strides towards open markets over the past 50 years, industries such as agriculture, textiles, transport by air and shipping remain highly protected. Many tariffs are still high. New trade barriers keep appearing. On the other hand, EU directives on the free trade of services are subject to much disagreement in many countries today, especially when former Eastern Europeans are prepared to work in countries like France at significantly lower salaries than the local population, particularly in industries like plumbing or transportation.

Booming industries such as computing and telecommunications are vulnerable from foreign competition. Notably through standards that handicap foreign firms. Even e-commerce can be subject to trade restrictions. A new effort to open markets is needed both in the services and in the goods sectors.

As shown in Chapter 1, each firm is exposed to macro environmental factors that play a crucial role determining market entry. In an international context the same environmental factors apply:[10]

- Demographic environment;
- Regulatory environment;
- Economic environment;
- Technological environment; and
- Social (and cultural) environment.

We discussed these factors in Chapter 1. Here, in the international context, we would like to pay some more attention to the issue of national culture. National culture is an important driver of a service firm's internationalization strategy and actions. Some other facts will be discussed in addition to what has already been said in Chapter 3 on culture and its impact on customer behaviour. One important task for the global services marketer is to discover culturally universal models of behaviour (or understand the differences). Cultural universals are, according to the anthropologist George Murdock: athletic sports, cooking, dancing, decorative art, education, medicine, family feasting, ethics, residence rules, property rights, status differentiation and trade.

Edward Hall has suggested a concept of high and low context culture to assist in understanding different cultural orientations.[11] In a low context culture there are clear messages and the words consist of all the information. In high context culture there is less information in the verbal part of the message. The high context countries (Japan, Saudi Arabia) require less legal paperwork (and smaller contracts) while large and detailed contracts are essential for low context countries (USA, Germany). In high context cultures, deals are made with much less information, related to background and character of the participants. For example, much more reliance is placed on the words and numbers in the loan application.

Knowledge and understanding of cross-cultural differences are crucial for instance during negotiations and in performing market research. This determines how negotiations should or can be done. In cross-cultural marketing studies of social variables such as values or attitudes, it is often assumed that differences in scores can be compared at face value. However, a study conducted in six EU countries shows that response styles such as acquiescence may affect answers, particularly on rating scales. It confirms that ignoring national differences in response styles may lead to invalid inferences in cross-cultural research.[12]

One of the ways in which organizations can achieve international coordination is to use a 'common language' with respect to, for instance, etiquette, norms and values, and communication methods. Focussing on a shared, common culture ensures that people start thinking and acting in the same manner.[13] Besides, a common culture helps to ensure that a similar approach is adapted to clients everywhere, which makes large (international) or 'mobile' clients feel more at home. Organizations differ in the extent to which their culture is shared within and between countries.

Culture is not only something that exists outside the walls of the company. Corporate culture is often a strong intangible asset of world-class service providers revealing their market orientation toward the care of people. Some organizations – for example HSBC, the global local bank or McDonald's – are known for their 'strong' or homogeneous (management) culture, with common characteristics worldwide that help facilitate decision making among managers. Other organizations, such as trading firms, operating in various markets, typically have many different sub-cultures when they do not have their own green field operations but co-operate for instance with subsidiaries or agencies.

Culture is probably not the most simply manageable coordination mechanism, although many organizations work hard at it through universal codes of conduct, joint introduction programmes for new personnel and stimulation of the convergence of norms and values through cross-cultural and cross-functional operation teams.

7.3 Managing the Basic Characteristics of Services Internationally

In Chapter 2 we mentioned five basic characteristics of services:

- Intangibility;
- Inseparability;
- Inconsistency;
- Inventory; and
- Inability to own.

We will discuss each of these characteristics briefly in the context of internationalization.

Intangibility

As service firms primarily deliver intangibles, the impact of differences in perceived risk may affect the way a service's intangibility will be perceived. Service quality and consistent delivery over time are both crucial aspects. To cope with these aspects it is important for international service firms to institutionalize the knowledge gained abroad by means of procedures, manuals, improved service processes and IT solutions, and disseminate this knowledge among the service workers to learn from, so as they can avoid the same mistakes occurring elsewhere in the world.

Collecting, analysing, interpreting and disseminating (and thus institutionalizing) knowledge on foreign markets is a capability in its own right. This is a basic feature of market oriented international service organizations. It relates to the firm's customer-based assets and outside-in capabilities. For that reason, service companies have to invest in their major asset, employees. Recruiting internationally experienced staff is one way to acquire the necessary knowledge to operate successfully across borders. It is critical that firms planning to internationalize consider how locally employed staff live the organization's brand, and the subsequent impact that this will have on the organization's international image.

Fuelled by high wages in western countries, competitive wages abroad, the high costs of expatriates, ICT, improved education and the fast growing middle class in many emerging markets, service firms have been forced to change their approach to business. Currently service firms must pay ample attention to recruiting foreign staff, using local knowledge and developing relationships in the hope that this will provide them with a competitive advantage, in the event that other international firms will seek to move into the same market.

Citigroup is a company that wants to use the advantage of its resources and act quickly when opportunities arise, as you can see in Service Practice 7.3.

SERVICE PRACTICE 7.3

Citigroup Moves Quickly

Citigroup, the world's largest financial services firm, aims to move quickly and project its operations and services globally. The group unveiled smaller and seemingly riskier ventures such as the $US2.73 billion (€2.23 billion) acquisition of Kor Am Bank, a midsize South Korean lender, and in China, the rollout of the first credit card issued by a foreign bank that can be settled in the local currency, yuan.

The willingness of the group to internationalize is based on several trends:

- 95% of the world's population live outside the USA and Canada.
- 65% of the world's gross domestic product is generated outside of the USA and Canada.
- 35% of Citigroup's earnings are generated outside the USA.

In consideration of these trends, Citigroup sees two big opportunities. First, to aggressively expand its consumer banking presence outside the USA in order to boost profits. Second, to leave behind rival American banks only now moving to copy the Citigroup's model of marrying domestic corporate and consumer banking in the USA.

The main competitors of the Group in the push to expand internationally aren't US banks. London-based HSBC Holding plc boasts that its earnings are already spread around the globe more evenly than Citigroup's and General Electric Co. Insurance giant American International Group (AIG), already has considerable consumer finance business around the globe.

HSBC also aims to expand its consumer finance operations in emerging markets and has purchased financial firms in Mexico and Brazil. Citigroup sees advantage before the other American competitors who are busy with large domestic mergers. The group plans to invest further overseas and develop as a bank that could serve businesses and wealthy individuals far beyond the US border. The opportunities to tap into the enormous new middle class emerging in developing economies from Poland to India to China are also taken into consideration.

But going global is not always easy. Citigroup was harmed by some earlier incursions like the Latin America debt crisis, and making a substantial loss in 1998 from the market turmoil stemming from Russia's debt default and two years later in Argentina. China's credit card culture is in its infancy and that is associated with risk for the Citigroup with its current efforts of internationalization.[14]

Inseparability

Inseparability refers to the simultaneous production and consumption of services. This has two major consequences for internationalization of services:

- The problem of customer accessibility to the service delivery system; and
- The problem of difference in culture.[15]

The first issue on accessibility implies that service firms usually have to be in foreign countries while it is quite hard to export services. If Warner Brothers wants to grow, more film parks have to be set up in other countries. Deutsche Bank is a latecomer on the Chinese investment banking scene but seems to be quite successful in their operation since they hired Lee Zhang who 'has focused on trying to land China's corporate heavy-weights seeking to raise capital or to obtain merger-and-acquisition advice, rather than trawling for higher-volume but less-lucrative clients'.[16] It seems to be necessary that local management is present to run the business.

Participation during the servuction process involves two aspects which are of concern when services firms internationalize. These concerns are physical presence and the distinction between high and low contact services. This may also be called the distinction between soft and hard services. Analysing these provides a helpful tool to judge the extent that export of services is possible or if a physical presence is needed directly in the country that the firm is seeking to move into. These issues are related.

With respect to the physical presence of the customer, two kinds of service firms can be distinguished: soft and hard services firms.

1 *Soft service firms* are those service providers for whom it is impossible to decouple production and consumption. Usually such firms provide high contact services. The physical presence of both parties during the service encounter is necessary. Hairdressing, restaurants, hotels, car rental and accountancy firms belong to this category.

2 *Hard service firms* are those firms where it is indeed possible to separate production and consumption. This is usually the case in low (personal) contact services. E-tailing and software fall in this hard category.

Typically, soft service firms cannot export (unless they send their staff abroad), whereas hard service firms can. This again is based on the location bound character of some services.[17] As a result service firms seeking to internationalize should envisage clearly how to manage this degree of interactivity between the client and themselves.

The discussion here emphasizes what we already noted in section 7.2, the basic distinction between strategies of international service firms has to be made between 'client following' and 'market seeking'.[18] Client following means that the service firm enters foreign markets primarily to serve the foreign subsidiaries of their domestic clients. Most international brokers and auditing firms use such a strategy. Sometimes they are forced to follow clients, not only because of new business in a foreign country but also so as not to lose the existing business in the home country.[19] Market seeking occurs when the service firm enters foreign markets primarily to serve new foreign customers. You may understand that these perspectives will impact on the content of relationship marketing in those countries.

Inconsistencies of Service Delivery

Usually, market opportunities are defined in terms of the purchasing power for products and services, margins, lack of competition and competitive advantage. Putting a great emphasis on service quality and customer satisfaction we believe market oriented service firms can also apply these issues in analysing foreign market opportunities. For instance, the German Customer Barometer, which measures quality and satisfaction in many industries, signalled in the mid-1990s clear opportunities for upgrading existing services. On the question: 'How satisfied are you with the service of your main supplier altogether?' many suppliers got poor to average marks. In particular, the human side of the service encounter needed much improvement in Germany at that time. That is *the* service quality attribute for incumbent firms to achieve in Germany.[20]

While we discussed the issue of perceived risk in a previous section on intangibility, we stress here the impact of culture on customer expectations, a topic highly relevant in defining and measuring service quality. Service quality in turn defines customer satisfaction. International service firms have to take into account that countries may differ in what is considered to be the desired, acceptable or ideal level of expectations and actual experiences.[21] Thus, the zone of tolerance and service surprises may differ between countries.

When service firms are internationalizing, they will be confronted with different beliefs about the meaning of service quality in different cultures. This can be further understood through analysing the servuction process.[22] This process consists of three sets of resources; each of them may impact differently on the final service quality during and after the servuction process:

■ Customer resources and their style of participation in the service encounter;

- Contact resources (contact persons of the service provider and their style of delivering the service); and
- Physical resources.

The interaction between the first two sets of resources is at stake here. It hinges upon the participation style of the customer and the service style of the company employees. There should be a link between these styles of customers and employees to avoid mismatches and dissatisfaction, given the framework of the physical resources and environment (the service encounter). Four dimensions can be used in describing and explaining differences in these service styles. These are:

1 Empathetic versus non empathetic. This dimension deals with the degree of empathy shown by service providers in their approach to the customer;
2 Efficient versus inefficient. This dimension refers to the efficiency of the service production process as seen from the customer's point of view;
3 Remote versus close. This dimension indicates how customers perceive and assess service employees; and
4 Attentive versus inattentive. This dimension refers to the speed with which contact employees react to the customer's needs.

These dimensions can be used to explain various service styles that are (or should be) practised in various parts of the world because they fit the best to the cultural characteristics of those countries:

- The Oriental service style (OSS) will be practised in the Far East, Japan and India; its nature is empathetic and remote;
- The American service style (ASS) is extremely close and friendly; contact persons try to be attentive and friendly toward customers;
- The European service style (ESS) is made up of many sub-styles because Europe does not have a common culture. In general, the European style is not as efficient as the American one and not as attentive as the Oriental one. The cultural map of the world in Chapter 3 may give you more information on what styles may fit to which parts of this map.

Service firms intending on internationalizing should take these cultural differences into account and if deemed necessary may consider changing their strategies and their service encounter scripts. Approaches found to be effective in one market need not be effective in other markets. Worldwide standardization (uniform offer across cultures and countries) may not always be appropriate, in which case services firms will need to adapt their services to local circumstances. The major advantages of adaptation are: overcoming barriers to entry; consumption patterns; physical environment such as climate; stage of economic development; industry conditions; competitive practices; marketing institutions and distribution channels; legal restrictions; technical requirements; and cultural factors. The obstacles to standardization are summarized in Table 7.3.

From this discussion, you may have the impression that it is difficult to standardize service businesses and that the only thing that counts is customization. However, we think there is a converging trend. Customization was traditionally achieved through interaction with people,

Table 7.3   Obstacles to standardization in international marketing strategies

Factors limiting standardization	Product design	Pricing	Distribution	Sales force	Advertising & promotion: branding & packaging
Market characteristics					
Physical environment	Climate Product use conditions		Customer mobility	Dispersion of customers	Access to media Climate
Stage of economic and industrial development	Income levels Labour costs in relation to capital costs	Income levels	Consumer shopping patterns	Wage levels, availability of manpower	Needs for convenience rather than economy Purchase quantities
Cultural factors	'Custom and tradition' Attitudes toward foreign goods	Attitudes toward bargaining	Consumer shopping patterns	Attitudes toward selling	Language, literacy Symbolism
Industry conditions					
State of product life cycle in each market	Extent of product differentiation	Elasticity of demand	Availability of outlets Desirability of private brands	Need for missionary sales effort	Awareness, experience with products
Competition	Quality levels	Local costs Prices of substitutes	Competitors' control of outlets	Competitors' sales forces	Competitive expenditures, messages
Marketing institutions					
Distributive system	Availability of outlets	Prevailing margins	Number and variety of outlets available Ability to 'force' distribution	Number size, dispersion of outlets	Extent of self-service
Advertising media and agencies				Effectiveness of advertising, need for substitutes	Media availability, costs, overlaps
Legal restrictions	Product standards	Tariffs and taxes	Restrictions on product lines	General employment restrictions	Specific restrictions on messages, costs
	Patent laws	Antitrust laws	Resale price maintenance	Specific restrictions on selling	Trademark laws
	Tariffs and taxes	Resale price maintenance			

but can now also be achieved with remote communication. For instance, in service industries such as computer services, software and shopping, telephone and electronic links are rapidly growing as an addition to or replacement of more conventional ways of delivering services. Call centres, home shopping and Internet banking are forms which are all quite new and growing.

International service firms are now able to operate parallel modes in different countries, and even within one particular country. The growing knowledge of combining the three relevant production factors in services, namely human capital, physical capital and information technology, offers many opportunities to combine standardization and customization.

Inventories of Services: Stock Keeping in an International Context

The increasing technological component within services not only has a tremendous impact on the opportunities to internationalize but also on the choice of entry mode. Technological advances may avoid the necessity of the physical presence or physical proximity during the service encounter and thus impact on the inventory problems. Once a service firm does not have to have its complete offering on a particular site, it simplifies operations. In turn, this will make it easier to cope with the risks connected with servicing foreign markets.

A call centre may easily service clients abroad. It is not necessary for the company to establish sales or service centres in the individual countries. The technological component influences all the five I's. Technology may help intangible products to become less heterogeneous, in other words, to ensure that the service quality is at a consistent high level across markets. The way in which the service is delivered, for example, the degree to which the services are embodied in or delivered through tangible goods, determines the manner the inventory of services should be managed. Software or music embodied in CDs will need a different logistics policy than software or music transferred via the Internet. And these different logistics are dependent on and determine the way services are 'stored'.

A classification scheme for internationalizing services can be based on a six-sector matrix (see Figure 7.2).[23] It originates from the idea that modes of service internationalization are based on decisions about:

■ The nature of the service (mainly the degree of interaction between service provider and customer during the service encounter); and
■ The way in which the service is delivered (for instance, the degree to which the services are embodied in or delivered through tangible goods). And this delivery is partly determined by the way logistics and inventories are managed.

The vertical axis in Figure 7.2 represents the relative involvement of goods in a service. The horizontal axis depicts the degree of consumer/producer interaction (which is low in sectors 1, 2 and 3 and high in sectors 4, 5 and 6). Services in sector 1 are limited in international potential in their present form unless you start a new operation in those countries. Sector 3 services are easy to export from the country of origin, because these services are (almost)

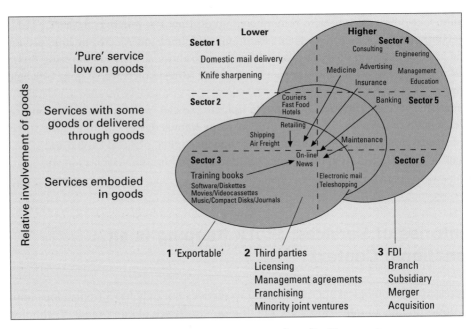

Figure 7.2 Towards a new internationalization mode.

Reproduced from 'The internationalization of services', S. VanderMerwe and M. Chadwick, 1989, *The Services Journal*, January.
By permission of Frank Cass Publishers.

fully embodied in goods. Sector 4 services encompass labour intensive and almost completely intangible customer and business services like consulting, advertising, medical services and insurances. These services have high experience and credence attributes, requiring personal interaction in the servuction process and are thus relatively difficult to store and export. Sector 6 services require a significant interaction with a physical good. Interaction is always (at least) a two-way phenomenon. However, here it often takes place through machines rather than people, for example electronic diagnostics and tele-shopping. With the development of new information technologies in-house which can be used to customize services, this sector is likely to become more globally significant in the future. Help desks situated in one country can service many medical and computer equipment all around the globe.

Inability to Own and Internationalizing Services

Not owning a service may create a lot of insecurity about the service, especially when perceived risk is high (which may vary per country). Leasing and other forms of ownership may be an alternative here. Trust is a critical factor in relationship marketing and creating bonds between the service provider and the customer.

Relationship marketing strategies should emphasize the honour of maintaining long-term relationships with a trusted supplier. Relational exchange occurs within a framework of rules and norms. National governance systems can be placed, for instance, on a continuum ranging from predominantly legally based to predominantly morally based systems. A service firm developing international relations should understand the basis of buyer–seller governance in overseas markets.

Relationship marketing, a form of interactivity often used for selling personalized services and B2B services, is not a universal model suited to uniform global application. Formulations of relationship marketing based on contemporary western interpretations may fail if transplanted to other countries, where the cultural and economic environments differ significantly from the country for which a relationship marketing policy was originally formulated.[24] Therefore, in developing a relationship marketing strategy it is important to look at the cultural distances as revealed in Figure 3.4 and decipher how that might impact on the issue of ownership (or the lack of ownership).

It is dangerous to apply a strategy of 'management by assumption' implying that one presumes to know what will be normal practice in other countries (for example with respect to this issue of lack of ownership), without proper verification.[25] The attitude and willingness towards creating, maintaining and enhancing relationships as well as towards the acceptance of financial, social or structural bonds may therefore differ in various societies. These will be established quite automatically in the more collectivistic societies, while a lot of effort must be put in creating loyalty programmes, as is done in Western Europe and North America these days (the more individualistic societies).[26]

In some cultures, social aspects of exchange form a relatively important part of the whole exchange process. Service providers trying to attract new business only on the basis of stressing the tangible benefits of services or creating financial (and not social) bonds may therefore fail in such cultures. You should not be surprised that this requires a set of unique assets and capabilities in international service firms.

7.4 Assets and Capabilities of Market Oriented International Service Providers

Internationalization requires a commitment of resources, regardless of the size of the step or whether it is the first or an additional move. In order to complete the journey successfully most service firms have to develop special assets and capabilities to face and deal with expected and unexpected business situations. Handling such situations in the foreign market makes the firm reflect on the experience it gains, and teaches it about doing business internationally.[27] So, now we turn to the issue of which assets and capabilities as mentioned in Chapter 6 may be critical to gaining a competitive advantage.

You may recall from Chapter 6 that many of the assets and capabilities service firms have relate to the characteristics of market oriented service organizations such as managing relationships, collecting market intelligence and understanding the market, service quality as well as internal communication, new service development, the distribution channel and cost controlling. Many service firms have quite a competitive advantage with respect to the customer-based assets, outside-in capabilities and inside-out capabilities.

We are convinced these assets and capabilities also hold for those service firms operating in various countries. However, you may doubt whether that is enough to survive in this international business environment. We hold that superior marketing information systems (as an example of internal-based assets) is critical in understanding foreign markets (customers as well as competitors and cultures). The outside-in capabilities of using this information can be used to a full extent. In entering foreign markets successfully (and staying successful in those markets) all the alliance-based assets may be critical here as well, although the accompanying networking capabilities may differ depending on the various method chosen to enter a foreign market.

You may also recall that most of the assets and capabilities belonging to international service providers mentioned here to a large extent resemble the assets and capabilities of market leaders (mentioned in Chapter 6). Usually, the leaders are the ones who set the standards for the industry, change the future of the business. These firms are the firms that internalize first and exploit the new market opportunities given their ambition to be successful and grow. Then other service firms may challenge them or just have to follow these leaders, while others may find smaller niches in the international markets.

Just as not all firms are market leaders, not all service firms that internationalize are the same. They will also have different assets and capabilities. The next typology of international service firms helps to understand those differences. It also provides you with an integrated overview of topics to be discussed in the next sections.

Four different types of service firms in international markets can be found. This classification is based on whether the service provision is location bound or not, and whether standard or customized service packages are delivered. The findings are presented in Figure 7.3. Each cell provides an overview of the organizational profile, the behavioural profile, the attitudes towards internationalization, the entry mode and the international operations profile.

Value added customized services, such as executive search, market research, transportation, finance, insurance and IT, have the most international profile. Their clients often urge them to follow them in foreign markets or are tempted by unsolicited orders from abroad. They perceive high risks and high profitability in the foreign markets. So, capabilities in relationship maintenance are quite critical here.

Low management commitment to internationalization was found in companies offering *location-free professional services* and *location bound customized services* such as engineering. Government regulation in Asia often still prevents these companies establishing their own subsidiaries. Joint ventures are difficult to arrange since local partners are hard to find. Nevertheless, being able to start and manage strategic alliances here is a critical capability.

Direct representation via sales representatives is the leading mode in cells 1, 3 and 4. As one architectural and property development firm with offices in Auckland (New Zealand), Jakarta (Indonesia), Hong Kong and Port Moresby (Papua New Guinea) said: 'Personal contact with the client is crucial in this business.'

Service providers where services are typically bundled with goods (Hilton Hotels and recording companies) choose mainly a franchise, licensing or management arrangement for delivery and distribution of their services overseas. Their main motivation to internationalize is market-seeking and the vision and commitment of top management.

Well-established service firms, such as international banks, often have a preference for wholly or majority owned subsidiaries. In this situation they want to exercise management control such as steering the credit process. In markets with a high political or country risk, these institutions may begin by choosing a lower investment, such as an investment in a majority owned joint-venture bank. Many professional firms, including lawyers and auditors,

Low		High

Degree of tangibility	Cell 1 *Location-Free Professional Services* *Typical Firms:* Executive recruitment, Market research, Environmental science consulting, Transportation, Finance and Insurance, Product design services.	Cell 2 *Location-Bound Customized Projects* *Typical Firms:* Project management, Engineering consulting, Management consulting, Human Resource Development consulting, larger Market Research firms, Legal Services.
Pure services	Organizational Profile: • Degree of customization: Firm Size: Small (median size = 25 employees). Foreign ownership 14%. Behavioral Profile: • Moderate risk perceptions regarding internationalization; Preparedness to invest and competitive intensity in foreign market is not as much of a hindrance to internationalization: Modest managerial commitment to internationalization; Client 'chasing' and unsolicited orders are only moderate motivators to internationalization. Attitudes to Internationalization: • Perceives moderate benefits to internationalization; Perceive low costs or internationalization; Considers profitability in internationalizing equivalent to domestic market. Entry Mode Profiles: • Direct representation 61%; Agency relationships 21%. International Operations Profile: • Low international business intensity: International business as % of sales = 21%: High international performance: Moderate satisfaction with international performance: High propensity to continue in international markets.	Organizational Profile: • Degree of customization: High: Firm size Largest in sample (median size = 160 employees). Foreign ownership 9 %. Behavioral Profile: • High risk perceptions regarding internationalization; Preparedness to invest and competitive intensity in foreign markets hindering internationalization; Modest managerial commitment to internationalization; Client 'chasing' is moderate motivation to internationalize; Unsolicited orders are low motivator. Attitudes to Internationalization: • Perceives moderate benefits to internationalization: Perceive moderate costs: Profitability equivalent to domestic market. Entry Mode Profiles: • Direct representation 35%: Local presence (branch) 38%. International Operations Profile: • Moderate international business intensity: International business as % of sales = 25%: High international performance: Moderate satisfaction with international performance: Very high propensity to continue in international markets.
Services bundled with goods	Cell 3 *Standardized Service Packages* *Typical Firms:* Software development, Installation/testing of new hardware/ equipment. Development of distance education courses. Compact disks. Organizational Profile: • Degree of customization: Firm Size: Small (median size = 40 employees). Foreign ownership 13%. Behavioral Profiles: • Moderate risk perceptions regarding internationalization; Preparedness to invest and competitive intensity in foreign markets is not as much of a hindrance to: Modest managerial commitment to internationalization: Client 'chasing' provides only low motivation: Unsolicited orders provide moderate motivation. Attitudes to Internationalization: • Perceives moderate benefits to internationalization; Perceives low costs: Profitability equivalent to domestic market. Entry Mode Profiles: • Direct representation 46%: Local presence 13%: Agency relationship 21%: Franchising, Licensing, Management agreements 13%. International Operations Profile: • Low international business intensity: International business as % of sales = 22%: Moderate international performance: Moderate satisfaction with international performance: High propensity to continue in international markets.	Cell 4 *Value-Added Customized Projects* *Typical Firms:* On-site training, Computer hardware consulting, Facilities management, Accommodation services, Catering, Software training and support. Organizational Profile: • Degree of customization: Firm Size: Medium (median size = 55 employees). Highest incidence of foreign ownership 21%. Behavioral Profiles: • High risk perceptions: Preparedness to invest and competitive intensity in overseas markets are barriers to internationalization. High management commitment to internationalization: Client 'chasing' and unsolicited orders are moderate motivators to internationalization. Attitudes to Internationalization: • Very high perceived benefits in internationalization; Perceive moderate costs: High profitability relative to domestic markets. Entry Mode Profiles: • Direct representation 37%: Local presence (branch) 26%: Agency relationship 22%: Franchising, Licensing, Management agreements 12%. International Operations Profile: • Moderate international business intensity: International business as % of sales = 36%: very high international performance: High satisfaction with international performance: Very high propensity to continue in international markets.

Figure 7.3   A typology of service firms in international markets

seem to have a preference for partnerships with established colleagues in mature markets. In fast-developing countries, besides partnerships a green-field investment is often a logical choice. In a green-field investment the professional firm would have to invest heavily in people by means of hiring, remuneration, training and development. In any case, the services firm has to introduce its own procedures and service standards in the foreign market. Human resource management is only one part of a firm's critical assets and capabilities.

7.5   Internationalization: Reasons and Theories

This section discusses some well-known internationalization theories. You might get the impression that internationalization is a new buzz word and subsequently is quite easy to do. Is the world really one marketplace with easy access? According to Ted Levitt (1983), customer needs, values and customs are converging all over the world. Human nature is becoming more uniform in its needs for universal values such as the need for security, the need to experience self-worth and materialism. This argument supports the attraction of the global market place, in which case segmentation should no longer be based on geographics, culture or language as such, but global segmentation should be based on the convergence patterns occurring.[28] Is it really that simple? We do not think so. Therefore, we pose the questions: Why should a service firm internationalize? Is it wise to internationalize or could a company better pursue other strategic options to survive and grow? Thus, why not simply stay at home and grow in that market?

Internationalization Versus Other Growth Strategies

There are benefits and opportunities associated with internationalization as well as risks and pitfalls. Therefore, it will be of no surprise that service providers should not start their activities abroad prematurely. The sequence, according to which a firm develops a growth strategy, is a function of:[29]

1   the expected value of profitability, measured by the return on investment of each strategy; and
2   the risk or expected variation in profitability.

The impact of five risk areas (finance, market and competition, compatibility of marketing programs, technical requirements and government regulations) should be estimated for each of three possible growth strategies. These strategies, phrased in terms of the Ansoff matrix from Chapter 6, are:

1   New service development: developing new services for that specific country;
2   Market development: entering out-of-country markets; and
3   Diversification, especially concentric diversification.

Concentric diversification and service development bear approximately the same risk. Out-of-country market expansion is considered to be of greater risk.

Financial management is the most important risk factor experienced by service firms seeking to internationalize. First, they risk that the reimbursement period for the service operations is long. Second, the exposure to currency fluctuations is great for service marketers because of price inflexibility and the inability to transfer easily the site of production. This issue is of less importance in Europe since the introduction of the euro. As they have to face the customer from day one, the service firm has significant personnel requirements. Expatriate management particularly in the start-up phase and specialists from abroad will be needed to succeed in the foreign marketplace. Newly hired local staff will need to be trained in procedures, systems and become acquainted with the corporate culture of their new firm.

In an expanding international marketplace, service firms are sometimes proactive in terms of their ambition to internationalize, however in many cases they are also very reactive. Services firms internationalize because they want to increase their profitability. To give you a further idea of why service firms internationalize, we developed Table 7.4,[30] which provides a

Table 7.4 Motives to internationalize	
Reactive motives	*Proactive motives*
• Following customers • Unsolicited foreign orders • Competitive pressures • Formal and informal networks of customers • Small and saturated domestic market • Export market incentives and disincentives • Proximity to international customers (also as psychological distance) • Overproduction/excess capacity	• Managerial initiative • Formal and informal networks to spot foreign market opportunities • Unique competences or products based on technology • Economies of scale

brief overview of two kinds of motives to internationalize, the reactive ones and the proactive ones.

At first glance you could say that the reactive motives fit to a strategy of client following, while the proactive motives relate to a strategy of market seeking. Is it easier to follow existing clients than to develop new markets on your own since the list of reactive motives is much longer than the list of proactive motives? Looking at different reasons to internationalize will give you some more insights in this process.

Reasons to Internationalize

Reasons to internationalize can be derived from the international environmental factors and analysing the macro, industry and specific market trends as described in Chapter 1. We will present an overview of five different categories of reasons found relevant.[31] These five driving forces are:

■ Top management ambition and commitment to internationalize;

■ Knowledge and skills that are exported or imported;

■ Market threats at home markets;

■ Market opportunities elsewhere; and

■ Finance, risks, cost and profits.

All these reasons are briefly circumscribed in Table 7.5.

There are benefits and risks to internationalization. The benefits of internationalization can be considerable to the service firm. A 'positive circle' can result from successful internationalization.[34] The perceived and realized benefits would then outweigh the anticipated risks.

Table 7.5 Reasons to internationalize for service firms	
Top management ambition and commitment	The ambition of top management counts as the single most powerful driving force behind internationalization. Such a personal spirit or entrepreneurial vision may encourage the whole firm to think and act internationally. Meeting other cultures, acquiring new ideas and technologies that may be implemented in the home operations, are arguments underlying this ambition.[32] A strong international flavour will then be part of the corporate culture.
Knowledge and skills	Based on its assets and capabilities, a service firm may have developed a managerial superiority and/or organizational superiority over the local firms in the market about to be entered. Existing knowledge about such issues as back office procedures, service quality, implementing customer friendliness, market orientation, shelf space allocation, in-store marketing, electronic data interchange, may be applied in foreign markets to get a competitive advantage over there. It is also possible that a service firm buys foreign companies possessing the assets and capabilities they themselves lack, but like to have to create competitive advantages. Both kind of reasons are applied by Dutch Ahold in their international retail activities.
Market threats at home markets	Based on an analysis of the DRETS factors, more and more companies experience market threats at home which drive them abroad. As demand reaches its peak or competition is heating up, companies start looking for alternatives to survive and/or grow. The development of new services, adding additional services to existing services, providing distinctive service quality, diversification and market development are then viable options. Alternatively, unbundling services and increasing efficiency are other means to restore profits in the saturated home market. This 'domestic push' to internationalization can thus be caused by intense local competition, small home markets, saturated home markets, declining purchasing power or diminishing consumer sentiment in one country (while not, at present, in other countries). In the retail world, it can also be the answer to the concentration and internationalization among manufacturers. Then, internationalizing retailers can be a countervailing power against these large manufacturers.
Market opportunities elsewhere	Multinationals and other firms operating internationally may ask their service providers to serve them abroad once they enter foreign markets. This client following motive is a kind of international 'demand pull' or 'client chasing'.[33] Successful service organizations may draw attention from local authorities, individuals, firms or other organizations in an unsolicited way. Their mere presence and way of working may lead these bodies to invite them to do business. So, this demand pull motive is initiated by these bodies in that foreign country.
Finance, risks, cost and profits	This group of drivers of internationalization hinges upon the financial side of doing business. First of all, risks may be spread when a firm is doing business in different countries with different economic climates, but, differences in time may also spread the risk of doing

business. Brokers, financial consultants and other firms may benefit from selling and buying stocks and shares at the many stock exchanges all over the world. Via IT, it can be done 24 hours a day.

The cost of capital and the related ease of access to capital may differ in various local financial markets. Interest rates may differ, depending partly upon differences in exchange rates. In some instances, financial institutions may prefer to finance international service firms than local ones. At present, local and foreign banks in Central and Eastern Europe are eager to finance McDonald's whereas the local 'pop and mom' restaurant will have great difficulties finding money outside the close circle of friends and family to invest in their own restaurant.

SERVICE PRACTICE 7.4

The Brabant Sensation in Hungary[35]

The logistics firm Rynart is based in Brabant, a province of the Netherlands located on the border with Belgium. In a short period of time, the young entrepreneur who started the company has conquered the distribution market in Eastern Europe.

Currently, there are three Rynart branches established in the Netherlands, Hungary and Turkey. The Hungarian branch has been established under Frank Rynart, an energetic 30-year-old, third generation transporter. From two trucks and one old hangar near the airport of Budapest in 1993 to the dazzling present distribution park near the capital with 450 brand-new heavy Scania trucks, Frank and his company have won 75 multinational clients such as Philips, Shell, Tesco and Metro in Hungary. Everybody does business with Frank Rynart. In ten years the company has conquered half of the distribution market; the company's 2003 turnover reached €100 million.

Until the mid 1990s, Rynart could not find financial backers. The Hungarian banks would not lend, particularly following the fall of communism. The Dutch banks were not eager to back adventurers. The breakthrough came in 1996 when Frank Rynart got into contact with representatives of the Dutch Investment Bank (NIB) and succeeded in getting a little more than €1 million, the maximum support for such type of business.

Rynart can offer competitive prices on the basis of having 'return loading'. With the enlargement of the European Union the branch in Budapest became a strategic centre for the western flank of Middle Europe. Outside Bucharest is the first pile to begin a new distribution complex, which will serve the eastern part of Romania and the northern part of Bulgaria. Sofia (Bulgaria) and Belgrade (Serbia) are also targeted as locations to set up representative offices.

Rynart has his own measure of whether or not to start a business. He argues that if you see a modern petrol station being built then it means that the country is ready for his type of business. 'Our most important challenge is to find a business structure where everything fits', he says.

Internationalization Theories

Several theories can be applied to explain the process of internationalization of service firms. We will discuss six theories briefly.[36] These theories are:

- The Swedish-based behavioural approach called the Uppsala model;
- The transaction cost analysis as developed by Nobel prize winner Coase;
- The way station model as developed by Johansson and Vahnle;
- The network model;
- Bron globals; and
- The ad hoc approach.

These models are summarized in Table 7.6.

Each of these theories and models emphasize different aspects of the internationalization process; such as experience, knowledge, cost advantages, relationships and networks, and vision to select small niches. You can imagine that the ad hoc opportunistic approach is not our favourite. However, an entrepreneur's intuition should not be underestimated. On the other hand a systematic approach to researching the barriers to enter a particular market or country and the selection criteria to enter a specific country will be helpful in structuring the activities and in trying to avoid mistakes. As such it is not a guarantee for success.

Table 7.6   Six theories on internalization

Internationalization theories	
The Uppsala model	The basic notion is that firms intensify their commitment towards foreign markets as their experience grows.[37] Swedish and other European companies usually appeared to develop their international operations in small steps, as a continuous process of incremental adjustments to changing conditions in the firm and the environment. The two key terms in this theory are: 'knowledge' and 'commitment'. Knowledge obtained in and about foreign markets drives the decision to commit more resources to those markets. The firm's present knowledge base is a result of its previous experience.[38] The experiential knowledge that firms gain in the early years of internationalization is extremely important for their subsequent resource commitments in the international market. Once the international decisions are implemented, the increased commitment enables the company to continue gathering improved knowledge. The model can be characterized as a combination of deliberate (or systematic) and emergent (or ad hoc) approaches.[39]
Transaction cost analysis (TCA)	This model dictates that a firm tends to expand until the cost of organizing an extra transaction within the firm will become equal to the cost of carrying out the same transaction by means of an exchange on the open market.[40] The firm relies on the domestic or international market for those activities in which independent outsiders have a cost advantage over the other suppliers.[41] The TCA framework is based on the premise that cost minimization explains structural decisions, e.g. regarding internationalization. Transactional difficulties and transaction costs increase when transactions are related to the specificity of the assets (and capabilities) and to the frequency of the transactions. If the required assets and capabilities abroad are very specific (especially when the associated risks are high), an entry strategy via wholly owned subsidiaries is obvious.

The way station model	This model assumes that when a firm is considering moving into international markets, it must first gather relevant knowledge (part 1) and then must take a commitment of resources (part 2).[42] This process can be split into two parts and six different way stations:

Part 1
1 motivation and strategic planning;
2 market research;

Part 2
3 market selection;
4 selection of entry mode;
5 planning of contingencies; and
6 post-entry strategic commitment.

The first part containing the first two way stations deals with acquiring knowledge and getting ready for 'the big jump'. Firms must use this knowledge to define their strategies for commitment of resources (in part 2).[43]

The network model	Relationships between firms as well as between one group of firms and other groups of firms keep the network together. These relationships can be based on technical, economical, legal and/or personal ties. In such a situation, managers' personal influence on relationships is strongest at the earliest stage of establishment. Routines and systems become more important later on in the process. Within such a network, individual firms are autonomous and at the same time, they are dependent on resources controlled by other firms. 'Business networks will emerge in fields where there is frequent coordination between specific actors and where conditions are changing rapidly'.[44] For example, the internationalization of ICT companies and the contacts based on ethnic roots between Chinese entrepreneurs. The foreign firm's position in a domestic network can be used as a connection to other networks in other countries. The internationalizing service provider can benefit from such a direct or indirect connection to other countries as an entry to new markets.
Born globals	These firms deliberately remained small since they entered international markets. They are managed by visionaries who consider the world as a marketplace without boundaries. Often born globals use a specialized network to govern their sales and operate on the market. They must often choose homogeneous business areas, because of their dependency on a single service: a limited service provider in a niche market. Their success is based on assets and capabilities like:[45]

- flexibility (shorter response time; fast adaptation to local tastes);
- born globals can streamline their processes very efficiently, leading to lower costs and highly competitive prices;
- born globals can disseminate the market intelligence more efficiently than larger companies; and
- born globals' global networks with distributors, trading companies, etc. build up strong long-term relationships with foreign partners.

Ad hoc approach	This ad hoc or opportunistic approach implies that the internationalization of the service firm does not follow a predictable pattern. Many of the internationalization steps occur more or less accidentally. Once started abroad without a sound and systematic plan, future decisions that have to be taken to stay in that country or not will probably also not be taken in a systematic way.

7.6 Barriers to Entry and Selecting the Entry Mode

Any organization that intends to start activities in a foreign country has to overcome the obstacles that might hinder them in entering their targeted market. Thus, part of the decision 'to go international' is to investigate these obstacles and see how these can be met in a creative way.[46]

Barriers to Entry

The barriers to entry, or the challenges to be met in internationalizing the business, are well known from the literature on international management or international marketing. These include barriers at a general level and at the industry level, as shown in Table 7.7.

Cultural hindrances are usually mentioned as one of the important barriers to entry. We certainly will not underestimate the relevance of this argument. In Chapter 3, we illustrated which cultures are similar and which are very different and in what way. Still, the impact of cultural differences should not be overestimated. History may also play a role, as the failure of the Telenor-Telia merger in Scandinavia revealed. The adaptation of marketing strategies to national or local cultures is also possible.[47] The country-of-origin bias may work out in a positive as well as in a negative way.

Tariff barriers are widespread and are an effective way to block newcomers. Also, non tariff barriers such as licences, legislation, taxation, non provision of access to public procurement and not being allowed to bid for public contracts and competition from the public sector, may exist for protecting home industries.

Internal resistance within a company to going international may also be a barrier to entry, especially when top management cannot convince other stakeholders that it is wise to do so. It may be that some stakeholders in the company show resistance to going international and are not willing to invest time and/or money in foreign activities. For instance, shareholders may find internationalization not an attractive option for growth, as it would require long-term commitment, low short-term revenues and decreasing return on equity. Such a 'negative' way of thinking, combined with a corporate culture of avoiding risks as much as possible, is not really in line with a market oriented firm that is in need of creating value in the long run.

Many industry barriers refer to the unique assets and capabilities of firms in the domestic service market or may be due to governmental regulations. These barriers are indeed barriers when a firm does not possess opportunities to exploit them. For instance, decreasing unit costs per service is very important in the international hotel business. Having no experience in doing business in other countries means that a hotel for example lacks this operational knowledge. The lodging company may feel this more strongly if it lacks knowledge about which technologies can be used to improve housekeeping efficiency. Moreover, issues like paying expatriates and well-skilled locals higher salaries to attract them, investing in language training programmes, high rents for offices and apartments, may be other cost disadvantages which need to be considered.

Table 7.7 Barriers to entry

General barriers	Industry level barriers
• Cultural, customs and language hindrances • Tariffs, quotas • Law, rules, tax • Costs of logistics and communications • Reaction of local competitors including entry to existing distribution channels • Internal company resistance to go abroad	• Economies of scale • Economies of scope • Experience effects • Service differentiation • Capital requirements • Technological requirements • Switching costs • Access to distribution channels • Cost disadvantages independent of scale • Competitive intensity

Service differentiation (whether perceived or actual) is an important means local firms can use to build relationships with their customers and clients. When moving into highly differentiated markets, new entrants have to spend a lot of resources to overcome this. Buyers of the service of the new entrant have to face switching costs when they leave their 'old service provider'. Changing from an established supplier to a new one may require the buyer to train staff, purchase new equipment, hire technical help, and change procedures and ways of working. Seemingly unimportant issues may have large consequences here. Think of changing banks, leading business clients to printing new letters and invoices with the new bank account. In essence, it implies the new customer must be convinced that the established service provider cannot deliver the service (now or in the near future) as promised by the new service provider.

Being excluded from established distribution channels might be a major threat to foreign companies. Sometimes the existing domestic firms have made (unwritten, informal) arrangements among each other to block the newcomer. Here again, creativity may solve the problem. A large insurance company operating in many countries around the world had problems in building a traditional network of intermediaries in Japan. To overcome this barrier, the company decided at first to use petrol stations as its distribution channel to sell standard policies. In Japan, petrolgas stations offer an extensive range of products and services. That is why this distribution channel was appropriate. Moreover, petrol stations in Japan are typically known for their high level of personal service, which fits the insurance business.

These barriers to entry should be taken into account when selecting the proper entry mode.

Selecting an Entry Mode

The previous sections indicated a wide variety of topics to be taken into account when a service organization intends to internationalize its activities. When the analysis of all these

It is important to recall that the actual location and the physical surroundings, the servicescape, are important to take into account when internationalizing services. Some service providers have little choice; they have to establish themselves in the foreign market right from the start; they need to have a local delivery system. In particular, resource-based industries, such as hotels, restaurants and hospitals, belong to this category. In this respect, an important distinction between three kinds of services can be made: people-processing services, possession-processing services and information-based services.[55]

People-processing services involve tangible actions to customers and require that customers themselves are present during the service encounter, for the customers are part of the servuction process and a high degree of contact with front office personnel is needed. Consequently, the service provider has to maintain a local geographic presence in order to deliver the service.

Possession-processing services involve tangible actions to physical objects to improve their value to the customer. Consequently, the object is part of the servuction process; customers need not necessarily be a direct part of the servuction process.

Information-based services encompass collecting, manipulating, interpreting and transmitting data to create value. Customer participation in the servuction process is often reduced to a minimum. Consequently, the local requirements of the service provider will be very limited; often only a computer terminal, telephone or fax is enough when such service firms start foreign operations. Hence, internationalization is quire easy here.

The greater the knowledge of and experience in a foreign market, the more confident a firm tends to be when making real commitments to activities abroad. It also appears that such firms are more confident about the risks they take in starting this 'adventure'. Relevant knowledge and experience should provide important feedback in the process. One of the key issues in the process of selecting the optimal entry mode then, is how to obtain management control. As many services are dependent on the quality of people rendering the service, the most obvious way to control this process is by full ownership of the service process, quite a strict management contract or a hard franchise. Such entry modes facilitate the control of many of the risks inherent in servicing foreign markets. These modes are often attractive from many points of view, not the least being that rendering services is still a 'people's business'; in many instances local circumstances, entry barriers or even the perception of country risk will lead to a different approach to exercising management control. For example, regulation may require the participation of local partners, as majority or minority owners.

7.7 Internationalization strategies

Now that we have seen the challenges of coping with the barriers to entry and choosing the best entry mode, we can continue with the specific strategies to be applied in internationalizing in the service business. Consistency in strategy is always an important issue. However, this does not mean that the service firm has always to adopt the same (entry) strategy in every country. This will depend on all the topics discussed before leading to different contingencies in every country.

The Decision to Select the Internationalization Strategy

Methods of overseas expansion, which minimize costs and risks, may well be essential. In particular, business service firms may set up a reciprocal arrangement with a firm in the overseas market or participate in a joint venture. Through this type of arrangement the firm can gain experience and knowledge of the foreign market, thereby reducing the risks and uncertainty involved in the process of internationalization. As the firm becomes more committed to an overseas market it may choose to increase its ownership share in the local presence.[56] This may indeed be required if, as commitment increases, intangible assets are shared. Increased ownership will facilitate greater control over the foreign presence and thus ensure the protection of the market oriented service firm's assets and capabilities. This is particularly notable where the knowledge assets being shared with overseas subsidiaries are non codifiable as is often the case for business service firms who deliver customized services to their clients.[57]

As shown in this chapter, when managing the basic characteristics of services appropriately, service firms are able to internationalize successfully. Some strive for a position as market leader while others challenge the leader in some high profit foreign markets or just follow the leader. Niche players are always interesting companies as the born globals and LSPs have shown. Some firms choose to apply a strategy of cost leadership (low cost positioning in every country like discounters) or a differentiation strategy (different offers adapted to local tastes). Some firms just have to follow their clients while others seek new markets abroad. Despite the strategy chosen, an issue of growing importance to all these service firms is 'how to select a country which is interesting to enter?'. Many criteria for this selection process can be found. These criteria can be divided in four groups. Table 7.8 elaborates on that.[58]

As a final point of comment on this schematic, it is important to note that when the complexity of the information supplied by the client is low, the probability of entering countries which are culturally distinct from the home country may be high. More complex information implies that customers and suppliers have to interact more closely during the servuction process. The formal and informal structural arrangements that have been made at home should be reviewed to check whether they need adaptation when going abroad.

Due to the characteristics of the service encounter, the service organization intending to internationalize has to check whether the service should be delivered personally or not (whether face-to-face interaction between supplier and customers is needed). Second, they have to ask themselves whether a physical outlet is needed to perform the service. If the answer to both questions is negative, in principle there is no reason why they should not export the service, provided there is a market and no other major obstacles exist, such as legislation prohibiting exports or imports. However, before starting an internationalization strategy it pays to prepare an analysis focussing on the strengths and weaknesses of the firm, opportunities in the selected market(s), including internal and external barriers. Moreover, it is necessary that all costs and benefits of obtaining and retaining control in a specific situation must be carefully weighed against each other. The most efficient (entry) mode is the one with the highest benefit-to-cost ratio.[59]

What we have said so far is that services are considered to be location bound (although IT allows us to transport services more easily around the globe), the barriers to entry and the chosen entry mode, the decision making process to internationalize or not could follow the hierarchical order of the road map as presented in Figure 7.4.[60]

Table 7.8 Selecting a country to enter	
Four groups of criteria in selecting a country to enter	*Explanation or examples*
Corporate goals	What benefits can be offered to potential customers in other countries? How does it impact on the company's goals? What quality levels exist in the foreign countries under investigation? What quality levels do customers expect or desire in those countries? What contribution can the company make in increasing the desired quality level in that country (or for a specific segment in that country)?
Market-related factors	How large is the host country market? How large is the intensity of competition and the degree of fragmentation in the market? What growth rates and profits are present or can be expected? What kind of economies of scale or scope can be achieved? How similar are home and host market in terms of physical and cultural distance or consumer behaviour, especially in coping with perceived risk, uncertainty avoidance and power distance?
Infrastructure	What does the economic, physical and IT infrastructure look like (advanced or old-fashioned)? Which trade barriers and governmental regulations do exist? Can they be met? How large is the country risk, be it political or economic?
Interaction between the service provider and the customer	Can the service encounter in the home country be transferred to another country? In what way should it be adapted to fit local norms, values and culture? In what way can long-term relationships be built, if any?

Figure 7.4 rests on three service characteristics being of utmost relevance in the international context:

1   Are the services transportable or location-bound?
2   Are the transportable services exportable or should they be delivered through mobile production units? and
3   Are the services traded through their symbiosis with the merchandise trade or are the services exportable through remote communications?

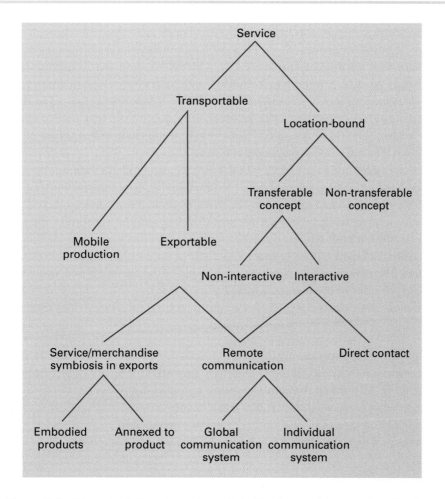

Figure 7.4   Characteristics of services globalization and internationalization

Reprinted from *Marketing Strategies for Services*, Kostecki, M. pp. 204, Pergamon Press, Copyright 1994 with permission from Elsevier

The first variable at the top of the figure depicts a dichotomy between 'transportable' and 'location-bound' services, i.e. services that have to be consumed at the place of production. Globalization of the latter category of services (e.g. supermarket retailing) calls for the location of a service provider abroad. Also, the transferability of the service concept is an essential variable in assessing the attractiveness of globalization by means of franchising, establishing an agency, direct investments or other forms of participation in another country. Service and process innovation encouraged by technological change renders a large number of services transportable, especially in financial services and back office services.

The second variable distinguishes between transportable services, which are exportable, and those that are delivered through mobile production units (e.g. airlines or an orchestra on tour). The latter form of service delivery is encouraged by improvements in travel services. The increased tradability of numerous new financial products (e.g. securitized loans) was made possible because of information technology.

The third variable differentiates between services which are exportable through remote communication (e.g. data processing or TV shows) and those which are traded because of their symbiosis with the merchandise trade (e.g. a filmed art show that is exported together with the supporting video tape). All merchandise trade relies on a range of annexed services – in most cases marketing services. Sometimes, the service component is limited to the 'shipment' of a product or to 'port services' which are linked to the transport of cargo and people in foreign ports. These additional services may also include a wide range of distributing services, after sale services and the like.

Remote communication is the central variable in the current globalization process, and many service firms emphasize the management of technology and information as a strategic resource in their international expansion. To banks, insurance companies or travel agents, the telecommunications network provides a 'lifeline' to customers and constitutes the key delivery mechanism in both domestic and foreign operations. In tourism or air transportation, access to a global network of tour operators like TUI or airlines like the Sky alliance is a *sine qua non* condition of successful marketing (this is one of the alliance-based assets and networking capabilities of the market oriented service firm).

Alongside these three distinctions, it is relevant to take the following issues into account:

■ Client/producer relations can be divided in interactive and non interactive relations;
■ The interaction between customer and service provider can be direct or remote;
■ The client can be reached through a global or an individual network;
■ The service may be transferable or non transferable;
■ The flexibility or rigidity in responding to national needs; and
■ The extent to which the service bundle can be divided while internationalizing.

The determination of these issues will provide firms with some well-documented support for assisting them in making the decision to internationalize. Having made the decision to internationalize the service form must then determine which of the various entry modes best suits the organizational objectives. In services, franchising is favoured given its flexibility to adapt to local circumstances and the possibility of having operations run by local management (with their knowledge of the local market, customs, culture, customer buying habits, language, taxes, governmental system, human resource policy).

Internationalization and Franchising

Franchising has become a major driving force in the globalization of service businesses. It has been accelerated through the changing patterns in the macro environment. The trend to a global consumer influenced by international experiences, travelling, watching TV and films, the growth of the Internet, the changing economic conditions in many countries, the favourable political and socio-cultural environments, the lower cost of air fares and a shift from manufacturing to service-based economies have all played an important role here. Developments in both the macro environment and meso environment have contributed to the globalization of marketing activity. Retailers with international franchise operations may be the result of different motivational factors. A study by Quinn and Alexander indicates that retailers, having expanded at home through franchising, may enter international markets as a result of predominantly pull rather than push factors.[61] For example, foreign entrepreneurs approach the firm in order to require a franchise licence for their own country, whereas the retailer that has expanded organically in the domestic market may expand through franchising in the international market because of limited opportunities, and hence push factors in the domestic market but limited pull factors in the international market.

British clothing retailers such as Mothercare, Jaegar, Next and Mulberry, without extensive international operations and operating from a non franchise domestic base, have employed franchising to enter new markets in Asia Pacific and the Middle East. For international retailers and other service sector companies the movement to diverse markets is made easier to some extent by the use of master franchising arrangements. With this strategy, used by international retail companies such as the Body Shop, 7.Eleven, Marks and Spencer, Knickerbox, Storehouse and Next, the foreign franchisee carries out most of the work involved in expanding the operation into the new market, and also acts as a source of information on cultural and language barriers, bureaucratic red tape and political problems. International franchise expansion usually takes place first in culturally close markets at a slow and steady pace, followed only then by assessment of global opportunities and movements to markets beyond the traditional, developed economies.[62]

Franchising is also an attractive option for international retail companies that have not had domestic experience of franchising and wish to explore the potential of international markets rather quickly. Given the increasing acceptance of franchising as an organizational form in many countries, there may be good local commercial reasons for exploring that option.

Internationalization and Retailing

Retailers in the food as well as in the non food business are active in many countries of the world. Just think of companies like Ahold, Lidl, Aldi and Spar or Hennis and Mauritz, Toys R Us, Ikea and Dixons. Companies like Wal-Mart, Carrefour, Asda offer food and non food worldwide. Sometimes they use their own name all over the world (Walmart, Aldi), sometimes they keep on using the local names, like Ahold did in the USA and Spain.

A recent study among various Dutch and UK international retailers found some interesting differences between those retailers that successfully entered a foreign market and those who ran into trouble while entering the market some years later. On reading the study it is easy to conclude that some of the findings are self-evident and simple. Perhaps this is the reason why companies pay insufficient attention to them.[63] The general conclusion was that 'a strong focus on gaining market access in the short term harboured the danger that conditions for building up a sustainable market position were ignored. International retailers were insufficiently aware of this danger.' In more detail, the main conclusions found that:

drivers for success as well as pitfalls were identified for the short term, so with an impact on performance for market entry. A high degree of:

☐ *vertical integration,*
☐ *innovative power,*
☐ *entrepreneurial drive,*
☐ *strong motivation*

were consistent success factors of a controllable nature.

Coupled with a focussed growth strategy, these factors were preconditions for taking the retail format abroad and establishing operations for a period of up to two years and beyond. Uncontrollable factors found to have a determining effect were social and economic trends in the markets entered, resulting in consumer buying behaviour patterns. A frequently observed pitfall in the early stages of internationalization was the failure to conduct market studies, particularly of future competitors. In addition, selection procedures of locations or foreign partners in the case of shared-control operations proved to be a stumbling block.

The study found two key success factors which had long-term impacts. These were positioning strategy and willingness to change. Both factors involve a willingness to learn from developments in the foreign market, and finetune retail operations accordingly. Pitfalls confronting the international retailer in the long term were found to be numerous. Sector developments often weakened the retailer's original competitive advantage. Efficiency of organizational structure, communication with foreign outlets and planning and control systems behind the scenes were frequently reported as weak areas. Furthermore, a lack of understanding of what was happening at local market level, both as regards the consumer and the employees, led to depressed performance. The pitfalls identified here mainly concerned issues of corporate culture and management and control, within the retailer's controllable internal environment.

7.8   Final Considerations

Despite the commonly accepted characteristics of services such as their intangibility and location boundedness, services firms can internationalize and can export their services to other countries, both near and far, physically as well as culturally. The service industry is in transition from a local industry to an international or global industry.[64] Various reasons are cited as to why this trend is occurring. First, deregulation in key industries like telecommunications and banking has spurred international competition in those industries. Second, as manufacturers go international, so have their service providers (they have been forced to follow). Finally, technology is making national boundaries borderless. The Internet makes distant services available. Whether it is renting a holiday house or downloading software, personnel in foreign countries may perform payment services and send them off wirelessly. These trends counterargue the risk of being distant from the customer in the service encounter and the problems of maintaining effective quality control at the point of service delivery.[65] Being a worldwide market oriented service provider might overcome these problems. It means, for instance, that such a service firm must be willing to take the risk of internationalizing and consider this risk as an acceptable one inherent in normal company behaviour (so, comparable to the risk taking behaviour of market oriented firms in general).

Since we have seen that the physical presence is not always necessary during the service encounter (see for example services delivered via the Internet), the traditional arguments given for not being able to internationalize may change in particular service circumstances. Consequently, the dynamics in service industries may affect the internationalization mode. What had been a proper entry mode at one time may be out-dated by another.

Research among small and medium sized service firms in Australia shows that the selection of an appropriate operation mode designed to enhance and protect the competitiveness of the firm is dependent on an amalgam of specific factors. These factors are:

- the nature and 'uniqueness' of the firm's competitive advantage and resource availability;
- industry-specific factors in target markets such as the level of market concentration;
- the extent of barriers to entry, or effective entry;
- location/country-specific factors such as the extent to which products/services need to be adapted to meet local requirements;
- host governments' policies on tariffs, subsidies.

The success of internationalization is attributed greatly to the commitment and vision of one or more executives. So, managers considering internationalization must realize that this seems to be a prerequisite for successful foreign market entry. Furthermore, it is abundantly clear that services in their international context are far from being homogeneous.[66]

Once a company has decided to start its own operations offshore, it is self-evident that it has to cope with far more issues than just marketing. To give the reader an idea about what a bank has to deal with, while establishing itself in one foreign market, we have produced a 'basis' for a more detailed checklist in Table 7.9.

Table 7.9   A basis for a bank branch development checklist in a foreign market*

1 Identity
   - demographic, regulatory, economical, technological, social (DRETS) factors in general view of the potential establishment
   - potential customers/target group
   - range of products offered (in line with local regulations/license restrictions)
   - competitors

   Based on market research (total market, market % to be obtained, present performance of comparable units) an estimate/target can be made with respect to volume and kinds of transactions/products.

2 Based on the outcome of 1. a pessimistic and an optimistic scenario could be made with respect to the projected development. The scenario selected finally (pessimistic, realistic or optimistic) should be the starting point for commercial, organizational, operational and logistical requirements.

   All commercial risks should be covered (as much as possible) by means of structural, procedural and risk control measures. The maximum investment risk can be estimated by means of a worst case scenario.

Table 7.9 (*cont.*)

3 Commercial aspects
  ● product descriptions (purpose and nature), marketing strategy, pricing, etc.
  ● authorizations/segregation of duties
  ● install limits (credits to customers, credits to banks, positions in foreign country, etc.)
  ● identity credit authorities
  ● guidelines with respect to selecting correspondent banks
  ● identify corporate responsibility guidelines (+ influence on forms and contracts)
  ● codes of conduct (money laundering, private business restrictions, etc.)
4 Organizational aspects
  ● identity number of commercial staff, management, back-office functions and support functions. Develop structure taking into consideration: optional support of business functions, segregation of duties, no conflicts of interest, efficiency aspects, etc.
  ● signing authorities (+ recording all delegated authorities)
  ● staff recruitment procedures/aspects (local staff/expatriates)
  ● job descriptions
  ● training of staff (ind. risk management)
  ● segregation of responsibilities between branch(es) and Head Office
  ● communication of address, etc.
5 Operational aspects
  ● tax rules/responsibilities
  ● local rules/regulations regarding commercial activities/reporting requirements
  ● audit rules/regulations
  ● reporting requirements (lay out/frequency/subject) to Head Office/Local Central Bank/Central Bank in home country
  ● accounting system/procedures (incl. accounting structure/reconciliation rules, etc.)
  ● capital requirements
  ● remittance of profits/dividends
  ● registration guidelines for swift/telex/fax/messages
6 Logistical aspects
  ● premises (office purchase/rent, location, conditions of the contract)
  ● office lay out
  ● staff housing/remuneration
  ● safety aspects
  ● office equipment (incl. communication equipment)
  ● EDP systems
  ● office supplies

The above-mentioned items are the basis for a more comprehensive checklist

*The authors gratefully acknowledge W.F. Hogewoning (ABN/Amro Bank) for providing the first draft of this checklist

Summary

A periodical assessment of the global service environment in which the service firm operates is a valuable tool to management both for analysing the impact of the external (and internal) change drivers and to get a feeling which markets and areas might be attractive to enter. Of course, there are still service industries where local players dominate the competition but the trend seems to be competing with an international dimension. In many countries and in numerous service industries, local entrepreneurs will meet ever increasing competition from internationals, foreign franchise formats, multinationals and globals during the coming years. The more fragmented or (state) monopolized a service industry is, the more attractive such a market may become for a service provider with a clear formula plus sufficient scale, scope, experience and resources.

Let us not forget the goal of internationalization. It is not a goal in itself nor a hobby of top management. As a growth strategy of the company it should, in the first place, generate value for our (new) customers and lead to the creation of adequate value for the shareholders. For this reason it is necessary to allocate the firm's assets and capabilities effectively. In this chapter we have looked at this issue from a perspective of managing the basic characteristics of services:

- Intangibility, the degree of (in)tangibility;
- Inseparability, the degree of interactivity between the customer and the customer;
- Inconsistencies of service delivery, managing the degree of heterogeneity;
- (Non)inventory of services, managing perishability; and
- Inability to own.

Expansion abroad is often driven by the needs of international customers ('following customers abroad') – the awareness that international experience in the long run will enhance the competitive advantage of the firm and/or chances abroad. Saturated home markets and more intensified competition in many industries force thriving companies to look for new frontiers. Market-seeking is another strategy here. Globalization has made customers more demanding and competition fiercer. The main internationalization theories and strategies have been discussed in this chapter. Internationalization theories are: the Uppsala internationalization model, the transaction cost analysis (TCA) model, the way station model, the network model, born globals and the ad hoc approach.

With the changes in the nature of service delivery systems, firms may find themselves changing the existing entry mode, or operating in more than one mode. For managers, it is no longer enough to think of their service business as one business. Around the world, each part of the service may be delivered differently. Combinations of mode can be used. The influence of the changing technology on the internationalization process of service firms is huge. This new mode will require a new thought process, more flexible organizations and more flexible managers. The role and the control or coordinating functions at head office will change. Linkages between the two and between all branches will become increasingly important. The transfer of knowledge will take place face to face and via technology. New managerial formats will be needed to manage a new hybrid type of global operation in which a geographical separation between front office and back office will become more and more prevailing.

A firm may be at different stages of international development within different foreign markets or regions. With increased internationalization, service firms, especially knowledge- and skills-based in contrast to resourced-based service firms and manufacturers, establish a foreign presence more rapidly, with less need for caution and with higher levels of market commitment from the beginning.

Developing an international marketing strategy is a fruitful process for the whole organization. It assists the company to concentrate on differences, not just on averages. What differentiates our company from our local and international competitors? Institutionalizing knowledge sharing and establishing centres of excellence are tools to stimulate the implementation of great ideas throughout the organization. However, marketing matters to everybody in the company. It is everyone's business. The question is: To what extent to standardize or adapt the marketing strategy and service concept? It appears that high cost savings are possible by somehow standardizing, while other arguments are in favour of adaptation to local needs. However, in most cases of globalization a certain degree of adaptation to local conditions will be necessary to be successful in the global market.

Technical progress in information technology, communications, production and logistics has made it possible to better accommodate clients. International service suppliers are now able to customize services more to local needs and even to individual tastes. This is more evident in service industries where personal touch, voice-driven information, Internet applications or sophisticated delivery systems can be easily tailored to the needs of the customer. Services, once seen as typically local, labour intensive and low cost activities, are now often exportable as a result of changes in technology, deregulation, asset structure and the ambition of managers.

Questions

1. Describe the macro level drivers to the internationalization of services.
2. Explain the motives that might influence service firms to internationalize.
3. Demonstrate which assets and capabilities are critical to manage the five I's of services.
4. Describe the difference between a standardization strategy and a strategy that requires the services to adapt to local circumstances. What strategy best suits a cost leader?
5. Describe the internationalization theories discussed in this chapter. Use companies that you are familiar with to illustrate how these theories have been applied.
6. Explain what is meant by the term 'franchising'. How does franchising work to reduce the risk of internationalization?
7. Illustrate how you consider that information technology might affect the internationalization process and entry mode of service firms.
8. Explain why physical proximity is not always necessary in service firms that operate internationally.
9. Describe what is meant by the term 'excellent service quality'. Can you argue that the term has the same meaning in different countries?
10. Describe the difference between a client following strategy and a market-seeking strategy. Illustrate the difference using examples.

Assignments

1. When you combine Table 1.1 and Table 7.1, which countries have the largest share of imports and exports of services as related to GNP?
   a Are there any commonalities between all the net exporters versus the net importers in services as shown in Table 7.1?

   b Does a particular pattern occur when you position these net importers and net exporters in the cultural map of the world as developed in Chapter 3?

   c What developments have taken place when you compare the data from Table 1.1 and Table 7.1 with the most recent OECD data?

2. A number of airlines have formed strategic alliances with one another. Sky team or Star Alliance are a couple of these alliances.

   a Make a list of all the alliances.

   b List the airlines which form part of these alliances.

   c Describe how the structures and participation in the alliances has changed over the past five years.

   d What do you expect to happen in relation to these alliances in the near future and why?

   e What can you conclude from these developments?

   f What is the impact of these alliances on the customer?

3. Make a list of five hard and five soft service firms in your country that have internationalized.

   a Describe how they internationalized.

   b What entry mode did they choose when they internationalized?

   c Justify why you think they choose a particular entry mode.

4. Check the *Wall Street Journal* or *Financial Times* for the past year and make a list of which European, American and Australian banks, insurance companies or hotel chains have tried to expand their business in the BRIC countries (Brazil, Russia, India and China).

   a What kind of entry mode have they used?

   b What barriers to entry have they had to overcome?

5. Make a list of the fashion retailers in your own country.

   a List separately all the foreign fashion retailers present in the domestic market.

   b List which countries they originally came from.

   c Describe their strategy; for example are they discounters or specialty stores (or do they have another retail format)?

   d Illustrate how successful you think they are relative to the local competitors.

   e Describe how you measure success.

   f Describe how the foreign competitors are positioned relative to the domestic retailers.

   g Describe the segments that the foreign competitors are targeting.

Endnotes

1 Slater, 2004, p. A3; Malik, 2004, pp. 72–79.

2 Kostecki, 1994, pp. 220–221.

3 This chapter has been partly based on the masters' thesis of two of our students. Saskia Veendorp's thesis, Globalization of marketing approaches: A literature study, analysis of globalization activities in seven companies, and interviews with employees within the ABN (1989) was prepared during her internship with ABN Bank in 1989. Ringo Janssen's thesis, The internationalization of business services, satisfying clients through

relationship marketing and service quality (1996) is based upon his internship at ABN AMRO Insurances and their planned international activities.

4 *OECD Observer*, 2003, p. 45; *OECD in Figures*, 2004. For more information on OECD work on statistics of international trade in services go to www.oecd.org/std/trade-services.

5 VanderMerwe and Chadwick, 1989.

6 Buckley, Pass and Prescott, 1992.

7 This is the basic idea. Just as we have seen in Chapter 2 that many services can be produced without the actual presence of the customer, there are also some exceptions to this rule.

8 Masurel, 2001.

9 *The Economist*, 27 November 1999; and Van der Heijden, 2003, p. 29.

10 This part is based on Hollensen, 2001, pp. 123–152.

11 Evans *et al.*, 1989; Bartlett and Ghoshal,1994; Handy, 1995.

12 Van Herk, Poortinga and Verhallen, 2004, pp. 346–360.

13 Hoeksema and De Jong, 2001.

14 Pacelle, 2004, p. M1.

15 Van Looy *et al.*, 1998, p. 407.

16 See Geiger 2005, p. M1.

17 This argument was found in Ringo Janssens's (1996) MBA thesis about the international insurance brokerage industry.

18 Erramilli,1992; Erramilli and Rao, 1990, 1993.

19 This section is based to a large extent on Jean Pierre Schreurs MBA thesis on international retailing (1992). The arguments given for the retail sector will also apply to the services sector in general. See also Kasper, 1994.

20 Kasper, Van Helsdingen and De Vries, 1999, pp. 384, 385.

21 See also Johansson, 2006, pp. 432–438.

22 See VanderMerwe and Chadwick, 1989; Bradley, 1995.

23 VanderMerwe and Chadwick, 1989; Segal-Horn, 1993.

24 Palmer, 1995, p. 471.

25 Bonoma, 1985.

26 'In studies in international marketing based on the relationship marketing paradigm of the Industrial Marketing and Purchasing Group, it appeared that a company's ability to break down cultural barriers and establish close social and business relationships with

clients, is a major factor for success in international industrial marketing.' David Ford, 1984 and 1997.

27 See Johansson and Vahlne, 1977; Bilkey and Tesar, 1977; Cavusgil and Nevin, 1981; and Erramilli, 1991.

28 See also Chapter 3 on consumer behaviour and the sections on culture and segmentation.

29 Carman and Langeard, 1980.

30 This figure is based on Lommelen and Matthyssens, 2005, pp. 99–102.

31 The previous sections have indicated that technological changes may make the internationalization of services possible. These dynamics may transform traditional soft services into hard services.

32 On the other hand, the danger of ego-boosting may also occur. Then irrational arguments dominate the internationalization process, while the real arguments, advantages and disadvantages are woven/swept away.

33 Sometimes such a strategy is called 'client chasing'. We do not think this is the proper wording when a service organization wants to be a market oriented one. Following the client expresses a better attitude to the market. Still, one should not regard that as a 'client followers' strategy. It is good that the service firm takes a proactive role in following the client.

34 Normann, 1984.

35 Postma, 2004, p. 11.

36 See for a comprehensive overview e.g. Hollensen, 2001, pp. 45–72; and Coviello and Martin, 1999, pp. 42–54.

37 Hollensen, 2001, p. 47, referring to Johansson and Wiedersheim-Paul, 1975; Johansson and Vahlne, 1977.

38 An empirical investigation, which used a sample of 362 Swedish service firms, showed that the first international step has an important impact on a firm's current experiential knowledge structure, and therefore the ability of building its capabilities (to operate successfully abroad). See als Hollensen, 2001, pp. 47–49.

39 Hollensen, 2001, p. 47.

40 Coase, 1937, p. 395.

41 Hollensen, 2001, p. 52.

42 See Johansson and Vahnle, 1977; or Johansson, 2006.

43 Some of the coefficients from second, third and fourth way stations to the two dependent variables are negative, but their standard error is so high (z statistics less than 1 in both cases) that this negative value must be taken as obtained by chance. Any other set of data might give a positive and still non significant value for this coefficient.

44 Hollensen, 2001, p. 70.

45 Hollensen, 2001, pp. 67–70.

46 A similar idea about the capabilities and skills of customers and front and back office personnel in order to participate in the service encounter and accomplish the market orientation of the service firm will be developed and applied in Chapter Fifteen. The terminology used here was originally developed by Uolevi Lehtinen.

47 Peter Wright, Charles Pringle and Mark Kroll, 1992 say that many of the factors, mentioned as barriers to entry in internationalizing the business, count also when entering a new business or industry in the home country. Then, it is a matter of creativity and corporate culture to deal with these issues and challenges (and not call them problems or barriers right away).

48 For a very detailed overview of the literature see Kennedy (2005).

49 Usunier, 1993.

50 Benito and Welch, 1994.

51 *The Economist*, 28 February 2004, special report, pp. 73–75.

52 The literature on market entry mode strategy is, according to Doherty and Quinn (1999, p. 381) essentially descriptive rather than theoretical. The categorization stems from her. See also the paper of Barry Quinn and Nicholas Alexander, 2002.

53 See Ulmer in Kostecki, 1994, p. 171.

54 Kostecki, 1994; Benito and Welch, 1994. This section is based on the ideas of M. Kostecki, 1994. We have added some new points to it.

55 This distinction is based on Lovelock and Yip, 1996; and is also presented in Chapter 2, when we classified services.

56 Johansson and Vahlne, 1977, pp. 23–32.

57 Buckley and Casson, 1976.

58 Erramilli and Rao, 1993.

59 Kostecki, 1994, pp. 204–208.

60 Kostecki, 1994.

61 Quinn and Alexander, 2002.

62 Quinn *et al.*, pp. 274–276.

63 This section is based on Marjolein Hinfelaar (2004), p. 284.

64 Patterson and Cicic, 1995.

65 Patterson and Cicic, 1995.

66 Patterson and Cicic, 1995.

Part 3
Delivering Value through the Actual Service Experience

This book is about services marketing management. Services marketing is about caring about people; employees, customers and other stakeholders. The final part of this book focusses on the actual delivery of services. It hinges upon the service experience that ultimately creates value to all these stakeholders. We can now discuss this subject because the building blocks have been made in the previous parts on understanding and creating value. In this part the five guiding principles become more concrete and operational. These were:

1 The service organization's market orientation;
2 The service organization's assets and capabilities;
3 The characteristics of services;
4 Internationalization in the service sector; and
5 Value created in the actual service experience.

The delivery of value through the actual service experience will be discussed in this, Part 3. A wide variety of subjects are needed to create value through those service experiences in terms of the elements of the marketing mix. Because we discussed the relevance of relationships in creating and delivering value already in the previous Part 2, we can now focus on the Ps of the marketing mix:

- services (be it traditional services or e-services);
- service innovations;
- people;
- processes;
- physical evidence;
- place;
- promotion;
- price;
- and, the final implementation and control.

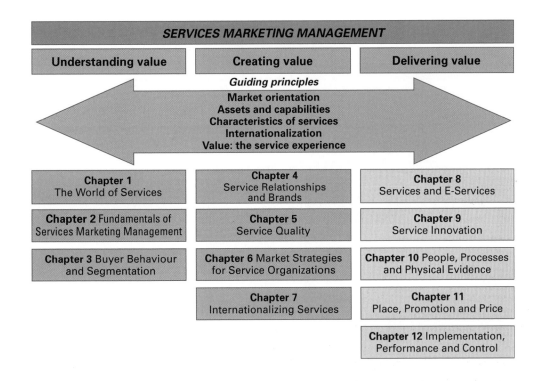

Figure P.3   Contents of Part 3 related to the other parts of the book

Chapter 8

Services and E-Services

Co-authored by Allard van Riel

Introducing new 'Royal Silk Class'. A journey...not the same

Feel the revolution in our ultra modern 'Lie flat' 170 degree seat, ergonomically designed to give the most individual comfort. Relax in a serene cabin with chic new Thai contemporary interior design and cabin lighting that can gradually dim to minimize jetlag. Every seat is equipped with a personal screen for you to enjoy a variety of entertainment. And taste our world-class international and Thai cuisine accompanied by our award-winning wine list.

And you can rest assured that while we revolutionise the way you fly, one thing will always remain the same: our legendary Royal Orchid Service - world class service from the heart that is distinctly THAI.

THAI. Smooth as silk.
Royal Silk Class has been introduced on selected flights on the London-Bangkok and worldwide routes.

www.thaiairways.co.uk

Reproduced by permission of Thai Airways International Company Limited

Learning objectives

At the end of this chapter you will be able to:

1 Describe what is meant by the term 'services lifecycle'

2 Describe what is meant by the term 'service hierarchy'

3 Illustrate how the services lifecycle and the hierarchy of services can be used to develop services strategy

4 Describe the difference between a service strategy and a service tactic

5 Understand the role of different kinds of after sales services

6 Expound the increasing importance of electronic services

7 Explain how electronic services can create sustainable competitive advantage

8 Explain the different ways in which electronic services create customer utility

9 Define electronic services and distinguish them from traditional services

10 Explain the different roles electronic services play in the economy

11 Appreciate the importance of regular evaluation and control

12 Describe the problems of measurement, in assessing electronic service performance

8.1   Introduction

1 Traditional and Electronic Services by Accor[1]

In 2003 the France-based Accor group provided a wide range of hotel services and other businesses like leisure and tourism, distribution, entertainment, and food and on board train services.
  In their portfolio of hotels are well-known brands for various segments of the market, e.g.:

- [ ] upscale segment: Sofitel;
- [ ] midscale segments: Suite hotel, Mercure, Novotel; and
- [ ] economy segment: Formule 1, Motel 6, Etap, Red Roof Inns and Ibis.

When you compare some of these service concepts, you will automatically come across the impact of electronic services in this business. The main features of the Sofitel brand are, according to their 2003 annual report:

- [ ] locations in major international cities and prestigious vacation resorts;
- [ ] rooms equipped with all the features you expect in a world-class hotel;
- [ ] expressing a distinctly French *art de vivre*, unique among international upper upscale hotels;
- [ ] restaurants supervised by outstanding chefs, featuring fresh, top quality ingredients, original recipes and respect for local culinary traditions;
- [ ] refined service, personalized customer care and access to the latest technological amenities.

The main features of the Formule 1 hotels are:

- [ ] functional rooms featuring basic comforts and a television;
- [ ] reception desk open from 6.30 to 9.30 a.m. and from 5.00 to 9.00 p.m. (hours may vary depending on the day or the country). At other times, rooms can be paid for at automated terminals outside the hotel;
- [ ] self-service, all-you-can-eat breakfast buffet;
- [ ] a price/cleanliness commitment to customers;
- [ ] Formule 1 guarantees the market's lowest rates within a radius of ten kilometres and the highest cleanliness and hygiene standards.

Accor is constantly improving their technological solutions. The 2003 annual reports states among others:

- [ ] 'the development of magnetic strip cards to replace paper vouchers and the more extensive use of the Internet for online ordering and sales' (p. 26). These magnetic strip cards and microchip cards are used today in a wide range of countries: Argentina, Brazil, China, France, Italy, Mexico, Sweden, Turkey and Venezuela;

□ 'In hotels, the technological 'leap forward' carried out in the past few years enabled Accor to take full advantage of the Internet's potential as a powerful sales driver. Now more user-friendly, the **accorhotels.com** website and the different chain sites (like **novotel.com** and **sofitel.com**) received 44 million visits in 2003. For the year, electronic sales totalled more than euro 300 million, a 47% increase over 2002.' (p. 28);

□ 'by streamlining customer interfaces with the Internet and travel agency booking systems (Amadeus, Galileo, Sabre, WorldRes and Worldspan), Accor Hotels' Travel Accor Reservation System (TARS) can respond much faster to fluctuations in demand.' (p. 28);

Accor acknowledges that 'the Web not only simplifies relations with existing customers but creates openings to markets that were previously untapped because too fragmented, such as small companies and self-employed professionals' (p. 29). Easy, personalized access to information can be provided via call centres, Web centers, Web portals and dedicated intranets.

The development of an organizational service strategy requires us to pull together many of the principles described in previous chapters. The link between the previous chapters and the service policy will be clarified in section 8.2. We will then illustrate how a service is applied as an instrument of the marketing mix within the framework of the relationship approach mentioned previously. It will be demonstrated how marketing, operational activities and human skills and resources interrelate when a service is provided. The interrelating of these activities focusses on process, in particular routines and capabilities. Ultimately, this comes down to the technical, functional and relational quality of services.

The discussion of the service hierarchy and the concept of a life cycle for services, which can be found in section 8.2, provides us with a springboard for a more in-depth study of the service concept (8.3), after sales services (8.4), e-servicing (8.5) and the development of new services (Chapter 9). We end this chapter with some final remarks (8.6; see Figure 8.1).

The purpose of the section on electronic services is to introduce and highlight an emerging type of services: electronic or high technology services. The differences between traditional and electronic service and different categories of electronic services will be explained. This chapter will identify various ways in which high technology services allow business firms to create competitive advantage, and explain how customers in turn can also take advantage of various increases in utility.[2] A better understanding of the differences between traditional

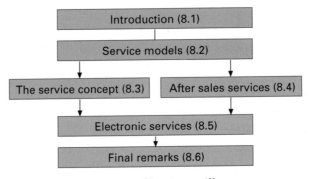

Figure 8.1 Chapter outline

face-to-face services and electronic services in terms of customer perceptions will help you to develop adapted design, evaluation and control strategies for the different types of e-services. The chapter concludes with a window on possible future developments.

In the international service sector, a modular approach is utilized to export services and adapt them to local circumstances. Regular visitors of international hotels and car rental companies recognize this standardization of services easily. Paraphrasing Jeannet and Hennessey, we could state that global services offer the potential to answer similar needs among similar market segments, and as transnational services they also allow for adaptations to cope with national differences.[3] In general, however, companies without the ability to develop such a line of ideal global services follow an extension strategy or an adaptation strategy when moving into foreign markets with services already developed in their home markets.

An extension strategy for service development requires more care and accumulation of background information on the different situations marketers find themselves in. This will include information covering opportunity costs and entry costs of each service. A 'one size fits all approach' must be handled with care.[4] Too often, managers fall back on a generic approach to service development because they are torn between the demands and costs of missing a fast-moving market, and the risk of entering a market with the wrong service. If the risk of developing a new service, for example, is high and the cost is low, then the goal is to create a service that is 100% right at market launch time rather than miss a fast-moving market window. In order to make the right decisions, extensive testing is required in the early stages of research and development, allowing customers to review concepts and make sure that the design concept meets the individual preferences being addressed.[5] If opportunity costs matter less than entry risk, there may be advantages in testing a service in a market niche outside the normal range of activities. This allows the organization to keep mature technology in the profitable larger markets without delay while experimenting with new products. Others, fighting high opportunity costs without much entry risk, may see a competitive advantage for services which can be quickly introduced without delay. If entry risk matters less than the opportunity costs, then there may be pressure to enter the market directly with a new service, thereby cutting the development costs and reducing opportunity costs.

An adaptation strategy is applied when some changes are required to fit the new market requirements. Due to the nature of many services (i.e. financial, professional) it seems more plausible that service features and elements will have to be adapted to some degree in the different legal and cultural environments. Those changes could be minor or quite major. Certain basic financial services such as credit cards, personal loans and current accounts can be promoted in almost every market. However, the more sophisticated financial services, particularly in the investment and insurance areas, will require a thorough re-examination of the marketing approach. For that reason, the marketer should look not at what services they would like to sell, but at what services the public would like to buy.[6]

In all instances, whether services are provided on a national or international basis, it is important to decipher how closely the planning, creation, delivering and evaluation assessment of services are linked. Feedback and forward planning are indispensable to the delivery of excellent service quality by market oriented providers. So, it will be clear that we focus in this chapter especially on customer-based assets (like company or brand name and reputation, and superior levels of customer services and support) and all the outside-in capabilities to understand customer needs and 'translate' them into 'concrete' services.

SERVICE PRACTICE 8.2

Perceived Security and the Use of Electronic Payments

It has proved difficult to convince customers of electronic commerce that online credit card payments are safe. Well known e-tailers, such as Amazon, etc. obviously use their reputation to reduce their customers' risk perceptions. Especially the less known and smaller online retailers have had great difficulty, however, in convincing their customers of the security of their systems. They make increasingly use of certification by companies such as Verisign, who provide encryption software solutions. Financial service providers are currently using various different techniques to offer secure access to their services. Next to the use of data encryption and secure connections, most banks are using card readers, digipass, or other client authentication tools, produced by companies such as Vasco (**www.vasco.com**).

8.2   Service Models

Various thoughts have influenced the theory about services as the 'P' of product. Here we will elaborate on three issues:

■   The coherence between planning, creating, delivering and evaluating services;
■   The hierarchy of services; and
■   The lifecycle of services.

The Coherence between Planning, Creating, Delivering and Evaluating Services

The marketing mix has to be implemented in the same way as the corporate and marketing strategy with respect to targets, planning, the organization's market orientation, desired quality of the service provided, choice of positions in the various matrices as developed for the classification of services, choice between core services and augmented services, choice between customized services and standard services, and target groups, market segments and market position. National and international external opportunities and risks have been taken into account at corporate and marketing planning, as well as the organization's internal strengths and weaknesses. The people, assets, capabilities, routines, resources and possibilities the organization needs to actually realize its plans were discussed before; now we turn to the 'service' itself. The strategic targets and plans, together with the (limited) resources, determine the contents of the service concept from a strategic point of view, in the same way as they determine the service concept in a more tactical or operational sense. Both concepts will be reflected in the way the services will be delivered. Finally, the performance of the service and the process of providing it needs to be evaluated. This process is summarized in

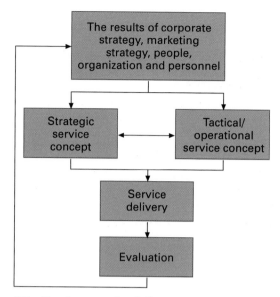

Figure 8.2   To plan, create, deliver and evaluate services

Figure 8.2. In it, we primarily intend to show the coherence between and the need to coordinate all these components from an organizational and process oriented viewpoint.[7]

The strategic service concept is very much based on the market orientation the organization has opted for; the needs and desires of the customer with regard to service and provision. In other words, the focus has to be on the desired benefits of the service, its function and its position relative to the competitors. In giving actual content to the tactical or operational service concept, the geographical range and organization of the activities is, among other things, determined. It indicates when the consecutive components of the service providing system must be ready to fulfil their specific tasks. The strategic service concept as well as the operational service concept influence the decision that shapes the process of delivering the services. The service provider must find practical answers to operational questions such as: the order of the various steps taken during the delivery process: where, when and at what speed should these steps be taken; the actual division between front and back office activities; the level of delegation (are tasks like information and reservation left to others or contracted out, or do we handle things ourselves?); the nature of the contact and the process between client and service provider; and the instructions for handling the scarce capacity (reservations, waiting and such), atmosphere and ambience (scripts for personnel, variation in the setting, lights, music and such).

When the service has actually been delivered, the performance can be determined and evaluated. This performance assessment primarily covers the extent the customer perceived quality matches the expectations. It goes without saying that other interested parties apply different standards. Staff will pay attention to the working atmosphere, opportunities for career development and remuneration. Shareholders will measure the performance and value of the service company by means of its profits, increase in value and/or dividend per share or other index numbers.[8]

All the strategic, procedural and organizational components in an organization need to be coordinated to actually fulfil the expectations of its clients and other interested parties. This is based on the idea that internal service quality will co-determine external service quality, and that strategy and operations should not be separated.

The Hierarchy of Services

As with goods, services may be defined at different levels. This hierarchy is important to give meaning to services at different strategic and operational levels. We distinguish seven levels of services: need family, services family, service class, service form, service type, brand, and service variation.[9] With the exception of level 6 (brand), every hierarchic level constitutes the sum of the parts of the consecutive level. Thus, together, the service variations constitute one service type. All different service types that are strongly interrelated combine into one service form, just as all service forms combine into one service class, and services may have a different life cycle at each of these levels. The strategic choices refer mainly to levels 1–4, while the tactical choices mainly refer to levels 4–7. So, level 4 may possess characteristics of both levels. An example is given in Service Practice 8.3. One should be aware of the fact that a brand name has great strategic value. A brand can have strategic value for the firm in terms of its brand equity[10] or for the customers in terms of visibility and image, thereby reducing perceived risk. Moreover, it has been mentioned before that brand name, image and reputation are among the key success factors and successful customer-based assets of service providers.

Life Cycle of Services

The life cycle of a service can be developed at any level. The introduction of new services or service variations may also give new impetus to the turn-over (profits) and/or extend the life cycle. The service hierarchy and the life cycle concept imply that the organization must make several choices as to its service policy. This is sometimes called managing services by means of their life cycles.

During the introduction phase at the beginning of the life cycle, emphasis will be put mainly on developing the primary demand for the service (class). Different pricing strategies may then be pursued. When a new restaurant has been established, one can see that, initially, prices are kept low to attract a sufficient number of curious visitors. Prices will go up once a regular group of people begin to visit the new establishment frequently.

The growth phase is characterized by a rapid increase in sales. Opinion leaders and early adopters are readily prepared to use new services. Competitors are attracted by the new offering because prices and margins are high and/or because some services can be imitated relatively easily, trying to lure clients by offering additional services. The pioneers will now have to aim at perfecting their service concept, check whether the service lives up to the clients' expectations, make improvements if necessary, develop additional services along with the core service, and so forth. New target groups and distribution channels may now become more important. Advertising, once focussed on an overall service (single-premium assurance policy, supplementary pension schemes, cash dispensers and debit cards, for example) can now be aimed at one's own specific service. All this is done as the first mover advantages seem to erode.

SERVICE PRACTICE 8.3

The Hierarchy of Life Insurances

Level	Definition	Example
Need family (type of need)	The core need forming the basics of the service	Old age security
Services family	All service classes which are more or less effective in satisfying the core needs	Savings and income
Service class	A group of services within the family of services which can be recognized as belonging to one class. It concerns essential basic services which cater to clearly outlined generic needs	Financial services
Service form	A group of services (comparable to the 'product line') within the service class that are closely related to each other, either because they function in the same way, or because they are being sold to the same group of clients or are distributed through the same channel or come into the same price-range (the 'service line')	Life insurance
Service type	All parts of a service form that have one or more characteristics of the service in common	Capital insurance or endowment life insurance policies
Brand	The name connected to one or more objects within the service form, used to determine the origin or character of these segments	American Express, AIX Insurance, Swiss Life, Aegon Insurance or Citigroup
Service variation	A distinct unit within a brand or service line that can be distinguished by way of size, price, or other common attributes/characteristics	The male/female insurance policy of Nationale Nederlanden, American Express Life Insurance, etc.

During the early phases of the service's adulthood, saturation, or maturity, the efficiency of the internal and external service delivery process becomes more important. This is related to some of the firm's internal-based assets and inside-out capabilities. Often, there is still the ability to add additional services. At the same time, room becomes available at the bottom of the market for consumers who, for price technicalities or other reasons, prefer to use the core service only (for example, flights with no on-board service). This relates to the 'wheel of servicing' (Chapter 6).

Firms that concentrate only on service upgrade, which tends to increase both service complexity and service divergence while increasing costs, are ignoring a still growing share of the market. This creates opportunities for new entrants (who offer little service) at the bottom of the market. Alongside this, there are other well-known strategies to survive during the saturation phase. These strategies are e.g. modification of the many elements of the service's marketing mix and market modification. The service organization can try to enlarge the market for its brands and services by influencing the two factors that determine the turnover (volume = number of users x quantity used per client) and service innovation.

Finally, at the end of the life cycle and during the decline phase of a service, a maximum effort will be made to limit all marketing mix expenses. This is sometimes called the passive sale of a service. It means that the service will be provided only if the client explicitly asks for it. Often, the service is deleted from brochures or price lists. In the end, it will be removed from the assortment completely. As in retail firms, every service organization may apply its assortment policy to detect each brand's market share, contribution margin, quality, customer satisfaction, etc. This is an essential part of the service policy. Another possibility is to modify the service in such a way that a new life cycle starts. Of course, entering new foreign markets is a way to cope with the decline in a particular country's service market.

Moreover, you may recall the concept of the relationship life cycle. The process of developing, maintaining and enhancing relationships may (but does not need to) go along with this services life cycle.

8.3 The Service Concept

A market oriented service policy must be directed at putting into practice all the benefits a service provider is able to offer to its clients. These are the general benefits of doing business with the organization as a whole, but include also the brand name, the assortment of services available and the actual range of services. This addition makes the general formulation somewhat more operational, but before a tangible service can be offered it must be given a more concrete form. This is about the 'translation' of our four matrix positions, opted for in Chapter 2, into a concrete service and the actual service delivery process. Here, again you have to distinguish between choices of a strategic, tactical or operational level.

As far as the tactical/operational level is concerned, choices will relate mainly to brands and the actual offering and delivery of all sorts of services. The composition of this offering is based on the assortment. The difference between strategic and tactical cannot be taken in the absolute sense here, sometimes there is only a difference of degree. Figure 8.3 depicts the major elements of the service to be discussed in this section.

The Strategic Service Concept

The decision taken by an insurance company not to limit themselves to issuing only life insurance policies but instead to extend their services to property insurance and savings is an example of a strategic decision. Within the limits of the strategic service concept the organization intends to develop services for one or more specific market segments. This can be represented as a positioning strategy. A positioning strategy will assist an organization in developing a strategic service concept which can be distinguished from those of the organization's major competitors.

Decisions on the core service(s) of an organization will be taken at company or strategic business unit (SBU) level. If one knows what the client considers to be the core benefits, the service can be expanded by adding additional services, or limited by deleting them. This distinction also serves as an aid for improving current services or developing new services and service delivery processes.

Important make or buy decisions, too, should be taken at company or SBU level. Here, the

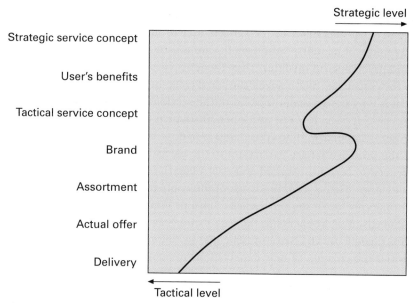

Figure 8.3 Services at a strategic and tactical level

focus is mainly on the internal service processes, in the sense that the organization always has a choice: do we produce it ourselves or do we buy it elsewhere? In this context, a distinction is made between three functions of a service:

■ The function of production;
■ The function of direction; and
■ The function of distribution.

The function of production refers to the actual 'production' of the service. Do we produce the service ourselves or do we buy it on the market? The function of direction refers to the assessment of the needs of the internal clients and translates these into a list of requirements. The function of distribution facilitates the maximum convergence of supply and demand. The question to be asked is whether this should be realized through internal service providing processes or by ordering the services from an external supplier. At present, more and more service providers ask themselves whether they are able to upgrade their (internal) services, should privatize them (hive them off), or buy them in as external services from third parties. This means that the production function may sometimes be contracted out; the function of direction and distribution, however, cannot. In the computer industry especially, but also in the airline industry, we see an increasing number of third party maintenance organizations.

User Benefits

'What's in it for me?' Irrespective of whether it is a marketing class or a cinema ticket, the (personal) benefit to the prospective user must be clear. For this reason, John Bateson (1995, p. 25) alleges that a service can only be defined from the point of view of the user's benefit:

'It is perceived service which matters, not the actual service.' The key issue of a service's *raison d'être* is: 'what benefits does the service offer to the prospective user?' Services can be defined as a bundle of benefits; these benefits are mostly a combination of functional, efficiency and psychological qualities. These benefits can only occur when the service is available to the consumer, that is when the service can be actually provided at a particular location. That is why design and operation of the service delivery system is a key element in defining a specific service. It is the user's benefits which determine what elements within this service delivery system have to be considered as crucial in quality control. Particularly, those elements in the process that are paramount to the user's final assessment (key success factors) will need to be both checked and controlled to ensure that they come up to the desired quality level. This is a consequence of the company's market orientation.

To transform expected or desired 'benefits' into profitable services may prove difficult. For example the needs of and benefits to the user cannot always be clearly investigated. The user's benefits change in the course of time, due to, among other things, good or bad experiences and the creation of new expectations influenced by environment and so on. Even if the client's needs and the benefits a service offers to the user have been listed, it may still be difficult to measure these benefits; and customers may focus more on the perceived risks than on the perceived benefits. These issues require a great deal of attention from both the marketing department and the operations staff of a company. Defining and analysing the user's benefits in time is of vital importance to all decisions concerning design and delivery of a service.[11]

When applying the idea of enhancing user benefits for the service strategy, it is also important to draw a distinction between attributes and benefits of a service, which is significant because a supplier will try to adapt the benefits of a service to correspond with the user's needs. Its further objective is to make a central presentation of these benefits in the sales promotion phase. It is important to acknowledge that what is useful to one person is not automatically advantageous to another. The measure of benefits, considering the subjective nature of a services, is difficult to assess by all involved; service providers try to get a better understanding of this by carrying out market research. Market segmentation and targeted promotions, by way of recommending certain advantages to individual customers or target groups, may help service providers to emphasize the benefits that can be reaped by the customer. To illustrate this, we have summed up various attributes (or features) and (possible) benefits of credit cards in Table 8.1.

The Tactical Service Concept

The tactical or operational service concept contains a description of the service package sold to the customer, as well as of the relative value of this package to the user. This definition enables the marketer to take into account the influence exercised by non tangible aspects which are difficult to measure and often implicitly influence the consumer's decision to purchase a concrete service.

The relative importance of the package of services to the customer also includes the actual, generic benefits an organization can offer. A service organization with an excellent market reputation is able to charge a larger fee compared to unknown service providers in the same

Table 8.1 Distinction between features of a credit card and its possible benefits to credit card users

Attributes/Features	Benefits
1. Small	1. Easy to carry
2. Plastic	2. Durable
3. Legal tender	3. Buy now, pay later. Less money in one's pockets, leading to better cash management
4. Can be used abroad	4. Less need for traveller's cheques and less need for cash money on a journey
5. Distinctive colour	5. Prestige: colour is linked to income and credit-worthiness of customer
6. Monthly debit notices	6. Proper administration of expenses and spending facilities
7. Credit facilities	7. More spending facilities, self-regulation of the extent of cash position
8. Can be used to pay with in many places	8. Increases usability
9. Insured against loss. Money-limited liability in case of abuse	9. More security as compared to cash theft
10. Receipt of copy of each liability	10. Better management of all transactions

industry.[12] In other words, when determining the tactical service concept the service provider must answer the question: taking our organization as a whole, how do we cater to the demands of the market? Again, this issue is closely related to the position the service provider intends to create and maintain in the market and thus to the strategic service concept. Now, it is made more 'concrete'.

Brands

Brand awareness, brand loyalty, brand personality, brand name and image have become important (non tangible) company assets. In Chapter 4, we have already pointed out the importance of the service company's name, brand or image as key success factors and the functions of brands to the customer and the service provider. Brands help to stabilize the relationship between customers and the service provider; however, recently, things seem to have subsided. On the one hand, a declining economic climate, more price sensitive and well-informed consumers and the rise of retailer brands is causing a decline in power of manufacturer brands in a number of industries; on the other hand, well-known service companies in the retail sector such as Wal-Mart, Marks and Spencer and Ikea create an aura of security with their own brand (private labels) which was previously only attributed to manufacturers' brands. We can assume that in the financial and travel sector the image of the distributor (a reputable bank or a chain of travel agencies), is replacing the labels of an insurance company or a tour operator. The service sector only recently discovered the value of developing a brand strategy in connection with improving its market position, offering security and creating a good relationship with the customers and employees.

Brand management is a hard job, especially, since it has been found that brand parity is high in some service industries. This means customers perceive no or hardly any difference between service brands. The advertising agency BBDO, for instance, has found that in Europe brand parity for credit cards is about 80–90%.[13] This means that only 10–20% of Europeans perceive (and are aware of) differences between the well-known credit cards like Visa, MasterCard, American Express and Diners card. Clearly, in these cases, brand management has not resulted in a distinctive positioning of these companies. It seems to be quite difficult to create global brands in retail financial services, not so much in the wholesale and professional financial services. Probably, only American Express and the French insurance company Axa have a global brand in their retail financial services although Citigroup attempts to. Such a brand can be built relatively quickly only 'if the company is committed to the task, and has a simple story to tell'.[14]

For a greater part, choosing a specific brand name is a strategic matter too, just as the choice between a family brand or individual brands is. A separate brand policy is followed particularly if major differences in market segment, price, quality and envisaged image exist; the distribution strategy necessitates this. A large market share, for example, makes the brand too dominant within a distribution channel or market area. By introducing a second brand, it becomes possible to implement more intensive distribution of the service in the same market area. Examples of this are the consumer financing and leasing that are offered by general banks as well as subsidiary companies which carry a different label (and different conditions); sufficient means are available (advertising budget, operational and management budgets); and there is a good chance that dissatisfaction with one particular service will adversely affect the sale of the remaining services. Another example refers to Virgin Atlantic Airways, which is giving names to its individual upper-class flights that travel from various US cities to London's Heathrow and Gatwick airports: Miami–London flights will be known as The Trance Atlantic for instance.[15]

The choice of a family brand, on the one hand, opens the way to a more consistent handling of all services and, on the other hand, necessitates this. From a customer's perspective, it helps in reducing risk. It also facilitates the efficiency of operational activities and advertising efforts. The generic investment funds of Fidelity, Templeton and Invesco are examples of company policies to develop a family or umbrella brand. However, a family brand policy is not a static one. For instance, the investment banking activities of Deutsche Bank and ABN AMRO have changed their names. Where the brand names of the banks were once carefully associated with the old merchant banks they had acquired (like Deutsche Bank, Morgan Grenfell or ABN AMRO Hoare Govett), these names have been dropped, e.g. ABN AMRO Securities. The new name reflects the business they are in. It all has to do with ways of accomplishing brand extentions. Brand extension occurs when service providers try to use the goodwill of the existing (family) brand for the benefit of the new service.

Assortment

When we discuss the assortment policy, it is self-evident to pay attention to the width and depth of the assortment. Then, a portfolio of services and brands can be accomplished and offered to different target group customers. Within the limits of their restricted service assortments, firms like McDonald's carry a rather wide range of service variations. In the case of McDonald's, these are the kinds of hamburgers and in case of a building society, the various types of mortgages. Therefore, we can label this assortment as small but deep.

In service organizations, assortment strategy plays a major role. What a portfolio of services brands should be composed of in an actual situation depends on the strategic and tactical service concept. The portfolio's build-up of services can also be linked to the relationship or familiarity with the organization; the service delivery process; and/or the sales.[16] As to relationship with the organization, one can think of the deployment of one organization or distribution channel for various forms or types of services (offering various kinds of package tours, for example). Relating services is usually aimed at increasing efficiency during the consecutive phases of providing services. Bundling services is a way of making this more concrete.[17] The transportation sector offers a number of examples. From this point of view, shipping, transportation and logistic services can be combined. For a transportation firm, it is paramount to cater to the needs of the clients by way of various logistics and distribution concepts instead of thinking from a procedural and organizational angle.

A service provider may complete the renowned Boston Consulting Group matrix (with the axes constituting the relative market share and market growth) for service brands that are available in the service provider's assortment. A similar matrix can also be composed for other levels of the service hierarchy, such as the service class, the service form, the service type and also, naturally, the service variation. This depends on the level at which one wishes to carry out such analyses about the positions of a company's services.

The Actual Service Offer

The last part of the service concept is the actual service offer and the supporting service delivery processes (its provision in particular). These delivery processes will not be discussed here; that will be done in other chapters on the service experience. The actual offer of services is a specific and detailed form of the service concept and assortment. The service offering is determined at an operational company level and can be regarded as the answer to many management questions, such as what services will be offered; what will be their definite form; when will these services be offered; how will they be offered; where are they offered; who is going to offer the services; and what costs do these services entail to the organization? Those responsible in an organization for defining the final service offer should at all times take into account three supply aspects when making decisions. These are the service elements, the final design of a service, and the level of service provision.

The service elements are the ingredients of the total supply of core services and additional services. Together, these elements form the one-off package of tangible and non tangible matters that actually constitute the augmented service offer. However, the success of a service or the consumer's judgement on the quality of the service, naturally, depend on many other things. The success of a holiday is determined not only by the elements the tour operator is responsible for, but also by group interaction, the people you meet, the amount of snow or sunshine, one's mood and unexpected events.

Managers in the service sector have to deal with a number of challenges when defining their offer to the client. Often, it is difficult to give a detailed summing-up of all tangible and non tangible elements which constitute the service offer. Usually, the tangible elements are easier to point out than the non tangible ones. In addition, calculating the cost will be difficult in both cases (just as the expected revenues); an offer not only consists of the service assortment (such as current accounts, mortgages, etc. by a bank) but also includes matters such as opening hours, the location of the branch and the like. The servuction process hinges upon the interaction between the clients. This will also affect service offerings and the quality of services as perceived by the consumer. So, a broad and integrative perspective is needed to design the 'perfect offer'.

The process of looking for the final form in which a service will be presented is aimed at a minute examination of the various options that exist for every service element. The decision on the precise structure of every service element (and so of its final design and the service delivery process) is based on factors such as market demands, competitors' policies, the need to balance the various elements within each service and all the competing services in the same branch. Service providers can make this as complex or as simple as they like. Naturally, the paramount questions are what the client desires and what the competition (already) does. Here, in a very concrete manner, substance is given to the firm's market orientation and the positions opted for. Low cost and differentiation now have to become a reality in service offers and brands. Upon determining the service offers, it is also necessary for every service, service variation and servuction process to decide at what level of service provision one should operate. Just as is the case with the other elements of the service provided, here too the service level, level of reliability and operational feasibilities have to harmonize with the positioning and competitive strategy opted for. If a company feels strongly about cost reduction it will, for example, limit the possibilities to provide customized services by means of human interaction. In addition to the available means, routines and capacity, naturally, play a role in this.

8.4 After Sales Services

The relevance of after sales services can be formulated as follows:

> *After-sales support is a litmus test of a firm's intention towards its customers. In effect, the customer judges the company by its willingness to stand behind its products and provide satisfaction to even the most unreasonable buyer.*[18]

First of all, after sales service will be among the additional services added to the core service. However, in turn, our four types of services can also be applied to the after sales services domain for, to some companies, this after sales service provision will consist of a standard service, to others it will be customized. Consumers will tend to use after sales services when core services or goods are not up to standard. The supplier must realize that the consumer's perception and state of mind will have a strong influence on the perceived quality of the after sales service. The same techniques and line of approach used to measure the quality of services and satisfaction that were previously mentioned are applicable when measuring the quality of after sales services.

After sales service can be described as the philosophy and all accompanying activities that can help to maximize consumer satisfaction following the purchase or the use of a good or a service by the consumer. After sales services receive a lot of attention these days (see also Chapter 5). Both consumers and firms consider them very relevant to developing and maintaining relationships and create new sources of value. It is important to consumers because it:

■ Is a means to gather information from the supplier;
■ Is a means to solve problems;
■ Makes it possible to settle complaints;
■ Is an essential part of the overall offer/proposition; and
■ Is an additional service.

For service providers, it is an essential part of their strategy because it:

■ Creates competitive advantages;
■ Forges or consolidates a bond with the clients;
■ Creates or consolidates brand loyalty and leads to repeat purchases;
■ Generates feedback from clients (particularly in case of complaints);
■ Provides more precise standards for the design of goods and services;
■ Provides services when a problem arises (service recovery);
■ Forces the organization to focus on the client and their needs and desires; and
■ Emphasizes the image of a market oriented organization.

In many B2B companies, after sales services hinge upon the technical oriented 'break and fix services'. For them, it is critical to add more of the after sales services we mention in the next section, if the customers ask for it. Moreover, they may have to switch from a technical orientation to a more social, interaction oriented one. This requires new and other skills, as you can imagine. These skills are the typical skills of market oriented service companies mentioned in the previous chapters.

Many Kinds of After Sales Services

It is important to know whether after sales services are based on people or machinery, how the client and the organization meet (who goes to whom?) and whether goods or services are concerned. In addition, there is another distinction between support services, on the one hand, and feedback and restitution services, on the other.[19] Guarantees, repairs, maintenance, availability of spare parts, replacements, delivery, installation, instruction, directions for use, user's help (help desk of computer suppliers and software houses), training, help in replacing spares, information, advice, etc. can be counted as support services. The feedback and restitutions category, for example, includes handling complaints, solving problems, refunds, telephone numbers for information, reactions to service staff's undesirable behaviour, dispute resolution, service recovery, returning products, etc. For both groups of after sales services, the quality will be determined by the perceptions and expectations of the client. Here, too, the well-known what, how and by whom determines after sales service quality.

With respect to after sales services, it is for service providers necessary to identify what causes the problems (if any): is it the service around the product or the product itself? That answer gives management information as to what should be done to solve the problem and avoid the problem in the future (prevention). Four types of situation might occur:

- The unbeatables: product is good and after sales is good;
- Walking wounded: product is good and after sales is poor;
- Time bombs: product is poor and after sales is good; and
- Dead on arrival (DOA): product is poor and after sales is poor.

It will be self-evident that only unbeatables will deliver excellent total service. On the other hand, great after sales services may sometimes be accepted in the short term as a remedy for imperfect goods. In the long run, however, no firm can survive with such a strategy. Then the time bomb will go off. Also, poor after sales services and good products will not be a viable situation in the long run; not to mention the DOA situation.

Investigating After Sales Services

Just as with any services discussed in this book, the quality of after sales service can be investigated in many ways. All the ways mentioned in Chapter 5 can be applied. It all hinges upon creating excellent after sales services. A special issue here, however, is that in many cases after sales services have to be used to solve consumer problems because something has gone wrong. So, after sales services are important as a way to solve customer dissatisfaction. As discussed in Chapter 5 you should avoid 'a double deviation scenario' in this respect.

Also, in general, when customers do not have any problems, after sales services are essential. For instance, in the automobile industry, satisfaction with the after sales services of the dealer (check-ups, 'normal' repair and maintenance, etc.) often appear to have a larger impact on dealer loyalty and brand loyalty than satisfaction with the car itself. This has turned out to be the case for many European, American and Japanese brands.[20] Since this service is also a people business, the way these service employees behave is often decisive in the perceived after sales service quality. As you will see in Chapters 10 and 12, these people live up the brand. The B2B world is no exception to this rule. Many people working in the B2B sector have a technical background and often pay less attention to social skills and social interactions in the customer–supplier relationships. However, it turns out that the 'soft skills' are most important in this industry. No one should forget that – even in this often technical world – issues like responsiveness, credibility and trust are crucial in the assessment of service quality. How technicians behave and interact with the customer is crucial from a marketing point of view. These part-time marketeers are often decisive in repeat buying decisions. This is one of the reasons why it may be so difficult to manage B2B services.[21] In the industrial world too, it is important to know whether customers have the same ideas, opinions and expectations about excellent after sales quality as the company offering this service. If this is not the case, the first cause for a lack of quality can be found, according to the SERVQUAL-model.

You may recall we have stated it is important to segment the market when buying services. This holds for after sales services as well. Significant differences of perceived after sales service quality exist between different segments of industrial customers. Differences in importance score for various items occurred among these segments as well.[22] We have experienced that the segmentation based on buying products or services does not need to be the same as for buying after sales services. Consequently, both need to be researched.

SERVICE PRACTICE 8.4

An Example of E-Loyalty

PhD candidate Sue Johnson desperately needed a book on a new statistical method from a small US publisher, as the deadline for the submission of her thesis was approaching rapidly. The local bookstores she had visited all told her that it would take about six to seven weeks to obtain a copy. They could not guarantee a delivery date, and were also not certain about the price. Needing the book earlier, Sue had done a search via Google and found out that the book was actually available from a large number of e-tailers. Although a number of them offered the book at a somewhat lower price, Sue decided to return to her favorite e-tailer, Amazon. The reasons for her choice to use Amazon were multiple. In her own experience, any information Amazon had provided her with had always been very reliable. They had informed her regularly of estimated delivery dates, and the precise amount her credit card was charged with. Their website was very intuitive and user-friendly, and the customer reviews the company provided her with had more than once helped her to decide, when she was in doubt about purchasing a book or CD. Moreover, they had a very clear return policy, and customer service. Sue ordered the book via Amazon, and when it arrived after two weeks, in the euphoria of being able to finalize her thesis, she wrote in the acknowledgements that she would never use another e-tailer again.

8.5   E-Services

PRACTICE 8.5

Tension Between Quality and Commercial Interests

Many commercial service providers have noticed the existence of a conflict between the e-service quality perceptions of their customers and related revisiting behaviour and other commercial interests such as advertising on their sites, and perceive their design decisions as a genuine balancing act. Portal sites, such as Yahoo! and MSN, have had to balance the e-service quality dimensions of accessibility of their services, navigability of their websites and design aesthetics – all known to be contributing to customer satisfaction and loyalty – with commercial interests, such as offering advertising space on their websites. The addition of banners, endless lists of links to sponsors, pop-up banners, etc. are known to negatively affect customers' quality perceptions and satisfaction, and their loyalty to sites. Although some rules of thumb are currently used in determining the amount and type of advertising acceptable to customers, the issue is very complex, and the only way to really know if the use of parts of the website for advertising is not leading to defection is to survey the customers regularly.

The Emergence and Increasing Importance of Electronic Services

In the recent past, a number of interrelated socio-economic and technological trends have led to the emergence and continuous growth of electronic forms of service, as you have seen in Chapter 1. A range of major breakthroughs and achievements in information and communication technology have paved the way for the development and commercialization of a wide range of new, technology-based services. Alongside this there has been an increased globalization which has resulted in the transparency of product and price information. This has led to an increase in rivalry in many industries.[23] This rivalry has increased the need for cost reductions. Finally, customers have become much more aware of price and quality differences between similar products, have become much better informed decision makers, and have in general become much more demanding with respect to value. The knowledge revolution, or the fast growth of knowledge, has increased the need for the exchange of information from a variety of sources, many of which are geographically spread.[24] High technology services are becoming increasingly important in different formats, to the extent that they can create substantial added value for the providers of the services as well as for their users and consumers.[25] The commercial use of the Internet and electronic commerce are steadily on the rise in all western economies, according to the US Census Bureau in 2003.

Recent research in high technology service innovation has provided a number of remarkable findings.[26] The high technology service industry is sometimes compared to other high technology industries, where many companies follow a technology push in their innovation strategies. However, important high technology service innovation success factors have been found, for example in a market orientation of the innovating firm, which stresses the important role of investigating, understanding and addressing actual customer needs and requirements, rather than the purely technology driven introduction of entirely new services.

Electronic Services and the Creation of Competitive Advantage

While electronic services provide a number of advantages to both the consumer and the provider of the service, the use of high technology services can create a sustainable competitive advantage in a number of ways. First, through the substitution of labour, considerable cost reductions can be realized by the service provider. Cost reductions can create a direct competitive advantage for companies that follow a low cost strategy, i.e. in all industries where service has become a commodity-like product.[27] Apart from realizing cost savings, the use of modern information and communication technology has also shown to increase the quality and the value added of existing services. This is especially important for firms that compete by differentiating their offer by providing high quality service.[28]

A familiar example from the financial services sector, demonstrating the power of information and communication technology to substantially improve the productivity of services, is the substitution of bank counters with ATMs and online banking services.[29] Other sectors of the services industry, such as insurance, the stock exchange, the travel industry, media, telecommunications and IT-service providers, are currently tapping into the potential of ICT-based services. Not for profit services, such as governmental services, community services and library services are also increasingly using high technology solutions. Electronic services also play an increasingly important role in the support of high technology products, as they enable producers to provide their customers with patches or updates (software) or sell upgrades or new versions. Many services contain these kinds of embedded software.

Electronic Services and the Customer Experience

If a new type of service is to be successful, it has to offer some extra value to the customer, or provide higher levels of utility at a lower price. In other words, what are the advantages in terms of extra value offered by high technology services to the customer? One of the most cited reasons for the success of e-commerce in general is the creation of time utility; the services are available around the clock, seven days of the week, without requiring the customer to travel to a service outlet. Another important reason is the creation of place utility, the convenience of being accessible from many different places, or virtually everywhere, e.g. by mobile phone. Another type of utility created by e-services is what could be called content or form utility: electronic services are considered to be very rich in content, in terms of the amount and detail of information they provide.[30] Finally, electronic services create price utility to the customer: part of the cost reduction realized by the service provider can be shared with the customer, which can make electronic service attractive to certain segments. Apart from these different traditional types of utility, technology creates innovative opportunities for entirely new types of service, which could attract new customer markets.

SERVICE PRACTICE 8.6

Personalization and Privacy

Excelling in the quality dimension of personalization, but making a large effort in respecting their customers' privacy, **Amazon.com** abundantly uses the option to customize Web pages and other electronic communication means, such as e-mail. By recording all purchases, and asking customers to rate their purchases, but also by recording all the pages their customers visit, the links they click on and the articles they browse, the company is able to personalize the pages the customer sees and the mail they receive. The extra information, based on the identification of complex patterns in the data, assists the customer in retrieving their previous interests, and to obtain recommendations based on their interests. Although many customers do appreciate the customized information and recommendations, there is a clear tension between the use of the browsing and purchasing behaviour of the customer and privacy. Privacy is mostly guaranteed by including a disclaimer at the bottom of the page, while customers are often asked to accept the privacy statement of the company, before being allowed to use the services.

Different Types of Electronic Services

Electronic services, also known as high technology services, can be defined as knowledge intensive services or composite service offers, interactively co-produced by the customer, through or with the help of electronic communication media. The medium used to provide the service can be a relatively simple (computer-) terminal, connected to the service provider via a telephone line, an intranet, the Internet, local area network (LAN), or wide area network (WAN) systems, or wireless communication systems such as a mobile phone, wireless application protocol (WAP), GPRS, 3rd Generation (3G) or Blueberry™ system. To develop an understanding of the diversity of electronic service types, and to understand the different opportunities service categories offer, a categorization of electronic services is useful. We have listed the most important categorizations of e-services in Table 8.2.

Distinguishing Electronic and Traditional Services

Not only is it important to be able to distinguish between different categories of electronic services, but it is also important to develop a good understanding of how electronically offered services, or e-services, differ from traditional services. These differences play a central role in the way customers perceive the services, and in the way they develop attitudes such as satisfaction with the service and loyalty to the service providers.[33] Developing a better understanding of the differences between these categories may help in identifying antecedents of success or failure of e-services, and may help e-service designers capitalize on the unique features of electronic services, instead of simply trying to substitute traditional services with similar electronic ones.

What is the result of a comparison between electronic and traditional services on the five I's distinguished in Chapter 2? The inability to own a service counts even harder for electronic services than for traditional services, for they are harder to grasp and depend completely on invisible technology. On the other hand, it may be easier since you can see the outcome of the service on the screen, which makes it more tangible. It can be observed that, on the dimensions of simultaneity and perishability, the differences between electronically provided services and traditional face-to-face services are relatively limited. In contrast with most consumer goods, electronically offered services are generally produced during an interaction between the service provider's computer system and a customer. They can therefore be considered to be simultaneously consumed and produced, similar to most traditional services. Electronically offered services are also perishable, since customers generally need to (re)connect to the service provider's computer network, and remain online in order to be able to use the service. This implies that communication bandwidth, the equivalent of staff in an electronic context, is needed when customers demand the service.

With respect to heterogeneity, a distinction can be made between two types of heterogeneity:

1 variance in quality perceptions between different customers; and
2 variance in quality perceptions between different usages of the service by a single customer.[34]

Table 8.2 A typology of electronic services	
Electronic service	
E-service autonomy	Electronic services can be launched and marketed as entirely independent or self-contained services, such as electronic banking. In a composite service offer these services play the role of a core service.[31] They can also be services intended to support or complement other products or services (e.g. a voice-mail service, offered by a telecommunication services provider).
E-service purpose	The strategic purpose of offering an electronic service, next to or instead of existing services, is determined by the service provider. In the first place, objectives such as cost reduction or an increase of value added could play a role. Furthermore, the e-service could be offered for promotional reasons, for example to increase traffic on a website or to promote a brand. Services can also be offered electronically to increase the number of distribution channels to expand the market for a service to remote areas that would be difficult to reach otherwise, or for purely lucrative reasons, being one of the company's core businesses; for example, ABI-Inform, one of the world's largest online library information services.
E-service directionality	The e-service can be provided one-directionally, from a service provider to a customer, but in most cases the use of technology will allow bi-directional real-time communication. However, one-directional service is often still part of the modern service offer, in the form of product catalogues and price lists. Two-sided, interactive communication via Internet is coming up.
E-service environment	Electronic services can be provided in a B2B or B2C environment, as well as in a consumer-to-consumer (C2C) or peer-to-peer (P2P) environment. B2B services facilitate functions in the supply chain such as purchasing, distribution or transportation, directly or indirectly.[32] Indirectly supported business functions and strategy are consultancy services, training is also a B2B service, and application service providers (ASP) provide online office applications. ASPs play an important role in the outsourcing of (functions of) IT departments, next to data storage and back-up services.
Transactional/ informational e-service	This is related to the degree to which a direct connection exists between the e-service and monetary transactions between the customer and the provider. Either the e-service supports transactional facilities with or without online monetary exchange, for example in the case of e-commerce, or the service is limited to the exchange of information, such as in the case of supporting services of other types of commerce.

Important heterogeneity will exist in both online and offline situations. In a traditional service context, both types of heterogeneity are largely caused by variations in staff performance on the one hand and customer mood and attitudes on the other. Online, the second type of heterogeneity can be attributed to variations in the technical functionality of the provider's Web server (e.g. caused by high traffic density) on the one side, and the quality

Table 8.3 Causes of heterogeneity in e-service performance

Type Locus	Between customers (type 1)	Between consumptions (type 2)
Provider	Offline: provider staff performance Online: technical matters	Offline: provider staff performance Online: technical matters
Customer	Offline: mood and attitude Online: Internet literacy and technical issues	Offline: mood and attitude Online: technical issues

of the (Internet) connection on the other. In this situation, heterogeneity does not occur as a result of customer behaviour. When heterogeneity occurs as a response to the customer's behaviour, for example in the case of variance in quality perceptions due to differences in technology readiness,[35] or other customer-related issues, an opportunity is created for service customization. In a traditional service context, employees can tailor the service offer almost completely to the specific needs or preferences of the customer, thereby potentially creating customer delight.[36] In an e-service context, customizability is currently still limited by the design of the service on the one hand and the degree to which customers can or are prepared to adapt the service to their particular needs on the other. Therefore, there is less heterogeneity between online customers.

Table 8.3 presents the sources of the heterogeneity based on two dimensions: the locus of heterogeneity (with the provider or with the customer) and the type of heterogeneity (between customers of the same service, or between customer experiences, i.e. the same customer experiencing different service consumptions from the same provider). This table shows the main causes of heterogeneity in e-service performance.

Service provider staff performance and especially their moods and attitudes are difficult to control. Technical problems are easier to identify and to control. Therefore, the use of online services can potentially limit heterogeneity in terms of quality perceptions.

Differences between traditional and electronic services can also be observed in their degree of intangibility. Online services are almost entirely intangible, although the design of the website, the colours used and the size and shape of icons and fonts, etc. are objectively visible and could be considered tangible elements. Contents of the service, like fact sheets, can be printed and could also be seen as a tangible aspect of online services.

Besides the five I's, two other dimensions, related to the origins of the provider, have been introduced to help distinguish different categories of e-services.[37] First, the perception of e-services differs with respect to the extent to which their providers have their origins in the physical world. Most traditional service providers exist in a so-called brick-and-mortar format; that is they have accessible premises in the tangible world. E-service providers having origins as a dot.com can be distinguished from those having a more traditional provenance. For service providers that have their origins in the tangible world, electronic services are an extension of their offline activities, while for dot.com starters the e-service portal represents the brand. Another dimension is related to the type of products sold. Some e-service providers sell tangible goods or traditional services; in such a case the electronic part of the services mainly functions as a channel for providing information to the customer and for

		Origin	
		Virtual	**Physical**
Product	**Virtual**	*E-portals* • Google • Yahoo • ICQ	*Company portals* • MSN • CNN
	Physical	*E-tailers* • Amazon • Dell	*E-sellers* • Barnes & Noble • Apple

Figure 8.4   E-services and their origin

Reprinted from 'Extending electronic portals with new services: Exploring usefulness of brand extension models', A. Van Riel and H. Ouwersloot, *Journal of Retailing and Consumer Services*, Copyright 2005 with permission from Elsevier.

realizing orders and transactions. In contrast, other e-service providers sell intangible products: search engines, communication services, information services and software. Combining the two dimensions, a matrix can be constructed (see Figure 8.4[38]). The lower compartments correspond to brick-and-mortar and click-and-mortar service providers. In the upper cells a distinction is made between clicks and bits, for portals that only provide online services, and 'bricks in bits', for providers who transformed their traditional service (bricks) into an electronic one (bits). Examples are provided in each cell of the matrix.

Different Functions of Electronic Services

Related to the strategic purpose of launching the service, electronic services, like traditional services, are used to perform many different functions. They are used to provide pre- or post-purchase product information, to supply product and customer support, to facilitate payments, and increase choice, or to deliver virtual or digitized products. They are also used as complementary channels for existing services.

The customer can perceive online services as core, facilitating, supplementary or complementary services. Core services are defined as self-contained Internet-based applications that let consumers conduct transactions, complete tasks, or solve problems, and also engage other (supplementary) e-services in the process, in order to complete higher level transactions.[39] Making a clear distinction between complementary, facilitating and supporting services is difficult in an online context, and often impossible. Especially in highly composite service offers it is difficult or even impossible to identify a clear core service.[40]

Web Portals

A unique phenomenon, which came into being with the introduction of electronic services, consists of Web or WAP portals. A collection of resources and services, like e-mail, forums, search engines and on-line shopping malls are bundled or made available via a common access point, home page, or a so-called portal site.[41]

Internet service providers (ISPs) and Internet directory services first introduced Web portals, simply offering access to an arbitrary mix of service categories and service providers on their own home page. These general portals (Yahoo!, MSN, AOL, etc.), expanded their service provision as a strategy to secure the user-base and lengthen the time a user stays on the portal. Game, chat, e-mail, news and other services were also introduced to make users' stay longer, thereby increasing revenues from online advertisements.[42]

A more recent generation of thematic and often highly focussed portals addresses specific customer segments. Examples are manufacturer portals (Hewlett-Packard, Benetton, Clarks), travel and tourism service portals (Virgin Express, **travel.com**), financial service portals (Visa, American Express, Bank One), retailer portals (Wal-Mart), news media and information portals (BBC, CNN, Lexus-Nexus, Lycos, InfoSeek, Google), and special interest group or niche portals (Planet-Pets, **Garden.com**, **Nanosig.org**). Most portals also provide various forms of content, in the form of relevant news and information. They often provide links and many other services like message boards, discussion forums, (free) e-mail or Web space and the possibility to order products or to execute transactions. Locating desired information and service providers can be a time-consuming task for customers. Therefore, a well-composed Web or WAP service portal can add substantial value and important potential benefits to the customer.[43]

On the Internet or in a WAP environment, service offers are regularly extended with new types of services. The extension of a portal site with a new service category has important similarities with a brand extension.[44] For example, when introducing new services on a Web or WAP portal, the perception of complementarity with the original service(s), or with the portal, appears to play a very important role in determining the customer's propensity to try the new service. In a traditional service or product extension context, customers also relate the quality of the new product to the presence of particular skills in the producer.[45] In an electronic service context, the expectation of the customer that the provider has the skills to provide this extension does not appear to play a major role in the success of the new service. This may not be valid, however, for providers associated with very specific skills, in which case the opposite may hold: they will probably be more successful when they make use of their specific expertise. Electronic service providers should therefore concentrate on extensions that are perceived to be highly complementary to the current service offer. They should also preferably focus on extensions that customers perceive to be presenting a challenge for the provider, and not on simple extensions that do not honour the quality reputation of the provider.

Domains of Electronic Service

Most of the traditional service domains have gained an online presence. The competitive success of the online version depends very much on the extent to which providers have been able to capitalize on the specific attributes of online services. We will mention and quickly describe the areas where online services are increasingly complementing or even substituting existing traditional service delivery methods.

Customer support services, often distinguished into pre-transaction, transaction and post-transaction services, are an area where the introduction of electronic services can help firms to realize large cost reductions, while at the same time customer service levels can be improved by using multiple channels that are adapted to the type of support required.[46] Customers appreciate the information richness, facilitated by the use of multimedia, the responsiveness and the search facilities offered by online databases in support services. Emerging extensions of online customer support are *customer forums*, organized by many high technology firms, where experienced customers take over a number of tasks from their help desks, and provide useful feedback.

Online health services, where customers pay for medical information and advice, are becoming increasingly important in remote areas, where direct access to medical assistance is very complicated, difficult or very costly.[47]

Bibliographic and content services are an increasingly important domain of online activity. The extensive search possibilities and the speed with which electronic documents can be retrieved and accessed make this a very attractive domain for customers of publishers and other content providers. Highly customized information can be provided through focussed professional portals[48] and many academic library services.

Communication services are taking advantage of the unlimited connectivity and the increasingly inexpensively available bandwidth of electronic means of communication, like the Internet and mobile communications. Successful examples are one-way communication entertainment services, such as streaming audio and video broadcasts, Web-based e-mail, and Web-based SMS. Two-way communication services, such as instant messaging, and Voice over IP (VoIP) are increasingly substituting traditional telephone services. This was the cover story in *Newsweek* of 26 September/3 October 2005.

Financial services, such as e-banking and mobile banking, provide functions such as online money transfers, account management and investing.

A sector that has been fundamentally impacted by the recent innovations in ICT is the financial services industry.[49] E-banking initiatives have been developed by nearly all large banks and the subject has been extensively studied by academics. Some interesting conclusions from a recent article are summarized in the following paragraphs.[50]

Adoption of electronic financial services occurs both in the industry and in consumers. Much academic research in the area of online financial services has focussed on the identification of these adoption factors. From a managerial point of view, understanding the factors that influence user adoption of online financial services is of primary importance. In the following discussion, we will first focus on the customer side.

Hospitality and tourism services (where the activities are traditionally performed by travel agencies), are another sector that has been fundamentally changed by the revolution in ICT. Leisure travel as well as business travel sectors are equally impacted by the emergence of electronic services. Booking and reservation of flights and hotels as well as the sale of complete holiday packages have become one of the most important e-commerce sectors.

Knowledge intensive services, such as training and high tech support, and consultancy services increasingly discover the advantages of online services. Especially in very dynamic areas where it is essential to provide accurate information that is up-to-date, the role of the Internet is increasing.

Electronic auction services are very popular today. You may think of EBay and other services. In internationalizing this kind of services, it is not always that easy. For instance EBay faces tough challenges in China and these challenges are becoming tougher, mainly due to a local rival called Alibaba.[51]

The Demand Side

Which factors persuade consumers to start and continue using electronic financial services? In the first place, perceived convenience, ease of use and usefulness induce consumers to start using online financial services. Overall trust in the bank and in the security of the electronic system have been identified as major conditions of financial service adoption. Customer attributes such as a positive attitude to change and experience or the previous use of similar applications also stimulate adoption. Overall access to the Internet, cost of investment and time spent on the Internet will also positively affect adoption.[52]

The Supply Side

The main drivers of electronic service adoption by firms in the financial services industry appear to be cost reductions, margin improvement and a strengthening of the competitive position.[53] Buzzachi *et al.* have highlighted that the development of online financial service offers may give rise to network externalities as defined by Shapiro and Varian; the value of the offer increases with the number of banks participating to the project.[54] This leaves few appropriation possibilities. It might actually be in the interest of the more innovative banks to transfer their know-how to the less dynamic ones. The locus of development thus tends to move from the leading banks to bank associations or institutions such as central banks.

An important step in the design of the online offer is the choice between a pure on line offer and a 'click-and-brick' offer. Improving brand recognition and increasing the perception of security in the customer are some of the advantages of a combined offer.[55] For other authors factors inhibiting adoption may come from company employees, who fear that the electronic service could threaten their job.[56]

Despite the fact that Internet-based technologies offer significant opportunities to create value, online financial services may not yet capture their full potential in the near future, as a result of customers' resistance to change or a lack of perceived benefits. Various services may show asymmetrical growth and development, with an early emphasis on payment services rather than on intermediation or insurance.

E-Service Evaluation and Control

Evaluation and control are part of each manager's job. Electronic services systems, whether they are used for supporting other products or for autonomous service delivery, for single services or for bundles of services, can contribute significantly to customer satisfaction and loyalty. At the same time, they require important investments in the supporting technology and in the maintenance of the system. The extent to which various electronic services contribute to the strategic goals of the company or the organization needs to be evaluated and controlled. Service quality is considered an important factor determining customer behavioural intentions, explaining about 50% of customer satisfaction. In traditional and electronic service contexts alike, customer satisfaction is driving loyalty, and is thus considered an important indicator of financial return.[57]

In order to evaluate traditional service performance, various service quality measurement instruments have been developed, mostly based on the SERVQUAL model. In an electronic service context, the customer does not interact with an employee of the service provider, but with the service provider's computer system, and the dimensions used in the SERVQUAL model are therefore not directly applicable in an electronic services context.[58] The interaction in an e-service context or m-commerce setting takes place through the mediation of what has been called a user interface.[59] A number of service quality models have been proposed in recent research, some of them attempting to adapt the existing service quality dimensions to this new context[60] and others trying to develop new distinctive e-service quality dimensions.[61] An important consideration when developing a method to assess electronic service quality is the contingency of the choice of the quality dimensions upon the type of service. Models have been developed to measure the quality of electronic service in an e-tailing context, such as the e-servqual and e-tailq models, but also in the broader context of electronic service delivery.[62] In the process of developing these new service quality instruments, it has become clear that some dimensions are not present in some electronic contexts, while some new dimensions needed to be introduced in others.

You may recall from Chapter 3 that a great many factors play a decisive role in using electronic services. This holds also with respect to evaluating the quality of e-services, e-service satisfaction and the quality of e-service recovery. Convenience or ease of use seems to be the major determining factor here. Because no clear patterns of factors explaining e-service quality and thus satisfaction and dissatisfaction have been found in the literature, we will give you some examples of results found recently.

In the USA, Internet retail service quality appears to consist of five dimensions:[63]

■ Performance means how well does an online retailer perform in terms of meeting a customer's expectations regarding physical fulfilment of an order. It also includes the amount of time and hassle to complete the whole online transaction;
■ Access refers to a consumer's ability to purchase a wide variety of products from anywhere in the world through a specific online retailer;
■ Security relates to the financial (conveying financial information on line like credit card number) and non financial security (revealing personal information like a telephone number);
■ Sensation: refers to the online consumer's ability to interact with the product as well as with other individuals during the shopping experience;
■ Information relates to the information quantity and credibility.

In this US study on Internet retailing, the scores on these five dimensions were summated into one scale that correlated highly and positively with satisfaction, word of mouth, likelihood of future purchases and even with the likelihood to complain. Performance and information were the factors online consumers were most concerned about. Or, stated a little bit differently, convenience and site design are the most important drivers of e-satisfaction in the USA and in Germany with respect to Internet shopping and Internet finance; service providers should provide additional value on these dimensions to online consumers.[64]

With respect to online securities brokerage services the most important quality dimensions were responsiveness, service reliability, ease of use, competence, access, systems reliability, timeliness and security. Ease of use is the only major driver of both customer satisfaction and dissatisfaction. Internet service satisfaction is mainly determined by responsiveness, service reliability and competence, while Internet service dissatisfaction is strongly related to information and systems quality dimensions.[65]

Recently, the E-S-QUAL Scale has been developed.[66] It was tested with respect to the Internet buying of a wide variety of products like apparel, books, CDs, computer software and hardware, drugs, electronics, flowers, groceries and toys. It consists of four dimensions:

- Efficiency: the ease and speed of accessing and using the site;
- Fulfilment: the extent to which the site's promises about order delivery and item availability are fulfilled;
- System availability: the correct technical functioning of the site; and
- Privacy: the degree to which the site is safe and protects customer information.

With respect to the quality of electronic service recovery, three dimensions existed:

- Responsiveness: effective handling of problems and returns through the site;
- Compensation: the degree to which the site compensates customers for problems; and
- Contact: the availability of assistance through telephone or online representatives.

The Role of B2B Electronic Services

In B2B services the role of cost reductions and quality improvement are at least as important as in B2C services. The purpose of introducing electronic services in the business-to-business environment was initially the reduction of costs in all sorts of inter-company exchanges, especially in the purchasing process. From the introduction of relatively simple one-to-one and one-to-many electronic data interchange (EDI) services, more complicated, many-to-many forms have evolved, such as online auctions. The use of online auctions reduces the cost of searching for customers or suppliers, and increases information transparency with respect to pricing and service quality, which at the same time increases the quality of purchasing decisions. Many different forms of online purchasing or intermediary services have been developed since. Next to cost reductions and increased transparency, an important advantage of electronic services is considered the reduction in human errors, and the speed with which information and documents can be exchanged.

Other types of B2B services that are gaining ground in online formats are corporate banking, outsourcing of administrative and accounting services, personnel management related services, distribution and transportation services, application service providers (ASPs) and other IT outsourcing.

8.6 Final Remarks

If only one thing should have become clear in this chapter, it is probably the observation that electronic services are different. They are different from traditional goods and services, in the way they are produced, used and consumed. They are very different in the way they are perceived, experienced and appreciated by consumers. They create different feelings and attitudes in consumers, and they create them in different dimensions and in different ways. They are also very different in the way they can be used to create competitive advantage for companies, for example by bundling complementary services in a service portal. The extent to which they can involve customer co-production is different, and they are in a very early stage of their development. This implies that many new e-service types, currently difficult to imagine, can be expected to emerge in the coming years. Research in the domain of electronic and other high technology services is also in its very early stages, and much remains unknown.

Although the growth of electronic commerce appears to be stagnating in a number of B2C sectors, there is little doubt in the minds of most researchers and executives that in the coming years the importance and role of electronic services will continue to increase. Electronic services already occupy an important share in the financial services industry, in travel booking, and in professional knowledge intensive services. As the development of communication technology will continue, companies in a growing number of industries will attempt to reap cost advantages created by the substitution of labour intensive traditional services by electronic services. At the same time, many new opportunities will arise to exploit the advantages high technology services can offer. For customers the main drivers of the use of electronic services remain convenience and ease of use.

Summary

The purpose of this chapter was to introduce and to highlight traditional services and an emerging type of services, the so-called electronic or high technology services, and to help you understand the differences between traditional and electronic service types on the one hand, and between different categories of electronic services on the other. In terms of the market oriented service firm's assets and capabilities, this chapter focusses especially on some of the customer-based assets (company brand name or reputation and superior levels of customer support) and all the outside-in capabilities (mentioned in Chapter 6) relevant to understand customer needs and translate them into concrete services.

The hierarchy of services revealed seven levels exist:

- need family;
- services family;
- service class;
- service form;
- service type;
- brand; and
- service variation.

We also distinguished between the strategic and the tactical service concept. Both consist in total of the following seven aspects:

- strategic service concept;
- user's benefits;
- tactical service concept;
- brand;

- assortment;
- actual offer; and
- delivery.

We made a large number of categorizations of the traditional services, aftersales services and electronic services, in order to better understand them and to see how each of them could be positioned best to create a competitive advantage. All of them can be monitored and evaluated according to the well-known concepts of service quality and satisfaction.

Much attention has been given to the newly emerging electronic services. Ease of use appears to be one of the critical factors determining electronic service quality and thus satisfaction with electronic services. Many more factors affect this quality and satisfaction. Some of them are similar to the ones affecting quality and satisfaction with traditional services, others are different. These factors are in line with the critical factors determining consumer behaviour with respect to electronic services and Internet retailing mentioned in Chapter 3.

Questions

1. What difference is there between features and benefits of a service? Why is it important to make this distinction in a service strategy?
2. What is the relationship between the service hierarchy and the differences between the strategic and the tactical service concept?
3. How can service firms impact on demand and supply? What strategies can be used to that end?
4. What are the functions of brands mentioned in Chapter 4? How can you relate them to what has been said about brands in this chapter?
5. Why is it relevant that coherence exists between the planning, creating, delivering and evaluating of services (traditional or electronic ones) and after sales services?
6. Where do quality expectations come from in customers of electronic services?
7. What would be the main causes of poor service quality perceptions in electronic services?
8. Is the role of trust different in electronic services from traditional services? And how about its role in after sales services?
9. Which types of electronic services can be distinguished?
10. Do you expect a convergence between e-servqual and servqual as more and more service firms offer both offline services and online services?

Assignments

1. Make a diagram that depicts how the family of services, classes and forms, the type of services and the service variations interrelate in the transportation sector.

2. Provide some examples of how service firms that you know actually manage their capacity.

3. Discuss how Internet retailers could organize a process to assess, control and improve electronic service quality.

4. Is it possible to apply the zone of tolerance model in an unchanged way to measuring electronic service quality? If not, what would you adapt? If yes, why?

5. Compare what has been said about consumers' use of the Internet (or barriers to using it) in Chapter 3 with what has been said about e-service quality and e-service satisfaction in this chapter. What do you conclude in general? What do you conclude e-tailers should do to improve e-service quality and e-satisfaction of first-time Internet buyers of books, computers and airline tickets?

Endnotes

1   See Annual Report 2003 Accor Group.

2   Stock and Lambert, 2001.

3   Jeannet and Hennessy, 1988, p. 340.

4   Krubasik, 1988.

5   See also Chapter 9 on service innovation and new service development.

6   Jeannet and Hennessy, 1988, p. 8 ; in both (extension and adaption) strategies of service in the international context, communications will play a major role in making the public aware of these services and reducing perceived risk. As soon as either a service or its communications needs to be adapted, qualitative research must be available which focuses on groups in order to generate ideas for the essential features of new services and their acceptance. For example, they can throw light on new service ideas. Such surveys should include testing of benefits, attitudes and promotional appeals (advertising, sales or personal selling) toward that particular service.

7   The diagram is based on one of Lovelock's (1991) models which we have adapted to our own ideas.

8   A large number of (financial) performance indicators have already been mentioned in Chapter 6; others will be mentioned in subsequent chapters.

9   Based on Kotler, 1991, p. 431.

10   Aaker, 1991.

11   Next to 'perceived benefits', 'perceived risks' are a major factor in the process of buying services. The literature on marketing of professional services, for example, shows that the purchase of many professional services actually comes down to a purchase intended to reduce risks.

12   The surcharge well-known accountant firms could attain in New Zealand has been shown by Firth (1993).

13   As told by Andy Mosmans at a 1996 conference on International Service Management, Maastricht, The Netherlands.

14 Martin, 1998, says American Express, Axa and Citibank have a global brand in retail financial services.

15 Lawton, 2005.

16 A more detailed overview of these factors is given by Hurts and Van Mechelen (1997).

17 See the Chapter 11 section on price bundling.

18 Lele and Sheth, 1987, p. 98.

19 The various criteria for classification used in Chapter 2 can be applied to after-sales services as well.

20 This has been shown by Bloemer and Lemmink (1992) for a Japanese brand and by Bloemer and Kasper (1996) for two German brands. See also Bloemer and Kasper, 1998.

21 See, for instance, Homburg and Garbe, 1996; Venetis, 1997.

22 Kasper and Lemmink (1988, 1989) also found that the segmentation criteria applied in segmenting the market for the copying equipment itself (the apparatus) is not necessarily the same as those used in segmentation of the after sales service market for this equipment. Both segmentations may lead to different groups of customers. The most important managerial implication of this finding is that the firm should not offer one type of after sales service for each copying machine but have the customer choose from a variety of after sales service options (at a particular price, of course). That will enhance perceived service quality and customer satisfaction.

23 Porter, 2001.

24 Chichilnisky, 1998.

25 Van den Ende and Wijnberg, 2001.

26 Van Riel, Lemmink, and Ouwersloot, 2004; Van Riel and Lievens, 2004.

27 Porter, 1985, 2001; Bitner, Brown and Meuter, 2000.

28 Normann, 2001.

29 Meuter, Ostrom, Roundtree and Bitner, 2000.

30 Electronic services are considered to be content-rich, but they lack the face-to-face human interaction of traditional services. This makes them perfectly suitable for some types of services, while they are less suitable for others.

31 Grönroos, 2001.

32 Lucking-Reiley and Spulber, 2001.

33 Zeithaml, Parasuraman and Malhotra, 2000.

34 Van Riel and Ouwersloot, 2005.

35 Parasuraman and Colby, 2000; see also Chapter 3.

36 Rust and Oliver, 2000.

37 Van Riel and Ouwersloot, 2005.

38 Adapted from Van Riel and Ouwersloot, 2005.

39 Borck, 2000.

40 Van Riel, Semeijn and Pauwels, 2004.

41 Rust and Kannan, 2003.

42 Wikipedia, 2005 (an online encyclopaedia).

43 Amor, 2002.

44 In early brand extension research (Aaker and Keller, 1990), focussing on tangible product categories and their extensions, it was found that the quality perception related to the original product was transferred to the new product, to the extent that the customer would perceive a fit or similarity between the two products. Aaker and Keller (1990) distinguished several fit dimensions that all played a role in determining customer perceptions of the quality of the extension. The mechanisms determining customer acceptance or adoption of the new online service category appear to be comparable, although some differences exist in the roles of the various fit dimensions (Van Riel and Ouwersloot, 2005).

45 Aaker and Keller, 1990.

46 Van Riel, Lemmink, Streukens and Liljander, 2004.

47 See, e.g., Gummerus, Liljander, Pura and Van Riel, 2004.

48 Van Riel, Liljander and Jurriëns, 2001.

49 Buzzacchi, Colombo and Mariotti, 1995.

50 Gailly and Philippart, 2005.

51 Mangalindan, 2005.

52 See Eastin, 2002; Sadiq Sohail and Shanmugham, 2003; Suh and Han, 2002.

53 See Orr, 1999; Simpson, 2002 ; Aladwany, 2001.

54 See Buzzacchi, Colombo and Mariotti, 1995; Aladwany, 2001.

55 Capiez, 2001.

56 Venard, 2001.

57 Reicheld and Schefter, 2000; Reicheld and Teal, 1996.

58 Liljander, Van Riel and Pura, 2002.

59 See Meuter, Ostrom, Roundtree and Bitner, 2000; Parasuraman and Grewal, 2000; Parasuraman and Zinkhan, 2002; Kleijnen, Wetzels and De Ruyter, 2004; Davis, 1989; Davis, Bagozzi and Warshaw, 1989.

60 Bitner, Brown and Meuter, 2000; Liljander, Van Riel and Pura, 2002.

61 Parasuraman, Zeithaml, and Malhotra, 2005; Wolfinbarger and Gilly, 2003; Zeithaml, 2002.

62 Parasuraman, Zeithaml and Malhotra, 2005; Wolfinbarger and Gilly, 2003; Zeithaml, 2002; Dabholkar and Bagozzi, 2002; Grönroos, Heinonen, Isoniemi and Lindholm, 2000; Zeithaml, Parasurman and Malhotra, 2000; Zeithaml, Parasuraman and Malhotra, 2002.

63 Janda et al., 2002.

64 Evanschitzky et al., 2004.

65 Yang and Fang, 2004.

66 Parasuraman et al., 2005.

Chapter 9

Service Innovation

CA software enables

22million

split-second securities trades a day for three of the world's leading investment firms.

Huge order volumes are executed swiftly and securely across platforms around the globe. It all happens when CA software automates systems and processes. To manage your customers' transactions with this kind of speed and reliability, call a CA representative on **01753 242 679** or visit **ca.com/uk/didyouknow**.

ca

© 2006 Computer Associates International, Inc. (CA) All rights reserved.

Reproduced by permission of Computer Associates and Getty Images

Learning objectives

At the end of this chapter you will be able to:

1 Understand the importance of service innovation to developed economies

2 Appreciate the problems of measurement, heterogeneity and the environment in assessing service innovation performance

3 Distinguish between service innovations which are breakthrough services, new to the world, new to the market and new to the organization

4 Identify the key steps in taking a service innovation to market

5 Describe the process of new service development

6 Understand the importance of generating a service culture

7 Describe the role of cross-functional teams in the service innovation process

8 Explain the process of consumer adoption of innovations

9 Understand how service organizations approach innovation activity

10 List the causes of success and failures in B2B new service development

9.1   Introduction

SERVICE PRACTICE 9.1

Innovations in the Air[1]

Competition is very hard in the airline industry. Airlines have to come with innovations to attract customers. These innovations may be of a very different nature.

From the previous chapter you may recall that Virgin Atlantic Airways branded specific flights on the trans-Atlantic routes.

Two new airlines plan to launch an all-business class service on the routes between London and New York. Despite the cut-throat competition on this route, Eos Airlines and Maxjet Airways plan to have fewer seats in their planes and charge higher fares. Both companies will fly to Stansted Airport and not to Heathrow. It is easy travelling from Stansted to the City. Although some failures have occurred in the past, these two companies will try it anew. Eos will have 48 seats on an airplane that usually will carry 180 seats.

Seats will fold down into beds 198 centimeters long, outfitted with cashmere blankets and cotton sheets. Instead of tray tables, Eos seats will have large credenza-like surfaces, and 'companion seats' for in-flight meetings. Fares will be . . . about 20% below the high end of existing business-class fares.

Maxjet will have 102 seats on a more-than-200-seats plane. It will be more like a standard business class. Maxjet plans to sharply undercut standard business-class ticket prices.

If pressing demands of business rob you of time to organize your wedding, you could always ask your airline of choice to do it for you. Or, if heavy traffic threatens to prevent you catching your flight, you could call for a helicopter to pluck you from the jam. But in either case you will need to be a very important customer . . . Perhaps the most visible example of special care and attention given to high premium travellers is a terminal opened by Lufthansa at Frankfurt airport last winter that is reserved for first-class passengers and top-tier frequent flyers. The airline plans to open a second next year, in Munich. Customers using the terminal have personal assistants at their disposal, private offices with phones and laptop connections or luxury rooms with baths and showers. They are driven to the aircraft in a Mercedes or a Porsche. Such services may prove more productive in attracting subsequent business than the occasional extraordinary measure.

Successful market oriented service organizations never stay still; they are constantly changing, trying to develop better ways of doing things, better ways to serve their markets, and develop better resources and knowledge. This whole process of change is referred to as 'innovation' but captures a whole range of organizational activities such as new service development, human resource selection and training, reassessing organizational structures, preparing communications and improving delivery.

Innovation can be defined as the conversion of knowledge and ideas into a benefit, which has commercial or social value, and which is evidenced by new or improved products, processes, or services and is key to competitiveness. As we have established so far, organizations have at their disposal a variety of assets and resources which can be transformed into market-based advantage. Equally they have a range of processes, knowledge and skills which represent capabilities. These assets and capabilities refer typically to what we have labelled in Chapter 6 as the service organization's copyrights and patents (as one of the internal-based assets), the alliance-based assets (especially the ones on shared technology and access to strategic partners' managerial know-how and expertise), all four the outside-in capabilities, and the spanning capabilities on the ability to launch successful new services and effective new service development processes. The danger for any organization is that many of these assets and capabilities have a short life. This is due to two effects; the first is that some assets and capabilities naturally degrade over time, for instance market knowledge if not maintained becomes out of date and increasingly useless. The second effect is assets and capabilities can be copied in the long run, other organizations can develop them or acquire them. In both cases organizations which intend to maintain their competitive advantage must constantly maintain and reinvest in their assets and capabilities in order to survive. This is true whatever the industry, but depending upon market and competitor conditions the drive toward innovation is either strong or weak. In strongly innovative industries such as IT, telecommunications, and business services a failure to innovate would mean a swift end to the company. As a consequence organizations require a steady flow of new and innovative service products. By contrast, industries such as civil engineering, public services, security services and education exhibit a weaker drive for new products and services and the innovation activity is less intense. A failure to innovate will not immediately threaten the company's survival but will slow down its ability to grow.

If innovation is so ubiquitous why should we consider it in a book about services? The first answer to this question is the emerging evidence that within an economy it is service innovations which contribute toward economic growth and therefore innovation must first be viewed from a macro economic perspective. The second answer to this question is that service innovations and particularly new service development is an emerging area of study.[2] We have already identified that services are quite different in many respects from physical goods and products. However the process of innovation associated with services is only just beginning to be investigated and while the fundamentals remain common, there are some quite distinct differences that separate services from traditional new product development processes. The final answer to this question is that often service innovations aren't fully appreciated or recognized because they happen continuously across the organization. It is only when innovation starts to slow down that managers start to consider the importance of an innovation culture and look for ways to encourage it. But you should also remember that the innovation and learning perspective are essential features of a market oriented service organization.

These themes provide the basis of this chapter on service and innovation. We start by considering the economic importance of services in tying together different parts of the economy. Second, we discuss the meaning of the famous word 'new'. Then we look at a typical new service development process and next we will examine the aspects of the

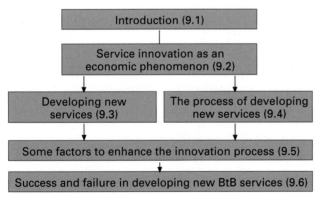

Figure 9.1   Chapter outline

organization which can both encourage and discourage innovation. We end this chapter with some typical success and failure factors when developing new services in the B2B sector (Figure 9.1).

9.2   Service Innovation as an Economic Phenomenon

The service sector is well recognized as the main growth driver for jobs and economic performance. While historically services have been viewed as a separate economic sector, increasingly the difference between services and other economic sectors is narrowing through the utilization of technology. While this narrowing has not yet reached the point where customers can enjoy the experience and atmosphere of a restaurant without actually going to one, or obtain medical intervention without physical presentation, information technology enables customers to participate in a growing number of services experiences in real or delayed time, making them closer to inventoried products. For instance, copies of films, and other entertainment can be recorded, stored and distributed on demand much like manufactured products. This approach marks a radical departure from previous assumptions about the relationship between service providers and customers where a product which is not mass produced can nevertheless be mass consumed.

While the distinctiveness of the services sector has been the focus in the past, a new debate is emerging about the macro importance of services to the economy and the interdependence of traditional manufacturing and service. According to the OECD, the arguments are first that services will reach a naturally imposed constraint on their growth since they are ultimately dependent upon manufacturing to survive. Opposing this view is that services growth will continue with manufacturing shifting in location to countries where the service sector is well developed and able to support manufacturing activity. This debate is still unresolved but what it highlights is the services cannot be seen as separate from manufacturing from an economic policy viewpoint. Without the demand for transportation there would be no demand for trucks, buses, aircraft and transport infrastructure. Similarly without the demand for

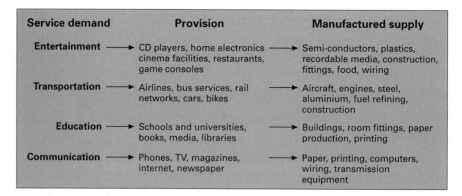

Figure 9.2   Relationship between service demand and manufacturing supply

information services and entertainment there would be no demand for CDs and DVDs, computers, semi-conductors and screens. Similarly manufactured products incorporate the value derived from many services, for instance a new TV is the embodiment of many design, transport and management services, or a new food product the result of research services, capital investment services and distribution. The point here is that it is difficult to consider the macro policy issues of encouraging industrial innovation without automatically considering services innovation and as such the distinction between the two is arbitrary at best (Figure 9.2).

When considering innovation in the service sector there are three problems that are consistently cited: measurement, heterogeneity and competitive environment. These issues taken together go some way to explaining why service innovation has been largely ignored by economists.[3]

Measurement

When trying to assess whether particular sectors are exhibiting evidence of innovation there are a number of key indicators which are used. The first indicator is research and development expenditure (R&D), which measures the amount of capital investment organizations are making in researching new ideas and developing new products. The problem with this approach for services (and especially organizations which are service dominant such as financial institutions) is that there is rarely an R&D department or research function. In engineering, pharmaceuticals or manufacturing, R&D expenditures are a common part of the company accounts with formalized processes and accountabilities. Even if a research structure exists it is unlikely to have, as a part of its remit distribution, internal service provision, marketing, environmental design or HR. These activities are often subsumed under headings such as business process re-engineering or business development.

The second problem associated with measurement is that service firms tend not to invest heavily in their own research and development but often buy it in. By this we mean they utilize existing technologies and adapt them to their operations rather than developing technologies in their own right. Consider for a moment the recent innovations in consumer banking, in particular the launch of Internet banking. In reality this innovation was enabled by the existence of the Internet, personal computers and software, all of which were already available and adapted to the specific service configuration. As a consequence banks wouldn't invest in developing their own Internet or personal computers although these developments would feature in current product focussed measures of innovation. Alternative measures of innovation such as patents, which are common in manufacturing and bio-engineering, are also rarely used in services. It is simply not possible to patent a service but other protections can be put in place such as registering copyright, using trademark protection, or intellectual property. These forms of protection don't always appear in national indices. Even if they did, they only relate to market visible activity and wouldn't capture the constant innovation in processes that goes on continually in organizations but which is not visible.

The final measurement issue is in capturing the multiplier effect of service innovation specifically the role of services in prompting innovation in other sectors of the economy. Business services such as consulting and communications can have the effect of stimulating connectivity between agents, sharing learning experiences, and enhancing the exchange of knowledge and ideas which help to improve innovation across the economy.[4] Some services, especially technology-based services, play an extremely important intermediary role in innovation activity across the economy.[5] Further, such services are particularly well networked into systems so that they may themselves promote innovation, such as large supermarkets forcing the adoption of EDI in supply chains, or banks promoting smart card technology. The problem is to capture this activity and not double count it when R&D expenditures are assessed.

Heterogeneity

The second major issue in relation to innovation in services is the degree to which natural development can be considered innovation. Services tend not to have any independent or identifiable physical existence and so service innovation is often invisible.[6] Because services are interactive by nature and often co-produced, the originator of any innovation is difficult to identify. Increasingly customers are being used as a key part of the production and development of new services, often as originators as well as developers. Similarly because we know that service events tend to be unique to the parties concerned, it is often difficult to distinguish between a service innovation (something new), a service addition (a new service added), a service variation (an enhancement), or a service update (periodic quality review). Services by their nature are constantly evolving and adapting themselves in response to customer demand for increasingly specific solutions and experiences (unless organizational structure and/or policies block it). The fact that one service provider of a specific service product can distinguish themselves from any other through the leveraging of organization specific assets and capabilities is indicative of a wide variety of potential service offers. The varying combinations of physical assets, human knowledge and skill, as well as customer involvement in the servuction process, mark services as a peculiarly dynamic but heterogeneous sector.

The traditional views of innovation as based upon discontinuity are shown in Figure 9.3.[7] The introduction of a new product or process is a discrete event and improves service quality incrementally. This is shown in graph (a). By contrast there is some evidence to suggest that

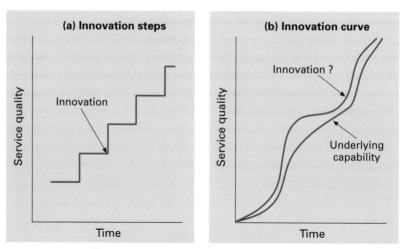

Figure 9.3   Alternate innovation paths

Tether, B. (2005), Do Services Innovate (Differently)? Insights from the European Innobarometer Survey? *Industry and Innovation*, Vol 12, No. 2, p. 157, Routledge.

the innovation process in services is more closely associated with the dynamics of underlying capability and resources. As knowledge increases the service improves; as staff leave or decisions made about resource focus change, then this impacts upon service quality. Service organizations tend to view innovation as an organization-wide phenomena, whereas in manufacturing, innovation was isolated in product or unit silos. In addition service firms tended to focus their innovation investment upon the skills and abilities of their workforce while manufacturers tended to focus upon the acquisition of advantage through technology.

Competitive Environment

The third issue in relation to innovation in the service sector is based upon the competence-based theory of the firm, a close relative of the resource-based view.[8] This argument is based upon the recognition that within any particular economic sector there are a wide variety of innovation trajectories. The extent to which organizations exhibit variation in the path of their innovation is a function of the competitive environment. In some markets there is a focus upon technical product features, making sure that the attributes of the product are better than others available. In other sectors, where products are increasingly difficult to differentiate, service innovation is taking over from price and quality. When looking at innovation generally, or innovation in the service sector specifically, it is important to take into account the competitive environment since this will determine the extent to which services or indeed other areas are the focus of innovation. Therefore it would be inadvisable to compare one sector with another and conclude that service innovation is higher or lower without also considering the competitive circumstances. Just because in telecommunications competition is increasingly service-based does not indicate that service innovation is greater or lesser here than in any other sector.

Copy Cat Can't be Stopped[9]

The airline industry is considered to be both highly fragmented and highly competitive with service organizations trying desperately to differentiate themselves from each other. As a result, airlines are always monitoring their competitors to see if innovations can be copied. NorthWest Airlines decided to reduce its costs by restricting meal access on its short haul flights. This meant a reduction in cost and less complexity at aircraft turnaround. The market responded well and within a few weeks Lufthansa decided to copy this innovation which subsequently spread to many airlines across the world.

These three issues provide some understanding of why innovation in services is relatively unreported at a macro economic level. This is important because without this macro data it is difficult to estimate the contribution of service innovation to the economy as a whole. We know that it is taking place, we know also that services are a dynamic and ever changing sector but perhaps we must be content not knowing the precise innovative state of services and instead focus upon innovation at the level of the organization and try to understand the underlying process of service innovation (Figure 9.4).

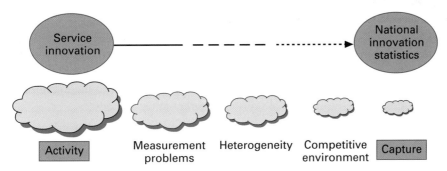

Figure 9.4 From innovation to national statistics

9.3 Developing New Services

There is substantial literature to indicate that in the face of rapidly changing technology, economic uncertainty, fierce competition and more demanding customers, service firms must innovate to survive (see Easingwood and Storey, 1996; Lovelock, 2001). To these external drives we can add a series of internal drives such as client demand, operational constraints such as cost reduction, the need for improved margins, or the emergence of new technology or delivery options. We must also recognize managerial action in pursuing new market segments, responding to declining sales, the activities of competitors or changes to the organizations strategic intent. We will focus our discussion upon new service product development since most service marketing managers use the terms 'innovation' and 'new product development' interchangeably and also don't distinguish between service and non service product development. This focus allows us to explore the role of customers, employees and the wider stakeholder community at different points in the innovation process.

Totally New? New? or Just Never Seen Before?

Before we examine innovation in the services context it is important to define our terms. Perhaps the most important is to understand what represents an innovation or more specifically what we mean by 'new'. This is important because we need to focus upon service innovations rather than service adaptations. This is due to the fact that adaptations will often be undertaken as a direct response to customer request and are therefore difficult to generalize. On the other hand, you should realize that market oriented service organizations do listen to their customers well enough to adapt their services gradually according to trends in customer preferences. By contrast, truly innovative service development is the result of a planned and usually well-documented process which provides a basis for understanding how firms accomplish the innovation task. Alam (2003) provides a summary of a number of newness classifications used and this is repeated in Table 9.1. The first thing to note is the amount of variation represented here and the difficulty in allocating service innovations to the various classes.

As you can see from Table 9.1 there are a variety of different 'new' services which can be considered, some more new than others. In fact we are really interested in the first three levels since these provide the greatest management challenges.[10] To generalize, service innovations are either new to the world, new to the market, or new to the organization and each requires a different set of internal skills and market entry strategy.

Breakthrough Services

A new category, on its own, is service breakthroughs.[11] Breakthrough services are so new, so different from the existing services that they have caused a revolution in the particular industry. Completely different standards are set to exceed customer expectations and needs (or meet them). This is all done in a very systematic way. Sometimes, there are high quality services having high process, sometimes such high quality is delivered at very low prices. Breakthrough services change the 'rules of the game' fundamentally: the development of a whole industry is changed. Breakthrough services are:

> *significantly differentiated from competition both on matters important to customers and the manner in which it achieves its results, whether that be through a well-defined, focused, and positioned service concept; a high-commitment organization; a comprehensive data-base; a hard-to-duplicate network or technology; clever financing arrangements; or other methods.*[12]

Table 9.1 Classifications of new services product innovativeness

Avlonitis et al., 2001	Booz, Allen and Hamilton, 1982	Crawford and Di Benedetto, 2002	Kleinschmidt and Cooper, 1991	Examples
Service new to the market	New to world products, new in the eyes of the customer	New to world products, i.e. inventions	Highly innovative	Mobile phones, Internet service providers, service consolidators (**lastminute.com**)
Service new to the company	New product lines, products that represent new challenges to the firm	New category entries, products new to the firm but not new to the world	Moderately innovative	Online banking, retailer credit cards, budget airlines
New delivery process	Additions to the existing product lines, new products that supplement a firm's established product lines	Additions to product lines Products that are line extensions within the current market	Low innovative products	Self-checkin at airports, pre-pay mobile phones, online brokerage
Service modifications	Improvement and revisions to existing products, products that provide improved performance	Product improvements, current products made better		Full year travel insurance, smartcard rail tickets, 24/7 maintenance contracts
Service line extensions	Repositioning, existing products that are targeted to new market segments			Wireless Internet for the home, personal share trading, direct airline bookings
Service repositioning	Cost reductions, new products that offer similar performance but at lower cost	Repositioning, products that are targeted for a new use or application		Budget airlines owned by major carriers, self-service options

Adapted from Alam (2003). Reproduced by permission of Westburn Publishers Ltd

So, they create a completely new kind of value, both to customers and the company.

In other words, some innovations are so revolutionary that they represent what is called a discontinuity, a major step forward as opposed to a small improvement. Sometimes these new to the world innovations aren't really that radical but they capture the market's interest and often change the direction of whole industries. Certainly the application of the Internet to service delivery in recent years has provided some radical new to the world innovations such as online banking, direct book retailing, and medical advice, but it must be remembered that most of the services we see today at some time were innovations. Supermarkets were an innovation in their time, as were automatic car washes, self-service restaurants and credit cards. It is estimated that approximately 10% of new products introduced are new to the world at the time of introduction, a very small proportion.

New to the World

An alternative way to assess whether a service innovation is new to the world is to look at the impact the service innovation has on the behaviour of customers. If customers experience a massive change to behaviour then we can consider the innovation to be new to the world. Examples might include self-service restaurant formats, outsourced IT management, digital television, or in-home computer repair, or help desks for medical equipment in hospitals. In many countries auctions are quite normal. EBay and Marktplaats are new in the sense that they are auctions organized via the Internet providing a large degree of market transparency. Unexpected rivals in China for instance have blocked the growth of EBay in that country.[13] Clearly where a major change in behaviour is required, the marketing effort must be focussed upon teaching individual customers (or households) and B2B customers how to use the service and the benefits associated with it. When automatic teller machines were first introduced the marketing effort was focussed on making them understandable and easy to use. The ongoing reluctance of customers to deposit money in an ATM is testament to the importance of focussing upon reducing the perceived risk associated with an innovation and explaining the benefits of a new service process. A failure to do so will stifle the success of a newly introduced service.

New to the Market

An alternative way to assess newness is to look at the innovation relative to current offerings in the market. The existence of stored value cards in Europe doesn't make their subsequent introduction in Australia new to the world, but new to the market. Clearly, for large organizations it is often not possible or even desirable to introduce new services in all markets at the same time. Indeed there may be benefits in delaying introduction to ensure that the service processes and staff are fully competent before approaching a new market. New to market innovations are mostly visible at the 'new country' level, where an innovation is slowly introduced into different global regions. The European launch of 3G phones in 2004 was two years behind their introduction in Japan and 3G is some way off introduction in North America. By contrast the introduction of fast-food services in the USA was ahead of their introduction in Europe, and automated road tolling was first introduced in Asia. Once a new to the world innovation has been commercialized the next step is to consider the new market potential. Not all service innovations are equally appropriate for all markets and their success is often dependent upon the existence of particular infrastructure (communications and telephones), demographic concentration (supermarkets and airline services) as well as regulatory control (online banking and gambling). When introducing an innovation into a new market, service managers must consider whether it is compatible with prevailing market conditions and not just expect its introduction to be replicated from its first market entry. There may be cultural, regulatory or technological issues to resolve before the new service can be successfully commercialized.

New to the Organization

This describes a situation where a service already exists in the market but is not provided by the organization. There may well be strategic or operational reasons which make the innovation attractive and now the organization must organize for its introduction. Marks and Spencer is a large retailer in the UK but it also provides insurance, investment services and loans. When these services were introduced they were not new to the market but for them to be provided by a food and clothing retailer was innovative. Similarly Virgin, whose core business is music and entertainment has introduced a range of new services including an airline, a credit card, a mobile phone service, bridal registry and Internet service provision. In each case the new services were considered to be strategically attractive and the task for the organization was to develop the resources and processes to deliver the service. In these circumstances it may be that the service is acquired, i.e. by buying a company that already provides it, it may be that the service is outsourced to another company in the initial stages to reduce the risk of failure, or there may be a need to enter an alliance to acquire the necessary capabilities. Whatever the configuration there is likely to be considerable change associated with the introduction of the new service.

9.4   The Process of Developing New Services

Research into new service development was initially based upon the well documented new product development process.[14] There is some debate though as to whether the nature of services means that these approaches are incompatible. There are three fundamental differences which might suggest that the application to services might be problematic.[15] The first is that due to inseparability, there is a simultaneous innovation occurring both in the product form and in its delivery each time the product is consumed. Second, that there is no separation between service innovation and organizational innovation since services are the result of organization-wide capability. Third, that there is no distinction between the creation of the service offer and the activity of production/commercialization. For these reasons there is increasing support for the notion of new service development as distinct from new product development (NPD). We distinguish between sequence models and organizational environmental models.

Sequence Models

The early research on NPD, used a sequence-based approach to understanding innovation.[16] This viewed the NPD process as organized into a planned sequence of steps starting with the idea and flowing through to the finished product. The task was to establish an optimum sequence. The most recognizable form of this approach was presented by Cooper (1994) as the 'stage-gate' model. Clearly, this was a good place to start for the early research into new service development (NSD).[17] A representation of the stage-gate sequence model is shown in Figure 9.5.

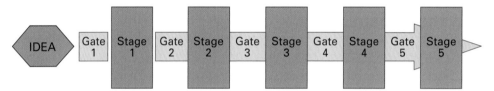

Figure 9.5   Example of sequential approach: stage-gate

Cooper, R. (1994) (Example of Sequential Stage Gate Model), Third Generation New Product Processes, *Journal of Product Innovation Management*, Vol. 11, pp. 3–14, Blackwell Publishing.

The problem with sequence models is that they appear to be overly bureaucratic and appear to slow projects down which is a problem in industries which require innovations to quickly get to market, such as IT and telecommunications. Second, in order to avoid problems early in the development many organizations were making use of cross-functional teams to steer projects through quickly and collapse the different stages. In reality NSD projects were the outcome of collaborative work rather than a single managerial champion following the process. Finally, that the sequence approach doesn't define the outcomes of each stage, and in reality each step in the sequence is more about finding solutions to problems within the whole process rather than signing off on separate completions.

Organizational Environment Models

These models look to aspects of the organization's climate to understand innovation focussing upon such things as functional differentiation, centralized/devolved structures, managerial attitude, resources, and administrative intensity. By investigating how an innovation is structured within an organization, research has confirmed that the way a development team is organized influences the overall efficiency of the development process.[18] These organizational dimensions appear to be a better candidate to help understand NSD due to the nature of service organizations which treat innovation as organization-wide rather than project-based.[19] This research has evidence links between innovation activity and management practices, cross-functional team communication, and decision making. As yet there have been few presented revisions to the sequential framework other than that of Johnson *et al.*, 2000, who provide a cyclic model of new service development, which is shown in Figure 9.6.

Given the division in the literature and the current state of knowledge regarding new service development we will focus our discussion on the sequential approach, but will allude to variations presented by the characteristics of the new service development context.

In simple terms the task in commercializing an innovation is to identify or develop new service opportunities that will effectively leverage current assets or capabilities and then take these ideas through a developmental process and if viable on to market. However, such a simple process hides a number of important steps which impact upon the overall success of innovations. Many new ideas fail, often because they prove to be too expensive to introduce, the company can't deliver them consistently or in all areas, they cannibalize existing markets or simply because there is insufficient demand. Even those which are actually introduced often fail with failure rates as high as 50%. With time and resources at stake it is important for service managers to minimize the chances of failure and to constantly review development to ensure that the final service innovation will have market acceptance. However, excessive time

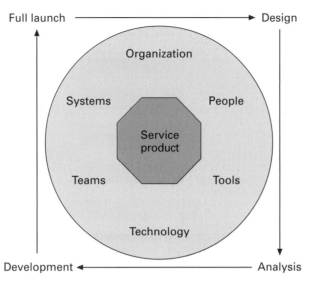

Figure 9.6 Alternative organization factors model of innovation

Johnson, S.P., Menor Lj, Chase, R.B., and Roth, A.V. (2000) A critical evaluation of the new service development process: Integrating service innovation and service design. In: Fitzsimmons, J. A. and Fitzsimmons, M.J. (eds) *New Service Development, Creating Memorable Experiences*, Copyright 2000, Sage Publications. Reproduced by permission of Sage Publications Inc.

investment may have negative effects, such as missing a receptive market, not being able to capitalize upon first mover advantage, and the possible upstaging of the innovation by competitors.

Strategic Intent

The first and often overlooked start point in any innovation process, and common in any context, is the setting of a strategic direction. This will be derived from both the corporate and marketing strategies of the business. Driven by a need for a quick solution to a problem many service organizations fail to fully appreciate the importance of an innovation direction. Simple strategic questions like

■ What business are we in?; and
■ What business do we want to be in?

can be used to develop a range of strategic options around an existing product portfolio. These will often focus upon growing market share, reducing churn, i.e. increasing repeat business, introducing line extensions or entering completely new markets. The identification of objectives and a strategy provides the end point or goal which the organization is trying to achieve. This will aid in keeping the innovation activity focussed upon the precise objectives.[20]

Once the direction has been broadly set the subsequent innovations should be linked back to this strategic direction. The most common approach to the problem of directed innovation, is to approach the innovation as a project management task – specifically to proceed through a number of well-defined stages which represent development hurdles. In theory if a hurdle is passed then the innovation can proceed to the next stage and so on until

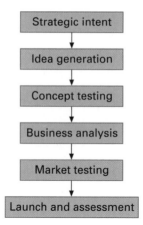

Figure 9.7   Generic new service product development process

it is ready for market. This ensures that only the very best service innovations actually require market launch. In summary these stages are: idea generation, concept testing, business analysis, market testing, launch and assessment, and are shown in sequence in Figure 9.7.

Clearly the first step must be the generation of ideas which seems obvious but service organizations often have no formalized process of generating new ideas. Remember we identified above the common lack of a research and development function in service organizations which in manufacturing often appears as a dedicated role. As a consequence there needs to be some other mechanism for capturing new ideas, staff feedback, customer involvement or regular external scanning of the market. The second generic stage is to sort these ideas into those which will progress to development and those which may be of interest but need to be stored for future use. The third stage is to take the developed concepts through a formal business case analysis to look in detail at whether they make business sense in terms of costs, resource availability and likely market acceptance. Following this step is the need to market test the innovation before the final launch and introduction. What is often forgotten though is that this is not the end. Service innovations must also be assessed as to their performance which requires some setting of performance criteria. We will consider each of these broad steps in turn.

Idea Generation

Service organizations have a variety of sources of innovative ideas from which to generate new services. The issue is to capture these ideas and feed them into a process for review and possible development. The main sources of ideas are shown in Figure 9.8.

The first source is the organization's own staff especially front line employees who have direct market contact. These employees have to work the service process and are often able to identify ways to streamline delivery and also recognize opportunities for completely new services by listening to customers, responding to complaints or requests, and analysis of customer requirements. Service personnel also interact with distribution channel partners, experience other services in their lives as customers, and interact with colleagues in other

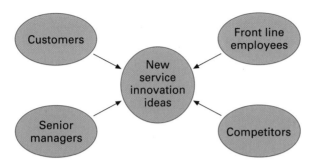

Figure 9.8   Sources of ideas for new service innovation

sectors and organizations. More senior or specialized staff may detect changes in technology, government policy or infrastructure availability which all provide opportunities for service innovations. In capturing these ideas companies often initiate service quality forums to look at improvements, 'blue sky' or 'scoping' events which let employees think about future products or simple suggestion systems which allow staff to submit ideas to a core assessment group. Whether staff actually become involved will depend to a great extent on whether they are motivated to do so, because the culture is innately innovative and there is social pressure to contribute to the organizations future, because there are incentives provided, or whether staff can see that something actually happens as a result of their suggestions.

SERVICE PRACTICE 9.3

Incentivizing Innovation[21]

Trying to get staff to generate innovative ideas is a common problem. In Pennsylvania, the state Social Services Board instituted a programme to enhance the creativity of its staff by focusing upon incentives to innovate. The programme involved the creation of a special fund managed by staff that awarded small grants in response to staff initiated projects. In response to this initiative, in the first three years 27 projects aimed at service improvement were funded.

Another prominent source of ideas is current customers and increasingly those service organizations which rely on a steady stream of innovative products are involving current customers not just in idea generation but throughout the whole process. Fujita (2000) in his study of the success of i-mode in Japan ascribes much of the success to users coming up with killer ideas for new services. This approach has also been used in the Swedish telecommunications sector and by Sony Ericsson.[22] The evidence would suggest that 'lead users' can generate more original ideas than professional developers. The use of lead users is also a feature of developing business-to-business service innovations and their early involvement in idea generation rapidly accelerates the likelihood of market adoption.

The final source of new ideas is imitation, that is copying an already deployed service innovation from another company. Imitation in the service sector is common but often the imitator can apply new knowledge and their own specific assets and capabilities to improve on the original idea. There are some problems associated with imitation such as reducing perceived differentiation by customers and accelerating conformity within a sector, but it has to be recognized as a common idea generation technique.

Concept Testing

Ideas generated can be very unformed, often little more than 'we could offer a service that does "x"'. This is clearly insufficient for an organization to do anything with and so the next phase of new service development is to flesh out the idea and move toward a more well-defined service proposal. One of the features of services is that they rely heavily upon the coordination of a variety of resources and processes to come together in the service delivery. In small service firms, arranging these will prove to be relatively easy but in large organizations coordination of tasks can be very complex. It may involve negotiation with other parts of the organization or indeed other organizations to assess whether they can provide the necessary technological, physical or human capacity. In order to fully explore the requirements associated with an innovation and to obtain the necessary buy-in from those who will ultimately have to provide the new service, the idea must be concept tested. This involves a full specification of what is involved, the likely utilization of resources and the likely impact of the new service upon the existing offer. Often these concepts in the form of specific proposals will need senior management approval and an assessment of whether the innovation is strategically attractive. Clearly at this stage, development funds may need to be attached to the project and this too will require some assessment as to likely commercial viability. Customers too might be involved in concept testing and are used to assess whether they understand the idea, whether they like it and whether they will be likely to prefer it to existing services.

The outcome of this phase is likely to be a concept plan with a proposal document which would be used to obtain senior management approval as well as the basis for consulting with other parts of the organization or other companies who may be involved. In addition this may be the first time the proposed innovation is made available to lead users to assess likely reaction.

A major service innovation cannot advance without a clear and document-based description. This document will then become a working document with amendments, and changes incorporated as more parties become involved in the development. It may be that at this stage the innovation will fail, possibly because other parties can't co-operate, the service isn't considered viable either strategically or operationally, or the development budget isn't available. Other reasons are because the likely changes required to the service process are too difficult or costly to engineer, alternative priorities are being pursued or services need to be deleted before capacity is available. Although an innovation may stop at this point the concept document should be stored and a regular review of 'held but failed' concepts should be undertaken. Many successful innovations were rejected on numerous occasions and only progressed when the time was right. For example, microwave technology for home cooking was available for many years before it was finally commercialized. Even early mobile phone technology was available for many years before it was introduced to the mass market.

Business Analysis

The next step along the path to commercialization is to undertake an objective business analysis of the concept. By this stage the innovation is likely to have been assessed as sound strategically, has a development budget allocated, may even have a team appointed to steward the process to market. This phase of the innovation process is dominated by financial modelling. In simple terms the organization must consider two key questions. The first is whether the innovation is financially viable, i.e. whether the number of people or companies using the service will pay for it over a sufficiently long period of time to recoup the costs of its development. The second issue is the likely impact of the new innovation upon the firm's resources.

SERVICE PRACTICE 9.4

iFly[23]

People Express Airline founded in 1980 brought with it low fares, and unparalleled employee involvement. It lasted a very short time as the major airlines attacked the fledgling which was involved in over expansion coupled with poor management. But Donald Burr the People Express founder is now back with a new business idea: tiny jets which will shuttle executives on demand to small airports. The idea is called 'iFly Air Taxi'. The service is aimed at high paying business travellers who want to get somewhere fast rather than a mass market. While many of these executives are using private charter jets, or buying shares in a jet, this new service aims to offer that same convenience at a fraction of the cost. The planes are likely to be four- or five-passenger jets costing about US$1 million, half the cost of a normal private jet. In this way the economics could ensure survival on the likely small demand. The service concept was released to potential investors and the company initially managed to secure US$6.3 million in convertible stock.

The problem with releasing the concept before development was that the planes are still to be designed and built, and haven't been certified to fly by the FAA nor any orders placed with the major manufacturers. Some analysts are also questioning the economics of the venture especially aspects of the business model. Most important it requires a critical mass of planes to be successful so that it can serve the mass market as well as entering a less developed market. Unfortunately that means heavier investment and higher risk. One solution is to use older planes which could be sourced second-hand and linked into an existing airline.

Recent developments have seen the FAA reject the name 'taxi' since it could be confused with 'taxi clearance' instructions from air traffic control. Also Atlantic Coast Airlines which recently rebranded itself as Indepedence Air has used the slogan Flyi as its main communication identifier causing the threat of legal action.

Early release of a concept may be required for funding and lobbying purposes but a release of an unformed concept can backfire.

The financial assessment of an innovation is very difficult to undertake quite simply because it doesn't yet exist. One of the enduring problems for service businesses is accurately estimating revenues and allocating costs to a specific service. Quite often, as is our experience, sales estimates in the business plan are too optimistic or not sufficiently documented. For instance if there is a single service outlet and three services are offered, how are the building and facility costs allocated?

Equally if the same staff deliver a number of services, should an equal proportion of their salary be allocated to each service or should the cost allocation be made according to the time spent on each service, or the number of customers served? The costs of a manufactured product can be allocated according to raw materials, costs of machines, and costs of staff divided by time or production output, etc. Questions arise, such as the likely number of staff, their physical location, the need for specific technology, training or special skills, where the service will be delivered, how long it will take and of course the necessary marketing and logistics. The same problem arises in estimating the likely revenue yield from the new innovation. Revenue is impacted upon by price charged and service volume and so pricing is a complex issue even when the service already exists. In most cases simple modelling should be able to identify breakeven figures based upon differing volume and price and these will be used to get a feel for the target price and the likely revenue for different patronage volumes.

The business analysis is also applied to resources associated with the proposed innovation, specifically, whether the firm is capable of delivering the innovation. There may be a need for more staff, more facilities, different technology and if the service is successful there needs to be some planning associated with scalability. This will mean going back to the various functions associated with delivery and getting their costings and capacity limits. At this point a service blueprint will be developed, specifying each step of the service process, tracking what happens if the service fails, customers exit or staff are faced with unpredictable requests. The service blueprint will also aid in the identification of appropriate staff training, new or revised software or booking systems and documentation for both employees and customers. At the end of the business analysis phase the organization should have both a clear concept plan and a financial viability model. At this point the proposed innovation will need top management approval and will need resources allocated to move it through the next development step.

Market Testing

Although some lead users will be aware of the proposal and in business-to-business services they may also have been involved in the concept development and business analysis phases, the next step is a proper market test. In the case of physical products this is simply choosing a test market and supplying the product to see whether the take-up is as predicted. In services, market testing will require identification of target customers and the choice of a test site. At this stage the innovation will be revealed to the market so care must be taken in communications. Some organizations prefer not to publicize an innovation until it has been fully tested. As a consequence it relies upon selecting current customers with personal communication. Other organizations possibly with rapid innovation cycles need to publicize the innovation as soon as possible to create sufficient demand to conduct a test.

SERVICE PRACTICE 9.5

Patient Experience Improved via Web-enabled TV

The hospital TV is now becoming a patient communications centre and a gateway for clinical information. A number of trials are being conducted to Web-enable patients' TV sets. The new systems allow for the TV to be used to view patients in their beds, patients can order food or view treatment information and, using a password system, for clinicians to view updated medical records and drug regimes. The tests have identified a number of enhancements such as linking the TV via Bluetooth technology to doctors' hand-held computers for updating direct from the patient's bed.

The market test also places a demand upon assessment of its performance, both from a customer and an employee perspective. This may involve independent research through market research agencies, or internal observation and monitoring to quickly detect problems and resolve them. Organizations are also likely to document the market testing, identifying actual fail points, suggestions for improvement, or likely changes to the service which will enhance its market appeal. The market testing of the innovation is a critical point in its survival and needs to be managed carefully. Insufficient funds, badly briefed staff or unreliable technology can jeopardize the market test and assign a potentially profitable and successful innovation back to the drawing board. Equally customer response must be assessed not only as to whether they found the service worthwhile but also whether they would actually use it again. If all goes well the organization will have learned a great deal from the market test. It will allow assessment of the business analysis exercise, and provide real data upon which to model likely take-up and future revenue streams. The analysis of the market testing will add another chapter to the innovation documentation which will again need to be reviewed. At this point the innovation is likely to reach the higher levels of the organization, often reviewed by the board or executive group to get the final decision as to whether the innovation should proceed to market launch.

Launch and Assessment

The innovation is now ready for introduction to the market and this again is a critical step. Any failures in planning, resourcing or performance can jeopardize future success. Customers in today's market environment are not going to be forgiving of a badly designed and delivered service even if it is new. The bad experiences and negative word of mouth can impact directly upon the organization's brand, other services and staff morale. The launch itself must be carefully planned and appropriately resourced. Organizations which undertake successful launches devote more than twice as many people to the launch as those allocated by organizations whose innovations subsequently fail.[24] This gives an indication of how many organizations underestimate resource requirements. Innovations in financial services, education, and online services, have been known to attract new customers and enquirers well beyond what was expected and therefore having access to extra capacity, such as a call centre or redundant servers, can reduce the likelihood of disappointed customers.

The market launch is a replication of the market test but on a larger scale. Clearly the lessons learned from the testing phase will need to be resolved and the communication issues addressed. It is often insufficient just to publicize the existence of the new service although this is clearly necessary, but depending upon the 'newness' of the innovation different communication will be required. For 'breakthrough and new to the world' innovations customers will need some idea of the benefits associated with the new service, how it is different from other services and most important, depending upon complexity, how to use the service. The introduction of broadband Internet services faced this launch problem, where customers were impressed by the speed of the new service, but less convinced of the comparative benefits to existing services given the pricing, and even more confused as to how to access the service. Compare this problem with that of a 'new to organization' innovation where the market will often already know a great deal about the innovation and will focus more on the comparative benefits obtained from different suppliers.

It must be remembered that this whole process of innovation has a very great risk attached to it and for this reason service organizations may decide to launch the new service using a different organization entirely. For instance, if the innovation is new to the world and the capabilities are not those currently held it is often wise to host the innovation in a start-up company under independent ownership even if it will be marketed under a common brand. When Virgin Airlines entered the South East Asian market the airline was set up as a new company 'Virgin Blue', which was a joint venture involving Virgin plc and a local company Patrick Corporation, and was quite distinct from the European entity.

One of the final considerations after initial launch will be how and for how long assessment of performance will be undertaken. Organizations which have spent a great deal of time and effort going through the previous stages are very reluctant to withdraw a service regardless of its market performance.[25] The decision to withdraw is clearly a difficult one but relies heavily on detailed performance criteria and a well-founded business plan. Against any underperformance must be placed the difficult task of managing withdrawal. It is not just the case of stopping the service. There may be customers 'signed up' to whom you have a responsibility and you may need to transfer them over to an alternative service. You also have to factor in the confusion among staff, the market effect of a service no longer available, and a degree of loss of morale as employees begin to question how the service got to market if it is such a disaster. Often organizations will 'leap frog' a failing service innovation by quickly bringing to market an alternative offer and migrate customers to it very quickly thereby reducing their exposure.

9.5 Some Factors to Enhance the Innovation Process

While the innovation process within different service organizations is likely to be different, there is a general consensus that there are a number of things which can help an organization in pursuing innovation. The first of these is to have a healthy innovation culture to provide a continuous source of innovation ideas such as incentivizing staff or customers to provide insights into how a service might be improved. The second is to use wherever possible cross-functional teams which enhance the transparency and also the effectiveness of the path from innovation to commercialization. Third, organizations must have a clear understanding of the customer innovation adoption process and input this knowledge at every stage of development. We will consider each of these in turn. Because technology is often referred to as an innovation facilitator in its own right, and could be described as the major innovative pathway for services we considered technology more explicitly in Chapter 8.

Innovation Culture

Many organizations struggle with the issue of creating and maintaining an innovation culture. It is far easier for managers to concentrate upon day-to-day operational decisions and forget about the task of creating change, leaving innovation as something that will happen on its own. The task for those concerned with innovation is to create what has become known as an innovation culture. This is where innovation is positioned as a clear priority and communicated as such throughout the entire organization. More specifically it's where employees are encouraged and rewarded for taking risks with company systems and processes in order to improve customer experience. Such a culture is supported by performance metrics and reward structures that are aligned to guide people so that their behaviours are focussed, and incentive structures are such that innovative behaviour is rewarded and encouraged. At the centre of the innovation culture is a system of norms and values that are adopted by all employees which accepts change and directs improvement in their work effort. That relates to the corporate culture. And we have seen in Chapters 2 and 6 that the culture of a market oriented service provider is among other things characterized by a positive attitude towards risk taking, a learning organization and incremental steps in service improvements. This aligns with breakthrough services only once those service providers have an excellent market intelligence, be it based on facts or intuition.

Establishing and maintaining an innovation culture can seem as an overwhelming task for managers when confronted with a stagnant and prescriptive culture and it takes a special kind of management that can truly empower employees, and trust that they will operate the freedom they are given in the organizations in its customer best interests. There are two key benefits of striving for an innovation culture.[26] These are protection of competitive advantage and shareholder, employee and customer satisfaction. The first benefit emanates from gaining unique advantage that arises from offering services which greatly surpass competitor's current offerings and providing a ready source of differentiation from existing services. In this way innovation provides a long-term insurance policy for competitive advantage and enables small accelerations in growth through small increments to margins. The second advantage arises from the impact of the successful development of new services which will simultaneously provide additional revenue and consistently delight customers and employees. Positive word of mouth and market reputation contribute to enhanced growth and productivity which directly feedback to shareholder value.

Some essential components that allow progress towards an innovation culture include top management commitment, a clear innovation direction and customer awareness. The first component is critical to success since innovation must be considered as a whole organization responsibility especially in services. If chief executives and senior managers try and delegate the responsibility there will be a lack of consistent action. Some companies may appoint innovation directors, or development directors to ensure that innovation is a consistent and real activity, allowing employees to feel supported as they try new things and, make decisions about new customer solutions.

SERVICE PRACTICE 9.6

CCD Industrial Cleaning – Culture Clash

CCD an industrial cleaning service wanted to energize some of its key employees to be more innovative and creative. They sent 60 senior employees on a series of challenging development programmes. The initial results for the staff when they returned were good with many small but significant adjustments made. After two or three weeks everything stopped. The organization couldn't work out what happened. They discovered that the newly innovative employees were deluged with operational decisions, couldn't get senior managers to take ideas seriously and found that suggestions about improvement to colleagues were seen as criticism. The senior employees started to become frustrated and within six months the company had lost 40% of its senior staff who were so frustrated they decided the company couldn't provide them with the innovative and creative work environment they now desired.

It is important to recognize again that innovation must be directed, otherwise the organization can become destabilized by employees who appear out of control and desert the day-to-day operation of the business in pursuit of more and more outlandish ideas. As a consequence some sort of innovation strategy must be set to steer innovation activity in the right direction. This strategy must set broad guidelines of what the organization needs to accomplish and some time horizon. It should define what innovation means and, where the company wants to direct innovation activity, and link these to financial goals. This strategy provides a test or benchmark to assess innovation activity and allows senior managers to set realistic expectations as to what is required. The final component is the need for customer awareness, that is to ensure that innovations actually benefit customers. The benefits from pursuing a customer perspective are numerous; it can be used as a screening mechanism, it ensures that innovation is focussed upon revenue enhancing activity, it helps employees to familiarize themselves with real customer issues, and it provides an opportunity to involve a customer voice such that it becomes a natural part of the innovation process.

You might like to consider the problem faced by senior mangers in visualizing and appreciating customer issues in service usage. How many senior executives at a car manufacturer actually buy their own cars like normal customers? How many executives who work for mobile phone suppliers actually buy their own phones, or bank employees queue up for service? It is a natural process for managers to become insulated from customer experience in their own service sector and organizations must fight to provide their managers with first-hand experience of how customers interact with the service and some of the problems customers face.

Cross-Functional Teams

In shepherding the development of an innovation it is critical to ensure that it is seen and experienced as a truly organizational activity which benefits from the full range of knowledge, and resources of the company. As said before, an opportunistic culture of only pursuing a person's or a department's self-interest is lacking in market oriented service providers. One way to achieve this lack of self-interest opportunism is through the use of cross-functional teams. This simply refers to a collection of individuals within an organization who are drawn from different functional backgrounds. Cross-functional teams are a feature of many innovation programmes and occur at many different stages in the development process. Some large financial services organizations have introduced departments dedicated to cross-functional development such as American Express, Chase Bank, Chubb Insurance, Merrill Lynch and Morgan Stanley. The different team members bring with them a range of backgrounds, experiences and skill sets. When these are applied to a new service development problem, they can be a powerful tool in both obtaining buy-in from across the organization as well as ensuring that the innovation isn't hampered by parochialism or conflict between different parts of the organization.[27] There are many benefits associated with cross-functional teams; some are obvious such as the benefit of exchange with people from different areas, the creativity that's engendered through learning and problem solving, as well as ensuring that in developing a service which necessarily involves many different people and systems that no unexpected problems arise. There are also a number of less obvious benefits, such as creating horizontal links within an organization which are often based upon functional silos, highlighting different priorities and ways of working, as well as improving members' experiences of coping with diversity. Some cross-functional teams operate well, others can merely be a collection of individuals who have nothing in common other than their employer. In practice a cross-functional team is a change from a parochial functional view of the organization in which functionally developed values and goals are dominant, to a collective 'we're in this together' view of the organization. As a consequence to get the best out of a cross-functional team a number of issues need to be addressed (Figure 9.9).

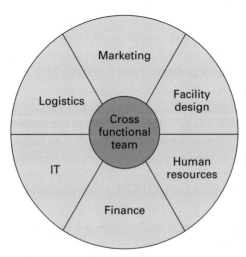

Figure 9.9 Cross-functional teams

The choice of team leader may seem insignificant, but in reality can shape the way a team operates. A team led by a technical expert may have difficulty dealing with aspects of design, ambience, or brand. A team led by a leader from finance may focus too much upon profitability and cost, at the expense of marketing and staff training. As a consequence the team leader must have a wide experience, and be able to cope with technical detail as well as softer issues such as employment practice, motivating staff and customer sensitivity. You may recall from Chapter 6 what we have said about leadership in a market oriented service organization to better understand how that style may affect the effectiveness of these teams.[28] A 'service-champion' (as the alternative to the product-champion) could be the leader of such a team. The second key issue is the setting of goals; these must be clear and unambiguous but not so restrictive as to divert attention away from the bigger picture. Depending upon responsibility, teams may focus upon idea screening and so the goal may be to come up with concept development plans for a single innovation, analysis of the business case, or a plan for launch and introduction. Specific goals must be set and achievement rewarded and recognized. The final issue is to ensure the team has sufficient authority – budgetary, personnel and top management support – to enable it to achieve its outcomes despite any lack of co-operation.

Many teams fail due to their being viewed as non aligned without recognizable lines of authority and managerial responsibility. Although many companies use cross-functional teams they struggle to implement them successfully.[29] It was found that team members focussed upon new product development tasks were often neglected by other members who viewed their tasks as more important and more immediately relevant to organizational goals.

Customer Innovation Adoption

The third factor which can enhance innovation success is a clear understanding of the customer innovation adoption process. In Chapter 3 we elaborated already on some of the reasons why some customers do accept new services and others do not. Typical examples were given for the adoption of buying services via the Internet. The theory of the diffusion of innovations is a well-established framework which explains how innovations spread across individuals within a social system. The original model was presented by Rogers (1962) and although a number of variations have been suggested the essential components are still relevant today. The model has been applied to technology-based service innovations,[30] to self-service innovations[31] and to financial service innovations.[32]

There are seemingly two parts to this understanding. The first is that there is a group of customers out there who will naturally gravitate toward any innovation. This gravitational tendency is focussed upon a comparatively small number of customers, existing and potential. Larger numbers will be in the second phase of adoption and still larger in the general customer base. As a start therefore innovations must be focussed upon a gradual process of diffusion and service companies must understand the characteristics of first, second and subsequent adopters.

The second part of the framework is directed toward the innovation itself and how customers evaluate the innovation as compared to existing provision. Many service innovations in today's market rely heavily upon technology, either in enhancing choice such as online consolidators, customization of the product such as in tourism, or in delivery such as home entertainment or mobile technology. Therefore the first consideration is the issue of access to the technological platform. This might be facilities for electronic data interchange between companies, adoption of specific technical standards, cabling in the home, or even a home computer with an Internet capability. A sound innovation can fail if customers can't access it. Consider the problems of introducing online banking innovations in economies which have no technical infrastructure to deliver it, no consumers with home computers, and unreliable if any telephone systems. The problems are not associated with the innovation but with the market's ability to access the innovation.

Assuming access is a foregone issue, then a series of characteristics of technical innovations which form the basis of a comparative assessment by potential users relative to existing provision, can be pointed out. The first is the perceived usefulness of the innovation or its relative advantage. Does it provide an improvement in the service from the customer's point of view? Specifically does it enhance convenience, speed or reduce price? Second, is it reliable? This is a consistent fail point of technical innovations which are rushed to market and are incompletely tested. Failures in systems, or processes are irretrievable from a customer's point of view.

Third, whether the innovation is complex. Innovations which require considerable customer learning have slower take-up. Take for example Internet banking which requires a considerable degree of intellectual input by the user, or collaborative design technology which requires changes to existing processes.

Fourth, to what extent is the service innovation trialable? We already know that services are difficult to trial, but perhaps it is possible to allow the customer to interact with the innovative service without having to change to it. One month's free access, in home/company presentations, and automatic upgrades are tools which are applied to encourage trial. Clearly they are not universally applicable. Insurance innovations are difficult to trial, as are educational service innovations.

Finally, there is some evidence that observability has an impact upon the diffusion of the innovation. If users can be observed as having access to a service innovation this encourages others to find out more and trial. Consider for example airline services where members of a frequent flyer programme have different check-in desks, or the introduction of mobile phone cameras which can be shown and used with non users. Where a service innovation is unobservable, such as a new type of superannuation, a different booking process, or personal services like counselling and healthcare, there is likely to be little knowledge of the innovation outside the user group and innovations can often be introduced without customers being aware of it.

<hr>

SERVICE PRACTICE 9.7

ITC and e-Choupal[33]

In a country where 200 million people are engaged in farming or related activities, ITC is developing its internationally competitive agricultural business by empowering, not eliminating, the independent small farmer. The company is setting up of a network of Internet-connected kiosks, known as e-Choupals, through which farmers can receive all the information, products and services they need to enhance their farming productivity and receive a fair price for their harvest. Through the choupal, ITC sources the farmer's produce directly, reducing its procurement and transaction costs. Currently ITC has set up 4300 e-Choupals covering six states and 25,000 villages. By 2010, the e-Choupal network plans to cover over 100,000 villages, representing one sixth of rural India, and create more than 10 million e-farmers.

The importance of customer innovation adoption will need to be recognized and acted upon at every stage of the development process. This will ensure that benefits are clearly communicated to potential users. It will ensure that processes and systems are robust before introduction. It will aid in focussing attention upon usability and ensure that it is designed into the service. Finally it will help enhance marketing through a clear understanding how the social system becomes aware, interested, and trials the innovation.

9.6 Success and Failure in New B2B Service Development

Much of what has been said about new service development applies to new customer services. But how about the development of B2B services? In this chapter we have already pinpointed at the critical co-operation with lead users and to have customers involved in the NSD process. But there is more.[34] We can think of:

- The firm's market orientation;
- The existence of a formal service development process (many firms lack such a process – also when we look at manufacturers with respect to their after sales services);
- Project synergy; and
- A truly superior new service offering.

Ulrike de Brentani's 2001 research indicates:

> *there are a small number of 'global' success factors which appear to govern the outcome of new service ventures, regardless of their degree of newness. These include:*
>
> ☐ *Ensuring an excellent customer/need fit;*
> ☐ *Involving expert front line personnel in creating the new service and in helping customers appreciate its distinctiveness and benefits; and*
> ☐ *Implementing a formal and planned launch program for the new service offering.*

But there were also some differences depending on the degree of newness.

> *For low innovativeness new business services ... managers can enhance performance by:*
>
> ☐ *Leveraging the firm's unique competencies, experiences and reputation through the introduction of new services that have a strong corporate fit;*
> ☐ *Installing a formal 'stage-gate' new service development system, particularly at the front-end and during the design stage of the development process; and*

☐ *Ensuring that efforts to differentiate services from competitive or past offering do not lead to high cost or unnecessarily complex service offerings.*

For new-to-the-world business services, the primary distinguishing feature impacting performance is the corporate culture of the firm: one that encourages entrepreneurship and creativity, and that actively involves senior managers in the role of visionary and mentor for new service development. In addition, good market potential and marketing tactics that offset the intangibility of 'really new' service concepts appear to have a positive performance effect.

It may be that these low innovative new business services greatly resemble what is going on in Vendors, while the new to the world service that may change the whole industry typically refer to the Game changers we discussed in Chapter 6. They all create value in their own unique way and via different ways of introducing new services. It will be self-evident that processes are different in those companies.

Summary

In this chapter we started by considering the importance of innovation and how the innovation activity of individual firms contributed towards the performance of the economy as a whole. The recognition of the importance and dominance of the service sector has often meant that it has been viewed as separate from other areas of the economy. To a large extent this has caused it to be ignored by mainstream economists, but in reality it is highly interdependent with other sectors. Part of the reason for the lack of understanding of service innovation are the problems of measurement, the problems associated with heterogeneity, and the fact that service organizations are difficult to compare with non service organizations. But perhaps the common theme here is that services are constantly changing and innovating and it's important to understand a hierarchy of effects in relation to new services. We distinguish new to the world services, new to the market services and new to the organization services which allow a degree of differentiation when looking at commercialization, next to breakthrough services.

Notwithstanding these problems new service development processes do have a number of common features already identified in relation to physical goods. These steps are used to explore the role of employees, customers and other stakeholder groups in steering the innovation to market. Cross-functional teams and a strategic agenda to new service development are critical to success.

Finally in this chapter we examine three issues which impact upon the success of the innovation process. The first of these is the development and maintenance of an innovation culture which if established can provide an environment where innovation is seen as a core activity of all employees rather than a special periodic task. The second is the use of cross-functional teams which can coordinate the input of expertise from across the organization and help to ensure that all resources are aligned as the commercialization process progresses. The final issue is the necessity to fully understand the market adoption process and be aware of the interplay between social networks and innovation characteristics as the innovation diffuses through the market place. All these topics are means to operationalize the market oriented service organization's assets and capabilities that are critical here, namely the service organization's copyrights and patents (as one of the internal-based assets), the alliance-based assets (especially the ones on shared technology and access to strategic partners' managerial know-how and expertise), all four the outside-in capabilities, and the spanning capabilities on the ability to launch successful new services and effective new service development process.

Questions

1. Define what is meant by the term 'innovation'.
2. Describe the three problems that make service innovation difficult to capture for national governments.
3. Describe the four different types of 'new' service.
4. Illustrate where ideas for service innovation might come from.
5. Describe the techniques that you might use to encourage suggestions from customers and employees.
6. Describe the common steps through which an innovation goes from idea to market launch.
7. Explain what an innovation culture is, detailing how you might encourage such a culture in an organization.
8. Describe what is meant by a cross-functional team. What are the benefits of cross-functional teams in developing a service innovation?
9. Why should an understanding of consumer innovation adoption be important?
10. Illustrate how customers assess a new service innovation as compared to an existing service.

Assignments

1. Using the national statistics, find out how much research and development activity is going on in your country. What measures are used to determine these figures?
2. How might you design a system for measuring the amount innovation taking place in a service organization? Write down a list of measures you might employ.
3. What alternative models have been published which describe a new service development process? How different are they from the models of new product development?
4. Examine advertisements for 'new services'. What category of 'new' do they fall into?
5. Choose a service organization that you use. What innovations would improve the service for you? Write to the company and detail the improvement you have designed. What is their response? What does this tell you about their innovation culture?

Endnotes

1 This Service Practice is based upon Lawton, 2005; McCartney, 2005; and Bray, 2005.

2 Johne and Storey, 1998.

3 Coombs and Miles, 2000.

4 OECD, 2000.

5 Miles, 2001.

6 Gadrey *et al.*, 1995.

7 Tether, 2005.

8 Tether, 2005; Metcalfe, 1998.

9 Jones, 1995.

10 Avlonitis *et al.*, 2001.

11 Heskett, Sasser and Hart, 1990. Their ideas are more or less in line with the new strategic thinking and competitive strategies developed by Hamel and Prahalad in their 1994 bestseller *Competing for the Future*.

12 Sasser, Hesket and Hart, 1990, p. VII.

13 Mangalindan, 2005.

14 Booz, Allen and Hamilton, 1982; Cooper, 1990; Baker and Hart, 1999.

15 Callon *et al.*, 1996.

16 Cooper and Kleinschmidt, 1987, 1991.

17 Reidenbach and Moak, 1986; Edgett and Jones, 1991.

18 Garel *et al.*, 1999.

19 Fitzsimmons and Fitzsimmons, 2001; Stevens and Dimitriadis, 2005.

20 Scheuing and Johnson, 1989.

21 Cohen, 1999.

22 Magnusson, Mathing and Kristensson, 2003.

23 Zellner, 2004; *Business Week*, 22 April 2004; Gilbert, 2004; *AIN*, July 2004.

24 Cooper, 1999.

25 Boulding *et al.*, 1997.

26 Kuczmarski *et al.*, 2003.

27 Damanpour, 2003.

28 For a fuller exposition of the impact of team background in the effectiveness of teams, see Randel and Jaussi, 2003.

29 Barczak and Wilemon, 2003.

30 Lee, Lee and Eastwood, 2003. This section draws heavily on this paper.

31 Bitner, Brown and Meuter, 2000.

32 Lee and Lee, 2000.

33 *digitaldividend.org* (accessed 23 June 2005).

34 This section heavily draws upon Ulrike de Brentani, 1989 and 2001.

Chapter 10

People, Process and Physical Evidence

Learning objectives

At the end of this chapter you will be able to:

1 Describe the role of the service process in creating the customer experience

2 Understand the distinction between the core customer process and associated sub-systems

3 Describe the main decisions in service process design

4 Understand the relationship between designed and delivered service

5 Understand how service blueprinting or mapping can aid managers in appreciating elements of the service process

6 Identify common problems in managing service employees' roles

7 Appreciate the importance of service employees and partial employees in creating the service experience

8 Identify the importance of the physical environment as a context in which the service delivery takes place

9 Describe the features of the service environment

10 Appreciate that service environments can be both physical and virtual

10.1 Introduction

Slowing Down Domino's Pizza's Turnover[1]

This Domino's Pizza story is a wonderful example of the HRM function in a company and how decreasing the turnover of employees will affect employee satisfaction, cost and consequently company profit.

When Rob Cecere became regional manager for eight Domino's Pizza stores in New Jersey four years ago, his boss gave him a mission: slow down turnover. Store managers in the region were leaving every three to six months. Without a steady boss, workers there who answered phones, made pizzas and delivered orders had a turnover rate as high as 300% a year.

In fact this means that on average every four months a completely new team was present in an outlet. Think about the way they were trained on the job and how much this would cost. What does it say about working climate? How many companies can afford such a situation? How does it affect employee satisfaction and retention, and customer satisfaction and loyalty?

Turnover is a chronic and costly headache for fast-food businesses, which rely on an army of low-paid workers. A harsh boss, a mean colleague, or a boring day can cause workers who earn around the minimum wage – which is $5.15 (or €3.95) an hour nationally but slightly higher in some states – to quit for similar pay elsewhere. Average turnover for most large and midsize companies is about 10–15%. But at fast-food chains, rates as high as 200% a year for hourly workers aren't unusual.

Some companies are tackling the problem with a higher starting wage. Starbucks Corp. says it pays hourly store workers more than minimum wage, although the rate varies in different markets. The company says its turnover rate for such workers is 80–90%. Starbucks says it also focusses on friendly workplaces and good managers, but higher wages make a difference. 'If we did all these other things, but paid minimum wages, I bet our turnover would be higher', says Dave Pace, Starbucks' executive vice president for partner resources.

Domino's has a different view. The company is willing to try all sorts of tactics to retain hourly employees – except paying them significantly more. 'If we had increased everybody's pay 20%, could we have moved the needle a little bit to buy a little loyalty? Maybe, but that's not a long-term solution', says Domino's chief executive officer, David A. Brandon.

He says that while pay is a factor, 'You can't overcome a bad culture by paying people a few bucks more.' He believes the way to attack turnover is by focussing on store managers – hiring more selectively, coaching them on how to create better workplaces, and motivating them with the promise of stock options and promotions.

High turnover hurts the bottom line. It costs money to recruit, hire, and train people, and undercuts service when inexperienced employees don't work as efficiently. It costs Domino's about $2500 each time an hourly store worker leaves and about $20 000 each time a store manager quits, the company estimates.

One of the first things Mr Brandon did when he joined the company was renaming the human resources department into 'People First'. And he found out in research that the single most important factor in an outlet's success was the quality of the store manager. So, that is where it all starts to get a high quality outlet: it is the manager, the leader and his/her role model.

Republished with permission of Dow Jones from: To keep its imployees, Domino's Pizza decides it isn't all about pay, White, E., *The Wall Street Journal Europe*, February 18–20, pp. A1 and A8. Copyright 2005. Permission conveyed through the Copyright Clearance Centre Inc.

The most critical focus for service managers is the experience of the service by its customers. This is where people, service processes and the physical environment co-operate together in producing the service product. The coordination of these elements into something which provides value to a customer provides many opportunities to effectively align these service elements into something that will truly delight customers, and provide supportive and positive reinforcement to the brand. Equally, there are many opportunities for misalignment, inconsistency and contradictory events which can severely damage a customer's experience. This volatility describes the knife edge that front line service managers walk every day, and also hints at the complexity involved in dealing with people, technology, rules, procedures and physical spaces, to continuously produce an outstanding service product.

Clearly, every service organization will attempt to combine its particular set of assets (e.g. human capital, technology, physical capital) and capabilities (e.g. process knowledge, design, system integration) differently. As a consequence organizations will always produce slightly different service products and experiences, not least because they will design different processes, engage different service personnel, and may deliver the service in a different place.

Any service outcome for customers is the result of many different activities, experiences and events brought together by the service organization. In order to ensure the coordination of these resources, service organizations build plans for how these resources are to be utilized and the sequences in which they are applied, and this is referred to as a process. In general a process is defined as a series of coordinated actions, changes or functions bringing about a predetermined result. In simple circumstances, a service process should be easy to design but in practice the coordination task can become very complex even for simple outcomes.

For example, imagine a customer phoning your company to book a sales visit to their home. How would you describe the sequence of activities to make this event happen? You might need to ask the customer a few questions, like their name, address and telephone number. You might also need to ask what products or services they were interested in. Then you might need to arrange a suitable time and date for the visit. At this point you would need to check your salesperson hasn't already been booked on a different sales visit and then in confirming the date and time with the customer you would need to forward these details to the sales person. Such a simple thing as arranging a sales call actually comprises quite a complex series of steps; receiving the call, obtaining information, checking availability, confirming date and time, and this is only part way to ensuring that the visit actually takes place. What happens if the sales person falls ill two days before the agreed time? Who is responsible for arranging a replacement or rescheduling?

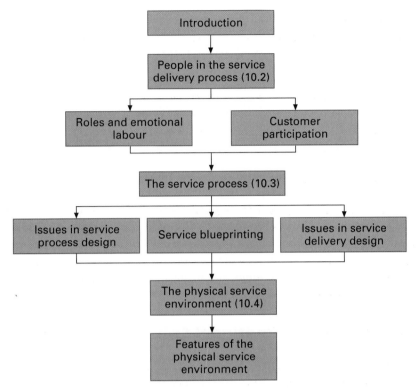

Figure 10.1 Chapter outline

Service organizations have long understood the importance of getting the service process right since this forms the platform upon which the service product is built. Once a process is embedded in the organization, people, technology and physical environments can then be built around it. In this chapter we explore the nature of the service experience through the activities of people, process and physical evidence and how the three components can interact to provide the customers' service experience. Consequently, we focus mainly on some of the internal-based assets (e.g. cost advantage in the servuction process), all the outside-in capabilities and some of the inside-out capabilities (especially effective human resource management and good operations management expertise). This does not say the other assets and capabilities are not relevant here; accents may differ.

10.2 People in the Service Delivery Process

The first step in our consideration of creating the service experience is to look at the involvement of people. If we consider a service organization and its customers as two separate entities, where they interact can be referred to as a 'boundary'. Those service employees who interact with customers are referred to as 'boundary spanners'. In reality these boundary spanners are any employee who has contact with a customer and they play a crucial role in creating the customer service experience. It is they who deliver on the service promise embodied in the service brand and in services marketing. It is they who represent the organization and promote the firm's service products. It is they who have to work in a market oriented way and have the customer participate in the servuction process, finally delivering actual excellent service quality and value.

Employees can be instrumental in supporting a weakly designed service process as well as sabotaging a well-designed process. In short, they are the most important people in any service business. Remember that services can't be seen and therefore the service provider is sometimes one of the few tangible elements of the service. Their appearance, behaviour, demeanour, social interaction and expertise, etc. impact directly upon customers' evaluation of both the service and the service organization. One way to understand their importance is use the metaphor of a theatrical performance where customers are the audience, employees the actors and the service environment is the stage. This dramaturgical perspective allows for the addition of other parts of the metaphor, such as costume, performance, roles and scripts, audience participation, etc. Following this approach we will now consider three key issues which relate to people in creating the service experience: employee roles and their emotional labour, generalized employee management, and finally customers as partial employees.

Employee Roles and Emotional Labour

The idea of an employee performing a role is not a complex one. Much like an actor in a stage play they have a set of tasks to perform, which are defined by the service process and which can be likened to the script of a play. The organization will predetermine much of the employee's role, which will appear in a formalized job description and, depending upon the service delivery process, will be more or less well-specified. Some organizations specify the role exactly, including where to stand, what to say and the tasks associated with the performance of the service. Consider a fast-food service where the server performs the same set of actions, uses the same questions and stands in the same place. Compare this approach to a service employee performing a business consultancy where they have almost complete discretion about the nature of the service they deliver. While the idea of a role is not new or complex we have come to understand that roles have a number of consequences for the individual employee and these provide some understanding of why and how different employees perform in service delivery. These consequences relate to role conflict, role ambiguity and role overload, factors that were mentioned as relevant causes for gap 3 in the SERVQUAL-model. In addition the role the employee performs may require a degree of 'acting' where the employee must suppress their own personality and social behaviours to such an extent that they must effectively work to control their own emotions; this is called 'emotional labour'.

Role Conflict

For front line employees their roles are divided between responsibility to their employer and to the service delivery process as well as to providing customer service. In most cases you might think that these are wholly compatible but in certain circumstances they can conflict. For example, the service delivery process requires them to serve a customer every 45 seconds, and the customer wants to talk about the service and possibly to find out more about it. In these circumstances the employee is caught between the needs to maintain process speed and to provide good service to a customer. A similar example might be where the employee knows that the service won't provide the customer with what they require but a competitor's service will. Do they serve the customer anyway or help the customer obtain the outcomes they are looking for? In general terms the organizational interest should dominate, but in reality good service providers especially those with experience tend to become psychologically close to customers with whom they interact on a daily basis. When faced with role conflict, service employees look for solutions such as working harder to recover average throughput times in the first example, and to serve more customers to compensate for the lost customer in the second example.[2] If it is not possible to reconcile the demands of the organization and those of customers the employee may start to experience frustration which may reveal itself through distress, anxiety and increasing uncertainty.

SERVICE PRACTICE 10.2

Determinants of Lateness[3]

Recent research looking at the causes of lateness (turning up to work late) among employees has highlighted the importance of attitudes to work. While males are generally more late than females, private sector workers more late than public sector workers and service sector employees more late than non service sector employees, the key cause was something much more significant. Although lateness is a function of incentives to be on time, and the monitoring of and sanctions for lateness, the research found that the lack of job satisfaction was a major cause of lateness and absenteeism.

Role Ambiguity

One common cause of role conflict is role ambiguity which refers to a situation where organizational expectations of the service employee are inadequately defined. This may be evidenced by a lack of clear direction, a lack of decision making authority or inappropriately tailored performance assessment. In circumstances of role ambiguity employees have a sense of being out of control and left to their own devices. This may not be a bad thing where their role requires dealing with a diverse range of customer requirements. However in other circumstances the employee can feel unsure about what to do, fail to make appropriate decisions, and undertake actions or behaviours which merely increase time rather than improve service performance. For managers, role ambiguity among front line staff needs to be handled carefully to avoid circumstances where the employee is operating 'off script' and to avoid service staff creating their own roles which are inconsistent with the service delivery process and overall strategic direction.

Role Overload

Front line service staff in services which are subject to large variations in customer traffic may be susceptible to role overload. This occurs where the staff member is inundated with demands upon their time and resources, often accompanied with a failure in the service delivery process. Airline check-in staff are often faced with hundreds of angry and disgruntled customers when a plane is delayed. Similarly a single software engineer can be overwhelmed if a company IT system collapses at a critical time. In these circumstances the employee may cease to operate, simply run away or make mistakes under pressure. For service managers overload situations need to be predicted and necessary resources brought to bear on the problem, such as more staff being brought in, offsetting customers to other service outlets, or in extreme cases suspending service for a short period.

Emotional Labour

Emotional labour is the management of an individual's own feelings to create a publicly observable display.[4] This encompasses simple functions such as a happy greeting when the service provider is tired or angry, as well as more complex displays such as associated with personal care, counselling or medical trauma. This range of emotional masking is more pronounced in professional service situations although even in more mundane services there will be expectations from the service organization as to appropriate facial and emotional responses: a welcome smile, cool detached demeanour, direct eye contact, etc. That is not to say that these overt displays are deceptive, just that the service employee is empathizing with the customer or following social norms as to appropriate behaviour which they may or may not feel.

There are two levels of emotional labour which are called 'surface acting' and 'deep acting'. Surface acting is where the service employee simulates emotions that they do not actually feel using verbal or non verbal techniques.[5] Non verbal responses might include a sad facial expression, a soft or sympathetic tone of voice or specific gestures such as shock, dismay or surprise. Note that surface acting also includes situations where emotions actually felt are suppressed such as shock, revulsion or anger. In simple terms the emotional and behavioural responses by a service provider are different from their real emotional or natural behavioural response.

Deep acting is where the service provider attempts to emulate emotions which are expected by putting themselves in a particular frame of mind. It is well known that actors can make themselves cry by thinking of sad events, or happy by imagining themselves in joyful ones. In deep acting the service provider attempts to deceive themselves as well as the viewer.

For service managers, emotional labour has a number of positive attributes; it can enhance customers' experience, it provides a means for service employees to self-regulate the stresses of constant interaction and can help bind service employees together.[6] Emotional labour and its consequences can also be negative, leading to long-term stress, appearing insincere to customers and instilling a sense of unreality among those serving customers. Finally, emotional labour cannot be 'mandated' or 'required' of employees, and is ultimately outside management control.

Generalized Service Employee Management Issues

A general approach to service employee management can be summarized with reference to four key concerns: selection, training, performance and reward (Figure 10.2). In other words:

Figure 10.2 Generalized staff management framework

'hire intelligently, train intensively, monitor incessantly, and reward inspirationally', which is a good phrase for service managers to remember.[7]

Selection

Not everyone makes a great service provider; some have exemplary technical skills but no social skills, some have outstanding social skills but no technical skill and therefore finding the right people with the right balance of attributes and service attitude or service mindedness is challenging. Service managers need to think carefully about how they select staff and should avoid at all costs the approach that says 'it doesn't really matter' and recruit just to fill vacancies. Techniques to improve selection are quite time intensive, and can be demanding upon the organization but should be viewed as an investment rather than a cost, as you may recall from Service Practice 10.1. Activities such as multiple interviews, on-job scenarios, task tests and role playing extreme situations can all help in identifying those who will make good front line employees. Above all, those who are selecting potential employees must have a clear and well-documented idea of the range of skills and attributes they are looking for and avoid imposing subjective assessments.

Training

From the above discussion of roles it is clear that service employees must be trained to undertake the roles they will be allocated to. This is not just at the time of appointment but should continue throughout their time with the firm, updating, developing and stretching employees. Although initially this training will usually be on standard processes and familiarization with resources such as record keeping, databases and interdependent process points, subsequently it can extend to more advanced training such as dealing with angry customers, techniques for cross- and up-selling, or ways to cope with stress and improve performance. As service personnel become more experienced it may be desirable to rotate them through other roles so that they eventually experience the complete service process. This can instill a deeper appreciation of the interdependencies within a service delivery process and offer opportunities for innovation. Without adequate training, service providers can be a liability when put in front of customers, much like an actor who doesn't know their lines. While service personnel definitely contribute to overall service evaluation, poorly trained and prepared staff can damage the customer's experience and in time the organization's reputation.

SERVICE PRACTICE 10.3

Hyundai[8]

At a Hyundai car dealership in the USA, the service manager noticed that the customer satisfaction scores for his dealership were falling. The dealership was not greeting customers promptly, and some cars were being returned unwashed.

As Hyundai makes improvements in vehicle quality and its sales continue to climb the company wants to ensure that its dealer service help improve the brand image and so increased traffic at dealers needs to be managed more effectively. Hyundai provided a series of training modules for its dealer employees directed at common failings in customer service and built them around specific process failures. The training modules specify a revised service process, which managers can print and communicate to their staff, based upon current research.

Employees at the dealership started to come in at 7.30 a.m. to greet customers dropping off their cars for service, got them coffee and sat with them to speed up the booking-in process. The customer satisfaction scores improved dramatically. About 80% of Hyundai dealerships now use the training modules.

Performance

In order to assess a service employee's performance there must be some sense within the organization of the criteria to be applied. That might seem obvious but most service organizations have quite underdeveloped performance criteria which leads to confusion among service providers and among service managers and supervisors. The criteria selected will to a certain extent dictate employees' behaviour. For instance if performance is to be assessed according to positive customer feedback employees will expend greater effort on ensuring a customer is fully satisfied. Alternatively if performance is measured according to the number of customers served in an hour then they will ensure they follow processes or meet targets associated with the number of customers served. Some organizations rely upon 360-degree feedback from customers, colleagues and supervisors to assess performance, while others rely upon management observation, or speed in delivering service events, or simply 'hours sold' as in consultancy. In general, the greater the number of sources consulted the more complete the picture. But whatever the method, the form of assessment and the criteria used must be clear to service staff.

Reward

It is important that front line service staff are rewarded appropriately, not just in terms of prevailing market pay, but for examples of outstanding service which represent signals to other employees of excellent performance. Rewarding appropriate behaviour will increase the likelihood that they will be repeated by the staff member concerned and others. The rewards may be monetary (such as a bonus, or incentive payment) or non monetary (such as a monthly employee of the month prize, or invitation to an event). Whatever the form of the reward it must be of value to the employee concerned and some companies are now asking employees themselves to nominate the form that a reward will take. It is intended to create true employee loyalty.

Customer Participation

In some service situations the customer is not expected to be an interested bystander but to become involved with the service personnel in helping to deliver their own service. This may be in the form of selecting specific events (such as excluding or including steps in the process of car maintenance), sharing knowledge (such as describing symptoms to a doctor), entering data (as in the case of hotel registration), or even by supplying their own labour (such as transferring luggage in a hotel, assembling furniture, or returning dirty dishes in a cafeteria). The degree of customer participation can vary from nil, such as in the case in viewing a film, to total as in the case of self-service. Where a customer participates, a number of authors have referred to them as 'partial employees' of the service organization since they are working albeit unpaid to achieve the performance of a service.[9] While almost all services require some provision of resources in the form of information or effort, physical presence is not a necessary requirement. Online services might require the entry of passwords or personnel data, and therefore partial employment should be viewed as widely as possible and does not mean that the customer walks behind the counter.

SERVICE PRACTICE 10.4

Participation Software[10]

Using customer participation software a number of companies are trying to involve customers in their service. American Airlines, Northwest Airlines and United Airlines are all using proprietary software to facilitate customer involvement in their processes. The most useful feature of these implementations is being able to automatically contact customers when a flight has been delayed. Before flying the passenger can customize the contact policies on the airline homepage. When a flight is postponed or cancelled, the customer has the opportunity via two-pager or SMS to choose an alternative flight and the booking is amended. This is an extension to the current 'flight alert' service and focusses more on resolving the customer's problem through interaction and participation.

The overall view is that customer participation is beneficial for both parties. From the organization's point of view partial employees can alleviate for the organization the performance of some tasks, both speeding up the process and reducing staff density. Clearly the introduction of customer service technology into a service delivery process is a means of partially employing customers, i.e. getting them to do some tasks themselves. Follow-on benefits include reduced costs, speeding up the process and improving the likelihood of a satisfactory service outcome since customers would have to take some responsibility if it were unsatisfactory. However, there is a disadvantage which while less obvious is just as important to consider.

There is an assumption that the customer is competent, motivated, willing, capable and has the time to carry out their part of the service. In some cases that is a fair assumption but in others, such as the operation of machinery or financial management, this assumption may be too great. This may point to the need to adopt the generalized service employee management principles but applied to customers – selecting customers who can participate, training them, monitoring their activity and even rewarding them. The implications of incomplete customer activity are also worthy of consideration since it will require less service quality and additional input form service staff to complete the service process. In these circumstances the activities of customers may directly conflict with those of service providers, promoting role conflict and role ambiguity, increasing their workload and the complexity of their task.

On the other side of the service, customers may not want to become involved in their own service delivery. Therefore when considering introducing or increasing customer participation some understanding of customer demand must be obtained. However opportunities for customer management through charging higher prices for full service or discounts for partial self-service can be employed to resolve this problem.

10.3 The Service Process

At the core of a service process is the organization's design of how it will apply its resources to delivering the customer's service experience: how customers are received into the process, the sequence of steps required to provide the service outcome and the receipt of money or revenue. Around this core are built a series of facilitating systems which help employees, customers and information progress through the service. In design, the core service process might require customers to make an appointment with the service provider, such as a doctor, lawyer or business consultant. As a consequence a process which allows bookings to be made must also be designed. Similarly, customers may be offered a choice with respect to some element of the service and so different processes for each available choice must be designed. It is therefore misleading to think of just one 'process' but a collection of many processes, each integrated into an overall framework. This overall, comprehensive framework we can call the 'customer service delivery process'. This is likely to be relatively permanent. In order that this overall framework operates effectively, the service organization will utilize a series of sub-systems focussed upon specific steps. This is shown in Figure 10.3. We have taken a simple customer service delivery process which is represented by the central spine of activity. These are the broad steps that the customer experiences. The associated systems, which are represented either side, exist as separate sub-systems each integrated into the core. The benefit of viewing a service process in this way is that the redesign of a sub-system can be accomplished without the need to redesign the whole service product. Many service innovations are actually based upon changes to sub-systems. In our example it may be that in a new sub-system bookings are made over the Internet or by phone, allowing for some customers to by-pass the reception sub-system.

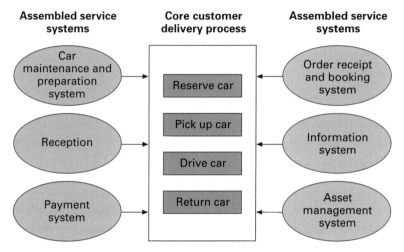

Figure 10.3   Core and integrated service systems

Depending upon the complexity of the core customer delivery process there will be more or less need for facilitating sub-systems. Where services are very complex such as medical services the assembled service systems will need to be quite comprehensive to support the complex diagnosis and treatment options. By contrast, ordering a taxi over the phone is a relatively simple delivery process and will have fewer facilitating systems associated with it.

SERVICE PRACTICE 10.5

Daimler Chrysler[11]

In an attempt to improve the experience of customers whose cars were being serviced, Daimler Chrysler implemented a 'service analyzer' product which aims to find out from customers in a structured way the problems they were asking their vehicle repairers to solve. At present many 'problems' require a technician to examine the car, then a follow-up visit, and then a repair visit while the problem is identified. This wastes a great deal of time and is frustrating and inconvenient to customers. For example, an owner notices their car is 'pulling to the right' and decides to book their car in for repair. The question for the service department is whether this is a steering problem, a tyre problem or a wheel alignment problem, further whether this occurs when braking, accelerating or all the time. The customer may never have thought to analyse this for themselves. Service analyzer is an intelligent Web enabled questionnaire which focusses a series of questions to the customer prior to repair booking. The system allows customers to achieve 'fix it first time' satisfaction and generates data for the company on persistent or emerging car problems.

It is worth noting here the interdependence of core service processes, sub-systems and customer perception. Even if a service is efficient and meets all the customer's required outcomes the service manager will have to contend with the reality of customer's perceptions. The process may be as fast as is practicable but nevertheless the customer may perceive it to be slow and cumbersome; it may provide the customer with considerable scope for customization and payment options, but the customer may perceive it to be confusing and overly bureaucratic. As a consequence service managers will always be trying to streamline the service, to review the steps, the timing and outcomes to enhance the customer's experience. It may mean deleting redundant sub-systems or adding new ones. For example, many airlines now don't issue physical tickets to customers booked onto their flights. The adding of the customer's name to the central reservation computer is sufficient for the issuing of a boarding card. The physical ticketing process is now redundant. Alternatively, many online customers of banks now have the opportunity to also talk to a service provider if they are experiencing problems.

In the following section a distinction is made between the design and assembly of the process, and how a customer experiences it in the form of a service product.[12] The process of service design and assembly comprises the definition and delineation of steps, tasks, procedures, etc. necessary to 'render the service'. This includes the core customer delivery process and the associated sub-systems. This is where the organization decides how to configure its assets and capabilities to the service product. One might think this is all that is needed but in fact a customer's service experience is not just dependent upon the sequence of steps but on a number of other factors which go beyond what was designed in the service assembly. This captures the service duration, the efforts of employees and ultimately the reliability of the service in delivering customer outcomes (Figure 10.4).

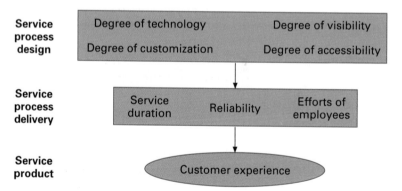

Figure 10.4 Issues associated with service design

Issues in Service Process Design

When service managers start to consider how a service process is constructed they have a number of decisions to make. These are often constrained by the resources, assets and capabilities they are able to bring to bear upon the service. However there are five key areas of design that not only need consideration but can also be used to discriminate between service processes.

The Degree of Technology Utilized

The growing application of technology to services has presented a number of opportunities for managers in designing the service process. Applying technology can mean making the service completely 'self-service' (i.e. the introduction of self-service ATM technology in banking, or the application of self-check-in booths at airports) and provides an alternative to face-to-face service. Other forms of application include direct information access for service employees to customer records, automated reception through smart card readers, tracking systems for packages and parcels, and documentation provision via websites and downloadable forms. Clearly the choice to apply technology to the assembly process must consider customer reaction, customer competence to use the technology, and that some customers will always avoid technology in favour of human interaction.

The Degree of Visibility

Much of what happens when a service is delivered is hidden from customers. The distinction in visibility is often referred to as a difference between front office (what the customer sees) and back office (what the customer doesn't see). A number of service delivery frameworks such as the servuction framework incorporate this approach in understanding service processes.[13] In some service settings this is desirable (i.e. smell, heat and noise from food preparation) but service managers have to decide upon the appropriateness of visibility and whether some systems should be visible and others hidden. Customers in banks were used to seeing employees behind the counters, dealing with paper and phone calls, but now these operations take place hidden from customers. By contrast, some restaurants have decided to make the kitchen activity part of the restaurant experience for customers. Again, customer reaction needs to be considered, some customers want to see nothing of the service processes which lie behind their service experience, while others like to see them just to ensure that they are being done, such as car maintenance and repair services.

Degree of Customization

In designing a service assembly process the degree of customization offered is an important decision which impacts upon the degree of process complexity (the number of steps involved in delivery) and the degree of process divergence (the amount of variety in processes).[14] In some services it is either not feasible, not economic or not convenient to allow customers to customize their service. For instance, it would not be possible to allow airline passengers to individually choose their exact departure time, or in fast-food restaurants to choose how well done your burger should be. But in some services customization may be desirable: when getting hair cut, or when companies purchase maintenance services, or in signing up to a mobile phone contract. Customization impacts upon service personnel since in highly rigid processes, which provide no opportunity for customization, employees have no discretion and their jobs are highly routinized. By contrast in high customization settings, service personnel are given extensive latitude to decide themselves how a service is to be delivered, such as medical or business consulting services.

Degree of Accessibility

In designing a service process the service organization must estimate customer problems in accessibility and decide whether these problems need resolving. Where the service is to be located at a specific place such as a retail outlet, office or premises then accessibility refers to the ease of arrival or departure. This accessibility may be focussed upon parking, pedestrian access or other issues associated with the location such as proximity or airports for tourist locations. Multiple locations may be desirable with a highly dispersed customer base but not if customers are densely located in a specific place. Once the customer is physically present it also encompasses how the service outlet is laid out, where queues are to be located or eliminated, seating for cinemas and theatres, arrangement of tables in food outlets, etc. In recent years accessibility as a process design consideration has also meant access to technology and the degree to which technological steps are included in the service process design. For example, a financial service might put large amounts of information on a customer website but access may be limited to those with a home computer. As an alternative a call centre may be set up, to allow phone users to access the service. Either solution enhances accessibility to the service by allowing customers to potentially interact from all over the world. This consideration may apply to the whole service process or to distinct stages in the process. For example it might be desirable to allow customers to access their account balances via the Web or phone, but clearly not to make deposits.

Accessibility can also be applied to decisions of how to reach the market, since it is also associated with distribution decisions, for instance whether to use Internet booking or ordering facilities, whether to franchise, etc. Depending upon the distribution decisions made service managers will have to consider how their own process will integrate and interact with other companies. Consider for a moment a hotel accepting bookings from travel agents, directly from online booking services such as **lastminute.com**, or via phone to a call centre as well as directly to the hotel. Each of these sources of booking, which enhance customer accessibility to the hotel, will also require some customization to the process to accommodate the booking source.

Degree of Interaction

This design consideration refers to a continuum which describes who conducts elements of the service process: the customer or the service employee. At the extreme customer end of the continuum are self-service processes where all the actions are conducted by the customer. For example, obtaining a drink, petrol or train tickets from a vending machine. In these circumstances there is no service interaction. By contrast at the other end of the continuum are services which are delivered by the service employee interacting with the customer. For example, business consulting, personal grooming, sexual services or professional services such as doctors or lawyers. The positioning of a particular service along this continuum depends upon the design decisions made and consequently how much self-service is designed into the process. Clearly there are many considerations here, not least whether a customer can self-service; it is applicable to retail services, but maybe not to professional services. Customers may need specialized information or facilities to undertake a self-service process such as buying a train ticket. There are many advantages to self-service processes, especially cost savings, but many disadvantages such as opportunities for self-induced service failure, or lack of ability to customize. High interaction services are expensive to provide but the interaction itself is often a key part of the service product and shouldn't be jettisoned on the basis of cost; the actions of service employees can make an average service process outstanding, and can in times of service failure lead to immediate service recovery.

Issues in Service Process Delivery

The application of these various process design criteria will result in the designed service process. Of itself, the process is merely an understanding of a series of steps which must be performed to arrive at a defined outcome for the customer. However, as we have seen above, only when the process becomes 'live' does it transform into a service product. A transition from service assembly to service delivery involves consideration of what can be referred to as 'the expressive performance of the service'.[15] This is highly variable due to the interaction between the assembled service (i.e. the designed process), the service employees, service customers and the service situation. The service delivery process varies according to three criteria: its duration, the effort of employees and the reliability of service delivery.

Duration

If we compare two service processes side by side, while they may be identical the speed at which the process steps are executed may differ. Consider our car rental example above which consists of four core steps: reserve car, pick up car, drive car and return car. For customers of one firm, the first three steps of this process might be completed within a few minutes; a mobile phone call from an airport arrival lounge, credit card payment and a shuttle bus to the car pound. Other service firms may require cars to be booked in advance, payment to be made in person with licence and identity checks, then car pick-up from another location. Technology can speed the service delivery process considerably. Five key elements of service process duration[16] are:

1 task times (how long it takes for each step in the process);
2 total process time (the aggregation of task times which require completion);
3 customer contact time (how much time is spent in direct customer interaction);
4 throughput time (the duration of the total customer experience); and finally
5 waiting times (time to commence the service and the time spent waiting for the next step in the process).

Clearly, the decisions by service managers as to staff density, requirements for data collection, the number of steps in the process and issues such as appointments and availability of equipment will impact upon these time metrics. Customer queueing presents a number of issues for service managers.

When we think of a queue we automatically think of a physical line of people standing in front of a service provider waiting to be served. But queues can also be a collection of people sitting at a computer waiting for dial-up access to their Internet provider or people listening to 'hold music' while they wait to talk to a service provider on the phone. Customers perceive time differently depending upon factors such as whether they are in or out of process. Waits involve two major customer issues. The first is the actual wait time. Managing actual wait times is a balance between the costs of waiting against the costs of serving. Among the costs of waiting are the costs of abandoned shopping trolleys, lost customers who go elsewhere, reduced customer satisfaction, reduced revenues, etc. For these reasons it is important to keep the queue as short as possible and that the queue is designed to allow flow as quickly as possible. The second issue is managing the perception of waiting time, i.e. how long it feels to be in the queue. Waiting in a queue to be served for instance can feel longer than waiting for the next service event, or waiting in a line that is moving and with entertainment to pass the time can feel shorter than waiting in a quiet room. Service managers can affect the perception of service delivery process time by reducing the number of separate process steps, reducing between steps waiting, dividing queues, or setting strict interaction time limits. Sometimes this is called the 'subjective waiting time'.

One important criteria in queue management is trying to understand the different types of service that the queueing customers require. Do they have a standard service request, or a special service request? Are they queueing to make a transaction or to ask for advice? Can the service provider cope with all requests or are they trained to deal with only the basic requests and have to pass the customer to someone else? Triage systems which select customers according to the service they require or on the basis of importance can help to reduce queueing and make customers feel special at the same time (Figure 10.5).

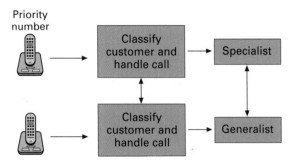

Figure 10.5   Simple telephone triage for customer service calls

Given these remarks on waiting and queueing, it will be no surprise that these two subjects are receiving more and more attention. Effective organizing of waiting lines and minimizing waiting times have a profound impact on the customer's quality perception of the whole service. This is because waiting quickly causes irritation and dissatisfaction. Waiting is related to, among other things, the service provider's capacity, the predictability and forecasting of consumer behaviour (= demand) and the planning within the service organization (the service delivery process). Waiting is also typical for services, since they cannot be produced on stock. Waiting times create many more problems today than in the past when customers were not that much in time constraints. But not all waiting times are the same. We have to distinguish between various kinds of waiting times and delays.[17] Customers may have to wait before, during or after a transaction. There are various kinds of 'pre-process waits':

■ Pre-schedule waits: the customer arrived too early and on purpose;
■ Delays: post-schedule waits when the dentist's treatment starts 15 minutes after the time agreed upon; and
■ Queue waits: lining up due to being served on a first-come-first-go basis.

In general we can conclude that longer delays result in lower evaluations of service. Overall service evaluations are directly affected by evaluations of punctuality, uncertainty and anger created by delay. Anger and uncertainty are affected directly by the length of the delay and degree to which time is filled during the delay. Anger is also related to the degree of control the service provider has over the delay.[18] The subjective evaluations of punctuality are in line with many things we discussed before about the reliability in performance and its impact on service quality. Subjective feelings of uncertainty and anger are partly related to perceived risk: uneasiness, unsettledness, anxiety, annoyance, irritation and frustration play a critical role here. This also indicates that the subjective evaluation of waiting time is so important.

Efforts of Employees

The service delivery process can also be impacted by the efforts of employees. As shown earlier in this chapter, employees' actions will impact upon the delivery process. A service employee's ability and motivation to engage in empathy, responsiveness and assurance will either enhance or detract from the customer experience.[19] The degree to which an employee can empathize with a customer (i.e. understand their requirements, select the appropriate delivery process), provide appropriate responsiveness (i.e. execute process steps speedily and competently), and provide assurance (i.e. display appropriate skills, and professionalism) are issues which depend largely upon individual employees' efforts. Customers' assessments of the service delivery process are highly correlated with their assessments of employee effort. Again, decisions made at the assembly stage will impact directly upon employee effort through the provision of adequate resources such as the number of staff, provision of adequate training and skills development as well as adequate equipment such as terminals, medical equipment or physical capacity.

Reliability

The service delivery process is directed toward providing customers with the outcomes they expect and those which the organization can provide. Reliability refers to the consistency, dependability and integrity of the process in achieving this objective. If a customer is promised an insurance policy in the post in five days then the process must be able to ensure that they receive it. Process reliability is one of the main drivers of perceived service quality.[20] Some service managers take reliability of their service delivery process as the main performance measure. To a large extent they are correct to focus upon it since it defines the core customer experience. While 'reliability' is the term we use, we should not forget the words 'consistency' and 'dependability'. Consistency may be desirable in some services settings but undesirable in others. For instance, when paying money into a bank account consistency is highly important. However, consistency may be undesirable in circumstances which have a high entertainment or theatrical component, where customers return to obtain a similar but not identical experience. Dependability refers to the strength of the process to cope under pressure, and often overlaps with the idea of customization and responsiveness. The most robust a process, the more dependable it is and the more customers trust that the outcome will be achieved.

Understanding the Service Process through Blueprinting

One technique to be able to understand how service process design and service process delivery come together to produce the customer's experience is through holistic analysis of the service product. Blueprinting (also known as service mapping) is such a process mapping technique.[21] A service blueprint is a pictorial representation of the service process with service events linked through a series of lines which represent dependencies. There are many formats for drawing the service blueprint and the one shown in Figure 10.6 includes both the staff who perform the functions and a total time line. Note in particular the line of visibility; the patient will only see relatively few service events.

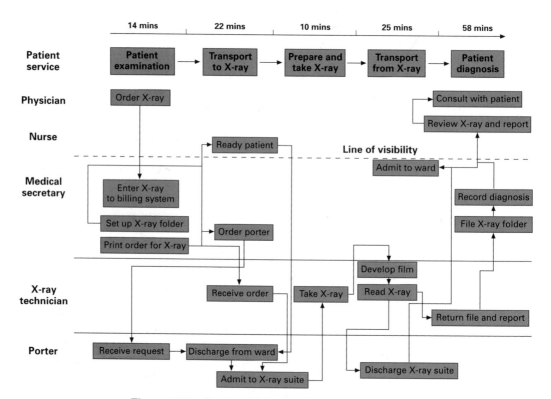

Figure 10.6 Service blueprint for X-ray department

In preparing the service blueprint such as this, there are four key steps: sequencing, visibility, timing and tolerances. We have outlined the important issues in Table 10.1.

Service blueprinting is a complex task to undertake, with many different decisions the service manager has to make. For instance, what level of detail to specify? Where to obtain the tolerance and timing data? Are steps required or do they hint at some forgotten process? Nevertheless, this approach can be used for a variety of different analyses and is sometimes a useful start point in both understanding how the current service operates and identifying opportunities for innovation. Different approaches which add lines of interaction, where the customer area is separated from the supply area, and lines of internal dependence, such as data entry and tracking, can also enhance analysis.

Table 10.1 The four key steps in preparing a service blueprint		
Key step	*Content*	*Remarks*
Sequencing	As you think about the service and all the various stages that are required to complete the service delivery process you can imagine how complex even a simple service like obtaining an X-ray in hospital will be. For slightly more complex events such as a loan approval, a restaurant meal or buying an airline ticket the number of steps and the involvement of different parts of the organization grow exponentially.	Once the main sequence is identified, the interface with associated systems such as databases, financial systems and stock and ordering can be added.
Visibility	The line of visibility can be drawn at different levels within the blueprint depending upon how much of the process the service manager wants to reveal to the customer. Some service steps are fairly mundane, such as the transmission of the order for the X-ray in our example, while others such as the consulting with the doctor and transportation to and from X-ray have to be visible.	In mapping the process, software can allow service managers to move components above and below the line of visibility.
Timing	In the X-ray example, the customer visible process has timing associated with it, which is the aggregation of the timing associated with each service step and the delays between service steps. A more comprehensive blueprint might include actual time down to the second, as well as average times for the last month. Moreover, waiting for the physician to re-examine and consult with the patient might be an area where a new service step, such as 'notify physician that patient has returned' might be added.	Timing can be affected by the number of steps so it is important in streamlining the service process to look for events which are relatively simple but take a long time to execute.
Tolerance	The final thing to add to the service blueprint is some sense of how variable the timings can be, from best to worst as well as the average time. This will indicate some degree of variation and can be used to focus attention on causes. Equally, tolerances might be included as to what the customer is prepared to accept and when the wait becomes too long.	In this way actual service time can be compared and where it is greater than the customer is prepared to accept this too can be a focus for greater examination.

10.4   The Physical Service Environment

We now move to the third component which creates the customer service experience and that is the environment where the service takes place. The ability of the physical environment to influence the behaviour of those exposed to it has been a feature of the environmental psychology literature for many years. Its relevance for marketing and for services in particular has led to increasing interest in the physical environment from those designing hotel and tourist destinations, restaurants, retail outlets and other customer contact environments such as professional services, hospitals and government buildings. The early focus of interest in physical settings was retail environments;[22] later on it was applied to wider service environments.[23] But perhaps the most influential work was published by Bitner (1992) whose article describing aspects of the 'servicescape', highlighted its importance in providing customers with cues to service quality, and influencing employee productivity and satisfaction. This work highlights two important effects of the service environment: an impact upon individual behaviours and an impact upon social or exchange behaviours.

Individual behavioural responses can be categorized as two opposing reactions to a physical environment: approach and avoidance.[24] Environments which prompt approach behaviour mean that people wish to spend time there, explore aspects of the environment, find them stimulating and motivate social exchange. By contrast avoidant environments prompt people to stay away, not explore and avoid social interaction. The key is to identify those aspects of the environment which are associated with each response and adjust the environment to enhance its positive appeal such as in the case of background music.[25] Part of the difficulty in making this link is that individual responses can be:

■ Cognitively based (such as appreciating the functionality of a layout such as a supermarket or an Ikea store, finding adequate signage in an airport, or recognizing people through their uniforms);
■ Emotionally based (where an environment's design might take your breath away, or make you laugh); or
■ Physiologically based (such as feeling cold or hot, or stressed by noise or large numbers of people).

Accounting for all these possible sources of reaction is extremely difficult as they often conflict (i.e. great design but very hot and stuffy) and they are also quite transient. You might be impressed the first time you walk in but as an employee your emotional response might give way to more cognitive assessments over time. Physical environments also prompt the playing out of social roles.[26] People associate certain behaviours with certain environments and by designing in the props and features associated with that behaviour its likelihood will increase. We generally approach a desk or service window, but avoid what appear to be employees' personal spaces in some cultures. Similarly, in many cultures, we tend to join queues, sit in waiting rooms, wait to be seated at a restaurant reception podium, or pick up a tray in a self-service cafeteria; in other cultures this is not that self-evident. Using this information service managers can use physical equipment, props, signage, etc. to promote desired individual behavioural responses.

While the individual behaviours of customers is important, due to the nature of services the impact upon social exchange is equally relevant. Some environments enhance exchange while others discourage it. Simply arranging waiting seats in rows will discourage communication among those waiting, while arranging seats around tables will encourage it. The design of the environment may be used to impact social interaction between customers, between employees, or between customers and employees. In the case of customers, opposing seating or circulation areas can encourage social contact when this is leveraged with the service process in activities such as getting customers to undertake joint tasks together (i.e. self-service restaurants, check-in, or form filling) or spending extended periods in close proximity (airline passengers on long haul flights, tourist excursions or college classes). Encouraging employees to interact with each other can also be enhanced by environmental design such as open plan service areas or offices, communal areas such as tea rooms, or staff working in close proximity. For the service organization customer–employee interaction is critical and so a focus upon serving areas, the ergonomics of equipment and physical positioning to remove 'avoidant' attributes is important. By combining behavioural cues and the actions of staff, customers can be guided into a narrow set of possible behaviours and the service process can be commenced (see also Figure 2.3).

Features of the Service Environment

Three dimensions of the service environment can be identified.[27] The three groupings are:

- Atmospherics;
- Physical layout; and
- Tangible service evidence.

These are groupings of characteristics which are controllable by the service organization and can be used to create both the customers and the service employees' experience. In designing an environment there are two issues to be aware of. The first is the competing interests of customers and employees. Consider a retail outlet in Vancouver. In the winter the temperature can drop to as low as −20°C and so customers coming in from the street will be wearing very warm clothing. Employees in the heated store will be wearing normal working clothes. How hot should the temperature be? Too hot and customers will find the transition from outside to inside stifling, too low and employees will find it too cold to work. The second issue is to understand that different customers have different expectations and responses. You might think it strange to have dance music playing in a lawyer's office, or classical music in a car maintenance garage. Customers expect different atmospherics according to the type or category of service outlet fitting to the preferred identity and actual image of the store. Similarly, different market segments respond differently to stimuli. Loud music and lots of noise discourage older customers, 'lift music' or 'muzak' can discourage younger customers. There are a number of companies that now specialize in choosing music appropriate to different outlets and target customer groups. While it is difficult to estimate the relative impact of environmental attributes it is possible to see how they combine to provide an overall environmental experience.

Atmospherics

Atmospherics refers to those background environmental conditions such as heat, light, sound and smell. As you can see they generally impact upon people through the five senses and are often physiologically experienced. In the marketing literature, the main studies have related to music.[28] Variations in music selection, tempo, and volume were found to have an effect upon work rate in manufacturing and similar effects (walking speed, length of stay) have been noted in supermarket studies. Temperature, light intensity, colour and noise have also been found to elicit behavioural responses and there is some evidence to suggest that effects are magnified when the atmospherics are consistent.[29] And better atmospherics have customers stay longer and spend more in general as we indicated in Chapter 3.

SERVICE PRACTICE 10.6

Hotel Indigo[30]

While some people call it a W Hotel for the middle class, InterContinental Hotels Group likes to refer to its new Hotel Indigo chain-to-be as an aspirational brand that plugs into the psychographics of its existing and potential customers. At a recent press conference in New York, IHG executives provided further details on the background and specifics of its new boutique-like conversion flag that debuts later this year. 'For the first time in the hotel industry, we're defining customers by mindset rather than a price point,' explained Steve Porter, president for the Americas. He said the company borrowed heavily from the world of retail to 'cater to middle-market consumers who are trading up to higher levels of quality and taste, but still seeking value'.

To nurture the concept, IHG worked with Back Lot Productions, an Atlanta design firm that specializes in retail environments but has no hotel experience. The result is a look and service style that mimics attitudes more common at The Gap than at Holiday Inn. As in retail stores, the design components of Indigo properties will change periodically. In guestrooms, artwork, area rugs and slip covers will rotate to give guests what the company calls a 'renewed environment'. Art, signage and paint in public spaces will change, too. Guest agents will greet guests on the lobby floor, not from behind traditional front desks. The first Hotel Indigo, a conversion of a 141-room property in midtown Atlanta, will open by the end of the year.

Spatial Layout

Service environments are different to many others since they are built around a specific purpose. Hospitals are not designed to be appealing or enjoyable to those that use them, but functional and to allow the service tasks to be completed. As a consequence, the physical layout of offices, consulting rooms, laboratories and pharmacies are as much a consideration as patient waiting areas, toilet facilities and service desks. The same can be said about airports, schools and many public buildings. That being said, service environments can be differentiated quite dramatically by the use of spatial elements. Different furniture, modern or old, can be used to give the impression of conservatism and reliability versus liveliness, fun and enthusiasm. The use of space and the configuration of functional (desks, terminals, phones) and non functional (plants, artwork and lighting) can be used to achieve similar effects.

Tangible Service Evidence

Any service where customers and the organization interact will have some tangible components to it, even if it is only the service provider. In physical environments the arrangement of tangible/physical items provides a rich and complex set of communication signals to those observing them. The most direct form of communication from a service environment to its occupiers is signage: the name of the company, instructions, directions and conditions of use. Clearly some environments with large customer traffic (stations, airports, hotels, etc.) will require more intense signage than those with few (lawyers' offices, hairdressers, travel agents). Less direct communication to customers and employees can be seen in the use of different quality materials, finishes and colours. White linen tablecloths versus plastic tables, linoleum floor coverings versus carpet, rich curtains versus blinds, or plastic cutlery versus silver all convey meaning. One high quality, high service, and the other lower quality and less service. Similarly bright dynamic colours convey fun, intensity and excitement, while pale blues and greens are meant to relax those in stressful environments. Around these symbols and the messages they communicate are built customers expectations of the service.

Marketspace

A final consideration, under place, is to consider the role of the Internet as a service environment. This approach is still in its infancy but for some service organizations, this is the only 'service environment' they have. In general we can apply the same set of design considerations to websites as we have discussed in relation to physical service environments. Ease of use appeared to be the main driver of success of websites and Internet use, as we saw in previous chapters. Specifically, that a website must encourage 'approach' rather than 'avoidance' response, to encourage users to explore the site, rather than leave. It must provide sufficient signage to allow for easy navigation. It must combine functional components such as ordering and payment facilities with non functional content to enhance enjoyment, lingering and visual stimulation. Finally the overall design, colour scheme and feel of the site should be consistent with the message being communicated. Sites which are providing expensive services to more mature customers should avoid gimmicks, flashing lights and animations more appropriate for a younger target market. The World Wide Web as a service environment is likely to attract increasing interest as more and more services put all or part of their offer into this medium. The benefit of this environment for service managers is that experimentation with different designs is far easier than with physical spaces and it can be changed dynamically to suit the wide range of possible users.

As with all components of the design of service settings, actual response can be very different to that planned or theorized. Peterson (2003) points to elements of a recently opened and highly regarded hotel. Designed features such as open foyers and glass backed elevators were considered dizzying by customers, sameness in hotel rooms was considered 'prison-like', glass walls considered dangerous, corridors like a freeway, and exposed concrete within the interior 'brutal'. While a lot has been written about the impact of service environments upon customers and employees there are few consistent and normative findings to guide service organizations and, while ensuring the functionality of the space is paramount and achievable, the higher considerations of aesthetics, socio-spatial consumption and hyper-modernity are less conclusive.

Summary

In this chapter we have identified three elements of the service which directly contribute toward the customer's service experience. We started by considering the service process and identified how the series of steps, events and activities need to be designed in order to coordinate the organization's efforts. We also distinguished between the core customer delivery process which comprises the consumption steps for a customer and how the organization articulates this with a number of sub-systems or processes. In considering how managers might construct a service experience, two key steps were identified: those associated with designing the service and those which impact directly upon its operationalization. We noted how a designed process can be enhanced in the customer's eyes by the efforts of employees, perceived speed or duration and its reliability. Service blueprinting was described as a technique which gives managers a holistic tool for considering a service process and the opportunities it presents for diagnostic analysis.

The second key element in the customer's service experience is employees, and in particular how service employees often suffer through role conflict, role ambiguity and role overload as well as the constant pressure of emotional labour to act in a market oriented way to provide value to the customer. We presented a generic framework for managing service employees with a focus upon selection, training, performance and reward. The final part of this chapter considered the physical environment as a key part of the customer's experience and how it can impact upon individual and social behaviour. We identified atmospherics, spatial layout and tangible evidence as opportunities for managers to adjust environmental impact. Finally we presented the Internet as a service environment which presents many similar design issues.

All these issues give more concrete content to the assets and capabilities deemed relevant to creating the service experience based on the people, processes and physical environment: some of the internal-based assets (e.g. cost advantage in the servuction process), all the outside-in capabilities and some of the inside-out capabilities (especially effective human resource management and good operations management expertise).

Questions

1. How is process defined?
2. What five issues need to be considered in service process design?
3. Why is service duration important to the customer's service experience?
4. Explain the four key steps in service blueprinting.
5. What is meant by the term 'emotional labour'?
6. How does 'role conflict' come about? And what should be done about it?
7. What are the four generic issues in managing service employees?
8. Who or what is a partial employee?
9. Characterize 'approach' versus 'avoidance' behaviours with respect to service environments.
10. Explain the three main features of a service environment.

306, 340, 370, 140, 112,
114, 216, 314, 465.x

Service Marketing Management
Strategic Perspecti...

GET WOW!
MONDAYS AT
BROOKLYN

SKINT
TUESDAYS AT
PEACOCK & MOLOKO

TERMINAL→
WEDNESDAYS AT
LEVEL

DIRTY ANTICS
THURSDAYS AT
HEEBIE JEEBIES

SCAN YOUR CAMERA OVER ME
TO JOIN OUR SOCIAL MEDIA!

RUNWAY
FRIDAYS AT
INK

LOCATION
FRIDAYS AT
54

TOYBOX
SATURDAYS AT
LEVEL

PANDAMONIUM
SATURDAYS AT
ELECTRIK

Assignments

1. Using a theatrical metaphor, explain how a single act play can be likened to a single service experience. Pay special attention to scene changes, audience participation and scripts.
2. You are a service manager selecting new staff for the position of waitress in an up-market restaurant. Write the skills you think would be essential for the new staff member and reflect these in the design of a selection process for three candidates.
3. Using either the process of ordering a pizza over the telephone, or a cup of coffee at your local café, map the complete customer service process into a blueprint. Identify any facilitating sub-systems you are assuming exist. What issues have you encountered?
4. In a group, get one person to select a short period of time, say 2 minutes and 40 seconds, without telling anyone else. Get the timekeeper to say start, and wait in silence until they say finish. Guess how long you have been waiting. You might want to try the same exercise where you can read, or watch TV, or talk to others and assess whether the perceived waiting time is different in each case.
5. Design a physical layout for a car rental outlet. What features would you introduce to improve the customers experience?

Endnotes

1 White, 2005.

2 Weatherly and Tansik, 1993.

3 Adapted from Clark *et al.*, 2005.

4 Hochschild, 1983.

5 For a fuller explanation of non verbal communication in service encounters, see Gabbott and Hogg, 2000, 2001.

6 Ashforth and Humphrey, 1993; and Shuler and Davenport-Sypher, 2000.

7 Fisk, Grove and John, 2000.

8 Adapted from Harris, 2002; and *Automotive News*, vol. 76, no. 5977.

9 Gummesson, 1987; Bettancourt, 1997; Kelly, Donnelly and Skinner, 1990; Hsieh, Yen and Chin, 2004.

10 Ploskina, 2002; and *Interactive Week*, vol. 8, no. 20.

11 Based on Accenture Consulting.

12 Booms and Bitner, 1981; Shostack, 1992; Mayer, Bowen and Moulton, 2003.

13 Langeard, Bateson, Lovelock and Eiglier, 1981.

14 Shostack, 1987.

15 Grönroos, 1984.

16 Stuart and Tax, 1997.

17 Taylor, 1994.

18 Taylor, 1994; Casado Díaz, 2005.

19 Parasuraman, Zeithaml and Berry, 1988; and Mohr and Bitner, 1995.

20 Grönroos, 1990a.

21 This idea was originally developed by Shostack, 1982; later on it was further developed by Kingman-Brundage, 1989, 1995.

22 Grossbart *et al.*, 1975; Donovan and Rossiter, 1982; Kotler, 1973.

23 Baker, 1986; and Aubert-Gamet, 1992.

24 Mehrabian and Russell, 1974.

25 Milliman, 1986; and Oakes, 2000.

26 Forgas, 1979; and Barker, 1968.

27 Bitner, 1992.

28 These studies draw heavily upon the scientific management tradition of Taylor (1911), and the work done by Mayo on the Hawthorn Studies; see Mayo (1945).

29 Matilla and Wirtz, 2001.

30 Based on *Lodging Hospitality*, 2004.

Chapter 11

Place, Promotion and Price

Hamburg Süd. The cutting edge.

Hamburg Süd's worldwide network services Europe and the Mediterranean, all coasts of North and South America, the Caribbean, Australia/New Zealand, the Pacific Islands, South Africa, India and the Far East.
For more, visit us at www.hamburgsud.com

No matter what.

Reproduced by Hamburg Süd. Advertisement designed and produced by Myriad Marketing Communications, Sydney, Australia

Learning objectives

When you finish this chapter you should be able to:

1 Describe the issues which must be considered when formulating distribution, communication and pricing objectives

2 Illustrate the difference between strategies and these objectives

3 Describe how communication can strengthen the relationship between the service organization and customer

4 Prepare a communications plan

5 Describe how communication can reduce the perceived risk inherent in services

6 Describe the foundations of pricing strategy

7 Illustrate what is meant by the term 'value-based pricing'

11.1   Introduction

SERVICE PRACTICE 11.1

The 'Wow' Effect: How One Restaurateur Continues to Delight Customers[1]

The restaurant, Old San Francisco, continues to delight its customers. The restaurant's success is attributed to the delivery of the '*wow* effect'. The *wow* effect is the culmination of the efforts of the management group to keep the restaurant chain fresh and exciting for both customers and employees. It is the dividend received for constantly innovating and caring for, delighting and exceeding the expectations of those who make the business a success; the managers, the employees, the customers and the community.

The *wow* recipe for success is the delivery of the unexpected. *Wow* moments are 'high touch'. Whenever a manager or servers believe that a table has been waiting too long for their meals, servers will descend on the table with the offer of free drinks and appetizers. They do not wait for the guests to complain about slow service. This 'wait party' is a terrific way to generate *wow* and it can be delivered at minimal cost.

Modern marketers must give people a reason to leave their comfort zones. This means learning about the community, listening to their needs, putting in effort to reach the clients. This process is sometimes called 'reverse cocooning'.

☐ *Wow yourself*: The principal concern at Old San Francisco is that the products and service will be consistently excellent, not necessarily consistently the same. The general managers take the time to be innovative. By encouraging innovation at the restaurant they intend to be one step ahead of the customers expectations.

☐ *Wow your employees*: There is a firm belief in empowering the employees. The empowerment is a dividend of providing ownership to the employees. Ownership is the employee 'buy-in' to the company, their financial or psychological investment in the business. Financial ownership occurs when employees are financially invested in the company. In some industries, employee ownership is the norm; the longer the employee works for the company the more stocks they are entitled to. This practice is not usual in the restaurant industry. The only exception is Starbucks Coffee. The service at Starbucks is extremely good, partly because of its employee-ownership policy. Psychological ownership is extraordinarily important to motivating employees. It means the employer cares about the employees and makes them an integral part of the company.

☐ *Wow your customers*: *Wow* style empowerment is the result of everyone working together on every aspect of the concept, and not just having the people on the front line working while the manager sits back. The customer service gospel is called 'QAPS' – quality, amount, properness and spirit.

- ☐ *Quality*: Old San Francisco is focussed on the quality of the ingredients, original presentation and unusual menu. It has taken years to find suppliers who can meet the standards. Quality is linked with originality. The products served cannot be found anywhere else. If you fill your menu with items that the customer could find down the street at a casual dining chain you will not gain repeat business.

- ☐ *Amount* is another important issue and not just the amount of food. *Wow* people with big portions but impress them also with the amount of service they receive.

- ☐ *Properness* means doing things the right way. Whenever new employees come to the company, they should understand what 'the right way' for the company means, before they encounter a single customer.

- ☐ *Spirit* is the final major component of QAPS customer service. The restaurant's 'mood' is the third most important factor to the customers, after food and value. Customers want a restaurant to exude a positive spirit, so the employees mood is important.

- ☐ *Wow your community*: The restaurant must participate in the community. A story illustrates this point. A group of teenagers went to Atlanta for jobs during the Olympic Games, expecting to pay off the price of the trip and to earn a decent amount of money. Some of them spent all of their savings for the ticket. Unfortunately there were no job offers, instead they were completely stranded. The manager of Old San Francisco heard about their dilemma and took care to arrange their return tickets via Continental Airlines. When the kids were home he gave a party at the local restaurant. This action made the evening news. This deed has been generating an inestimable amount of goodwill and publicity for the restaurant. Its total cost for the action has been less than one large newspaper ad. Traditional advertising simply does not create this effect.

- ☐ *Wow your competition*: The competitors should never be ignored. In Old San Francisco, the approach is thinking one step ahead. This means trying to shake things up before anyone else does.

Cohen, Barry, 'The "WOW" effect: How one restaurateur continues to delight customers', *Cornell Hotel and Administration Quarterly*, Ithaca, April, Vol. 38, Iss. 2, pp. 74–82, Copyright 1997 Sage Publications. Reproduced by permission of Sage Publications Inc.

The *wow* effect leverages important elements of relationship marketing and the marketing mix instruments, place (distribution), promotion and price. Moreover, it combines these elements with the marketing instruments discussed in Chapter 10 (personnel, process and physical evidence). Appropriate leveraging of these elements should result in the delivery of a customer *wow* experience, a service experience about which people are talking. Figure 11.1 provides an overview of this fourth chapter on creating service experience.

11.2   Organizing the Distribution

Place or distribution embraces all of the strategic and operational activities that make the service available to target customers. It considers the channels used, outlet locations and

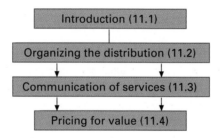

Figure 11.1   Chapter outline

methods of transportation. Prior to developing a distribution strategy it is important to consider the following questions.

1   Is it only possible to distribute services at the point where they are produced?
2   What should the supply chain look like?
3   Are there still some possibilities to store the service?
4   Does the internationalization of the service firm add complications to distributing excellent quality services in different countries?
5   What is the impact of IT?
6   Does the use of IT cannibalize existing channels?

Distribution and the Characteristics of Services

All these topics relate to the specific features of market oriented service organizations as well as to some particular assets and capabilities, like the four distribution and supply chain assets mentioned in Chapters 2 and 6, namely,

■   Good relationships with suppliers;
■   Extent or nature of the distribution network;
■   The uniqueness of the distribution approach;
■   The relationship with distribution channel intermediaries; and
■   Networking capabilities like the ability to manage relationships with suppliers.

This section aims to add to these by giving you more information on how to create value based on these assets and capabilities.

SERVICE PRACTICE 11.2

Bulgaria: Worldwide Investing at the Touch of a Button

Local investors can buy shares on the International Stock Exchange via online brokers. A few years ago the International Stock Exchange was a place reserved exclusively for big players such as merchandise and investment banks, insurance companies and pension and hedge funds. Individuals and smaller investors were able to buy stocks only through their own bank via a personal account manager. The delay to effect the transaction ranged from a couple of hours to a couple of days.

Now the picture is totally different; approximately 60% of International Stock Exchange deals are completed online. It only takes a second to transfer the order to the Stock Exchange. Individuals and other smaller corporate clients can easily become shareholders in multinationals. They can trade freely with futures, options or other stocks.

The daily exchange rate difference of these stocks provides the opportunity for those with access to such information to make considerable profits without running high risk exposures. To buy a Wall Street quoted company for example, you need only to have access to an online broker and a computer.

This is a much cheaper way compared to the same service offered via a bank where the commission fees vary from €18 to €25 on average to open or close short positions and this can be very expensive. Online brokers can be found in many places around the globe and are accessible from Bulgaria and elsewhere.

Taking into account the environmental forces discussed in Chapter 1, the market opportunities and risks resulting from the external analysis, the service provider will have to clearly position its service offer. The positioning of the service will be supported in part by the distribution strategies. Distribution strategies must be consistent with and support the organization's corporate and marketing objectives. Prior to identifying the organization's distribution strategies the organization should take the following into account:

1   What degree of coverage in service distribution is the service provider aiming for?
2   Who travels to whom, and in what manner should the client participate during the service encounter?
3   What kind of visibility is required?
4   Does the service delivery take place individually or collectively?

First of all, the purpose of the intended distribution coverage has to be determined. Therefore, the initial question that needs to be answered here is whether large distribution coverage is desirable. If the answer is negative, the number of locations will be limited. If the answer is positive, it is most likely that new outlets will have to be founded. It is of paramount importance to make a principal choice of the desired coverage of the distribution network (outlets) first, before further dealing with the question of 'how to reach this goal'. The intensity of distribution (exclusive or intensive) is at stake here. The answer to the first question will influence the options the marketer has for tackling the other three distribution issues.

In response to question two, in general when a service is provided the customer and the producer may get in touch with each other in three ways:

1   The customer goes to the producer;
2   The producer visits the customer;
3   No physical contact is involved and the customer and producer meet at arm's length.

Buying a holiday, theatre tickets, banking, insurance or the services of the tax consultant does not always require the customer's presence during the service encounter. The 'degree of visibility' in the servuction process is marked by a certain degree of flexibility. It is part of the marketing toolkit that is used to create the service experience. An individual value delivery often requires perfect accessibility. If a service is to be delivered personally and if the customer is required to travel then a high number of outlets will be necessary. Customized service and personal delivery can maintain 'exclusivity' provided the sales area remains local or regional.

The situation with respect to collective deliveries constitutes more of a problem. On the one hand it is logical that more outlets are opened when collective delivery is aimed for; on the other hand collective delivery (in practice) is usually a result of the choice made to set up a limited distribution system. This, in turn, depends on the specific service; examples would be tourism or a concert. In regard to booking facilities we notice that with the change of personal services towards ICT-based (24/7) services, the impact of physical booking facilities is becoming less important.

Distribution Channels and Supply Chains

Usually, the distribution function emerges as the way to solve imbalances between demand and supply. Since both occur simultaneously in services, distribution is not the only way to meet this problem. Chapter 12 summarizes the options of the marketing mix to influence supply and demand. In order to make a service available to its customers, a company should build a network, not only with its customers but also with the main suppliers and resellers in the chain. A supply chain consists of upstream and downstream partners in the distribution channel. Traditionally, marketers focus their attention on the downstream marketing channels and distribution channels. Here the focal point is on sales. The supply chain, however, resembles the idea that all upstream and downstream partners work together to deliver superior value to the customer. A critical prerequisite to accomplish this is that all the partners in the distribution channel have given the same content to their philosophy of being market oriented.[2]

The success of a company is dependent not only on the company strategy but also on the performance and competitive abilities of the other supply and marketing partners in the chain. These partners can also be part of the supply chains of other companies. As the supply chain concentrates on 'make and sale' it would be better to speak of a demand chain. If this view were to be adopted then the organization would need to start off by scanning the consumer (B2C) and/or the business (B2B) demand. The reaction of the firm and the planning of assets and capabilities of the firm are then organized in such a manner that the needs of the target market become central and the company builds profitable client relationships. With the guiding principle of understanding, creating and delivering value, the value delivery network offers yet a broader view than the demand chain. The value delivery network consists of the firm, suppliers, distributors and in the end the customers that work in partnership to improve the performance of the total system. The value delivery networks of big companies consists of a growing number of supply chains including B2B websites, electronic purchase and e-auction sites such as EBay.

The simplest distinction in distribution and marketing channels are twofold. First it depends on whether the distribution channel is direct or indirect. Second, the ownership of the distribution channel is an issue.

A direct distribution channel is characterized by the absence of intermediaries between the producer of the service and the customer. A lawyer having one office in a city serves that community with his advice directly. Direct writers in the insurance industry communicate and deal directly with their customers without any brokers. In an indirect channel, one or more middlemen are present in bridging the distance between the service producer and the customers in order to deliver excellent service quality. These distances may be geographical, but they can also be of a social or psychological nature. This is especially the case when middlemen are needed to lower thresholds to meet a service provider. Direct distribution implies that the 'original' service supplier delivers directly to the 'end-user'. A short distribution channel is characterized by having one intermediary, a long channel by various middlemen.

The decision as to what kind of distribution channel a service provider should choose depends on many things. In general, it is accepted that it is a matter of costs versus benefits. It will also depend on what the chosen market segments, the potential customers, view as value. For this reason we advise you to look at the overall scheme of this book, where this first part of the figure refers to understanding value. In our view, at least one other factor should be taken into account. Do the distribution partners possess the critical assets and capabilities to be market oriented, deliver excellent quality and hence value to the customer? If not, bad quality, dissatisfaction (also with prices), complaints and customer switching will occur, eventually leading to unintended images and loss of sales.

The ownership issue in the distribution channel of the 'intangible services lacking ownership' has to do with the opportunities and means to manage the distribution channel according to the goals set by the service provider. The control of a fully owned distribution channel will be different from controlling a distribution channel with many, independent middlemen all seeking to pursue their own interest.[3] For that reason, some service providers state explicitly in their marketing strategy that their objective is 'to control the end-user'. For example, if such a service firm wants to form a strategic alliance with another company it will never give up this control.

Figure 11.2 illustrates the various forms of distribution channels and supply chains that may occur. There are many ways to organize distribution. The service supplier may use various forms of distribution channels simultaneously. A multichannel strategy fits a differentiated marketing strategy aimed at reaching different market segments and target groups. It might also be that the various channels compete with one another. They may also 'quarrel' when margins, prices, conditions and the way of dealing with the customer differs per channel. The risk of channel conflicts is then a reality. Powered relationships between the parties determine the power of the channel. In the insurance business, in some countries, brokers and middlemen have a long standing position in the distribution channel of insurances. In other countries, this has not been the case. The emergence of the Internet has made the contents and prices of services more transparent. It also created better informed customers. And, with the growing acceptance of the Internet also marketing mix issues connected with direct distribution and multi-channel distribution are becoming increasingly a dilemma to traditional service providers.

The enthusiasm for running many distribution channels simultaneously may be tempered

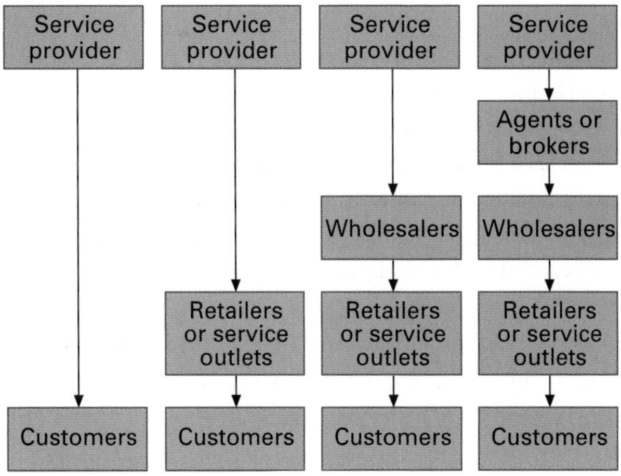

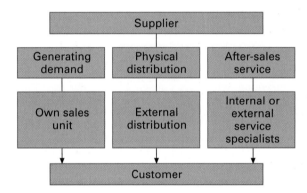

Figure 11.2 Typical distribution channels

Figure 11.3 Compound channels

Source: De Vries & Van Helsdingen, 2005, p. 403

by the risk of channel conflicts, especially when services are the same, but prices (and conditions) are different. Then it will be easier to use different brand names in different channels, which would also avoid cannibalization.[4]

Recently, the number of compound channels has been growing. We speak of compound channels when the original service provider and the channel partners divide the execution of the service according to a horizontal task allocation. The first one is busy with sales, negotiations and generating client orders, while the second one is responsible for the physical distribution as well as to execute the orders. The other members can specialize in functions like providing services after the purchase. In this way, as shown in Figure 11.3 everybody is working together delivering the service.

Distribution Strategies

You may recall distribution strategies can be labelled as intensive, selective or exclusive. Intensive distribution is a strategy directed at developing as many outlets as possible. This strategy is the result of an objective directed at a high coverage rate in the distribution network. Intensive distribution is often necessary when convenience in services is deemed relevant by customers (banks, fast food). If the distribution is limited to a few branches or even only one, then the selective and the exclusive methods of distribution form strategic alternatives. These strategies apply, respectively, to convenience, shopping and speciality services. However, considering the specific features of services, we can basically distinguish between the following distribution strategies developed by multi-site strategy, multiservice strategy and multisegment strategy.[5] While the hybrid strategy is a combination of two or three of these strategies, the network concept emphasizes the possibilities of remote and/or non-personalized servicing. This is summarized in Table 11.1.

Hybrid Strategies

Naturally, a hybrid variety has its advantages and disadvantages. We speak of a hybrid variety between multisite and multiservice if a service provider directs its activities at different market segments and has various outlets at its disposal. The great advantage of this hybrid variety is extended market coverage. If a service provider has more than one branch, its service can cover a larger sales area. The possible disadvantage of this hybrid variety is the risk to the organization of losing part of its identity.

Quite often, service providers who have chosen a particular positioning via their multisite or multiservice strategy are further tempted to develop their business. Adding new sites or services to the existing ones may be detrimental to the existing image. For service providers with a clear cut position in the mind of their target group (e.g. McDonald's), this may end in a much vaguer and consequently less recognizable formula by increasing the number of services ('product line') for a multisite company.

The opposing strategy is such that a company that is recognized in the market as a multiservice company wants to increase its outlets in an attempt to increase profits. By doing so it has to make hefty investments because these companies are typically resource- or information-based. The question now will be: can these investments be covered by the additional outlets?

In the case of Euro Disney, we have seen that the start-up period, in terms of number of visitors (paying an attractive entrance fee for the company and spending reasonably during their visit) was extremely long in comparison with both the US and Japan Disneys. In these instances developments may cause problems to the multisite company, because of its natural tendency to add services (and therefore to create a diffused image) and to the multiservice as it is tempted to invest in new locations (by doing so it invests too heavily and offers lower than expected returns). As a final consequence, companies may eventually disappear if they are not really aware of what is happening/might happen. Sasser (1976) has called this the danger of the Bermuda Triangle. In Figure 11.4, we have shown this process towards an imaginary Bermuda Triangle for McDonald's and Disney.

Networks

The servuction process differs for each service. Therefore, some services require a physical outlet to be produced, while others do not; for example, providing information via computer

Table 11.1   Three basic distribution strategies

Distribution strategies	Explanation	Examples
Multisite strategy	Consists of repeating one particularly successful basic formula at several other outlets or locations. Possible differences in environmental factors are hardly significant here. The formula is and remains standard and there is no, or hardly any, reason for adaptations. This can actually be defined as a standard service and holds for both core and augmented standard services. Franchising is an example of a multisite strategy. The only question that needs to be solved in the field of marketing is: 'Will it catch on here?'	Hotel and catering business; fast-food chains excel in standardization: McDonald's hamburgers in San Francisco have almost the same taste as those in Moscow. However, in the Philippines the McDonald's hamburgers are spicier there (local adaptation).
Multiservice strategy	Is designed particularly to provide various services: service differentiation. Relying on the existing goodwill of the consumers and the firm's thorough knowledge of them in one particular area, the service provider begins offering new and different services to the existing assortment. It is a kind of new service development and service innovation. Essentially, a pure multiservice strategy would consist of one outlet, which targets its various services in a particular market segment. This is an example of an exclusive distribution strategy.	Many software houses, in particular those focussing on a specific target group, frequently offer three core activities: innovation, developing new programmes; maintenance of existing application programmes or machine software; and technical management.
Multisegment strategy	From one particular location, a particular service is targeted at several market segments. This strategy is often applied in situations in which part of the capacity remains unused and the fixed costs in providing the service are relatively high. If this unused capacity is structural, the service provider will be inclined to use it, and usually a different target group is opted for. In a pure multisegment strategy this is, once again, an instance of exclusive distribution as the number of establishments could be limited to one.	Amusement parks target several segments from one location with one service (entertainment). Disney World or Euro Disney Paris have to make considerable investments each year to maintain their appeal for various target groups or increase the number of visitors. In extending their assortment of services, they also offer hotel facilities with different offerings, services and prices to attract different market segments during the week and weekends, during the business season and the holiday season.

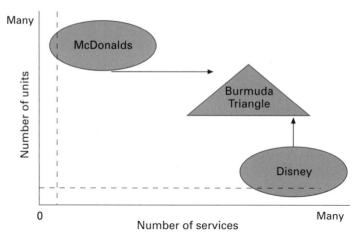

Figure 11.4   Multisite multiservice

networks or telephone, consequently offering the possibility of remote service delivery.[6] Consumers may use a network in different ways. Some may use just one branch of a bank or food retailer in their neighbourhood while others use (and value) many branches of the same bank or retailer in various cities.

Information technology now makes it possible to trace consumer behaviour and see which outlets customers use and when. In assessing the relevance and performance of an outlet it is important to define the outlet's function in the network precisely what pattern of concentration holds for this particular outlet in attracting and keeping customers.[7] Managing these network relations well is a specific feature of market oriented service providers.

When the three basic distribution strategies from Table 11.1 are combined in Ansoff's well-known growth matrix, then the relationship as depicted in Figure 11.5 emerges. This also shows the link between the distribution strategy and the opted-for location. The multi-site strategy demands new choices of location, whereas multi-segment and multi-service do not. In the latter case, a new location is only required if the strategy is applied in a hybrid form with multisite. Market innovation in the form of internationalization, with a new branch being opened abroad, is therefore a hybrid form of multi-site and multi-segment. If any element of the forms is hybrid, then diversification may occur.

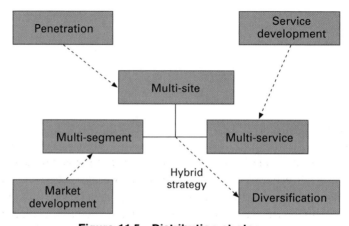

Figure 11.5   Distribution strategy

Choice of the Location

If clients come to the service provider the physical surroundings in which they will then find themselves play a role in their (subjective) assessment of the service. But the impact of a location goes further. Not only the client but also the service provider can benefit from an attractive service environment. Just imagine what will happen when airports get crowded because of the large number of passengers and airplanes, in the near future. Delays will increase and overall travel satisfaction will decrease.[8] The importance of the service environment, therefore, depends on, among other things:

■ Who is present in this environment?
■ How complex is the physical environment?
■ What is the influence of the client and service provider?
■ How to select a site? and
■ How can atmospherics contribute to the service experience?[9]

As Chapter 10, on the physical service environment, showed: in choosing a location, the marketer should also look at the impact of the physical environment on the client and the service provider. The literature on retail management pays a great deal of attention to developing a retail location strategy. The basics of selecting a store site can also be applied to selecting the location of a travel agency, a bank, a hospital, a university, etc. The marketing strategy chosen is the starting point for decisions about three issues relevant to the spatial environment where the services will be delivered. These are regional analysis, areal analysis and site evaluation itself.[10]

Regional analysis refers to 'the identification of regional markets such as cities, towns, and metropolitan areas in which to locate new' service outlets. Since the competitive entironment may differ spatially, areal analysis 'focuses on the immediate area surrounding potential sites' (trade area). The emphasis should be on the characteristics of the target group of clients or customers. Finally, evaluating the site 'focuses on the characteristics of the sites at which a new store may be located. The characteristics of each site are analyzed in detail with respect to traffic flow, access patterns, compatibility, and terms of occupancy.' Indexes of buying power or saturation (e.g. how many outlets already exist) may be applied here, next to the potential of the market and the competitive situation, in order to forecast the sales of a particular outlet.

11.3　Communication of Services

Internal and external communications of services should be embedded within the company goals, the marketing objectives and the chosen target group. Great internal and external communication is typical for market oriented service organizations. You may recall for instance that horizontal communication was critical in creating excellent service quality. The external communication is for instance aimed at creating the firm's desired image among its target groups. So, communication relates to customer-based assets like company or brand name and reputation, credibility with customers, and to the assets on starting, maintaining and enhancing the relationships with customers and partners in the distribution channel. It also hinges upon many of the outside-in capabilities and the spanning capabilities of communicating internally across the organization. This section will provide you some more information on how 'communication works' to accomplish this.

Communication should not be isolated from the other elements of the marketing mix. In contrary, it should create a coherent image of the service company and its offering. Here we will deal with external communication. For internal communication we refer to the sections on personnel and internal marketing.

SERVICE PRACTICE 11.3

Be Different and Stand out from the Competition

Jordan Furniture sells more furniture per square foot than any other furniture store in the USA. Jordan Furniture transformed their family owned business into a multimillion dollar corporation by following a principle called 'shopper entertainment'.

To surprise employees and customers, Barry and Eliot Tatleman dressed up like the Lone Ranger and Tonto and rode horses in their parking lot. They built an Imax theatre inside one store to entertain children while their parents shopped. When you drive around to pick up your furniture they provide you with free hotdogs and wash your car windows.

Communication and the Characteristics of Services and Service Quality

Communication of services has to be aimed at more than just stimulating demand. External communication is one of the ways to manage expectations. Communication about services will impact on the perceived quality of the service in the eyes of the beholder: the consumer. So, communication will affect the various dimensions of service quality as well as the overall service quality.

You may recall that in the SERVQUAL model customer expectations are strongly affected by four factors; these are word-of-mouth communications, personal needs, past experience and external communications to consumers. Two of these four factors directly relate to communication. However, only one factor (the external communications) is under the direct control of the service provider, the other three are not. Problems in the horizontal communications and 'over promising' have been called the major causes for gap Four.[11] In fact, five key reasons can be found.[12] These are:

■ Inadequate management of service promises;
■ Inadequate management of customer expectations;
■ Inadequate customer education;
■ Inadequate internal marketing communications; and
■ Differences in policies and procedures across countries, branches or units.

Table 11.2 contains an overview of these reasons and the possible way to solve them.

Table 11.2   Reasons and solutions to overcome communication problems in services

Reasons	Solutions	Examples
Inadequate management of service promises due to the vows made by salespeople, service employees and advertising or other ways of communication	Create effective services advertising; coordinate external communication; make realistic promises; offer services guarantees; keep customers informed about changes; negotiate unrealistic expectations; set prices to really match quality levels	Don't be too general; be specific in defining the service offering. Document performance. Present actual case histories; visualize the service encounter, have the external ad agencies inform the own company before the ad is launched, etc.
Inadequate management of customer expectations due to unrealistic expectations created and overpromises	Resetting expectations via offering choices; create tiered-value service offerings; communicate criteria for service effectiveness; negotiate unrealistic expectations	Develop new offerings at different times and costs having a different value to customers; have customers know how to evaluate the service offering's effectiveness; provide information and show that no value can be delivered at the price one is willing to pay
Inadequate customer education: customers do not know their role nor how to perform their role in the service encounter. This holds especially to high credence services or first-time buyers	Prepare customers for the service process; confirm performance to standards; clarify expectations after the sale; teach customers to avoid peak demand periods and seek slow periods	Tell customers exactly the script and what they are expected to do themselves; tell customers the service actions have been done (it is fixed/repaired); tell customers what is actually offered; offer customers better or cheaper services in off peak periods
Inadequate internal and horizontal marketing communications causes employees not to know their role nor how to perform in the service encounter	Create effective vertical communications; create effective horizontal communications; align back office personnel with external customers; create cross-functional teams	Use memos and newsletters for effective downward communications about new plans and sales actions; have effective and open communications between all functional departments (cross-functional teams are effective in that); have back office people meet the real customer (to avoid that internal rules and procedures set the tone instead of the external customer); external customers can be used to evaluate back office people

continued

	Table 11.2 *(cont.)*	
Reasons	*Solutions*	*Examples*
Differences in policies and procedures across countries, branches or units implies inconsistencies occur creating insecurity and a diffuse image of the company among customers	Communicate clearly when services are standardized or when they are adapted to local circumstances; control the image and service quality of the company in various markets carefully; building worldwide consistent brands requires a centralized organizational structure in communications (either by the company itself or by the agency taking care of the integrated communications strategy). However, such a strategy allows insufficient flexibility to adequately meet local needs.	Have clear guidelines on the positioning of the company in different markets; control it strictly; define differences beforehand and act accordingly; communicate that throughout company and explain; do comparative research on service quality in various markets and countries; McDonald's is a good example of having a consistent brand image worldwide combined with a considerable local autonomy for local advertising and sales promotions.[13]

Guidelines for Effective Services Communication

To be even more specific than in the previous section we developed Figure 11.6 showing some guidelines for effective services communication.

Because intangibility is a feature of services, the risk that goes with the purchase of a service is generally high. Although the service itself stays intangible, adding tangibles may help to decrease the risk perception of the consumer. The use of figures (for example; 'Forty-five per cent of our pupils pass the driving test in one try!') or the 'personification' of a service by using celebrities in promotions may be effective in creating consumer confidence. The protection offered by an insurance company can be made visible by using an umbrella in its promotion or logo. For services with a greater perceived risk and/or services with little search attributes, this is of major importance.

To find the right doctor, hairdresser or school, consumers will rely on the opinion of others who already have had experience with these service providers. In general, two communication techniques can be used for the purpose of stimulating word-of-mouth-communication; these are using satisfied consumers to provide testimonials or bloggers in the case the Internet, or the use of celebrities to affect the trend setters or opinion leaders. Both aim at enhancing credibility.

Some other guidelines for successful and effective communication in services are:

- Making services understandable;
- Having external communication directed to employees;
- Performing what has been promised;
- Stimulating word-of-mouth communications;

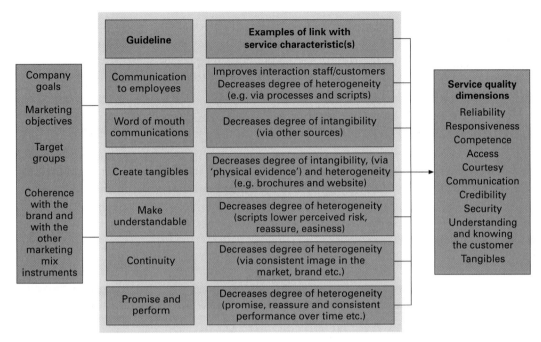

Figure 11.6 Guidelines for effective communication and service quality dimensions

■ Continuity in communication; and
■ Integrating communication with the other elements of the marketing mix.[14]

Some Basics

A service provider can create continuity by the frequent use of the brand name and same slogans, themes and symbols in advertising. Positioning a brand in the minds of the customers is a task typically performed by communication about the brand, e.g. by advertising. When service providers act globally, customers everywhere will know what the service will be about. A consistent service image can assist customers in developing consistent expectations about the services.

Continuous repetition of the symbols and slogans should help form the packaging of the service. Therefore, the ideal situation for a service provider is that a consumer is able to associate the advertisement with the service organization without mentioning the name of the organization in the advertisement. Continuous repetition can also result in a 'corporate personality';[15] in the long run helping the customers to see the organization as a person they know well and trust.

The relevance of external communications to one's own customers is clear. However, it also has a critical role to play to one's own employees. The acceptance of the role model's portrayed in advertisements can be increased by involving employees in the advertising campaign.

Word-of-mouth (WOM) communication is an intriguing phenomenon. It is the power of both satisfied and unsatisfied customers. The satisfied consumers are capable of spreading positive WOM regarding the services that they use and love. The acceptance of a new service depends on external marketing efforts for example advertising. However, beyond the early stage of the growth cycle of the product, the effectiveness diminishes and the information dissemination is dominated by word of mouth rather than by advertising.[16] The power of negative WOM relates to the spread of negative experiences. Weblogs can be very powerful in spreading negative WOM.

Communicating Services Online

Online advertising is becoming a serious rival to traditional sorts of communication. Google's new advertising service makes the Internet an even more valuable marketing medium. Worldwide ad revenue on the Internet grew by 21% in 2004. However, many big firms still allocate only 2–4% of their marketing budgets to the Internet, although it represents about 15% of consumers' media consumption.

SERVICE PRACTICE 11.4

The Online ad Attack[17]

Many young people already spend more time online than they do watching TV. The combined advertising revenues of Google and Yahoo! compete with the combined prime-time ad revenues of America's three big television networks, ABC, CBS and NBC.

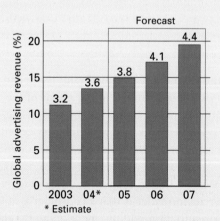

Reproduced by permission of ZenithOptimedia,
Advertising Expenditure Forecaster, April 2005

   Google has begun testing a new auction-based service for display advertising using keyword search-terms which deliver sponsored links to advertisers' websites. This has proved to be particularly lucrative. Advertisers like paid search because, unlike TV, they only pay for results; they are charged when someone clicks on one of their links.

   Both Google and Yahoo!, along with search-site rivals like Microsoft's MSN and Ask Jeeves, are developing much broader ranges of services. Google, for instance, already provides a service called Ad Sense. Ad Sense works rather like an advertising agency automatically placing sponsored links and other ads on third-party websites. Google splits the revenue with the owners of those websites, who can range from multinationals to individuals publishing blogs, as online journals are known.

Stages in the Buying Process

In Chapter 3, the process of buying services was broken down into three stages: pre-purchase, consumption and post-purchase stages. The communication objectives in all three phases differ. This is illustrated in Figure 11.7.

In the pre-purchase stage, consumers are not yet aware of the service provider as such or of its services, thus awareness has to be created. The quality image of the company may help in reducing the perceived risk associated with buying particular services for the first time. Besides the intrinsic image of the service itself, the corporate image of a service organization and the service industry can play an important role in 'tangibilizing' quality. Positive word-of-mouth communications is an excellent method of influencing the consumer's attitude here. In internationalizing services, applying the attributes of the country of origin that are associated with reliability may ease entry to that country.

During the consumption stage, front-office employees usually communicate with customers about the service to be provided and about the actions customers have to take. The image may clarify the script and the roles to be performed. The employees' way of communicating will affect the functional and relational quality. In the end, it will impact on customer satisfaction in a positive (or even in a negative) way.

In the post-purchase stage communication can, if necessary, help in reducing cognitive dissonance or dissatisfaction by reassuring customers that they have still bought the right service. During and after the consumption stage, consumers evaluate the performances of the service provider. These (past) experiences affect expectations and impact on decisions to continue the relationship or not. It may stimulate positive word-of-mouth communication, increase brand loyalty, repeat purchases and correct (if necessary) and strengthen the firm's quality image. It will add to deepening the relationship by giving rewards or incentives (such as air miles, coupons or discounts for loyal customers), or by enhancing commitment.

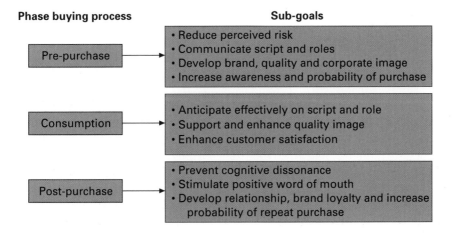

Figure 11.7 Sub-goals of communication per phase of the buying phase[18]

The Communications Mix

The exact content and implementation of a communication plan depends on the type of service and the goals set, but in general a communication plan involves the steps presented in Figure 11.8.

Although most tools are already known, we think that it is useful to pay attention to a number of components of the communications mix. We will focus not only on the tools themselves but also stress the clarity of the message and the effectiveness of the tools. First of all, it is always necessary to define the target audience and objectives as precisely as possible. These should be in line with the general objectives of the corporate and marketing strategy.

For customized or personalized services, *personal selling* is considered to be the backbone of communication in services marketing. Personal selling is expensive and can only be used where there are a limited number of customers; a small market; a high purchase price; a long-term obligation; where there needs to be adjustments to individual needs; where explanation is required by the customer; where there are negotiations about the price; and a strong relationship with the existing supplier. In one-on-one relationships, expectations can be managed before, during and after the service encounter. Personal contact offers the opportunity for a dialogue with customers.

Advertising can be used to influence or manage customer expectations, especially with respect to standard or core services aimed at mass markets. However with advertising it is important to consider the second target audience. Employees are responsible for determining quality and therefore have to be motivated and willing to deliver the service on levels as shown in the ads. It is essential to design clear messages in advertisements, because a message must meet several expectations of both customers and employees.

To a certain extent, *publicity and word-of-mouth* communication can be influenced by the effective use of public relations (PR). Publics embrace any group with common

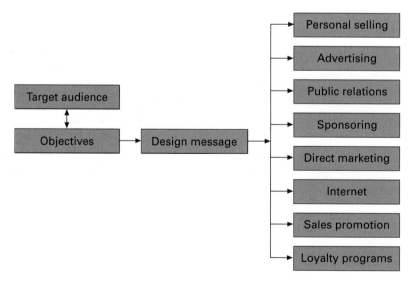

Figure 11.8 Steps in developing a communication plan: from target audience to determination of the communication mix

characteristics with which an organization needs to communicate, including the media, government bodies, financial institutions, pressure groups, etc. as well as customers and suppliers.[19] So, the core of the PR lies in promoting mutual understanding.

Sponsoring works indirectly. It does not aim to change the perception of the organization or service by means of a frontal attack. The effect of sponsoring on consumer behaviour is often determined by visibility. The effect should be measured by asking questions such as:

■ How long were names or logos visible in a TV sports programme, during a football game on TV?
■ Does someone in the target audience notice a logo on the background during a match or interview?
■ Does someone know which brand the sponsor is of a certain team or event? or
■ Is there any change in brand perception of the target group as a result of the connection of the sponsored party or event and the organization?

Direct marketing is a specialized form of marketing that aims at building and maintaining a relationship between a seller and a selected buyer. Direct marketing tactics are telemarketing, direct mail, mail order teleshopping and e-communication. Direct marketing can be applied both as a form of distribution and as a promotion tool.

The *Internet* fulfils three functions: it is a communication medium, an information medium and a distribution medium (see also Chapter 9). The communication function of Internet started with e-mail. The commercial applications of Internet communication such as advertising are increasing rapidly, as Service Practice 11.4 showed. Interestingly, this computer-based communication system is no longer a one-way communication, but an interactive (two-way) communication.

Sales promotion focusses on stimulating impulsive purchases and brand switching. It can be used effectively where services have a low perceived risk, which are bought frequently, which are familiar to the customer and which differentiate themselves from competing services by price.[20] In other words, sales promotion is mainly used for quite standard and/or core services.

Loyalty programmes are designed to enhance repeat purchases among current customers. What has been started as a frequency programme, as part of a sales promotion activity, is used more and more as a strategic device to create loyalty within the framework of a relationship marketing strategy. American Airlines was the first airline which started a frequent flyer programme, in 1981; the AAdvantage. Today, almost all airlines have such a programme. Consequently, the competitive advantage that American Airlines once had has disappeared. Such a programme was easy to imitate. If customer commitment to the brand is high, real brand loyalty will occur. So, loyalty programmes should add to increasing this commitment.

11.4 Pricing for Value

The word 'pricing' may be a little confusing, because the term 'price' is seldom used in the service sector. More often, we find terms like premium (insurance), rent (house), fare (railway), honorarium (legal advice), rate (tourist guide) and tariff (barber). Despite all these different names, the fact remains that a customer has to pay for most services. The marketing term 'price' will be our focus point, whereas service providers often use other terms. Each customer in fact needs to answer the question: does the overall value derived from my benefits of the service experience exceed the costs of acquiring these benefits?

Customer Value = Customer Benefits – Cost of Purchase

As the customer has to bear monetary cost (actual price to be paid) and non monetary costs (search time, hassle, collecting information, studying results of comparative testing, etc.), the cost of purchase is usually more than just the price.

This section hinges upon the spanning capability of the service provider on setting such prices as to attract customers and create value to the firm (in terms of financial goals) and to the customers (quality and satisfaction). To the extent that prices are based on company costs, internal-based assets as cost advantage in the servuction process or superior cost control systems are critical to the firm's financial performance, especially in the case of cost leaders. But also other firms have to accomplish selling prices being higher than costs to make a profit in the long run. Inside-out capabilities of strong financial management are relevant here as well.

Pricing and the Characteristics of Services

Due to all the characteristics of services, pricing is quite complex in the service business. That may explain why simple methods of pricing are often applied in pricing services. As in every business, pricing is an important management tool to achieve the objectives of the service organization. These strategic objectives partly determine the freedom a service provider has in setting the price (= tactics).[21]

SERVICE PRACTICE 11.5

Charges of Auditors

In a study among US certified public accounting (CPA) firms and their way of setting prices, it appeared that two thirds of the respondents either do not set pricing objectives or do so informally. Where objectives are established (in one-third of cases) the objectives fit a number of reasons, and include:

- ☐ short-term profits   84.3%;
- ☐ be competitive   81.2%;
- ☐ long-term profits   73.9%;
- ☐ attract new business   64.7%;
- ☐ encourage demand for services   44.8%;
- ☐ image   43.3%;
- ☐ market share   14.4%.[22]

In reality, many professional service providers base their price on the time and materials (covering the cost) involved in providing the service or they set a fixed fee. Only in a few instances has a 'pay-for-performance' (no win: no fee) pricing policy been applied.[23]

We will elaborate on that complexity by discussing some topics about services' transparency and the link between front and back office. Because of the intangible nature of services, it is important to introduce two concepts of transparency:

- The price transparency of services (which can be high or low); and
- The transparency of the service utility (which can also be high or low).[24]

The term 'transparency' embraces the customer's insight in the various cost and quality components. When both types of transparencies are low, the service provider has the most freedom to set prices. In the opposite position, where both features are high, customers will know everything about prices and quality. The Internet has enhanced the transparency of service pricing. Price differences must reflect differences in costs or quality. Otherwise, customers will switch to other, cheaper suppliers. As an example, market research may reveal that for certain people the safety image of an airline and not price is the main reason for buying a ticket. The marketers of Qantas, Australia's national airline, with a reputation as one of the safest airlines in the world, could use this in their advertising campaigns, although they have a deliberate strategy of not using safety in their advertising campaign as it would surely backfire if the airline did have an accident. It is important to remember that pricing in the service sector is less influenced by cost than it is by the customers' perception of 'value' or 'worth'.[25] In all instances, it is essential to realize that quality and price are linked together, indicating the value of the service to the customer. As such Qantas will use price to reflect their perceived high value.

Pricing is also complicated by the back office and front office processes that are often entangled. This applies in particular to service providers with high fixed costs. It complicates cost allocation and thus the attempt to specify exactly the cost price of individual items. Typically, when calculating correctly it may happen that one service (partly) subsidizes the other. Moreover, 'the intangible character of the service itself makes it difficult to understand what the package consists of'. Strange enough, even customers sometimes use the price as an indicator of quality (instead of the other way round), assuming 'a higher price must imply a better quality'.

Foundations of Pricing

There are many foundations of pricing. The determination of the final price will be done against the background of our view on market oriented services marketing management, namely the adequate managing in an organization of:

1 The concept of value;
2 The basic characteristics of services;
3 The organization's market orientation; and,
4 The organization's assets and capabilities.

In setting prices, knowledge of competitors' prices, customer preferences (especially 'what the market can bear'), the company's own corporate strategy and objectives, marketing

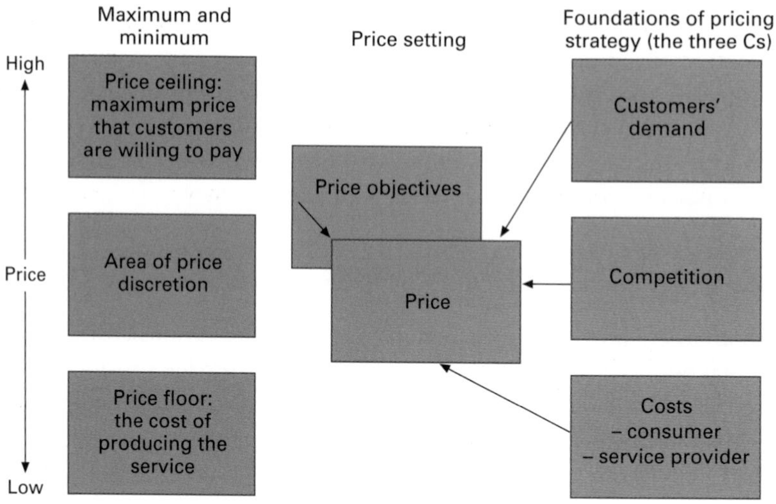

Figure 11.9   Key factors influencing price decisions

strategy and objectives and financial strategy and objectives but most of all customer's perceived value play a decisive role. Usually, the tripod – customers, costs and competition – forms the foundation of pricing. This is shown in Figure 11.9.

When a service provider wants to perform a market oriented pricing policy, the price must be based on the so-called pricing triangle:[26]

■ Customer demand or value to consumer;
■ Company cost; and
■ Competition, including substitution factors.

You may recall that this approach refers to both the competitor and the customer orientation which are part of an organization's market orientation. These three Cs – the customers' demand schedule, the cost function and the competitors' price – often are combined to set the final price. So, we will examine this combined method at first to show you the complexity of pricing in services. Later on, we will focus on each of the three components separately. Only when a service provider has a clear understanding of these three fundamentals can the limits of the field within which the service provider has to set his price be defined roughly. A possible upper limit of price can be determined by a clear understanding of how demand has developed in the past, whereas the lower limit of the price is determined by the organization's costs. The final price must be set between these limits.

Value-Based Pricing

Value-based pricing is highly valued by many service providers intending to apply it in today's competitive markets. It is also the most difficult pricing policy to apply. Nevertheless, if you can master value-based pricing, then you have created a competitive advantage. Then you have shown how to master the market oriented way of pricing and creating value to the customer. Basically, this pricing policy is based upon the idea of 'what is the customer willing to pay for this particular service?'.

Value may have different meanings for different groups of customers. For a customer, the value of a trip depends strongly on the reason for that trip. A honeymoon will be more valuable to a consumer than a business trip. This point of view is therefore not based on costs but on the value of a service as perceived by a customer. Zeithaml gives the following definition of 'value':[27]

■ Value is a low price;
■ Value is what is desired;
■ Value is quality, that I get for the price; and
■ Value depends on what I give and what I sacrifice.

In many cases, value is a very personal reflection of what people assess as good or bad. So value, or what one is willing to pay, is very subjective. It may even deviate from actual costs, for instance. It is critical to outweigh cost by adding benefits.[28]

Value-based pricing strategies can be attractive to service providers given that they know their costs, have efficient operations, provide excellent service and the service is hard to assess by the customer in every detail. Lovelock developed the notion of 'net value' as the difference between all perceived benefits minus the perceived costs,[29] including non monetary costs. The perceived benefits may increase or decrease as the (social) image is positive or negative.

You may recall from Chapters 3 and 6 that we have identified four types of customers and service providers in the B2B sector. These four different customers all want to get a particular value from their suppliers, but 'need a different price'. In case of Vendors, a low or the lowest price must be the case. Game changers may charge a premium price. Specialists may charge a high but acceptable price, while Total solutions providers may charge a high but competitive price to their customers.[30]

Berry and Yadav suggest 'three distinct but related pricing strategies for capturing and communicating the value of a service:

■ Satisfaction-based;
■ Relationship-based; and
■ Efficiency pricing'.[31]

Each of these pricing strategies utilizes one or more of the concepts to be discussed in this chapter. The difference, however, is the starting point, which is now value, meaning benefits for 'burdens endured' (monetary and non-monetary costs). In this sense, marketing thinking is shifting from trying to maximize the service firm's profit from each transaction to maximizing the mutual profit from each relationship.[32] These value strategies can be either applied separately or in a combination. They are explained in Table 11.3.

Value: Quality, Cost and Price

The transcendent vision of quality in Chapter 5 involves high quality costs. Quality viewed from this angle is defined as 'the best' or 'very good'. But you may question whether this view

Table 11.3 **Pricing strategies for capturing and communicating the value of a service: satisfaction-based, relationship, and efficiency pricing.**

Type	Focus	Clarification
Satisfaction-based pricing Forms of benefit pricing include: ● success-fee pricing, ● incentive pricing ● flat pricing	Alleviate uncertainty (and perceived risk) To allow people and businesses to do business in a 'one-off' fashion Apply success-fee pricing It is the service provider that shares in the benefits for its client	Service guarantees, for example promising delivery within a certain time or return of money if the buyer is not satisfied with the performance. Success-fee pricing: an IT-consultant or lease company could link its (increased) price – according to some agreed formula – to demonstrated results in performance and/or savings. Health insurance policies stimulate customers to participate in activities (e.g. prevention visit or exercising programmes) or non participating (e.g. no smoking of cigarettes).
Relationship pricing	Enter into, maintain and enhance the relationship with (potential) profitable clients Reward long-term clients with lower tariffs and/or additional service Key idea is to convert 'shoppers' into 'loyals' by adding (relevant) value to the client	As customer relationships become more remunerative over time, this method decreases the substantial costs connected with acquisition of new customers. To optimize profit, it is crucial to base price considerations, manage costs and concentrate efforts of all parties within the firm on those customers offering the best potential profit over the relationship's lifetime. Long-term contracts and/or price bundling are at the core of relationship pricing. Some services are billed as a lump sum at the start or at intervals. These services are very attractive because the fee is paid before the service is performed.
Efficiency pricing	Understanding, managing and reducing costs	To be effective, the leaner cost structure must be difficult to imitate in the short term. Furthermore, cost savings passed on to customers must genuinely enhance their value perceptions. Cost trimming that results in less expensive but unsatisfactory service will not be successful.

Source: Berry and Yadav, 1996.

is the right one. We hold a value-based quality orientation implies lower costs. Value-based pricing mostly refers to choices – whether the increase in quality is still worth the effort in the eyes of the buyer. Here, the trade-off is between quality and price. Striving for excellent quality implies costs which should be incorporated in the price. Thus, focussing on higher quality often leads to price increases or rates higher than those of the competition. As a consequence, it creates openings for limited service providers ('no frills') in mature markets.

The ultimate goal of quality control and quality cost reporting is optimizing total quality costs. How this should be obtained is not always clear. Roughly speaking, most of the literature distinguishes between two basic views on the optimum level of quality costs:[33]

■ One school of thought favours the idea that the optimum level of quality costs is a trade-off between prevention costs and assurance costs, on the one hand, and failure costs, on the other hand; whereas

■ The other school of thought believes the optimum level can be achieved by zero defects (high costs on prevention, however high costs with after sales services and retention). Shortcomings detected at an early stage entail fewer expenses for the organization than quality shortcomings showing up at a later stage during the service delivery. The conclusion is that by reserving more financial resources for prevention activities, not only inspection but also internal and external costs may fall (and therefore rates can be decreased).

Customers' Demand

For a service provider, it is desirable but also very difficult to understand exactly if and how responsive demand would be to a change in price. It takes a lot of research to get a clear understanding of consumers' behaviour. This research is not feasible or profitable for many small service providers. Subjective estimation of customers' *price sensitivity* may solve this problem. Also, adding services focussing on aspects that enlarge personal loyalty via personal contacts often result in inelastic behaviour. If prices are somewhat lower elsewhere, customers won't drop the supplier. Then loyalty functions as a kind of buffer to avoid switching. However, having insight into the degree of price elasticity of demand for a particular service is a must for any market-oriented organization. If a service is elastic, a relatively small price decrease leads to a substantial increase in demand for that service. A price increase results in a relatively large drop in demand for this service.

$$E(p) = \frac{\% \text{ Change in quantity demanded}}{\% \text{ Change in price}}$$

Price elasticity becomes even more relevant in the case of standard core services without too many complexities for the customer. Customers can compare the service with competitors' offers and the number of substitutes for the service is larger than for a customized augmented service. In general, we assume that price elasticity of a service increases as: the service is more a standard service (a 'commodity'); the service includes not too many customized augmented services; the number of substitutes is larger; and/or the price covers a relatively larger share of income per household. Having insight in the price elasticity of the various market segments and demand fluctuations, which can be predictable or random, the service provider is able to increase its ability to manage demand and supply.

The *level capacity strategy* aims at producing a better match between demand and supply by affecting demand. For years, the tourist industry has been used to regulating demand. Low prices are set to attract tourists during off-peak periods, whereas during peak periods the price is much higher. The use of different pricing strategies is just one tool of the level-capacity strategy the service provider can apply. The other 'tools' include:

■ Differential pricing (based on different cost prices, for example, by providing augmented services along with the standard service);

■ Discriminatory pricing (the same service is sold at different prices which are not based on similar differences in costs);

■ Maintain the price, but develop waiting lists/reservation systems, which can shift demand from peak to off-peak periods;

■ Develop complementary services, which will entice customers to purchase more from the same organization; and/or

■ Price bundling.[34]

Price bundling may occur in a number of forms. If bundling occurs to such an extent that the services cannot be bought separately, it is pure bundling. One may think of a tailormade augmented service belonging to a core service. Both services are sold as a package and, therefore, cannot be bought separately. Mixed bundling occurs when services can be bought as a package but also separately. Mixed bundling takes two forms: mixed leader and mixed joint bundling.

Mixed leader bundling means that a buyer gets a discount off the price of a second service, if this is bought together with a leader service. Mixed-joint bundling occurs when the package price is lower than the total price of the individual services. Customers do not know exactly where the price difference is to be found and it is, in fact, irrelevant to them. The extent to which this form of bundling really works depends largely on economies of scale, which can be accomplished by stimulating demand and, of course, on how consumers value the bundling (and do not consider it as an unattractive form of cross-selling).

With regard to the price of a service bundle, consumers benefit from a bigger search efficiency when a service bundle is characterized by search attributes and demand is elastic. There is no need for the customer to search after two separate services. Services that are characterized by experience and credence attributes will, if bundled, profit from the service provider's images – provided that the image is positive. In addition, price elasticity of a service determines the choice of the type of price bundling (mixed leader or mixed joint). To choose the mixed leader bundle, the leader service must be elastic. To choose the mixed joint bundle, demand for both services must be elastic.

Recently, we have seen successful initiatives for *unbundling*. Unbundling air travel means that catering and newspapers are not available in the plane or should be paid for separately. Decoupling financial services implies that a bank is no longer cross-subsidizing its products. So, the price of providing payment transactions will be not subsidized by the income of investment products. An Internet bank client who also wants to receive printed statements by mail will have to pay for this service. At the same time, we observe profitable initiatives in the same industries to bundle services. For example, Internet-based travel companies that offer travel packages for various destinations. Flight, hotel and rent-a-car are combined in one service offering.

In order to optimize profit, the pricing strategies discussed are most profitable if directed towards clearly defined market segments. *Segmented pricing* looks first and foremost at the question whether different market segments are willing to pay different prices. Segmented pricing and level capacity are both strategies aiming at the same area: matching supply and demand by effectively applying the price instrument. In employing the price differentiation tool, marketers need to be careful. Then, segments need not only be defined clearly; they also have to be separated. Bateson distinguishes six conditions to be fulfilled if a firm wants to apply price differentiation and discrimination successfully.[35] These criteria also indicate that separating the segments (and keeping them separated) is not an easy task. These are:

- Different groups of buyers must value the service differently and respond differently to price;
- Management should be able to identify the segments and approach these segments with various tariffs;
- Buyers should not have access to lower or higher segments;
- The size of the segment should be large enough;
- The costs of price differentiation (or price discrimination) must not be higher than the expected additional revenues; and
- Price differentiation (or price discrimination) should not be confusing to the potential buyers.

For service industries with high fixed costs, such as transport, hotel, amusement parks, cinemas and hospitals, segmented pricing is often essential. Within the airline industry, it is common knowledge that business travellers prefer to return home before the weekend or at least on a Saturday. For that reason, most airlines offer substantial lower rates to travellers if they include a Saturday night in their journey when applying segmented pricing. Airlines and hotels, utilizing pricing tactics, differentiate distinctly between 'holiday passengers' and business travellers. Holiday or leisure travellers are often prepared to make advance commitments, accept varying quality levels, are quite flexible in location and destination, are indifferent to prestige, have a high price elasticity and stay for a long time.[36] The opposite holds for most business travellers. However, exceptions to the rule always exist and require tailor made offerings.

Segmented pricing enables a company to develop profitable pricing strategies. Potential customers who are less price sensitive or more costly to serve, or less well served by competitors, can be charged more without the loss of buyers who the firm can serve more profitably at a lower price. The pricing tactics are based on the following eight segmentation variables:[37]

- Buyer identification;
- Purchase location;
- Time of purchase;
- Purchase quantity;
- Service design;
- Service bundling;
- Metering; and
- Membership.

Table 11.4 considers various tactics of effective segmented pricing.

	Table 11.4 Effective segmented pricing tactics	
Pricing tactic	*Description*	*Example*
Buyer identification	The challenge here is to obtain information about the segments and to identify the (prospective) buyer in many respects. Sometimes, segmenting is easy. Sound marketing research is needed to identify price sensitive market segments. This aims at inducing buyers of any product or service to reveal their price sensitivities. Sometimes, salespeople are in the best position to judge the proper tariff in a sales talk. Within the limits set by management, they then evaluate the well-known price affecting factors, such as demand, competition and costs, and set the final charge. For barbers, simple observation and experience are an easy guideline. In other service industries, buyer identification is not so easy.	Barbers charge different prices for short and long hair because long hair is usually more difficult to cut (price segmenting in combination with activity based pricing). They also cut children's hair at substantially lower rates because parents view home haircuts as acceptable alternatives to costly barber cuts for their children (price segmenting under influence of substitution factors; activity-based pricing would lead to a price that is too high). Examples include (after sales) service contracts and consumer services where management has delegated some authority regarding pricing to contact personnel.
Purchase location	In a wide range of service industries it is common practice to charge different prices at different locations. Client switching from the higher price to the lower price location is minimized by differences in the convenience, ambience or prestige value of different locations. Many countries put legal constraints on geographical price differences. Price dumping – offering services under the integral cost price – typically aimed to undercut local suppliers, is forbidden in most countries.	In some countries, dentists, doctors and lawyers tend to set prices according to their clients' price sensitivity. A doctor treating patients in a hospital may demand a different remuneration from a patient in the doctor's private clinic. In the lodging industry, hotels may offer rooms – which are of the same size or even larger – outside the main building at lower rates.
Time of purchase	Customers in different markets may buy at different times. Firms use this information for pricing by time of purchase. The purpose is to attract price sensitive people to use seats or beds otherwise unoccupied. In this context, fixed capacity costs are important for setting prices at peak times. However, as the cost of capacity up to the amount used at peak times is mostly unavoidable, fixed capacity costs should be ignored	Theatres segment their markets by offering midday matinées at deep discounts. Chinese restaurants in residential areas have cheap lunches on their menu while having the same food priced higher during dinner time. Tickets on airlines and railways are less expensive during off-peak times. Hotels in city centres offer weekend packages to families or couples at substantially lower rates than during week days.

	when determining prices in non peak periods. In non peak periods, variable operating costs, such as fuel for aircraft, food ingredients for restaurants electricity and cleaning costs after a film performance or a stay at a hotel, should be used in profitable decision making.	
Purchase quantity	Quantity discount tactics are commonly used in the service sector and include volume discounts, order discounts, step or block discounts and two-part pricing: ● volume discounts are aimed at retaining business of large customers and promoting volume; ● order discounts encourage customers to place few (infrequent) large orders instead of small (frequent) orders; ● step or block discounts seduce customers to buy more services as every next block of volume is bought at a lower price (these discounts do not apply to the total quantity purchased); ● two-part pricing consists of separate charges to consume a single service. In each of these cases, heavy users pay less than do light users for the same service since the fixed price is spread over time.	Tour operators purchasing high volumes of rooms in hotels and seats in aircrafts are naturally offered lower rates than ordinary people renting one room or buying a few tickets. Banks quote big enterprises lower interest rates for their loans than small businesses or consumers. Examples of two-part pricing include: amusement parks sometimes have an entry fee plus a ticket charge for each ride (at i.e. the incremental costs), car rental companies have a daily rate plus a mileage charge, and racket clubs have an annual membership plus charge on court time.
Service design	Some of the most effective segmentation strategies involve offering different versions of the service with hardly any or no difference in production costs. In particular, with standardized or semi-standardized services, there is frequently little or no cost difference in the different versions.	Segmenting by service design is easy when selling services such as air travel, because the seller can easily limit resale of the service. If airline tickets were not issued to specific passengers, firms would soon spring up to buy discounted tickets in advance for resale to businessmen closer to departure times.
Service bundling	Both customers and suppliers can benefit from bundling. The price of the bundled service should be (perceived as) lower than the sum of the separate items. Price and convenience are both significant benefits to the purchaser. The service provider may sell more without bundling, optimize its yield	Manufacturers or retailers bundle goods with (free) services. Shopping malls offer free parking for one hour. Restaurants combine menu items into fixed price dinners. Concert halls bundle diverse concerts into season subscription tickets.

continued

	Table 11.4 (*cont.*)	
Pricing tactic	*Description*	*Example*
	management and also enjoy the benefit of convenience. Generally, bundling is optional. Thus, customers can purchase the service also separately, although at a higher total price.	
Metering	Metering segments buyers by useage. By offering car rentals with metering, customers are attracted by hiring a car for convenience rather than for long distance trips.	Free mileage offerings typically attract a category of drivers that travel longer distances.
Membership	At the scale of temporary versus permanent relations between clients and organizations in Chapter 2, membership is one of the most permanent. Members of all kinds of clubs, profit and non profit organizations pay their fee periodically. Frequently, the core service is free. Members then have to pay for additional services in full or may obtain them at a lower rate. The attraction for the service provider lies in coverage of the (fixed) costs.	In some instances, membership of an organization features privileges such as 'ensured' tickets for a concert or sports event.

Source: Adopted from Nagle, 1986, pp. 156–162.

The challenge for the supplier is to find a homogeneous group among the prospects that is large enough to justify each of the pricing tactics.

To understand the effects of price fluctuations on revenues, the values of ARGE might be helpful. ARGE stands for 'asset revenue-generating efficiency' and measures the extent to which the organization's assets are achieving their full revenue-generating potential.[38] The ARGE index is composed of the yield percentage and the occupancy rate. The yield percentage reflects the extent to which the maximum price is received. To compute this percentage, the actual price is divided by the maximum price. The maximum price can be seen as the highest posted price. If a group is offered a 20% discount off the maximum price, the yield percentage is 80% or 0.8. Of course, the yield percentage can only be computed if the highest posted price is known.

The second component, the occupancy rate, reflects the extent to which total capacity is used. If the capacity utilization rate is 50% or 0.5, only half of the hotel beds, or seats are sold. Such occupancy rates are important in cost accounting, setting prices and calculating break-even points. There are three ways to derive an index of ARGE (see Figure 11.10).

If a service provider has a number of options, the ARGE index may be useful to make the right choice. Of course, a service provider has to consider other variables as well, for instance: the costs incurred by the consumer should be the same; the relationship between

$$ARGE = \text{Yield percentage} \times \text{occupancy rate} \ (\times\ 100\%)$$

$$ARGE = \frac{\text{Actual selling price}}{\text{Maximum selling price}} \times \frac{\text{Sold capacity}}{\text{Total capacity}}$$

$$ARGE = \frac{\text{Total revenues}}{\text{Theoretical maximum revenues}} \times 100\%$$

Figure 11.10 Three ways to calculate ARGE

direct and indirect costs of the service provider; and the relationship between total costs and revenues of the service provider.

Cost of Service Providers

This section refers to some specific assets and capabilities of market oriented service organizations in setting prices. You may recall that cost refers to the cost leadership strategy part of market orientation: own cost compared to competitors'. Competitive cost advantages are essential to those service providers offering standard services. The service provider can reduce (service) unit costs through the efficient organization of its internal structure (the inside-out capabilities of good operations management expertise). It can do so by organizing its operations to exploit economies of scope, scale and experience. Controlling costs is an ongoing activity in any successful company (the internal-based assets of superior cost control systems and cost advantages in the servuction process). Controlling the business must be a continuing process because various parties are involved, including both employees and external suppliers, who have a vested interest in seeing certain costs rise.[39] Three pricing methods are often used in services in which different kinds of 'costs' play a role:

■ Cost-plus pricing;
■ Rate of return pricing; and
■ Direct costing.

In *cost-plus pricing*, the firm determines the price by adding a (standard) mark-up to their costs (full costs or a part of all costs). Thus, the company cost determines the price, ignoring demand and competition. The aim of *rate of return pricing* or target return pricing is to achieve a given rate of return on investments (ROI) or assets.[40] *Direct costing* centres on the difference between the selling price and direct costs, called the contribution margin. This margin is used to see whether a particular selling price contributes to cover the direct costs. If this is the case in the short run, the order can be accepted. This basis of setting prices is often referred to as 'marginal costing'. Direct costing is a very specific method not really suited for calculating selling prices in general. In the servuction processes a lot of activities have to be performed where both parties interact. We have said before that may be difficult to allocate cost properly and that the distinctions of fixed/variable or direct/indirect do not solve all those problems. However, when we analyse the service firms' activities we may get a better hold on the cost involved. *Activity-based costing* (ABC) is a useful technique here. ABC differs from other costing systems in its allocation of indirect costs.[41] ABC not only results in more accurate cost prices but also provides better insight into the cost structure as well as into the cost-causing factors. Information about these cost-drivers is essential in determining whether to separate or bundle standard services and customized augmented services. Putting it simply, ABC traces the costs of services through all the service-generating activities. This method relates activities to costs. Then, it becomes important to have an adequate insight in those activities leading to the strategic cost drivers in the value chain.[42] In addition, ABC helps the marketer to apply bundling or unbundling services more profitably.

Because ABC is based on activities, costs are also collected per activity. These activities are the key in this approach to cost calculation. On the basis of a thorough analysis of the activities involved in producing a service, dynamic production processes of services can be mapped. Expensive activities may be reconsidered: is it still necessary to perform them ourselves or at all? Should they be priced differently? Analysing and reconsidering activities related to the production of the service (especially from an IT perspective) is called 'business process redesign'.

For a better understanding of the impact of total costs on prices, examining the costs incurred by the service provider and the costs incurred by the customer are both necessary.

Customers' Costs

As said, consumers of a service face more costs than just monetary costs. This is particularly so when it concerns services requiring the presence of a customer, services directed at the customer as a person and services of which the level of participation intensity can be classified as high (or active). The single fact that a customer needs to be present during a service delivery requires cost and effort on the consumer's side, in order to be present at the location where the service is delivered. Therefore, in determining consumer costs, a service provider has to take into account more than just its own financial costs. Besides monetary costs, the following non monetary costs may be incremental:

- Opportunity costs;
- Physical costs;
- Sensory costs; and
- Psychic or mental costs.[43]

Opportunity costs are the 'costs of the alternative foregone'. In money terms, it may be, e.g. a new car instead of a holiday abroad; a night at the theatre instead of a dinner in a restaurant. Time costs incur during the total consumption process. In other words, they are part of the opportunity costs, expressing that a customer is bound by time during consumption and therefore must leave other alternatives.

Physical costs occur when a consumer has to make physical efforts to make use of a service. These costs are sometimes hard to measure, because it is difficult to draw a line between physical effort and physical relaxation (a benefit).

Sensory costs are all inconveniences perceived by our sense organs throughout the service delivery. We can think of the smell of a hospital, exposure to draught, cold or heat. Irritating colours or noise nuisance are also included. Costs are closely connected with feelings of insecurity, which increase the perceived risk to such an extent that they are called mental costs. A consumer may be confronted with these costs before, during or after the service delivery.

A service provider must be alert to the *psychic or mental cost*, because consumers may decide not to use the service anymore based on these personal costs that are hard to grasp. Reducing perceived risk is critical again, but now in respect of these kinds of cost.

All these costs should be taken into account to determine the total costs the customer has to incur to get a particular value. This is particularly true when a service provider may economize his own costs, while (partly) shifting them on to the customer. Then the question is whether a consumer is willing to pay for it, considering the new quality–price relationship. The consumers themselves also have to invest in the service delivery.

Competition and Substitution

In setting prices, competitors also must be taken into account. Thus, competition and substitution are the third pillar of pricing. Here, we recall that part of our concept of market orientation consists of competitor orientation: their prices, offerings and thus their value relative to the value we offer customers.

To be able to determine the upper limit of prices, those suppliers that customers perceive as competitors must be identified. The identification may take place in terms of the service offered or the needs that the service fulfils as perceived by the customer. Starting from positioning models, competition occurs when the same service is offered at the same level of standardization and complexity. Examples of price setting of standardized services are 'going-rate pricing' or 'me-too pricing'. In these markets, where services are rather homogeneous and the number of suppliers is high, service providers cannot afford to price higher or lower. A higher price will result in a loss of revenue, whereas a lower price will lead to an unintended price war.

In services business, 'make or buy decisions' are often at stake. The purchaser's total monetary and non monetary costs of substitution by doing it oneself instead of buying the service should be taken as a benchmark in pricing. Parents may decide to cut their children's hair. The prices of gardeners, mutual funds and take-away food are also frequently compared with do-it-yourself. The increase of leisure time, the application of new technology in the garden, kitchen and online information to enhance stock-picking, may involve important changes for the respective service providers.

In this situation, 'competitive bidding' is often used as a pricing method. A buyer compares competitors' offers and prices and will then make a choice. A special form of competitive bidding is sealed bid pricing. This method is, for instance, mandatory for public funded services contracts. Tender documents of World Bank or EU contracts indicate, normally, the weight of prices within the overall judgement of the service offer.

Combined Pricing Strategies for Creating Value during a Service's Life Cycle

A service passes through four phases of the life cycle: development, growth, maturity and decline. Applying this knowledge to pricing services produces the following tips for improving profitable decision making on pricing over the service life cycle. At the end of this section we return to where we started, namely by showing how relevant the combination of the three Cs of pricing is in delivering value and in setting the upper and lower limit of the prices (see also Figure 11.9).

Relative product advantage and competitive advantage are critical in setting the price when launching new services. In other words if a new service has a substantial advantage in both areas there is no reason for a company to price its services (too) low. Moreover, during the first phase of market development, buyers are to a great extent price insensitive because they are not aware of the service benefits. Three pricing practices (value informed pricing, information on costs, competition) may help the firm to understand the boundaries of price of the price discretion.[44] This is shown in Table 11.5.

The more the service differs from that of the competition, and the more potential customers view the advantages of the new services valuable, the more space to ask for a high tariff.[45] Innovators are usually not that price sensitive. Price sensitivity can also be quite low in this phase because consumers are not fully aware of the service benefits. This impacts on the decision whether a skimming or penetration strategy should be applied.

A *market skimming* strategy is remunerative if there are clearly divided sizeable segments that value the service more highly than other segments. This price discrimination or price differentiation approach allows the firm to reap early profits. As imitation is relatively easy in most service industries, penetration pricing can be used quickly to obtain a large market share before competitors wake up. *Market penetration* pricing is an appropriate policy for establishing and exploiting industry-wide cost leadership. In markets which are not price sensitive, penetration pricing will not enable a firm to gain enough of a share to achieve or

Table 11.5 Three pricing practices to set the boundaries of prices	
Pricing practice	*Explanation of the pricing practice*
Value informed pricing	Compare the advantages of the service to the competitors' services in terms of the customer's perceived value, the advantages of the new service offered to the customer, the balance between advantages of the service and price, the advantages of the service compared to substitute services
Information on costs	Possess the variable costs of the service; know the price necessary for break-even; calculate the investments in the new service; beware of the share of fixed costs in total cost
Competition informed pricing	Know the price of competitor services, the competitor's current price strategy, the estimation of competitor's strengths to react, the market structure (number and strength of competitors, the degree of competition on the market, the competitive advantages of competitors on the market)

exploit a cost advantage. In those circumstances, neutral pricing is the most appropriate pricing strategy. At the same time, this strategy can still be quite consistent with the successful chasing of cost leadership.[46] Sometimes, penetration pricing results in loss leading pricing. Of course, loss leading pricing can be only applied in the short term. Typically, it aims at building a defensible market share or cross-selling other services. Penetration is not the right strategy if the real demand (during peak times or more permanently) is larger than anticipated. Often, at this initial stage, operational systems cannot handle the demand. In conclusion, there is generally no need to apply penetration pricing, other than in the case of preventing competitors entering the market or enlarging their market share.

Promotion, personal experiences or feedback from the first users (innovators) spread the information about the service and its features more broadly. Combined with the entrance of new – previously lagging – large competitors, prices tend to be from stable downwards. In particular, this is true if market growth is limited, capacity constraints are limited and buyers are price sensitive. However, adding features, auxiliary services and differentiating the core service from competitors may still strengthen the profit margins during this phase.

By now, repeat sales are material for the cash flow. Most buyers are familiar with the service. In industrialized countries, many service industries operate in *mature markets*. Banks, insurance companies, health services and lodging are all facing saturated demand and rivalry. In a mature market, the drive towards lower prices, a lower cost base and a more diverse supply will need an integrated marketing mix approach in order to create lasting relationships, to avoid diffuse images and to protect the market share of the established firm. Relationships and loyalty may avoid cut-throat competition and switching.

During the final phase of *decline*, suppliers are leaving the battlefield. The need to reduce prices further now depends heavily on the remaining competition, the demand and the internal cost structure of the firm. In most service industries, flexibility at the supply side is now a necessary element to meet demand and keep costs low.

Final Remarks on the Cs of Pricing

For every organization it is important to avoid setting prices too high or too low. Cost informed pricing helps to understand the lower boundary of the price discretion. This is 'best practice' when the competition is strong and 'bad practice' when the competitive intensity is low. Competition informed pricing helps to understand the upper limit of the price discretion. This applies especially when relative service advantage is low. If relative advantage is high, competition oriented pricing can be considered 'bad practice'. Like competition informed pricing, value informed pricing provides a better understanding of the price ceiling.

As a result of competition and high price elasticity, the price of standard services is based mainly on the company's costs including, among others, full costing, activity-based costing, mark-up (cost-plus) pricing and target return pricing. Despite their single focus on costs, the two last mentioned methods are still used frequently in the service sector. These pricing methods give the company an initial impression about the final price. However, if more services are added, there is more room in price setting. If a customized augmented service offered by Game changers leads to a high degree of differentiation, even a more than proportional increase in price is possible. Mostly, adding (peripheral) services means a less transparent price for the buyer. Trust in the service provider is, however, more than necessary; otherwise the customer will not perceive a fair price and will feel cheated. A good example of an open (= transparent) price strategy (and also benefit driven pricing incentives to the client) is Lease Plan, a leasing company operating predominantly in Europe and Australia, offering fixed operational leasing rates for cars. By keeping track of all costs, Lease Plan will return money to customers when actual costs are lower than the projected costs. This approach stimulates organizations – as it concerns mainly company cars – to economize in the usage of their cars. Thrifty drivers then contribute to the credit notes their companies are receiving from the leasing company. This open method of calculation has proved to be a successful marketing tool in the international expansion of Lease Plan.

For internationally oriented service firms, pricing is mostly determined locally. *The Economist*'s annual 'Big Mac' comparison, indicating the value of currencies, is a good example of this. However, globalization of demand and supply, and the growth of the World Wide Web make prices increasingly comparable and thus transparent. Service firms feel this impact on their business. Moreover, in international business, transfer pricing is a hot issue, next to the risks incurred in fluctuations in exchange rates.[47] Reasons are the policy of expansion of multinationals and the continuing economic uncertainty. Transfer pricing is not only a tax issue but also a means to evaluate business units on their performance and to motivate management. In addition it appears that management control systems (and as a consequence transfer pricing systems) should be in line with the structure of an organization. This helps determining how transfer prices are computed as well as determining to which country sales and profits should be assigned when a subsidiary in country A gets a job to be performed in country B where the company also has a subsidiary. Apart from international transfer pricing, the same question arises when two business units or subsidiaries within one country are dealing with each other. Service firms may choose to split fees through the regular accounting system or by allocating a service fee of e.g. 10% to the subsidiaries initiating or hosting the deal (or project). They believe this direct approach is often more effective than dividing sales and profits in a detailed way between these units (for instance based on 'hours spent on the job'). In these matters, it is imperative to remember that the service firm still pays full attention to the customer and does not forget the customer here by paying too much attention to the internal accounting.

Summary

Organizing and managing the service experience that drives client value should be used to distinguish a company from its competitors. Distribution, communication and pricing are completing the tools – the marketing-mix – which a service provider has at its disposal to create an excellent service experience. Value can be created via service offerings based on a cost leadership or a differentiation strategy; both topics are parts of our definition of market orientation. Phrased differently, distribution, communication and pricing are part of a set of assets and capabilities service organizations posses to create value to its stakeholders. In this chapter we focussed on elements of all four capabilities of market oriented service organizations and almost all of the assets, as shown in Table 11.6.

Table 11.6	Assets and capabilities of market oriented service organizations	
Section on	*Assets*	*Capabilities*
Distribution	Distribution or supply chain assets (all)	Networking capabilities (especially those on managing relationships with suppliers)
Communication	Customer-based assets (image, reputation relations)	Outside-in capabilities and those spanning capabilities referring to internal communication
Pricing	Internal-based assets of cost advantage in servuction processes and superior cost control systems	Spanning capabilities of setting good prices and inside-out capabilities referring to good financial management

The specific characteristics of services raise some specific opportunities and threats with respect to distributing, communicating and pricing services. On the one hand, the non storability of services seems to cause a serious problem. On the other hand, the direct contact between customer and service provider can also be regarded as an opportunity since there is hardly any need to think about 'storing services'. The intangibility of services may create a high perceived risk. Communication can be used to decrease that perceived risk tremendously. Overpromising can be a disaster, however. The servuction process with its back and front office and consumer participation makes a proper cost allocation quite difficult. It also offers the opportunity to use activity-based costing to detect the real cost drivers among the monetary and non-on monetary cost involved in setting prices and creating value.

Organizing the distribution of services is a central issue. This refers to the delivery of services: making them available at a particular place in the local environment, domestically or internationally. In distributing services, a company should answer the question: 'who travels to whom?' The answer determines to a great extent the importance of the location decision to the service provider which, in turn, affects the final servicescape characteristics, especially the atmospherics. Usually, this place is a physical place. Changes in information technology offer opportunities to distribute services in such a way that the customer does not always need to be physically present in delivering services, nor the service provider. Especially in the delivery of services internationally, this may prove to be an attractive idea. Many forms of direct and indirect distribution may occur simultaneously (and may be a source of potential conflict).

Distribution strategies can be categorized by the well-known concepts of intensive, selective and exclusive distribution which hold for convenience, shopping and speciality services. This distinction can be applied also to our typology of standard core services, standard augmented services, customized core services and customized augmented services. In turn, it was shown how this coincides with the distinction between single and multisite, single and multiservice and single and multisegment distribution strategies. In practice, these purely strategic alternatives present themselves in a hybrid form. They can be linked to the four service strategies from the famous Ansoff matrix. Market penetration strategies and multisite are then combined, while service and market development strategies go along with multiservice strategies and, respectively, multisegment strategies. Diversification occurs when a combination of these strategies is looked for. Changing positions in this figure can be dangerous when it results in creating a more diffuse image of the service provider that is not clear to the customer.

Communication can play a major role: in reducing perceived risk, in providing clarity about the roles to be played by customers and employees in service encounters, in getting the necessary information from customers about their needs, in creating the desired image, in attracting the right employees, in gaining sales, etc. Many topics about information are closely linked to quality issues. That is why we made explicit links between communication and the dimensions of service quality. Not only is external communication to customers relevant but also the internal communication within the service organization (to motivate employees). Often, external communication is also aimed at influencing employees.

Many factors affect customer expectations. Corporate image and brands are very relevant to service industries in this respect. Here, we have focussed on those factors related to communication in the various stages of the consumption process of services. In order of importance to services, we have discussed:

- personal selling;
- advertising;
- public relations;
- direct marketing;
- the Internet;
- sales promotion;
- sponsoring; and
- loyalty programmes.

The chapter contains several guidelines for the effective communication of services. These are:

- direct communication to employees;
- stimulate word-of-mouth communications;
- provide tangibles;
- make a service understandable;
- aim at continuity; and
- do as you promised.

The final part of the service experience centres on price. It is difficult for the client to judge tariffs and for service providers to set the right price. Due to that complexity, some quite simple pricing tactics are being used, like mark-up pricing just based on time and materials involved. Pricing strategies and pricing depend strongly on the organization's objectives. Value-based pricing is valued highly these days; it hinges upon the idea what the customer is willing to pay for the service. Insight in the three Cs – customers, costs and competition – form the foundation of strategic pricing. Real understanding of what the customer views as 'value' is essential. Lots of other factors also play a role in setting the final price. In practice, the outcome results in some form of combined pricing strategy. Since customers participate in the servuction process, activity-based costing may provide adequate information on the actual cost drivers, both at the company side of the process as well as on the customer side of the process. Customer cost involves both monetary and non-monetary cost.

Questions

1. Describe how the distribution of services is affected by innovations in information technology?
2. Illustrate what makes the complexity of a service environment grow?
3. Describe the various distribution strategies.
   a Why will hybrid forms emerge?
   b In what way are these distribution strategies linked to 'coverage'?
4. Describe why the servicescape and atmospherics are important in determining service quality.
5. Describe how the four basic issues in communication can be distinguished. Provide examples of each in the service industry.
6. Illustrate how communication goals differ per stage in the process of buying services.
7. Explain the various elements of the communication mix in services. Describe what is important in determining the effectiveness of communication in services.
8. Identify whether marketers can use price bundling as part of a level capacity strategy.
9. Describe in what way a service firm's market orientation will ideally be reflected in its pricing policy.
10. Define what is meant by the terms 'ARGE' and 'ABC'. Why it is useful to apply these concepts?

Assignments

1. Using Figure 11.4 as a guide, prepare a list of service firms (from your home country), that you consider to be excellent in utilizing the various positions illustrated. Describe why you consider them to be excellent.
2. Select a number of competing airlines (or universities or banks).
   a Analyse their communication mix.
   b Describe which elements do they use and why.
   c Describe how different are their activities.
   d Identify whether their communication is in line with their strategy and other elements of the marketing mix.
   e Describe how their communication strategies fit their positioning.
3. Our discussion on the relationship loyalty perception model (RLM model) in Chapter 3 revealed that four types of customers exist: friends, acquaintances, sympathetics and functionalists. Communication can help to move customers from one segment to another, if deemed relevant.
   a Develop a communications plan for a fitness chain, being not satisfied with their present customer base and setting targets for the future.
   b Describe how would such a communication plan look likely to transform the customer base as shown in Table 11.7.
4. Discuss the following hypothesis. 'The increasing use of ICT in services will diminish the personal communication in services. This will have a negative effect on service quality since the personal interaction is crucial.'

Table 11.7 Segmentation

Segments	Present customer base	Future customer base
Friends	10%	50%
Acquaintances	50%	–
Sympathetics	25%	20%
Functionalists	15%	30%

5. List three services with a high pricing transparency. List three services with a low pricing transparency. Describe what both types of pricing transparencies imply for the supplier's freedom to determine prices.

Endnotes

1 Cohen, 1997, pp. 74–81.

2 See e.g. Langerak, 2001.

3 Probably this extreme situation is not realistic when the service provider has established long-term relationships with the other organizations in the channel. This will depend partly on the kind of relationship management being practised between the middlemen and the service provider.

4 Such a conflict also occurred among others in the struggle between Fidelity Mutual Funds and Charles Schwab, king of the discount brokers, who wanted to halt the selling of some of Fidelity's most popular funds like Magellan and Contrafund (see Wyatt, 1996).

5 Bateson, 1976.

6 Coyne and Dye, 1998, p. 101. This section is based to a large extent on this Coyne and Dye article.

7 Guglielmo, 1996.

8 See an article in *The Economist*, Delays can be expected, 27 July 1996.

9 Bitner, 1992.

10 Ghosh, 1994, pp. 249–313.

11 See our discussion of the SERVQUAL model in Chapter 5.

12 This section relies heavily on Zeithaml and Bitner, 1996, ch. 16; and Zeithaml, Bitner and Gremler, 2005, ch. 16. We have added some of our own ideas to it.

13 We have seen in many instances in this book that a clear vision and goals are necessary as the framework within which employees and business units are entitled to work and be empowered. This is typical for market oriented firms.

14 George and Berry (1981) have developed the six points of this overview. They have focussed on the guidelines for successful and effective advertising in services. We have broadened the scope to communication in general.

15 Firestone, 1983.

16 Goldenberg, Libai and Muller, 2001, pp. 211–223.

17 27 April 2005, from *The Economist* printed edition.

18 This figure is based on Kurtz and Clow, 1998, p. 417. The present authors have adapted the figure slightly.

19 Institute of Public Relations definition, Brassington, Pettitt, and Gossery, 2003, p. 1107.

20 Lovelock, 1991.

21 Nagle, 1987, p. 7.

22 Thor, 1996.

23 See Alexander, 2004, p. 26.

24 Simon, 1992.

25 Normann, 1991, p. 126.

26 See also Lovelock, 1991, pp. 236–245.

27 Zeithaml, 1988.

28 See Alexander, 2004.

29 Lovelock, 1991.

30 Alexander and Hordes, 2003, pp. 84–86.

31 Berry and Yadav, 1996.

32 See also the recent books and courses of Philip Kotler in which this idea has been worked out.

33 See, for example De Heer *et al.*, 1990, pp. 27–33.

34 Price bundling is just one of the means firms can use to implement bundling. Bundling can also be regarded as a cheap, low risk form of innovation (Eppen *et al.*, 1981; De Brentani, 1995; Simonin and Ruth, 1995). Then existing products and services are combined in a new bundled form. Bundling can also be seen as a form of standardization. When services are completely tailormade and/or new, it is hard to convince the prospective buyer about the (benefits of the) new service, especially when it is hard to assess the new service on search attributes. A bundled form of services may provide the customer with more attributes or tangibles. Then the purchase decision may become easier to the customer. Bundling can also be seen as a way to strengthen relationships with customers by providing them full packages of products and accompanying services. In this respect, Eppen *et al.* (1991) even discuss the concept of 'loyalty bundling' as a form of bundling primarily aimed at preventing customers to switch.

35 Bateson, 1995, pp. 366–376.

36 Adapted from Rutherford, 1995, p. 102.

37 Nagle, 1987, pp. 175–176. To a large extent, this section about segmented pricing is based on chapter 7 of Thomas T. Nagle. We have added the membership variable to the seven variables for segmentation Nagle mentions.

38 Lovelock, 1991, pp. 122–127.

39 Nagle, 1987, p. 217. See for a more detailed explanation of the importance of competitive cost advantages and external/internal cost efficiencies, Nagle, ch. 9.

40 ROI represents the required rate of return or the cost of capital. It does not fully represent a 'cost approach'.

41 Roozen, 1991.

42 Porter, 1985; Govindarajan and Shank, 1989.

43 Compare for example Lovelock, 1991, p. 236.

44 Ingenbleek *et al.*, 2003, p. 300.

45 Ingenbleek *et al.*, 2003, p. 300.

46 Nagle, 1987, p. 153.

47 See, for example, the biannual Ernst & Young Transfer Pricing, 2003, Global Survey; Antić and Jablanović, 2000.

Chapter 12

Implementation, Performance and Control

That's the effect of Société Générale financial services.

Choosing an innovative bank means gaining the freedom to imagine anything. Driven by its ability to look ahead, Société Générale now has a workforce of 93,000 in 80 countries and has become steadily stronger in its three key fields, offering its customers ever more occasions to broaden their perspectives. With more than 17 million customers[1] in retail banking, 326 billion euros[1] managed by global investment management and services and a confirmed worldwide leadership in corporate and investment banking (euro capital markets, derivatives and structured finance), Société Générale has become a first choice partner for its customers around the world. If you too, have a taste for growth, you will soon see what the "Société Générale red and black effect" can do for you. (1) at 31/03/05. www.socgen.com

Société Générale is authorised by Banque de France and the Financial Services Authority, and is regulated by the Financial Services Authority for conduct of UK business. In the United States, certain securities, underwriting, trading, brokerage and advisory activities are conducted by Société Générale Group's wholly-owned subsidiaries SG Americas Securities, LLC, and SG Cowen & Co., LLC, both registered broker-dealers and members of NYSE, NASD and SIPC.

Red, black and rising.

Learning objectives

At the end of this chapter you will be able to:

1 Translate the assets and capabilities of market oriented service organizations in to a marketing plan

2 Integrate and use various models presented in previous chapters in to developing a marketing plan

3 Formulate strategies to manage demand and supply which create and deliver external value

4 Understand the role of marketing planning in a service organization

5 Develop a marketing plan for each segment

6 Understand the links between the various chapters of this book, the service guiding principles and the contents of a marketing plan

7 Realize that the goals set in the marketing plan set the framework for the financial and non financial criteria for evaluating actual service performance

8 See the need to apply the concept of internal marketing in easing the implementation of marketing strategies and the implementation of the marketing plan

9 Discern the unique problems of implementation of the marketing strategy in a market oriented service firm and formulate ways to avoid these problems and/or solve them

10 Define and measure performance and control strategies in service industries

12.1   Introduction

SERVICE PRACTICE 12.1

Quality over Quantity[1]

The slogan 'Quality over quantity' is one of the leading principles in the ten most admired companies in the world. If we observe the top ten positions, it stands out that six of them earn the major part of their revenues though selling services.

Comparing the results of 2004 and 2003 you will see that GE regained No. 1 from Wal-Mart, Dell moved up from place 6 to place 3. Toyota (the most profitable car maker) moved up three positions higher to No. 5, making it once again the highest ranking non US company on the All Stars Top 10 list.

Position				
2004	2003	Company	Industry	Country
1	2	General Electric	Electronics	USA
2	1	Wal-Mart Stores	General merchandiser	USA
3	6	Dell	Computers	USA
4	3	Microsoft	Computers	USA
5	8	Toyota	Motor vehicles	Japan
6	9	P&G	Household & personal products	USA
7	4	Johnson & Johnson	Pharmaceuticals	USA
8	10	FedEx	Delivery	USA
9	7	IBM	Computers	USA
10	5	Berkshire Hathaway	Property and casualty insurance	USA

To be admired a company should have:

1   Superior management;
2   Industry leadership;
3   Technological progress; and
4   Innovativeness.

The most admired companies fulfil all of these four criteria. Other important criteria on which the 357 global companies are ranked include: use of corporate assets, globalness, financial soundness, long-term investment value, social responsibility, quality of products and services.

Profit making is not the most important criterion when you evaluate your competitor in order to admire him. Exxon Mobil, America's most profitable company, ended up at position 41 for 2004 compared to 32nd place in 2003. The judgement of the toppers and losers was done, of course, from those who know them the best: their competitors.

Why do these companies (and many of them are US companies) score so well? These are the main reasons:

☐ They have responded very well to the competitive challenges and taken advantage of the opportunity to globalize, 'Tapping markets and talent around the globe', as Robert Hormats, Vice Chairman of Goldman Sachs, a global Investment Bank Intl., said.

☐ They are constantly innovating; and

☐ Their slogan has been and is: 'Quality over quantity'.

Source: *Fortune Magazine*, Marth 7th 2005, No. 4, p. 41

In previous chapters, we have discussed many issues of a strategic nature. At those points some practical hints deemed relevant to efficient implementation were given. In this chapter, the focus is on the final stages of the marketing planning process aimed at accomplishing the goals set. These final stages hinge upon implementing and controlling the service marketing effort in concert. Basically, the most critical questions to be raised here are for instance:

■ What assets and capabilities make companies great and admired?

■ What assets and capabilities make companies different from competitors?

■ What creates great service providers, or breakthrough service providers?

An insight into the characteristics of these kinds of service providers (what they think, what they actually do and how they create value) may function as a benchmark other service providers may use for comparison purposes.

The marketing plan is an essential vehicle to accomplish that implementation. What we have discussed before will be integrated here in quite an operational way to make strategies work. In fact, that is what implementation is all about: making strategies work.[2] A common way to translate a strategic 'management agenda' into action is to agree with managers on 'management contracts' and with other employees on their 'personal performance plans' and 'personal development plans'. Usually, these plans include well defined tasks, responsibilities and targets. Establishing objectives – by means of key performance indicators (KPIs) based on the key success factors, assets or capabilities in the six blocks of our balance scorecard – is helpful to manage implementation at an organizational level in an integrative way. Other arguments for this integration are based on the idea that the quality of internal processes determines not only the final external quality and value on the market but also the power and control structure within the company.

Value refers to a great many things. You may think of service firms understanding the opportunities to create value to the various stakeholders but also to the value created during the service delivery. Then the excellent quality service experience occurs. Therefore, the value concept can also be interpreted here as a continuous cyclical process consisting of identifying, defining and delivering value (and then again identifying value opportunities, etc).

Creating shareholder value implies in our vision that the company should first understand, create and deliver value through the eyes of the client. Assuming that a company serves a profitable market segment and customers, in turn this will lead to value for the shareholders.

A special league of fast-growing companies, such as Starbucks, the Swedish fashion chain Hennis & Mauritz, the Spanish fashion chain ZARA, Google, E-Bay and Yahoo to mention a few, fall into the category of breakthrough service providers. They set the standard for a new way of providing services. This may vary from introducing 13 collections a year (one for every month and the Christmas season while other fashion retailers think in terms of the autumn, winter, Christmas, spring and summer season) with a radical change in design and logistics processes (H&M) to auctions and selling via the Internet (even – or especially? – second-hand goods).

Section 12.2 examines the tools a service provider has to manage supply and demand in order to deliver excellent service quality and create value. The marketing strategy and the marketing mix can be used to give content and meaning to the relationships the service organization and the customers want to establish, maintain, enhance and, if necessary, want to end. Section 12.3 focusses on the four types of services we developed. The development and implementation of the marketing plan is the topic of section 12.4. Many issues have turned out to be important in the relationships between a service provider and its (B2C and B2B) customers in order to assure excellent service quality. Managing all of them properly, effectively and efficiently is a complex task. Implementation counts many obstacles. These obstacles and possible solutions are the focus of section 12.5. With respect to the part on performance and control, this chapter discusses, among others, the relationship between control, strategy and the service concept and measuring performance in services (section 12.6). It pays off to be market oriented for it has been shown that the more market oriented service organizations are, the better their non financial performance and their financial performance are. The chapter is visualized in Figure 12.1.

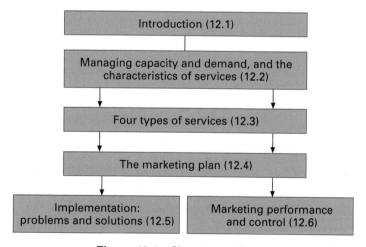

Figure 12.1   Chapter outline

12.2   Managing Capacity and Demand and the Characteristics of Services

As in every business, managing demand and supply is critical. In services this process has an extra dimension due to the specific characteristics of services. Because they cannot be owned or stored usually, managing demand and capacity (= supply) has its own uniqueness in the service business. Creating stock means it is often impossible to resolve fluctuations in demand or supply, for, services are consumed at the time of production. Or, should we challenge this notion and say that stock keeping is not necessary since production and consumption take place simultaneously? Here you may think back to our discussion on the inability to own services from Chapter 2.

So matching demand and supply at a particular moment in time is an essential part of the management job which in turn is a major determinant of profitability. It requires specific assets and capabilities in managing e.g. waiting times and being out of stock.

In previous chapters we have focussed on four particular assets and four particular capabilities of market oriented service organizations. These were

- Customer-based assets;
- Internal-based assets;
- Distribution or supply chain assets;
- Alliance-based assets;
- Inside-out capabilities;
- Outside-in capabilities;
- Spanning capabilities; and
- Networking capabilities.

These assets and capabilities are critical in matching demand and supply of services resulting in the unique delivery of excellent service quality, making your service organization admired by your customers and different from your competitors. You may recall that reliability, responsiveness, assurance, empathy and tangibles were the dimensions of service quality.[3] In the B2B sector these dimensions are also applicable. However, when you focus specifically on the relationships between customers and service providers which are so important in the B2B sector, it appears that interaction dimensions like product/service exchange, financial exchange, information exchange, social exchange, co-operation and adaptation play a decisive role in determining professional service quality.[4] But also commitment and trust are critical as we have seen in Chapter 3. Professional service firms too are often faced with severe and increasing competition and thus lower prices. In such a situation, they still have to deliver excellent quality in ever more shorter times to perform the assignment. At the same time, their employees also expect 'value in their jobs' otherwise it will be difficult for the firm 'to keep them on board'.[5] Job satisfaction and customer satisfaction are linked together according to the service profit chain. So, many issues are linked together in a service business emphasizing the need for such an integrative action during the implementation stage; however, this does not mean that integration should be left over to this stage. It is critical during the whole planning process.

The assets and capabilities are also important in implementing our view of market orientation in which among others the differentiation strategy and cost leadership strategy for a particular market segment are combined. Although the differentiation part is typical for marketers, the cost and efficiency part of running the business (the typical focus of managers with a background in accounting, finance or engineering) should not be overlooked. Both parts of market orientation offer different opportunities to match demand and supply (differentiation in services' content versus price differentials) and are critical in determining a service organization's performance. And we have seen that the more market oriented the business is, the higher the non financial performance and the financial performance are.

The motto 'once the plane has left, the chance to earn has gone' counts in most 'fixed assets' dominated service industries. The crux for these service providers is to find market segments or niches that are of sufficient size and price sensitive enough to get high occupancy rates. In this context, fixed capacity costs are important for setting prices at peak times. However, as the cost of capacity up to the amount used at peak times is mostly unavoidable, fixed capacity costs should be ignored when determining prices in non peak periods. In non peak periods, variable operating costs, such as fuel for aircraft, food ingredients for restaurants, electricity and cleaning costs after a film performance or a stay at a hotel, should be used in profitable decision making.

In fact, all parts of the marketing mix in services, and the relationships a service provider wants to have with its clients, can be used in matching demand and supply.[6] They will have a different content given the strategy to manage demand and supply. These two strategies are: 'chase demand' and 'level capacity'.

The chase-demand alternative is often selected where demands are highly volatile and unpredictable, the cost structure can be managed on a highly variable basis, and there is a ready supply of relatively low-skilled labour for jobs requiring limited training ... In contrast, level-capacity strategies may be employed where demand is less volatile and more predictable, the consequences of a poorly performed service are serious, and the need for expert providers requiring substantial training (or expensive, complex, specialized equipment) high.[7]

This is further elaborated upon in Figure 12.2.

The size of fluctuations in demand, the speed of these fluctuations and their predictability as well as the cost structure, the cost of poor service quality and the cost of lost business are important issues in determining whether we have to employ a chase-demand or a level-capacity strategy. So, managing demand and supply is more than just manipulating one part of the marketing mix, the price. Smart service providers, confronted with volatile, unpredictable demands (as with chase-demand strategies) modify their strategies by, for instance,

maximizing service delivery during peak periods, using part-time employees or renting/ leasing equipment, cross-training employees to perform two or more jobs with different demand patterns, sharing capacity among businesses, and increasing consumer participation in the delivery of service. In addition, through advanced facility planning, excess capacity of hard-to-change features may be built into service facilities when they are constructed. Finally, even if none of these possibilities exists, humans are able to deliver what we often call superhuman efforts for short periods of time.[8]

Operating responses that can be made to the problems of managing chase-demand or level-capacity strategies refer to, among other things, the percentage of peak business that will be covered by the base capacity, the division of labour, the required level of labour skills, the job discretion, the compensation rate, the working conditions, the training required for each employee, the amount of supervision required, and the type of budgeting and forecasting required. This is also summarized in Figure 12.2.[9]

Condition encouraging:	Chase-demand	Level-capacity
Size of fluctuation in demand	Large	Small
Speed of fluctuation in demand	Fast	Slow
Predictability of fluctuation in demand	Unpredictable	Predictable
Cost structure	Highly variable	Highly fixed
Cost of poor service	Low	High
Cost of lost business	High	Low

Operating responses	Chase-demand	Level-capacity
Percentage of peak business covered with 'base capacity'	Low	High
Division of jobs	High	Low
Labour skill level required	Low	High
Job discretion	Low	High
Compensation rate	Low	High
Working conditions	Sweat shop	Pleasant
Training required per employee	Low	High
Amount of supervision required	High	Low
Type of budgeting and forecasting required	Short-run	Long-run

Figure 12.2 **Conditions encouraging chase-demand and level-capacity strategies and characteristics of some operating responses**

In implementing a strategy, a lot of strategic and operational actions have to be performed and integrated. Starbucks is an example of a company that keeps up with the growing market opportunities (strategic issue). At the same time this coffee house installs automatic espresso machines and offers prepaid Starbucks cards for automatic espresso machines to speed up service. Thus, they manage capacity and demand at an operational level. The Starbucks (service) experience is a result of branding, relationships (loyalty) and service quality – complete with a smart design and execution of the marketing mix.

SERVICE PRACTICE 12.2

Starbucks: 'To Keep up the Growth, it Must Go Global Quickly'

Starbucks has grown from 17 coffee shops in Seattle about 15 years ago to 5689 outlets in 28 countries in 2002. Sales have climbed an average of 20% annually since the company went public

12 years ago, to $2.6 billion in 2001, while profits bounded ahead an average of 30% per year, hitting $181.2 million in 2001. Starbucks' name and image are connected to millions of consumers around the globe. It was one of the fastest-growing brands among the top 100 survey of *Business Week* in August 2002. Its stock has soared more than 2200% over the past decade, surpassing Wal-Mart, General Electric, Coca Cola, Microsoft and IBM in total return.

In Manhattans' 24 square miles, Starbucks has 124 cafes. This means one for every 12 000 people. So, there could be room for even more. In coffee-crazed Seattle, there is a Starbucks outlet for every 9400 people, considered from the company as the upper limit in coffee-shop saturation. The crowding of so many stores so close together has become a national joke. The company admits that while its practice of blanketing an area with stores helps achieve market dominance, it can cut sales at existing outlets. Starbucks plans to reach worldwide the number of 10 000 stores. But global expansion is always related to more risk. For one thing, it makes less money on each overseas store because most of them are operated with local partners. While that makes it easier to start up on foreign turf, it reduces the firm's share of the profits to only 20–50%.

By relying on mystique and word of mouth, whether in the USA or overseas, the company saves a bundle on marketing costs. She spends $30 million annually on advertising, or approximately 1% of revenue, just for new flavours of coffee drinks in the summer and product launches, such as its new in-store Web service.

It is cheaper to deliver to and manage stores located closer together. But Starbucks is large enough to absorb losses at existing stores as new ones open up, and soon overall sales grow beyond what they would have with just one store. The firm is still capable of designing and opening a store in 16 weeks or less and recouping the initial investment in three years.

What is important is that Starbucks has proven to be highly innovative in the way it sells its coffee. It has installed automatic espresso machines in 800 locations to speed up service and offering prepaid Starbucks cards, priced between $5 and $500, which clerks swipe through a reader to deduct a sale. This cuts the transaction time. Another innovation has been pre-paying for a service via the website Starbucks Express. The client just makes a call or clicks the mouse before arriving at the store, and his drink will be waiting with his name printed on the cup. Starbucks executives have the hope that with such innovations they can attract the next generation of customers: the younger coffee drinkers. The management philosophy holds, inviting creative conflict and debate: 'If there is no tension, I do not think you get the best result.'

Reproduced by permission of *Business Week*

12.3   Four Types of Services

In the previous section we have been discussing matching demand and supply in the services business in general. You may recall that we have developed four kinds of services in our typology:

- Standard core services;
- Customized core services;
- Standard augmented services; and
- Customized augmented services.

This typology fitted quite well to another typology, especially fitting to the B2B sector encompassing respectively the vendor, total solutions provider, specialists, and game changers. In Chapters 3 and 6 we elaborated on the latter typology of service providers. Here we provide you with an integral overview of the basic characteristics of the firms in our typology. Once you have seen this overview, it will ease your way of looking at the implementation of strategies to be discussed in the rest of this chapter.

Standard Core Services

Standard core services are usually characterized by large-scale cost effective production. This is possible due to its standard character of serving an unsegmented market (or very large segments in a market). It is a typical production line organization (also in terms of empowerment) for the front office employees. The standardization in work procedures means high (and top) management exercises direct control. Relatively low skilled jobs are present.

The services offered consist of a wide but not so deep assortment of core services including some (simple) facilitating services. Brands are not that relevant in this mass market (they may become more important in order to differentiate from competitors in mature markets or when these services become 'a commodity'). Personal contact in the service encounter is quite low (often replaced by computers and machines, e.g. ATMs). Advertising and direct marketing are appropriate means of communication between service provider and customer/client. These convenience services are provided via intensive distribution. The choice of the location to which the customer has to travel is an important issue. Prices are quite elastic. Monetary costs are relatively high to the customers while the non monetary costs are quite low.

Customized Core Services

Customized core services are standardized services which are differentiated to a certain extent to meet the needs of some specific segments in the market. This differentiation, via some facilitating and/or supporting services, is used to give deeper meaning to the relationship intended between service provider and customer. Standardization in work procedures is high, although some form of personal involvement of front line personnel is at stake. Top management not only exercises direct control but also has a supporting role. The personal interaction during the service encounter is low to medium. The assortment of services offered is wide, not deep. This fits quite well into these shopping services offered via a selective distribution strategy. Prices are probably not so elastic and the quality perception of prices is quite high.

Standard Augmented Services

Standard augmented services are dominated by the standardization character. Again, cost efficient production of these services is at stake. Differentiation via some standard, additional, facilitating service leads to this kind of augmented service. Some broad market segments have been defined for which this offering is intended. The standardization in work procedures is moderate, empowerment is taking place via a high job involvement and a supporting or initiating role of top management. The assortment of these convenience and shopping services is not so broad and has some depth. Selective distribution via a multiservice, multisite policy and high contact personal interaction are crucial in the servuction process. This explains why personal selling and quite high labour skills are crucial here. Prices are rather elastic and the quality perception of prices is low, mainly because of the dominant feature of standardization within these augmented services.

Customized Augmented Services

Highly differentiated, complex services consisting of a core service plus a wide variety of facilitating and supporting services defined for a very specific market segment or even individual customers are the main features of the customized augmented services. Highly qualified and empowered front office employees, coached by their top managers, provide services with hardly any strict or standardized work procedures. They have high contact situations during the service encounter and 'sell and market' the services personally. These specialty services are offered via a strategy of exclusive distribution. The service organization does not have that many outlets. However, in each outlet a multitude of services can be 'produced'. Psychological pricing is at stake, the quality perception of prices is high (meaning a higher price will be regarded as providing better quality because experience and credence attributes play a crucial role here).

Now that you have seen this overview, it is important to know how we can accomplish such an integrative situation in reality. How can we translate strategy into action and take care of all the relevant interdependencies? In what way can the marketing planning be instrumental to accomplish that goal?

12.4 The Marketing Plan

The process of value delivery can be analysed and defined along the lines expressed in our strategic pathway. Stated differently, via strategic analysis (market segmentation, target marketing and resource analysis), strategic choice (market positioning) leads to execution and implementation (marketing programme, marketing plan and implementation).[10]

This section discusses one part of marketing planning: developing a specific marketing plan for a chosen market segment. Marketing planning in market oriented organizations requires focussing on customers and competitors by definition. However, yet another dimension has to be added to this statement. Since delivering services is generally people-based, this 'asset' of a company should be fully equipped to provide the service planned to external customers. Therefore, it is necessary to have performed all the 'missionary and motivational work' within the company (the internal market of employees, departments and the like) about the new plans or new ways of working before it is communicated to the market. Commitment within all organizational layers has to be present.

From Gap 4 in the SERVQUAL model, you will remember how seriously service quality can be harmed when employees do not know what customers do know or when promises cannot be met. Therefore, external and internal marketing planning processes are needed and should be well coordinated. The different components of both models should be integrated into the overall marketing planning process. Both the internal (= to the company) and the external (= to the customers and competitors) marketing strategy have to be fine-tuned and in the implementation stage the two are combined (meaning both are completed). Both should be coordinated simultaneously as indicated in Figure 12.3. This figure not only demonstrates the contents of the marketing plan but also the link with the service guiding principles and the chapters in this book. In that sense, you see all the building blocks of the marketing plan together.

The marketing plan or marketing programme has a planning horizon of mostly six to 18 months. It is shorter than the planning horizon of strategic marketing programmes which companies use (mostly a couple of years). Many companies have (operational) marketing plans aimed at a one-year period. These are typically called the (annual) marketing plans or commercial plans.

The content of the marketing plan may consist of nine topics:

■ Management summary;
■ Marketing audit;
■ Market segmentation;
■ Strategic analysis, choice and market position;
■ Implementation of the marketing mix;
■ Internal marketing;
■ Finance and accounting;
■ Activity planning; and
■ Business cases.

This list may give you the impression that each step should be taken after the previous one has been taken to a full extent. In reality, this is not such a hierarchical process. Quite often, many steps are worked on at the same time. Interactive planning, in which bottom-up procedures are used effectively in combination with top-down communicated frameworks, can be applied here. The most important thing is that you apply all of them and finally report on them in a logical order. In the next sections, we will elaborate on each of these stages.

Management Summary

The management summary should be brief, reflect the highlights of the marketing plan and should not exceed two pages. The management summary highlights the corporate and marketing objectives of the organization. It indicates the scope of the marketing plan and the place/position of marketing in the service organization (= power position). Scope and

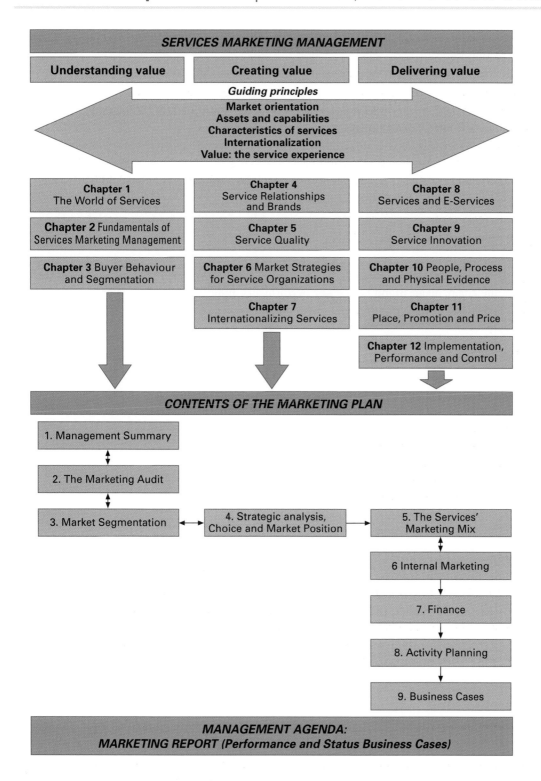

Figure 12.3 **The contents of the marketing plan: linking guiding principles, chapters and
sections of the marketing plan**

position can be described along the marketing audit, the strategic choices and our guidelines for creating value.

The marketing audit reveals the opportunities for value delivery by pinpointing:

■ The most significant opportunities and threats based on the DRETS factors in the macro, meso and micro environment of the service organization;
■ The service provider's most significant assets and capabilities (strengths and weaknesses); and
■ The strategic issues (e.g. alignment with corporate strategy, multichannel distribution).

The strategic choices refer to the organization's value definition, market targeting and positioning in terms of e.g.:

■ Competitive strategic choices (e.g. the type of relationships aimed at the parties in the value chain, major brand issues, key performance indicators and the major activities to reach these objectives, proposed major commitments, mentioning of most significant activities);
■ The position (leader, challenger, follower, niche player);
■ Target segments (based on value management);
■ The positioning (actual and desired, overall and per segment in case of differentiated marketing strategy);
■ The service delivery process (e.g. major proposed efficiency and/or service quality improving projects), linked to the type of service according to our classification of services (see also section 12.3).

Before the marketing team starts writing the management summary it is important that they check whether the marketing plan has fully covered the five strategic management guidelines of

■ Understanding, creating and delivering valuable service experiences;
■ Effectively managing the basic characteristics of services;
■ Enhancing market orientation;
■ Managing the impact, challenges, risks and opportunities of internationalization; and
■ Enhancing the 'assets and capabilities' management.

through its three phases of

■ Understanding;
■ Creating; and
■ Delivering value to all the stakeholders through excellent service experiences which are worth the money (and efforts) of sufficient profitable clients.

Thus, the activities in the marketing plan should deliver external value for customers (client value) and the other stakeholders (in particular shareholder value) of the company.

It will be self-evident that this management summary can only be made after all the eight steps of the marketing plan have been taken, starting with the first one, the service marketing audit.

The Service Marketing Audit

The mission, corporate goals and corporate strategy have to be considered as given when a marketing planning process starts. Defining them is part of determining the strategic context of the organization (see Chapter 6). A clear strategic vision should be the basis for a strategy; that is one of the major lessons in the service sector.[11] The marketing planning process starts with a systematic analysis of the situation relevant in the marketing environment.[12] For the service sector, we developed a service marketing audit consisting of five different analyses (see Figure 12.4). The components of the service marketing audit are analysing:

- The macro environment;
- The specific service industry;
- The market;
- The competition and their strategies; and
- One's own service organization/firm.

These five issues should not be regarded as separate items but should be taken together. They are not independent from one another. Chapter 1, the environmental impact analysis, forms the input for the first four issues of the marketing audit. At this point it is worthwhile that marketers fully realize that while factors and trends are the same for every company, the impact of these two can be different for every firm. In terms of systems, the organization should ensure that this information is stored in the central database (which is one part of the marketing information system) and is easily accessible to other departments. A thorough competitive analysis is a special issue here.

The *analysis of the macro environment* contains the present demographic, regulating, economic, technological and social (DRETS) factors and the expected changes in each of them. It analyses the impact of (changes in) the macro factors for the service marketing audit. Trend extrapolation, expert opinions, scenario building, watching television, reading magazines and 'just looking around' are means to decipher what is going on in the various environments that have to be analysed in the marketing audit.

For instance, the ageing of the population can be used in many ways to develop particular services. Many publishers produce magazines for the 55+ generation. Railways have special tickets, prices and arrangements for the 60+ age group. In Arizona (USA), new towns are built for the 55+ generation where the atmosphere is relaxed, nobody is in a hurry and where the service and merchandising in supermarkets is suited completely to the needs of this target market. This includes the medical infrastructure. Also environmental concerns may offer opportunities for new products and services like environmentally friendly tourism.

The *analysis of the trends and developments in the specific service industry* could focus on, among other things, internationalization, buy-outs, outsourcing and offshoring, economies of scale, self-service, co-operation, franchising, vanishing differences between lease, rent and

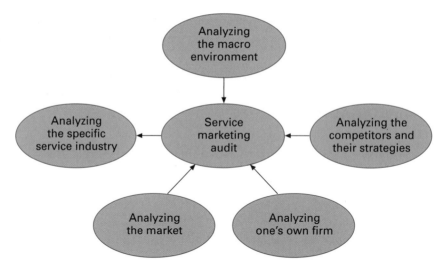

Figure 12.4 The service marketing audit

joint common property. For instance in finance, banks merge within one country to become larger and subsequently internationalize. On the other hand, new niche players see new opportunities in a particular industry because some segments cannot be served satisfactorily by large chains. In the hotel industry, the good quality, small, family hotels and pensions are still successful (and less expensive than many of the large hotel chains). In many industries, limited service providers are challenging general service providers.

The market segments and services defined by the service organization are the starting point of the *analysis of the market*. It is of great importance to define market segments properly and understand the benefits a target segment is looking for and the extent to which these benefits are satisfied. The clear description of the organization's mission is crucial here. Positioning techniques are key tools to accomplish it.

In *analysing competitors and their strategies*, our typology of four generic service strategies can be helpful: standard core service; customized core service; standard augmented service; and customized augmented service. The description of these four types in section 12.3 reveals on what topics you can compare competitors. This step in the whole process of the services marketing audit is aimed at analysing what kind of services competitors are offering and how. It is important to see who those firms are that should be taken into account, and what customers perceive or actually consider as alternatives for the firm under consideration. So, the firms customers do perceive as competing do not need to be the ones that the firm itself considers as their competitors, but are, in fact, the peer competitors. With respect to those peer competitors, it should be analysed what kind of strategy they apply, how it is implemented, how it is valued by their customers and how the firm under consideration scores on relevant benchmarks, like customer satisfaction, service quality, customer loyalty, sales, market share, distribution coverage, costs, profits, market orientation (the cultural side as well as the marketing topics deemed relevant), employee satisfaction and the like. Who are the most important competitors? What blank spots can be found to offer new services or new ways of providing services? It is also interesting to look at who may become competitors in the (near) future (especially when they could come from unexpected industries).

The marketing audit must reveal whether your *own firm's* marketing aspirations and the available resources can be balanced. Analysis of the internal factors focusses on the service process and the five guidelines of our book. It reflects your own belief in your own strengths as a service provider. Corporate analysis then deals with the marketing instruments, the resources and capabilities of the service organization. It reveals what the content of the internal marketing strategy should be in order to actually execute all these skills.

The *links between the five elements of the service marketing audit* can be established in many ways. One can think of many tools, methods or concepts like:

■ The analysis of strengths, weaknesses, opportunities and threats (SWOT);
■ The service life cycle (SLC as counterpart to the well-known product life cycle PLC);
■ The service portfolio theory (as counterpart to the well-known product portfolio; and growth share matrix) developed by the Boston Consulting group; and
■ Multiple factor portfolio matrices as they are developed by the McKinsey company, General Electric and Shell (the directional policy matrix).

A SWOT analysis combines the main issues in the firm's external environment that can be regarded as opportunities and threats with its own strengths and weaknesses. These issues are put together in a grid. When this is done properly, it is our firm belief and experience that the strategic (and operational) solutions easily follow from this overview.[13] Different options will result; then you have to apply your own criteria on what is probably the best option to choose.

The marketing opportunities can be defined in terms of their attractiveness and their success probability. Both can be high or low. The various combinations in this 'opportunity matrix' that can be made now reveal what opportunities are among the most attractive and profitable ones. These should be nurtured especially.[14] Another way of looking at the environmental forces is to evaluate each of the opportunities and threats in terms of a major opportunity, minor opportunity, major threat or minor threat. When this is combined with the probability that they will actually occur, the seriousness of these opportunities and threats can be assessed for the various options found.

With respect to portfolio planning, service firms can offer more than one service to more than one target group of customers to spread risks or (seasonal) cycles in their activities. In the matrix of the Boston Consulting Group, relative market share and market growth rate are the two variables to be considered.[15] Four categories of services can then be detected: stars, problem children (sometimes called question marks), cash cows and dogs. Special strategies should be developed for each of these four. General Electric developed a grid matching the internal strengths of the company with the opportunities in the environment (= attractiveness). This consists of a 3×3 matrix since each factor is divided into three components:

■ Industry attractiveness: low, medium, high; and
■ Business strength: weak, average, strong.

Again, companies, business units or services can be positioned in each of the nine cells of this matrix. Special development strategies apply for each of them based on the other results from the service marketing audit and objectives set.[16]

Before a service firm chooses one of the strategic alternatives, some assumptions have to be made. These assumptions should be mentioned explicitly. Then you all know what you expect or have taken for granted and different scenarios could be developed. These assumptions could refer to forecasting demand, changes in gross national product, inflation rate, change in regulation, changes in consumer taste, differences in national cultures and the like. The content of most of these assumptions will be depicted in the marketing audit. These assumptions have to be made for the whole market as well as for specific target groups. Moreover, a service firm should realize that planned and actual figures are compared to one another in the first stage of the marketing planning process. This takes place via the evaluation at the end of the planning cycle. Control is important to that end. The results of the marketing audit, assumptions and comments on or explanations for the deviations between planned and actual figures are reported in the marketing report.[17]

The marketing audit has been discussed thoroughly because a great many relevant topics should be analysed at this stage. Information for the next stages should be collected here and the value of that information determines the quality of the rest of the planning process. Here, it is important to realize that 'garbage in' means 'garbage out'; a wrong analysis results in defaults in strategy. Moreover, it is important to set down these assumptions and starting points. This makes clear to everybody what assumptions are made. That is important to know, for instance, in controlling the marketing performance of the service firm.

Otherwise, it is difficult to structure and implement the strategy development process, which is very simple in its basic structure, as Figure 12.5 shows.[18]

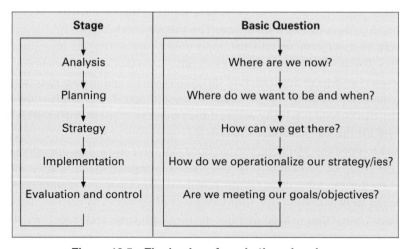

Figure 12.5   The basics of marketing planning

Market Segmentation

The target group of the organization is determined in this second stage of the external marketing planning process. In large organizations the input for this section is obtained during the strategic analysis. It contains the findings of two exercises:

■ Identify customer needs and segment the market in a unique way; and
■ Develop profiles of the resulting segments (i.e. via research).

The application of market segmentation brings the service organization closer to its target group. Hence, it is important to know what are the best criteria for segmentation. In Chapter 3, we discussed many of these variables, in particular the advantages of benefit segmentation and domain specific segmentation. Also, the kind of relationships (and intensity) a service firm wants to have with their customers or clients can be a criterion for segmentation, next to the relationship the customer wants to be engaged in. In general, we maintain that the classification criteria mentioned in Chapter 2 can be applied as ways to segment service markets. A few specific criteria will be dealt with now; they are closely linked to the specific features of services.

Since customers have to participate in the service encounter, the degree of participation can be a criterion to segment the market.[19] An obvious example is the difference between self-service restaurants and restaurants where the guests are being served. As a consequence, customers must be willing, capable and motivated to participate. So, their ability to perform generic consumer tasks or to participate in specific servuction processes can be used as another criterion to segment the market. This customer competency can be defined as: 'the goodness of fit between customer inputs (skills, knowledge and motivation) and customers' corresponding task roles in the service delivery system of the firm'.[20]

A prerequisite to successful implementation of market segmentation is that the service organization itself is structured around these market segments. The minimum requirement is that the information systems in the service firm (be it market intelligence or book keeping) are structured around these segments.[21]

Strategic Analysis, Choice and Market Position

This third stage contains the development of the marketing goals and strategy, estimating the expected results and identifying alternative mixes. This is all within the framework of the generic, corporate strategies developed to go to market and the (actual and intended) relationships with customers. Now, the marketing instruments are defined on the strategic level. Long-term activities (when, how, where, who) are mentioned in this section and budgets are set. These long-term activities, often in the form of business cases, are explained in the final section of the marketing plan. At a later stage each business case will be sent to senior management within the firm for approval. This programme anticipates the actions of competitors. Scenarios may be developed to that end as well as estimates of the sensitivity of the company results to the expected actions of competitors.

When you return to the previous chapters you will recall that many models, techniques, concepts, etc. are mentioned that can easily be applied to the various stages in the process of developing and planning strategies to go to market. The management of a service organization should in any case acknowledge the three strategic Ws:

■ What do we want and can we achieve;
■ What are the opportunities on the market; and
■ Which way to go in order to achieve the goals?

Each service provider can define these Ws. The elements that may assist the company at this journey in unknown territory are summarized in Table 12.1.[22] By ticking the boxes in the

Table 12.1 The process to develop market strategies		
Elements of the process analysed successfully	*Output*	*Specific models, techniques and theories used*
The strategic pathway ☐	Market choices: definition of the market; clearly defined market segments and target groups; attractiveness of the market and position in the market	Market research, business intelligence, trade press, SWOT analyses, product or service life cycle, RFM
	Value proposition: clear description of chosen value discipline; stimulating mission statement; differentiation from other service providers; own and unique marketing assets	matrix, Boston matrix, General Electric matrix, analysis of internal processes
	Key relationships: well-defined description of present and preferred relationships with customers, competitors, collaborators and co-workers/employees	
Competitive advantage ☐	Assets and capabilities that are hard to imitate Employees and managers Customers Legal protection	Research among competitors
Competitive positioning ☐	Customization Quality/price ratio Uniqueness of the service Level of supporting services Innovation	Research among competitors
Assets ☐	Customer Internal structure Distribution/supply or demand chain Alliances	Internal research
Capabilities ☐	Inside-out Outside-in Spanning Networking	Internal research
Generic strategies to go to market ☐	Clear choice on what generic strategy will be followed: cost leadership, differentiation or focus in general as the basis for the final decision on offering low cost services, highly differentiated low cost services, highly differentiated higher priced services or tailor made services for a focussed market or choosing among our four types of service	Porter, Ansoff, Heskett, Hamel and Prahalad, value-based management (VBM)
	Clear choice on what growth strategy will be followed: market penetration, services development, market development or diversification	

Choice on whether a company wants to depart from it's own skills and competence (or is looking for market opportunities or a combination of both)

Answer the question to what extent creating shareholder value should overhaul other principles (VBM)

1. Product/market growth ☐	Rules of thumb: • The penetration strategy concentrates in one stable market on price and/or increases the costs of promotion • Product development or product innovation has an impact for the process of service delivery and/or product. New services and/or service providing processes should be implemented in order to achieve growth • Market development or market innovation has big consequences for personnel, place and process. New relationships should be established. All customers are per definition prospect in a new market. This costs time, efforts and cash collection capabilities of the personnel • Diversification makes everything new. All the Ps from the marketing mix should be defined anew during the diversification process as well as the content of the newly intended relationships	The Ansoff growth matrix
2. Competition ☐	The essence of the formulation of a competitive strategy lies in the positioning of a company in its social-economic environment. The rules of the competition game and the available strategies a company can use are highly influenced by the structure of an industry. The competitive intensity in an industry depends on five forces: 1 entry and exit barriers, 2 the power of the customers, 3 substitutes, 4 the power of the suppliers, and 5 the competition, rivalry on the market. The market and the positioning of the service provider should fit ('strategic fit'). Based on the five-forces analysis, generic competitive strategies can be formulated	Competitive strategy by Porter and Heskett
3. Competence ☐	Here we follow the idea that the way organizations get access to new markets and market possibilities is critical. Own	Resource-based view of the firm (Hamel and Prahalad; Hunt and Morgan)

continued

Table 12.1 *(cont.)*

Elements of the process analysed successfully	Output	Specific models, techniques and theories used
	skills, competences and resources that are difficult to be copied by others are the starting point for the strategy. Hamel and Prahalad suggest that advantage in competition should not be searched in a unique market position but in the capabilities of the company itself. See also the section on internal marketing	
4. Value propositions ☐	The customer decides after comparing service where to buy: to stay with the present supplier or to switch to another service provider or to an alternative service. That's why the price of a service is an indicator of value of a service. This value can be represented in terms of result, service (delivery), price and acquisition efforts. In order to excel, usually, a company chooses for a period of at least some years one of the following three value disciplines to excel, while from a viewpoint of the customer operating at the other two dimensions at a 'satisfactory' level: operational excellence, product leadership or customer intimacy The value disciplines and the generic strategies can be combined to a certain extent showing which Ps from the marketing mix are dominant in each combination:	The value positions of Treacy and Wiersema; generic strategies; marketing mix; relationship management

- *Operational excellence and cost leadership* pushes to standardization in offerings and processes. Simultaneous consuming and producing is more often increased but still kept on a very simple level, because this combination often leads to personalized or standardized services
- *Product leadership and differentiation* requires creativity. Products (services) and process are continuously renewed. The exact word is innovation. It is obvious that there are higher costs involved because of R&D. These higher costs often require a premium price.
- *Customer intimacy and client partnership or focus/niche* requires a lot of interaction between the client and

	the organization. The client partnership requires often account management and personal sales. In addition, the personnel and the processes should be so flexible that the wishes of the client should be individually responded to	
5. Value based management ☐	Value-based management is predominantly based on the idea that all activities of the companies should create sufficient shareholder value. Sufficient can be measured in absolute terms or in relative terms, such as in the top three of our (well-defined) peer group within a period of four years. In this view client value is an intermediate value that is needed on the route towards shareholder value	Value-based management; focus on shareholder value
Marketing strategies to develop, maintain or enhance a position in the market ☐	Well-defined statement on being a market leader, challenger, follower or niche player for each of the services offered in particular markets	Kotler, Ries and Trout and RFM matrix
	Clearly formulated statement on the application of defensive, offensive, flanking or guerrilla tactics for each of the services offered in particular markets	
	Clearly formulated policy on the desired relationships with the customers for each of the services offered in particular markets: clear choices on which customers will be treated as friends, sympathetics, functionalists or acquaintances	

first column the marketer indicates that all the elements of the process have been analysed successfully. The second column illustrates the output management may expect from every element. The last column of Table 12.1 demonstrates the specific models, techniques and theories managers and their assistants in the marketing department could use to obtain the strategic output.

Once the marketing audit, the selection of the market segments and the strategic choice have been completed the organization should choose its positioning strategy. Positioning is the way in which your organization's brands, relationships, service quality, service concepts and individual product offerings attempts to achieve a sustainable, financially attractive position vis-à-vis competitors in the minds of the customers. This perception or image should encourage target customers to prefer your services over competing and alternative services, brands or organizations. The essence of the market positioning is usually described in a positioning or brand concept or statement. So, branding and creating a brand personality in this people's business is crucial. To serve as a guideline through the marketing planning process a positioning should clearly:

- Demonstrate the core value and benefits the company offers its customers;
- Demonstrate differences between the company and its competitors;
- Be consistent; and
- Be a meaningful reference point for executing the marketing strategy and plan.[23]

This positioning is relevant not only to the customers in the external market but also to the employees and departments within the company. This positioning is also a basis for the internal marketing strategy to 'educate your employees' (if necessary) or help them change to a new policy or action.

Thus, in this third step of the marketing plan relationships, branding and service quality will come to the floor in and outside the service organization. It is about the relationship with the client and the employee and the quality they expect. That's why the quality and relationship should be discussed at this stage.

In order to apply quality perception into organization, it is helpful to consider once again Grönroos' model: it is logical that the value discipline of customer intimacy fits better in a user-based quality vision than in the product-based angle of incidences. Here we add explicitly a third dimension to the Grönroos model from Chapter 5, for it is very important to consider how the quality image has been built up:

- *What* quality has been delivered? – the technical quality;
- *How* has the quality been delivered? – the functional quality; and
- *Who* has delivered the quality? – the relational quality.

Then, the question is: to what degree do the What, How and Who qualities contribute to the quality perception of the client? Studies on service quality will reveal the importance of all three qualities in the overall quality evaluation that in turn determines customer satisfaction. And satisfaction or dissatisfaction is the basis for future customer behaviour (being loyal or switching, voicing word of mouth, etc.). If problems occur and improvements are needed the company will have to adjust its marketing-mix mix. So, knowledge of the customer (an essential part of market orientation) is needed. Basically, while analysing the client the following questions can arise:

- What expectations do our clients have? and
- Which risks have our clients taken before, during or after the purchase of the service?

In consumer markets it may be the individual customer who can provide the answer to these questions in a research project. That is different from in B2B markets. Then it is worth utilizing the following models as input for the development of the marketing plan:

- Decision making unit (DMU) with all your customers or only the most important clients (A and B accounts);
- The Kraljic purchase portfolio, indicating how and whether your customers appreciate your product or service. Would a customer have ample alternatives to leverage their purchase position?

- Wallet sizing estimating the market share of your business with your (big) clients;
- Switch behaviour influencing profits. If the customers switch frequently, it will negatively affect turnover as well as profit margins (as long as profitable customers leave). The danger is that while new clients come through the 'front door' (high acquisition costs), profitable existing ones leave through the 'back door'.

We have said before that the service life cycle is an interesting model to decipher in which phase of the life cycle the service is and what strategies, relationships and mix instruments fit best to that particular phase. Mentioning this phase explicitly in the marketing plan and making plans accordingly is obligatory.

We have mentioned a lot of methods, models, techniques and tools that can be used in this stage of the marketing planning process. You should realize that the mere application of each model does not automatically lead to the best strategy. A lot of your own creativity, brain-storming and thinking is needed to develop some interesting options and make the decision that leads to a unique service offering and positioning. Remember that all these topics are linked together and cannot be solved on their own. Eventually, each strategic choice has consequences for the marketing mix.

The Services' Marketing Mix

The implementation of the service experience is executed with a selection of instruments within the marketing mix. Management has to choose the right actions to create value. It requires that all the marketing mix instruments are congruent with the firm's strategy and support the service experience which represents the value proposition to the clients. The marketing mix of the service provider consists of seven Ps: personnel, product (= service), process, physical evidence, place, price, and promotion.[24] The international service organization of course should know to what extent local law, tax, customs, language, etc. impact on these seven Ps.

Personal relationships have proven to be very effective (but often also very costly) in service industries. You could even say that *employees* live up the brand. In the Dolci chain of excellent service quality conference resorts in the USA and Europe, the employees are called 'associates' indicating from a cultural perspective how the company perceive their staff. They have the skills to deliver excellent service quality in this highly competitive business. Consequently, you will understand why the mere fact of introducing the function of 'account manager' is not sufficient to create loyal customers and high retention rates; more needs to be done to make the whole organization market oriented and work in a market oriented corporate culture.[25] In many service businesses, the professionals (be they doctors, dentists, veterinarians, lawyers or accountants) have to change attitudes in order to cope with the laws of the market today (face competition, advertise, etc.). They have to realize that their own professional (technical) quality is often not the decisive factor in determining service quality.[26]

A study about marketing relationships in personal banking in New Zealand revealed:

the personal banker strategy facilitates the development of customer–bank relationships – where customers are satisfied with their personal banker's performance. Contact with personal bankers builds positive perceptions and word of mouth, yet is not significantly correlated with retention.

This final notion is indicative of the complexities and depth of relationships. You probably are only sure of the fact that once you have no relationships, you will have no business. But the ultimate effect of relationships is often hard to predict.

As was said before, HRM (recruitment, training, assessment, career development and rewards/incentives) is an important part of company activities in order to be or become market and value-oriented. Marketing this HRM side is sometimes called 'internal marketing'. Next to this, practical issues related to implementing the 'P' of personnel, can be mentioned, such as:

- The notion of considering employees as part-time marketers and consumers as part-time employees;
- The notion of the outside-in and inside-out orientation of the employees and the relevance of the other critical assets, capabilities, skills, competencies, etc.
- The content given to the service attitude and the leadership style in a service organization;
- The analysis of the total service delivery process by means of e.g. flow charts and blueprints and the role (e.g. scripts and procedures) of the employees in this process;
- Costs, revenues of employees vis-à-vis cost-saving ICT-solutions, client value and shareholder value;
- Balancing front office and back office;
- The presence of employees during the service-encounter; and
- Managing customer demand and supply with regard to personnel (peak demand e.g. hiring of part-time employees).

The specific characteristics of *services* imply that experience and credence qualities will tend to dominate, whereas search qualities dominate in the choice of tangible products. Management can also influence credence qualities in terms of the marketing of services. Since customers cannot evaluate a service before consuming it, it is important to provide clues as to what can be expected during the service delivery process so that customers can make some kind of pre-purchase evaluation of the service. A new service concept and service experience should embed the knowledge of these three categories or qualities. For example, a service concept may include some sort of service guarantee ('not satisfied – money back' or 'no cure – no pay'). The service guarantee may work as a 'trust factor', 'pull demand' and 'differentiator'.

Considering this P from product there are a few questions that should be answered in the marketing plan:

- How does the individual service contribute to the overall service concept?

■ How can the intangibility, perishability, simultaneity, heterogeneity and lack of ownership issues be solved and reduce perceived risk?

■ What degree of customization and differentiation should be established to create external value?

■ Which brand policy is suitable for a certain service?

■ Which assortment approach has your organization?

■ Which new services survive at the end and are launched?

■ In which manner can the adoption of new services be ensured? Did we apply the five mental steps the consumer makes according to Rogers: awareness, consideration, intention, continued use and eventual rejection? Did we already allocate some promotion budget in our marketing plan for these new services? Product innovation, the P from product, the P from process and the P from personnel are quite often the basics for service innovations;

■ How are service recovery and complaint management structured? How visible are they for our customers to solve their complaints as quickly and efficiently as can be in order to improve service quality and satisfaction again? What skills do our employees need to solve complaints properly?

The performance of the *process* is clearly determined by both the performance of the employees and ICT in this process. However, focussing on the individual employees is not enough: organizations should also consider how people interact in the process. This is also a function of the other resources: tangible resources such as equipment or building, but also the information provided. It is also a function of the way the various activities interact, how the processes are improved and how customers perceive the processes they are part of. Processes are particularly important because in many services the process is the product. It is therefore important to map the process before performance measures are defined. The different activities that make up a service process are made explicit and related to each other with process mapping. With the help of operations management processes can be structured to increase efficiency. But then your service organization needs these (mathematical) skills to re-engineer processes.

In the service business, the interaction with the customer is an extremely important aspect influencing both productivity and quality. The customer is an important source of the heterogeneity in the service delivery process and if the process is not planned enough, problems might occur. Mapping the service process and the different service encounters allows the company to identify the critical issues.

■ Which procedures may leapfrog the competition, decrease costs and enhance the service experience?

■ Should the company differentiate itself here or follow common practice?

■ How to keep track whether procedures are followed by the personnel, customers and ICT – and why not?

■ Can these activities be improved?

■ What to do, when things go wrong?

■ Which procedures have to be in place to prevent mistakes and to limit the damage if a mistake is made?

Considering these questions about structuring processes up-front, before developing the service design, will definitely affect the service quality perceived by the customer in a positive way. A 'benchmark study' is an effective way to optimize the service design. Certifying is also an option, but it means standardizing. The company should think about whether they would like this option or not.

Another process-related issue is: how may technology enhance value for the various stakeholders? And to what degree is the consumer prepared to use technical innovation or not? If we consider two innovations, that are the same or very similar, often the result will be the consumer will choose the one that is most easy to use. In this context we could mention five forms of service convenience: decision convenience, access convenience, transaction convenience, benefit convenience and post-benefit convenience. Since many consumers have a huge preference for convenience, this topic should not be overlooked in the marketing plan.

Since services are so intangible, the *physical environment* outside and inside the service outlet is very influential in communicating an image and in shaping customer expectations. Services high on experience and credence attributes have few intrinsic features upon which customers can base their evaluation of quality. Therefore, the customer uses cues about the building, décor, employees' attire, background music, physical surroundings and location to infer quality. The environment in which the service takes place is part of the service experience and should support the needs and preferences of the customer. Some important dimensions are:

■ Ambient conditions referring to all the elements of our environment that affect our five senses;
■ Spatial layout and process refer to the elements of the physical environment that are often closely related to the core element of the service. You may think about machinery, equipment and furniture that are necessary to deliver the process, the way they are arranged and their physical and psychological effect on the customer;
■ Signs, symbols and artefacts serve as explicit or implicit communications to its users about the place. Signs such as labels on doors or instructions on how to proceed are used for directional purposes, or to communicate rules of behaviour.

Choosing the location is one important point of the marketing mix element *place* and distribution. The related questions here are for instance:

■ How intensively would you like to offer your services?
■ How accessible is the location for customers and employees?
■ Who is present in the location: only the employees, the client or both?
■ Do you offer only one service to a certain target group or do you choose a mixed form?
■ Do you sell also via Internet?
■ Do you travel to the client personally as service provider?
■ What is the cost of the location, as such and compared to traffic (= number of customer walking alongside)?
■ How much space do you need for back and front office?
■ How are the logistics organized?

■ How is facilities management structured (facilities management is concerned with all the physical aspects of the service delivery system)?

Price is a crucial marketing tool to deliver external value. It is the only marketing instrument that costs no money up-front. Here relevant questions are:

■ What objectives would we like to achieve with price setting?
■ Do we wish to achieve profit maximization (a public utility's goal however may be linked to political convictions)?
■ To what extent do current prices contribute to external value?
■ To what extent are prices based on company cost, customer preferences and competitor prices?
■ Which costs do you experience as service provider? Can these costs be lowered without decreasing the value of the service experience and/or the competitive advantage?
■ What is your break-even turnover?
■ Are you aware of customer profitability analysis (CPA), customer lifetime value (CLV) or the strategic advantage?

As we have seen, customers not only pay the price of the service but often have to make their own monetary and non monetary cost to get the service. Customer value is based on comparing the service experience and quality with all the costs made. The pricing decisions reflects on the total service concept consisting of all the Ps.

Promotion may be expensive in services. In order to get value for its communication expenses every service provider should pay a lot of attention to this topic. Because the quality of the service is very often based on the motivation of the personnel, external communication is also focussed on their own employees. Company pride and culture play a critical role here.

The communication mix consists of advertising, personal sale, sales promotion, public relations, sponsoring, Internet, direct marketing, etc. All kind of combinations are possible. In the case of loyalty programmes it is recommended that costs and revenues are estimated as well as the internal use of this market information. It may be a rich source of market information. However, when the company does not have the skills or computer programmes to analyse this data, collecting them is useless. As with all kinds of market information, the service company should critically look at the way this information can be used for decision making purposes. Also, existing loyalty programmes should be evaluated periodically to see whether they still provide valuable information.

Internal Marketing

Internal marketing is the process of planning and executing marketing activities aimed at the creation and improvement of exchange processes within the organization, with the objective of accomplishing organizational and personal objectives and processes in a more efficient and effective way. In this definition, three important statements emerge:

■ Internal marketing is applied to exchange processes within the organization;
■ It deals with HRM activities, for which internal marketing instruments are used; and

■ It is a process of planning and executing aimed at satisfying the objectives of both parties in the service encounter (if we apply it to service organizations).[27]

Internal marketing can be defined briefly as getting the new way of working and new ideas accepted in the organization. It is a way of marketing these new issues in the organization. Therefore, it is important to check whether persons, procedures, routines, knowledge, structures, competencies, skills, capabilities and the like really fit into the new way of working or to the new requirements for the future (or need some adjustment). So, internal marketing facilitates the external marketing; before the new marketing strategy can be implemented and executed in the external market, the internal organization must be well equipped to perform as they should do in the new situation. That is why you see the double arrow in Figure 12.3 between the boxes with the marketing mix and internal marketing. Moreover, internal marketing is a way of showing that the firm consists of individuals and departments that can be considered as each other's clients.[28] The service organization can start developing the internal marketing planning process when the strategic goals for the external marketing strategy and plans are set.

Table 12.2 contains a brief overview of the steps to be taken in the internal marketing planning process and the models, techniques and theories to be used.

Today, increased competition and the growing need for market orientation and value creation contribute to the growing relevance of internal marketing.[29] The increase in competition makes the role of the customer-based assets and the boundary spanning role of front office employees more important. Other causes for this growing interest are its potential for easing the implementation of marketing strategies and the on-going urge for cost reduction and quality improvement.

Finance and Accounting

This section of the marketing plan elaborates on the financial budgets and targets that are connected with the marketing function and the activities. The estimated (financial and non financial) advantages of the marketing activities should preferably exceed the objectives of the company; at least they have to meet the budgeted revenues and cost. Without going into too much detail, for competition reasons, the information on suppliers and partners regarding the various activities is useful to adequately estimate cost and revenues. Of course, the budget associated with a marketing plan differs from company to company and from year to year. However, to succeed in calculating approximately the separate costs and revenues of the marketing function and each activity (try to use activity based costing), it is helpful that the marketer gains financial insight in the variables that are vital to implement services marketing.

At this stage the financial underpinning of the marketing actions is made. Usually it is not such a problem to estimate costs, especially not when – as in many service industries – fixed costs make up a large part of total cost. It can be debated whether some expenses should be regarded as expenses for a particular period or as an investment that should be spread over a couple of years. A promotional campaign to invest in the brand image can be regarded as an

Table 12.2 The internal marketing planning process

Stages in the internal marketing planning process	Output	Models, techniques, theories used
Defining required skills, knowledge, assets and capabilities	Clear overview of necessary skills, knowledge, assets and capabilities to meet the requirements of the new strategy to go to market and the specific external marketing strategy as well as to meet the requirements of internal clients	Market segmentation Internal market research Human resource management (e.g. research on job satisfaction, internal structure and efficiency in work processes) Operations research in analysing processes
Defining the internal marketing strategy	Focussed internal marketing strategy for each department, internal entity or employee	Consistency with corporate strategy and external marketing strategy, goals, objectives Methods to measure resistance to change
Developing internal marketing programmes	Overview of planned activities to teach the new skills and to get the new ideas accepted before new external marketing strategy will be implemented	Techniques to overcome resistance to change Responsibilities, budgets, individual or group training; appointing service champions
Organization and implementation	Coherent overview of coordinated strategies and actions of external and internal marketing strategies; at company level, at SBU level or in sales units. *Now, you have accomplished the internal conditions to introduce the new plan or service to the market effectively and avoid Gap 4 of the SERVQUAL model.*	Plans, budgets, internal structure (centralized, decentralized; SBU, departments, etc.), market orientation of front and back office employees

investment as well as the start of a CRM programme. Training employees is also an investment in this critical asset of each company.

In reality it is more difficult to make a good estimate of potential revenues and sales than of costs. Quite often we experience that companies are too optimistic in estimating sales. It will be helpful to define target markets as specifically as can be to best understand consumer behaviour and translate it into sales figures. Better estimates can be made once the administrative system of the company is organized around customers. Then the service provider knows which are the profitable customers or customer segments. Scanning data offer a lot of information on individual consumer behaviour. This offers the opportunity to forecast a consumer's reaction to specific marketing actions. This way of structuring the firm's administration is typical for market oriented service providers. It also requires educating accountants in this way. On the other hand, we have also experienced that marketers do not think that much in terms of the financial consequences of their plans. Quite often they do not pay enough attention to the financial resources available (or needed) to execute their plans. So, an excellent finance–marketing interface needs to be present in every service organization to avoid too risky adventures. One simple check in the marketing plan thus refers to checking the financial resources and the impact on the statement of income and losses or the balance sheet.

Activity Planning

Activity planning gives an overview of the activities, people, budget, other required resources and evaluation and control in the short run and in the long run. Long-term and operational actions can be plotted against a time line. In the right order these activities define the critical path, for example activities that can only start when others have been finished. They are crucial to the continuation of the project. For each activity a particular time frame is set in which it should be implemented. Moreover, each activity is linked to some employees being responsible for that action and to the colleague having the final responsibility (the service champion).[30] Table 12.3 shows the basic structure of such an activity planning.[31]

Business Cases

Business cases and special projects are the operational issues important to accomplishing the entire organization's goals. They are of a strategic nature. Due to its integral nature, many departments are always involved in business cases. Such plans as, for instance, the introduction of a new service concept, development of a new distribution channel or creation of a new television campaign will be argued in the strategic and annual marketing plan. In approving these plans, managers have approved the preparations for these projects. Still, the actual start (or kick-off) of such a business case or project requires a careful planning of its expected risks (but also the risk of not doing this project), costs, benefits, required

Table 12.3 Activity planning

Activities	People	Other resources	Budget	Timing	Evaluation and control
Identification of activities and tasks involved to realize the marketing plan	Identification of (a) project champion and other people involved, including a specification of responsibilities and authority	Capacity and time required from other persons and departments, for example, the ICT-department, commitment of a senior manager	Financial means and allocation of means to execute the activities	Time frame for execution of the activities (including deadline)	Programme and time frame for evaluation and control; ensure measurable outcomes (e.g. KPIs, budget, projected revenues)

skills, capabilities and other resources. This calls for a separate proposal for approval from senior management of such a project. Sound project management and excellent internal marketing are needed here. Again, this is to prevent the horizontal communication problems mentioned as one of the causes of Gap 4 in the SERVQUAL model.

What has been said about internal and external marketing plans at corporate level in the service organization or at the business unit level applies equally to the level of the sales unit, outlet or branch. This is the level in the service organization where it should all come true. Stores, offices of travel agencies, banks or hotels, being part of a large, international chain, have marketing plans for each of these local units. Such marketing plans exist at the strategic and operational level (annual plan). In essence, making these plans occurs at the same stages as in the marketing planning process described in this chapter. However, the scale of the activities is much smaller than at corporate or business unit level. The analysis and activities are much more focussed on the direct, local environment of the sales units. Goals, about the kind of customer relationship desired and the content of the marketing mix, are more predetermined at higher levels in the organization. The freedom of action in such fields as service development, price policy and advertising policy is very limited at this sales unit level. Most of the time, adjustments to local circumstances are necessary and allowed by headquarters. Stores, local sales units of banks and travel agencies have to adjust their sponsoring and assortment to local circumstances, demographics and tastes. This is self-evident if one thinks of the differences between Kensington Gardens and Tottenham Court Road in London, the 'Village' and Fifth Avenue in New York, for these plans end up as local plans for marketing in action. In many cases, local banks sponsor local events to increase consumers' brand awareness. It may go to an even lower level in that account managers define their own year plan with commercial activities in their branch, for instance by stating goals about the number of new accounts to visit and about the percentage of turning these prospects into new clients. Other goals with respect to activities of front office employees may be defined as well. The most important thing to realize at this sales unit level is that these plans are very concrete and operational by nature. Here, the money is being made/earned.

12.5   Implementation: Problems and Solutions

'Making strategies work' is possibly more difficult than making plans and arranging budgets, especially in service organizations in which 'caring about people' is critical (see Chapter 2) to be really market oriented. For, usually, such a service organization heavily depends on people (employees and participating customers) and their resources, assets, capabilities, (core) competencies, possibilities and routines. So, implementation is quite hard to accomplish although it may have sounded simple and logical in the last sections you have studied. Let us share some examples. Service Practices 12.3 and 12.4 show some of the barriers confronting Citigroup, Internet start-ups and RTL Group. The examples also reveal that disciplines other than marketing affect the proper implementation of the marketing strategy as well, for instance finance and human resource management.

SERVICE PRACTICE 12.3

Different Causes and Different Situations!: Different Strategies in a Changing Corporate Environment[32]

Enough is not enough for Chuck Prince, Citigroup's chief executive since October 2003. The world's largest financial services group has been hit repeatedly by scandals that have cost it billions of dollars in fines and compensation, blighting its reputation. Mr Prince has announced plans to change Citi's culture to avoid such lapses, but he will face a difficult task in a group that is complex to manage and embodies serious conflicts of interest.

The common thread running through many of the scandals at Citigroup is the pursuit of short-term profit at the expense of long-term reputation. This is a consequence of the way in which the group was created, by a series of mergers and acquisitions during the 1990s that brought together diverse businesses. Throughout this period, the emphasis was on reducing the cost of back-office activities, while setting tough profit targets for the operating subsidiaries that were given considerable autonomy. Executives who cut corners to hit profit targets could earn large performance bonuses.

Mr Prince wants to build a corporate culture for the group that balances short-term operating profit against its long-term health. Some of his measures are relatively trivial – a film on the group's value aspirations, an ethics hotline to report dodgy deals and sending managers on one-day annual courses on 'franchise training'.

Others are more substantial, however. A common appraisal system is to be introduced for senior managers to replace about 50 different systems inherited with acquisitions. Performance pay is to be linked to the group's overall performance as well as to the profits of individual businesses.

The changes needed at Citigroup are very fundamental and relate to the company's culture, its short-term cost focus and rewarding system, as Service Practice 12.3 indicates. Just think about how these features relate to our vision on market oriented service companies.

SERVICE PRACTICE 12.4

Different Causes and Different Situations!: Different Strategies in Service Start-Ups and Turbulent Markets

Michael Moritz, a Silicon Valley venture capitalist, talks about the lessons he has learnt in how to create business winners – and losers – in the Internet economy. The

lessons he draws for building a business from scratch sound disarmingly simple. One is to pick the right market – and the right basis for competition. And being in a fast-growing market is essential.

Moreover, quite a large customer base is attractive, avoiding a company being too dependent on a small number of users. Another lesson is: think big and don't be put off.

You need unrealistic expectations. If you don't have unrealistic expectations, you're going to fallshort. The paradox for any start-up is that its financial projections can seem hopelessly unrealistic – until sudden success shows them to be too cautious. Most start-ups may not make it past the early stages, but the ones that do well often far exceed their founders' hopes.'[33]

RTL Group, Bertelmann AG's television arm, is forging plans to launch pay-TV channels in selected European countries, a fundamental shift in strategy that comes as the broadcaster faces a rapidly changing television landscape across the region. Using a mix of subsidies and political pressure, a number of European countries, including Germany, Italy, the UK and France, have been prodding broadcasters and viewers to switch from analogue systems to digital television, which offers a crisper picture and more channels. The result, analysts say, will be a fragmented television market similar to what has evolved in the USA, where the growth of cable and satellite forced the once-dominant broadcast networks to compete with scores of niche channels.

To avoid losing viewers in a more splintered market, RTL Group, which operates a network of 31 television channels spanning 10 European countries, wants to supplement its free-TV offerings with pay channels, RTL Group Chief Executive Gerhard Zeiler said in an interview. The success of the plan, which could cement RTL Group's position as Europe's top broadcaster, is crucial to the future of Bertelsmann. RTL Group generates more than 40% of Bertelmann's profit and is its biggest division.[34]

The example about Michael Moritz relates to starting a business in high tech services industries as companies like Google and Yahoo did. Fundamental topics underlying the implementation of a strategy seem to be very simple indeed. Nevertheless, you just should not forget to think about these basics. They are that self-evident as they are, as Service Practice 12.4 on service start-ups shows, you can easily forget to pay attention to them. The third example shows new services have to be launched to survive in a turbulent marketplace. Increasing competition may be counter-attacked by introducing new technologies in the European TV market. It shows also that management should be aware of the pressure of shareholders and not focus only on the value to external customers.

After having read these three examples, you can imagine that introducing a new strategy is not only a matter of developing it, but also a matter of getting it accepted by the employees who have to execute the plans. They have to change their existing way of working and thinking. Then it will not be surprising when some kind of resistance to these changes comes up. Barriers may be built to avoid changes in the present working procedures, for instance. It is important to know those barriers but also how to overcome them. Internal marketing can be instrumental here. Since the personal interaction is so important in the servuction process, a closer look at the employees and customers is needed to avoid one of the barriers to implementation. This is what we call the 'service triad'.

The human side of the service business should not be underestimated. Since the service business is a people's business, many problems during the service encounter, where the customer and the employee interact, can be solved or prevented when the idea of the service triad is applied. This specific triad consists of the customer, the front office employee and the back office employee in a service organization. They all three interact in a particular environment and together they determine the final service quality. In general they should fulfil the following requirements to perform well in the servuction process of a market oriented service provider and create a high quality service experience:

The customer is

- able;
- motivated; and
- has the opportunity to participate in the service encounter.

The front office (or contact) employees are

- able;
- motivated; and
- have the opportunity to work in a market-oriented way.

The back office (or other) employees are

- able;
- motivated; and
- have the opportunity to work in a market-oriented way

in order to create a high value service delivery resulting from a great service experience. This idea has been visualized in Figure 12.6.

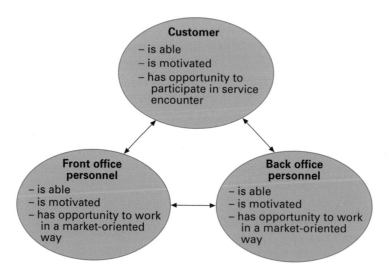

Figure 12.6 Three triads facilitating the implementations of a market-oriented marketing strategy in a service organization

But many more barriers can be found in the management literature and in actual business life. Also a lot of remedies have been found to exist. An overview of such barriers and solutions/remedies is provided in Table 12.4.[35]

Once you know these barriers and the way to solve them, a change of management and internal marketing can be helpful to have the employees accept the new ideas and ways of working and get the new initiatives implemented. The external marketing strategy is – of course – aimed at getting the new services and servuction processes accepted by customers.

Table 12.4 Barriers and remedies to marketing planning in services

Barriers to marketing planning	Remedies to the barriers
The gaps in the SERVQUAL model arise at different levels in the service organization. The barriers in Gap 1 and Gap 2 are more of a strategic nature	At strategic level (Gaps 1 and 2): • culture of market orientation and quality awareness • clear objectives • flat and informal organization • more and better market information • co-operation, information exchange and bottom-up communication • mapping the process
The gaps in the SERVQUAL model arise at different levels in the service organization. The barriers in Gap 3 and Gap 4 are more of a tactical nature	At tactical/operational level (Gaps 3 and 4): • working conditions, atmosphere • teamwork • fit person, job and equipment • delegation and empowerment • selection and training • realistic promises • the triad of market orientation
Confusion between marketing tactics and strategy	Formulate strategy before tactics; focus on the analysis of the external environment
Isolating the marketing function from operations	Situate marketing within operations
Confusion between the marketing function and the marketing concept	Shared values about approaching the market and the organization's market orientation determine the organization's attitude of mind about marketing more than just some activities
Organizational barriers – the tribal mentality, for example to define strategic business units correctly	Organize company activities around customer groups rather than about functional activities; have marketing planned and executed in the SBUs
Lack of in-depth analysis	Scan the external and internal environment thoroughly; have the right analytical skills
Confusion between process and output	Translate information into intelligence and summarize it in SWOT analyses
Lack of knowledge and skills	Ensure that all those responsible for marketing in the SBUs have the necessary marketing knowledge, skills, assets and capabilities for the job
Lack of systematic approach to marketing planning	Systematize the process by means of a set of written procedures and clear format for marketing planning
Failure to prioritize objectives	Sequence objectives and prioritize them according to their impact on the organization and their urgency. Secure that resources are allocated accordingly
Hostile corporate cultures	Style of leadership (often coaching) and culture of market oriented organizations (open, caring, people and results oriented, etc.) should fit to the stage (of the organizational life cycle and market situation) the organization is in

12.6 Marketing Performance and Control

The implementation of the marketing strategy and tactics will lead to a particular performance. How can this performance be measured in order to check whether the goals set are accomplished? This latter issue is relevant with respect to the control of the marketing performance in services.

Usually, performance is defined in financial and quantitative terms like profits, sales, market share, profitability, return on investment and the like. One may wonder whether this applies to the service business as well; are these criteria sufficient?[36] Especially, when the creation of service quality and added value is important, the performance of the service organization should be measured in terms directly associated with those concepts, for instance total value added or value added per employee, respectively service quality, satisfaction or return on quality (ROQ).[37] In the ROQ approach, a model has been developed to allow managers to determine where and how much they should spend to improve customer satisfaction and service quality, and the likely financial impact of those expenditures.[38]

Since the service business is a people's business, non financial performance indicators like quality, customer satisfaction and loyalty or employee satisfaction and loyalty may be relevant performance indicators as well. It seems that the magnitude of these non financial performance indicators have a great impact on the magnitude of the financial indicators.[39] Recent research indicates that the more market oriented service firms in the United Kingdom, Ireland, Australia, New Zealand and Austria are, the better their performance. Moreover in that study, the relationship between market orientation and non financial performance indicators was stronger than the relationship between market orientation and financial performance indicators.[40] This conclusion holds irrespective of these service firms' generic strategy or market position held.

In many countries, performance measurement is closely linked with two aspects:

1 behavioural change; and
2 alignment to assist employees and management to improve performance in a coordinated way.[41]

Therefore, the indicators should be accepted, understood and owned across the entire organization in order to have effective performance measurement.[42] Performance indicators, or rather key performance indicators (KPIs) are measures that serve as the basis for performance evaluation. Preferably they are closely linked to the service firm's key success factors. The purpose of KPIs is to enable measurement of project and organizational performance, and in our case marketing performance.[43] To obtain and capture the involvement and co-operation of all contributors, only a limited, manageable number of KPIs should be maintained for regular use and the data collection must be made as simple as possible. Having too many or too complex KPIs will not only be time- and resource-consuming, it will also meet with considerable aversion from the ones involved.[44] A great difficulty in applying performance indicators is that they can not always be quantified into numerical format.[45] Then creativity is needed to define the proper performance indicators in monetary or non monetary terms. And you have to realize that they cannot be added to one another as a simple mathematical calculation resulting into one final figure.

In developing marketing plans the inclusion of KPIs is needed to justify the funding asked for the projects to be executed and the evaluation of the marketing performance later on. After the evaluation, this can be new input into the planning process.

Measuring Marketing Performance

In Chapter 6 we developed the balanced score card and indicated it could be used for two purposes, namely to develop strategies and to control the business. Before we go on, have a look at Dutch ABN Amro bank to see how they measure their performance.

SERVICE PRACTICE 12.5

Performance Measurement at ABN Amro Bank

In general, today's ABN Amro bank performance criteria can be divided into external and internal performance indicators. The external performance indicator is the leading one. This external indicator is translated into a number of internal performance indicators. How is this going on exactly?

External Performance Indicator
The leading external performance indicator the bank has applied since 2001 is total return to shareholders (TRS). This indicator reflects the extent to which ABN Amro is able to create external value to its shareholders. In more operational terms, this TRS is a combination of two factors, namely the increase in share value at the stock market and the amount of dividends paid to the shareholders.

The bank has set up a long-run target for this value creation. ABN Amro compares itself with a group of 20 competitors with similar TRS positions and follows the TRS development of this group on a daily basis. In terms of value creation they want to be among their competitors in the top 25 of banks in the world.

Internal Performance Indicators
Next, the bank's ambition in terms of long-term external value creation is translated into a number of internal performance indicators. The bank recently performed an internal study to identify the correlation of the external value creation (TRS) with core financial figures such as efficiency ratio, growth of revenue as well as return on equity. The most significant relationship between long-term external value creation and these financial indicators was expressed via two indicators:

☐ Cumulative economic profit (EP) that can be defined as the net profit corrected for the costs for required capital. Companies that have generated a higher cumulative EP within a certain period scored higher on their TRS; and

☐ Return on equity (ROE): the higher the ROE, the higher the TRS.

Next, these indicators are used in order to define internal targets and check long-term plans as well as the ambitions of the bank. When you take a look at all the indicators discussed so far, it appears that financial numbers play an important role in evaluating the performance of this commercial organization. Then, the next question becomes: to what extent do marketing aspects play a role in this performance measurement and control?

The bank acknowledges that their role is crucial. After defining the strategic directions of the organization, these long-term objectives are translated into commercial plans which the bank calls 'implementation initiatives'. These implementation initiatives are the application of the way in which the bank intends to accomplish its strategy. An example of such an implementation initiative is the formulation of a new retail strategy within one of the home markets, e.g. the use of Internet banking next to the selling via brick-and-mortar outlets.

In defining the implementation initiative it is very important to identify the concrete and feasible figures that can be used to measure the degree in which the implementation initiative is on track with respect to its realization. Then, within ABN Amro two kinds of key performance indicators (KPIs) are used in reporting on this progress: strategic KPIs and financial KPIs.

The strategic KPIs consist of non financial figures related to the implementation initiative. An example is customer satisfaction. Consequently, the development and evaluation of a new strategy for a particular segment of customers is based on the development of client satisfaction.

The financial KPIs consist for example of the growth in customers' volume, margins and revenues. The financial KPIs are measured on the level of the implementation initiatives as well as on the level of the total result of the business unit.

On a quarterly basis the progress of the most important implementation initiatives and related KPIs are discussed and measured. On the basis of KPIs the plans of the business units are discussed.

A wide spectrum of variables can (or must?) be used in measuring service performance. All these measures are needed to measure the performance in the process of delivering excellent service quality.[46] Kullvén proposed that in services performance is and must be measured from three perspectives, namely the market (= satisfying the customers), the workplace (= satisfying the employees), and a financial perspective (= satisfying the owners). However, this approach does not fully match our view on market oriented service delivery because performance is not yet measured from all stakeholders' perspectives. Moreover, you have to realize that many performance indicators are industry specific such as occupancy rates in the lodging and airline industry. They have a quantitative and a qualitative nature as well as a financial and a non-financial (behavioural) background. This combination is in line with our suggestions about the perspectives to be used in measuring performance in a service organization based on the notion of the balanced score card as developed in Chapter 6:

- The financial perspective;
- The customer perspective;
- The internal business process perspective;
- The learning, innovation and growth perspective;
- The employee perspective; and
- The strategic perspective.

The combined use of a wide variety of instruments to measure corporate performance in services also comes to the fore in a US study by the International Benchmarking Clearinghouse.[47] That study revealed CEOs in service businesses like insurance, banking, transport, retail consumer services, utilities, health, consulting and the government mostly use the following measures to evaluate their performance:

■ profitability (net operating income or contribution, budget variance, ROE/ROC/ROI/ROA, revenue, revenue growth, after tax net income);
■ customer satisfaction (customer satisfaction surveys, competitive comparisons, customer perception of service, complaints/complaint resolution, on-time delivery, customer retention, inactive accounts, customer acquisition, customer loyalty, profit per customer, expenditure per customer);
■ workforce issues (employee satisfaction, employee turnover, cost of benefits, suggestions, inclusion in incentive programmes, diversity targets, safety results, training amount or cost, health or cost of health, job rotation);
■ marketplace (market share, target market penetration, service development cycle time, share of customer, number of new services, presence in distribution channel);
■ productivity (labour productivity, cost per unit of service, inventory turnover, equipment utilization);
■ quality (cycle time, error rate/sigmas, supplier performance, training/competency, cost of poor quality, score on quality assessment, scrap/rework, supplier profile); and
■ community and environment (community involvement, public image, corporate citizenship evidence, environmental results).

Lately, the external value, in particular the creation of 'client value' and 'shareholder value' has become a relevant indicator of financial performance.

Marketing Control

Once the performance of a service organization can be measured, it becomes possible to control this performance, and to compare objectives or budgets with actual outcomes. A basic prerequisite to do such a comparison is that the goals set must be as clear as possible. The more diffuse goals are, the more difficult it is to measure and control them and to pinpoint employees on the fact that goals have or have not been met. In this stage of the marketing planning process, you will encounter all the problems and pitfalls once goals are not formulated according to the SMART principle.[48] Goals or objectives should be:

■ Specific;
■ Measurable;
■ Accepted;
■ Realistic; and
■ Timely.

The financial objectives as well as the non financial objectives can be formulated according to this SMART principle.

The comparison between planned results and actual results can be done by just comparing the two or by a simple analysis of variance in which one looks for the explanation for the differences found. The necessary feedback can then be provided and corrective actions (if needed) can be taken. It then becomes necessary to control the efforts efficiently and effectively by means of all kinds of organizational structures and processes. A service organization should not forget to explicitly pay attention to their personnel (their service attitude, leadership style, knowledge, ability, skills, etc.), hence human resource management (HRM) and the role of the customer in accomplishing the goals set on service quality for instance.

The factors useful in controlling a service organization will refer partly to the output of the organization (for example, the number of policies closed, train tickets sold and customer satisfaction; often the technical quality). They will also refer to the input used (professional skills of employees, equipment, etc.) and to the 'throughput' (how does the service process work, the service attitude; in short, the functional and relational quality).

Another important distinction that has to be made is the difference between formal control mechanisms (focussing on the above mentioned input, throughput and output measures) and the informal control mechanisms (self-control, social control, control via e.g. colleagues, and cultural control; control via the existing corporate culture).[49] Moreover, the service company should define not only its key success factors and its key performance indicators, but also its key control variables (they may be different).

An important part of this control process is measuring, just like giving feedback. Control and giving feedback can take place on a formal and/or informal basis with the help of processes and structures that characterize the service delivery.

In this final stage, the marketing planning process and the marketing plan, are evaluated. Such an evaluation can be done from an internal and external perspective. The internal perspective assesses whether the goals set are actually accomplished and our five service guidelines are followed. The external perspective assesses whether the organization has been capable of really satisfying customer needs, delivering service experiences and external value. The outcome of the evaluation is written down in a report to top management. These results are the input for an adjustment procedure or change in the marketing strategy or marketing programme and are of great importance to the next marketing plan which is aimed at generating value to all the stakeholders in the next time period.

Summary

Matching demand and supply is essential to the success of a service organization. Marketing planning can be helpful in that matching process. The marketing planning process consists of an external and an internal part. It is important to realize that decisions made about the characteristics of services as discussed in Chapter 2 now show their impact on the service firm's strategic room for manoeuvre. This also determines what skills the front and back office employees and the customers should possess (or should learn if not available right now). They all must be able, motivated and have the opportunity to perform the role they have to play in the script during the servuction process. Therefore, we developed the notion of the service triad.

The marketing plan consists of the following nine elements:

- Management summary;

- The marketing audit;
- Market segmentation;
- Strategic analysis, choice and market positioning;
- Implementation of the marketing mix;
- Internal marketing;
- Finance and accounting;
- Activity planning;
- Business cases.

The aspect of internal marketing is very important in the service sector. Human beings rather than production processes are key in delivering services. Somehow, service marketing is less hard than marketing of (fast-moving) goods. Tangible products are of minor importance. This calls for a great human effort to make things work. So, the coordination of activities through internal marketing is vital.

In our opinion, it is key to check whether the marketing plan conceals the five strategic service marketing management guidelines of:

- Understanding, creating and delivering valuable service experiences;
- Effectively manage the basic characteristics of services;
- To enhance market orientation;
- To manage the impact, challenges, risks and opportunities of internationalization; and
- To enhance 'assets and capabilities' management;

through its three phases of

- Understanding;
- Creating; and
- Delivering

value through excellent service experiences. These service experiences should be worth the money (and efforts) of (profitable) customers.

Implementation refers not only to developing the marketing mix in services according to the service provider's mission, goals and strategy 'on paper' in such a way that all parts logically fit together. In fact, implementation hinges upon actually 'making strategies work' and making relationships come true. In other words, the required investments in equipment and employees should be completed, employees should be convinced of the new strategy, plans, actions, ways of working, etc. accept them and act accordingly.

The resulting performance should be measured. The specific features of services (intangibility and the like), impose special requirements on these measurements as such and, in particular, with respect to assessing the performance achieved. It also affects the way performance can be controlled. Since the service encounter and the processes that take place in it are crucial to providing services and delivering excellent service quality, measuring and controlling this process and the activities of the actors (front office personnel and the customer) should be crucial elements in measuring and controlling this performance. So, throughput measures are vital here, next to input and output measures. Also, informal control mechanisms can be applied. The added value can be looked at from three points of view: the customers', the employees' and the owners' point of view. The six perspectives mentioned in our balanced score card, key performance indicators, key control indicators and value-based management, are useful means to that end.

In marketing control, financial as well as non-financial and behavioural variables can be used. As such, planning and the way the marketing department is organized are also means to (formally) control the marketing performance. It has been shown that the relationship between market orientation and performance is a positive one. The relationship is stronger for the link between market orientation and non financial performance than for the link between market orientation and financial performance.

Questions

1. What is the link between Figure 12.2 and our four types of services as described in section 12.3 and the four types of B2B service providers (vendor, total solutions provider, specialists and game changer)? What is the possibility of utilizing personal interaction and capacity management with these four generic strategies of service typology?
2. What can be said about the importance of internal marketing within the marketing planning process?
3. What is unique to measuring performance and exercising control in service businesses?
4. What is unique to marketing services in mature markets?
5. Why is the implementation and organization stage so important in marketing planning in service companies?
6. What is the link between the chapters of this book, the service guidelines and the content of the marketing plan? Make a one-page note on this.
7. What are the solutions to overcome the implementation problems in the more strategic gaps of the SERVQUAL model? What are the solutions to overcome the implementation problems in the more operational gaps of the SERVQUAL model?
8. What is the SMART principle? Why is it so important in formulating and controlling objectives?
9. What are the building blocks of the service marketing audit?
10. Why should the nine elements of the marketing plan not be carried out in an hierarchical order?

Assignments

1. Chapter 4 contains a number of causes underlying the implementation problems at the strategic level (Gaps 1 and 2 of the SERVQUAL model) and at the tactical level (Gaps 3 and 4). Put these causes in a diagram distinguishing between the strategic and tactical levels.
2. Make a scheme in which you combine the six perspectives of our balanced score card with the seven measures used in the International Benchmarking Clearinghouse study mentioned in section 12.6. What conclusion can you draw? In what respects do the two match?
3. Do you know some examples where the execution of the marketing strategy in service firms is not in accordance with what they claim in, for instance, advertising campaigns? Elaborate on these examples and try to find an explanation.

4. Perform a service marketing audit for the university or school where you study now. What kind of strategies do competing schools apply? Or, perform a service marketing audit for any other service firm you like (dentist, hospital, charity, accountant, food store (or chain), bank, insurance company, travel agent, hotel, bar, airline, building society, etc.). How does your chosen company differ from its main competitors?

5. Describe briefly the marketing steps of the marketing plan for a transport company that focusses on transport of clothing in your country.

Endnotes

1 *Fortune*, 2005.

2 Bonoma, 1985.

3 We mention here the five dimensions. You have seen in Chapter 5 that it is also possible to define ten dimensions.

4 Woo and Ennew, 2005a, 2005b.

5 For more on strategic management in professional service firms, see Lowendahl, 1997.

6 The remainder of this section is largely based on James Heskett, W. Earl Sasser Jr and Christofer Hart, *Service Breakthroughs* (1990).

7 Heskett, Sasser and Hart, 1990, p. 150.

8 Heskett, Sasser and Hart,1990, pp. 152–155.

9 The authors of the text have based their figure on Heskett, Sasser and Hart (1990, p. 151), but also made some modifications to it.

10 Nijssen and Frambach, 2001, p. 116.

11 See Heskett, 1987.

12 However, the different lengths of the sections do not imply that length equals importance of the stages in the whole planning process.

13 Such an analysis also can be done at corporate level. Then the result will be a (new) corporate and marketing strategy. We discuss it here in order to incorporate all the relevant marketing issues to deliver excellent service quality.

14 The discussion of these issues about SWOT, opportunity matrix, etc. is largely based on Palmer, 1997, ch. 3.

15 Of course, more factors are deemed relevant to assess markets and services than just these two. One should remember that in completing this matrix. One of the authors once applied this matrix successfully in positioning on the one hand all Dutch universities to decipher the positions of Maastricht University and all schools at

Maastricht University on the other hand. The well-known strategies for each of the four segments could be developed easily for our university and the various schools.

16 The strategies are well known and can be found in every textbook on marketing management.

17 In fact, the marketing audit can be part of the corporate audit, containing for instance also a financial, production, personnel and IT audit. See Palmer, 1997, p. 50.

18 This figure is a slight adaptation from Palmer's Figure 3.1, p. 47. This simple structure is the foundation of the more complex figure – the overall marketing planning process.

19 Faes and Van Tilborgh, 1984, pp. 107–112.

20 Canziani, 1997, p. 8. In this paper, an interesting classification of new customers has been developed: virgin newcomers, virtual newcomers, value switchers and vagabond switchers. It would go too far here to elaborate on it in detail.

21 See e.g. Homburg and Pflesser, 2000.

22 The summary of the generic strategic models is adopted from: De Vries and Van Helsdingen, 2005, pp. 149–151 and 525–527.

23 Nijssen and Frambach, 2001, p. 114.

24 This part is largely based on De Vries and Van Helsdingen, 2005, pp. 532–539.

25 However, in our consultancy work we have quite often experienced that companies think that introducing such a position in the company would (almost) lead to being market oriented. That is a huge mistake.

26 Bell and Fay, 1991.

27 Grönroos, 1990b.

28 See also Stauss, 1991.

29 This section is largely based on a report written for the NIMA (the Dutch Marketing Institute) by Wolter Kloosterboer (under supervision of Prof. Dr Jos Lemmink and Prof. Dr Hans Kasper). This report is based on his MBA thesis about Internal Marketing, University of Maastricht, 1992.

30 Usually these people are called 'product champions'; you will understand that in this text on services marketing, we call them 'service champions'. In other instances, especially when something has gone wrong, these people are called 'problem owners'. We find that term too negative to use over here.

31 The overview and figure is based on Nijssen and Frambach, 2001, p. 140. KPIs indicate key performance indicators – they are linked to key success factors.

32 NN, 2005.

33 Waters, 2005.

34 Karnitschnig, 2005.

35 This figure is based on various sources, like McDonald and Payne, 1998; Bonoma, 1985; and Kasper, De Vries and Van Helsdingen, 1999.

36 Edvardsson, Thomasson and Ovretreit, 1994.

37 Rust, Zahorik and Keiningham, 1995.

38 Research is forthcoming to validate this model empirically. That's why we cannot elaborate on the empirical findings obtained (see Rust, Zahorik and Keiningham, 1996).

39 Ittner and Larcker, 1998; Banker *et al.*, 2000; Nager and Rajan, 2001.

40 Kasper *et al.*, 2006a. In the regression equations it turned out that FP = constant + 0.25 MO (with adjusted R2 of 0.062) and NFP = constant + 0.35 MO (with adjusted R2 of 0.119).

41 Permenter, 2004, p. 103.

42 Collin, 2002, quoted by Chan and Chan, 2004, p. 205.

43 Chan and Chan, 2004, p. 205.

44 Collin, 2002, quoted by Chan and Chan, 2004, p. 205.

45 Campbell, Campbell and Ho-Beng, 1996, p. 261.

46 See also Kullvén, 1996.

47 Thor, 1996.

48 We have come across many service organizations (especially in the public sector) where goals are very vaguely formulated, often because of the different political interests that have to be taken into account. This makes the control of the policies initiated very difficult. However, we realized that mentioning in advance that goals should be very clear in order to evaluate progress was not that much accepted by politicians. Afterwards they do realize that it should have been done before. Because the impact of mentioning these SMART principles is greater when control does not work out as easily as expected, we have mentioned these principles here (and not in Chapter 6).

49 The basics about control in a marketing setting are presented in Jaworski (1988). A comprehensive overview of management control is presented in Merchant (1995). Insight into the accounting and control implications of the various characteristics of services, is still rare. Sven Modell (1996) developed a framework to that end. However, this framework has not been tested yet.

Chapter 13

Case Studies

Case Study 1

Risk Has No Religion[1]

Traditionally Islamic banks are not allowed to charge interest to their customers. This makes it quite difficult for them to operate in the international financial world and compete with their (Islamic and other) competitors. This case shows how the Bank Aljazira has solved this problem.

Mishari al-Mishari worked for two decades at international banking titan Citibank before he became chief executive of Bank Aljazira. He hired western-trained expatriates to fill management ranks at Aljazira, which has been posting significant gains.

The key to Bank Aljazira's recent success is a plaque displayed near the elevators at its headquarters. It is a brass copy of a certificate signed by a board of Muslim scholars, testifying that the institution now works in strict compliance with Islamic religious laws.

With his profits soaring in the Arab world's biggest economy, Mr Mishari spotted an early trend that is reshaping the financial landscape of the Middle East and beyond: Islamic banking.

Islam's Sharia laws severely limit the practice of charging or paying interest. But a new generation of Islamic banks have found ways to make products mimic the western originals, from floating-rate infrastructure loans to Islam-compliant credit cards issued by visa. The paperwork, however, is Islamic. 'Risk,' Mr Mishari says with a smile, 'has no religion.'

In the past decade, Islamic banking has matured from a tiny, sometimes controversial backwater into an important current of global finance, especially as western bankers and borrowers compete for the new funds gushing into the Persian Gulf because of higher oil revenues. Citigroup Inc. now operates what is effectively the world's largest Islamic bank in terms of transactions. Some $6 billion, or about €4.6 billion, of Citibank deals have now been structured and marketed in conformance with Islamic laws since starting out in 1996. HSBC group, Deutsche Bank, ABN Amro, Société Génerale, BNP Paribas and Standard Chartered also have established Islamic banking units in the past few years.

In 1999, there were just a dozen Islamic-branded investment funds; now there are at least 150 around the world. In Malaysia, Islamic financial instruments now account for 10% of the country's public and private financial dealings, up from 6% in 2000, according to the Malaysian central bank. In Turkey, the biggest economy in the Muslim world, market leader HSBC Turkey arranged $438 million of loans for companies last year, up from $50 million in 2001.

Western borrowers are tapping the trend. Citibank sold a €100 million Islamic bond last September for the German state of Saxony-Anhalt. The deal involved investors buying the state's tax office buildings and then leasing them back for a revenue stream. The return on investment was from ownership, not interest payments. It was thus Islamic and attracted Middle Eastern money.

Even the US Treasury Department has noted the increasing popularity of Islamic mortgages and investment indexes in the USA and Europe. It appointed its first Islamic banking scholar-in-residence last June. 'Islamic finance is coming of age,' says Mahmoud al-Gamal, chairman of Islamic economics at Rice University in Texas, who filled the Treasury post last year.

Britain has gone further, actively encouraging Islamic banking to help defuse Islamic extremism in its Muslim minority and keep funds within its own regulatory framework. A high-ranking British finance official travelled to the Persian gulf in 2002 to ask Arab investors to help capitalize one of the first stand-alone, deposit-taking Islamic banks in the West. The Islamic Bank of Britain opened in November and has raised more than $100 million in a private placement and an initial public offering in London. Although eight out of ten of its investors are in England, 80% of the money behind the bank has come from the Persian Gulf, the bank says. The project also has attracted interest from neighbouring European countries that are struggling to integrate large Muslim populations. Says Michael Hanlon, the bank's chief executive, a 60-year-old veteran of Barclays and a Christian: 'Why can't we bring Islamic banking into the western world?'

Regulation remains a big concern, partly because so much involved with Islamic banking is so new. There isn't any unified Islamic banking authority – comparable, say, to the Bank of International Settlements in Switzerland – and no universal view of what exactly qualifies as an Islamic product. Several competing bodies in Bahrain and another in Malaysia are working on new rules over Islamic financial accounting, bank governance and lending standards.

Still, in Saudi Arabia, Islamic banking is already challenging the long-standing dominance of western-style financial institutions. At the national Commercial Bank, mainly owned by the Saudi state and the largest bank in the Arab world, the lending portfolio shot up last year alone to 80% compliant with Islamic law from 16%, according to the bank's senior economist Nahed Taher. The bank is now considering going all-Islamic, like Bank Aljazira. 'There's huge demand,' says Nahed Taher.

Bank Aljazira, while far smaller, already has capitalized on the trend. From 2002, when its all-Islamic strategy gained traction, the bank has doubled its profits each year. Mr Mishari arrived from Citibank in 1993, lured by a group of Saudi financiers who wanted to rebuild the then-struggling bank. The bank operated completely on Western banking conventions back then. 'In Saudi Arabia, there was only one bank concentrating on Sharia-compliant products,' says Mr Mishari, a graduate of the University of Oregon. 'We saw very little innovation.'

Mr Mishari's team decided Islamic products would be perfect for attracting a distinct group of potentially lucrative customers: middle-class Saudis who thought Islamic banking meant earning no return or dealing with financial products that were unimaginative, backward and designed only for highly religious Muslims. In Saudi Arabia, in particular, Mr Mishari's team now saw low-hanging fruit: nearly half of Saudi bank deposits were kept in non interest bearing savings accounts.

In 1998, the bank decided the best strategy was to brand itself as a high-class, all-Islamic bank. But Mr Mishari didn't want to jettison the suit-and-tie westerners he had hired; they still feature prominently in the bank's annual report, and Mr Mishari, who favours the traditional Saudi robe and headdress as attire, often turns to them to work out the finer points of Islamic finance.

The bank's first step was setting up a Sharia board – made up of three to five Islamic authorities who vet the bank's documentation and certify that products comply with Islamic law. This religious approval could be vital: One adviser to the Sharia board took two months to persuade the owner of a building in a Saudi provincial city to accept Bank Aljazira as his tenant.

Mr Mishari's team first approached the board with a leveraged stock-trading mechanism that lets customers trade as much as $2\frac{1}{2}$ times the value of stocks in their accounts – an Islamic version of the margin-trading account. It made Bank Aljazira rocket to the No. 1 spot in stockbroking in 2000, which it held onto in 2001. 'People say there's something lucky about coming to Aljazira,' said Saud Mira, a 42-year-old professor of engineering visiting a plush new Bank Aljazira branch for after work speculation.

Next, the bank plunged into developing all-new Islamic life insurance. Western-style insurance is a tricky product for Islamic bankers. For a start, some Muslims also view insurance as betting against God's will, and thus a failure of faith. That problem was quickly overcome. 'The scholars agree that we are put down on Earth with free will,' explained Dawood Taylor, a British convert to Islam who heads the insurance project. 'When asked the question: "Shall I tie up my camel or leave his fate to the will of Allah?" they answered: "Tie up your camel and then look to the will of Allah."'

But the Sharia board rejected Mr Taylor's first attempt to mimic the way traditional insurance companies profit from controlling customers' premiums. So Mr Taylor developed an Islamic version of the mutual insurance, which was acceptable to the Aljazira Sharia Board because it pools funds from policy holders.

The bank now has 2500 individual and 12 500 corporate policyholders for the insurance plan. This breakthrough has caught the eye of traditional insurance giants like France-based AXA SA. 'So far our business in Saudi Arabia is minuscule. We'll have to think about something like that if we want to stay in the market,' an AXA spokeswoman said.

Case Questions

1. Which DRETS factors have caused Bank Aljazira to develop these special Islamic banking services.
2. What is your opinion of the role of the Sharia Board in the bank's operations, in general, and in its process of developing new services, in particular.
3. In what way or to what extent are the characteristics of the Aljazira Bank in line with our statements on a market-oriented service organization? Explain.

Endnote

1 This case is based on Hugh Pope, 2005.

Case Study 2

Scanning Blogs for Brand Insights

One of the main problems that service organizations face in the management of their customer relationships and their brands is gaining accurate and up-to-date information upon how their customers feel. Traditional market research can take months from customer to board room and often the answers themselves reveal little about customers underlying motives and responses. As one bank employee recently stated, 'Ask a customer the most important thing about choosing a personal loan and they will say "interest rate" but only 20% of customers with personal loans actually knew what rate they were currently paying.' One solution is to use the growth in 'blogs' and establish this form of 'online anthropology' as a direct and quick insight into customers real and often secret lives.

The word 'blog' is a contraction from the term 'Web log'. This is an online diary or journal which is published and shared with others on the Web by an individual, who is known as a 'blogger'. 'Blogging' has now become a very popular publishing method on the Web as the software does not require any technical knowledge to use and provides an opportunity to understand daily experiences of individuals. Blog watching has now become part of the research effort undertaken by advertising and brand development agencies to gain insights into brands and their communities, partly because the research is quick, cheap and less biased than other research forms.

Blog watching services, which utilize sophisticated technology to draw inferences from blogs, chat groups, message boards and other electronic forums, are at the forefront of this development. Using natural language analysis, target customers can be identified from their speech format, subject matter and the use of acronyms. OMG (Oh my God), POS (parent over shoulder) are acronyms highly associated with Generation Y girls, while FUBAR (fouled up beyond all recognition) identified the blogger as a male Baby Boomer.

Charging US$30–100 000 the services are useful for getting the lay of the land and picking up market sentiment. Many service companies are now using these services to inform them about new product opportunities and to assess how they respond to market changes. One service called Intelliseek has a free web site called BlogPulse which allows its customers to enter up to three key words and see where their company sits. Before the latest *Star Wars* film was released mentions of Natalie Portman (one of the stars of the film) briefly topped mentions of Paris Hilton, which was evidence that the pre-launch marketing campaign was getting through to the target group.

Advertising giant WPP crafted a new promotion aimed at teenagers using blog watching. Using technology which is able to identify demographic groups based on speech patterns and discussion topics, the company found that teens were really anxious about exceeding their cellular minutes, often because parents make them pay if they talk too much. The teens also resented being ambushed by incoming calls that pushed their talk minutes up. The campaign called 'call me' minutes was launched in January 2005 and the following press release describes the service product and how it related to the blog research:

U.S. Cellular has recently introduced CALL ME minutes, providing its customers with unlimited free incoming calls, from anyone, anywhere, anytime – landline or wireless – to a U.S. Cellular customer in their local calling area. U.S. Cellular is the first cellular carrier in the United States to offer this feature. CALL ME minutes are not deducted from package minutes, leaving customers with more 'anytime' minutes to place calls. CALL ME is available to new customers and to those renewing service with U.S. Cellular. 'As consumers rely more and more on their cell phones, we give our customers more value and the freedom to answer incoming calls without worrying about going over their allotted minutes,' said Alan D. Ferber, vice president of marketing for U.S. Cellular. 'The reaction from our customers has been excellent,' added Ferber.

Some blog watching services are able to spot trends before they emerge in mainstream media. For instance blog watchers 'Intelliseek' were able to identify the impact of claims against the presidential candidate John Kerry some three weeks before the Kerry campaign addressed them.

For a Japanese car maker, the blogs revealed a shift in market preferences. Families said that their young children loved the new minivan format and the kids often said that it was like 'a playhouse on wheels'. By contrast the teen bloggers regarded the minivan format as 'lame' and wanted their parents to get a sports utility vehicle instead. The response from the manufacturer was to recognize the potential damage from families 'trading up' as their children got older. They instituted a loyalty programme to persuade current minivan owners to trade up to the company SUVs rather than looking elsewhere or trying to sell them another minivan.

But not everything that bloggers says about brands is necessarily reliable though. One agency was monitoring Burger King and the introduction of the Angus Burger. The blogs gave the new burger a bad review and derided the company for its tongue in cheek TV ads that called the burger a diet food. Notwithstanding the Angus burger has become a hit. While the information is interesting there are many questions yet to be answered about the collection of the information and the reliability of the data generated.

Case Questions

1. How might the marketing manager of a service firm use this type of service?
2. Does the blog phenomenon pose any threats to an organization?

Case Study 3

Linking Core Competencies to Customer Needs: Strategic Marketing of Health Care Services[1]

ADK Research Corp. and Clinical Trial Services

The principals of ADK Research Corp. had, over a period of ten years, developed expertise in data collection, database management and networking technologies for large-scale, government-funded, clinical trial research projects. Unique, customized systems were developed that integrated leading-edge mini and micro computing hardware with customized software applications. The systems reduced data entry errors, enhanced data processing, and provided greater research efficiency (in data collection through report generation) while improving data accuracy. ADK's goal was to expand into the private sector. Market research was needed to determine if ADK's systems could be successfully marketed to the private sector. Target customers included pharmaceutical, biotechnology, and device manufacturers in need of clinical trial research services.

The clinical trial services required for developing a new drug or device are: clinical centre review and selection; protocol development; clinical centre management; data collection; statistical analysis; research report generation; and FDA report generation.

Most manufacturers do not have the facilities or capabilities to manage all of their clinical trial work in-house. While some services may be conducted by the company developing the new product, others however are contracted to an outside clinical trial research supplier (CTRS).

Previous research in health care settings has shown that service quality, customer satisfaction and subsequent market behaviour are interrelated. ADK was concerned that its perceptions of consumer CTRS expectations might differ from actual expectations. Any expectation gaps would likely result in ADK developing and implementing ineffective marketing programmes.

Of interest to ADK was the value firms would place on their hardware and software innovations. Specifically, information was desired regarding the (1) importance of CTRS technical capabilities relative to other criteria and (2) degree of satisfaction with current CTRS services, particularly dimensions related to the application of technology. Such information would help ADK determine if and how its core competencies could be translated into benefits sought in the marketplace.

Research Design

To provide ADK with insights into the CTRS market, a research study was developed that had three components. The first was information on the criteria firms use to select a research supplier. The second component included information on the evaluation of and satisfaction with prior CTRS use. These two components would provide insights into the CTRS selection and evaluation processes used by pharmaceutical firms. The third component entailed linking ADK's technological strengths with the selection and evaluation criteria. Establishing such links would identify the ways in which ADK could offer potential customers greater satisfaction while highlighting how ADK should market its services.

A questionnaire was designed to determine criteria used to select CTRS and satisfaction with CTRS use. Questionnaire items were developed following (1) a service quality literature review, (2) analysis of competitive CTRS marketing communication, and (3) exploratory indepth interviews with clinicians and/or researchers with clinical trial decision making responsibilities.

Survey participants were sought from pharmaceutical, biotechnology and device manufacturers. The informants were typically vice presidents or directors of R&D, product development or clinical research. Each informant was mailed a description of the study and a questionnaire. A reminder letter and questionnaire were mailed if the original had not been returned after three weeks. In total, 27 useable responses were collected for a 46% questionnaire return rate.

Of the 27 responses, 11 were from pharmaceutical companies, eight each were from biotechnology and device firms. All of the firms in the sample had moderate to extensive experience using CTRS.

Results

CTRS Selection Criteria

Table 1 shows the attribute evaluations, ordered in terms of importance. The five more global benefits associated with each attribute (image, credentials, expertise, cost, and technology) are also listed.

ADK's chief concern was the relative importance of its core competencies – the attributes related to technological benefits. The three technological attributes – data management systems, telecommunications capabilities, and hardware and software configurations – were perceived to be relatively unimportant attributes.

Table 2 shows the relative importance of the six CTRS benefits, both overall and for each industry sector. CTRS' technological capability is one of the least important benefits when it comes to selecting a CTRS.

Table CS3.1 Attributes used to select CTRS

Selection factor	Benefit	Importance score*
Overall reputation	Image	6.33
Private sector/pharmaceutical industry experience	Credentials	5.73
Expertise in treatment/application area	Expertise	5.33
Price	Cost	5.13
FDA experience	Credentials	4.80
Prestige of clinical centre(s) provided	Image	4.47
Prior NDA/PMA preparation experience	Credentials	4.43
Data management system	Technology	4.00
Telecommunications capabilities	Technology	3.36
Clinical research publication experience	Credentials	3.29
Hardware and software configurations	Technology	3.21
Location of supplier	Convenience	3.00
University affiliation	Credentials	2.93

Note: *Mean importance score across all respondents using CTRS. All attributes measured on seven-point scales, where 1 = not at all important, and 7 = very important.

Table CS3.2 Benefits sought from CTRS by industry sector				
		Industry sector*		
	Total	Pharmaceuticals	Biotechnology	Device
Image	5.40	5.56	4.63	6.25
Expertise	5.33	5.33	4.50	6.70
Cost	5.13	5.00	5.25	5.50
Credentials	4.50	4.71	4.20	3.80
Technology	3.52	3.78	3.42	3.34
Convenience	3.00	3.22	2.50	3.00

Note: *Mean importance score across all respondents using CTRS. Importance score for each benefit represents average of all related attributes. Attributes measured on seven-point scales where 1 = not at all important and 7 = very important.

ADK's innovations, its technological competencies, were not highly sought by CTRS decision makers. Other benefits, particularly the CTRS' image, application expertise, cost and certain of its credentials seemed to guide the selection process. Hence, ADK's core competencies are not perceived by customers as providing any differential advantage (Tables 3 and 4).

Past CTRS Satisfaction

Table 3 shows respondents' satisfaction with past CTRS on six service dimensions. Four service dimensions were evaluated very similarly, yielding moderate satisfaction: data accuracy, staff responsiveness, and quality of reporting to clients and the FDA (the Federal Drug Administration). The remaining two dimensions – flow of communicaton and performing deliverables – only resulted in neutral levels of satisfaction.

Also, respondents assessed their overall satisfaction with CTRS services, and the resulting mean score was 4.64. From the service satisfaction measures shown in Table 3, the only dimensions with significantly lower satisfaction scores, compared to the overall satisfaction variable, were performing deliverables and flow of communications.

Given that satisfaction with CTRS seemed to be moderate at best, it should be explored why this might be the case. A useful way to understand relationships between attributes or

Table CS3.3 Satisfaction with CTRS service dimensions	
Service dimension	Satisfaction score*
Data accuracy	4.93
Responsiveness of study staff	4.92
Quality of reporting to client firm	4.76
Quality of submission for NDA/PMA	4.75
Flow of communications	4.29
Performing deliverables/meeting deadlines	3.92

Note: *Mean satisfaction score across all CTRS users. All dimensions measured on seven-point scale where 1 = not at all satisfied and 7 = very satisfied.

Table CS3.4   Relationship between CTRS service satisfaction dimensions

	Pearson correlation coefficients*					
	Data accuracy	Meeting deadlines	Comm. flow	Staff responsiveness	Quality of reporting	Quality of submission
Meeting deadlines	0.165					
Comm. flow	0.590	0.752**				
Staff responsiveness	0.667**	0.513	0.776**			
Quality of reporting	0.702**	0.498	0.866**	0.645		
Quality of NDA/PMA submission	−0.372	0.567	0.298	0.365	0.000	
Overall satisfaction	0.389	0.878**	0.890**	0.804**	0.675**	0.683

Note: * $n = 27$. All dimensions measured on seven-point scales, where 1 = not at all satisfied and 7 = very satisfied. ** Statistically significant relationship, one-tailed t-test, at $p < 0.01$.

dimensions is to explore intercorrelations. Table 4 shows correlation analysis results for the service satisfaction dimensions (including overall satisfaction). Table 4 shows four dimensions correlate very highly with overall satisfaction: performing deliverables, communication flows, staff responsiveness and quality of reporting. The relatively low overall CTRS satisfaction is due in part to poor CTRS performance on meeting their deadlines and establishing good communications with their clients.

Communication flows appear to be highly correlated with performing deliverables on time, staff responsiveness, and reporting quality. Hence, communication flows may be a key dimension through which to facilitate quality service delivery.

Case Questions

1. In what way do ADK's own perceptions of customer satisfaction differ from customer's own perceptions?
2. How do you evaluate the market research study ADK performed?
3. What would you suggest that ADK do to become a market oriented company (and lose its technology orientation)?

Endnote

1 This case is based on the Roth and Amoroso (1993) study about CTRS.

Case Study 4

Driving Online Legal Services at Minters[1]

By David Rymer, Director of KnowHow, Minter Ellison

From Bricks to Clicks

Minter Ellison is one of Australia's leading legal practices. Since 1995, Minter Ellison has doubled in size and now has over 2000 people working in seven countries with annual revenue of over $340 million. In a recent *Business Review Weekly* survey, it was ranked second in Australia in fees generated.

Initially, online legal services were seen as a threat to a profession that rejoiced in its traditional approach to client service. Now these products and services are very much part of the legal landscape.

Demand Drivers behind Online Legal Services

Minter Ellison's adoption of online legal services was driven by its appreciation of three compelling forces to change:

■ client demand
■ productivity/cost considerations and
■ competitive pressures.

Client Demand
Clients who have undergone an extensive organizational change process increasingly look for professional service organizations who mirror their own efficiency. Without IT investment and streamlined internal systems, it is difficult for clients to achieve the benefits offered by online legal services or to utilize the online products effectively.

Productivity Cost Considerations
Like other sectors of the economy, Australia's legal companies are rationalizing in search of economies of scale. A large company can afford to invest in the IT infrastructure investment required to deploy cost-effective, sophisticated online legal technologies. Client extranets, portals and information systems are very cost-effective ways of delivering client contact details, legal information and administrative updates.

Similarly, dedicated online products such as SAFETRAC provide low cost delivery systems in areas of the law where the ability to adapt standardized legal documents quickly and efficiently are major considerations in choosing a legal representative.

Competitive Pressure
As legal companies grow larger and ever more international in their orientation, the provision of legal services through online technologies has come to be viewed as simply yet another pragmatic investment decision.

In seeking to compete locally with larger Australian-based companies and globally across Asia, the United Kingdom and the United States, Minter Ellison has sought to differentiate its brand from its competitors by being a technology enabled and knowledge-management-rich company. By doing this, the company hopes to achieve the optimum blend of personal and online legal service.

Delivering this differentiation demands an understanding of the drivers behind client demand, sophisticated revenue and cost modelling and an insight into end-to-end value chain support.

Minter Ellison's online legal product and service portfolio

Over the past two years, Minter Ellison has deployed a portfolio of online legal services including:

- SAFETRAC: an award winning online risk management training and evaluation product designed to deliver best practice compliance;
- LeaseKeeper: an online commercial leasing software and documentation package designed to standardize documents, sign-off procedures, matter management and compliance facilities;
- virtual case rooms: designed to support litigation teams, facilitate the discovery process and enable online document sharing in a secure environment;
- client extranets: facilitate clients' access to contact details, matter management documents, client bulletins and continuing legal education; and
- information services: online delivery of continuous updates on legal issues, judgements, trends and background briefings.

So why online legal services?

First, Minter Ellison increasingly operates on a national and international basis. Online legal products are an essential tool in operating a global business effectively. Second, its focus on national clients requires innovation to deliver productivity and efficiencies. Third, Minter Ellison operates in an increasingly complex information environment. Online legal services help to simplify this wall of information.

Most importantly, however, Minter Ellison's clients are changing. Clients are increasingly sophisticated in the way they source professional services. They are looking for advisers who have creative problem solving skills that add value to their business as well as the traditional technical legal expertise. At the same time, they want to simultaneously reduce costs and accelerate turnaround times.

In developing its online legal services strategy, Minter Ellison has been highly conscious of the need to optimize the mix between its traditional approach to legal services and the new opportunities for delivering value to clients via Web-based tools.

Moving forward

Effective online systems demand more than technology. They demand a clear business strategy and an economic model. In Minter Ellison, the development of online legal services is being driven by the desire to deliver economic value to our clients in the form of:

- ease of access
- convenience
- cost savings.

Online legal services involve cultural change that will facilitate the day-to-day operation support for these technologies within the company. To do this, Minter Ellison must develop innovative processes that will leverage the company's proprietary intellectual capital (IP) to deliver unique value to clients via online distribution channels.

Leveraging IP online with clients enables the company to:

- reduce costs and speed up response times on client matters;
- create opportunities to value-bill;
- identify new revenue streams;
- compete effectively against our competitors.

Thus, online legal services in many ways complement our traditional approach to client service.

Three key questions

In commercializing its online legal services strategy, Minter Ellison asked three basic questions:

- How well positioned is the firm to learn from its experience?
- How readily can the firm convert its experience and expertise into proprietary intellectual property (IP)?
- How fast can the firm apply its IP to clients and prospects to deliver value online and differentiate its brand?

Finally, the success of any online legal services programme rests with the company's culture and values. Firms that are able to learn and develop have a far greater chance of successfully using online legal services to grow the company's collective wealth.

Case Questions

1. Three main drivers influenced Minter Ellison's adoption of online legal services. Which one do you think would be the most important? Why?
2. Minter Ellison has deployed a portfolio of online legal services. Go to its website (**www.minterellison.com.au**) and find at least three of these services. Provide an evaluation of each in terms of ease of access, clarity and usefulness.
3. In what ways do changing client needs affect Minter Ellison's online strategy? How do you think it is able to track these changes?

4. What are the three key questions for Minter Ellison in commercializing its online legal services strategy? Can you think of any other questions it should ask?

Endnote

1 This case is from McColl-Kennedy (ed.), *Services Marketing: A Managerial Approach* (2003), John Wiley & Sons.

Reproduced by permission of David Rymer.

Case Study 5

Low Cost, No Frills Airlines[1]

By Sanna Sutter

In November 1995 the Greek businessman Stelios Haji-Ionnou started the low cost airline, easyJet. easyJet offers the choice of 183 routes to 57 big airports throughout Europe. With a fleet of 94 planes they transport more than 24 million passengers a year and the number of passengers is still growing. easyJet offers flexible and low cost flights to key destinations promising the best service despite their focus on low costs. Ideal for business travellers and holidaymakers, easyJet is one of the best low cost airlines in the world. In the case below, the sustainable competitive advantage achieved by such low cost airlines will be explained.

Historically, the airline industry has been one of the most heavily regulated and protected sectors. In the European Union, the deregulation of air services began in 1987, embedded in the much broader attempt to create the Single Market. After a long transition period, complete liberalization of intra-European Union air services was achieved on 1 April 1997. Deregulation, or liberalization as it has been termed in Europe, involves the effective removal of many regulations affecting civil aviation. Under regulation, airlines were not allowed to set their ticket prices at will and this form of price regulation produced two adverse consequences. On the one hand, airlines had no incentive to reduce costs by streamlining operations and increasing productivity. On the other hand fare levels in general were extremely high. These two consequences disappeared after the deregulation. Now government approval is no longer required for airlines to set fares or launch new services. Any European Union airline can, in theory, start domestic services in another member country. Liberalization has brought about numerous advantages to European travellers, both in terms of higher quality offered by airlines and drastic price reductions. One of the main and most interesting aspects of the free market has been the entry in the industry of low cost airlines. No frills airlines, also known as low cost airlines and budget airlines, are scheduled carriers with significantly lower cost than mainstream airlines who can therefore offer much lower average fares. Table CS5.1 shows that the low cost airlines maintain a cost level about 40–45% of the traditional airlines that fly on the same route.

Low-cost airlines have some important characteristics as shown in Table CS5.2.

Pricing

Airline pricing is so distorted that often a full-fare paying passenger is seated next to a passenger who paid more than 300% for his or her ticket. What makes this situation so exasperating is that each passenger is receiving the same quality of seat and in-flight service, regardless of the airfare paid.

Most companies have so far ignored the crucial importance of innovative pricing strategies as a tool to create sustained competitive advantages over rivals. Pricing is the only tool in the marketing mix that generates revenues directly whereas, at least initially, all others only cause costs to rise. Passengers always value price of airfare and travel time convenience over any

Table CS5.1 Cost advantages of low cost carriers on short haul routes

Carrier type	Cost reduction (%)	Cost per seat
Conventional scheduled carrier		100
Low cost carrier		
Operating advantages:		
Higher seat density	−16	84
Higher aircraft utilization	−3	81
Lower flight and cabin crew salaries/expenses	−3	78
Use cheaper secondary airports	−6	72
Outsourcing maintenance/single aircraft type	−2	70
Product/service features:		
Minimal station cost and outsourced handling	−10	60
No free in-flight catering	−6	54
Marketing differences:		
No agents' commissions*	−8	46
Reduced sales/reservation costs	−3	43
Other advantages:		
Smaller administration costs	−2	41

Note: *Assume 100% direct sales and none through agents

Rigas Doganis, *The Airline Business in the Twenty-first Century*, 2001, p. 150. Reproduced by permission of Thomson Publishing Services.

form of product differentiation. The higher quality in-flight amenities, emphasized by the major airlines, play very minor roles in determining the choice of airline. The primary reason for a passenger to select a particular airline is based on the cheapest airfare and the most convenient departure and arrival times. From this it becomes clear that it's important to offer a low fare.

Generally, the pricing of services requires a separate and different treatise to the issue of product pricing because of the atypical nature of services. If the source of an item's core benefit is more tangible than intangible, it should be considered a product, and if it is more intangible than tangible, it should be considered a service. The low cost airlines offer a service because the source of the product's core benefit, the flying, is more intangible.

One problem with a service is perishability. When a plane departs, unused seats are lost forever. To solve this problem airlines try to maximize their profit per passenger by using yield management, a tactical price strategy based on segmentation. Yield management tends to fill capacity by partitioning time into discrete periods, charging discount prices in early periods, and reserving capacity by restricting sales in these periods.

Segmentation by low cost airlines only occurs based on two variables:

1 The date of booking; and
2 The effective demand for specials flights.

Because of these variables there are two market segments for low cost airlines. Once each passenger's willingness to pay has been determined, the airline can then adjust fares

Table CS5.2	Characteristics of low cost airlines
Pricing structures	No frills airlines tend to use simplified pricing structures based on demand regulated single fares or flexible return tickets without the high cost premium fares required by mainstream airlines for fully flexible travel.
Service levels	In-flight services on most flights are curtailed or even eliminated, thereby reducing costs and labour. Faster airport turnarounds are also facilitated in this way. These are often no more than 30 minutes. Beverage service, where offered, is usually charged to customers and on international flights duty-free sales are promoted as sources of revenue generation. The fare only includes basic transportation in a single-class cabin. In-flight entertainment is often excluded from the package. Frequent flyer programmes (FFPs) are usually not offered.
Free seating arrangements	By offering free seating arrangements boarding times are reduced. Plastic, re-useable boarding cards are often used, again improving turnaround times.
Rapid turnaround times	Free seating arrangements are not the only reason for faster turnarounds, as reductions in service levels and other factors are relevant. The outcome is increased aircraft utilization.
Distribution	A major saving made by low cost carriers is that they tend not to maintain offices in the cities they serve. The direct purchase of tickets by telephone and with payment by credit card is encouraged by budget airlines keen to cut out the middleman and avoid paying commission to travel agents.
Load versus yield	Seats are usually sold on first come, first served basis with the cheapest seats being sold first as opposed to the traditional approach of trying to sell as many high revenue tickets as possible.
Booking restrictions	In addition to competitive fares, low cost airlines generally offer fewer restrictions.
Aircraft	Low cost carriers tend to lease rather than purchase aircraft.
Departure points	Most of the new carriers utilize airports such as Stansted and Luton for reasons of cost and faster turnarounds. Low cost carriers offer non stop point-to-point services to and from uncongested airports instead of connecting flight via a hub airport.
Labour costs	Further savings include reduced labour costs, as new airlines have labour costs that are about 40% of those of the big carriers. Staff productivity at the low cost carriers is substantially higher due to systematic outsourcing and longer daily, monthly and annual working hours (close to the legal maximums).

according to the types of passengers purchasing tickets. This results in groups of travellers with lower price elasticity paying a higher airfare than those with higher price elasticity, which clearly represents price discrimination. According to the economics literature, price discrimination occurs whenever identical goods or services are sold to different consumer segments at different prices. In order to implement price discrimination in the market the following assumptions must hold true:

1   The service provider or the seller must have price setting capability;
2   The markets for the services can be well segmented; and
3   The elasticity of demand must be different for each of these markets.

The low cost airlines meet all three assumptions. From this it becomes clear that yield management represents nothing more than a technical term for successful market segmentation followed by price discrimination.

Sustainable Competitive Advantage

The fundamental basis of the long-term success of a firm is being able to achieve and maintain sustainable competitive advantage. The definition of sustainable competitive advantage is the prolonged benefit of implanting some unique value-creating strategy not simultaneously being implemented by any current or potential competitors along with the inability to duplicate the benefits of this strategy. A conceptual model of sustainable competitive advantage in service industries is presented in Figure CS5.1. Here a firm's distinctive organizational skills and resources are viewed as the source of a business's

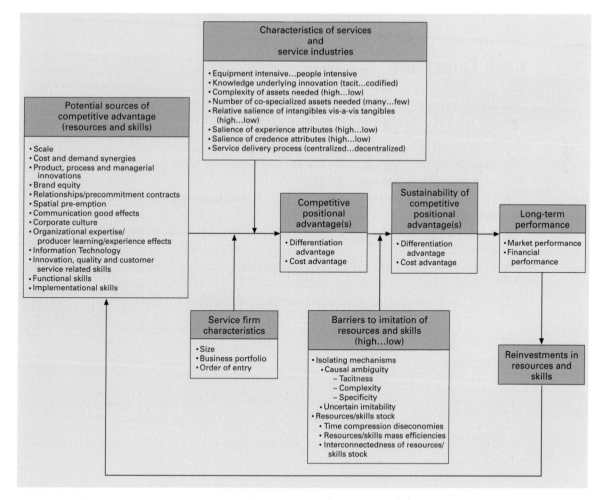

Figure CS5.1   A contingency model of sustainable competitive advantage in service industries

Reprinted with permission from the *Journal of Marketing*, published by the American Marketing Association. Bharadwaj, Varadarajan and Fahy, 'A contingency model of sustainable competitive advantage in service industries', October 1993, p. 84.

competitive advantage in the marketplace. The characteristics of services are shown as moderating the skills and resources underlying a business's competitive positional advantages. The model further suggests that sustainable competitive advantages are the key to sustained, superior long-term performance.

Researchers generally distinguish between two broad sources of competitive advantage – unique resources (assets) and distinctive skills (capabilities). These two broad sets of sources enable a business to perform the various primary and secondary value activities that make up its value chain either at a lower cost or in a way that leads to differentiation. They facilitate the attainment of competitive positional advantages in the form of:

1 Superior customer value through a differentiated product/service; and/or
2 Lower relative costs through cost leadership.

Differentiation leads customers to perceive a consistent difference in important attributes between the firm's offerings and its competitors' offerings. Cost leadership means performing most activities at a lower cost than competitors while offering a parity product.

Case Questions

1. What kinds of factors (trends) are influencing the airline? Describe what kind of influence these trends have for the airline industry.
2. What pricing strategy is used by low cost airlines?
3. Describe the two major segments that can be found in the airline industry and the ways airlines work with yield management.
4. What strategy, as described by Porter (1980), is used by airlines that provide low price airfares?
5. What strategy, as described by Hamel and Prahalad (1994), is used by airlines that provide low price airfares?
6. Explain how the low cost airlines can come to sustainable competitive advantage through the conceptual model of sustainable competitive advantage in service industries.
7. What conclusion can you reach by your answers of questions 4, 5 and 6?

Endnotes

1 This case is based on Pender and Baum, 2000; Knorr and Žigová, 2004; Kons, 1999; Holden and Nagle, 1998; Mitra and Capella, 1997; Hoffman, 2000; and Bharadwaj, Varadarajan and Fahy, 1993.

Case Study 6

Starbucks[1]

By Hendrik-Jan Lugtmeijer

Introduction

Starbucks Corporation is a coffee company based in Seattle, USA. This corporation buys, roasts and sells whole bean specialty coffee drinks through an international chain of retail outlets. Starbucks started in 1971, selling packaged, premium specialty coffee and exotic teas. By August 2005, Starbucks had evolved into a company with 9671 retail outlets (with 6888 in the United States), making them one of the fastest-growing companies in the USA. Over a ten-year period starting in 1992, the net revenues increased at a compounded annual growth rate of 20%, to 3.3 billion in fiscal 2002. Starbucks has turned coffee from a commodity to an experience to savour and has changed the perception and consumption of coffee for people around the world. Starbucks has emerged as one of the fastest-growing companies and one of the 75 global brands of the 21st century.

Background

In 1971, Jerry Baldwin, Zev Siegl and Gordon Bowker started selling whole bean coffee at Pikes Place Market in Seattle. They named this store after the coffee loving first mate Starbuck, from the 1851 novel *Moby Dick*. In 1982 the company had grown to five stores, one roasting facility and a wholesale business selling coffee to local restaurants. That year Howard Schultz (current Chairman, ex CEO) entered the business. He believed, following a trip to Italy, that this Seattle-based company could become a national chain of coffee houses styled after the Italian coffee bars. Nevertheless the owners did not want to be in the coffee bar business, so Howard Schultz started his own coffee bar, Il Giornale, in 1985. This concept was an overnight success and another two were opened soon after. Within two years this company had three stores and in 1987 it took over the Starbucks Company for $4 million. After the acquisition, the Il Giornale coffee bars changed their name to the more easily pronounced name of Starbucks with a new logo and nine new stores. The expansion first spread to Chicago, and went on to New York City, Boston and Atlanta and eventually numbered 161 stores in total in 1992. This was also the year that the Starbucks company went public and raised their capital for further national expansion.

The history of the coffee industry in the USA

The commercial market for coffee originates 500–1000 AD when Arab traders brought coffee to Europe. During the European imperial expansion, coffee was imported to the USA and the demand for this commodity soared immediately. In the first 20 years of its American introduction (1670) it replaced beer as New York's favourite breakfast drink. While the basic coffee business stagnated, the market for specialty coffee took off. The retail sales volume of specialty coffee rose from $45 million in 1969 to $2 billion in 1994. The sales of specialty coffee in 1994 accounted for 19% of the coffee sold in the USA.

The Starbucks Model

One of the main goals of Starbucks Corp., according to Howard Schultz, is to:

establish Starbucks as the premier purveyor of the finest coffee in the world while maintaining uncompromising principles as we grow.

This strategy has paid off; during the period of 1987 to August 2005 the number of shops increased from 17 to 9671 and since 1992 the business has shown a growth rate of 20% and a profits rate of 30%. To maintain growth, Starbucks searches for new areas in which to build hub and spoke infrastructure, where a city serves as a 'hub' and the surroundings as a 'spoke'. With this expansion the strategy is to blanket the area totally even if one shop cannibalizes another. The 'Starbucks everywhere' approach helps to cut down delivery and management costs, shorten customer lines at individual stores, and increases foot traffic for all the stores in the area. Overall, with this clustering strategy, Starbucks can better develop a Starbucks culture in the newly opened stores. Nevertheless each site has been carefully selected; the new site has to be in a visible, accessible and high traffic location. Significant criteria for these locations are the population density, median age, education level, estimated household income and the density of local competition.

The tremendous growth of the Starbucks locations has been facilitated by the strong relationships with the real estate representatives across the USA and the other locations around the world. This strong relationship facilitates the growth for Starbucks because they franchise rather than lease all the properties. Each location maintains their existing structure and therefore has a different size and shape. This diversity means that each site has to be transformed individually. Starbucks has very high standards, with their own in-house team of architects, designers and construction managers employed to transform the site. This includes the design of each space, including layout, lighting and furnishings. To reduce the average store opening costs, Starbucks centralize their buying, consolidating the work from contractors with costs control practices, and also consolidating products needed from vendors so they can achieve discounts up to 30%. This centralized and consolidated buying approach decreased the average store opening costs from $350 000 in 1995 to $315 000 in 2003.

Starbucks Distribution

Starbucks' main brand strength is their high quality standard for their coffee. In the coffee market there are two beans: the high quality arabica and the lower quality robusta beans. In their attempts to offer the best possible quality of coffee they purchase arabica beans directly from the producing countries. In 1992 Starbucks collaborated with Narino Supremo Bean Corp., guaranteeing to purchase their entire yield. This enabled Starbucks to be an exclusive purveyor of Narino Supremo, purportedly one of the best coffees in the world. Beside the bean, the roasting process is another crucial element of high quality coffee. Starbucks currently operates multiple roasting facilities. The coffee is roasted in a gas-fired drum roaster that is controlled by a computer that guarantees consistency. After roasting, the end product is finally sold through a range of distribution channels, not just the regular Starbucks sites but also hospitals, banks, office buildings, supermarkets, shopping centres and even in the air. Starbucks made a supply arrangement with United Airlines, providing them with coffee for 75 million passengers annually. Furthermore Starbucks established a licensing agreement with Kraft Foods Inc. to offer their coffee in grocery stores in the United States.

The Starbucks Experience

According to Howard Schultz

We're not just selling a cup of coffee, we are providing an experience.

The Starbucks brand relies heavily on the customer experience and therefore their biggest promotion is by word of mouth and the appeal of the shop fronts. The traditional advertising and promotion budget is rather small; in fact, in its first 20 years of existence only $20 million had been spent on this traditional advertising. The locations sell themselves by achieving the feel of an Italian coffee bar with each site being distinctive in size and format. The Starbucks brand name is also perceived as reliable, safe and consistent and the stores tend to be found in high traffic locations, such as shopping centres and busy streets corners. The motto for building this ambience was 'everything matters', so the store's fixtures, merchandise displays, colours, artwork, banners, music and aromas all create an environment that lends itself to drinking coffee. All these elements allow the customer to escape from the crowded streets and enjoy a relaxed atmosphere created by jazz or opera music in the background, good lighting and pleasant surroundings.

Another very important element of the Starbucks experience is its people. The employees called *baristas* at Starbucks are the ones who can directly affect the quality of the product and are part of the customer experience in the stores. Starbucks employees are considered partners in the business. This means they are offered excellent employee training, generous benefits programmes (health care), and a stock ownership plan. This system pays off, reflected in the fact that the *barista* turnover at Starbucks is 60% compared with 140% or more for workers in the fast-food business. The advantage of this relatively low employee turnover is the savings on training costs but more importantly the *baristas* get familiar with the regular customers, knowing their name and preferred drinks.

Starbucks Globalization

By 2004 business analysts observed that the US coffee bar market was reaching saturation. The only way to grow within the USA was to snap up their smaller competitors. Global expansion has become Starbucks' major opportunity for growth and therefore they established a subsidiary called Starbucks Coffee International Inc. Franchising has always been an opportunity for expansion but the management were afraid of losing control of the quality of the coffee. Therefore Starbucks used other mechanisms like joint ventures, licences and company owned operations in order to facilitate their global expansion.[20] The first overseas stores opened their doors in Tokyo and Singapore in 1996 and following this shops opened all over the Asian Pacific area, chosen due to their heavy concentration of world population.[21] By August 2005 Starbucks had 6888 locations within the USA of which 4666 are company operated and 2222 licensed (the total number changes with approximately three to four new sites per day). Outside the USA there are 2783 locations of which 1049 are company operated and 1734 are joint venture and licensed operations. We see a higher percentage of joint venture and licensed operations outside the USA because Starbucks chose to select local business partners to capitalize on local knowledge of recruitment and suppliers. There are still plenty more opportunities for Starbucks; in fiscal 2004 only 15.2% of the total revenues was created outside of the USA. In the future Starbucks will focus on Europe and Asia with plans to open 1000 new sites in China.

Case Questions

1. The direct promotional expenditure of Starbucks is relatively very low ($20 million in the first 20 years). Explain Starbucks marketing strategy with the help of the marketing mix.
2. Explain why Starbucks uses joint venture partnerships and licensing instead of franchising for their expansion strategy. (See also *www.starbucks.com*)
3. a Starbucks wants to control the end product and wants to teach people how to drink the specialty coffee. Explain how from the beginning Starbucks have driven their markets.
   b Give one example from the case in which Starbucks became market oriented and has changed one of their products according to customer demands.
4. Starbucks has a relatively low employee turnover. Explain, according to Figure 10.2, the generalized staff management framework and how each of the elements contributes to the low employee turnover.
5. Starbucks believe that 'everything matters' to create a good atmosphere within their stores. Give an example of how each sense can be experienced at Starbucks.
6. The service process design (Figure 10.4) can be used to discriminate between service processes. Give an example of Starbucks for each of them.
7. Prepare a service blueprint of the Starbucks coffee experience.

Endnotes

1 This case is based on *http://www.starbucks.com/aboutus/Company%20Fact%20Sheet%20Apr05.pdf*; *Business Week*, 2002, pp. 100–110; *http://www.bizjournals.com/seattle/stories/2000/07/17/daily22.html*; Thompson and Gamble, 1999: *http://www.mhhe.com/business/management/thompson/11e/case/starbucks.html*; Kotha and Glassman, 2003; Dittakavi and Thota, 2003; *Business Week* online, 6 August 2001; Schultz, 2001, p. 18; Fortune, 1996; Annual Report 2004, Part 2, p. 20: *www.Starbucks.com*; *New York Times*, 2005.

References

Aaker, D.A. (1990), How will the Japanese compete in retail services?, *California Management Review*, vol. 33, no. 1.

Aaker, D.A. (1991), *Managing Brand Equity: Capitalizing on the Value of a Brand Name*, The Free Press, New York.

Aaker, D.A. and Keller, K.L. (1990), Consumer evaluations of brand extensions, *Journal of Marketing*, 54, no. 1, 27–41.

Abell, D. (1980), *Defining the Business: The Starting Point of Strategic Planning*, Prentice-Hall, Englewood Cliffs, NJ.

Ahmed, S.A. and d'Astous, A. (1994), Comparison of country-of-origin effects on household and organizational buyers' product perceptions, *European Journal of Marketing*, vol. 29.

Al, D. (1997), *Dienstenbranding*, GVR-monografie, Genootschap voor Reclame, Amsterdam.

Aladwany, A.M. (2001), Online banking: a field study of drivers, development challenges and expectations, *International Journal of Information Management*, vol. 21, no. 3, 213–225.

Alam, I. (2003), Innovation strategy, process and performance in the commercial banking industry, *Journal of Marketing Management*, vol. 19, 973–999.

Alexander, J.A. (2004), *The State of Professional Services II: An Industry Comes of Age*, Alexander Consulting, St James City, Florida and AFSM International, Fort Myers, Florida.

Alexander, J.A. and Hordes, M.W. (2003), *S-Business, Reinventing the Services Organization*, SelectBooks Inc., New York.

Alexander, J. and Hordes, M. (2005), Everybody sells services, *Sbusiness*, vol. 29, no. 1, January/February, 65, 66, 92.

Alsem, K.J. and Hoekstra, J. (1994), *De Marketingoriëntatie van het Nederlandse Bedrijfsleven* (The Marketing Orientation of Dutch Companies), SUM Research Report, Groningen University, Groningen.

Ambler, T. and Barrow, S. (1996), Employer brand, *Journal of Brand Management*, vol. 4, no. 3, 185–206.

Amor, D. (2002), *The E-Business (R)evolution: Living and Working in an Interconnected World*, 2nd edn, Prentice-Hall PTR, New York.

Anderson, E.W. and Mittal, V. (2000), Strengthening the satisfaction-profit chain, *Journal of Service Research*, vol. 3, no. 2, November, 107–120.

Anderson, J., Hakansson, H. and Johanson, J. (1994), Dyadic business relationships within a business network context, *Journal of Marketing*, vol 54, no. 4, 1–14.

Ansoff, H.I. (1965), *Corporate Strategy*, McGraw-Hill, New York.

Antić, L. and Jablanović, V. (2000), Ernst and Young transfer pricing: criteria for evaluating transfer pricing methods, *Economics and Organization*, vol. 1, no. 8.

Arnott, R.D. and Casscells, A. (2003), Demographics and capital market returns, *Financial Analysts Journal*, March/April, vol. 59, no. 2.

Ashforth, B. and Humphrey, B. (1993), Emotional labour in service roles: the influence of identity, *Academy of Management Review*, vol. 18, no. 1, 88–115.

Assael, H. (1987), *Consumer Behavior and Marketing Action*, Kent Publishing, Boston, MA.

Aubert-Gamet, V. (1992), Le design d'environment commercial: un outil de gestion pour les enterprises de service, *Proceedings of the 2nd International Seminar in Service Management*, La Londe Les Maures, pp. 2–23.

Automotive News, vol. 76, no. 5977.

Avlonitis, G., Papastathopoulou, P. and Gounaris, S. (2001), An empirically-based typology of product innovativeness for new financial services: success and failure scenario, *Journal of Product Innovation and Management*, vol. 18, no. 5, 324–342.

Axelsson, B. and Wynstra, F. (2002), *Buying Business Services*, John Wiley & Sons, Ltd, Chichester.

Babakus, E. and Boller, G. (1992), An empirical assessment of the SERVQUAL scale, *Journal of Business Research*, vol. 24, no. 3, 253–268.

Bagozzi, R.P., Gopinath, M. and Nyer, P.U. (1999), The role of emotions in marketing, *Journal of the Academy of Marketing Science*, vol. 27, no. 2, 184–206.

Baker, J. (1986), The role of the environment in marketing services: the consumer perspective, in Congram, C., Czepiel, J. and Shannahan, J. (eds.), *The Services Challenge: Integrating for Competitive Advantage*, AMA, Chicago, 79–84.

Baker, M. and Hart, S. (1999), *Product Strategy and Management*, Prentice-Hall, Hemel Hempstead.

Baker, P. (1994), *Europe in 1998*, ERECO, BIPE Conseil, Paris.

Baker, W.E. and Sinkula, J.M. (1999), The synergistic effect of market orientation and learning orientation on organizational performance, *Journal of the Academy of Marketing Science*, vol. 27, no. 4, 411–427.

Bakewell, C. and Mitchell, V-W. (2004), Male consumer decision-making styles, *International Review of Retail, Distribution and Consumer Research*, vol. 14, no. 2, April, 223–240.

Balls, A. and Swann, C. (2004), Skill shortages seen as key in outsourcing, *Financial Times*, 31 March, 4.

Banker, R.D. *et al.* (2000), An empirical investigation of an incentive plan that includes non-financial performance measures, *Accounting Review*, vol. 75, no. 1, 1–49.

Bansal, H.S., Irving, G.P. and Taylor, S.F. (2004), A three-component model of customer commitment to service providers, *Journal of the Academy of Marketing Science*, vol. 32, no. 3, Summer, 234–250.

Barczak, G. and Wilemon, D. (2003), Team member experiences in new product development: views from the trenches, *R&D Management*, vol. 33, no. 5, 463–480.

Barker, R. (1968), *Ecological Psychology*, Stanford University Press, Stanford, CA.

Barksdale, H.C. and Darden, W.R. (1972), Consumer attitudes toward marketing and consumerism, *Journal of Marketing*, vol. 36, no. 4, 28–35.

Barksdale, H.C., Pereault Jr, W.D., Arndt, J., Barnhill, J., French, W.A., Halliday, M. and Zif, J. (1982), A cross-national survey of consumer attitudes toward marketing practices, consumerism and government regulations, *Columbia Journal of World Business*, vol. 17, no. 2, 71–77.

Barlow, R.G. (1992), Relationship marketing: the ultimate in customer services, *Retail Control*, March.

Bartlett, C.A. and Ghoshal, S. (1994), Linking organizational context and managerial action: the dimensions of quality of management, *Strategic Management Journal*, vol. 15, no. 5, 91–112.

Bateson, J.E.G. (1992, 1995), *Managing Services Marketing*, Dryden Press, Orlando, 2nd and 3rd edns.

Beatty, S. (2005), In spa industry's makeover, some tough regimens, *Wall Street Journal Europe*, 21–23 January, A5.

Beckers, P. (2003), Creating the perfect consumer experience in Peru: a case study in destination image and identity, MBA thesis, Universiteit Maastricht, Maastricht, the Netherlands.

Beckett, A. (2000), Strategic and marketing implications of consumer behaviour in financial services, *Service Industries Journal*, vol. 20, no. 3, July, 191–208.

Bell, J.D. and Fay, M.T. (1991), From the gentlemen to the marketer: the changing attitudes of the profession in New Zealand, *International Journal of Advertising*, vol. 10.

Benito, G.R.G. and Welch, L.S. (1994), Foreign market servicing: beyond the choice of entry mode, *Journal of Marketing*, vol. 2, no. 2, 7–28.

Bergadaà, M. (1991), The role of time in the action of the consumer, *Journal of Consumer Research*, vol. 17, December, 289–302.

Bergeron, P.B. (2003), *Essentials of Shared Services*, John Wiley & Sons, Inc., New York.

Bergner, K., Deifel, B., Jacobi, C., Kellerer, W., Rausch, A., Sabbah, A., Schätz, B., Sihling, M., Vilbig, A. and Vogel, S. (2002), *The Future of Information Technology: An Interdisciplinary, Scenario-based Approach*, FORSOFT, Technische Universität München, *http://www.forsoft.de*

Berkowitz, E.N., Kerin, R.A. and Rudelius, W. (1986), *Marketing*, Times Mirror/Mosby College Publishing, St Louis.

Berry, L.L. (1995), *On Great Service: A Framework for Action*, The Free Press, New York.

Berry, L.L. (1999), *Discovering the Soul of Services*, The Free Press, New York.

Berry, L.L. and Parasuraman, A. (1991), *Marketing Services, Competing Through Quality*, The Free Press, New York.

Berry, L.L. and Parasuraman, A. (1993), Building a new academic field: the case of services marketing, *Journal of Retailing*, vol. 69, no.1.

Berry, L.L. and Yadav, M.S. (1996), Capture and communicate value in the pricing of services, *Sloan Management Review*, Summer.

Berry, L.L., Seiders, K. and Grewal, D. (2002), Understanding service convenience, *Journal of Marketing*, vol. 66, July, 1–17.

Berthon, P., Hulbert, J.M. and Pitt, L.F. (1997), *Brands, Brand Managers, and the Management of Brands: Where to Next?*, Report no. 97–122, Marketing Science Institute, Cambridge, MA.

Bettancourt, L. (1997), Customer voluntary performance: customers as partners in service delivery, *Journal of Retailing*, vol. 73, no. 3, 383–406.

Beverwijk, A. (2002), *Time orientation of customers*, MBA thesis, Universiteit Maastricht, Maastricht, the Netherlands.

Bharadwaj, S.G. and Menon, A. (1993), Determinants of success in service industries, *Journal of Services Marketing*, vol. 7, no. 4.

Bharadwaj, S.G., Varadarajan, P.R. and Fahy, J. (1993), Sustainable competitive advantage in service industries: a conceptual model and research propositions, *Journal of Marketing*, pp. 83–99.

Bilkey, W.J. and Tesar, G. (1977), The export behavior of smaller-sized Wisconsin manufacturing firms, *Journal of International Business Studies*, vol. 8, no. 1, Spring, 93–99.

Biswas, A. (1992), The moderating role of brand familiarity in reference price perceptions, *Journal of Business Research*, vol. 25, 69–82.

Bitner, M., Brown, S. and Meuter, M. (2000), Technology infusion in service encounters, *Journal of the Academy of Marketing Science*, vol. 28, no. 1, 138–149.

Bitner, M.J. (1990), Evaluating service encounters: the effects of physical surroundings and employee responses, *Journal of Marketing*, vol. 54, no. 2, April, 69–82.

Bitner, M.J. (1992), Servicescapes: the impact of physical surroundings on customers and employees, *Journal of Marketing*, vol. 56, April, 57–71.

Bitner, M.J. and Hubbert, A.R. (1994), *Encounter Satisfaction versus Overall Satisfaction versus Quality: the Customer's Voice, in Service Quality: New Directions in Theory and Practice*, Sage, Thousand Oaks, CA.

Bitner, M.J., Booms, B. and Tetrault, M.S. (1990), The service encounter: diagnosing favourable and unfavourable incidents, *Journal of Marketing*, 54, no. 1, January, 71–84.

Blackwell, S.A., Szeinbach, S.L., Barnes, J.H., Garner, D.W. and Bush, V. (1999), The antecedents of customer loyalty, an empirical investigation of the role of personal and situational aspects of repurchase decisions, *Journal of Service Research*, vol. 1, no. 4, May, 362–375.

Blanchard, K.H., Zigarmi, P. and Zigarmi, D. (1985), *Leadership and the One-Minute Manager: Increasing Effectiveness through Situational Leadership*, William Morrow & Co., New York.

Bloemer, J. and Kasper, H. (1995), The complex relationship between consumer satisfaction and brand loyalty, *Journal of Economic Psychology*, vol. 16, 311–329.

Bloemer, J. and Ruyter, K. de (1999), Customer loyalty in high and low involvement service settings: the moderating impact of positive emotions, *Journal of Marketing Management*, vol. 15, 315–330.

Bloemer, J.M.M. (1993), Loyaliteit en levredenheid, PhD, Universiteit Maastricht, Maastricht, the Netherlands.

Bonoma, T.V. (1985), *The Marketing Edge: Making Strategies Work*, The Free Press, New York.

Booms, B. and Bitner, M.J. (1981), Marketing strategies and organisation structures for service firms, in Donnelly, J. and George, W. (eds), *Marketing of Services*, AMA Chicago.

Booz, Allen and Hamilton (1982), *New Product Management for the 1980s*, Booz, Allen Hamilton, New York.

Borck, J.R (2000), Transforming e-business: e-services, *Infoworld*, vol. 22, no. 41, pp. 75–76.

Boulding, W., Morgan, R. and Staelin, R. (1997), Pulling the plug to stop the new product drain, *Journal of Marketing Research*, vol. 34, February, 164–176.

Bouts, J.M. (1989), Het Buitenlandse Merk, *Tijdschrift voor Marketing*, vol. 23, no. 12.

Bradley, F. (1995), The service firm in international marketing, in Glynn, W.J. and Barnes, J.G. (eds), *Understanding Service Management, Integrating Marketing, Organizational Behavior, Operations and Human Resources Management*, John Wiley & Sons, Ltd, Chichester.

Bray, R. (2005), Fly higher than the first-class flock; airlines will go to extraordinary lengths to impress – and secure the loyalty of – big spending passengers, *Financial Times Europe*, 29 September, 8.

Brentani, U. de (1989), Success and failure in new industrial services, *Journal of Product Innovation Management*, vol. 6, 239–258.

Brentani, U. de (1995), New industrial service development: scenarios for success and failure, *Journal of Business Research*, vol. 32, no. 2.

Brentani, U. de (2001), Innovative versus incremental new business services: different keys for achieving success, *Journal of Product Innovation Management*, vol. 18, 169–187.

Brown, K., Ryan, N. and Parker, R. (2002), New modes of service delivery in the public sector – commercializing government services, *International Journal of Public Sector Management*, vol. 13, no. 3, 206–221.

Buckley, P.J. and Casson, M. (1976), *The Future of the Multinational Enterprise*, Macmillan, London.

Buckley, P.J., Pass, C.L. and Prescott, K. (1992a), *Servicing International Markets, Competitive Strategies for Firms*, Blackwell, Oxford.

Buckley, P.J., Pass, C.L. and Prescott, K. (1992b), The internationalization of service firms: a comparison with the manufacturing sector, *Scandinavian International Business Review*, vol. 1, no. 1.

Burns, L.R. (2000), A research agenda for health services management, *Health Care Management Review*, Fall.

Burrows, N. (2005), Hanging out on-line, *Virgin Express* inflight magazine, March/April/May, p. 3.

Business Week (2002), Planet Starbucks, 9 September, pp. 100–110.

Buttle, F. (1996), SERVQUAL: Review, critique, research agenda, *European Journal of Marketing*, vol. 30, 8–32.

Buzzacchi, L., Colombo, M.G. and Mariotti, S. (1995), Technological regime and innovation in services: the case of Italian banking industry, *Research Policy*, vol. 24, pp. 151–168.

Buzzell, R. (1968), Can you standardize multinational marketing?, *Harvard Business Review*, November, 102–113.

Callon, M., Laredo, P. and Rabeharisoa, V. (1996), Que signifie innover dans les services? une triple rupture avec le modele de l'innovation industrielle, *La Recherche*, February.

Cameron, M.A., Baker, J., Peterson, M. and Braunsberger, K. (2003), The effects of music, wait-length, and mood on a low-cost wait experience, *Journal of Business Research*, vol. 56, no. 6, June, 421–430.

Campbell, D. and Frei, F. (2004), The persistence of customer profitability: empirical evidence and implications from a financial services firm, *Journal of Service Research*, vol. 7, no. 2, November, 107–123.

Campbell, D.J., Campbell, K.M. and Ho-Beng, C. (1996), Innovation through performance analysis: Team-building and the development of performance indicators, *Journal of Product Innovation Management*, no. 3, 261–262.

Canabal, M. (2002), Decision-making styles of young South Indian consumers: an exploratory study, *College Student Journal*, vol. 36, no. 1, March, 12–20.

Cano, C.R., Carrillat, F.A. and Jaramillo, F. (2004), A meta-analysis of the relationship between market orientation and business performance: evidence from five continents, *International Journal of Research in Marketing*, vol. 21, 179–200.

Canziani, B.F. (1997), Leveraging customer competency in service firms, *International Journal of Service Industry Management*, vol. 8, no. 1.

Capiez, A. (2001), Banque à distance et pilotage bancaire, *Gestion 2000*, November/December.

Carman, J.M. and Langeard, E. (1980), Growth strategies for service firms, *Strategic Management Journal*, vol. 1, no. 1, 7–22.

Caruana, A. (2002), Service loyalty, the effects of service quality and the mediating role of customer satisfaction, *European Journal of Marketing*, vol. 36, no. 7/8, 811–828.

Casado Díaz, A. (2005), *Customers' Responses to Service Failures: Empirical Studies on Private, Voice and Third-Party Responses*, PhD, Universidad de Alicante.

Casado Díaz, A. and Más Ruíz, F.J. (2002), The consumer's reaction to delays in service, *International Journal of Service Industry Management*, vol. 13, no. 2, 118–140.

Cavusgil, S.T. and Nevin, J.R. (1981), Internal determinants of export marketing behavior: an empirical investigation, *Journal of Marketing Research*, vol. 18, no. 1, February.

Chakrapani, C. (1998), *How to Measure Service Quality and Customer Satisfaction*, American Marketing Association, Chicago.

Chan, A.P.C. and Chan, A.P.L. (2004), Key performance indicators for measuring construction success, *Benchmarking*, no. 2, 203.

Chay, D. (2005), New segments of boomers reveal new marketing implications, *Marketing News*, 15 March, p. 24.

Che, K-J. and Liu, C-M. (2004), Positive brand extension trial and choice of parent brand, *Journal of Product and Brand Management*, vol. 13, no. 1, 25.

Chebat, J.-C., Davidow, M. and Codjovi, I. (2005), Silent voices: why some dissatisfied consumers fail to complain, *Journal of Service Research*, vol. 7, no. 4, May, 328–342.

Chernatony, L. de and Dall'Olmo-Riley, F. (1999), Experts' views about defining services brands and the principles of services branding, *Journal of Business Research*, vol. 46, 181–192.

Chernatony, L. de and McDonald, M. (2003), *Creating Powerful Brands*, 3rd edn, Elsevier, Oxford.

Chernatony, L. de and McDonald, M.H.B. (1992), *Creating Powerful Brands: The Strategic Route to Success in Consumer Industrial and Service Markets*, Butterworth-Heinemann, Oxford.

Chernatony, L. de, Drury, S. and Segal-Horn, S. (2004), Identifying and sustaining services brands' values, *Journal of Marketing Communications*, vol. 10, no. 2, 73–93.

Chichilnisky, G. (1998), The knowledge revolution, *Journal of International Trade and Economic Development*, vol. 7, no. 1, 39–54.

Christopher, M., Payne, A. and Ballantyne, D. (1991), *Relationship Marketing, Bringing Quality, Customer Service and Marketing Together*, Butterworth-Heinemann, London.

Chu, W., Gerstner, E. and Hess, J. (1998). Managing dissatisfaction: how to decrease customer opportunism by partial refunds, *Journal of Service Research*, vol. 1, no. 2, 140–155.

Coombs, R. and Miles, I. (2000), Innovation, measurement and services: the new problematique, in Metcalfe, S. and Miles, I. (eds), *Innovation Systems in the Service Sectors: Measurement and Case Study Analysis*, Kluwer, Dordrecht and London, 85–104.

Cooper, R. (1990), Stage-gate systems: a new tool for managing new products, *Business Horizons*, vol. 33, no. 3, 44–54.

Cooper, R. (1994), Third generation new product processes, *Journal of Product Innovation Management*, vol. 11, 3–14.

Cooper, R. (1999), The invisible success factors to product innovation, *Journal of Product Innovation Management*, vol. 16, no. 2, 115–133.

Cooper, R. and Kleinschmidt, E. (1987), New products: what separates the winners from the losers?, *Journal of Product Innovation Management*, vol. 4, no. 3, 169–184.

Corporate Executive Board (2000), *Shared Service Centers: Fulfilling the Promise of Cost Reduction and Service Excellence*, Washington DC.

Coviello, N. and Brodie, R. (1998), From transaction to relationship marketing: an investigation of managerial perceptions and practices, *Journal of Strategic Marketing*, vol. 6, no. 3, 171–187.

Coviello, N.E. and Martin, K.A. (1999), Internationalisation services SMEs: an integrated perspective from the engineering consulting sector, *Journal of International Marketing*, vol. 7, no. 4, 42–66.

Coviello, N.E., Ghauri, P.N. and Martin, K.A.-M. (1998), International competitiveness: empirical findings from SME service firms, *Journal of International Marketing*, vol. 6, no. 2.

Coyne, K.P. and Dye, R. (1998), The competitive dynamics of network-based businesses, *Harvard Business Review*, January/February.

Crawford, M. and DiBenetto, A. (2002), *New Product Management*, McGraw-Hill, Boston, MA, 7th edn.

Crimp, M. (1985), *The Marketing Research Process*, Prentice-Hall, London, 2nd edn.

Crompton, J. (1979), Motivation for pleasure vacations, *Annals of Tourism Research*, vol. 6, 408–424.

Cronin Jr, J.J. and Taylor, S.A. (1992), Measuring service quality: a reexamination and extension, *Journal of Marketing*, vol. 56, no. 3, July, 55–68.

Cronin Jr, J.J. and Taylor, S.A. (1994), SERVPERF versus SERVQUAL: reconciling performance-based and perception-minus-expectations measurement of service quality, *Journal of Marketing*, vol. 58.

Crosby, P. (1983), *Quality is Free*, McGraw-Hill, New York.

Curran, J.M., Meuter, M.L. and Surprenant, C.F. (2003), Intentions to use self-service technologies: a confluence of multiple attitudes, *Journal of Service Research*, vol. 5, no. 3, February, 209–224.

Dabholkar, P.A. and Bagozzi, R.P. (2002), An attitudinal model of technology-based self-service: moderating effects of consumer traits and situational factors, *Journal of the Academy of Marketing Science*, vol. 30, no. 3, 184–201.

Damanpour, F. (2003), Structure correlates of innovation: a meta analysis, *Academy of Management Review*, vol. 34, 555–590.

Danaher, P.J. and Mattsson, J. (1994), Customer satisfaction during the service delivery process, *European Journal of Marketing*, vol. 28, no. 5, 5–16.

Davern, F. (2005), You said I'd get a room with a view, *Travel Trade Gazette*, vol. 25, March, 7.

Davies, G. and Chun, R. (2002), Gaps between the internal and external perceptions of the corporate brand, *Corporate Reputation Review*, vol. 5, no. 2/3, 144–158.

Davis, F.D. (1989), Perceived usefulness, perceived ease of use, and user acceptance of information technology, *MIS Quarterly*, vol. 13, no. 3, 319–340.

Davis, F.D., Bagozzi, R.P. and Warshaw, P.R. (1989), User acceptance of computer technology: a comparison of two theoretical models, *Management Science*, vol. 35, no. 8, 982–1003.

Dawkins, W. (1997), New policy delights for foreign insurers, *Financial Times*, 21 January.

Day, G.S. (1990), *Market Driven Strategy, Processes for Creating Value*, The Free Press, New York.

Day, G.S. (1994), The capabilities of market-driven organisations, *Journal of Marketing*, vol. 58, no. 3, 37–52.

Day, G.S. (1999), *The Market Driven Organization, Understanding, Attracting, and Keeping Valuable Customers*, The Free Press, New York.

Deal, T.E. and Kennedy, A.A. (1982), *Corporate Cultures: The Rites and Rituals of Corporate Life*, Addison-Wesley, Reading, MA.

Delener, N. (1996), Beware of globalisation: a comparative study of advertising agency–client relationship, *Services Marketing Quarterly*, vol. 14, 167–176.

Dessler, G. (2002), *A Framework for Management*, Prentice-Hall, Upper Saddle River, NJ.

Diamantopoulos, A. and Hart, S. (1993), Linking market orientation and company performance: preliminary evidence on Kohli and Jaworski's framework, *Journal of Strategic Marketing*, vol. 1, no. 2, 93–122.

Dibb, S., Simkin, L., Pride, W.M. and Ferrell, O.C. (1994), *Marketing, Concepts and Strategies*, 2nd European edn, Houghton Mifflin, Boston, MA.

Dick, A.S. and Basu, K. (1994), Customer loyalty: toward an integrated conceptual framework, *Journal of the Academy of Marketing Science*, vol. 22, no. 2, 99–113.

Dittakavi, P. and Thota, V.K. (2003), *Starbucks: Evolution of a Global Brand*, ICFAI Knowledge Center.

Dobree, J.S. and Page, A.S. (1990), Unleashing the power of service brands in the 1990s, *Management Decision*, vol. 28, no. 6.

Doherty, A.M. and Quinn, B. (1999), International retail franchising: an agency theory perspective, *International Journal of Retail and Distribution Management*, Bradford, vol. 27, no. 6.

Dolen, W. van, Ruyter, K. de and Lemmink, J. (2004), An empirical assessment of the influence of customer emotions and contact employee performance on encounter and relationship satisfaction, *Journal of Business Research*, vol. 57, no. 4, April, 437–444.

Donovan, R. and Rossiter, J. (1982), Store atmospherics: an environmental approach, *Journal of Retailing*, vol. 58, no. 1, 34–57.

Doyle, P. (2000), *Value-Based Marketing, Marketing Strategies for Corporate Growth and Shareholder Value*, John Wiley & Sons, Ltd, Chichester.

Duboff, R.S. and Sherer, L.U. (1997), Customized customer loyalty, *Marketing Management*, vol. 6, no. 2, 20–27.

Durrande-Moreau, A. and Usunier, J.-C. (1999), Time styles and the waiting experience, *Journal of Service Research*, vol. 2, no. 2, November, 173–186.

Durvasula, S. and Lysonski, S. (1993), Cross-cultural generalizability of a scale for profiling consumers' decision-making styles, *Journal of Consumer Affairs*, vol. 27, no. 1, Summer, 55–65.

Dwyer, F., Schurr, P. and Oh, S. (1987), Developing buyer–seller relationships, *Journal of Marketing*, vol. 51, April, 11–27.

Easingwood, C. and Storey, C. (1996), Determinants of new product performance: a study in the financial services sector, *International Journal of Service Industry Management*, vol. 7, no. 1, 32–55.

Eastin, M.S. (2002), Diffusion of e-commerce: an analysis of the adoption of four e-commerce activities, *Telematics and informatics*, vol. 19, 251–267.

Easton, G. (1995), Comment on Wensley's 'a critical review of marketing': market networks and interfirm relationships, *British Journal of Management*, vol. 6, 83–86.

Echtner, C.M. and Ritchie, J.R.B. (1991), The meaning and measurement of destination image, *Journal of Tourism Studies*, vol. 2, no. 2, 2–12.

Economist, The (1996), Delays can be expected, 27 July.

Economist, The (1999), 27 November.

Economist, The (2004), Special Report, 28 February, pp. 73–75.

Economist, The (2005), 27 April.

Edgett, S. and Jones, S. (1991), New product development in the financial service industry: a case study, *Journal of Marketing Management*, vol. 7, 271–284.

Edvardsson, B., Thomasson, B. and Øvretveit, J. (1994), *Quality of Services, Making it Really Work*, McGraw-Hill, London.

Eiglier, P. and Langeard, E. (1987), *Servuction*, McGraw-Hill, Paris.

Ende, J. van den and Wijnberg, N. (2001), The organization of innovation in the presence of networks and bandwagons in the new economy, *International Studies of Management and Organizations*, vol. 31, no. 1, 30–45.

Eppen, G.D., Hanson, W.A. and Kipp Martin, R. (1991), Bundling new products, new markets, low risk, *Sloan Management Review*, no. 7.

Eriksson, K., Majkgard, A. and Deo Sharma, D. (2000), Path dependence and knowledge development in the internationalization process, *Management International Review*, vol. 40, no. 4, 307–328.

Erramilli, M.K. (1991), The experience factor in foreign market entry behavior of service firms, *Journal of International Business Studies*, vol. 22, no. 3, 479–501.

Erramilli, M.K. (1992), Influences of some external and internal environmental factors on foreign market entry mode choice in service firms, *Journal of Business Research*, vol. 25, no. 4, 263–277.

Erramilli, M.K. and Rao, C.P. (1990), Choice of foreign market entry modes by service firms: role of market knowledge, *Management International Review*, vol. 30, no. 2, 135–150.

Erramilli, M.K. and Rao, C.P. (1993), Service firms' international entry-mode choice: a modified transaction-cost analysis approach, *Journal of Marketing*, vol. 57, no. 3.

Es, E. van (2004), *Consumentenbeslisstijlen en de Aanschaf van Eenvoudige Bankdiensten onder Jong volwassenen*, Masterthesis Katholieke Universiteit Nijmegen, Nijmegen.

Esteban, Á., Millán, Á., Molina, A. and Martín-Consuegra, D. (2002), Market orientation in service, a review and analysis, *European Journal of Marketing*, vol. 36, no. 9/10, 1003–1021.

Evanschitzky, H., Iyer, G.R. Hesse, J. and Ahlert, D. (2004), E-satisfaction: a re-examination, *Journal of Retailing*, vol. 80, 239–247.

Fabien, L. (2005), Design and implementation of a service guarantee, *Journal of Services Marketing*, vol. 19, no. 1, 33–39.

Faes, W. and Tilborgh, C. van (1984), *Marketing van Diensten*, Kluwer, Antwerpen/ Deventer.

Fan, J. and Xiao, J. (1998), Decision-making styles of young-adult Chinese consumers, *Journal of Consumer Affairs*, vol. 32, no. 2, 275–294.

Fang, T., Fridh, C. and Schultzberg, S. (2004), 'Why did the Telia-Telenor merger fail?', *International Business Review*, vol 13. no. 5, October, 573–594.

Firestone, S. (1983), Why advertising a service different, in Berry, L.L., Shostack, L. and Upah, G.D. (eds), *Emerging Perspectives on Service Marketing*, AMA, Chicago.

Fisk, R., Grove, S.J. and John, J. (2000), *Interactive Services Marketing*, Houghton Mifflin, Boston, MA.

Fitzsimmons, J. and Fitzsimmons, M. (2001), *Service Management, Operation, Strategy and Information Technology*, 3rd edn, McGraw Hill, New York.

Fitzsimmons, J.A. and Fitzsimmons, M.J. (1994), *Service Management for Competitive Advantage*, McGraw-Hill, New York.

Ford, D. (1982), The development of buyer–seller relationships in industrial markets, in Hakansson, H. (ed.), *International Marketing and Purchasing of Industrial Goods*, John Wiley & Sons, Inc., New York.

Ford, D. (1984), Buyer/seller relationships in international industrial markets, *Industrial Marketing Management*, vol. 13, no. 2, 101–113.

Ford, D. (1990), *Understanding Business Markets*, Academic Press, London.

Ford, D. (1997), *Understanding Business Markets: Interaction, Relationships and Networks*, 2nd edn, The Dryden Press.

Ford, D. (ed.) (2004), *The Business Marketing Course, Managing in Complex Networks*, John Wiley & Sons, Ltd, Chichester.

Forgas, J. (1979), *Social Episodes*, Academic Press, London.

Fortune magazine (1996), 9 December.

Fortune magazine (2005), 7 March, no. 4, 41.

Foxall, G. and Greenley, G. (2000), Predicting and explaining responses to consumer environments: an empirical test and theoretical propositions, *Service Industries Journal*, vol. 20, no. 2, 39–52.

Francese, P. (2002/2003), Top trends for 2003, *American Demographics*, vol. 24, no. 11, 48–52.

Friman, M. and Edvardsson, B. (2003), A content analysis of complaints and compliments, *Managing Service Quality*, vol. 13, no. 1, 20–26.

Fujita, J. (2003), Docomo bets US users will see beyond tiny screen, quoted in Magnusson *et al.*, op cit.

Furrer, O., Shaw-Ling, L.B. and Sudharshan, D. (2000), The relationships between culture and service quality perceptions, *Journal of Service Research*, vol. 2, no. 2, May, 355–371.

Gabbott, M. and Hogg, G. (1995), Service dimensions and service quality: an asymmetric approach, in Kunst, P. and Lemmink, J. (eds), *Managing Service Quality*, vol. 3, Pub PCP, London.

Gabbott, M. and Hogg, G. (2000), An empirical investigation of the impact of non-verbal communication on service evaluation, *European Journal of Marketing*, vol. 34, 384–398.

Gabbott, M. and Hogg, G. (2001), Non verbal communication in service encounters: a conceptual framework, *Journal of Marketing Management*, vol. 17, no. 1/2, 5–26.

Gadrey, J., Gallouj, F. and Weinstein, O. (1995), New models of innovation: how services benefit industry, *International Journal of Service Industry Management*, vol. 6, no. 3, 344–367.

Gailly, B. and Philippart, A.-J. (2005), Internet banking and SME: an exploratory study, *Electronic Commerce Research and Applications*, forthcoming.

Gardyn, R. (2002), What's cooking, *American Demographics*, March, 29–35.

Garel, G. (1999), La mesure et la reduction des delais de developement des produits nouveaux, *Recherche et Application Marketing*, vol. 14, no. 2, 29–47.

Garvin, D. (1988), Managing quality: 'The Strategic and Competitive Edge', Free Press, New York.

Gaski, J.F. and Etzel, M.J. (1986), The index of consumer sentiment toward marketing, *Journal of Marketing*, vol. 50, no. 3, July.

Geiger, K. (2005), Deutsche Bank scores banking deals in China; after late start, firm gains on Wall Street rivals in corporate-advisory work, *Wall Street Journal Europe*, 12–14 August, M1.

Gelderman, C.J. (2003), *A Portfolio Approach to the Development of Differentiated Purchasing Strategies*, PhD thesis, Technische Universiteit Eindhoven, Eindhoven.

Gemünden, H.G. (1985), Perceived risk and information search: a systematic meta-analysis of the empirical evidence, *International Journal of Research in Marketing*, vol. 2, no. 2, 79–100.

George, W.R. and Berry, L.L. (1981), Guidelines for the advertising of services, *Business Horizons*, vol. 24, May/June, no. 4.

Gerstner, E. and Hess, J.D. (1998), Yes, 'Bait and Switch' really benefits consumers, *Marketing Science*, vol. 17, no. 3.

Ghose, S. and Balachanderand, S. (2003), Reciprocal spillover effects: a strategic benefit of brand extensions, *Journal of Marketing*, vol. 67, no. 1.

Ghosh, A. (1994), *Retail Management*, 2nd edn, The Dryden Press, Orlando.

Ghoshal, S. and Bartlett, C.A. (1994), Linking organizational context and managerial action: the dimensions of quality management, *Strategic Management Journal*, vol. 15, Summer, 91–113.

Goldenberg, J., Libai, B. and Muller, E. (2001), Riding the saddle: How cross-market communications can create a major slump in sales, *Journal of Marketing*, vol. 66, no. 2, April, 1–16.

Gounaris, S.P. (2005), Trust and commitment influences on customer retention: insights from business-to-business services, *Journal of Business Research*, vol. 58, no. 2, February, 126–140.

Govindarajan, V. and Shank, J.K. (1989), Strategic cost analysis: the Crown Cork and Seal Case, *Journal of Cost Management for the Manufacturing Industry*, vol. 2, no. 4.

Grant, R.M. (1991), The resources-based theory of competitive advantage: implications for strategy formulation, *California Management Review*, vol. 33, no. 3, Spring, 114–136.

Gray, B.J., Matear, S. and Matheson, P.K. (2002), Improving service firm performance, *Journal of Services Marketing*, vol. 16, no. 2/3, 186–200.

Greenland, S. and McGoldrick, P. (2005), Evaluating the design of retail financial service environments, *International Journal of Bank Marketing*, vol. 23, no. 2, 132–152.

Griffin, J. (1997), *Customer Loyalty: How to Earn it and How to Keep It*, Jossey-Bass, New York.

Grifford, Jr., D. (1997), Brand management, moving beyond loyalty, *Harvard Business Review*, vol. 75, March/April.

Grönroos, C. (1982a), *Strategic Management and Marketing in the Service Sector*, Research Report 8, Swedish School of Economics and Business Administration, Helsinki.

Grönroos, C. (1982b), An applied service marketing theory, *European Journal of Marketing*, vol. 16, no. 7.

Grönroos, C. (1984), A service quality model and its marketing implications, *European Journal of Marketing*, vol. 18, no. 4, 36–44.

Grönroos, C. (1987), Competitiveness in the service economy, *Ekonomiska Samfundets Tidskrift*, vol. 40, no. 3, 137–144.

Grönroos, C. (1990a), Relationship approach to marketing in service contexts: the marketing and organizational behavior interface, *Journal of Business Research*, vol. 20, no. 1, 3–11.

Grönroos, C. (1990b), *Service Management and Marketing: Managing the Moments of Truth in Service Competition*, Lexington Books, Lexington MA.

Grönroos, C. (2000, 2001), *Service Management and Marketing: A Customer Relationship Management Approach*, 1st and 2nd edns, John Wiley & Sons, Ltd, Chichester.

Grönroos, C., Heinonen, F., Isoniemi, K. and Lindholm, M. (2000), The Netoffer model: a case example from the virtual marketspace, *Management Decision*, vol. 38, no. 4, pp. 243–252.

Grossbart, S., Mittelstaedt, R., Curtis, W. and Rogers, D. (1975), Environmental sensitivity and shopping behaviour, *Journal of Business Research*, vol. 3, no. 4, 281–294.

Grove, S.J., Fisk, R.P. and Bitner, M.J. (1992), Dramatizing the service experience: a managerial approach, in Swartz, T.A., Bowen, D.E. and Brown, S.W. (eds), *Advances in Services Marketing and Management*, vol. 1.

Guglielmo, C. (1996), Here come the super-ATMs, *Fortune*, 10 October.

Gummerus, J., Liljander, V., Pura, M. and Van Riel, A. (2004), Customer loyalty to content-based web-sites: the case of an online health care service, *Journal of Services Marketing*, vol. 18, no. 3, pp. 175–186.

Gummesson, E. (1987) The new marketing – developing long-term interactive relationships, *Long Range Planning*, vol. 20, no. 4.

Gummesson, E. (2002). *Total Relationship Marketing*, Butterworth-Heinemann.

Gwinner, K., Gremler, D. and Bitner, M. (1998), Relational benefits in services industries: the customer perspective, *Journal of Academy of Marketing Science*, vol. 26, Spring, 101–114.

Hafstrom, J., Chae, J. and Chung, Y. (1992), Consumer decision-making styles: comparison between United States and Korean young consumers, *Journal of Consumer Affairs*, vol. 26, no. 1, Summer, 146–158.

Häkansson, H. (1982), *International Marketing and Purchasing of Industrial Goods*, John Wiley & Sons, Inc., New York.

Halinen, A. (1994), *Exchange Relationships in Professional Services – A Study of Relationship Development in the Advertising Sector*, Published Dissertation Project, Series A-6, Turku School of Economics and Business Administration, Turku.

Hamel, G. and Pralahad, C.K. (1994), Competing for the future, *Harvard Business School Review*, July/August.

Han, C. (1989), Country image: halo or summary construct?, *Journal of Marketing Research*, vol. 26, May, 222–229.

Han, J.K., Kim, N. and Srivastrava, R. (1998), Market orientation and organizational performance: is innovation a missing link?, *Journal of Marketing*, vol. 62, 30–45.

Handy, C. (1995), Making sense of the future, *Leadership and Organization Development Journal*, vol. 16, no. 6, 35–41.

Harris, L.C. and Reynolds, K.L. (2003), The consequences of dysfunctional customer behavior, *Journal of Service Research*, vol. 6, no. 2, 144–161.

Hart, C.W.L. (1988), The power of unconditional service guarantees, *Harvard Business Review*, vol. 67, no. 4, 54–62.

Hart, C.W.L., Heskett, J.L. and Sasser Jr, W.E. (1990), The profitable art of service recovery, *Harvard Business Review*, vol. 68, no. 4, July/August, 148–157.

Hart, C.W.L., Schlesinger, L. and Maher, D. (1992), Guarantees come to professional service firms, *Sloan Management Review*, vol. 33, no. 3, 19–29.

Hattink, R.J. (1995), Merken en merkenbeleid binnen dienstenmarketing, MBA thesis, Universiteit Maastricht, Maastricht, the Netherlands.

Heer, A. de, Ahaus, C.T.B. and Vos, A.M.A.M. (1990), *Kwaliteitskosten, wat baat het?*, 2nd edn, Kluwer Bedrijfswetenschappen, Deventer.

Heijden, C. van der (2003), *De Zegeningen van de Gloablisering*, NRC Handelsblad, January.

Hennig-Thurau, T., Gwinner, K. and Gremler, D. (2002), Understanding relationship marketing outcomes, *Journal of Services Research*, vol. 4, February, 230–247.

Herk, H. van, Poortinga, Y.H. and Verhallen, T.M. (2004), Response styles in rating scales: evidence of method bias in data from six EU countries, *Journal of Cross-Cultural Psychology*, vol. 35, no. 3, May, 346–360.

Herrington, J., Lollar, J.G., Cotter, M.J. and Henley Jr, J.A. (1996), Comparing intensity and effectiveness of marketing communications: services versus non-services, *Journal of Advertising Research*, November/December.

Heskett, J.L. (1986), Managing in the service economy, *Harvard Business School Press*, Boston, MA.

Heskett, J.L. (1987), Lessons in the service sector, *Harvard Business Review*, March/April.

Heskett, J.L., Jones, T.O., Loveman, G.W., Sasser Jr, W.E. and Schlesinger, L.A. (1994), Putting the service profit chain to work, *Harvard Business Review*, March/April.

Heskett, J.L., Sasser Jr, W.E. and Hart, C.W.L. (1990), *Service Breakthroughs: Changing the Rules of the Game*, The Free Press, New York.

Heskett, J.L., Sasser Jr, W.E. and Schlesinger, L.A. (1997), *The Service Profit Chain, How Leading Companies Link Profit and Growth to Loyalty, Satisfaction and Value*, The Free Press, New York.

Heung, V. and Lam, T. (2003), Customer complaint behaviour towards hotel restaurant services, *International Journal of Contemporary Hospitality Management*, vol. 15, no. 4/5, 283–290.

Hinfelaar, M. (2004), *Key Success Factors in International Retailing*, PhD, Universiteit Maastricht, Maastricht, the Netherlands.

Hochschild, A. (1983), *The Managed Heart: Commercialisation of Human Feeling*, University of California Press, Berkeley, CA.

Hoeksema, L. and Jong, G. de (2001), International co-ordination and management development: an application at PricewaterhouseCoopers, *Journal of Management Development*, vol. 20, no. 2, 145.

Hoekstra, J.C. (1993), *Direct Marketing*, Wolters-Noordhoff, Groningen.

Hoffman, N.P. (2000), An examination of the 'sustainable competitive advantage' concept: past, present, and future, *Academy of Marketing Science*, pp. 1–16.

Hofstede, G. (1991), *Cultures and Organizations, Software of the Mind*, McGraw-Hill, London.

Hofstede, G. (2001), *Culture's Consequences*, 2nd edn, Sage, Thousand Oaks, CA.

Holden, R.K. and Nagle, T.T. (1998), Kamikaze pricing, *Marketing Management*, pp. 30–39.

Hollensen, S. (2001), *Global Marketing: A Market-Responsive Approach*, 2nd edn, Pearson Education Limited, Harlow.

Holzmann, K. (1996), Leasing operations catalyze capital equipment purchases, *Development Business*, vol. 9, 16 October, p. 1.

Homburg, C. and Pflesser, C. (2000), A multiple-layer model of market-oriented organizational culture: measurement issues and performance outcomes, *Journal of Marketing Research*, vol. 37, 449–462.

Homburg, C., Krohmer, H., Cannon, J.P. and Kiedaisch, I. (2002), Customer satisfaction in transnational buyer–supplier relationships, *Journal of International Marketing*, vol. 10, no. 4, 1–29.

Hookway, J. (2005), A new frontier in outsourcing, *Wall Street Journal Europe*, 16 March, A3.

Hooley, G.J. (1992), *Marketing in the UK*, Aston Business School, Birmingham.

Hooley, G.J., Greenley, G. and Fahy, L. (2001), *Market-Focused Resources, Competitive Positioning and Firm Performance*, Working Paper, Aston Business School, Birmingham.

Hooley, G.J., Saunders, J.A. and Piercy, N.F. (1998), *Marketing Strategy and Competitive Positioning*, 2nd edn, Prentice-Hall Europe, London.

Hooley, G.J., Saunders, J.A. and Piercy, N.F. (2004), *Marketing Strategy and Competitive Positioning*, 3rd edn, Prentice-Hall Europe, London.

Horowitz, J. (2000), *The Seven Secrets of Service Strategy*, Prentice-Hall, Harlow.

Howcroft, B., Hewer, P. and Hamilton, R. (2003), Consumer decision-making styles and the purchase of financial services, *Services Industries Journal*, vol. 23, no. 3, May, 63–81.

Hsieh, A.T., Yen, C.H. and Chin, K.C. (2004), Participative customers as partial employees and service provider workload, *International Journal of Service Industry Management*, vol. 15, no. 2, 187–199.

Hughes, A. (1997), Customer retention: integrating lifetime value into marketing strategies, *Journal of Database Marketing*, vol. 5, no. 2, 171–178.

Hunt, S.D. (2001), Commentary: a general theory of competition: issues, answers and an invitation, *European Journal of Marketing*, vol. 35, no. 5/6, 524–548.

Hunt, S.D. and Morgan, R.M. (1995), The comparative advantage theory of competition, *Journal of Marketing*, vol. 59, April, 1–15.

Hunt, S.D. and Morgan, R.M. (1996), The resource-advantage theory of competition: dynamics, path dependencies, and evolutionary dimensions, *Journal of Marketing*, vol. 60, October, 107–114.

Hurley, R.F. and Hult, G.T. (1998), Innovation, market orientation, and organizational learning: an integration and empirical examination, *Journal of Marketing*, vol. 62, July, 42–54.

Hutt, M.D. and Speh, T.V. (1992), *Business Marketing Management, a Strategic View of Industrial and Organizational Markets*, 4th edn, The Dryden Press, Orlando.

Iacobucci, D., Grayson, K.A. and Ostrom, A.L. (1994), The calculus of service quality and customer satisfaction: theoretical and empirical differentiation and integration, in Swartz, T.A., Bowen, D.E. and Brown, S.W. (eds.), *Advances in Services Marketing and Management*, JAI Press, Greenwich, CON, vol. 3, 1–67.

Ingenbleek, P., Debruyne, M., Frambach, R.T. and Verhallen, Th.M.M. (2003), Successful new product pricing practices: A contingency approach, *Marketing Letters*, vol. 14, no. 4, 289.

Institute of Public Relations Definition (2003).

Interactive Week, vol. 8, no. 20.

Interview/IPM (1974, 1981), *Consumentisme, Een Onderzoek naar de Consument in een Veranderende Samenleving*, Schiedam/Amsterdam.

Ittner, C. and Larcker, D. (1998), Are non-financial measures leading indicators of financial performance? an analysis of customer satisfaction, *Journal of Accounting Research*, Supplement, vol. 36 no. 3, 1–35.

Jacoby, J.W. and Chestnut, R.W. (1978), *Brand Loyalty Measurement and Management*, John Wiley and Sons, Inc., New York.

Jacoby, M. and Pringle, D. (2005), Duopoly fate rings beyond Ireland, *Wall Street Journal Europe*, 21–23 January, A2.

Jain, D. and Singh, S. (2002), Customer lifetime value research in marketing: a review and further directions, *Journal of Interactive Marketing*, vol 16, no. 2, 34–46.

Janda, S., Trocchia, P.J. and Gwinner, K.P. (2002), Consumer perceptions of Internet retail service quality, *International Journal of Service Industry Management*, vol. 13, no. 5, 412–431.

Janiszewski, C. van and Osselaer, S. (2000), A connectionist model of brand quality associations, *Journal of Marketing Research*, vol. 37, 331–350.

Janssen, R. (1996), The internationalisation of business services, satisfying clients through relationship marketing and service quality, MBA thesis, Universiteit Maastricht, Maastricht, the Netherlands.

Jaworski, B.J. (1988), Toward a theory of marketing control: environmental context, control types and consequences, *Journal of Marketing*, vol. 52.

Jaworski, B.J. and Kohli, A.J. (1993), Market orientation: antecedents and consequences, *Journal of Marketing*, vol. 57, July, 53–70.

Johansson, J.K. (2006), *Global Marketing, Foreign Entry, Local Marketing and Global Management*, international edn, 4th edn, McGraw-Hill, New York.

Johansson, J.K. and Vahlne, J.-E. (1977), The internationalization process of the firm: a model of knowledge development and increasing foreign market commitments, *Journal of International Business Studies*, vol. 8, no. 1, Spring/Summer, 23–32.

Johne, A. and Storey, C. (1998), New service development: a review of literature and annotated bibliography, *European Journal of Marketing*, vol. 32, no. 3, 184–251.

Johnson, K. and Leger, M. (1999), Loyalty marketing: Keeping in contact with the right customers, *Direct Marketing*, vol. 62, no. 5.

Johnson, G. and Scholes, K. (1988), *Exploring Corporate Strategy*, Prentice-Hall, London.

Johnson, K. and Dunai, M. (2005), Weak flag carriers' sales don't fly, *Wall Street Journal Europe*, 29 April–1 May, pp. A1, A10.

Johnson, S., Menor L., Chase, R. and Roth, A. (2000), A critical evaluation of the new services development process: integrating service innovation and service design, in Fitzsimmons, J. and Fitzsimmons, M. (eds), *New Service Development, Creating Memorable Experiences*, Sage, Thousand Oaks, CA.

Jones, P. (1995), Developing new products and services in flight catering, *International Journal of Contemporary Hospitality Management*, vol. 7, no. 2/3, 24–28.

Juran, V. (1974), Basic concepts in Juran, J., Gryna, F. and Bingham, R. (eds), *Quality Control Handbook*, McGraw-Hill, New York.

Kahn, B.E. (1998), Dynamic relationships with customers: high-variety strategies, *Journal of the Academy of Marketing Science*, vol. 26, no. 1.

Kangis, P. and O'Reilly, M.D. (2003), Strategies in a dynamic marketplace: a case study in the airline industry, *Journal of Business Research*, vol. 56, no. 2, February, 105–111.

Kapferer, J. (1997), *Strategic Brand Management*, Kogan Page, London.

Kapferer, J.-N. (1995), *Les Marques, Capital de l'Enterprise, les Editions d'Organisation*, 2nd edn, Paris.

Kaplan, R.S. and Norton, D.P. (1992), The balanced score card – measures that drive performance, *Harvard Business Review*, January/February.

Kaplan, R.S. and Norton, D.P. (1993), Putting the balanced score card to work, *Harvard Business Review*, September/October.

Karnitschnig, M. (2005), Bertelsmann unit plans pay-TV move, *Wall Street Journal Europe*, 21 February, A1, A10.

Kasper, H. (1993), *The Image of Marketing: Facts, Speculations and Implications*, Working paper 93–104, Universiteit Maastricht, Maastricht, the Netherlands.

Kasper, H. (1994), Some trends in distribution and retailing in Europe, in Urban, S. (ed.), *Europe's Economic Future, Aspirations and Realities*, Gabler Verlag, Wiesbaden.

Kasper, H. (1995), *The Essence of a Market Driven Corporate Culture; Theory and Empirical Evidence*, METEOR Working paper 95-009, Universiteit Maastricht, Maastricht, the Netherlands.

Kasper, H. (1997), Remote service delivery, information technology will alter the distribution of service – if customers cooperate, *Marketing Management*, vol. 6, no. 3, Fall.

Kasper, H. (2002), Culture and leadership in market-oriented services organisations, *European Journal of Marketing*, vol. 36, no. 9/10, 1047–1057.

Kasper, H. and Bloemer, J. (2000), *Successful Service Start Ups in Business-to-Business Services*, Paper, QUIS7, Karlstad University.

Kasper, H., Bloemer, J., Kyriakoploulos, K., Hooley, G. and Greenley, G. (2004), *Marketing Assets and Capabilities, Competitive Advantage, Competitive Positioning and Performance in Service Firms*, Paper QUIS9, Karlstad University.

Kasper, H., Bloemer, J., Matear, S., Hooley, G. and Greenley, G. (2005), Market positions and the relationship between market orientation and (non-) financial performance: the Dutch case, paper at EMAC Conference, Milan.

Kasper, H., Bloemer, J., Matear, S., Hooley, G. and Greenley, G. (2006a), Generic strategies, market positions and the relationship between market orientation and (non-) financial performance: evidence from the UK, Australia, New Zealand, Ireland and Austria, paper at EMAC Conference, Athens.

Kasper, H., Bloemer, J., Matear, S., Hooley, G. and Greenley, G. (2006b), Generic strategies, market positions and the relationship between market orientation and (non-) financial performance: evidence from the service industry in the UK, Australia, New Zealand, Ireland and Austria, paper at Frontiers in Services Conference, Brisbane.

Kasper, H., Helsdingen, P. van and Vries Jr, W. de (1999), *Services Marketing Management, An International Perspective*, John Wiley & Sons, Ltd, Chichester.

Kasper, H., Strepp, Y. and Terblanche, N. (2005), An exploratory qualitative study of brand associations as a means for brand extensions, *South African Journal of Economic and Management Science*, Part 1, vol. 8, no. 3 and Part 2, vol. 8, no. 4.

Keaveny, S.M. (1995), Customer switching behaviour in service industries: an exploratory study, *Journal of Marketing*, vol. 59, April.

Keegan, W. (2002), *Global Marketing Management*, 7th edn, Pearson Education Inc., Upper Saddle River, NJ.

Keegan, W. and Schlegelmilch, B. (2001), *Global Marketing Management An European Perspective*, Pearson Education Limited, Harlow.

Keiningham, T.L., Perkins-Munn, T. and Evans, H. (2003), The impact of customer satisfaction on share-of-wallet in a business-to-business environment, *Journal of Service Research*, vol. 6, no. 1, August, 37–50.

Keller, K. (2002), *Strategic Brand Management*, Prentice-Hall, New York.

Keller, K.L. (1993), Conceptualizing, measuring, managing customer-based brand equity, *Journal of Marketing*, vol. 57, no. 1.

Kelly, S., Donnelly, J. and Skinner, S. (1990), Customer participation in service production and delivery, *Journal of Retailing*, vol. 66, no. 3, 315–335.

Kennedy, A. (2005), Entry mode choice in service firms: a review of contemporary research, in Pauwels, P. and Ruyter, K. de (eds), *Research on International Service Marketing: A State of the Art*, Elsevier, Amsterdam, pp. 119–145.

Kiesler, C.A. (1968), Commitment, in Abelson P.A. *et al.* (eds), *Theories of Cognitive Consistency: A Source Book*, Rand McNally, Chicago., 448–455.

King, S. (1991), Brand building in the 90s, *Journal of Marketing Management*, vol. 7, no. 1, 3–13.

Kingman-Brundage, J. (1989), *'Blueprinting for the Bottom Line' in Service Excellence: Marketing's Impact on Performance*, AMA, Chicago.

Kingman-Brundage, J. (1992), The ABCs of service system blueprinting, in Lovelock, C. (ed.), *Managing Services: Marketing, Operations and Human Resources*, Prentice-Hall, NJ.

Kleijnen, M., Ruyter, K. de and Andreassen, T.W. (2005), Image congruence and the adoption of service innovations, *Journal of Service Research*, vol. 7, no. 4, May, 343–359.

Kleijnen, M.H.P., Wetzels, M. and De Ruyter, K. (2004), Consumer acceptance of wireless finance, *Journal of Financial Services Marketing*, vol. 8, no. 3, 206–217.

Kleinschmidt, E. and Cooper, R. (1991), The impact of product innovativeness on performance, *Journal of Product Innovation and Management*, vol. 8, 240–251.

Kloosterboer, W. (1992), *Interne Marketing, een Inventariserend Onderzoek*, NIMA, Amsterdam.

Knorr, A. and Žigová, S. (2004), *Competitive Advantage Through Innovative Pricing Strategies: The Case of the Airline Industry*, Universität Bremen, pp. 1–19.

Kohli, A.K. and Jaworski, B.J. (1990), Market orientation: the construct, research propositions and managerial implications, *Journal of Marketing*, vol. 54, no. 2, April, 1–18.

Kohli, A.K., Jaworski, B.J. and Kumar, A. (1993), MARKOR: A measure of market orientation, *Journal of Marketing Research*, vol. 30, no. 4, November, 467–478.

Kons, A. (1999), Understanding the chaos of airline pricing, *Park Place Economist*, vol. 8, 15–29.

Koopmans, A.J. and Versteeg, M.F. (1989), De Rol van het Industriële Merk: case-story IBM, *Tijdschrift Voor Marketing*, vol. 23, no. 12.

Kostecki, M.M. (1994), *Marketing Strategies for Services: Globalization, Client-Orientation, Deregulation*, Pergamon Press, Oxford.

Kotha, S. and Glassman, D. (2003), Starbucks Corporation: Competing on a global market, *UW Business School*, April, 2.

Kotler, P. (1973), Atmospherics as a marketing tool, *Journal of Retailing*, vol. 49, no. 4, 48–64.

Kotler, P. (1991), *Marketing Management, Analysis, Planning, Implementation and Control*, 7th edn, Prentice-Hall, Englewood Cliffs, NJ.

Kotler, P. (1994, 1997), *Marketing Management*, 8th and 9th edns, Prentice-Hall, Upper Saddle River, NJ.

Kotler, P., Brown, L., Adam, S. and Armstrong, G. (2004), *Marketing*, 6th edn, Pearson/Prentice-Hall, Frenchs Forest NSW, Australia, 753–766.

Kozlova, Z. (2003), *Dutch Young-Adult Consumer Decision-Making Styles: an Exploratory Study*, MBA thesis, Universiteit Maastricht, Maastricht, the Netherlands.

Kraljic, P. (1983), Purchasing must become supply management, *Harvard Business Review*, vol. 61, no. 5, September/October, 109–117.

Krapfel Jr, R.K., Salmond, D. and Spekman, R. (1991), A strategic approach to managing buyer–seller relationships, *European Journal of Marketing*, vol. 25, no. 9.

Krubasik, E. (1988), Customer your product development, *Harvard Business Review*, November.

Kuczmarski, T., Seamon, E., Spilotro, K. and Johnston, Z. (2003), The breakthrough mindset, *Marketing Management*, March/April, 39–43.

Kullvén, H. (1996), *Performance Measures for Service Processes*, in Edvardsson, B., Brown, S.W., Johnston, R. and Scheuing, E.E. (eds), *Advancing Service Quality: A Global Perspective*, Proceedings of QUIS 5, Karlstad.

Kumar, P. (1999), The impact of long-term client relationships on the performance of business service firms, *Journal of Service Research*, vol. 2, no. 1, 4–18.

Kurtz, D.L. and Clow, K.E. (1998), *Services Marketing*, John Wiley & Sons, Inc., New York.

Lado, N., Maydeu-Olivares, A. and Rivera, J. (1998), Measuring market orientation in several populations, a structural equations model, *European Journal of Marketing*, vol. 32, no. 1/2, 23–39.

Laing, A., Lewis, B., Foxall, G. and Hogg, G. (2002), Predicting a diverse future, directions and issues in the marketing of services, *European Journal of Marketing*, vol. 36, no. 4, 479–490.

Lam, S.Y., Shankar, V., Erramilli, M.K. and Murthy, B. (2004), Customer value, satisfaction, loyalty, and switching costs: an illustration from a business-to-business service context, *Journal of the Academy of Marketing Science*, vol. 32, no. 3, Summer, 293–311.

Lang, J. (2005), Partners in time, *Food Service Director*, vol. 18, no. 3, 51–53.

Langeard, E., Bateson, J., Lovelock, C. and Eiglier, P. (1981), *Services Marketing: New Insights from Consumers and Managers*, Marketing Science Institute, Cambridge, MA.

Langerak, F. (2001), Effects of market orientation on the behaviors of sales persons and purchasers, channel relationships, and performance of manufacturers, *International Journal of Research in Marketing*, vol. 18, 221–234.

Laroche, M., Bergeron, J. and Gouteland, C. (2001), A three-dimensional scale of intangibility, *Journal of Service Research*, vol. 4, no. 1, 26–38.

Laroche, M., McDougall, G.H.G., Bergeron, J. and Yang, Z. (2004), Exploring how intangibility affects perceived risk, *Journal of Service Research*, vol. 6, no. 4, 373–389.

Lasser, W., Mittal. B. and Sharma, A. (1995), Measuring customer-based brand equity, *Journal of Consumer Marketing*, vol. 12, no. 4, 11–19.

Lastovicka, J.L. and Gardner, D.M. (1978), Low involvement versus high involvement cognitive structures, *Advances in Consumer Research*, vol. 5, 87–92.

Lawton, C. (2005), Virgin gives names to flights in pursuit of brand loyalty; US ad campaign puts focus on perks package in trans-Atlantic travel, *Wall Street Journal Europe*, 7 April, A4.

Lee, E. and Lee, J. (2000), The acceptance and diffusion of electronic banking technologies, *Journal of Financial Counseling and Planning*, vol. 11, no. 1, 49–60.

Lee, E., Lee, J. and Eastwood, D. (2003), A two-step estimation of consumer adoption of technology based service innovations, *Journal of Consumer Affairs*, vol. 37, no. 2, 256–282.

Lehmann, D.R. (1998), Customer reactions to variety: too much of a good thing?, *Journal of the Academy of Marketing Science*, vol. 26, no. 1, 62–65.

Lemmink, J.G.A.M., Rohs, R.L.E.J. and Schijns, J.M.C. (1994), One-Price-Selling en de Relatie met Autodealer, *Tijdschrift voor Marketing*, vol. 28, no. 2.

Lewis, L. (1999), *Service Level Management for Enterprise Networks*, Artech House, Boston, MA.

Liljander, V. and Strandvik, T. (1995), The nature of customer relationships in services, in Schwartz, T.A., Bowen, D.E. and Brown, S.W. (eds), *Advances in Services Marketing and Management*, vol. 4, JAI Press, Greenwich, CON.

Liljander, V., Riel, A.C.R. van and Pura, M. (2002), Customer satisfaction with e-services: the case of an on-line recruitment portal, in Bruhn, M. and Stauss, B. (eds), *Jahrbuch Dienstleistungsmanagement 2002 – Electronic Services*, Gabler, Wiesbaden, 407–432.

Lodging Hospitality (2004), vol. 60, no. 9.

Lommelen, T. and Matthyssens, P. (2005), The internationalization process of service providers: a literature review, in Pauwels, P. and Ruyter, K. de (eds), *Research on International Service Marketing: A State of the Art*, Elsevier, Amsterdam, 95–117.

Looy, B. van, Dierdonck, R. van and Gemmel, P. (1998), *Service Management, An Integrated Approach*, Financial Times Pitman Publishing, London.

Lovelock, C. and Gummesson, E. (2004), Whither services marketing? in search of a new paradigm and fresh perspectives, *Journal of Service Research*, vol. 7, no. 1, 20–41.

Lovelock, C. and Wright, L. (1999), *Principles of Service Marketing Management*, Prentice-Hall, Inc., Upper Saddle River, NJ.

Lovelock, C.H. (1983), Classifying services to gain strategic marketing insights, *Journal of Marketing*, vol. 47, no. 3, 9–21.

Lovelock, C.H. (1991), *Services Marketing*, 2nd edn, Prentice-Hall, Englewood Cliffs, NJ.

Lovelock, C.H. (1992), *Managing Services: Marketing, Operations and Human Resources*, 2nd edn, Prentice-Hall, Englewood Cliffs, NJ.

Lovelock, C.H. and Yip, G.S. (1996), Developing global strategies for service businesses, *California Management Review*, vol. 38, no. 2.

Løwendahl, B.R. (1997), *Strategic Management of Professional Service Firms*, Handelshojskolens Forlag, Copenhagen.

Lucking-Reiley, D. and Spulber, D.F (2001), Business-to-business electronic commerce, *Journal of Economic Perspectives*, vol. 15, no. 1, 55–68.

Lysonski, S. and Durvasula, S. (1996), Consumer decision-making styles: a multi-country investigation, *European Journal of Marketing*, vol. 30, no. 12, 10–21.

Magnusson, P., Mathing, J. and Kristensson, P. (2003), Managing user involvement in service innovation, *Journal of Services Research*, vol. 6, no. 2, 111–124.

Maister, D.H. (2001), *Practice What You Preach, What Managers Must Do to Create a High Achievement Culture*, The Free Press, New York.

Malik, O. (2004), Cellphone market in India is poised for rapid growth, *Business 2.0*, July, 72–79.

Mangalindan, M. (2005), As Ebay tries to click in China, local rival makes new bid to grow, *Wall Street Journal Europe*, 12–14 August, A1 and A8.

Marketing (UK) (2005), 23 March, p. 2.

Martinez, E. and Pina, J.M. (2003), The negative impact of brand extension on parent brand image, *Journal of Product and Brand Management*, vol. 12, no. 7, 432–448.

Masurel, E. (2001), Export behavior of service sector SME's, *International Small Business Journal*, vol. 19, no. 2.

Matear, S., Osborne, P., Garrett, T. and Gray, B.J. (2002), How does market orientation contribute to service firm performance?, An examination of alternative mechanisms, *European Journal of Marketing*, vol. 36, no. 9/10, 1058–1075.

Matilla, A.S. (1999), The role of culture in the service evaluation process, *Journal of Service Research*, vol. 1, no. 2, February, 250–261.

Matilla, A. and Wirtz, J. (2001), Congruency of scent and music as a driver of in store evaluations and behaviour, *Journal of Retailing*, vol. 77, no. 2, 273–289.

Mayer, K., Bowen, J. and Moulton, M. (2003), A Proposed model of the descriptors of service process, *Journal of Services Marketing*, vol. 17, no. 6, 621–639.

Mayo, E. (1945), *The Social Problems of the Industrial Civilisation*, Ayer, New Hampshire.

McAlexander, J.H., Schouten, J.W. and Koenig, H.F. (2002), Building brand community, *Journal of Marketing*, vol. 66, no. 1, January, 38–54.

McCartney, S. (2005), The competitive class: two trans-Atlantic start-ups are set to add to majors' pain; cheaper fares and fewer seats, *Wall Street Journal Europe*, 20 September, A10.

McDonald, I. (2005), Barclays to expand Asian trading, *Wall Street Journal Europe*, 21–23 January, M.

McDonald, M. and Payne, A. (1998), *Marketing Planning for Services*, Butterworth-Heinemann, Oxford.

McNaughton, R.B., Osborne, P. and Imrie, B.C. (2002), Market-oriented value creation in service firms, *European Journal of Marketing*, vol. 36, no. 9/10, 990–1002.

Mehrabian, A. and Russell, J. (1974), *An Approach to Environmental Psychology*, MIT, Boston.

Merchant, K.A. (1995), *Control in Business Organizations*, Ballinger, Cambridge.

Metcalfe, J.S. (1998), *Evolutionary Economics and Creative Destruction*, Routledge, London.

Meuter, M.L., Bitner, M.J., Ostrom, A.L. and Brown, S.W. (2005), Choosing among alternative service delivery modes: an investigation of customer trials of self-service technologies, *Journal of Marketing*, vol. 69, no. 2, April, 61–83.

Meuter, M.L., Ostrom, A.L., Roundtree, R.I. and Bitner, M.J. (2000), Self-service technologies: understanding customer satisfaction with technology-based service encounters, *Journal of Marketing*, vol. 64, no. 3, 50–64.

Miles, I. (2001), Services innovation: coming of age in the knowledge based economy, *International Journal of Innovation Management*, vol. 4, no. 4, 371–389.

Miller, J. (1979), Studying satisfaction, modifying models, eliciting expectations, posing problems and making meaningful measurements, in Hunt, H.K. (ed.), *Conceptualisation and Measurement of Customer Satisfaction and Dissatisfaction*, Marketing Science Institute, Cambridge, MA.

Miller, J.W. (2005), Eastern Europe grows as call-center locale, *Wall Street Journal Europe*, 14 March, A10.

Milliman, R. (1986), The influence of background music on the behaviour of restaurant patrons, *Journal of Consumer Research*, vol. 13, September, 286–289.

Mintzberg, H., Lampel, J., Quinn, J.B. and Ghoshal, S. (2003), *The Strategy Process: Concepts, Contexts, Cases*, 2nd European edn, Pearson Education, Harlow.

Mitchell, V. and L. Bates (1998), UK consumer decision making-styles, *Journal of Marketing Management*, vol. 14, no. 1/3, April, 199–225.

Mitra, K. and Capella, L.M. (1997), Strategic pricing differentiation in services: a re-examination, *Journal of Services Marketing*, pp. 329–341.

Modell, S. (1996), Management accounting and control in services: structural and behavioral perspectives, *International Journal of Service Industry Management*, vol. 7, no. 2.

Mohr, L. and Bitner, M.J. (1995), Process factors in service delivery: what employee effort means to customers, in Swartz, T.A., Bowen, D.E. and Brown, S.W. (eds), *Advances in Service Marketing and Management*, vol. 4, JAI Press, Greenwich, CON.

Moller, K. and Halinen, A. (2000), Relationship marketing theory: its roots and direction, *Journal of Marketing Management*, vol. 16, 29–54.

Mooij, M. de (2004), *Consumer Behavior and Culture, Consequences for Global Marketing and Advertising*, Sage, Thousand Oaks, CA.

Moorman, C., Zaltman, G. and Deshpande, R. (1992), Relationships between providers and users of marketing research: the dynamics of trust within and between organisations, *Journal of Marketing Research*, vol. 29, August, 314–329.

Morello, G. (1988), *Business Requirements and Future Expectations in Competitive Bank Services: The Issue of Time Perception*, in ESOMAR, Research for Financial Services, Milan, Italy.

Morgan, R. and Hunt, S. (1994), The commitment-trust theory of relationship marketing, *Journal of Marketing*, vol. 58, July, 20–38.

Mowen, J.C. and Mowen, M.M. (1991), Time and outcome valuation: implications for marketing decision making, *Journal of Marketing*, vol. 55, 54–62.

Mulligan, P. and Gordon, S.R. (2002), The impact of information technology on customer and supplier relationships in the financial services, *International Journal of Service Industry Management*, vol. 13, no. 1, 29–46.

Nager, V. and Rajan, M.V. (2001), The revenue implications of financial and operational measures of products quality, *Accounting Review*, vol. 76, no. 4.

Nagle, T.T. (1987), *The Strategy and Tactics of Pricing, A Guide to Profitable Decision Making*, Prentice-Hall, Englewood Cliffs, NJ.

Narver, J.C. and Slater, S.F. (1990), The effect of a market orientation on business profitability, *Journal of Marketing*, vol. 54, no. 4, 20–36.

New York Times (2005), Starbucks aims to alter China's taste in caffeine, 21 May.

Nijssen, E., Singh, J., Sirdeshmukh, D. and Holzmüeller, H. (2003), Investigating industry context effects in consumer-firm relationships: preliminary results from a dispositional approach, *Journal of the Academy of Marketing Science*, vol. 31, no. 1, Winter, 46–60.

NN (2005), Ethics and business, changing Citigroup's corporate culture will not be easy, *Financial Times*, 18 February, p. 12.

Normann, R. (1984, 1991 and 2001), *Service Management: Strategy and Leadership in Service Business*, 1st, 2nd and 3rd edns, John Wiley & Sons, Ltd, Chichester.

O'Cass, A. and Grace, D. (2004), Exploring consumer experiences with a service brand, *Journal of Product and Brand Management*, vol. 13, no. 4, 257–268.

Oakes, S. (2000), The influence of the musicscape within service environments, *Journal of Services Marketing*, vol. 14, no. 7, 539–556.

Odekerken-Schröder, G. (1999), The role of the buyer in affecting buyer-seller relationships; empirical studies in a retail context, PhD, Universiteit Maastricht, Maastricht, the Netherlands.

OECD (2000), *Science and Technology Industry Report: The Service Economy*, OECD, Paris.

OECD (2002), *Expenditure on Health and Their Financing*, in OECD Health Data, Meeting of Experts in National Health Accounts, Paris, 10–11 October.

OECD (2004), *OECD in Figures, 2004 edition, Statistics on the Member Countries*, OECD, Paris.

OECD Observer (2003), No. 239, September, p. 45.

Oliva, T.A. and Lancioni, R. (1996), Identifying key traits of good industrial service reps, *Marketing Management*, vol. 4, no. 4, Winter/Spring, 44–51.

Oliver, R. (1977), Effect of expectation and disconfirmation on post-expense product evaluations: an alternative interpretation, *Journal of Applied Psychology*, vol. 62, no. 4, 480–486.

Oliver, R. (1980), A cognitive model of the antecedents and consequences of satisfaction decisions, *Journal of Marketing Research*, vol. 17, November, 460–469.

Oliver, R.L. (1997), *Satisfaction: A Behavioral Perspective on the Consumer*, Irwin/McGraw-Hill, New York.

Oliver, R.L. and Burke, R.R. (1999), Expectation processes in satisfaction formation, *Journal of Service Research*, vol. 1, no. 3, February, 196–214.

Olshavsky, R. and Miller, J. (1972), Consumer expectations, product performance and perceived product quality, *Journal of Marketing Research*, vol. 9, February, 19–21.

Onkvisit, S. and Shaw, J.J. (1989), *Service Marketing: Image, Branding and Competition*, Business Horizons, January/February.

Orr, B. (1999), ABAecom poised for e-commerce growth, *ABA Banking Journal*, vol. 91, no. 10, 84–91.

Osborne, P. and Imrie, B.C. (2002), Market-oriented value creation in service firms, *European Journal of Marketing*, vol. 36, no. 9/10, 990–1002.

Pacelle, M. (2004), Citigroup places bet outside US, *Wall Street Journal Europe*, March 15, M1.

Palmer, A. (1997), *Principles of Service Marketing*, 2nd edn, McGraw-Hill, London.

Palmer, A. (2005), *Principles of Service Marketing*, 4th edn, section 8.3, McGraw-Hill, London.

Palmer, A.J. (1995), Relationship marketing: local implementation of a universal concept, *International Business Review*, vol. 4, no. 4.

Papadopoulos, N. and Heslop, L.A. (1993), *Product Country Image: Impact and Role in International Marketing*, International Business Press, Binghamton, NY.

Parasuraman, A. (2000), Technology readiness index (TRI); a multiple-item scale to measure readiness to embrace new technologies, *Journal of Service Research*, vol. 2, no. 4, May, 307–320.

Parasuraman, A. and Colby, C.L. (2000), *Techno-Ready Marketing: How and Why Your Customers Adopt Technology*, The Free Press, New York.

Parasuraman, A. and Grewal, D. (2000), The impact of technology on the quality-value-loyalty chain: a research agenda, *Journal of the Academy of Marketing Science*, vol. 28, no. 1, 168–174.

Parasuraman, A. and Zinkhan, G.M. (2002), Marketing to and serving customers through the internet: an overview and research agenda, *Journal of the Academy of Marketing Science*, vol. 30, no. 4, 286–295.

Parasuraman, A., Zeithaml, V.A. and Berry, L.L. (1985), A conceptual model of service quality and its implications for future research, *Journal of Marketing*, vol. 49, Fall, 41–50.

Parasuraman, A., Zeithaml, V.A. and Berry, L.L. (1988), SERVQUAL: a multiple-item scale for measuring consumer perceptions of service quality, *Journal of Retailing*, vol. 64, no. 1, Spring, 12–40.

Parasuraman, A., Zeithaml, V.A. and Malhotra, A. (2005), E-S-QUAL; a multiple-item scale for assessing electronic service quality, *Journal of Service Research*, vol. 7, no. 3, February, 213–233.

Pas, J. van der (2004), *De Consumentenbeslisstijlen van Jong volwassenen bij Bankdiensten en de Invloed van deliberatie*, Masterthesis, Katholieke Universiteit Nijmegen, Nijmegen.

Patterson, P. and Cicic, M. (1995), A typology of service firms in international markets: an empirical investigation, *Journal of International Marketing*, vol. 3, no. 4.

Pauwels, P. and Ruyter, K. de (eds), Research on international service marketing: a state of the art, *Advances in International Marketing*, vol. 15, Elsevier, Amsterdam.

Payne, A. (1993), *The Essence of Service Marketing*, Prentice-Hall International, London.

Payne, A. and Clarke, M. (1995), Marketing services to external markets, in Glynn, W.J. and Barnes, J.G. (eds), *Understanding Services Management*, John Wiley & Son Ltd, Chichester.

Pender, L. and Baum, T (2000), Have the frills really left the European airline industry?, *International Journal of Tourism Research*, pp. 423–436.

Perea y Monsuwé, T., Dellaert, B.G.C. and Ruyter, K. de (2004), What drives consumers to shop online?; a literature review, *International Journal of Service Industry Management*, vol. 15, no. 1, 102–121.

Permenter, D. (2004), Performance measurement; crunchy KPI's: How measuring performance feeds success, *New Zealand Management*, 103–104.

Peter, J.P. and Olsen, J.C. (1993, 2002), *Consumer Behavior and Marketing Strategy*, 3rd and 6th edn, Irwin, Homewood, IL.

Peters, J. (2003), Viewpoint: Don't drink the bleach!, *Measuring Business Excellence*, Bradford, vol. 7, no. 2, 103–104.

Peters, M.A.M. (1997), *Brand Personality in Services*, MBA thesis, Universiteit Maastricht, Maastricht, the Netherlands.

Peters, T.J. and Waterman, R.H. (1982), *In Search of Excellence: Lessons from America's Best-Run Companies*, Harper & Row, New York.

Peterson, M. (2003), Report of special session: 'Incorporating consumer perspectives in the architectural design of servicescapes', *Proceedings of Advances in Consumer Research*, vol. 30, 208–210.

Petrof, J. (1997), Relationship marketing: the wheel reinvented?, *Business Horizons*, vol, 40, November/December, 26–32.

Pfeifer, P., Haskins, M. and Conroy, R. (2005), Customer lifetime value, customer profitability and the treatment of acquisition spending, *Journal of Managerial Issues*, vol. 17, Spring, 11–25.

Piercy, N. (1997, 2002), *Market-Led Strategic Change, Transforming the Process of Going to Market*, 2nd and 3rd edns, Butterworth-Heinemann, Oxford.

Pieters, R., Warlop, L. and Wedel, M. (2002), Breaking through the clutter: benefits of advertisement originality and familiarity for brand attention and memory, *Management Sciences*, vol. 48, no. 6.

Pine II, J. and Gilmore, J.H. (1999), *The Experience Economy*, Harvard Business School Press, Boston, MA.

Plas, S. (2005), EU cites Telecom-rule offenders, *Wall Street Journal Europe*, 15–17 April, A3.

Plutchik, R. (1980), *Emotions: A Psychoevolutionary Synthesis*, Harper & Row, New York.

Poiesz, T. and Raaij, F. van (2002), *Synergetische Marketing*, Pearson Education, Benelux.

Popcorn, F. (1992), *Trends van Overmorgen*, The Popcorn Report, Contact, Amsterdam.

Pope, H. (2005), Islamic banking takes its place globally as way to do business, *Wall Street Journal Europe*, 3 May, A1 and A6.

Porter, M.E. (1980), *Competitive Strategy*, The Free Press, New York.

Porter, M.E. (1985), *Competitive Advantage: Creating and Sustaining Superior Performance*, The Free Press, New York.

Porter, M.E. (2001), Strategy and the Internet, *Harvard Business Review*, vol. 79, no. 3, 63–78.

Postma, R. (2004), *NRC Handelsblad*, 20 February, 11.

Pritchard, M., Havitz, M. and Howard, D. (1999), Analyzing the commitment-loyalty link in service contexts, vol. 27, no. 3, 333–348.

Pujari, D. (2004), Self-service with a smile? Self-service technology (SST) encounters among Canadian business-to-business, *International Journal of Service Industry Management*, vol. 15, no. 2, 200–219.

Quinn, B. and Alexander, N. (2002), International retail franchising: a conceptual framework, *International Journal of Retail and Distribution Management*, Bradford, vol. 30, no. 5, 264–276.

Quinn, J.B. (1980), *Strategies for Change, Logical Incrementalism*, R.D. Irwin, Homewood IL.

Quinn, J.B. (1988), *Beyond Rational Management*, Jossey-Bass, San Francisco, CA.

Raaij, W.F. van and Verhallen, T.M.M. (1994), Domain specific market segmentation, *European Journal of Marketing*, vol. 28, no. 10.

Ranaweera, C. and Prabhu, J. (2003), The influence of satisfaction, trust and switching barriers on customer retention in a continuous purchasing setting, *International Journal of Service Industry Management*, vol. 14, no. 4, 374–395.

Randell, A. and Jaussi, K. (2003), Functional background identity, diversity and individual performance in cross functional teams, *Academy of Management Journal*, vol. 46, no. 6, 763–775.

Reichheld, F.F. and Schefter, P. (2000), E-Loyalty: your secret weapon on the Web, *Harvard Business Review*, vol. 78, no. 4, 105–113.

Reichheld, F.F. and Teal, T. (1996), *The Loyalty Effect: The Hidden Force behind Growth, Profits and Lasting Value*, Harvard Business School Press, Boston, MA.

Reidenbach, R. and Moak, D. (1986), Exploring retail bank performance and new product development: a profile of industry practice, *Journal of Product Innovation Management*, vol. 3, no. 3, 187–194.

Richins, M. (1983), An analysis of consumer interaction styles in the marketplace, *Journal of Consumer Research*, vol. 10, June, 73–82.

Riddle, D.I. (1992), Leveraging cultural factors in international service delivery, in Swartz, T.A., Bowen, D.E. and Brown, S.W. (eds), *Advances in Service Management*, vol. 1, JAI Press, Greenwich, CON.

Riel, A.C.R., Lemmink, J. and Ouwersloot, H. (2001), Consumer evaluation of service brand extensions, *Journal of Services Research*, vol. 3, no. 3, 220–231.

Riel, A.C.R. van and Lievens, A. (2004), New service development in high tech sectors: a decision making perspective. *International Journal of Service Industry Management*, vol. 15, no. 1, 72–101.

Riel, A.C.R. van and Ouwersloot, H. (2005), Extending electronic portals with new services: exploring the usefulness of brand extension models, *Journal of Retailing and Consumer Services*, vol. 12, no. 1.

Riel, A.C.R. van, Liljander, V. and Jurriëns, P. (2001), Exploring consumer evaluations of e-services: a portal site. *International Journal of Service Industry Management*, vol. 12, no. 4, 359–377.

Riel, A.C.R. van, Lemmink, J. and Ouwersloot, H. (2004), The role of information in high tech service innovation success: a decision making perspective. *Journal of Product Innovation Management*.

Riel, A.C.R. van, Lemmink, J., Streukens, S. and Liljander, V. (2004), Boost customer loyalty with online support: the case of mobile telecoms providers, *International Journal of Internet Marketing and Advertising*, vol. 1, no. 1, 4–23.

Riel, A.C.R. van, Semeijn, J. and Pauwels, P. (2004), Online travel service quality: the role of pre-transaction services, *Total Quality Management and Business Excellence*, vol. 15, no. 4, 475–493.

Riezebos, R., Vries Jr, W. de and Waarts, E. (1996), *Miles Mania, van Gratis Weggevertje tot Electronisch Sparen*, Wolters-Noordhoff, Groningen.

Robbins, S.P. and Coulter, M. (2002), *Management*, 7th edn, Prentice-Hall, Upper Saddle River, NJ.

Roberts, J. (2000), The internationalization of business service firms: a stages approach, *Services Industries Journal*, vol. 19, no. 4, 68–88.

Rogers, E. (1962), *The Diffusion of Innovations*, The Free Press, New York.

Roos, I. (1999), Switching processes in customer relationships, *Journal of Consumer Research*, vol. 2, no. 1, August, 68–85.

Roozen, F.A. (1991), Activity based costing, in *Handbook of Management Accounting*.

Rosenbloom, S. (2001), Sustainability and automobility among the elderly: an international assessment, *Transportation*, vol. 28, November, 375–408.

Rossomme, J. (2003), Customer satisfaction measurement in a business-to-business context: a conceptual framework, *Journal of Business and Industrial Marketing*, vol. 18, no. 2/3, 179–196.

Roth, M.S. and Amoroso, W.P. (1993), Linking core competencies to customer needs: strategic marketing of health care services, *Journal of Health Care Services*, vol. 13, no. 2, 49–54.

Roth, S. and Silberer, G. (2000), Urlaubsstimmung und Tourismus-marketing, *Planung & Analyse*, no. 2, 77–83.

Rust, R.T. and Kannan, P.K. (2003), E-service: a new paradigm for business in the electronic environment, *Communications of the ACM*, vol. 46, no. 6, 3–42.

Rust, R.T. and Oliver, R.L. (2000), Should we delight the customer, *Journal of the Academy of Marketing Science*, vol. 28, no. 1, 86–94.

Rust, R.T., Zahorik, A.J. and Keiningham, T.L. (1995), Return on quality (ROQ) making service quality financially accountable, *Journal of Marketing*, vol. 59, no. 2, April, 58–70.

Rust, R.T., Zahorik, A.J. and Keiningham, T.L. (1996), *Service Marketing*, Harper Collins, New York.

Rust, R.T., Zeithaml, V.A. and Lemon, K.N. (2000), *Driving Customer Equity, How Customer Lifetime Value is Reshaping Corporate Strategy*, The Free Press, New York.

Rutherford, D.G. (1995), *Hotel Management and Operations*, 2nd edn, Van Nostrand Reinhold.

Ruyter, K. de, Lemmink, J., Wetzels, M. and Mattson, J. (1997), Carry-over effects in the formation of satisfaction: the role of value in a hotel service delivery process, in Swartz, T.A., Bowen, D.E. and Brown, S.W. (eds), *Advances in Service Marketing Management*, vol. 6, JAI Press, Greenwich, CON.

Sadiq Sohail, M. and Shanmugham, B. (2003), E-banking and customer preferences in Malaysia: an empirical investigation, *Information Sciences*, vol. 150, no. 3/4, 207–218.

Sasser, W.E. (1976), Match supply and demand in service industries, *Harvard Business Review*, November/December.

Scheuing, E. and Johnson, E. (1989), A proposed model for new service development, *Journal of Services Marketing*, vol. 3, no. 2, Spring, 25–34.

Schiffman, L.G. and Kanuk, L.L. (1987), *Consumer Behavior*, 3rd edn, Prentice-Hall, Englewood Cliffs, NJ.

Schijns, J.M.C. (1996), Measuring relationship strength for segmentation purposes, in Parvatiyar, A. and Sheth, J.N. (eds), *Contemporary Knowledge of Relationship Marketing*,

Research Conference Proceedings, Center for Relationship Marketing, Emory University, Atlanta.

Schijns, J.M.C. (1998), *Het Meten en Managen van Klant-Organisatie Relaties*, PhD, Universiteit Maastricht, Maastricht, the Netherlands.

Schlesinger, L.A., Heskett, J.L. and Sasser Jr, W.E. (2003), *The Value Profit Chain, Treat Employees like Customers and Customers like Employees*, The Free Press, New York.

Schnabel, P. (1999), *Sociale en Culturele Verkenningen 1999*, Sociaal en Cultureel Planbureau, The Hague.

Schreurs, J.P. (1992), *International Retailing, Ambition, Skills and Knowledge*, MBA thesis, Universiteit Maastricht, Maastricht, the Netherlands.

Schriver, S. (1997), Customer loyalty: going, going . . ., *American Demographics*, September.

Schultz, H. (2001), Trust: How and why Starbucks build its brand through trust, not advertising, Spring, 18.

Schultz, M. and Chernatony, L. de (2002), The challenge of corporate branding, *Corporate Reputation Review*, vol. 5, no. 2/3, 105–112.

Segal-Horn, S. (1993), The internationalization of service firms, *Advances in Strategic Management*, vol. 9, 31–55.

Selnes, F. and Hansen, H. (2001), The potential hazard of self-service in developing customer loyalty, *Journal of Service Research*, vol. 4, no. 2, November, 79–90.

Shapiro, C. and Varian, H.R. (1999), *Information Rules: A Strategic Guide to the Network Economy*, Harvard Business School Press, Cambridge, MA.

Sharma, D.D. (1994), Classifying buyers to gain marketing insight: a relationship approach to professional services, *International Business Review*, vol. 3, no. 1.

Shaw-Ling, L.B., Furrer, O. and Sudharshan, D. (2001), The relationships between culture and behavioral intentions toward services, *Journal of Service Research*, vol. 4, no. 2, November, 118–129.

Shimp, T.A. and Sharma, S. (1987), Consumer ethnocentrism: construction and validation of the CETSCALE, *Journal of Marketing Research*, vol. 24, August.

Shostack, G.L. (1977), Breaking free from product marketing, *Journal of Marketing*, vol. 41, no. 2, April.

Shostack, G.L. (1987), Service positioning through structural change, *Journal of Marketing*, vol. 51, no. 1, 34–43.

Shostack, G.L. (1992), Understanding services through blueprinting, in Swartz, T.A., Bowen, D.E. and Brown, S.W. (eds), *Advances in Services Marketing and Management*, vol. 1, JAI Press, Greenwich, CON.

Shuler, S. and Davenport-Sypher, B. (2000), Seeking emotional labour management, *Communication Quarterly*, vol. 14, no. 1, 50–89.

Shusaka, Y. and Tessensohn, J. (2002), Japanese court refuses trade mark protection for retail services, *Managing Intellectual Property*, no. 117.

Siguaw, J.A., Simpson, P.M. and Baker, T.L. (1997), *The Influence of Market Orientation on Channel Relationships; A Dyadic Examination*, Working paper, Marketing Science Institute, Cambridge, MA.

Simon, H. (1992), *Preismanagement*, 2nd edn, Gabler Verlag, Wiesbaden.

Simonian, H. (2005), Troubled Swiss axes more jobs, *Financial Times Europe*, January 19, p. 21.

Simonin, B.L. and Ruth, J.A. (1995), Bundling as a strategy for new product introduction: effects on consumer's reservation price for the bundle, the new product, and its tie-in, *Journal of Business Research*, vol. 33, no. 3.

Simpson, J. (2002), The impact of the Internet in banking: observations and evidence from developed and emerging markets, *Telematics and Informatics*, vol. 19.

Skapinker, M. (2003), Contracted-out services may carry a high price, *Financial Times Special Report*, 24 November, p. 2.

Slater, J. (2004), Its global economy – so quit whining about outsourcing, *Wall Street Journal Europe*, 12 March, A3.

Slater, S.F. and Narver, J.C. (1994a), Does competitive environment moderate the market orientation-performance relationship?, *Journal of Marketing*, vol. 58, no. 1, January, 46–56.

Slater, S.F. and Narver, J.C. (1994b), Market orientation, customer value, and superior performance, *Business Horizons*, vol. 37, no. 2, March/April, 22–29.

Slater, S.F., Olson, E.M. and Reddy, V.K. (1997), Strategy-based performance measurement, *Business Horizons*, July/August.

Sproles, G. (1985), From perfectionism to fadism: measuring consumers' decision-making styles, in Schittgrund, K. (ed.), *Proceedings American Council on Consumer Interests*, ACCI, Columbia, 79–85.

Sproles, G. and Kendall, E. (1986), A methodology for profiling consumers' decision-making styles, *Journal of Consumer Affairs*, vol. 20, no. 2, Winter, 267–279.

Stauss, B. (1991), *Internes Marketing als Personalorientierte Qualitätspolitik*, in Bruhn, M. and Stauss, B. (eds), Dienstleistungsqualität: Konzepte-Methoden-Erfahrungen, Gabler, Wiesbaden.

Steenkamp, J.B.E.B.M. (1993), *Kwaliteit van Diensten, Enige Inzichten uit de Economische Theorie*, MAB, no. 12.

Steenkamp, J.B.E.B.M. and Dekimpe, M.G. (1997), The increasing power of store brands: building loyalty and markets share, *Long Range Planning*, vol. 30, no. 6.

Stevens, E. and Dimitriadis, S. (2005), Managing the new service development process: towards a systemic model, *European Journal of Marketing*, vol. 39, no. 1/2, 175–198.

Stock, J.R. and Lambert, D.M. (2001), *Strategic Logistics Management*, 4th edn, McGraw-Hill Irwin, Boston, MA.

Storbacka, K. (1994), *The Nature of Customer Relationship Profitability–An Analysis of Relationships and Customer Bases in Retail Banking*, PhD Swedish School of Economics and Business Administration, Helsinki.

Strandvik, T. and Liljander, V. (1994), Relationship strength in bank services: in Sheth, J.N. and Parvatiyar, A. (eds), *Relationship Marketing: Theory, Methods and Applications*, 1994 Research Conference Proceedings, Emory University, Atlanta, GA.

Strandvik, T. and Storbacka, K. (1996), Managing relationship quality, in Edvardsson, B., Brown, S.W., Johnston, R. and Scheuing, E.E. (eds), *Advancing Service Quality: A Global Perspective*, Proceedings, QUIS 5, ISQA, New York.

Strepp, Y. (2001), *A Study on Brand Extensions with Emphasis on Brand Stretching*, MBA thesis, Universiteit Maastricht, Maastricht, the Netherlands.

Streukens, S. (2005), *Return on Services, Empirical Studies on the Financial Consequences of Customer Service Evaluations*, PhD thesis, Universiteit Maastricht, Maastricht, the Netherlands.

Strikwerda, J. (2003), *Shared Service Centers*, Koninklijke Van Gorcum, Assen.

Stuart, F. and Tax, S. (1997), Designing and implementing new services: the challenge of integrating service, *Journal of Retailing*, vol. 73, no. 1, 105–134.

Sturm, R., Erickson-Harris, L. and St Onge, D. (2002), *SLM Solutions: A Buyer's Guide*, Enterprise Management Associates.

Suchard, H.T. and Polonsky, M.J. (1991), A theory of environmental buyer behaviour and its validity, *Proceedings American Marketing Association Educator's Conference*, Chicago.

Suh, B. and Han, I. (2002), Effect of trust on customer acceptance of Internet banking, *Electronic Commerce Research and Applications*, vol. 1, no. 3/4, 247–264.

Szmigin, I.T.D. (1993), Managing quality in business-to-business services, *European Journal of Marketing*, vol. 27, no. 1.

Taylor, F. (1911), *Principles of Scientific Management*, Harper, New York.

Taylor, S. (1994), Waiting for service: the relationship between delays and evaluations of service, *Journal of Marketing*, vol. 58, no. 2, 56–69.

Teas, K. (1993), Expectations, performance evaluation and consumers perception of quality, *Journal of Marketing*, vol. 57, October, 18–34.

Tether, B. (2001), The sources and aims of innovation in services: variety between and within sectors, *Economy Innovation and New Technology*, vol. 12, no. 6, 481–505.

Tether, B. (2005), Do services innovate (differently?) Insights from the European Innobarometer Survey, *Industry and Innovation*, vol. 12, no. 2, 153–184.

Thompson, A.A. and Gamble, J.E. (1999), *Starbucks Corporation, Student Resources*, McGraw-Hill.

Thor, C.G. (1996), Corporate performance measures in service industries, in Edvardsson, B., Brown, S.W., Johnston, R. and Scheuing, E.E. (eds), *Advancing Service Quality: A Global Perspective*, Proceedings of QUIS 5, Karlstad University.

Tiggelaar, B. (1999), *Internet Strategie, concurrentievoordeel in de digitale economie*, Addisson-Wesley, Longman Nederland BV.

Treacy, M. and Wiersema, F. (1995), *The Discipline of Market Leaders*, Addison-Wesley, Reading, MA and HarperCollins, London.

Tsikriktsis, N. (2004), A technology readiness-based taxonomy of customers: a replication and extension, *Journal of Service Research*, vol. 7, no. 1, August, 42–52.

Twyman, T. (2000), *International Journal of Market Research*, Winter, vol. 42, no. 4, p. 365.

Uncles, M., Dowling, G. and Hammond, K. (2003), Customer loyalty and customer loyalty programmes, *Journal of Consumer Marketing*, vol. 20, no. 4, 294–317.

Usunier, J.-C. (1992), *Commerce entre Cultures: Une Approche Culturelle du Marketing*, Presses Universitaire de France, Paris.

Usunier, J.-C. (1993), *International Marketing, A Cultural Approach*, Prentice-Hall, London.

Usunier, J.-C. and Valette-Florence, P. (1991), Construction d'une echelle de perception du temps: résultats préliminaires, in Chebat, J.C. and Venkatesan, V. (eds.), *Time and Consumer Behavior*, UQAM, Montreal.

Usunier, J.-C. and Valette-Florence, P. (1994), Individual time orientations: a psychometric scale, *Time and Society*, vol. 3, no. 2, 219–241.

VanderMerwe, S. and Chadwick, M. (1989), The internationalization of services, *Service Industries Journal*, vol. 9, no. 1, 79–93.

Varadarajan, P.R. and Thirunarayana (1990), Consumers' attitude towards marketing practices, consumerism and government regulations: cross-national perspectives, *European Journal of Marketing*, vol. 24, no. 6.

Vargo, S.L. and Lusch, R.F. (2004), Evolving to a new dominant logic for marketing, *Journal of Marketing*, vol. 68, January, 1–17.

Veendorp, S. (1989), *Globalization of Marketing Approaches, A Literature Study. Analysis of Globalization Activities in Seven Companies and Interviews with Employees within the ABN Bank*, ABN Bank, Amsterdam.

Venard, B. (2001), La trajectoire technologique de l'e-commerce: le cas de l'assurance, entre technique et innovation de marché, *Gestion 2000*, March/April.

Venetis, K.A. (1997), Service quality and customer loyalty in professional service relationships: An empirical investigation into the customer-based service quality concept in the Dutch advertising industry. PhD, Universiteit Maastricht, Maastricht, the Netherlands.

Venetis, K.A. and Ghauri, P.N. (2004), Service quality and customer retention: building long-term relationships, *European Journal of Marketing*, vol. 38, no. 11/12, 1577–1598.

Verschuren, K. (1996), Waarom maakt een consument geen gebruik van technologische innovaties in de dienstverlening, MBA thesis, Universiteit Maastricht, Maastricht, the Netherlands.

Virgin Express (2005), *Inflight Magazine*, March/April/May.

Vogler-Ludwig and Hoffmann (1993), *Business Services in Market Services and European Integration: Issues and Challenges, European Economy, Social Europe*, Commission of the European Communities, no. 3.

Vorhies, D.W., Harker, M. and Rao, C.P. (1999), The capabilities and performance advantages of market-driven firms, *European Journal of Marketing*, vol. 33, no. 11/12, 1171–1202.

Vries Jr, W. de and Helsdingen, P. van (2005), *Dienstenmarketingmanagement*, 4th edn, Wolters Noordhoff, Groningen.

Wackman, D.B., Salmon, C.T. and Salmon, C.C. (1987), Developing an advertising agency-client relationship, *Journal of Advertising Research*, vol. 26, no. 6.

Walsh, G., Mitchell, V. and Hennig-Thurau, T. (2001), German consumer decision-making styles, *Journal of Consumer Affairs*, vol. 35, no. 1, Summer, 73–95.

Wang, C.-L., Siu, N.Y.M. and Hui, A.S.Y. (2004), Consumer decision-making styles on domestic and imported brand clothing, *European Journal of Marketing*, vol. 38, no. 1/2, 239–252.

Ward, P., Davies, B. and Kooijman, D. (2003), Ambient smell and the retail environment: relating olfaction research to consumer behaviour, *Journal of Business and Management*, vol. 9, no. 3, 289–305.

Waters, R. (1995), *Financial Times*, 17 September.

Waters, R. (2005), Start-ups are 'a perceptual stroll into the fog', *Financial Times*, 16 February, 9.

Weatherly, K. and Tansik, D. (1993), Tactics used by customer contact workers: effects of role stress, boundary spanning and control, *International Journal of Service Industry Management*, vol. 4, no. 3, 4–17.

White, E. (2005), To keep its employees, Domino's pizza decides it isn't all about pay; chain attacks turnover by focusing on nurturing managers' performance; funny glasses and a pet fish, *Wall Street Journal Europe*, 18–20 February, A1 and A8.

White, L. and Yanamandram, V. (2004), Why customers stay; reasons and consequences of inertia in financial services, *Managing Service Quality*, vol. 14, no. 2/3, 183–194.

Wikipedia (2005), Electronic Encyclopedia.

Wilson, D.T. (1990), *Creating and Managing Buyer–Seller Relationships*, ISBM report 5-1990, Penn State University.

Wilson, D.T. (1995), An integrated model of buyer–seller relationships, *Journal of Academy of Marketing Science*, vol. 23, no. 4, 335–345.

Wing, H. (2004), Brand extension is not a low risk option that firms think it is, *Media Asia*, 27 August.

Wirtz, J. and Johnston, R. (2003), Singapore Airlines: What it takes to sustain service excellence – a senior management perspective, *Managing Service Quality*, vol. 13, no. 1, 10–19.

Wirtz, J. and Kum, D. (2004), Consumer cheating on service guarantees, *Journal of Academy of Marketing Science*, vol. 32, no. 2, 159–175.

Wolfinbarger, M. and Gilly, M.C. (2003), eTailQ: dimensionalizing, measuring and predicting etail quality, *Journal of Retailing*, 79, no. 3, 183–198.

Womack, J.P and Jones, D.T. (1996), *Lean Thinking: Banish Waste and Create Wealth in Your Corporation*, Simon & Schuster, New York.

Woo, K.-S. and Ennew, C.F. (2005a), Business-to-business relationship quality, *European Journal of Marketing*, vol. 38, no. 9/10.

Woo, K.-S. and Ennew, C.F. (2005b), Measuring business-to-business professional service quality and its consequences, *Journal of Business Research*, vol. 58, no. 9, September, 1178–1185.

Woodruff, R., Cadotte, E. and Jenkins, R. (1983), Modelling consumer satisfaction processes using experience based norms, *Journal of Marketing Research*, vol. 20, August, 296–304.

World Development Report (1993), *Investing in Health*, The World Bank, Washington DC.

World Development Report (1994), *Infrastructure for Development*, The World Bank, Washington DC.

World Development Report (2004), *Making Services Work for Poor People*, The World Bank, Washington DC.

Wright, P., Pringle, C. and Kroll, M. (1990), Strategic profiles, market share and business performance, *Industrial Management*, vol. 32, no. 3.

Wright, P., Pringle, C.D. and Kroll, M.J. (1992), *Strategic Management, Text and Cases*, Allyn & Bacon.

Wulf, K. de, Odekerken-Schröder, G. and Iacobucci, D. (2001), Investments in consumer relationships: A cross-country and cross-industry exploration, *Journal of Marketing*, vol. 65, October, 33–50.

Wyatt, E. (1996), Why Fidelity doesn't want you to shop at Schwab, *New York Times*, 14 July.

Yamamoto, S. and Tessenhon, J. (2002), Japanese court refuses trade mark protection for retail services, *Managing Intellectual Property*, London, March, p. 16.

Yang, Z. and Fang, X. (2004), Online service quality dimensions and their relationship with satisfaction, *International Journal of Service Industry Management*, vol. 15, no. 3, 302–326.

Yorke, D.A. (1988), Developing an interactive approach to the marketing of professional services, in Blois, K. and Parkinson, S. (eds), *Innovative Marketing: A European Perspective*, Proceedings, 17th EMAC Conference, Bradford.

Zeelenberg, M. and Pieters, R. (1999), Comparing service delivery to what might have been; behavioral responses to regret and disappointment, *Journal of Service Research*, vol. 2, no. 1, August, 86–97.

Zeithaml, V.A. (1988), Consumer perceptions of price, quality, and value: a means-end model and synthesis of evidence, *Journal of Marketing*, vol. 52, July.

Zeithaml, V.A. (2002), Service excellence in electronic channels, *Managing Service Quality*, vol. 12, no. 3, 35–38.

Zeithaml, V.A. and Bitner, M.J. (1996), *Services Marketing*, 2nd edn, McGraw-Hill, New York.

Zeithaml, V.A. and Bitner, M.J. (2003), *Services Marketing: Integrating Customer Focus Across the Firm*, 3rd edn, McGraw-Hill, New York.

Zeithaml, V.A., Bitner, M.J. and Gremler, D.D. (2005), *Services Marketing: Integrating Customer Focus across the Firm*, 4th edn, McGraw-Hill, New York.

Zeithaml, V.A., Parasuraman, A. and Malhotra, A. (2000), *A Conceptual Framework for Understanding E-Service Quality: Implications for Future Research and Managerial Practice*, Marketing Science Institute, Cambridge, MA.

Zeithaml, V.A., Parasuraman, A. and Malhotra, A. (2002), Service quality delivery through web sites: a critical review of extant knowledge, *Journal of the Academy of Marketing Science*, vol. 30, no. 4, 362–375.

Zeithaml, V.A., Parasuraman, P. and Berry, L. (1990), *Delivering Service Quality: Balancing Customer Perceptions and Expectations*, The Free Press, New York.

Index